MW00788745

A COMMENTARY ON
THE PSALMS

KREGEL EXEGETICAL LIBRARY

A Commentary on Exodus
DUANE A. GARRETT

A Commentary on Judges and Ruth
ROBERT B. CHISOLM, JR.

A Commentary on 1 & 2 Chronicles
EUGENE H. MERRILL

A Commentary on the Psalms, vol. 1 (1–41)
A Commentary on the Psalms, vol. 2 (42–89)
A Commentary on the Psalms, vol. 3 (90–150)
ALLEN P. ROSS

A Commentary on the Book of the Twelve,
The Minor Prophets
MICHAEL SHEPHERD

A Commentary on Romans
JOHN D. HARVEY

KREGEL EXEGETICAL LIBRARY

A COMMENTARY ON
THE PSALMS

Volume 1 (1–41)

Allen P. Ross

A Commentary on the Psalms: Volume 1 (1-41)

© 2011 by Allen P. Ross

Published by Kregel Academic, an imprint of Kregel Publications, 2450 Oak Industrial Dr. NE, Grand Rapids, MI 49505.

The English translations of the original Greek or Hebrew texts of the Bible are the author's own. The traditional renderings have been retained as much as possible because of the use of the psalms in churches, but the English has been modernized where appropriate.

Library of Congress Cataloging-in-Publication Data
Ross, Allen P.
  Commentary on the Psalms / Allen P. Ross.
    p. cm.
  1.Bible. O.T. Psalms—Commentaries. I. Bible. O.T. Psalms. English. New International. 2011. II. Title.
  BS1430.53.R67 2011
  223'.2077—dc22

                                                                2010028703

ISBN 978-0-8254-2562-2

Printed in the United States of America
21 22 23 24 25 / 8 7 6 5 4

To my aunt and uncle,
The Reverend Leonard and Beatrice Sukut,
for a lifetime given to ministering the Word of God
in exposition and music

CONTENTS

PREFACE
FOR VOLUME 1

For hundreds of years the Book of Psalms has been one of the richest resources for the expressions of worship and the development of the spiritual life, and at the same time one of the more complex and challenging sections of the Bible for expositors, to which the many commentaries attest. Even in the past few years several commentaries have appeared, as well as a steady production of literature on Psalms as a whole or on different aspects of individual psalms, and a number of new and interpretive translations. Each of these contributes to our understanding of the text, but there is no final word on the Book of Psalms. People who write on the psalms know this full well, for the subject matter is vast and many difficulties remain unsolved. There are so many ways that people have used the psalms in sermons, theological arguments, and pious devotions, beginning with ancient Israel and continuing to this day, that a complete study of the interpretation of the Psalter is most unlikely. Clearly, any commentary on the Psalms will be circumscribed by its purpose, and yet the challenge remains to be as thorough as possible while being concise.

My purpose in writing this commentary was to focus on the chief aim of exegesis, the exposition of the text. Many people preach or teach from the psalms, but too often take lines or sections from a psalm for the message, or limit their expositions to a select few psalms, perhaps those that are most often quoted in the New Testament. All the psalms should be carefully studied by believers and used in their meditations, prayers, and praises; but they should also be expounded in the assemblies of the churches for edification and exhortation, because as a part of Holy Scripture they are divinely inspired and must not be ignored. By exegetical exposition I mean that the exposition should cover the entire psalm, and that it should not only explain the text verse-by-verse but also show how the message of the psalm unfolds section-by-section. After all, a psalm is a piece of literature and therefore has a unified theme and a progression of thoughts developing that theme. Of course, the expositor will have to determine how much detail from the psalm can be included in the allotted time, but with the development of the message in mind that choice will be less arbitrary. If such expositions are developed for the church, the response will be enthusiastic because so many people have come to love the psalms, having learned to live by them in times of trouble and distress, as well as to celebrate with them in times of victory and blessing.

So I have written this commentary for pastors, teachers, and all serious students of the Bible who wish to develop their understanding of the Book of Psalms and to improve their ability to expound it with precision and depth. The format and contents of this commentary are then geared to my purpose and audience. Consequently, I have not included detailed discussions of all the different views down through the history of interpretation, and I have been selective with technical discussions of related matters and proposals for the resolutions of difficulties. I have tried to keep in mind my chief concern, that is, what a pastor or teacher needs to have for the development of an expository message. There are many things that would have been included if the purpose was more academic; but from my experience of teaching the exposition of the psalms in the seminary classroom and expounding them in the churches, I have a gained a fairly good sense of what needs to be explained and how it can be done in a limited period of time.

For those interested in studying the related questions and concerns in more detail, other works are available and can be consulted. In the chapter, "History of the Interpretation of the Psalms," I have given a basic bibliography of selected commentaries and helpful resources. At the end of Volume 3 I have provided a lengthy bibliography of specific studies, keyed to the relevant psalms.

The expositor should have several works on the psalms available, works that make their unique contribution and complement the study as a whole. My commentary is designed to move from the exegesis of the text to the formation of the exposition, that is, not simply commenting on lines and verses but putting the material together in an expository format. I do not expect expositors to put the material together in the way I have done or simply follow my outlines and points—although I would not object, but it is my hope that these arrangements will help expositors see how the material can be arranged and inspire them to develop their own expositions for their particular situations—albeit remaining true to the text.

In writing a commentary on the Psalms there are a number of things that had to be decided. In general, I wanted to write the commentary so that it would be easy to read, but not simplistic. It had to be thorough, and so that meant including necessary technical information, but in a way that would not disrupt the discussion. So I have kept technical terms and Hebrew words in parentheses in the commentary so that the English sentence is completely readable. In the footnotes on textual problems, I have put the Hebrew and Greek forms in the sentences but translated them so that the expositors who may not be up on the languages would still understand the variants and the arguments, and those that know the languages would have the information before them.

I have kept the translation of each psalm very close to the text and did not include too many clarifying words (which when used are in italics). I have tried to retain traditional renderings as much as possible because of the use of the psalms in the churches; but I have modernized the English. The figures of speech have not been decoded or given dynamic equivalents but retained in the poetry. At times there will be lines that seem cryptic or unusual. It is poetry, after all, and in a translation the poetry should be retained as much as possible. If paraphrases are used for the translations, the exposition may be once removed from what the text actually says, and this can influence how it is explained in the congregation. I have avoided doing this, although a degree of paraphrasing was necessary for understanding in some instances. The commentary discusses these cases.

13

Textual criticism is a necessary part of the study of a psalm. This should be obvious to those who have compared a psalm in different modern English versions, perhaps the one they brought to church and the one the expositor is using. There will be questions for sure—not a great number in a given psalm but some nonetheless, and on occasion it might be necessary to say we cannot be sure what the original manuscript had. I decided to note all the significant textual problems to help the expositor with these questions. With the more involved problems I have tried to explain the variant readings in an understandable way. In dealing with textual problems that were significant (that meant a change of meaning), I laid out the relevant material and offered my conclusion on the matter, whether it harmonized with the Hebrew text or the versions. In places where there was no clear solution for the textual problem, I presented the more plausible options and modern proposals. In such cases where the Hebrew reading was difficult but made sense, I retained it in the translation but left the material in the footnote for the expositor to decide what was the more probable reading. I have avoided the temptation to rewrite the text so that it makes better sense to me. Most of the difficulties centered around differences between the Hebrew text and the Greek version. In the commentary I refer to the old Greek version, popularly called the Septuagint, as simply "the Greek," or "the Greek version" or "the Greek translation." Later Greek revisions and translations are identified by name. In most cases the overall meaning of the psalm was not greatly changed by textual problems, but individual lines and expressions were. At least in having the difficulties laid out this way the expositor will be better equipped to explain why some modern versions have translated the passages the way they did.

In a number of places the word in the text seemed to be too difficult to make sense as to the original reading; in such cases numerous proposals have been made. Almost all these proposals made sense in the passage—that is what the commentators are trying to do after all—but often they required too many changes to be made in the text. I am inclined to be more skeptical where there is no evidence in Hebrew manuscripts or versions to support the proposed change; nevertheless, each textual problem had to be analyzed on its own merits and the choice explained. Expositors may disagree with my choice here and there, but at least they will have an easier time thinking through the problem with the variants explained.

In the Book of Psalms, the expositor also has to explain precise meanings of the words. In the psalms there are many rare words (and these often created textual difficulties); these have to be clarified, and that means considering proposals for etymological connections. Even with well-known words there may be a precise nuance in a psalm that has to be clarified. I have included a good number of word studies on the most frequently used terms in the Psalter. These are not full word studies in such a short space; rather, these are meant to help the expositor focus on the meaning of the word within its range of uses in the Bible. Each word will be discussed in a footnote in connection to the verse in which it is found; in other places where that word appears, a reference to the passage where the word study occurs is included in parentheses in the text. At the end of Volume 3 there is an index of all these word studies.

The psalms are filled with poetic language that needs to be explained clearly in the exposition. I have provided a very general survey in my chapter, "Literary Forms and Functions in the Psalms," and then throughout the commentary I explained the figures of speech and other poetic devices as they have bearing on the meaning of the text. Rather than refer to the figures in general terms, I have specified the precise figure being used and how it works in the psalm. If this kind of explanation is done well in the exposition, people will gain a much better understanding of the text.

One of the biggest challenges for translating and expounding the Psalms is the interpretation of the Hebrew tenses. Beginning Hebrew students quickly learn the range of nuances for the different tenses and how to decide when each should be used—the so-called perfect tense, imperfect tense, forms with sequential "and" (*wāw*), and volitional forms. That this decision remains a difficulty for us can be seen in a comparison of different English Bibles. Where there is disagreement in the translation (often a choice between an English present tense ["he judges"] and a future ["he will judge"], or perhaps a volitional mood ["may he judge"]), I have tried to work with each form in its context, preferring the more common nuances of the forms in difficult lines to the rare and perhaps questionable uses. Still, this is poetry, and so some unusual syntactical constructions do occur. And in Hebrew, some verbal forms may be spelled the same but have very different translation values in various contexts—it is often a translator's choice. At times the parallel structure of the lines of poetry may help in the choice of a translation, but that only works if the parallel lines are synonymous in some way; at other times the identifiable pattern of a psalm may help determine the translation of the verbs, but that too is not always possible since there are so many mixed types or passages that do not follow the praise or lament patterns. And the way the verb was translated in the versions often raises additional questions that cannot be answered apart from other evidence. When there is a difficulty with the tenses or other syntactical constructions, I have usually provided the options and then explained my choice. The change in tenses (from a present to a future, for example) may not make a great difference in the interpretation of the psalm, but then again it may. Where all the translations agree, that is good reason for caution before proposing a different translation.

The issue of higher criticism cannot be avoided in the study of any book in the Bible, and the Psalter is no exception. On the one hand, we might say that the date, authorship, and occasion of a psalm is not important to the interpretation because a poem stands on its own as a timeless piece of literature, and especially since we do not have this information for the majority of them. On the other hand, higher criticism often has a bearing on the interpretation of the psalms, as a brief survey of the commentaries will show. With many psalms, a superscription may supply the author, the occasion, or the use of the psalm in Israel's worship. While these notes were most likely added later when the psalms were being compiled, they nonetheless provide traditions that cannot simply be discarded. If a psalm is attributed to David, that should at least be given some consideration in the study; if there is no reason that David could not have written that piece, then the tradition may be considered reliable. This note of authorship may have no relevance to the exposition at all. Furthermore, if there is no other indication of the occasion in the psalm, one should be cautious in providing one and making it an integral part of the exposition. Modern scholarship generally places most of the psalms in the late pre-exilic time or post-exilic time, even though commentators do allow that many of the psalms were from the early monarchy period, or from David, even if they have been put to use in the last books of the collection. I see no reason to abandon the traditional view that David actually wrote many psalms, yet not all of them by any means, and not necessarily all that are traditionally attributed to him. Each psalm has to be studied on its own. The psalms that make up the collection seem to come from different times over a thousand years, and in most cases it is impossible to say when they were written or by whom. This issue will be an ongoing debate; in the commentary I have laid out the proposals for each of the psalms and where necessary responded to them. The expositor will soon discover that a good deal of time can be spent on matters of higher criticism, time that should be spent on the exposition of the text.

Another aspect of the study of the psalms necessarily requires correlating the material with the later revelation, especially the New Testament. The exposition must show how the theological message should be connected with New Testament revelation, even when the New Testament does not cite or allude to the specific psalm. At times the exposition will have to explain the ways of thinking or the activities referred to in the psalms in the light of the New Testament, for many of these have changed or been modified, even though the theology that informs them remains.

Correlation with later Scripture will, of course, focus on messianic elements in the psalms, whether prophetic or typological, but this has to be done carefully: the exposition must first develop the theological message of the psalm as it was written and then show how it came to fulfillment in the New Testament. In this way the continuity of Scripture will be maintained and the manner which the writers of the New Testament used the psalms better understood. I have attempted to follow this procedure in the messianic and eschatological passages.

Finally, the development of the exposition from the exegesis is basic to this commentary. For each psalm I have written a detailed exegetical outline to provide a clear analysis of what the different parts of the psalm are saying. Then this outline is changed into a homiletical outline that I have used as the headings of the commentary proper. In the conclusion I have provided a summary expository idea for the whole psalm, a short statement of the message of the psalm. The expositor will word these ideas differently for various purposes, but they do provide a sample of how the material can be unified and expressed in clear and relevant statements. I have explained this procedure more fully in my chapter, "Exposition of the Psalms."

My work in the Book of Psalms has been guided and inspired by a number of people. In particular for instruction in and inspiration for the study of the psalms, I owe a special debt of gratitude to Professors Bruce K. Waltke and John A. Emerton. Also, for years my colleague Donald R. Glenn was a reliable source of precision and clarification in the exegesis of the text. And over the years the work of my students has provided continual opportunities to think through the passages and find better ways to explain the meaning of the text. I am also grateful to Beeson Divinity School for much encouragement and help as well as a sabbatical along the way. And I wish to thank the folks at Kregel for taking on this project, Jim Weaver who was behind it from the start and Paul Hillman for his careful work with the commentary.

As I was working on the psalms, my mind easily ran to the innumerable saints who for centuries have sung, prayed, and expounded these passages. It was easy to identify with them because the study of the Book of Psalms immediately inspires meditation, prayer and praise, and the desire to teach them to the church so that worship and service may bring greater glory to God. In my own life I have had the privilege of praying and singing them in the worship services, drawing on them for my spiritual growth, and expounding them in many different congregations. By writing this commentary I want to honor all those who in prayer, praise, and proclamation make careful use of the Psalter.

ABBREVIATIONS FOR ALL VOLUMES

Symbols

//	parallel lines of poetry; the point of division between them
=	the equivalent of
<	derived from

A

A	Codex Alexandrinus (A), Greek uncial manuscript of the Bible, fifth century A.D.
AJBL	*Annual of the Japanese Biblical Institute*
AJSL	*American Journal of Semitic Languages and Literature*
ANET	*Ancient Near Eastern Texts* (J. B. Pritchard)
AnOr	*Analecta orientalia*
AO	*Archiv orientalni*
Aquila	Greek version made about 130 A.D.
ASTI	*Annual of the Swedish Theological Institute*
ASV	American Standard Version, 1901
ATR	*Anglican Theological Review*
AUSS	*Andrews University Seminary Studies*
AV	Authorized Version

B

B	See Vaticanus
BArch	*Biblical Archaeologist*

BASOR	*Bulletin of American Schools of Oriental Research*
BBR	*Bulletin for Biblical Research*
BDB	*A Hebrew and English Lexicon of the Old Testament* (F. Brown, S. R. Driver and C. A. Briggs)
BH3	Biblia Hebraica (Kittel)
BHS	Biblia Hebraica (Stuttgartensia)
Bib	*Biblica*
BibSac	*Bibliotheca Sacra*
BibV	*Biblical Viewpoint*
Bijdr	*Bijdragen Tijdschrit voor filosophie en theologie*
BiTod	*Bible Today*
BJRL	*Bulletin of the John Rylands Library*
BR	*Bible Review*
BSOAS	*Bulletin of the School of Oriental and African Studies*
BT	*The Bible Translator*
BTB	*Biblical Theological Bulletin*
BZ	*Biblische Zeitschrift*
BZAW	*Beihefte zur ZAW*

C

CBQ	*Catholic Biblical Quarterly*
CJT	*Canadian Journal of Theology*
CTJ	*Calvin Theological Journal*
CTM	*Concordia Theological Monthly*

E

e.g.	for example
EncBib	*Encyclopedia Biblica*
EncJud	*Encyclopedia Judaica*
ESV	English Standard Version
EvQ	*Evangelical Quarterly*
EvQ	*Evangelical Quarterly*
EvTh	*Evangelische Theologie*
ExT	*Expository Times*

G

GKC	*Gesenius' Hebrew Grammar*, ed. by E. Kautsch, trans. by A. E. Cowley
Greek	The Old Greek version, Septuagint

Greek^A	Greek, Alexandrinus
Greek^B	Greek, Vaticanus
Greek^S	Greek, Sinaiticus
Greek^L	Greek, Luciant
GTJ	*Grace Theological Journal*

H

HALOT	*The Hebrew and Aramaic Lexicon of the Old Testament* (Ludwig Koehler, Walter Baumgartner, et al)
HAR	*Hebrew Annual Review*
HBT	*Horizons in Biblical Theology*
HeyJ	*Heythrop Journal*
HTR	*Harvard Theological Review*
HTS	*Harvard Theological Studies*
HUCA	*Hebrew Union College Annual*

I

IB	*Interpreter's Bible*
ICC	*International Critical Commentary*
IDB	*Interpreter's Dictionary of the Bible*
i.e.	that is
IEJ	*Israel Exploration Journal*
Int	*Interpretation*
IB	*Interpreter's Bible*
IDB	*Interpreter's Dictionary of the Bible*

J

JANES	*Journal of Ancient Near Eastern Studies*
JAOS	*Journal of the American Oriental Society*
JBL	*Journal of Biblical Literature*
JBQ	*Jewish Bible Quarterly*
JBR	*Journal of the Bible and Religion*
JEOL	*Jaarsberichte v. h. Vooraziatische-Egyptisch Genootschop 'Ex Oriente Lux'*
JETS	*Journal of the Evangelical Theological Society*
JJS	*Journal of Jewish Studies*
JNES	*Journal of Near Eastern Studies*
JNSL	*Journal of Northwest Semitic Languages*
JPS	*Jewish Publication Society*

JQR	*Jewish Quarterly Review*
JRel	*Journal of Religion*
JPS	*Jewish Publication Society*
JQR	*Jewish Quarterly Review*
JSNT	*Journal for the Study of the New Testament*
JSOT	*Journal of the Study of the Old Testament*
JSS	*Journal of Semitic Studies*
JTS	*Journal of Theological Studies*
Jud	*Judaica*

K

kᵉthîv	what is written, the letters in the manuscript for words where the vowels are from the oral tradition (see also *qᵉrê*)
*KBL*³	*Lexicon in Veteris Testamenti Libros*, 3rd Edition (Ludwig Koehler and Walter Baumgartner)
KJV	King James Version

L

LSJ	*A Greek-English Lexicon* (ed. by Liddell, Scott, and Jones, Oxford: Clarendon, 1925–40; addenda and corrigenda, 1968; supplement, 1996)

M

ms(s)	manuscript(s)
MT	Masoretic Text, the received Hebrew text printed in BHS

N

NASB	New American Standard Version of the Bible
NBD	*New Bible Dictionary*
nd	no date
NEB	New English Bible
NIDOTTE	*New International Dictionary of Old Testament Theology and Exegesis* (ed. by Willem A. VanGemeren)
NIV	New International Version
NJPS	New Jewish Publication Society
NJV	New Jewish Publication Society Version

NLT	New Living Translation
NovT	*Novum Testamentum*
NRSV	New Revised Standard Version
NT	New Testament
NTS	*New Testament Studies*

O

Or	*Orientalia*, new series
OT	Old Testament
OTS	*Oudtestamentische Studiën*
OTSt	*Old Testament Studies*

P

PIH	*Psalterium iuxta hebraeos* (Jerome's translation from the Hebrew)
PTR	*Princeton Theological Review*

Q

Q	Qumran, as in 11QPs[a] (the Psalm a scroll found in Qumran, cave 11)
q^{e}rê	what is read, the oral tradition of a word represented by the vowels written with a different word in the text (see *k^{e}thîv*)

R

RB	*Revue biblique*
ResQ	*Restoration Quarterly*
RevExp	*Review and Expositor*
RSV	Revised Standard Version
RTR	*Reformed Theological Review*

S

SBL	Society of Biblical Literature
SBTh	*Studia Biblica et Theologica*
Sem	*Semeia*
SJOT	*Scandanavian Journal of Theology*
SJT	*Scottish Journal of Theology*
SP	Samaritan Pentateuch
StTh	*Studia Theologica*

s.v.	under the word, meaning see under
Symmachus	Greek version made near the end of second century A.D.
Syriac	the Bible of the ancient Syriac Church

T

Targum	ancient Aramaic paraphrases of the Hebrew Bible
TDOT	*Theological Dictionary of the Old Testament* (ed. by G. J. Botterweck and H. Ringgren)
Theodotion	Greek version made in the early second century A.D.
ThL	*Theologische Literaturzeitung*
ThT	*Theology Today*
ThZ	*Theologische Zeitschrift*
TynB	*Tyndale Bulletin*

U

UF	*Ugaritische Forschungen*

V

Vaticanus	Codex Vaticanus (B), Greek uncial manuscript of the Bible, 325–350 A.D.
VT	*Vetus Testamentum*
VT Supp	*Vetus Testamentum Supplement*
Vulgate	ancient Latin Bible, traced to Jerome

W

WTJ	*Westminster Theological Journal*
WW	*Word and World*

Z

ZAW	*Zeitschrift für die alttestamentliche Wissenschaft*
ZNW	*Zeitschrift für die neutestamentliche Wissenschaft*

VALUE OF
THE PSALMS

It is impossible to express adequately the value of the Book of Psalms to the household of faith. For approximately three thousand years psalms have been at the heart of the spiritual life of the people of God. The array of prayers, praises, hymns, meditations, and liturgies in the collection cover all the aspects of living for God in a world that is antagonistic to the faith. They have always been important for the expression of the faith, both privately and corporately. In Israel the collection of the psalms formed the hymn book of the temple, with many psalms being designated for regular use on certain days and at different occasions, including festivals and holy days. For early Christians, the psalms were also treasured because of their value in the prayers and praises of the people, but more so because of their application to Christ in the writings of the New Testament. Down through history wherever the psalms formed the prayers and praises of worshiping communities, they became well-known. In modern Christian congregations, however, the use of the psalms has almost fallen by the way to the detriment of the spiritual life of the church, and the prayers, hymns, and songs that have replaced the psalms in worship do not have the substance, power, and beauty that they have.

The change is significant in view of the importance of the psalms throughout the history of the faith. When combined with belief and understanding, the psalms were used to inform doctrine, inspire sermons, and provide the main resource for the development of the spiritual life. Kirkpatrick wrote:

> When men and women, forsaking their ordinary callings, dedicated their lives to devotion and prayer in monasteries and communities, the singing of the psalms formed a large part of their religious exercises. In course of time the recitation of the psalter became a clerical obligation as well. Various schemes or uses were drawn up. Fixed Psalms were generally assigned to certain of the canonical hours, while at the other services the remainder of the Psalms were recited "in course."[1]

Holladay illustrated this by surveying the structure of the psalms in the different religious orders, noting that the arrangement became the outline for the prayer life of the community.[2]

Throughout the history of the church, the great importance of the Book of Psalms has been recognized and proclaimed again and again. It is not my purpose here to collect scores of witnesses to the fact; but a few examples will serve to introduce the study of the book. For example, Augustine described the spiritual benefit he received from the psalms when he wrote:

> In what accents I addressed Thee, my God, when I read the Psalms of David, those faithful songs, the language of devotion which banishes the spirit of pride. . . . How I addressed Thee in those Psalms! how my love for Thee was kindled by them! how I burned to recite them, were it possible, throughout the world, as an antidote for the pride of humanity . . . .[3]

The psalms were so highly valued that a thorough knowledge

1. A. F. Kirkpatrick, *The Book of Psalms* (Cambridge: At the University Press, 1914), p. ci.

2. William L. Holladay, *The Psalms through Three Thousand Years: Prayerbook of a Cloud of Witnesses* (Minneapolis: Augsburg Fortress, 1993), pp. 176–77 (see pages 175–184 for a survey of the use of the psalms in the divine office).

3. *The Confessions of St. Augustine,* ix. 4, in *A Select Library of Nicene and Post-Nicene Fathers of the Christian Church*, ed. by Philip Schaff (Edinburgh: T&T Clark, 1994 reprint), p. 131.

of them was early on required for ordination. Kirkpatrick cited a few examples: Gennadius, Patriarch of Constantinople (458–471 A.D.), would not ordain anyone who had not been diligently reciting the psalms; the second Council of Nicaea (587 A.D.) concluded that no one was to be consecrated bishop unless he knew the Psalter thoroughly; and the eighth Council of Toledo (653 A.D.) ordered that no one be promoted to any ecclesiastical position who did not know perfectly the entire collection.[4] Praying these prayers and singing these hymns were recognized to be essential to the spiritual life of believers, especially any who would lead the churches in devotion and worship.

And this recognition of their importance continued in the Protestant world. Martin Luther said of the collection:

> You may rightly call the Psalter a Bible in miniature, in which all things which are set forth more at length in the rest of the Scriptures are collected into a beautiful manual of wonderful and attractive brevity.[5]

John Calvin said of the psalms:

> Here the prophets themselves, seeing they are exhibited to us as speaking to God, and laying open all their inmost thoughts and affections, call, or rather draw, each of us to the examination of himself in particular, in order that none of the many infirmities to which we are subject, and of the many vices with which we abound, may remain concealed.[6]

And Hooker wrote:

> The choice and flower of all things profitable in other books, the Psalms do both more briefly contain and more movingly

---

4. Kirkpatrick, *Psalms*, p. cii.
5. *Works*, ed. 1553, Vol. iii, p. 356. For a little more information, see Holladay, *The Psalms through Three Thousand Years*, pp. 192–195.
6. John Calvin, *Commentary on the Book of Psalms*, Trans. By James Anderson. 3 Volumes (Grand Rapids: Eerdmans, 1963 reprint), p. xxxvii.

express, by reason of that poetical form wherewith they are written.[7]

Several collections of verse were printed for the church after the Reformation, including selections from the Psalms, songs and hymns from other portions of the Bible, traditional medieval liturgical hymns, and original compositions patterned after Scripture. For example, one of the earliest and most thorough collections of biblical lyrics and comparable poems was *The Hymnes and Songs of the Church* (1623), designed to supplement the Psalter in the liturgy. The New England *Bay Psalm Book* (1640) included metrical versions of the Psalms; it became the authorized text for congregational singing in New England. The hymns of the church after the Reformation, then, were patterned after the kinds in the Book of Psalms—by 1640 there were over 300 editions of the Psalter in English.[8] Anyone studying the psalms in detail will understand why they became so important to the spiritual life of the church; Perowne said:

> We cannot pray the psalms without realizing in a very special manner the communion of the saints, the oneness of the Church militant and the Church triumphant. We cannot pray the Psalms without having our hearts opened, our affections enlarged, our thoughts drawn heavenward. He who can pray them best is nearest to God, knows most of the Spirit of Christ, is ripest for heaven."[9]

That the Psalter has for ages served as the book of praises and prayers for the worshiping community as well as for devout individuals in their private meditations should be enough to prompt churches of today to reconsider their place in the instruction and development of the spiritual life of the church. They should be the model for our songs of praise, the instruction for our prayers

---

7. Hooker, *Ecclesiastical Polity*, Book V, Chapter xxxvii, Par. 2.
8. See Coburn Freer, *Music for a King*, 14–15; and Terence Cave, *Devotional Poetry in France c. 1570–1613* (Cambridge, 1969).
9. J. J. Stewart Perowne, *The Book of Psalms* (Grand Rapids: Zondervan, 1966 reprint of the 1878 edition), I:40.

and meditations, and the inspiration for our quest for piety. They should also be considered for their benefit to our understanding of what worship is about, for they were inseparably bound to Israel's worship by divine inspiration. Since prayer and praise—indeed, worship—must be informed, these psalms must be interpreted correctly, taught clearly, and preached convincingly. The church is missing one of its richest experiences if it ignores the Book of Psalms or relegates it to a routine reading in a service without any explanation.

A clear explanation, however, does not come easily. Those who would expound the psalms for use in the spiritual life and worship of the people of God will find some challenges. They will first have to resolve textual difficulties; and this task is not made any easier by the fact that modern translations opt for one or another of the available readings.

Another challenge for the expositor comes from the different approaches taken in the study of the psalms in commentaries. These will have an influence on both translations and interpretations of many psalms; and so expositors will have to think critically when using the various resources.

Poetry itself presents a challenge for the interpretation and application of the psalms. It will take some practice for expositors to be able to work comfortably with the poetic structures and figures of Hebrew poetry. Some of the poetic language is universal and therefore fairly straightforward; but much of it is not obvious. To explain the imagery will require awareness of the use of biblical language as well as the culture of ancient Israel.

And finally, Hebrew grammar and syntax will pose a challenge to many expositors. It will be obvious to anyone who surveys how the various English Bibles translate the tenses of the verbs and other constructions of the language that some knowledge in this area is necessary. If expositors are not familiar with the forms and constructions of Hebrew, they will have to find reliable resources to help them understand the translations and commentaries. Since these are not always in agreement, expositors will have to weigh the arguments and decide what the precise emphasis of a given line of poetry should be, based on context and use in Scripture.

The following chapters will include discussions of these challenges in more detail and offer directives for the study of the psalms in these and other areas. The commentary itself will attempt to explain the meanings of the words, the biblical imagery, the constructions of the language, and the variations in translations and interpretations in the most important cases in the psalm so that the expositor will have more information with which to make an interpretive decision.

TEXT AND ANCIENT VERSIONS OF THE PSALMS

A brief survey of the texts and versions of the Psalms is always in danger of oversimplifying a complex issue, for which a thorough investigation would be helpful. From the following overview the expositor will gain some idea of the relationship of the texts and versions mentioned frequently in commentaries.[1]

THE MASORETIC TEXT

The Hebrew text used for our translations is the Masoretic Text (MT).[2] Although the extant manuscripts are comparatively late, evidence shows that the MT may preserve a text that can be traced back to pre-Christian times. The common theory is that the Hebrew manuscripts brought back from Babylon had been

---

1. See further E. Würthwein, *The Text of the Old Testament: An Introduction to the Biblia Hebraica* (Grand Rapids: Eerdmans, revised edition, 1995); R. W. Klein, *Textual Criticism of the Old Testament: the Septuagint After Qumran* (Philadelphia: Fortress Press, 1974); and Ellis R. Brotzman, *Old Testament Textual Criticism* (Grand Rapids: Baker Book House, 1994).
2. As those who have studied Hebrew will know, the Hebrew word *masorah* means "tradition," a tradition handed down. The scribes who preserved the text by adding the markings to represent the vowels they had learned to pronounce were called *masoretes* (they lived in the 8th–10th centuries A.D. around Galilee, especially the city of Tiberias, and so their system is called Tiberian). And the Hebrew Bible that they preserved with the vowel markings is called the *Masoretic Text*.

31

preserved more precisely than others and were accepted as authoritative. The Hebrew text of these manuscripts, frequently referred to as the Babylonian text, was standardized by about 100 A.D.[3] These were the manuscripts that were copied and preserved over the centuries until scribes known as Masoretes added pointing (a system of marking vowels and accents) to the text about the 9th century A.D. Their marks in the text simply recorded the oral tradition, the pronunciation, of the words. Although the text was faithfully preserved over the centuries, there are difficulties with many forms in the text, especially in the poetic passages.

In spite of such difficulties, this Masoretic Text is superior to any other text-type. This does not mean it always preserves the correct reading. When dealing with a textual difficulty, all external and internal evidence must be weighed before deciding on what the original text probably read. Very often when the form in the MT is difficult, commentators and editors will either suggest a preferred reading, or offer conjectural emendations in an effort to make sense out of the text. Because these solutions are at times helpful and at times not helpful, they must be evaluated critically, especially if they do not have manuscript evidence to support them. What makes the exposition of the psalms challenging is that many of these variant readings and suggested emendations have been incorporated into the different English translations. So, a comparison between the text and the translations most often used today has to be made line-by-line when preparing an exposition. Although the MT is not to be considered the inspired original text, it does display a greater reliability under textual evaluation than the versions.[4]

---

3. One explanation is that at the end of the first century Jewish teachers under Rabbi Aqiba concluded that the manuscripts of the Babylonian text type were the most rugged and therefore superior in the Pentateuch, and so that text became the standard text.

4. In theory we may say that in all probability we possess the original text; but in various places we are not sure which reading is the original and so have to do textual criticism. Modern translators, like ancient scribes, tend to make difficult readings smooth. On the one hand that may help the reader understand the line better, but on the other hand, that is how some of the textual variants arose. The Masoretic Text often preserves the more

THE GREEK TEXT AND OTHER VERSIONS

The oldest and most important version of the Psalms is the Greek translation, popularly known as the Septuagint (LXX), although that designation for the whole Old Testament is more convenient than accurate. In this commentary I shall refer to it simply as the Greek version or the Greek translation, whereas I shall identify other Greek versions and revisions specifically by name. The Greek translation of the Bible was begun about 280 B.C., the Pentateuch being translated first, and then the rest of the books over the next hundred or so years so that the work (or works) was completed by about 150 B.C. The Greek translation was based on a different Hebrew text (manuscripts referred to as the "Palestinian" text type) that was not preserved as rigidly as the text behind the MT (the "Babylonian" text type). The Greek version is preserved in uncial manuscripts from the 4th and 5th centuries A.D. and the first Latin and early English versions depended heavily on the Greek tradition for their understanding of the text.

The Greek translation underwent some revision almost immediately, so that the situation was rather fluid in the first Christian century as various manuscripts of different types were in use, as well as Christian writings that were quoting from the Greek Old Testament. One attempt to bring the Greek version into line with the standardized Hebrew text was made by Aquila around 135 A.D. Then, later that century, other revisions were made by Symmachus and Theodotion. On occasion the apparatus in the Hebrew Bible will refer to one or more of these different Greek versions.

Since these translations do not exist, we rely on other witnesses to what they had, such as Origen's Hexapla (which is also preserved largely in translation). Origen in the middle of the 3rd century made a column Bible of translations, including the Hebrew text transliterated into Greek, Aquila, Symmachus, Theodotion, and the old Greek "Septuagint." The reconstruction of the various readings using the existing manuscripts as well as the many treatises and sermons that quoted from the Bible was

---

rugged and difficult forms and constructions, which indicates that the text was not smoothed out by later scribes.

an amazingly complex task for scholars; fortunately, we today have many resources they provided that make our work in the text a little easier.

When textual variations surface in the psalms, they most often involve the Greek version and the Hebrew text. On occasion the Greek text will preserve the original reading, but for the most part it is a translation that tried to smooth out difficulties in the Hebrew, paraphrase readings that they did not fully understand, or generalize rare and unfamiliar words.[5] And on occasion we will see that the later Greek recensions differ from the old Greek version, often indicating what the standard Hebrew text of the time may have read. At times when the Greek translation differs from the Hebrew, it may not be a variant reading— the translators may simply have been interpreting the form or construction differently.

So, for textual problems in the psalms we must not simply assume the Greek reading is wrong; rather, we have to deal with every significant case carefully. Often a modern English translation will follow the Greek version because it makes a smoother reading, better sense, or closer parallelism. This may be the right way to deal with a given problem, especially if the Hebrew text is too difficult; but it may also perpetuate the kind of problem that led to the variant in the first place.

The Aramaic translation may at times be paraphrastic and verbose in places, given that its purpose was to make the meaning clear; its value for the determination of the reading in the text is that it often presents an interpretation of the word, clause, or verse in question. These interpretations were at first preserved orally, but then were written down a few centuries later, perhaps by the 4th or 5th centuries A.D. The Syriac also comes from this time. It was largely dependent on the Greek version, and therefore agrees with it much of the time. The Latin translations are also helpful at times for the study of the Psalms. The *Psalterium Romanum* (PR) is a revision of the Old Latin Psalter in accordance

---

5. For a more detailed discussion of the characteristics of the translations of the Greek and other versions, see James Barr, *Comparative Philology and the Text of the Old Testament* (Oxford: At the Clarendon Press, 1968), pp. 238–272.

with the old Greek; the *Gallican Psalter* is a revision of the Old Latin Psalter according to the LXX column in Origen's *Hexapla;* but the *Psalterium iuxta Hebraeos Hieronymi* (PIH) is a new translation Jerome made according to the Hebrew text. This one did not displace the familiar *Gallican Psalter* which is the text of the Vulgate. But it is occasionally instructive to see how Jerome rendered a text when working from the Hebrew.

DEAD SEA SCROLLS

A third text type besides the standard Hebrew (of the Babylonian or proto-Masoretic text type) and the Greek (or Alexandrian text type) is called the Palestinian text type. For the study of the Psalms, it is represented by the copies of the psalms from Qumran (11QPsa or Qumran, cave 11, Psalm scroll a).[6] These manuscripts of the Hebrew text do not always agree with the forms and arrangements in the MT; although they are still very close, there is enough difference to conclude that they represent a different text type, one that had made clarifications and revisions. In general this text type is inferior to the standard text we have in the MT. In many cases the Qumran manuscripts confirm readings in the MT that are in question, but at times they line up with the Greek translation against the reading in the MT. So where the form is readable in the Qumran material, it can be very important in solving a textual difficulty.

It should be clear from this that just because these other text types are said in general to be inferior to the text preserved in the MT that does not mean that the MT reading is to be automatically preferred. A problem is seldom solved on the basis of external evidence (manuscript witness) alone; it almost always requires the study of internal evidence (graphic, lexical, syntactical, and contextual considerations).[7] Here most expositors are

---

6. See further J. A. Sanders, *The Psalms Scroll of Qumran Cave 11, Discoveries in the Judaean Desert of Jordan, IV* (Oxford: At the Clarendon Press, 1965).

7. For a brief, practical introduction to the method (with samples), see Robert B. Chisholm, Jr., *From Exegesis to Exposition, A Practical Guide to Using Biblical Hebrew* (Grand Rapids: Baker Books, 1998), 20, 21. See also Kyle McCarter, Jr., *Textual Criticism* (Philadelphia: Fortress Press, 1986); and

dependent on commentaries for the discussion of textual problems. All commentaries that are exegetical in nature will discuss at least some of the textual problems and draw their conclusions, but they do not always give a full explanation of the different readings and the reasons for their choice. So if expositors have a serious problem to resolve, they must be sure to gather as much information as they can before making a decision. And then in explaining the problem in an exposition, they will have to use wisdom so that people will understand the issue and not lose confidence in their Bibles. But if people read different English translations they will quickly see that there are differences that need to be clarified. Now if the changes are merely translation choices ("houses" instead of "dwellings" or "delivered" instead of "saved") these are not textual problems and can be noted in passing; but if the changes are major, then more time will have to be given to the explanation. On the whole, the meaning of a psalm is not altered by variant readings; certain phrases or words may be but not the overall message.

In this commentary I shall note the significance textual variations in each psalm and discuss more fully those that make a significant difference in the meaning of the line. This will be done in the footnotes to the translation so that I can use the exact Hebrew and Greek words in the more technical discussions. In the commentary itself I try to keep the languages and technical jargon in parentheses so that the English sentence is readable. My approach to the textual problems will follow the established canons of textual criticism, even though they are not hard-and-fast rules to follow.[8] When a difficulty arises I shall explain the differences between the readings; if it is a significant problem I shall try to make sense out of the Masoretic Text and try to explain the variant readings and where possible suggest what might be behind them. From that I shall suggest the preferred reading. Where there is

---

Emanuel Tov, *Textual Criticism of the Hebrew Bible* (Minneapolis: Fortress Press, 1992).

8. These have been developed by those who work closely with the text and its variants. The cardinal guideline is: the reading that best explains the origin of the other is to be preferred. To determine this usually requires other criteria, such as difficult readings or shorter readings, as well as an awareness of scribal tendencies.

a need to find a better reading than what the Hebrew has, especially if there is manuscript evidence to support a variant reading, I shall make the change. Where there is a difficulty in the text and no clear resolution, only an array of readings in the versions and proposals by biblical scholars, I shall retain the Hebrew text if it makes sense but list what seem to me to be the most plausible suggestions with the least amount of change to the text, and let the reader decide if one is to be preferred over another. If there is a proposal to change the text primarily for a smoother reading, better parallelism, or clearer meaning, and there is no manuscript support, I shall mention it if it is helpful in the understanding of the line but also note where such a suggestion might be unwarranted. Even though I will make my preference known, by giving and explaining the differences each expositor will have enough information to make his or her own decision.

TITLES AND HEADINGS OF THE PSALMS

THE NAMES OF THE PSALTER

The Hebrew Title

In the Hebrew Bible the title of the collection is the *Book of Praises* (סֵפֶר תְּהִלִּים), abbreviated to *Praises* (תְּהִלִּים). The title is related to the verb "to praise" (הִלֵּל), most frequently used in connection with the temple service (1 Chron. 16:4), and commonly known in worshiping communities by the expression "praise the LORD" (הַלְלוּ־יָהּ). Although the word "praise" occurs many times in the Psalter, only one psalm (145) has the title "Praise" (תְּהִלָּה). The title *Book of Praises* may have originated with the use of the collection in the second temple (see Neh. 12:46).

Because the collection includes such a variety of psalms, no one term would adequately summarize them all, but no title could be more fitting for this collection, of which praise and thanksgiving are predominant characteristics, and which ends with the repetition of *hallᵉlû-Yāh* in increasing intensity (Pss. 145–150).

As we shall see, even psalms that form prayers or laments include an element of praise. Concerning this Westermann wrote:

> In the investigation of all the LI [individual lament psalms] of
> the Old Testament I found to my astonishment that there are
> no Psalms which do not progress beyond petition and lament.[1]

Thus, Praises (תְּהִלִּים) was and is an appropriate title.
Another title, apparently of an older collection of Davidic
Psalms, was Prayers (תְּפִלּוֹת) according to Psalm 72:20. Only
Psalms 17, 86, 90, 102, and 142 have this title. Prayer, in its
widest sense, includes the cycle of prayer and thanksgiving
(see 1 Sam. 2:1; Hab. 3:1). So this title seemed appropriate to
some compilers.

The Greek Title

Our word "psalm" comes from the Greek translation (ψάλμος)
of the Hebrew title used for many of the compositions (מִזְמוֹר),
which is a technical term for a song that was to be sung, perhaps with musical accompaniment. And so the collection was
called Psalms in LXX B (see Luke 24:44), or Psalter (*psalter* or
psalterion as it is in LXX A). The Greek words have come down
to us through the Latin *psalmus, psalterium* (and thus the
title Book of Psalms in Jerome). The classical definitions for
psalmos, "the music of a stringed instrument," or *psalterion*,
"a stringed instrument," were soon overshadowed by the use
of the terms for the Greek translation. *Psalmos* means "song
of praise."

NUMBERING AND THE PSALMS

The Psalms

It will soon be noticed that the Greek Bible, followed by the
Latin, differs from the Hebrew divisions of the psalms. The following chart will show the corresponding passages.

---

1. Claus Westermann, *The Praise of God in the Psalms,* tr. Keith R. Crim
   (Richmond: John Knox, 1961), p. 74.

Hebrew	Greek
1–8	1–8
9–10	9
1–113	110–112
114–115	113
116:1–9	114
116:10–19	115
117–146	116–145
147:1–11	146
147:12–20	147
148–150	148–150

This difference must be kept in mind when working with the Greek in textual or philological studies, as well as when using commentaries written by scholars following the Latin numbering (although most of them will use both numbers).

Qumran includes Psalm 151 in agreement with the supernumery psalm of the Greek and Psalm 151 in the Syro-Hexapla. The text is a midrash on 1 Samuel 16:1–7.[2]

The Verses

In the Hebrew Bible the numbering of the verses begins with the superscriptions, if present, whereas the English, like the Greek and Latin, does not. This means that in many psalms the verse numbers in the Hebrew will be one (or two) numbers higher than the verse numbers in the English. Many commentaries and books dealing with the Hebrew text will use the Hebrew system; they may or may not include the English in brackets afterwards. Of course, in public exposition where people will be

---

2. See J. A. Sanders, *The Psalms Scroll of Qumran Cave 11. Discoveries in the Judaean Desert*, IV (Oxford: Oxford University Press, 1965), pp. 54–64.

using the English text, the expositor must be sure to use the same numbers.

TRADITIONAL NOTATIONS OF AUTHORSHIP

Personal Names

Many of the psalms begin with a superscription that has traditionally been understood to attribute authorship to the passage; modern critical scholarship generally rejects the reliability of these notations.[3] Seventy-three psalms have in or as their superscription *leDāwîd*, (לְדָוִד), usually translated "of [by] David" (a few more in the Greek version have the title). The preposition used has a large number of meanings, but its most common translations are "to, for, of." It is used for psalms attributed to others as well: Asaph (Pss. 50, 73–83), Solomon (Pss. 72, 127), Moses (Ps. 90), Heman the Ezrahite (Ps. 88), and Ethan the Ezrahite (Ps. 89). The same preposition is used in the superscriptions (sometimes along with the notation with a name) to indicate that the psalm was "for the Chief Musician," or "for the sons of Koreh."

These prepositions with single names have been taken to record the authorship of the psalm. They were not part of the original composition; but they do record very early traditions about the individual psalms. Expositors who accept Davidic authorship for the psalms with this designation have taken support from Gesenius' comment that "the introduction of the author, poet, etc., by this *lāmed auctoris* (*lāmed of authorship*) is the customary idiom also in the other Semitic dialects, especially in Arabic" (GKC, #129c). Yet simply quoting a Hebrew grammar when convenient is insufficient argumentation. To make a convincing case for Davidic authorship for those psalms that have the superscription "of David," for example, would require several lines of argumentation. First, one would have to demonstrate that the *lāmed* preposition can be used for authorship. This would require verifying the grammatical point by usage. Within the Bible one could

---

3. For a more detailed discussion of the issue, see the introductions to the Old Testament, R. K. Harrison and Gleason Archer on the conservative side, Driver and Eissfeldt on the liberal side.

use a passage like Habakkuk 3:1 for support; outside the Bible one could use the Samaria Ostraca or the Lachish Letters, potsherds and dockets from the time of the divided monarchy, which use the preposition *lāmed* for the sender and the addressee (e.g., shipped "from/by" someone "to" someone). This would substantiate that the *lāmed* could indicate authorship.

The next step would be to show that it did refer to authorship for a particular psalm. Evidence for this would come from three lines of argumentation. First, one could muster the abundant evidence in the Bible that David was a writer of sacred poetry.[4] Second, one could compare the form and style of the ancient Ugaritic poetry (earlier than David) to see how early some of the features of Hebrew poetic are. And third, one could evaluate the internal evidence of the psalm itself to see how well it harmonizes with the superscription.[5] When all the material is considered, it will be clear that traditional notations in the superscriptions are on the whole defensible traditions. The expositor will still have to analyze the content of the psalm itself to see if there is anything there that would argue convincingly against the traditional ascription of authorship.[6]

An additional part of the study would be to consider the witness of the New Testament, the Lord Jesus Christ and the apostles, that supports Davidic authorship in several places. Many scholars have adopted the view that New Testament references to David, for example, are simply references to the Psalter in general, or accommodations to the popular understanding (right or wrong) that they are David's. A fair exegesis of Mark 12:35–37, Acts 2:24–36, Acts 4:25, or Acts 13:35 would indicate more than that. When they refer to David as a prophet writing something, or talk about David's tomb to indicate that the psalm he

---

4. See J. G. S. Thompson, "Psalms, Book of," in *New Bible Dictionary*, p. 1053.

5. See, for example, Delitzsch on Psalm 90 with regard to Mosaic authorship (Franz Delitzsch, *Biblical Commentary on the Psalms,* tr. Francis Bolton [Grand Rapids: Eerdmans, reprint of 1867 edition], III: pp 48–49).

6. Some commentators suggest approaching a psalm without any assumption about its authorship. This might work in favor of a focused exegesis of the passage. Unfortunately, in practical terms this often means denying David wrote psalms, a denial that violates the idea of approaching without making assumptions about the authors.

wrote had a greater fulfillment, then there is a stronger support for specific authorship. So Davidic authorship cannot be rejected so easily. Even if the superscriptions were added later than the composition of the psalm, they record ancient traditions about the psalms and therefore deserve serious consideration.

Historical Notices

The superscriptions also contain historical references to events in the life of David; these, too, will have bearing on the question of authorship in that they preserve an ancient tradition. The period of David's life covered in 1 Samuel 16 through 2 Samuel provides the setting for several psalms ascribed to him. The correlations are as follows: 1 Samuel 19:11 with Psalm 59; 1 Samuel 21:10–15 with Psalm 56; 1 Samuel 21:10–22:2 with Psalm 34; 1 Samuel 22:9 with Psalm 52; 1 Samuel 23:15–23 with Psalm 54; 1 Samuel 23:24–29 with Psalm 7; 1 Samuel 24 or 22:1–2 with Psalm 57 (Ein Gedi or Adullam); 1 Samuel 24 or 22:1–2 with Psalm 142 (same two caves possible); 2 Samuel 8:8, 13 and 1 Chron. 18:9–12 with Psalm 60; 2 Samuel 22 with Psalm 18; 2 Samuel 11, 12 (12:1–15) with Psalm 51; 2 Samuel 15–18 with Psalm 3; 2 Samuel 15:23 with Psalm 63; and 1 Chronicles 21:1–22:1 with Psalm 30.

Critical Discussion

Because some of these psalms do not fit neatly with the passages noted, modern commentators question the validity and value of the historical superscriptions, as well as the reliability of all the notations in the superscriptions. There is not complete agreement on these matters; modern critical writers range in views from the denial that David wrote any psalms to the allowance that he may have written some of them. On the whole, most commentators would consider the psalms to have come from periods later than David, perhaps early in the monarchy, but most likely from the late pre-exilic, exilic, or post-exilic periods. The reasons for dating psalms later is not always stated clearly in the commentaries in the discussion of individual psalms. The reader may simply be told that David could hardly have written this psalm, or the nature of the psalm requires a post-exilic date.

This means that in the commentator's view there are references and theological ideas that do not fit the time of David.

One common explanation of the superscriptions is that they were artificially developed after the return from the exile. Broyles presented this theory fairly clearly. He noted that when the people came back from Babylon, there was in addition to the restored temple a second locus for the revelation of the LORD, namely the Law. Accordingly, the psalms were now literary; as scripture they were correlated with the David of 1st and 2nd Samuel.[7] Broyles then explained that after the exile texts were identified with prominent figures; the Law was associated with Moses, and the Psalms with David.[8]

Goldingay built on this theory by saying that the psalms with historical notices were not written in those circumstances; rather, the object of the scribal activity was to link these psalms with events in David's life in such a way that they would function a little like the collocation of passages in a lectionary (the interest in David generated the headings). It was profitable to look at the Psalm and the passage in Samuel side-by-side. So the headings were more for the use of the psalms than for evidence about their origin. He concluded by saying that the nature of the headings reflects the way David became a hero for Bible readers![9]

This rather involved reconstruction of how the headings came to be—and how David became a hero—is fraught with difficulties.

1. There is absolutely no evidence for it, as Goldingay himself admitted (he said as a theory it just fits the evidence of these psalms in which parts can be connected with the events and parts cannot).

2. Since it is a theory without support, some of its basic assumptions need to be considered. This will have to be done

---

7. Craig C. Broyles, *Psalms* (Peabody, MA: Hendrickson, 1999), 4–5. He does not like to use the word "psalmist" because it suggests that a psalm is the personal expression of that individual; instead, he uses "liturgist, speaker" or "worshiper."

8. Ibid., pp. 27–29.

9. John Goldingay, *Psalms 1–41* (Grand Rapids: Baker, 2006), pp. 28–29.

psalm-by-psalm in order to deal with the passages that are said to be late; but, in general, some of the generalizations should be questioned. For example, there is sufficient evidence in Scripture to show that the Law was basic to Israel's understanding of divine revelation from the very beginning, so to say that after the exile the Law became prominent and the psalms became literary needs to be qualified and supported. Assumptions like this usually require other passages in the Old Testament that seem to indicate the Law was central to their understanding of revelation are also dated later. So the subject is too large for a thorough treatment here; it involves the higher criticism of several books of the Bible.

3. Taken to its natural conclusion, this theory is saying that David was falsely connected to the psalms and his high standing in tradition is artificial. This has repercussions in the New Testament references to David, not all of which can be easily dismissed as general references to the collection. One is left wondering if the biblical statements about David and the psalms (biblical texts and not superscriptions) are true or false.

4. Finally, if the superscriptions represent the deliberate attempt of the post-exilic folks to line up psalms with Davidic events, why did they do that with only fourteen psalms?

It seems to me that it is more plausible to say that knowledge about the occasion of some of the psalms was handed down traditionally and simply recorded where available. This would not be surprising since the Bible clearly shows David's connection with writing and singing psalms. And even if the psalms were put to use in the sanctuary for worship and edification, that does not mean they were not first the works of individual psalmists, or that they had to be late. Such uses of the psalms in Israel's worship appear to be much earlier than the exile.

In this commentary I am not bound simply to say a psalm is David's because a traditional note credited him with the psalm; but neither am I ready to dismiss the tradition without good reason. Each psalm must be studied individually, and then the traditional notes and the modern theories may be equally evaluated critically.

It is true that the message of the psalm does not require a knowledge of the author or of the circumstances, but the assumptions that are made about what is early and what is late will have to be dealt with, not just in a given psalm, but in the theology of the Old Testament as a whole. And while most commentators will state that the author and setting is not that important, they usually try to find settings for the psalm that are later rather than earlier.

In the final analysis, the message of the psalm will come from the exegesis of the psalm itself, without the need for a reference to a specific event. If a historical setting can be plausibly suggested, that would simply be illustrative of the kind of situation the psalm addresses. Poetry seldom references specific events, although some descriptions might hint at an occasion. If a theory of authorship or setting, whether traditional or critical, is made to be the controlling factor in the development of the message, the exegesis may be skewered. It is better to deal with the passages as pieces of literature in their own right and draw the message from what is said in the text.

TRADITIONAL NOTATIONS OF THE TYPES AND FUNCTIONS OF THE PSALMS

Part of the classification of the psalms into types and functions involves the considerations of other headings to the psalms.

Names Designating Types of Psalms

1. "Psalm" (מִזְמוֹר), the heading for fifty-seven psalms, refers to a musical composition; the verb connected to it (זָמַר) may have the sense of "singing praises accompanied by instruments." It became a technical term designating a song that is accompanied by a (stringed) instrument.[10]

---

10. Mowinckel, Sigmund, *The Psalms in Israel's Worship*, translated by D. R. Ap-Thomas (New York: Abingdon Press, 1967), p. 208.

2. "Song" (שִׁיר) is a common term for both cultic and secular songs. The term is used in some thirty titles, some of which are also labeled "Psalm" (e.g., Pss. 65, 75, 76, 92).

3. "A Contemplative Poem" (מַשְׂכִּיל) is found with thirteen psalms. There is little agreement concerning the translation of the term; the proposals include "an efficacious song" (Mowinckel), "a meditation" (Delitzsch), or "a skillful psalm" (Ewald). All of these draw on the etymological connection to the verb "be wise, prudent, successful" (שָׂכַל).

4. "An Inscribed Poem" (מִכְתָּם) is found in six psalms (16, 56–60). Its meaning is disputed: in later Hebrew (and the Greek) it means "inscription poem," "epigram," or "a poem containing pithy sayings." Mowinckel suggested it was "a song of atonement" because it appeared related to the Akkadian *katamu,* "to atone."[11]

5. "Prayer" (תְּפִלָּה) is the heading for Psalms 17, 86, 90, 102, and 142 (note also 72:20). It may denote more than prayer, sometimes referring to a prayer song that includes praise with the prayer (see Hab. 3:1 and Jonah 2:1).

6. "Praise" (תְּהִלָּה) is found only with Psalm 145, a psalm which is at the beginning of the great doxology to the whole collection, Psalms 145–150.

7. "A Song of Love" (שִׁיר יְדִידֹת) is the heading of Psalm 45 (literally "a song of loves"), which is a celebration of the royal wedding.

8. "Lamentation" (שִׁגָּיוֹן) is found only with Psalm 7. It may mean a psalm of "lamentation,"[12] but it may be connected with the root שָׁגָה, "to wander," and therefore characterize the song with irregular structure or variation of feeling.

---

11. Mowinckel, *The Psalms in Israel's Worship,* p. 209.
12. Ibid., p. 209.

Names Designating Functions

1. "For the Sabbath Day" (לְיוֹם הַשַּׁבָּת) is found with Psalm 92. This psalm in particular was designated for use at Sabbath services.

2. "For Acknowledgment" (or "For Thanksgiving," לְתוֹדָה) is the heading on Psalm 100. This psalm may have been used to accompany the *todah* sacrifice in the services (see Praise Psalms).

3. "To Remind" (לְהַזְכִּיר) heads Psalms 38 and 70. The term may be connected with the so-called "memorial" (אַזְכָּרָה) sacrifice (see Lev. 2:2, 9); if so, it would be related to the dedication of the psalmist. The title may have been intended to remind the LORD of the plight of the psalmist, or to remind the people of the works of the LORD.

4. "A Song for the Dedication of the House" (שִׁיר חֲנֻכַּת הַבַּיִת) is the title with Psalm 30. Various theories have been put forward for this note and the psalm, ranging from David's sin of presumption before the purchase of the site for the temple, to the cleansing of the temple and festival of lights in the Hasmonean period. See the discussion of Psalm 30.

5. "A Song of Ascents" or "A Song of Goings-Up" (שִׁיר הַמַּעֲלוֹת) is the heading for each of Psalms 120–134. The AV had "Song of Degrees," presumably thinking of the development of ideas in each psalm. Most commentators understand it to refer to the Israelites' "going up" to Jerusalem to the festivals, hence, "Pilgrim Song."[13]

6. "For Instruction" (לְלַמֵּד) or "to teach" (AV) is part of the title of Psalm 60. Kirkpatrick suggested it meant the psalm was to be learned by heart (cf. Deut. 31:19; 2 Sam. 1: 18) and

---

13. See C. C. Keet, *A Study of the Psalms of Ascents: A Critical and Exegetical Commentary upon Psalms CXX to CXXXIV* (London: Mitre, 1969), pp.1–17.

recited at public occasions.[14] Mowinckel doubted that it was liturgical; he suggested it was to encourage the people[15]

7. "A Prayer of the Afflicted When He Pines Away and Pours Out His Complaint before the LORD" is the heading for Psalm 102:

תְּפִלָּה לְעָנִי כִי־יַעֲטֹף וְלִפְנֵי יְהוָה יִשְׁפֹּךְ שִׂיחוֹ

THE COMPILATION OF THE PSALMS

The reader of modern translations of the Bible will notice other headings in the Psalter: "Book I" heads Psalms 1–41; "Book II," Psalms 42–72; "Book III," Psalms 73–89; "Book IV," Psalms 90–106; and "Book V," Psalms 107–150. This arrangement of the Psalter into five books is not a modern arrangement; it reflects the final editing of the collection in the post-exilic community. It is very difficult to reconstruct how the psalms came to be arranged this way. Some commentators simply say it is impossible, and others try to do it. The findings of such attempts are preliminary and sketchy, but they do demonstrate that the psalms were not arbitrarily added to the collection. The following summary is a hypothetical proposal, but there are enough hints in the psalms to suggest it is a defensible proposal.

Evidence of Earlier Collections

The Psalter is not the work of one single author, nor is its arrangement the result of one act of compilation. It is the product of various collections made over the centuries, although exactly how all that happened step-by-step is beyond reconstructing with any certainty.

The final and present arrangement of the collection is divided into the five books. Each of the books ends with a doxology: Book I in Psalm 41:13; Book II in Psalm 72:18–19; Book III in Psalm 89:52; Book IV in Psalm 106:48; and Book V in Psalm 150:6,

---

14. Kirkpatrick, *Psalms,* xxviii.
15. Mowinckel, *The Psalms in Israel's Worship,* p. 217.

after the grand doxology of several psalms. These doxologies are present in the Greek translation and so the fivefold division or basis of it is probably as early as that (by about 200 B.C.).

This five-book arrangement was a rearrangement of earlier, smaller collections. There are several clues for this in the book itself.

1. The Psalter contains a number of duplicates (Ps. 14 = 53; Ps. 40:13–17 = 70:1–5; Ps. 108 = 57:7–11 + 60:5–12). One original collection would probably not have retained such (unless for some liturgical purpose).

2. Psalm 72:20 says the prayers of David end, but the present Psalter has about 18 "Davidic" psalms after this note.

3. There is a noticeable change in titling at the beginning of the psalms. Most of the first ninety psalms are ascribed to various people, while most of the rest (91–150) are anonymous; there are also less musical and liturgical indicators in the second half of the book.

4. Some psalms show a preference for the name "Yahweh" and others for the title "God." In Book I (Pss. 1–41) "Yahweh" occurs approximately 278 times and "God" only 15 times; in Book II (Pss. 42–72) "God" occurs 164 times and "Yahweh" only 30. If we look at Psalms 42–83, the figures are 201 occurrences of "God" and 44 of "Yahweh." Furthermore, in Psalms 84–89 "Yahweh" occurs 31 times and "God" only 7 times. In Psalms 90–150 (Books IV and V), "Yahweh" occurs 339 times and "God" only 9 times. A. A. Anderson rightly said, "The variation can hardly be accidental and without any significance."[16] He suggested that the phenomenon represents editorial activity (compare Pss. 14 and 53), pointing to at least two older collections. Other commentators have suggested, however, that this difference may be due to the tendency to substitute the holy name (the *tetragrammaton* or four letters—יהוה)

---

16. A. A. Anderson, *Psalms 1–72* (Grand Rapids: Eerdmans, 1996), p. 25.

with other terms, but this would not fully explain the increased use of the name in the last two books if they reflect a post-exilic time. So the question remains as to why the name is in some psalms and not others.

The recovery of any early collections is practically impossible. We have clues in some psalms as to their place in the collections and their function in the sanctuary, but all we have is the final arrangement. And yet that in itself may give some ideas of the themes that were employed in earlier collections and how the emphasis changed in the later.

The Formation of the Collection

The Jewish explanation of the division into five books is expressed in the Midrash on Psalm 1, which says, "as Moses gave five books of law to Israel, so David gave five books of Psalms to Israel."[17] This may provide a helpful comparison since David dominates the Psalter as Moses does the Pentateuch; but the process of collecting, editing, and arranging the psalms was much more complex. Any attempt at reconstruction will have problems, but the following makes good sense.

Individual Poems

From the beginning individual psalms were collected in the sanctuary for use in regular worship, some written for the worship, and others written in individual, personal experiences. Not all psalms and songs were collected; the song of Moses and Miriam (Exod. 15), the song of Moses (Deut. 32), the song of Deborah (Jud. 5), and the song of Jonah (Jonah 2), are but a few samples of psalms that were not deposited in the Temple for use in worship. The song of David (2 Sam. 22 and Ps. 18) may provide an example of a song that was composed in a certain situation (2 Sam.) and then was adopted and slightly adapted (Ps. 18) for worship at the sanctuary. They were given over to the chief musician who would collect them

---

17. See William G. Braude, *The Midrash on the Psalms* (New Haven: Yale University Press, 1954); see another discussion of this structure in N. H. Smith, *Hymns of the Temple* (1951), pp. 18–20.

for temple use. First Chronicles 16:4 reports that various guilds were appointed to sing such psalms in the sanctuary.

Collections of Psalms

Collections of these songs were formed fairly early. Psalm 72:20 testifies to the existence of an early collection of the prayers of David; but some in the collection must have been moved to other books in the final arrangement. Then, according to 2 Chronicles 29:30, "Hezekiah the king and the princes commanded the Levites to sing praises to the LORD with words of David and of Asaph the seer." This may indicate that in Hezekiah's time (ca. 700 B.C.) there were two collections of psalms. Most of Asaph's works are in the present Book III (Pss. 73–83), but Psalm 50 is in Book II.

Psalms 120–134 form another collection known as "Pilgrim Psalms." However, since some of these psalms are post-exilic, the final, present form of this collection must be late, even though earlier collections of psalms for pilgrim festivals probably existed (Ps. 137 refers to the custom of singing the songs of Zion).

Collection into Books

The smaller collections of psalms were then reorganized into the five books with the addition of the later psalms. It may be that these five collections were formed gradually over a long period of time, but it seems more likely that they were arranged in the post-exilic period. This may have involved less rearrangement for the first two books than for the last three, because the last three seem to rearrange the psalms to reflect the destruction and restoration of the nation.

There does not seem to be an obvious argument running through the Psalter, but there is evidence of a design for the final arrangement that involves the messages of the psalms. This arrangement has been receiving a good deal of renewed attention in recent years, although not all the proposals are convincing. Due to the complexity of the psalms, the proposals have to generalize the messages of the psalms somewhat to see the patterns. So this needs refinement to be more convincing, but the research is still in the early stages.

Those who study the arrangement of the Psalter conclude that it was deliberately planned with theological and historical contexts in mind.[18] In general, Books I and II lay out the foundation of God's program in the Davidic monarchy, Book III reflects the failure of the monarchy and was shaped with the exile in mind, and Books IV and V present the restoration and the hope for the future with the LORD as king.

The final compilation therefore came after the traumatic experience of the exile and the joyous renewal of the faith in the restoration. The people no longer had a king, but they knew that eventually there would be one; they had seen their world collapse, but through it all they had come to a fresh understanding of Yahweh as their king, and their praises were broadened to reflect his sovereignty over all the nations. Back in the land they restored the Temple for worship, but they also restored the study of the Torah in a fresh way (it had fallen by the way as the nation slid into idolatry before the exile). The proposal for this arrangement of the collection is that it reflects in a very general way the sweeping changes in Israel's history, but because it does so by arranging psalms that have fitting messages into the different sections, there is no clear presentation of the history of Israel. For that one would read Chronicles. No, this is poetry arranged to reflect the periods. Each psalm retains its own meaning, but when placed in a specific section of the hymnal, it also applies to that context. It would be very easy to say the psalms were actually written at the times that each book reflects, but this is an unnecessary conclusion for the way the collection was arranged. For example, a psalm of praise for victory over the enemies that was written early could easily have been put with psalms of praise for deliverance from the exile.

Psalms 1 and 2 together form the introduction to the whole Psalter.[19] Psalm 1 introduces the human responsibility for remaining faithful to the Law of the LORD in a confusing and chaotic world; and Psalm 2 introduces the divine provision of a

---

18. See in particular Gerald Wilson, *The Editing of the Hebrew Psalter* (Chico, CA: Scholar's Press, 1985); and J. Clinton McCann, Jr., *The Shape and Shaping of the Hebrew Psalter* (Sheffield: JSOT Press, 1993).

19. They have often been joined together as the introduction because they have no superscriptions, which is unusual for Book I; but they have been joined as one in some copies. Each psalm has its own integrity. See Robert Cole, "An Integrated Reading of Psalms 1 and 2," *JSOT* 98 (2002): pp. 75–88.

king for safety and security in the world for the people of God. Kingship and the Law become the two dominant emphases of the Psalter.

For Books I–III the royal psalms[20] appear in significant places at the seams between books (Psalm 2 is in the introduction), and then each book ends with a royal psalm (Psalms 41,[21] 72 and 89). Books I and II reflect the times of the monarchy, but Book III is a turning point in the collection, giving every indication that the nation under the Davidic kings had failed. The emphasis on Davidic kingship gives way to the celebration of the kingship of Yahweh in Book IV. In the Old Testament the reign of the king and the reign of Yahweh were inseparably bound together; when there was no longer a human monarch, the faithful knew that Yahweh was still reigning, and that would guarantee that the Davidic covenant would be restored. These are some of the ideas that surface frequently in Book V.[22]

Book I

Book I is Psalms 1–41. The royal Psalm 2, the coronation of the king, lays the foundation for this book as well as the whole Psalter. These psalms have a general emphasis on the assurance of the LORD's protection from malicious enemies (Yahweh's special covenant with his king in Psalm 2 is demonstrated by David's protection in the LORD's presence). Many of these psalms record the struggles of the psalmist, traditionally understood to be David; but since his enemies are enemies of the LORD as well, as Psalm 2 makes clear, their opposition will fail.

---

20. The royal psalms focus on some high point in the life of the king. They include Psalms 2, 20, 21, 45, 72, 89, 110, 144, and possibly a few others. They were useful to any king who comes to the throne, and as a result they apply to Jesus the Christ as well, but in a much higher sense than in the original contexts.

21. Psalm 41 is not technically a royal psalm, but since it has several motifs in it that appear in Psalm 72, it functions in much the same way. Books I and II were united and did not need a major break between them.

22. In the New Testament the motifs of the LORD's reign and the reign of the Anointed One, the Messiah, come together in the teachings of the apostles on the incarnation of the Son of God.

Thus the assurance of protection and deliverance comes through in so many of the songs in Book I.

And yet there is also the reminder of the responsibility of the faithful to live in harmony with God's laws so their prayers, their worship, their lives would be acceptable to God. In the middle of Book I is Psalm 19, which extols the value of the Torah.[23]

Book I does not end with a royal psalm as Books II and III do. Psalm 41 has several themes that appear in the royal psalm, Psalm 72, that closes Book II. Both psalms lay out the king's responsibility to protect the people, and both promise the king deliverance from his enemies and security on the throne. The lack of a royal psalm at the end of the first book may attest to the editing of the two books into one large collection of Davidic psalms.

Book II

In Book II, Psalms 42–72, the same themes continue, but in a slightly different way. For example, in Psalm 44 the nation is losing a war, even though it has been faithful to the covenant, but throughout the book confidence remains strong. For example, Psalm 45, a royal wedding psalm, extols the power and righteousness of the king who would be victorious over the enemies. And then there are songs of Zion, the place of strength for the nation because the LORD is there (Ps. 46). The language of some of these psalms is reminiscent of Isaiah 7 and 8 and the great Assyrian invasion. In the center of the book attention is given to the responsibility of the people to follow the way of wisdom (Ps. 49), to restore pure worship (Ps. 50),

---

23. There appears to be a general chiastic arrangement in the heart of Book I that emphasizes the *Torah*:

> **Ps. 15** Liturgy at the Gate: "Who may ascend?"
>> **Ps. 16** God's Blessings for his People: "The LORD is my cup"
>>> **Ps. 17** A Prayer for Deliverance from the Enemies
>>>> **Ps. 18** A Royal Psalm concerning Battle
>>>>> **Ps. 19** The *Torah*
>>>> **Ps. 20–21** Two Royal Psalms concerning Battle
>>> **Ps. 22** A Prayer for Deliverance from the Enemies
>> **Ps. 23** God's Blessings for his People: "My cup runs over"
> **Ps. 24** Liturgy at the Gate: "Who may ascend?"

and to find forgiveness for sin (Ps. 51). There follows a return to the struggle with the world; a series of psalms review the psalmist's (David's) flight from enemies in which he holds fast to his faith and gains victory over the surrounding nations. At the end of this book the faith of the community is strong, inspired by psalms expressing the desire to be with the LORD in the sanctuary (Ps. 63), the celebration of the harvest (Ps. 65), praise for answers to prayer (Ps. 66), and the anticipation of people in the world coming to faith (Ps. 67). Psalm 68 recalls the heart of Israel's faith by tracing the procession of God from Sinai to Zion where he ascends on high as the conquering king. Book II closes with a series of prayers for help. Even the final royal psalm, Psalm 72, is a prayer for the reign of the king, that he will be victorious over the enemies, rule from sea to sea in righteousness, and champion the cause of the needy (perhaps implying that these were not being done). Psalm 72 reminds the reader that the Davidic covenant was to be passed on to the next generation.

Book III

Book III, Psalms 73–89, continues some of the same themes, but the disturbing picture of a nation in trouble emerges regularly. The LORD seems to be judging the nation by allowing other nations to inflict suffering on it. Psalms 73 focuses on the difficulty of living by faith in a prosperous but pagan world, and then Psalm 74 describes the devastation of the temple. The focus on divine judgment on the nation surfaces in Psalms 79, 80, 85 and 89 as well; so it is easy to see the selections might have been made to reflect the beginning of the exile. And yet, the sanctuary is still extolled as the lovely and desirable place (Ps. 84); in fact, Zion stands as the epitome of security (Ps. 87). So the psalms in this collection have an emphasis on national disaster set against the backdrop of the glories of Zion. The book ends with a royal psalm, Psalm 89, essentially the Davidic covenant in poetry. In it the psalmist expresses a concern for the future as he looks back to the covenant—he hopes for the restoration of the Davidic king in accordance with the promise of God. Now it seems that God has cast off the covenant, indicating that the future looked bleak.

Book IV

Book IV, Psalms 90–106, marks a shift in the messages of the psalms. Instead of recalling the faith and the triumphs of the monarchy (namely, David), this collection looks back in history to the time of Moses and the exodus—it is often referred to as the Mosaic collection. The collection reminds people of the answer to the dilemma indicated in Book III, namely, that God remains faithful no matter what happens to the nation or its king, for "the LORD reigns" over all the nations. So the section begins with a Psalm "of Moses" (Ps. 90) that laments how God was letting the people die because of their sins, a description of the wilderness wandering that would resonate with the people in the exile. And yet the message is positive: God is the everlasting God, he is still faithful. So this is followed by songs of trust (Pss. 91 and 92), affirming that there is protection from all dangers in the LORD. What is unique and striking about this book is the inclusion of the enthronement psalms, psalms that celebrate "the LORD reigns" over all the earth (see Pss. 93, 96, 97–99), a theme Isaiah declared as well for deliverance from exile (52:7). The enthronement psalms have an eschatological application; they anticipate the age to come in which the nations would come to serve the LORD and the LORD would rule the whole world with righteousness.

Through the exile and the restoration the people came to see the sovereignty of Yahweh in a new light. And the collection of psalms on this timeless theme were therefore placed in Book III. They did not abandon the idea of the Davidic Covenant in Jerusalem, but they saw a great kingdom now in which the LORD himself would come to reign in some way. And his appearance to reign is described in epiphany language taken from the experience at Mount Sinai: lightning, thick clouds, darkness, earthquakes, volcanoes and the like.

The book also includes didactic psalms based on history, such as the warning for people not to harden their hearts when they hear the word of the LORD, a warning based on the failure of the wilderness generation (Ps. 95), as well as instruction in God's faithfulness in protecting and caring for his people (Pss. 104–106).

The division between Book IV and Book V (Psalms 107–150)

is not as clearly distinguishable (Pss. 106 and 107 have similar elements). And there is no royal psalm ending Book IV, but there is a royal psalm near the end of IV (Ps. 101), one near the beginning of Book V (Ps. 110), another in the middle (Ps. 132), and another at the end (Ps. 144). Books IV and V flow together so well that some scholars have seen parallels between sections, such as Psalms 90–101 and 102–110.[24]

Book V

Book V expresses in general the hope of the people for the future, using David as the model (the book is bracketed with Davidic psalms, Pss. 108–110 and 138–145). It includes other collections as well, such as hallel psalms, Psalms 111–118, 135–136; the pilgrim psalms, Psalms 120–134, and the grand doxology, Psalms 146–150.

Psalms 107–117. Book V may be looked at in three parts and a doxology. The first part, Psalms 107–117, begins with the call to give thanks to the LORD for his loyal love (*hôdû*, Ps. 107:1), responding to the plea of Psalm 106:47, "gather us . . . in order that we may give thanks." Psalms 108 and 109 remind the people that faith relies solely on the LORD, and Psalms 111–117 continue the theme of reliance on God. These are praise psalms that later came to be used for the great festivals in Israel: Psalms 111 and 112 declare that Yahweh is worthy of trust, and Psalms 113–117 rehearse his exaltation as well as his trustworthiness.

---

24. See for example, Jinkyu Kim, "The Strategic Arrangement of Royal Psalms in Books IV–V," *WTJ* 70 (2008): pp. 143–57. The parallels are: Pss. 90–91 and Ps. 102 about mourning for the transitory nature of humans and the need to trust in the LORD (90 and 102 have superscriptions of prayer); Ps. 92 and Ps. 103 with a closing hymn of praise for God's care of his people, restricting previous words of transitory life; Ps. 93 and Ps. 104 are praises that focuses on Yahweh's handling of creatures and his just rule; Ps. 95 and Pss. 105–7 show that Yahweh's handling of history serves as spiritual instruction for the nation; Pss. 96–98 and Ps. 108 are prayers for Yahweh's reign over the world and the destruction of the enemies; Ps. 97 and Ps. 109 promise the reign of Yahweh; Pss. 99–100 and Ps. 109 offer the word of trust in Yahweh in Zion in the face of opposition; Ps. 101 and Ps. 110 are two royal psalms that come at the end of each sequence: the charter of the king (101), and the coming of the king-priest in conquest of his enemies (110).

He proved to be the true and living God in the exodus (Ps. 114), and he has no rival among the pagan gods (Pss. 115–116). The doxology (Ps. 117) calls for all people, Israelites and Gentiles, to praise him for his faithful covenant love. At the heart of this first part is the great royal Psalm 110. Putting a very old Davidic psalm in this section of the book delivered a much-needed message to the people: the victory over the enemies of God will be won in an eschatological warfare in which the great Messiah will come to conquer and reign as both king and priest forever. This is the conquest promised in Psalm 2 and hoped for in Psalm 45. So the Davidic Covenant is still operative, but it will be realized in a much grander way than ever before.

Psalms 136–145. If we look next to the third part of Book V, Psalms 136–145, we see that this section also begins with a call to give thanks (*hôdû*) in celebration of the loyal love of the LORD. Psalm 136, the initial praise of this part, repeats the reason for giving thanks line after line—"for his loyal love endures forever." Psalm 137 recalls the exile and raises the question of how can the suffering people of God sing the songs of Zion? While this was a rhetorical question offered in lamentation in the exile, the question is actually answered in Psalms 138–145; for it is David who shows people how to sing the songs of Zion in adversity. Psalm 138 is a burst of praise, and then the rest of the collection (Pss. 139–145, all prayers for deliverance) focus on Yahweh's benevolent protection of his people. Then the royal Psalm 144 picks up the theme of human frailty from Psalm 90, as well as the conquest of the king from Psalm 18, but focuses on God's plan of creation. The end of Psalm 144 provides another eschatological vision of the prosperity of the nation in the kingdom of Messiah (vv. 12–15). For the exiles and those returning from the exile, this last part of the collection would have been very inspirational.

Psalms 118–135. In between these two parts we have the central section of Book V, Psalms 118–135. Here again the section begins with a call to give thanks (*hôdû*) to Yahweh for his loyal love. The psalm is a celebration of the restoration of Israel to the land to become the center of God's program once again. Psalms 118 and 135 correspond in their emphasis on Yahweh's loyal covenant love, forming an *inclusio* for the section. In the middle of the central section of Book V is the massive 119th psalm which shows the primacy of the law in the people's relationship to Yahweh. How are the people to rely on him? The *Torah*! If Book V is in general an answer to the plea of the people to be regathered to the land and reconstituted as the people of God, Psalm 119 provides the means on the human side. Their renewal would depend on their faith; and their faith would be demonstrated by obedience to the law of God. The individual approach to God by faith and the meditation on and obedience to the law was not new; it was simply restated forcefully after the trauma of the nation's failure. Then, following this we have the pilgrim psalms, Psalms 120–134, which focus attention on going up to Zion to offer praise and thanksgiving. Here is a series of songs of faith in Yahweh alone, some having been written much earlier, and a few after the exile. Near the end of them is Psalm 132, which may not be a royal psalm proper, but focuses on David's vow to find a place for the ark, and Yahweh's vow to honor the Davidic covenant. In this place in the Psalter this psalm presents the prospect of the renewal of the Davidic covenant and all the blessings that were promised with it. In fact, Psalms 132–134 (as well as Ps. 125) bring back the centrality of Zion. So the promise of kingship and the focus on the Law bring Book V together.[25]

Psalms 146–150. Finally, the grand doxology of the collection is Psalms 146–150. Psalm 145 is the climax of Book V and the key to the doxology to follow. The theme is introduced in Psalm 145:21. Psalm 146 gives the answer to verse 21a, the individual's praise for the LORD. Psalm 147 includes Israel and Jerusalem in the chorus of praise; Psalm 148 includes the heavenly angelic hosts; Psalm 149 again calls the people to praise; and Psalm 150

---

25. Just as Books I and II were brought together, so Books IV and V seem to have blended. This may be seen in a general chiastic arrangement of their overall pattern:

  90–110 Several Davidic psalms and others that rehearse God's dealings with his people
    111–118 Hallel psalms for worship, ending with the messianic image of the stone
      119 The *Torah*
    120–134 Pilgrim psalms for worship, including the messianic hope (Ps. 132)
  135–145 Several Davidic psalms and others that demonstrate God's faithfulness to his people

calls everything that has breath to praise, answering the theme of Psalm 145:21b.

Conclusions

This, then, is a general summary of some of the findings in the studies of the present arrangement of the Book of Psalms. The observed relationships of the psalms by authors, themes, and repeated motifs are a positive beginning to the study of the arrangement of the Psalter, but as in any study like this there is the tendency to see connections and patterns that may not be there, or if they are there, are only slight. And until the details are worked out to satisfaction, if indeed they can be, it will seem to be artificial and forced. The main caution we have in working with this kind of study is to make sure we are not reading the patterns of Israel's experience reflected in the prophets into the arrangement of various psalms.

Studying the place of psalms in the collection may not have a direct bearing on the exposition of any given psalm because the exposition will be derived from the psalm itself. Studies like this will remind the expositor of the major theological themes of the Psalter, so that when psalms that focus on these themes are addressed they will receive proper attention. The central themes are found in the royal psalms with their focus on the Davidic king, the Zion Psalms with their focus on Jerusalem, and the enthronement psalms with their focus on the sovereign reign of Yahweh. These psalms not only keep the theology of the psalm in mind, but they keep the collection together as well. Expositors must expound the royal psalms especially, not only because they are critical to the arrangement but because they are basic to biblical theology. After all, they are the most frequently quoted psalms in the New Testament, because in the days of Christ the apostles had to discover again how God's timeless program for his king and his holy city would find fulfillment when there was unbelief, rejection, and exile. The apostles knew that the program had not ended, and neither were the passages to be spiritualized away. No, they saw the fulfillment of the royal psalms and the enthronement psalms in the second advent of Christ, the Lord.

And this study will also make expositors aware of how the psalms have been applied in different situations in Israel's history, and this in turn will contribute to applications for today.[26] In the flow of the psalms through the books, from the Davidic experiences to the universal reign of Yahweh over all the earth, prayers and praises and meditations have been gathered and arranged to establish the faith of the people in historical events, restore the faith of the people after traumatic experiences, and refocus their faith on a greater program that includes the nations in the fulfillment of the promises of God to Israel.

---

26. The Psalter is like our hymn books. There are hymns and songs that have been put to use for Advent, Christmas, Easter, the Mission of the Church and the like, whether that was the original intent of the song or not. Association with current worship does influence the way that we use music. For example, "Joy to the World" is a second coming song, but it is used at advent (which celebrates both advents), and in nonliturgical services for Christmas.

HISTORY OF THE
INTERPRETATION
OF THE PSALMS

APPROACHES TO THE STUDY OF THE PSALMS

In view of the complexity of the psalms and the diversity of the literature on them it is difficult to identify and describe the different approaches taken to the study of the psalms over the centuries in a few pages, but as a general introduction to the exposition of the book it is helpful to have some idea of what informs the interpretation taken in different commentaries.

For centuries the church interpreted the psalms in a dogmatic, theological, and messianic way. Patristic and medieval commentators, and even a number of modern commentators, interpreted the psalms with a primary interest in doctrine, notably Christ and his kingdom. On the whole they attributed the collection to David, but were interested more in David's greater son, Jesus. Since the liturgical calendar of the church correlated the feasts of Israel with the work of Christ, it was only natural for the official interpretations of the Psalter to be directed to the same end. What was lost in many cases was attention to the original setting or use of the psalms, as well as the historical development of revelation from the Old Testament to the New.

The psalms also became the pattern for biblical lyrical poetry. The church in different places translated the Psalter into the languages of their worship so that it might be their hymn book as it had been of the Temple. The collection was considered to be the compendium of all theological matter in the Scriptures, both

Old and New Testaments. In particular, through the Psalms God spoke to the church, and in turn, the church spoke to God. On the one hand God's revelation to his elect took the forms of instructions, exhortations, corrections, consolations, promises, and prophecies; and the church on the other hand spoke through the psalms to God through confessions, complaints, prayers, praises and thanksgivings. Thus the psalms were incorporated into the theology and liturgy of the church. On the whole this is one valid use of the psalms, but it has to be selective because not all of the psalms can be correlated easily to Christian theology and worship.

At about the time of the Reformation biblical scholars began to challenge the use of the psalms for dogmatic theology. Eventually, historical criticism came to dominate the scholarly study of the psalms from the 18th to the 20th centuries. Its aim was to determine the date, authorship, composition and unity of the psalms based on literary and analytical methods. It rejected the traditional ideas, especially those recorded in the superscriptions, because the contents of the psalms did not seem to fit the suggested occasion. Instead, by analytical criteria such as theological conceits, references to known events or conditions, poetic form, and language, most of the psalms were ascribed to periods much later than David, many even to the Maccabean period (ca. 150 BCE). In general, more attention was given to the meaning of the Psalter as the hymn book of the second temple.[1] Many of the conclusions that were drawn from this approach were seriously challenged by the emergence of form criticism and the expanding interest in archaeology.

Because this approach became rather subjective, it did not produce consistent results and was therefore unconvincing. And yet, while the more radical conclusions of this approach have not proved helpful, reading a commentary like Briggs' makes the expositors aware of the difficulties and problems in the text, so

---

1. Some of the writers who followed this approach were Duhm, Bernhard, Cheyne, Haupt, and Briggs (the ICC commentary on the Psalms). In addition to the introductions to the Old Testament, see Ovid Sellers, "The Status and Prospects of Research Concerning the Psalms," *The Study of the Bible Today and Tomorrow*, ed. H. R. Willoughby (Chicago: University of Chicago Press, 1947).

that they may try to find plausible solutions. Too many expositors are simply unaware of the difficulties in the text.

In response to the more radical conclusions of this approach, a number of commentators attempted to relate the psalms to Israel's earlier history, particularly the Davidic period, in view of the superscriptions and biblical evidence. They follow what may be termed a historical and literary approach. Even when the psalm does not specify a historical situation, these writers often tried to reconstruct from internal evidence what incident they thought lay behind it. At times their evidence is very sketchy, and at other times a bit more convincing, even though the conclusion might still remain only a working hypothesis. Conservative expositors have found these commentaries helpful because they present arguments against the old literary analytical method and offer plausible alternatives.[2] In using commentaries from proponents of this method, expositors must be careful not to use a hypothetical, reconstructed situation as the basis for the interpretation of the psalm, whether there is a superscription or not. The reconstructions may be correct, but they most often remain unsubstantiated. The message must come from the psalm itself, whether people think it is early or late.

The form critical approach to the psalms changed the way people worked with the psalms dramatically—almost every commentary now tries to identify the literary form and function of the psalm being studied. This approach was pioneered largely by Hermann Gunkel;[3] it seeks to identify the literary form of a psalm by analyzing its structure, vocabulary, and function. To determine the setting of the psalm, Gunkel started from the premise that at first every song in Israel's religion was written to accompany some ritual act (see Deut. 26:5; 1 Sam. 1:24–2:10; 1 Chron. 16:1–37; and Amos 5:21–23). Support for this idea came from liturgical titles in the psalms' superscriptions (e.g.,

---

2. Commentators such as MacLaren, Alexander, Perowne, and Delitzsch attempted to fit the psalms into the biblical period of the monarchy for the most part, by relating them to known events, especially in the life of David if the superscription suggested that connection.

3. Gunkel developed his approach in *Einleitung in die Psalmen*, which he did not live to finish. The work was finished by Joachim Begrich, whom he selected for the task before his death in March, 1932.

tôdāh, "thanksgiving," identified a psalm with the ritual of the *tôdāh* sacrifice; cf. Num. 10:35, 36; Lev. 9:22) as well as comparison with Babylonian hymns which were connected with specific cultic acts.[4] This idea has made the expositor more aware of the situations out of which the psalms grew, or how they were used in the ritual. It is doubtful, however, that every psalm was at first written for the temple worship, even though they all eventually were adapted to such use. Gunkel himself said that the earliest psalms were written by priests for the ritual, and then individual psalms were added to the collection. Still, it is not often easy to show this.

According to form criticism, psalms forming different types must share a common occasion, a common treasure of ideas and moods, common forms of expression, and common motifs. Using these considerations, the psalms have been classified into several types, and these have been expanded and clarified over the years.[5] The common classifications are:

1) Individual Laments (the psalmist prays);

2) Laments of the People (the nation prays);

3) Individual Thanksgivings (the psalmist praises for deliverance);

4) Hymns (the psalmist praises God);

5) Royal Psalms (the king is in the foreground);

---

4. In this the superscriptions were recognized as important to the understanding of the psalms, but the question remains whether they spoke to the origin of the psalm or its use.
5. Some of the better known form critics are Gunkel, Eissfeldt, Engnell, Kittel, H. Schmidt, A. Bentzen, Oesterley, Terrien, and Westermann, who is known especially for his simplification of the method for Psalm studies. For further information, see A. R. Johnson, "The Psalms," *The Old Testament and Modern Study*, ed. by H. H. Rowley, pp. 162–207; H. Gunkel, *The Psalms: A Form Critical Introduction* (Fortress, 1967); and Gene Tucker, *Form Criticism of the Old Testament* (Fortress, 1971).

6) Enthronement Psalms (the rule of Yahweh is celebrated);

7) and minor types: Pilgrim Songs (for pilgrimages to Jerusalem), Songs of Zion (extolling the holy city), Torah Songs (the Law is preeminent), Songs of Victory, Communal Thanksgivings, Psalms of Confidence, Prophetic Psalms, Dirges, Confessionals, and Wisdom Psalms.

Knowing the types of psalms with their patterns can be a great help. The synthesis of the psalms (especially outlining) is made easier when the structures and motifs are clear; lexical studies may be focused when found in different types of psalms; and the tone or mood of a given psalm may be identified more readily to capture the spirit of the passage in the exposition. In addition, the clarification of the translation of the Hebrew tenses has been made a little easier by knowing whether a section of the psalm is an expression of confidence or a prayer.[6] The danger of this approach to the psalms, however, is the tendency to force the psalms into strict forms or settings and not make allowance for the uniqueness of many psalms.

Subsequent work in the psalms has taken form criticism a step further, insisting that the psalms must be interpreted in the light of their function in the cult. Sigmund Mowinckel, the most influential writer in this approach, proposed for the psalms the single cultic setting of a fall festival that was patterned after the Babylonian festival. Guthrie said, "For Mowinckel the *Sitz im Leben*, the actual setting of worship, was the indispensable key to an understanding of formal, cultic songs such as those preserved in the Old Testament."[7] Advocates of this approach follow a traditio-historical method that seeks to reconstruct the occasion on which the psalm was used in the cult. They attempt to do a complete literary analysis, using

---

6. These benefits of form critical studies are not always obvious. Sometimes the proposal for the type of psalm leads to the way a verb or a word is translated, but if the psalm is taken differently, the translations might be different (such as translating a verb as a jussive, a prayer, or a future tense, a note of confidence.

7. H. H. Guthrie, *Israel's Sacred Songs: A Study of Dominant Themes* (Seabury, 1966), p. 15.

everything available to uncover the use, including compositional analysis and comparative religious studies.

Mowinckel compared this festival to the Babylonian Akitu festival, believing that such a festival was disseminated across the Fertile Crescent. He gathered comparable ideas and expressions from the psalms to attest that the same kind of festival was in Israel. His argument drew heavily on certain psalms that celebrated the fact that "the LORD reigns"; hints from postbiblical Hebrew literature that vestiges of some such festival did exist on the first day of the New Year; and the supposition that Israel patterned its cult after the festivals of the surrounding pagan nations. This idea does not stand up under close scrutiny; its theory is too broad, making all the different literary types fit one festival, and it lacks clear evidence, relying on passages selected from throughout the Psalter for the reconstruction.[8]

Mowinckel's demonstration that many of the psalms were associated with some aspect of ritual worship (e.g., Pss. 5:7; 51:9; 66:3; 68:24–27) has proven helpful in understanding the Psalms. However, if there was such an important festival every year in Israel, it is strange that the Old Testament nowhere mentions it.

Others have modified this approach considerably. Artur Weiser connected most of the psalms with a fall festival, but he argued that this festival did not celebrate the enthronement of Yahweh but a renewal of the covenant (cf. Josh. 24). This view, however, also depends on one setting, and that setting cannot account for all the psalms. Hans-Joachim Kraus took a similar approach but presented a more complex picture of the cult. He isolated three formative elements in the traditions of the cult: first, there was a "tent festival" that brought into remembrance Israel's wilderness wanderings; second, there developed a festival of covenant renewal that antedated the monarchy; and, third, there were added the conceptions of kingship and Canaanite mythology during the reigns of David and Solomon.[9] This approach

---

8. W. Brueggemann, *The Message of the Psalms* (Minneapolis: Augsburg, 1984), 18. For further discussion, see K. A. Kitchen, *Ancient Orient and Old Testament* (Inter-Varsity, 1966), pp. 102ff.

9. See H. J. Kraus, *Worship in Israel* (Knox, 1966), pp. 208ff. See also *Psalmen* in the *Biblischer Kommentar Altes Testament* (Neukirchen-Vluyn, 1966).

attempted to incorporate the more diverse elements of Israel's cult but still suffered from the lack of convincing evidence for the proposed cultic setting.

Other approaches have also made an impact on the study of the psalms. James Muilenberg proposed a rhetorical critical approach that would focus on the stylistic features of the individual psalms, but he did not write a commentary that would show how this emphasis informs the interpretation. Brevard Childs gave most attention to the final form of the Psalter to show how the meanings of the psalms were affected by their form and place in the canon (hence, canonical criticism). Gerald Wilson argued that the psalms were collected and compiled with theological intention, focusing more on the present form of the psalm than on a reconstruction of its history. And Walter Brueggemann presented a sociological approach to the psalms. He divided the psalms into three categories, psalms that show how things are supposed to be, psalms that demonstrate things are not as they should be, and psalms that explain how in the final analysis God makes it work. He then proposed a sociological analysis to explain these types.

Most modern scholarship on the Psalms draws from all these approaches in one way or another because they all make helpful contributions to the study. This commentary will also incorporate many of the suggestions of various approaches as they relate to the interpretation of each psalm.

SELECTED BIBLIOGRAPHY

Introductory Works

Anderson, Bernhard H. *Out of the Depths: The Psalms Speak for Us Today.* Philadelphia: Westminster, 1970.

Crenshaw, James L. *The Psalms, An Introduction.* Grand Rapids: Eerdmans, 2001.

Crim, Keith R. *The Royal Psalms.* Richmond, Virginia: John Knox, 1962.

Drijvers, Pius. *The Psalms, Their Structure and Meaning.* New York: Herder and Herder, 1965.

Estes, Daniel J. *Handbook on the Wisdom Books and Psalms.* Grand Rapids: Baker, 2005.

Gunkel, Hermann. *The Psalms: A Form Critical Introduction.* Trans. by Thomas M. Horner. Philadelphia: Fortress, 1967.

Holladay, William L. *The Psalms through Three Thousand Years, Prayerbook of a Cloud of Witnesses.* Minneapolis: Fortress, 1993.

Kraus, Hans-Joachim. *Theology of the Psalms.* Translated by Keith Crim. Minneapolis: Augsburg Publishing House, 1979.

McCann, J. C., Jr. *A Theological Introduction to the Book of Psalms: The Psalms as Torah.* Nashville: Abingdon, 1993.

Mowinckel, Sigmund. *The Psalms in Israel's Worship.* Translated by D. R. Ap-Thomas. New York: Abingdon, 1967.

Sabourin, Leopold. *The Psalms: Their Origin and Meaning.* New York: Alba House, 1974.

Sarna, Nahum M. *Songs of the Heart: An Introduction to the Book of Psalms.* New York: Schocken Press, 1993.

Seybold, Klaus. *Introducing the Psalms.* Edinburgh: T. & T. Clark, 1990.

Tsevat, Matitiahu. "A Study of the Language of the Biblical Psalms." Missoula, MT: *Journal of Biblical Literature* Monograph Series, Volume 9.

Westermann, Claus. *The Praise of God in the Psalms.* Richmond, VA: John Knox, 1965.

Commentaries

Alexander, Joseph Addison. *The Psalms Translated and Explained.* Grand Rapids: Baker Books, 1977 reprint of the 1873 edition.

Allen, Leslie. *Psalms 101–150.* Word Biblical Commentary. Volume 21. Revised Edition. Waco, TX: Word, 2002.

Anderson, A. A. *The Book of Psalms.* New Century Bible. 2 Volumes. London: Marshall, Morgan & Scott, 1972.

Braude, William B., editor. *The Midrash on the Psalms.* London: The Soncino Press,

Briggs, Charles A. and E. G. Briggs. *A Critical and Exegetical Commentary on the Psalms.* The International Critical Commentary. Edinburgh: T. & T. Clark, 1903.

Brueggemann, Walter. *The Message of the Psalms.* Minneapolis: Augsburg, 1984.

_____. *The Psalms and the Life of Faith*. Minneapolis: Fortress, 1995.

Broyles, Craig C. *Psalms. New International Commentary*. Peabody, MA: Hendrickson, 1999.

Buttenwiesser, Moses. *The Psalms*. Chicago: University of Chicago Press, 1938.

Calvin, John. *Commentary on the Book of Psalms*. Translated by James Anderson. 3 Volumes. Reprint. Grand Rapids: Eerdmans, 1963

Clifford, Richard J. *Psalms*. 2 Volumes. Abingdon Old Testament Commentaries. Nashville: Abingdon, 2002, 2003.

Cohen, A. *The Psalms*. Soncino Books of the Bible. London: Soncino, 1945

Craigie, Peter C. *Psalms 1–50*. Word Biblical Commentary. Volume 19. Second Edition. Waco, TX: Word, 2005.

Dahood, Mitchell. *Psalms*. The Anchor Bible. 3 Volumes. Garden City, NY: Doubleday, 1965.

Dalglish, Edward R. *Psalm Fifty-One in the Light of Ancient Near Eastern Patternism*. Leiden: E. J. Brill, 1962.

Delitzsch, Franz. *Biblical Commentary on the Psalms*. 3 Volumes. Translated by Francis Bolton. Grand Rapids: Wm. B. Eerdmans Publishing Co., reprint.

Eaton, John. *Psalms*. Torch Bible Commentaries. London: SCM Press, 1967.

Gerstenberger, Eberhard S. *Psalms and Lamentations*. Forms of Old Testament Literature. 2 Volumes. Grand Rapids: Eerdmans, 1988, 2001.

Goldingay, John. *Psalms*. 3 Volumes. Grand Rapids: Baker, 2006.

Goulder, Michael D. *The Psalms of the Sons of Korah*. Journal for the Study of the Old Testament Series 20. Sheffield: JSOT, 1982.

Gunkel, Hermann. *Die Psalmen*. Goettingen: Vandenhoeck und Ruprecht, 1926.

Jacquet, L. *Les Psaumes et le couer de l'homme. Etude textuelle, litteraire et doctrinale*. 3 Volumes. Gembloux: Duculot, 1975.

Kidner, Derek. *Psalms 1–72, Psalms 73–150*. 2 Volumes. London: InterVarsity, 1975.

Kirkpatrick, A. F. *The Book of Psalms*. The Cambridge Bible for Schools and Colleges. Cambridge: At the University Press, 1906. Reprint by Baker Books.

Kraus, Hans-Joachim. *Psalms 1–59, Psalms 60–150.* 2 Volumes. Minneapolis: Augsburg, 1988.

Leupold, H. C. *Exposition of the Psalms.* Grand Rapids: Baker, 1969.

Luther, Martin. *First Lectures on the Psalms.* 2 Volumes. Volumes 10 and 11 of *Luther's Works,* ed. by H. C. Oswald et al. St. Louis: Concordia, 1974–6.

Mays, James L. *Psalms.* Interpretation. Louisville: Knox, 1994.

McCann, J. Clinton. "The Book of Psalms," in *The New Interpreter's Bible,* Volume 4. Ed. by Leander E. Keck. Nashville: Abingdon, 1996. 639–1280.

Moll, Carl Bernhard. *The Psalms.* Lange's Commentary on the Holy Scriptures. Edited by John Peter Lange. Grand Rapids: Zondervan Publishing House, reprint of the 1869 edition.

Oesterley, W. O. E. *The Psalms.* London: S.C.K., 1962.

Perowne, J. J. Stewart. *The Book of Psalms.* 2 Volumes. Grand Rapids: Zondervan, reprint of 1878 edition.

Rogerson, J. W. and McKay, J. W. *Psalms.* 3 Volumes. The Cambridge Bible Commentary. Cambridge: Cambridge University Press, 1977.

Terrien, Samuel. *The Psalms.* Grand Rapids: Eerdmans, 2002.

Tate, Marvin. *Psalms 51–100.* Word Biblical Commentary. Volume 20. Waco, TX: Word, 1991.

VanGemeren, Willem. *Psalms.* The Expositor's Bible Commentary. Grand Rapids: Zondervan, 2008.

Weiser, Artur. *The Psalms: A Commentary.* Philadelphia: Westminster, 1962.

Wilson, Gerald H. *Psalms.* NIV Application Commentary. Grand Rapids: Zondervan, 2002.

The Psalms as Poetry

Alden, Robert. "Chiastic Psalms." *Journal of the Evangelical Theological Society* 17 (1974):11–18; 19 (1976):191–200; 21 (1978):199–210.

Alonso-Schoekel, Luis. *Estudios de Poetica Hebrea.* Barcelona: Juan Flors, 1963.

_____. "Hermeneutics in the Light of Language and Literature." *Catholic Biblical Quarterly* 25 (1963):371–386.

Alter, Robert. *The Art of Biblical Poetry.* New York: Basic Books, 1985.

Berlin, Adele. *The Dynamics of Biblical Parallelism.* Bloomington: Indiana University Press, 1985.

Boling, R. G. "Synonymous Parallelism in the Psalms." *Journal of Semitic Studies* 5 (1960):221–255.

Bright, John. *Jeremiah.* The Anchor Bible. Garden City, NY: Doubleday, 1965. cxxvi–cxxxviii.

Bywater, Ingram. *Aristotle on the Art of Poetry.* Oxford: At the Clarendon Press, 1909.

Bullinger, E. W. *Figures of Speech Used in the Bible.* Grand Rapids: Baker Book House, reprint of 1898 edition.

Caird, G. B. *The Language and Imagery of the Bible.* Philadelphia: Westminster, 1980.

Casanowicz, Immanuel M. *Paronomasia in the Old Testament.* Boston: Norwood Press, 1894.

Craigie, C. "Psalm 29 in the Hebrew Poetic Tradition." *Vetus Testamentum* 22 (1972):143–151.

Driver, G. R. "Poetic Diction." *Supplement to Vetus Testamentum* 1 (1953):26-39.

Empsom, W. *Seven Types of Ambiguity.* London: Chatto and Windus, 1947.

Engnell, Ivan. "The Figurative Language of the Old Testament." In *Critical Essays of the Old Testament.* Edited by John T. Willis. London: S.C.K., 1970.

Gevirtz, Stanley. *Patterns in the Early Poetry of Israel.* Chicago: The University of Chicago Press, 1963.

Good, Edwin. *Irony in the Old Testament.* London: S.P.C.K., 1965.

Honeyman, A. M. "*Merismus* in Biblical Literature." *Journal of Biblical Literature* 85 (1966):401–435.

Howard, David M. *The Structure of Psalms 93–100.* Biblical and Judaic Studies from the University of California, San Diego, 5. Winona Lake, IN: Eisenbrauns, 1997.

_____. "Recent Trends in Psalms Study." In *The Face of Old Testament Studies: A Survey of Contemporary Approaches.* Ed. by David W. Baker and Bill T. Arnold. Grand Rapids: Baker, 1999.

Jackson, Jared J., and Kessler, Martin. *Rhetorical Criticism. Essays in Honor of James Muilenberg.* Pittsburgh: The Pickwick Press, 1974.

Keel, Othmar. *The Symbolism of the Biblical World. Ancient Near Eastern Iconography and the Book of Psalms.* Translated by Timothy J. Hallett. New York: Seabury, 1978.

Kikawada, Isaac M. "Some Proposals for the Definition of Rhetorical Criticism." *Semitics* 5 (1977):67–91.

Kraus, Hans-Joachim. *The Theology of the Psalms.* Trans. by Keith Crim. Minneapolis: Fortress, 1992 (original date 1979).

Kugel, James L. *The Idea of Biblical Poetry.* London: Longman Group Ltd., 1969.

Laney, J. Carl. "A Fresh Look at the Imprecatory Psalms." *BibliothecaSacra* 138 (1981):35–45.

Lewis, C. S. *Reflections on the Psalms.* New York: Harcourt, Brace and World, 1958.

Longman, Tremper, III. *Literary Approaches to Biblical Interpretation.* Grand Rapids: Zondervan, 1987.

Lowth, Robert. *Lectures on the Sacred Poetry of the Hebrews.* Translated by G. Gregory. Andover: Codman Press, 1829.

Mays, James Luther. *The Lord Reigns: A Theological Handbook to the Psalms.* Louisville: Westminster John Knox, 1994.

McConville, Gordon. "The Psalms: Introduction and Theology." *Evangel* 11 (1993):43–54.

Muilenberg, James. "Form Criticism and Beyond." *Journal of Biblical Literature* 81 (1969):1–18.

_____. "A Study in Hebrew Rhetoric: Repetition and Style." *Supplement to Vetus Testamentum* 1 (1953):97–111.

Payne, D. F. "Old Testament Exegesis and the Problem of Ambiguity." *ASTI* 5 (1967):48–68.

Preminger, A., Warnke, F. J., and Hardison, O. B. *Princeton Encyclopedia of Poetry and Poetics.* Revised Edition. Princeton: Princeton University Press, 1975.

Rankin, O. S. "Alliteration in Hebrew Poetry." *Journal of Theological Studies* 31 (1930):285–300.

Roberts, J. J. M. "The Enthronement of Yhwh and David: The Abiding Theological Significance of the Kingship Language of the Psalms." *Catholic Biblical Quarterly* 64 (2002):675–86.

Robinson, Theodore H. "Hebrew Poetic Form: The English Tradition." *Supplement to Vetus Testamentum* 1 (1953):128–149.

_____. *The Poetry of the Old Testament*. London: Duckworth, 1947.

Saydon, "Assonance in Hebrew as a Means of Expressing Emphasis." *Biblica* 36 (1955):36–50; 287–304

Shepherd, John. "The Place of the Imprecatory Psalms in the Canon of Scripture." *Churchman* 111 (1997):27–47, 110–26.

Slotki, Israel W. "Antiphony in Ancient Hebrew Poetry." *Jewish Quarterly Review* 26 (1935):199–219.

Waltke, Bruce K. "Superscripts, Postscripts, or Both." *Journal of Biblical Literature* 110 (1991):583–96.

Watts, John D. W. "A History of the Use and Interpretation of the Psalms." In *An Introduction to Wisdom Literature and the Psalms*. Ed. by H. Wayne Ballard and W. Dennis Tucker. Macon, GA: Mercer University Press, 2000. 21–35.

Watson, W. G. E. *Classical Hebrew Poetry*. Journal for the Study of the Old Testament Supplement Series 26. Sheffield: JSOT, 1984.

Watters, William R. *Formula Criticism and the Poetry of the Old Testament*. Berlin and New York: Walter de Gruyter, 1976.

Westermann, Claus. *The Living Psalms*. Trans. by J. R. Porter. Grand Rapids: Eerdmans, 1989 (original date 1984).

Additional Resources for the Study of the Psalms

Anderson, G. W. "Enemies and Evildoers in the Book of Psalms." *Bulletin of the John Rylands Library* 48 (1965):18–29.

Beckwith, Roger T. "The Early History of the Psalter." *Tyndale Bulletin* 46 (1995):1–27.

Bonhoeffer, Dietrich, *Meditating on the Word*. Minneapolis: Augsburg, 1970.

_____. *Psalms, The Prayer Book of the Bible*. Minneapolis: Augsburg, 1970.

Borowski, Oded. *Agriculture in Iron Age Israel*. Winona Lake, IN: Eisenbrauns, 1987.

Braun, Joachim. *Music in Ancient Israel/Palestine*. Grand Rapids: Eerdmans, 2002.

Chisholm, Robert B., Jr. *From Exegesis to Exposition. A practical Guide to Using Biblical Hebrew.* Grand Rapids: Baker, 1998.

Cole, Robert L. *The Shape and Message of Book III (Psalms 73–89).* Journal for the Study of the Old Testament: Supplement Series 307. Sheffield: Sheffield Academic Press, 2000.

Day, John. *Psalms.* Old Testament Guides. Sheffield: JSOT Press, 1990.

Dell, Katharine J. "The Use of Animal Imagery in the Psalms and Wisdom Literature of Ancient Israel." *Scottish Journal of Theology* 53 (2000):275–91.

DePinto, B. "The Torah and the Psalms." *Journal of Biblical Literature* 86 (1967):154–174.

Eaton, J. H. *Kingship and the Psalms.* London: SCM, 1976.

Engnell, Ivan. *Studies in Divine Kingship in the Ancient Near East.* Uppsala, 1943.

Fensham, F. C. "Widow, Orphan, and the Poor in Ancient Near Eastern Legal and Wisdom Literature." *Journal of Near Eastern Studies* 21 (1962):129–139.

Finkelstein, L. "The Origin of the Hallel (Pss. 113–118)." *Hebrew Union College Annual* 23 (1950):319–337.

Fisher, L. R., editor. *Ras Shamra Parallels. The Texts from Ugarit and the Hebrew Bible.* 2 Volumes. Rome:AnOr, 1972. See especially "Literary Phrases" by Schoors, 1–70; "Ugaritic-Hebrew Parallel Pairs" by Dahood and Penar, 383–452; and "Flora, Fauna, and Minerals" by Sasson.

Gillingam, Susan E. *The Poems and Psalms of the Hebrew Bible.* Oxford Bible Series. Oxford: Oxford University Press, 1994.

_____. "Studies of the Psalms: Retrospect and Prospect." *Expository Times* 119 (2008):209–216.

Hareuveni, Nogah. *Desert and Shepherd in Our Biblical Heritage.* Translated by Helen Frenkley. Neot Kedumim, Israel, 1991.

Harmon, A. M. "Aspects of Paul's Use of the Psalms." *Westminster Journal of Theology* 32 (1969):1–23.

Hayes, John H., and Holladay, Carl R. H. *Biblical Exegesis, A Beginner's Handbook.* Atlanta: John Knox, 1982.

Hilber, John W. *Cultic Prophecy in the Psalms.* New York: Walter de Gruyter, 2005.

Hooke, S. H., editor. *Myth and Ritual. Essays on the Myth and Ritual of the Hebrews in Relation to the Cultic Pattern of the ANE.* Oxford: Clarendon Press, 1933.

Jaki, Stanley L. *Praying the Psalms, A Commentary.* Grand Rapids: Eerdmans, 2001.

Jenni, Ernst, and Westermann, Claus. Translated by Mark E. Biddle. *Theological Lexicon of the Old Testament.* 3 Volumes. Peabody, MA: Hendrickson, 1997 (original German edition, 1976).

Keet, C. C. *A Study of the Psalms of Ascents. A Critical and Exegetical Commentary upon Psalms 120–134.* London, 1969.

Knight, Jack C., and Sinclair, Lawrence A. *The Psalms and Other Studies on the Old Testament Presented to Joseph I. Hunt.* Nashotah, WI: Nashotah House, 1990.

Kraus, Hans-Joachim. *Worship in Israel.* Oxford: Clarendon Press, 1966.

Lamb, J. A. *The Psalms in Christian Worship.* London, 1962.

Lipinski, E. "*Yahweh malak.*" *Biblica* 44 (1963):405–460.

McCann, J. C. Jr., ed. *The Shape and Shaping of the Psalter.* Journal for the Study of the Old Testament Supplement Series 159. Sheffield: Sheffield Academic, 1993.

McKeating, H. "Divine Forgiveness in the Psalms." *Scottish Journal of Theology* 18 (1965):69–83.

McKenzie, J. L. "Royal Messianism." *Catholic Biblical Quarterly* 19 (1957):25–52.

Moreton, M. J. "The Sacrifice of Praise." *Church Quarterly Review* 165 (1964):481–494.

Morgenstern, J. "The Cultic Setting of the Enthronement Psalms." *Hebrew Union College Annual* 35 (1964):1–42.

Mowinckel, Sigmund. *The Psalms in Israel's Worship.* Translated by D. R. Ap-Thomas. 2 Volumes. Nashville: Abingdon, 1962. Reprint Eerdmans, 2004.

Pritchard, James. *Ancient Near Eastern Texts Relating to the Old Testament.* Princeton: Princeton University Press, 1969.

Rabinowitz, L. J. "The Psalms in Jewish Liturgy." *Historia Judaica* 6 (1944):109–122 (cf. *CBQ* 1945, 353).

Ross, J. P. "*Yahweh Seba'ot* in Samuel and Psalms." *Vetus Testamentum* 17 (1967):76–92.

Ross, Allen P. *Recalling the Hope of Glory*. Grand Rapids: Kregel, 2006. Pp. 221–292.

Rowley, H. H. *Worship in Israel*. London: SCM Press, Ltd., 1967.

Snaith, N. H. "Selah." *Vetus Testamentum* 2 (1952):42–56.

VanGemeren, Willem, ed. *The New International Dictionary of Old Testament Theology and Exegesis,* 5 Volumes. Grand Rapids: Zondervan, 1999.

Walton, John H. *Ancient Israelite Literature in Its Cultural Context: A Survey of Parallels Between Biblical and Ancient Near Eastern Texts*. Grand Rapids: Zondervan, 1989.

Weiss, Meier. *The Bible from Within: The Method of Total Interpretation*. Jerusalem: Magnes, 1984.

Wieder, Laurence, ed. *The Poets Book of Psalms. The Complete Psalter as Rendered by Twenty-Five Poets from the Sixteenth to the Twentieth Centuries*. Oxford: Oxford University Press, 1995.

Wilson, Gerald H. *The Editing of the Hebrew Psalter*. Society of Biblical Literature Dissertation Series 76. Chico, CA: Scholars, 1985.

Wolff, Hans Walter. *Anthropology of the Old Testament*. Philadelphia: Fortress, 1974.

Wright, G. E. *The Old Testament Against Its Environment*. London: SCM, 1950.

Yadin, Yigael. *The Art of Warfare in Biblical Lands*. New York: McGraw-Hill, 1963.

INTERPRETING
BIBLICAL POETRY

Expositors have to develop a keen understanding of poetic language when working in the Book of Psalms. This cannot be developed quickly; they have to "live" in the experiences of the poets to begin to see what they saw, feel what they felt, and think what they thought. And they will come to realize that poetic language does not simply embellish the text with pictures but serves to convey ideas in their fullest meanings.

THE NATURE OF POETRY

Poetry will take the reader beyond the straightforward meanings of words to their intellectual and emotional connotations. Poets want to excite in the reader or listener the ideas and feelings that they had when they wrote. In effect they recreate their emotional experience by the choice of words so that the reader may enter into the experience. To communicate such ideas and emotions necessarily requires the use of figurative language. People think in pictures and symbols, and their conversations are filled with such expressions.[1] Thus, beautifully written

---

1. It should be clear that poets use images drawn from their culture and experience. While some of these images will be universal, some will not. The expositor will be helped greatly by a good knowledge of the history and culture of the biblical writers. Books like Othmar Keel's *The Symbolism of the*

literature that employs effective figures of speech is both satisfying to the human desire for aesthetics and meaningful to the
human need for images.[2]

It should come as no surprise, then, that poetic language can
be found on almost every page of the Bible, both the Old and
New Testaments. God chose to communicate his truth to people
with high and low figure! Such language not only brings an aes-
thetic quality to the Scriptures but also a level of human experience so that the words may be fully understood.

It might help to think in terms of the poetic composition before discussing how the interpreter works from the finished composition back to the intended meaning. For example, the prophet
could have said the following in plain terms:

1. The powerful judge of the world is about to perform his
   work.

2. He will come and remove all evil from the earth.

3. He will separate the righteous people from the wicked
   people.

4. The righteous people will be taken to the place that he
   has prepared for them, but the wicked people will endure
   everlasting punishment.

Instead he chose to relate these truths to human activities
that his audience would know in order to engage their total intellectual and emotional identification with the truths. So he compared these truths with the agricultural activity of winnowing,
in which good grain is separated from the worthless chaff that is
mixed with it in the harvest. Thus, proposition #3 above would
say:

Biblical World (New York: Seabury Press, 1978) will provide descriptions
and pictures from archaeology that help the expositor "see" the image.

2. Of course, defining and describing poetic discourse is an enormous and
complicated subject. These few comments certainly oversimplify the
matter; they are merely intended to help clarify the task of interpreting
figurative language in the process of developing expositions.

3. He will separate the righteous people from the wicked people like a man who separates good grain from worthless chaff in the process of winnowing.

Propositions #2 and #4 would fall into place with comparisons:

2. He will come and remove all evil from the earth like a man who comes to his harvest to remove the worthless chaff.

4. The righteous people will be taken to the place that he has prepared for them like the wheat which is taken into the barn; but the wicked people will endure everlasting punishment like the chaff which is taken to be burned.

Since chaff is not burned forever, it was necessary to add that the punishment of the wicked would be everlasting. One way to do this was to qualify the comparison with fire in some way, such as by adding:

but the kind of fire the wicked face is different.

Proposition #1 announces the imminency of this judgment and so could be graphically illustrated as well:

1. The powerful judge of the world is about to perform his work like a man who picks up a winnowing fork in his hand to head for the threshing floor.

The comparison is a good one, but left in this form would be laborious and cumbersome. So the prophet suppressed all the original propositions and presented an *implied comparison* between the Lord God (in the realm of the spiritual) and winnowing (from the agricultural world). The purpose of the message (hardly to teach how to winnow), the context (the man is Messiah who comes), and a trace of evidence (besides the context) that something other than literal is meant (the fire is unquenchable) all reveal to us the language is figurative and that the implied message is like the picture. So we read Matthew 3:12:

And his winnowing fork is in his hand,
and he will thoroughly clean his threshing-floor,
and he will gather his wheat into the barn,
but he will burn up the chaff with unquenchable fire.

The expositor must work from the poetic language, which is often cryptic and figurative, to reconstruct the intended meaning. The poets do not fully explain their meanings because they are using images that communicate them to their readers, and in fact the literal meaning would not convey as much as the image does. By nature figures are elliptical and evocative, so it is the task of the expositor to supply the ideas that the figure conveys.

But what is the criterion for distinguishing when a word is literal or figurative? We might in general say that a figurative expression is one which, when its component words are employed in the usual or customary way, turns out to be either a patently false or a nonsensical statement (e.g., we are not sheep, the LORD is not a block of stone, and Jesus is not a piece of wood on hinges). In essence, figures exhibit a departure from some rule of usage.[3]

This criterion must be qualified by the following consideration. Poetic language is commonly employed as a device in expository and explanatory discourse—it is meant to help clarify and specify the subject matter. Therefore, figurative expressions must have paraphrases or translations that communicate the

---

3. This means that the expositor will first have to study the usage of the word. The process is fairly simple for the common words: the uses have to be surveyed and then categorized into classes of meanings. Words that deviate from their normal semantic range will then be discovered. For example, a study of the word *son* will show that in the Bible its common meaning is a physical descendant, but there will be passages where it does not retain the literal meaning. For example, it refers to the nation of Israel as God's son (so covenant language uses *son* and *father* terminology), or to the king who is crowned and declared to be the son (also covenant language, but for a different covenant), or to a political dependent (as in a genealogy where *sons* often refer to alliances, or where the king is called a son of the Assyrian king), or to people to describe their nature (as in a son of Belial) or religion (as in son of a false god). Such deviations from normal use have to be explained, and the classifications of the figures helps the expositor to do this.

literal sense, so the conclusion that poetic language is merely fancy and figurative on the one hand, or ambiguous and mystical on the other, fails to understand the nature of poetic language. These two conditions provide a basis for interpreting and evaluating figurative language: there must be an ascertainable point in the deviation from ordinary usage (the violation of usage must be deliberate), and there must be available a literal rendering of the expression in question. The procedure requires that expositors be able to identify the figure of speech used and to articulate its literal meaning as well as the ideas and feelings conveyed with it.

THE STRUCTURE OF HEBREW POETRY

Parallelism

Poetic language in the Book of Psalms is set within the structure of Hebrew poetry. The most frequent and obvious structure is parallelism.[4] This term refers to the recurrent use of a relatively short sentence-form that consists of two (or more) brief clauses (or phrases). Psalm 42:9 reads:

> By day the LORD sends forth his love //
> and at night his song is with me.

The two parallel parts are regularly separated by a slight pause (here represented by parallel lines //), because the second part is a continuation of the first and not a completely new beginning. The second or final part of the line ends in a full pause. It may be diagrammed as

---

4. The complete analysis of parallelism in the Bible (and in other texts such as Ugaritic) is a study in its own rights. This brief overview will present the basic meaning and types of parallelism to help the expositor think in terms of the structure of the verses. I am relying here on the major works on the subject, especially James L. Kugel, *The Idea of Biblical Poetry, Parallelism and Its History* (New Haven: Yale University Press, 1981); and Adele Berlin, *The Dynamics of Biblical Parallelism* (Bloomington: Indiana University Press,1985).

_____ // _____

In English the slight pause may be punctuated with a comma (if punctuation is required), and the full stop with a semicolon (since it is probably a line within a poem) or a period.

This is the basic pattern, but by no means the only one. Throughout the poetry there will be variations of this pattern. A line of poetry may have three brief clauses or even four.

A major interest of anyone who studies the Psalms is the understanding of how these units are related. To help in this pursuit the clauses that are said to be in parallel verse have been given a number of names. The most common description would be "parallel member," but that is cumbersome. They are also referred to as "half-verse" (when there are only two), or "colon" (hence, a line might be made up of two or three "cola"). Whatever they are called, they refer to the short units (clauses, but at times phrases) that make up the line of poetry. They are indicated in the Hebrew text by the use of accents with the words that end the units (although there are exceptions in the text). To scan the parallel construction of a line easily, one would first observe the disjunctive accents to see the divisions preserved by tradition (usually reflected by punctuation in English versions), and then observe the semantic notions of the parts or cola.

The line of poetry (or verse-line) normally will correspond to the English verse division. In the Hebrew text it is marked off by the strongest disjunctive accent, the _sillûq_ (‚), and the corresponding _sôph pāsûq_ (:), meaning "the end of the line," that is written with it. The main division in the verse (called the dichotomy) is marked off with the next strongest disjunctive accent.

If a line contains two of these parallel parts, it may be referred to as a bicolon or couplet. If it contains three, a tricolon (or triplet). And if there are three units, the major division or dichotomy could be after the first or second unit, depending on the meaning of the line. If the line of poetry contains four parallel units, it may be called a quatrain.[5]

---

5. See further Sigmund Mowinckel, _The Psalms in Israel's Worship._ Translated by D. R. Ap-Thomas. Vol. II (New York: Abingdon, 1962), pp. 165–66.

Types of Parallelism

Of course, these terms for poetic structure were not used by the Hebrews. They have been applied by modern scholars because of their use in other, comparable disciplines, to describe the structure of the poetry.

Robert Lowth is the man credited with the "discovery" of biblical parallelism (in 1753). He coined the phrase *parallelismus membrorum*, "the parallelism of the clauses," and set out the patterns of such parallelism for modern studies. He distinguished three types:

1. Synonymous parallelism became a way of saying the same thing twice;

2. Antithetical parallelism, marking a contrast, served to make a distinction;

3. Synthetic parallelism became sort of a catchall for what would not fit the others.

It is evident from Lowth's own examples that these titles are more convenient than precise descriptions of the relationships between the parallel parts. His categories will serve as a starting point for the analysis of parallelism, but I am following A. A. Anderson's variation of Lowth's categories.[6]

1. Complete Parallelism

There are verses where every accented unit (either one word, or in Hebrew words joined together) is parallel to an equivalent unit in the other. In the samples I use (/) to mark off the word or word unit and (//) to mark the division in the parallelism. There are several ways that complete parallelism can used:

a. Synonymous Parallelism

Normal Order. The idea expressed in the first half is repeated in the second with synonymous words. Psalm 105:23 reads:

---

6. A. A. Anderson, *The Book of Psalms*. New Century Bible. 2 Volumes (London: Marshall, Morgan & Scott, 1972), I: pp. 41–42.

Then Israel / came / to Egypt; //
Jacob / sojourned / in the land of Ham.

Inverted or Chiastic Order. Sometimes the word order is reversed in the second half of the synonymous parallelism for different reasons. The English translation may not be able to retain this arrangement. Isaiah 11:13b has:

Ephraim / shall not be jealous of / Judah, //
and Judah / shall not harass / Ephraim.

b. Antithetical Parallelism

The writer contrasts the idea of the first part with the second part. This is very common in wisdom literature. Psalm 90:6 has:

In the morning / it flourishes / and is renewed; //
in the evening / it fades / and withers.

c. Emblematic Parallelism

One parallel unit is a complete picture or emblem illustrating the idea expressed in the other. Psalms 103:13 says:

As a father / pities / his children, //
so the LORD / pities / those who fear him.

2. Incomplete Parallelism

The parallelism is incomplete when only some of the terms are paralleled in the other part. When this happens the interpreter must try to determine the reason for the variation. There are two kinds of incomplete parallelism.

a. Incomplete Parallelism with Compensation

In this type each half of the line has the same number of words or word units but the words are not all paired. Psalm 21:10 is balanced metrically, but the first word, the verb, and the last word do not match.

You will destroy / their offspring / from the earth,
and their children / from among the sons of / men.

Climactic Parallelism or Step Parallelism is a distinct type of this; the thought is developed by the repetition and builds to a climax with the additional material. Psalm 29:1–2 has:

Ascribe / to the LORD / O sons of / the mighty *One*,
Ascribe / to the LORD / glory / and strength,
Ascribe / to the LORD / the glory of / his name;
Worship / the LORD / in holy / array.

b. Incomplete Parallelism Without Compensation

In the other kind of incomplete parallelism one of the parts will have less accented words or word units than the other; the word that is not picked up with a parallel word does double duty. Psalms 6:2 has this:

O LORD, / rebuke me / not in your anger, //
and chasten me / not in your wrath.

3. Formal Parallelism

There is no parallelism here, only a metrical balance between the units. In formal parallelism the sentence simply continues through the second half of the verse. Psalm 2:6 has this:

I have set / my king //
on Zion / my holy hill.

Summary

Biblical parallelism is the predominant feature in the structure of Hebrew poetry, even though it is not actually a paralleling in the rigid sense. The expositor will soon realize that parallelism is far more complex than saying it is a way of repeating the idea but with different words. In practical terms, expositors will have to consider the parallelism of every verse and be able to explain those that are helpful or necessary for the understanding of the psalm. Some will be easy to explain at first glance, others more difficult. Kugel's emphasis that parallelism displays a sequence, chronologically, logically, or literally, is a helpful guideline to follow. Even if the verse uses synonymous parallelism, there is additional meaning supplied by the synonyms in the second part.

So when it is necessary or helpful, expositors will have to explain the relationship between the parallel parts as it contributes to the meaning. Kugel explained that the parallelism will display a sequence in the ideas when the second part makes a contribution to the whole; it may carry the idea further, echo it, define it, narrow it, restate it, contrast with it, or illustrate it—all basically seconding the first part. Yet it does it in a symmetrical pattern that is aesthetically pleasing and easily remembered. Its sequences of ideas, emphases, completions, cause-effect relationships, forms of differentiation, and differences in fixed pairs, all have a significant part in poetic expression.[7]

FIGURES OF SPEECH

As mentioned earlier, a figure of speech (or a trope) involves a deviation from the ordinary and principal signification of a word. At times a word is transferred from its normal semantic range into one that is foreign to it to provide a comparison, and at other times a word is used that describes something loosely connected to the subject matter. Expositors will have to be able to identify and explain the figures used in order to derive the intended meanings.

At times commentators will refer to a figure as *metaphorical,* meaning "figurative," without explaining what the actual figure is and how it is used. So from time to time literary critics have attempted to analyze and categorize these deviations in the use of words in order to gain better control over the intended thought and feeling of the author. As a result, expositors have resources like E. W. Bullinger's *Figures of Speech Used in the Bible* to help them, but this work needs to be used critically because Bullinger's choice of figures may not always be the best. On the whole this book and others like it help the expositor think about the ways words and expressions are used.

Following Bullinger's outline, we will survey the most useful figures of comparison, substitution, addition, and omission.

Figures Involving Comparison

In figures involving comparison a writer transfers a word into a

---

7. Kugel, *The Idea of Biblical Poetry,* p. 51.

foreign semantic field to illustrate or picture his or her thought and to evoke the appropriate feeling in the reader. In this way the writer draws a comparison between two things of unlike nature that yet have something in common. The subject matter is real, but that to which it is compared is present in the imagination. What the subject and things compared have in common is not stated and must be expressed and validated by the interpreter from other indications in the composition and from the use of the figure elsewhere in the literature.

1. Simile

The simile is the clearest expression of comparison; it uses "like" or "as." It is an explicit comparison between two different things that have something in common.

> He shall be like a tree planted by rivers of waters (Ps. 1:3).

The comparison is between an individual who meditates in the Law and a tree. Here, as is often the case, the simile is qualified: the tree produces fruit in season and does not wither because it is planted by water. The extended qualifications of the simile lead the expositor to conclude that the water represents the Law, and the fruit, righteousness; but the common thought between the tree and the person is life or vitality. The figure creates a positive feeling of desirability.

2. Metaphor

The metaphor is an implicit comparison between two different things that have something in common; it is usually a statement that one thing is or represents another thing. This description of metaphor will serve the purpose of this introduction, but it is a simplification of a major poetic device. Pure metaphors are essentially figures of transference.

> The LORD God is a sun and a shield (Ps. 84:11).

The LORD is here compared to both a "sun" and a "shield." Each metaphor supplies different information about the LORD. The "sun" conveys light, warmth, and provision for growth among

91

other things; the "shield" primarily represents protection. The common idea between the LORD and the sun concerns giving light and life; and the common idea between the LORD and a shield is protection. The line brings a feeling of security in God's provision of and protection for life.

3. Hypocatastasis

The hypocatastasis, or as it might be stated more simply, the *implied comparison*, is characterized by implication. The figure is an expression that implies a comparison between two different things that have something in common. Unlike the two figures above, in this one the subject matter intended must be inferred—the text will not state what the intended reality is.

> Dogs have surrounded me (Ps. 22:16).

The psalmist is comparing his enemies to dogs, but he does not say that. He simply says dogs have surrounded him. There are no dogs surrounding him; the context makes it clear that he means a company of evil-doers (this is where parallelism can be helpful). If he had used a simile, he would have stated explicitly "my enemies are like dogs." A straightforward metaphor would have said "my enemies are dogs"; but he simply says "dogs have surrounded me," and the expositor is left to determine if they are real dogs, and if not, what are they? Once this has been done, the study must ask why he compared them to dogs. Dogs in the ancient world were scavengers—they ran in packs and scoured for food. So the psalmist was saying a lot about his enemies, but he was also saying that he was almost dead because that is why the "dogs" would be surrounding him and nipping at his extremities.

4. Parable

A parable is technically an extended simile. It compares two things that are different but yet have something in common. As an extended simile it provides an anecdotal narrative designed to teach a lesson. The word *parable* is one translation of the word that usually means "proverb" (מָשָׁל); it is related to the verb meaning "to be like." Psalm 49:10 describes the fool who trusts in wealth as being like the beasts that perish. So the basic idea of a parable is found in the Old Testament, but the most famous examples are those found in the New Testament.

> The kingdom of heaven is like a man that sowed good seed in his field (Matt. 13:24ff.).

The parable is essentially a story based on a simile. It is not always easy to determine how much of the story should be interpreted as part of the simile. It is safe to say the main point of the parable is what was intended, but along the way other comparisons surface.

5. Allegory

An allegory is an extended metaphor (but the development and range of allegory needs to be studied more fully, especially as it came to be used in the allegorical interpretation of Scripture that often set aside the literal meaning of the passage). In the basic use of allegory, the writer might draw on something historical or cultural.

There are not many examples of allegories in the Old Testament; and of those that come to mind, the images are not drawn from historical events (e.g., the Allegory of the Vineyard in Isa. 5:1–7). In the Allegory of the Fig, Olive, Vine, and Bramble (Judg. 9:7–15), the narrative is based on an implied comparison (hypocatastasis). The trees of the forest meet to choose a king over them; all decline for very legitimate reasons, but the bramble bush, the worthless one, agrees to rule over them. In the context the story is told with Abimelech in mind—he is like the bramble bush (which takes up the water, offers no shade, and burns easily).

6. Personification

Personification is the investment of non-human subjects (e.g., abstractions, inanimate objects, or animals) with human qualities or abilities. Here, too, the things compared are different in nature, but the thing to which the comparison is made is always a person.

> Your rod and your staff, they comfort me (Ps. 23:4).

The human ability to provide comfort in time of trouble is ascribed to the LORD's rod and staff. Of course, "rod" and "staff" are also figures, carrying through the comparison of the LORD's activities with those of the shepherd. The line essentially affirms that the means of protection that the LORD uses brings comfort to the worried psalmist.

7. Anthropomorphism

This is an implicit or explicit comparison of God to some corporeal aspect of mankind. It overlaps with hypocatastasis somewhat but differs in that here the figure is true of all people. By making a comparison with humans or common human traits, the author wishes to communicate a truth about the person of God. The author will choose that part of human life which best corresponds to some characteristic of God's person: e.g., the face denotes his presence or favor, the eyes denote his awareness or evaluation, the ears signify his attentiveness, the nostrils signify his anger, and the heart speaks of his moral purpose. Revelation of the Godhead demands the use of human language to communicate the nature of God in language people understand.

> Incline your ear to me (Ps. 31:2)

This an expression that describes what humans would do to pay close attention, leaning over to listen more intently. God does not need to do this; nor does he have an ear that he lowers to hear one praying. Such anthropomorphisms are for our benefit. This one is an urgent appeal for God to hear the prayer.

The Scriptures are filled with anthropomorphic expressions about God that will have to be interpreted clearly (and carefully since many people take some of them literally).

God is described as having

everlasting arms,
saving hand,
consuming breath of his nostrils,
and feet.

He is portrayed as

sitting enthroned,
hurling a storm,
blotting out of a book,
and putting tears in a bottle.

These are only a few of the host of other figurative expressions from the human realm. They are all meant to reveal the person and work of the LORD in terms that we can understand and appreciate.

Some commentators distinguish *anthropomorphism* from the description of God's passion(s), which they designate as anthropopatheia, an implicit or explicit comparison between the nature of God and human passions; but this designation runs the risk of denying the reality of passions and emotions to God. It limits God's personality, traditionally defined as intellect, sensibility, and will.

In the pagan world similar expressions are used of other gods, but there are two very important differences. First, those descriptions include baser human instincts and sinful acts, which Scripture never does for God. And second, the Old Testament makes a distinction between the LORD and false gods in that he is a spirit. The other gods are all too human.

8. Zoomorphism

This is a comparison of God (or people) to the lower animals or their parts. If this classification is used to explain a verse, the explanation will show it is a figure of comparison.

In the shadow of your wings I used to rejoice (Ps. 63:8).

Of course, God is not a bird with wings, but divine (and human) protection is frequently expressed by the image of taking someone under the wing. It speaks of safety and security.

9. Idiom

An idiom is a name given to a regular occurrence of a figure of speech that achieves lexical status. In the exposition of the text while these expressions can be called idioms, they often need to be explained in terms of the figure of speech that became idiomatic. An idiom is also called a dead metaphor, low figure, or a common use of a figure. It may be easily activated if used in a different way.

The way of the righteous (Ps. 1:6).

"Way" is an idiom, meaning one's course of life or conduct, but it must be explained as an implied comparison, the word "road" or "way" being used in comparison to the pattern or direction of life. The expositor cannot assume that common biblical idioms will be generally understood.

Figures Involving Substitution

Comparison is not the point of figures of substitution. Here something related to the idea is stated instead of the idea itself; and because of the close connection, the figure is literal—there is just more to it. For example, when the psalmist says, "the grave cannot praise you," he means the dead person (himself) in the grave. He is not comparing himself to a grave; he is using something connected with the dead to say that if he dies and goes to the grave he can no longer praise.

10. Metonymy

This is a change of a noun (or any idea) for another noun that is closely associated with it (but not generically part of it). While it most often refers to a noun, it can also apply to a verb or a whole line. It involves the substitution of some attributive or related word for what is meant. We use this figure often in modern communication: "crown" for "royalty," "brass" for "military officer," "pen" for "writer," or "bad hand" for "poorly-formed characters."

Bullinger analyzed metonymy into four kinds; *viz.*, of the cause, of the effect, of the subject, of the adjunct. These are helpful, but this analysis does not always work neatly.[8]

a. Metonymy of the Cause

The writer states the cause but intends the effect. If it is a metonymy of cause, the interpreter must state what the intended effect is.

---

8. E. W. Bullinger, *Figures of Speech Used in the Bible* (Grand Rapids: Baker, reprint of 1898 edition), pp. 538–608.

(1) Example where the instrument is put for the effect:

And the whole earth was of one lip" (Gen. 11:1).

The idea is that everyone spoke the same language. "Lip" is the cause, the instrument, and the effect of using the lip is "language."

(2) Example where the thing or the action is put for the effect:

Pour out your anger upon the nations (Ps. 79:6).

"Anger" is the emotion behind the judgment. The psalmist wants God to pour out (also a figure, an implied comparison) acts of judgment. So the cause is stated, the effect (judgment) is meant.

(3) Example where the person acting, the agent or actor, is put for the effect:

They have Moses and the Prophets (Luke 16:29).

What is meant is that they have the Scriptures that Moses and the Prophets wrote. The cause is stated, the effect is meant.

b. Metonymy of the Effect

The writer states the effect but intends the cause producing it; this is the reverse of the first class. Sometimes one line of poetic parallelism will give both the metonymy of cause and the metonymy of effect to express the complete idea:

Then he will speak (cause) to them in his anger, and terrify (effect) them in his fury (Ps. 2:5).

(1) Examples where the effect is put for the thing or action producing it:

Entreat the LORD your God, that he take away from me this death only (Exod. 10:17).

Locusts! That is what the Pharaoh wanted removed, but if they were allowed to remain, they would utterly destroy the land and bring death.

> Cause me to hear joy and gladness (Ps. 51:8).

The entire line is a metonymy of effect. The psalmist desires to hear the oracle of forgiveness from the prophet so that he can once again join the congregation with shouts of praise to God. The intended cause is "tell me I am forgiven."

(2) Example where the effect is put for the material object from which it is produced:

> You split the springs and brooks (Ps. 74:15).

He split the rock, and water came out. The use of metonymies here is very economical, for it is obvious that God did not split the water. The reader would know that the cause, the rock, is intended, but the effect, water from the rock, is stated.

(3) Example where the effect is put for the person or agent producing it:

> But you, O LORD, be not far off; O my help, hasten to my assistance (Ps. 22:19).

The stated effect is help, what the psalmist will receive; the cause is the LORD.

c. Metonymy of the Subject

Here the container, or subject or thing, is stated but something connected with it is meant.

(1) Examples where the container is put for the contents:

> You prepare a table before me (Ps. 23:5).

The stated subject-idea is "table," but the intended meanings are food and drink on the table. The literal meaning of preparing a table, i.e., carpentry, would be inappropriate here, for the psalmist is enumerating spiritual and physical provisions.

The voice of the LORD shakes the wilderness (Ps. 29:8).

As a metonymy of subject "wilderness" signifies the flora and fauna in the wilderness. In the sentence "voice of Yahweh" is either a metonymy of cause for the storm (God commanded it), or hypocatastasis for the similarity of thunder to a voice.

(2) Examples where the thing or action is put for that which is connected with it (the adjunct):

"Soul" for desires, appetites;
"heart" for thoughts, understanding, courage, will;
"kidneys" for conscience, affections, passions;
"liver" for emotions, center of immaterial part.[9]

(3) Examples where the sign is put for the thing signified:

The scepter shall not depart from Judah (Gen. 49:10).

The point of the oracle is that Judah (here the tribe and not the patriarch [met. of cause]) will retain the tribal supremacy or rulership. The sign of the rulership is a scepter, so we classify that as metonymy of subject because it signifies far more than (literally) retaining a scepter.

Kiss the son (Ps. 2:12).

The stated idea of kissing the son has the intended meaning of submission, or showing homage.

d. Metonymy of Adjunct

The writer puts the adjunct or attribute or some circumstance pertaining to the subject for the subject itself.

---

9. See also Hans W. Wolff, *Anthropology of the Old Testament* (Philadelphia: Fortress Press, 1974).

(1) Example where the attribute is put for the subject matter (thing or object):

Then shall you bring down my gray hairs with sorrow to the grave (Gen. 42:38).

This is the opposite of the metonymy of subject. Here the adjunct—gray hairs—is put for the subject—old Jacob. More than the gray hairs will be going down to the grave.

(2) Example where the time is put for the thing done in it:

For the shouting for your summer (Isa. 16:9).

The intended idea is the harvest that takes place in the summer. By substituting summer the prophet has economized his description and conveyed more than "harvest" alone would convey. "Summer," the time of the harvest, is an adjunct idea.

(3) Example where the contents are put for the container:

And when they had opened their treasures (Matt. 2:11).

They opened the chests that were holding the treasures. Here the adjunct is stated (contents of the containers), but the subject is meant (containers).

(4) Example where the appearance of a thing is put for the thing itself:

His enemies shall lick the dust (Ps. 72:9).

This is a vivid description of the defeat of enemies. The intended subject-idea is that the enemies will be defeated, be in a state of humble prostration; but the stated description is an adjunct of that defeat, an act related to and signifying the defeat.

(5) Example where the thing signified is put for the sign.

Because the separation is on his head (Num. 6:7).

This expression comes from the chapter on Nazirite vows in which the person would not cut his hair. The intended sign of the vow would be uncut hair (the subject), but the thing that is signified is stated —separation. "Separation" is not a metonymy of effect because that would say long hair causes the vow.

(6) Example where the name of a person is put for the person:

May the name of the God of Jacob protect you (Ps. 20:1).

The stated title is "name," but the intended meaning is the LORD himself, or better, all the attributes of the LORD.

11. Synecdoche

This is the exchange of one idea for another idea that is actually connected. In this figure one word receives something from another that is unexpressed but associated with it because it belongs to the same genus. Like metonymy, the figure is based on a relationship rather than a resemblance, but whereas in metonymy the exchange may be made between related words belonging to different genera (and so only loosely connected by contact or ascription), in synecdoche the exchange is made between two words related generically. For example, "ends of the earth" as a metonymy of subject would mean the people living in the ends of the earth, but as a synecdoche it would mean distant geographical locations as part of a larger mass of land—soil, not people.

As a general guideline, one may use synecdoche for figures that are actually a part of the whole, or the whole for a part— more strictly connected to the thing intended than a metonymy would be. The use of Genus and Species may not be as frequent as Whole and Part, but is serviceable for those things actually related generically.

a. Synecdoche of the Genus

The genus is substituted for the species: e.g., weapon for sword, creature for man.

101

(1) Words of wider meaning for a narrower sense:

The glory of the LORD shall be revealed, and all flesh shall see it together (Isa. 40:5).

The general word "flesh" is used in place of the specific idea "mankind" (they stand in a genus-species relationship).

Preach the gospel to every creature (Mark 16:15).

The stated genus is "creature"; the intended species is "people."

(2) "All" for the great part:

All the people were gathered to Jeremiah (Jer. 26:9).

This use of "all" might just as easily be handled as a lexical matter. The stated genus here is "all the people," but the intended sense is "the greater number of the people."

(3) "All" for all kinds:

It contained all four-footed animals (Acts 10:12).

What is meant no doubt is that all kinds of four-footed animals (i.e., every kind) were represented.

b. Synecdoche of the Species

Now we have the reverse, the species is substituted for the genus, a part for the whole; e.g., bread for food, sword for weapon.

(1) Words of a narrower sense for a wider meaning:

I will not trust in my bow, neither shall my sword save me (Ps. 44:6).

This type of synecdoche is more helpful for the interpretation. In this psalm "bow" and "sword" are stated, but the intended meaning is all kinds of "weapons," including the bow and the sword.

(2) Species for genus proper:

A land flowing with milk and honey (Exod. 3:8, 17).

The intended genus is all luxurious foods.

Give us this day our daily bread (Matt. 6:11).

The intended meaning is "basic food." "Daily bread" is a species of the genus food.

c. The Whole Put for the Parts

Many of the samples we have for this category could be treated as lexical matters, especially when "all" is used for parts.

Behold, the world has gone after him (John 12:19).

The synecdoche of the whole is "world"; the intended meaning (the part) is people of all sorts.

Many of these figures also involve metonymy of subject— the container for the contents. Usually it is enough to classify it is a metonymy and then explain the meaning. That explanation will show that the whole is put for the part. It is worth noting that synecdoche is also frequently hyperbolic, or even understatement.

And he shall serve him forever (Exod. 21:6).

The whole is "forever"; the intended part is "as long as the slave lives." Again, this may be a lexical matter, or the way it has been translated that has to be discussed.

d. The Part for the Whole

For example, sail for ship, canvas for sail, foot for body. These could also be classified under "species for genus"; moreover, many of these are close to metonymy. This is the most common use of synecdoche.

(1) Part of man for the whole man:

Their feet run to evil (Prov. 1:16).

The part stated is the "feet"; the intended whole is "their entire bodies" = evil people. The point is that heart and soul they are into evil deeds.

The one who lifts up my head (Ps. 3:3).

For the stated part, "head," the meaning is the whole person being exalted with dignity—head held high; but if the line, "to lift up the head," is included, it may better be explained as a metonymy of effect or adjunct, i.e., restoration to dignity and honor.

(2) A part of the thing for the whole thing:

Your seed shall possess the gate of his enemies (Gen. 22:17).

The stated part is "gate," but the intended whole is the city. As a synecdoche "gate" represents brick and mortar—the actual city. If we think gate means people in the gate, then that is metonymy of subject, because people and gate are not generically connected.

(3) An integral part of men for others associated:

Before Ephraim, Benjamin, and Manasseh, stir up your might (Ps. 80:2).

By these parts the psalmist means the northern tribes, southern tribes, and tribes of Transjordan. In other contexts the patriarchal names could be metonymies of cause (e.g., "Judah gathered against him" means either the descendants of Judah [met. of cause] or the people living in Judah [met. of subject]—but not

Judah himself. Words like "seed" and "sons of" will receive similar considerations.

12. Merism

This is the use of two opposite statements to signify the whole; e.g., day and night, springtime and harvest, heaven and earth. Merism is a kind of synecdoche, parts for the whole.

> You know when I sit down and when I get up (Ps. 139:2).

The ideas of "sitting down" and "rising up" are opposites; the intended whole is all the activities including sitting down and getting up. It means, "You know every move I make"—including these. So the expressed ideas are literal, but more is meant.

> From the rising of the sun to the place where it sets, the name of the LORD is to be praised (Ps. 113:3).

This verse may form a double merism: it could mean everywhere—from east to west; and it could mean all the time—from sunrise to sunset.

13. Hendiadys

This word means "two through one"; it refers to the expression of one idea through two formally coordinate terms (nouns or verbs) instead of a noun and an adjective, or a verb and an adverb. One component then modifies the other.

> My soul shall be satisfied with fat and fatness (Ps. 63:5).

The single idea is expressed better by making one of the nouns a modifier: "abundant fatness." This is how to test the words to see if a hendiadys is involved.

14. Type

A type is a divinely prefigured illustration of a corresponding reality (called the antitype); it is a form of prophecy, the major difference with direct prophecy being that the passage can only be understood as prophetic once the fulfilling antitype has come into full view. This topic will be discussed in the notes on the royal psalms.

> My God, my God, why have you forsaken me? (Ps. 22:1).

The words of the psalm hyperbolically describe the suffering of David but become historically true in Jesus.

15. Symbol

A symbol is a material object substituted for a moral or spiritual truth, a visible sign of something invisible. The visible sign stands as a constant resemblance to some spiritual truth.

> I will appoint you . . . a light to the nations (Isa. 42:6).

"Light" becomes a symbol for spiritual and moral instruction (contrast "darkness" in the next verse). Actually, this symbol originated as a figure of comparison.

Figures Involving Addition or Amplification

16. Repetition

The repetition of the same word or words in the passage, or passages in a book. This phenomenon has many variations, and the expositor must state the type and purpose of repetition.[10]

> My God, my God, why have you forsaken me? (Ps. 22:1).

The intense pathos of the verse is enhanced by the repetition beyond what one expression would convey.

17. Paronomasia

This refers to the repetition of words similar in sound and frequently in sense or origin as well. If the words are etymologically connected, then it is a paronomasia in the classical sense; if the

---

10. See the rather extended section in Bullinger, *Figures*, pp. 189–263.

words are not so related, then it is a loose paronomasia, or, phonetic word play. This study requires the ability to work with the Hebrew words.

Now the earth was waste and void (Gen. 1:2).

The two words *tōhû wābōhû* are a phonetic word play. They sound like they might be related, but they are from different words.

Therefore, the name of it was called *Bābel,* because there the LORD confused (*bālal,* i.e., turned into a babble) their language (Gen. 11:9).

The name *Bābel* is not etymologically related to the Hebrew verb *bālal,* "to confuse"—they are different languages. *Bab-ili* is a Babylonian word that means "gate of God," but the verb in Hebrew captures the sounds of the name and makes a comment about it in the context.

18. Acrostic

This refers to the repetition of the same or successive letters at the beginnings of words or clauses, arranging a poem in alphabetical order. Psalm 119 is the passage with which most people are familiar; each line of each section begins with the sequential letters of the Hebrew alphabet. In Psalm 34, each verse is begun with a letter of the Hebrew alphabet in sequence, omitting the *waw* and ending with verse 21. Verse 22, beginning with a *pe',* is outside the series and probably stressed. Acrostics served mnemonic purposes as well as rhetorical ones.

19. Inclusio

The rhetorical figure in which a literary unit begins and ends with the same (or similar) word, phrase, or clause. This repetition serves as a framing device, iterating the theme of the section. It usually appears with chiastic constructions.

O LORD, our Lord, how excellent is your name in all the earth!" (Ps. 8:1, 9).

20. Hyperbole

This is the use of exaggerated terms for the purpose of emphasis or heightened effect; more is said than is literally meant.

> I am worn out from groaning; all light long I make my bed swim with weeping, and drench my couch with tears (Ps. 6:6).

Flooding and drenching the bed with tears is probably not literally true, but it certainly does signify a night of intense pain and uncontrollable weeping.

Figures Involving Omission or Suppression

21. Ellipsis

This refers to the omission of a word or words in a sentence.

> When you shall make ready [   ] upon your strings (Ps. 21:12).

"Your arrows" is not in the text; it must be supplied from the context. Sometimes words are left out because they are unnecessary to the context; other times they are left out for emphasis.

22. Aposiopesis

The breaking off of what is being said, with sudden silence (in anger, in grief, in promise) is aposiopesis.

> My soul is greatly troubled; but You, O LORD—how long? (Ps. 6:3).

The sentence is not complete because of the intense emotion involved. The psalmist simply breaks off the sentence and leaves it all in the care of the LORD.

23. Erotesis

This is the rhetorical question, the asking of questions without expecting an answer (to express affirmation, demonstration, wonder, exultation, wishes, denials, doubts, admonitions, expostulation, prohibitions, pity, disparagements, reproaches, lamentation, indignation, absurdities, or the like.

Why do the nations rage? (Ps. 2:1).

The psalmist is expressing amazement, possibly indignation, that the nations would rebel against the LORD.

24. *Meiosis*

Meiosis is a belittling of one thing to magnify another (also called litotes).

> And we were in our own sight as grasshoppers, and so were we in their sight (Num. 13:33).

Note that this is also a simile, comparing people to grasshoppers. The belittling is meant to enlarge the size and strength of the enemy.

25. *Tapeinosis*

Tapeinosis is an understatement, a lessening of a thing in order to increase it.

> A broken and contrite heart, O God, you will not despise. (Ps 51:17).

We would have expected "you will joyfully receive," but an understatement is used to express two ideas: (1) God will receive and take pleasure in a broken heart (the intended meaning) and (2) if one does not have a broken heart God will despise.

LITERARY FORMS AND FUNCTIONS IN THE PSALMS

LAMENT PSALMS

One of the most predominant themes in the Psalter is lament; this reminds us again and again that many of the psalms are prayer songs. Laments, or prayers, are cries to God in times of need, whether sickness, affliction, slander, war, or some other crisis. In ancient Israel, the worshiper could cry out to God anytime, anywhere; but if possible, he would normally go to the sanctuary to offer the petition, and in many cases the officiating priest might offer the prayer on his behalf. Laments form the starting point of the prayer and praise cycle found through the psalms, and so this survey of the types of psalms will begin with them.

The Parts of the Individual Lament

This outline of the pattern of lament psalms is basically drawn from the constructions of Claus Westermann. As he was careful to point out, these patterns are never stereotyped; there is a great deal of variation in the lament psalms. Knowing what lament psalms include helps the expositor understand the flow of the message through a psalm.

The Address and Introductory Cry
Lament psalms can be readily identified by their first words,

111

which include a turning to God for help: "O LORD, deliver me."
The cry to God need be no longer than the mention of the divine
name and then an imperative calling for help—but it could be
very long. Frequently, a lament psalm will have an introductory
petition and lament in anticipation of the formal sections of petition and lament. It is important for the expositor to keep this in
mind when arranging the structure of the exposition; and when
the introduction includes them, the reader has a clearer idea of
what the message of the psalm might be.

The Lament Proper

The main body of the psalm will contain a number of different
features. The order of the elements may vary considerably from
psalm to psalm, some of them even being absent, but a description of the distress or misfortune is the most important feature.

The expression of the lament may be very brief, such as one
verse, or extended and descriptive. Frequently the lament can
be subdivided into three perspectives: "my enemies," "I," and
"You, O God." For example, the psalmist's lament would say that
enemies have surrounded him, he is in trouble, and God has not
delivered him—all of which is lamentable.

The discovery of what is being lamented is important for the
exposition because it will provide the tension the psalmist faced
in the prayer. In modern exposition, then, the expositor looks for
comparable situations when applying the message of the psalm.

The Confession of Trust

Frequently the psalmist will contrast his plight with a statement of confidence in the LORD. This may begin with an adversative construction, "but as for me." The statement of confident
faith may be absent from lament psalms, but it may also be extended to the point of becoming the major part of the psalm. In
such a case commentators have been inclined to call the type a
"song of trust."

The Petition Proper

The actual prayer of the psalm, a prayer for help or deliverance,
will reiterate or further develop the introductory cry. It may be
brief or prolonged, but it will usually make two separate but

related requests, one for God to be favorable ("look," "pay attention") and the other for God to intervene ("save," "deliver").

One aspect of the petition that is instructive for prayer is the psalmists' frequent attempt to motivate God, that is, stating reasons why God should answer favorably. They might appeal to God because of the magnitude of the need (Ps. 54:3), or the nature of God (Ps. 86:2, 15), or the honor of God (Ps. 42:10), or the desire to praise God for this deliverance—which obviously would have to take place if the psalmist was going to praise (Ps. 6:5). In a few psalms there will be a confession of sin (Ps. 51:3) or a protesting of innocence as the reason for God's acting on the psalmist's behalf (Ps. 59:3). The reasons why God should answer prayer should be given special attention in teaching believers how to pray, for it makes them ask if they are praying according to the will of God or not.

The Vow of Praise or Declarative Praise

The most striking thing about lament psalms is that they turn to praise at the end.[1] The praise section may even follow the structure of the declarative praise psalm (see below).

This vow of praise must be understood: the petition is still open; the answer has not been given; and yet the psalmist promises to praise in the sanctuary when he receives the answer to the prayer. And this promise takes the form of a rehearsal of what actually will be said. When this praise section is patterned after the declarative praise psalms, there is simply an abrupt break in the mood of the psalm. The psalmist suddenly changes to a confident praise for the deliverance. It is this section that the psalmist vows to say or sing in the Temple when the thanksgiving sacrifice is offered. This too motivates God, for if God wants this said, he had to answer the prayer.

Once the prayer was answered, the psalmist was by duty bound to pay these vows, i.e., the vows of praise. In the Hebrew text the vows of praise are often begun with the use of the stronger volitional form, the cohortative, "I *will* praise."

There are several reasons that have been suggested for the

---

1. There are only a few exceptions: Psalm 42 does not, but then Psalm 43 was probably the last part of this psalm. Likewise, Psalms 9 and 10 were originally one. Psalm 137, a national lament, does not include a praise section.

sudden shift from prayer to praise in the laments. Some commentators have proposed that two psalms may have been deliberately or accidentally joined together, or that these psalms were actually declarative praise psalms and that the lament portion was simply a restatement of the cry from distress. But Westermann suggested that between the prayer and the praise there had been an "oracle of salvation," some indication from God that the prayer was heard. There were several ways this "oracle" might have been manifested. One way was that a priest or a prophet or some other individual was prompted by God to tell the one praying that God had received the prayer (and sacrifice) and would deliver (see for example, the account of Jehoshaphat in 2 Chron. 20:1–29).

The "oracle" need not come from a mediator. It could be that during the praying God revealed to the person praying some sign that the prayer would be answered—the circumstances began to change (Jonah 2), or God partially answered the prayer (Ps. 3), or God impressed on the heart of the one praying the conviction that the prayer was heard (Ps. 20). However it happened, the psalmists would break off their prayers to vow the praise that they would give to God. That kind of faith is exemplary to all who pray.

The Parts of the Communal Lament

National laments are less numerous than individual laments. They lament catastrophes that involve the nation, such as drought, plagues, and war. One can imagine the nation in such crises holding a national day of fasting and prayer (such as may be the background of Isa. 1; see also Jer. 36:1–10; Zech. 7). The elements of the national or communal lament do not differ appreciably from the individual lament:

1. The Address (an Introductory Petition to God)

2. The Lament Proper (often including the foes, the nation ["we"], God)

3. National Confession of Trust

4. The Petition Proper and Motivation (May God do this to our enemies, May God do this to us)

5. The Vow of Praise

Psalms that may be classified as communal laments include Psalms 44, 60, 74, 79, 80, and 83. Sometimes there is a spokesman for the congregation, but the description of the lament is broader in scope than an individual lament.

Imprecations in the Psalms

The fact that some of the psalms include curses in the prayers creates a tension for the modern believer. It is necessary, therefore, for the expositor to offer a few words of clarification on this issue. Fortunately, there are a number of resources available.[2] We are concerned here with imprecations (curses) in the psalms, not imprecatory psalms, because the imprecations form only a part of their content. There are about 18 psalms with such curses in them, and of the approximately 370 verses of those psalms about 65 include anything that might be called imprecation. Some of the psalms that include imprecations are Psalms 5:10; 10:15; 27:4; 31:17, 18; 40:14,15; and 140:9–10, but the three psalms that have the curses in their strongest form are Psalms 35, 69, and 109.

At first glance it looks like these imprecations reflect the psalmist's personal vengeance. One would then have to conclude that the Bible is recording what they said but not holding that up as a model for praying. Yet the psalms were hymns to be sung in public worship; they are not simply records of personal vendetta.

It also seems that they reflect a lower standard of morality that may have existed in the ancient Near East. However,

---

2. One of the most helpful discussion still is that of Chalmers Martin, "The Imprecations in the Psalms," *PTR* 1 (1903): pp. 537–553 (reprinted in *Classical Evangelical Essays in Old Testament Interpretation*, edited by W. Kaiser, pp. 113–132). See also J. Carl Laney, Jr., "A Fresh Look at the Imprecatory Psalms, *Bibliotheca Sacra* 138 (1981): pp. 35–45; and John Shepherd, "The Place of Imprecatory Psalms in the Canon of Scripture," *Churchman* 111 (1997): pp. 27–47, 110–26.

even the law of Moses forbad private vengeance and even commanded love for the enemies (Lev. 19:18), a standard reiterated in the New Testament. Paul, in Romans 12:19ff., forbad this very sin of a revengeful spirit by means of two quotations from the Old Testament (Deut. 32:35, "Vengeance is mine"; and Prov. 25:21–22, "If your enemy hunger, give him bread to eat"). The psalmists surely knew of such teachings. In fact, in some of the psalms with imprecations, the writer protests the kind feelings he had for those who were persecuting him (25:12ff., 109:4, 5). Neither personal vendetta or a lower morality satisfactorily explain these imprecations, but there are other possibilities:

1. The first thing to be kept in mind is that these are prayers to God, and that they are written in lyric poetry. Hyperbole is a frequent and loved figure of speech in the psalms. In the mentality of the psalmists, especially when suffering, feelings were expressed extravagantly.

2. These imprecations are the expression of the longing of the Old Testament believer for the vindication of God's righteousness. Their faith in God's goodness and righteousness was put to the test by malicious wickedness, and so they were left longing for vindication. Moreover, their imprecations made it clear that the wicked deserve their curse. Even in the New Testament we have the cry for the Lord to avenge the blood of his people (Rev. 6:10).

3. These imprecations are expressions of zeal for God and his kingdom. The monarchy was the earthly administration of the theocratic kingdom. It fell to the monarch, David, in the first place, and his righteous followers to protect the institutions of the nation against enemies who sought to overthrow them and the faith (e.g., Ahab and Jezebel). So if the king was God's representative, his enemies were not merely his enemies, but God's (see Ps. 139:19–22). Even Paul would advise, "If any man love not the Lord Jesus Christ, let him be anathema" (1 Cor. 16:22); but it was no longer the call for leaders to go to war to defend the faith.

4. These imprecations are the psalmists' expressions of their hatred for sin. The enemies who were actually attacking the righteous and taunting their faith were the embodiment of evil—vile people, in whom falsehood and treachery, cunning, greed, hatred, cruelty, arrogance, and pride had found full expression. Could David have pitied them and treated them with kindness? He did that, in so far as it was possible, but as a king he had to champion righteousness and punish evil-doers in order to safeguard God's program.

5. Finally, these imprecations form prophetic teachings about God's future dealings with sin and impenitent and persistent sinners. Of all the psalms that Jesus applied to himself, Psalms 69 and 109 appear frequently. David was a prophet; the psalms were inspired. And so there is nothing in these imprecations that is out of harmony with God's intent for the wicked. They are not, then, simply statements of that which the psalmists wish God to do but of that which God has done or certainly will do. There are no imprecations that lay upon the wicked anything more terrible than that which is laid up for them if they persist in wickedness and rebellion. In short, the imprecations address the ageless conflict of good and evil that will end in the triumph of righteousness. The psalmists wanted to make it absolutely clear where their loyalties lay.

The Prayers of Believers

Although there are helpful explanations for the imprecations, the emphasis in Christian prayers is different. And even though they may pray for the Lord to come, for his will to be done, which would mean judgment on the wicked, they are instructed to love their enemies and pray for them. Properly understood, these exhortations reflect the new focus of spiritual service in the new covenant. The prayer life of the believer today should be better than that of Old Testament believers (which is not to say it will be better, if people do not pray).

One consideration is that according to the New Testament believers today have a better relationship with God through the fulfillment of the promises in Christ Jesus. In both testaments believers are called servants (e.g., Psalms 132:2; 89:50; and 90:13, 16; and Acts 4:29 and Paul's salutations). Submission and dependence on God are therefore the attitudes of the servant appealing to the master, but the New Testament records more fully other descriptions of the believer's relation to the Lord introduced in the Old Testament. For example, Abraham is called the friend of God (Jas. 2:23) because of the personal relationship he had with God, but this finds a wider application and explanation in the New Testament (John 15:15). We have a close relationship through Christ and should be able to pray more intelligently (not because of our own knowledge, but because of the full revelation in Christ). The New Testament also develops the idea that believers refer to God as their Father. This was there in the Old Testament (Mal. 1:6); but in the New Testament it is explained in great detail. Believers are therefore exhorted to pray, "Our Father."

A second consideration is that the New Testament teaches that believers now have the full revelation of the grace of God. Old Testament believers certainly knew and experienced the grace of God, but they did not have the knowledge of how divine grace would provide salvation (see John 1:14, 16; Titus 2:11). So the believers today apply this full revelation to the attitude and the wording of their prayers so that what they pray is in harmony with the revelation of the grace of God in Christ.

For example, this is one reason why Christians do not pray imprecatory prayers as the leaders of the faith did in Israel; they pray for the salvation of the wicked. As long as evil exists, the name of the LORD is tarnished in the earth; and even though the righteous today long for relief from its presence, they pray for it in general when they pray, "Come quickly, Lord Jesus."

On the whole New Testament believers should pray with greater confidence because of the revelation and experience of the fullness of the grace of God (Rom. 8:32; Heb. 4:16), but more often than not, the confidence of the psalmists remains exemplary.

Third, in the new covenant there is a better priesthood. The book of Hebrews goes into some detail about this, but its significance for prayers is that believers today are able to pray with greater boldness and confidence because they have an eternal, sinless high priest who has passed into the heavenly sanctuary on their behalf. Moreover, the New Testament teaches that the Holy Spirit also makes intercession for believers, turning their attempts into proper prayers (Rom. 8:26). Further, the fact that we possess the complete canon, the oracle of our High Priest, nullifies our need for a word from a priest. We have the oracle from God; we have his Word. God has revealed more of his will to us than to them, and it is by that will we are to pray.

We can still learn from the prayers of believers in the Old Testament, for God has given them to us for our edification. Accordingly, the church has, with slight modifications here and there, adopted these prayers of Israel as part of its prayer life. There is much to be learned from studying these prayers.

1. We will find instructive the fact that the psalmists contrast their laments with their confidence, providing a much needed balance. The expression of confidence is important in building faith as well. As a result, they could rehearse their praise for the answer to their prayer before it actually was given.

2. We will also find it instructive that they motivated God to respond. Their petitions provided valid reasons why God should answer their prayers, and those reasons were always glorifying to God and his cause.

3. We will improve the prayers of the church if we include praise in them, the praise we want to give when he answers the prayers.

PRAISE PSALMS

The Nature of Biblical Praise

In both testaments believers are commanded to "offer unto God the sacrifice of praise" (e.g., Ps. 50:14 and Heb. 13:15). The fact that it is commanded means that it is a binding responsibility, not an option; and the fact that it is called a sacrifice means that it is a form of worship, an offering to be given to God. In Israel

119

believers were by duty bound to praise the LORD, and it always cost them to do so.

Praise, that is praise in the biblical sense, has fallen on hard times. Too often it is ignored completely, both in the assembly and in the daily life of the believer, or it is simply replaced by music.[3] Most believers would say that they are genuinely thankful for all that the LORD has done for them; but individual praise in the congregation is rarely a part of their gratitude.

Westermann provided a good study of the meaning of biblical praise in contrast to the modern practice of saying "thank-you."[4] He first noted that the simplified idea of "thanks" is not a primary meaning in many major languages, and there is no word in Hebrew that actually means "thank-you" or "thanksgiving" (although modern translations often use these words). From this observation he suggested that the custom of saying "thanks" (as we use it) may not be the most natural thing to do. He explained that pure praise makes the object praised the subject of the proclamation, whereas in saying "thanks" the speaker remains the subject (so praise involves looking away from oneself); praise is also a lavish description of that which is spontaneously enjoyed, whereas saying "thanks" can be a fixed duty with little description (so praise demonstrates a genuine appreciation); and praise is expressed in a forum, in the assembly, whereas saying "thanks" can be private or silent (so praise is telling others about the Lord, but saying "thanks" is addressed to the Lord). There is nothing wrong with saying "thank-you" to the Lord; but the gratitude should eventually be proclaimed to other people, thus encouraging and edifying them in the faith.

Along these lines C. S. Lewis described how natural praise is.[5] In any area of life one naturally praises what one appreciates—in fact, the praise is part of the enjoyment. To enjoy something fully one must speak of it. To praise God, then, means that

---

3. This is not to say that congregations should not use music to praise God; but music alone does not allow individuals to offer their praise in the congregation.

4. Claus Westermann, *The Praise of God in the Psalms* (Richmond, VA: John Knox, 1965), pp. 25–30.

5. C. S. Lewis, *Reflections in the Psalms* (New York: Harcourt, Brace and World, 1958), pp. 90–98.

people are enjoying his benefits. And when God calls people to praise him, he is calling them to enjoy his benefits, so that they will have cause to praise.

A study of the major words for praise in the Psalter brings further elaboration to these ideas. These will be discussed in greater detail in the commentary, but a survey here will provide some sense of the enthusiasm of biblical praise. The best known term for praise is *hālal* (הָלַל); it means "praise, shout for jubilation, sing praises, or extol." Its usage would indicate the praise is a natural response to something, a glowing report (for example, for Sarai's beauty [Gen. 12:15], Absalom's looks [2 Sam. 14:25], or a good wife by her works [Prov. 31:31]). The causes for the praise are things appreciated or enjoyed by those praising, and the manner of the praise seems to be extravagant descriptions and lavish reports.

There are many other words for praise that also inform the general concept. These terms show that praise was often done through singing, often to the accompaniment of instruments (*šîr* [שִׁיר], *zāmar* [זָמַר]), dancing (Ps. 149:3), and with all kinds of music (Ps. 150:1–5). They also show that the praise was loud and enthusiastic: *rānan* (רָנַן) means "to give a ringing cry" (referring to the shout or screeching made for joy), and *gîl* (גִּיל) is "to give a shout, exult, cultic cry." Other terms are *sippēr* (סִפֵּר), "to declare, tell"; *kibbēd* (כִּבֵּד), "to honor, glorify"; *higdîl* (הִגְדִּיל), "to magnify", *rômam* (רוֹמֵם), "to exalt"; *hizkîr* (הִזְכִּיר), "to remind, praise"; and *bērēk* (בֵּרֵךְ), "to bless, enrich by praise." All of these indicate that the praise was a public acknowledgment in one form or another.

Perhaps the most instructive word for praise, especially in the study of the first group of praise psalms, is the verb *yādāh* (יָדָה), usually translated with words for "thanks" or "thanksgiving." In the causative (*hiphil*) stem it means "to acknowledge," implying a public acknowledgment. The frequent call to praise has the imperative *hôdû* (הוֹדוּ), usually rendered "give thanks" (to the LORD). Expositors will have to work with the English translations, but their exposition should clarify that this is a call for a public acknowledgment of the person and works of God.

Key passages in Chronicles explain that the public praise was instituted in the worship center by David, entrusted to priests and Levites, and accompanied by the people (see especially

1 Chron. 16:4; 16:36; 23:30; 25:3; as well as 1 Chron. 16:36; 2 Chron. 8:14; 31:2; and 29:30).

The call to praise (using any one of these words) was a call for the worshipers of God to offer their spontaneous praise for that which they had received from God's hand. Praise was to the Hebrew a necessary condition of life. The reason that praise was so important to the life of the believer and to the congregational gathering is that it is essentially the public expression of loyalty to the covenant and the Lord of the covenant. This is why they could praise even in adversity.

Tôdāh (תּוֹדָה) became the technical term for the praise offering. According to Levitical laws, if an individual wished to offer praise to God for some reason, that public acknowledgment had to be delivered in the sanctuary and accompanied by a sacrifice, the peace offering (Lev. 7). Normally the peace offering would become a communal meal (if it was an animal). The one praising, the officiating priest, the friends of the worshiper, members of the congregation, and most importantly the poor and needy (as the commentary will show) would all share this communal meal. They would listen to the worshiper's public declaration while the animal was roasting—he was fulfilling his vow of praise. Thus, they would understand that they were sharing in God's bounty to this individual—they ate because God had blessed someone. Even in the New Testament when the writer to the Hebrews tells his audience to offer the sacrifice of praise, he instructs that they share with those who have needs (13:15–16).

It should be clear from the brief survey that praise was an integral part of the life of the worshipers. It was on of the major reasons they went up to the sanctuary at the great festivals (Ps. 122:4). Moreover, a study of the psalms will show the effect of praise on the edification of other believers, teaching them the ways of God and encouraging them in their prayers in times of need.

Declarative Praise Psalms

Biblical scholars may call this type of psalm a "thanksgiving psalm," or a "*tôdāh* psalm"; they also divide them into two groups, the praise of the individual and the praise of the community, but there is not an appreciable difference between the two—the essential elements are present in both.[6] The normal arrangement of the declarative praise psalm is as follows (although again it must be stated they are not tightly bound to this order):

Proclamation to Praise God

The psalm will begin with a clear intention to praise (a marked contrast from the lament's "Save me, O LORD"). This part will normally be expressed with a voluntative "I will praise." The essential nature of this type of psalm, then, is indicated at the very outset. In the proclamation the psalmist will state why he will praise ("because the LORD has. . . ."). This is what the psalmist promised to do. The vow of praise that was made during the prayer now is to be fulfilled in public. Because this type of praise psalm is experiential, it is essentially what many believers today call "testimony"—although it has far more substance.

Report of the Deliverance

The content of the praise will be given immediately, unless there is a burst of praise before it. The report will have two parts, a report of the dilemma, and a report of the deliverance. The introductory statement that summarized the reason for the praise will now be developed. The psalmist will look back to the time of need and report the distress, even repeating what he prayed at that time; then he will report that God delivered him. Throughout the praise the main elements present are "I cried . . . he heard . . . he drew me out (or whatever)."

Praise, or Renewed Vow of Praise

The psalmist now offers the praise. The psalm has told of the deliverance, the reason for the praise; now follows the praise proper which declares the saving deeds of the LORD.

Descriptive Praise or Instruction

Frequently the declarative praise will turn into a descriptive praise about God and his attributes; this will be included

---

6. Psalms that belong to this group include: 18, 21, 30, 32, 34, 40, 41, 66, 106, 116, and 138.

to explain the deliverance. This part too will fulfill the vow of praise since it focuses on the LORD.

On occasion the psalm will conclude with a didactic section that can be short or rather extended. Lessons drawn from the experience are taught to the congregation.

Descriptive Praise Psalms or Hymns

The distinctions between the two types of praise psalms are not always easy to discover, and some think they are essentially the same (because they often vary the elements); but the pure descriptive praise psalm when it appears differs substantially.[7] These are not personal reports of deliverance or answer to prayer; these are hymns that describe the nature of God (using examples of God's intervention for his people).

Prologue

Hall*e*lû Yāh! The psalm begins with some such expression.

Call to Praise

The beginning of the psalm will have an extended call for the congregation, or parts of the congregation, to offer praise to the LORD. Or, it may simply be the above "Praise Yah."

Cause for the praise

The second major section of these praise psalms is essentially the reason for and substance of the praise. The normal pattern has a summary statement of the cause for praise followed by specific illustrations of it. The summary statement usually has two parts: God's greatness (e.g., the LORD of creation) and God's grace (e.g., his dealings in history to save). In the description of God's greatness and grace, the psalmists frequently visit important themes, notably creation or the deliverance of Israel. A number of these psalms that focus on creation may be called "hymns to the creator."

---

7. Psalms that belong to this type include 28, 36, 105, 111, 113, 117, 135, 136, 146, and 147.

124

Conclusion

The psalm will close with a renewed call to praise for the reasons expressed in the psalm, or an exhortation, or a petition, or even a lesson.

Epilogue

Hall^e^lû Yāh! This expression may also appear at the end of the passage (although it is not always present).

Praise psalms are relatively easy to develop in exposition. The basic instruction in each one is to praise, but the reasons for the praising differ from psalm to psalm. Thus, an exposition of each praise psalm would concentrate on the reason for the praise and all that would imply—especially if the psalm develops a didactic element based on the praise. Once the reason for the praise has been identified and explained, whether something of the nature of God, or some act of deliverance, the immediate response expected is praise. And if the expositor has a biblical perspective of praise in mind, then praise cannot be isolated from faith and obedience. Praises should excite in the hearer the same devotion for and trust in the LORD that the one praising has. The hearer learns that if God could answer those prayers, or extend grace in such circumstances, he can do it for others as well. Thus, the patterns of praise psalms and the significance of praise make the exegetical exposition of these psalms fairly easy to develop.

In the declarative praise psalms, however, an additional point of contact will be available for the expositor. These psalms report the dilemma and the deliverance. Consequently the exposition can develop the whole cycle of prayer and praise from a particular kind of difficulty to the kind of praise voiced.

With the praise psalms expositors will need to be careful in making the divisions. Some psalms will fit all the parts of their type exactly; others may be missing major parts, or rearranging them, even though they still have the essential elements to fit one group. Expositors should use the patterns as a general guide, but they should not force the translation or the outline to fit parts that may not be there. Where the parts are discernible, expositors must explain them, especially if in a praise psalm the psalmist appears to be lamenting (in the report). The English translations sometimes obscure these divisions.

SONGS OF ZION AND PILGRIM PSALMS

A major focus of the psalms is the holy city, Jerusalem, the place of the central sanctuary, and so we have songs about Zion, and songs for the pilgrimages to Zion for the festivals. These are not literary types distinct from the prayers and praises; they are classified because of their function or central theme. They could also be laments or declarative praises or hymns.

The psalms classified as songs of Zion are at least Psalms 46, 48, 76, 84, 87, and 122 (which is also a pilgrim song). These songs extol Zion because it is the dwelling place of the LORD, the city of God, the holy mountain. They normally have the same form as hymns.

Zion is the name of the mountain in old Jerusalem on which the sanctuary was built.[8] It represents the city and all its important institutions; it therefore played a central role in the political, cultural, and religious life of Israel.

The pilgrim psalms (Pss. 120–134) have some of the same themes as the songs of Zion in view of the fact that they were sung on pilgrimages to the holy city (and Ps. 122 is both a Zion song and a pilgrim song). The pilgrim songs, like the songs of Zion, do not constitute a literary type; they were meant to provide inspiration to the pilgrims on the way.[9]

The identification of these songs as pilgrim songs comes largely from tradition, reflected in the fact that they are all grouped together and all have the same superscription, the word "song" joined with *hamma'ălôt* (הַמַּעֲלוֹת), the plural noun meaning "goings up," from the verb "to go up" So it would mean "a song of the goings up" There have been several explanations of the title presented by translations and commentaries:

---

8. Visitors to the site today may be confused; in later times the name "Zion" was given to a different section of the old city, the upper city. In biblical times it was the Temple Mount.

9. See C. C. Keet, *A Study of the Psalms of Ascent, A Critical and Exegetical Commentary upon Psalms 120–134* (London, 1969).

1. There is the old translation "a song of degrees." This may suggest the place where the songs were sung, perhaps the porch or the steps to the altar. We have the report that the Levites sang their songs on the fifteen steps of the portal of Nicanor (the Mishnah, *Middot* 2:6). However, this may be a later adaptation of the psalms and not an indication of the original meaning.

2. It has been translated "song of ascents." This may have been intended to convey the literary and rhythmical structure of the songs themselves, the last word of a verse or half-verse being repeated in the next (see Ps. 121); but this literary device is not common to all these psalms.

3. It has been taken to mean "song of the repatriated," i.e., when they ascended to Jerusalem after the captivity (Ezra 2:1; 7:7). If this was the point, it is not stated very clearly. Moreover, the idea would contradict other parts of the superscriptions in these psalms.

4. It seems most likely that these are psalms to be sung when "going up" to Jerusalem for the festivals ("a song for the goings up"), and so they are pilgrim songs. This finds support in the use of the verb "go up" (עָלָה) for the pilgrimages (Jer. 31:6; Mi. 4:2; and Isa. 30:29) and the nature of the songs with Jerusalem central. The third suggestion, "son of the repatriated," would certainly be a part of this, for a pilgrimage to Jerusalem after such a long exile would have been a significant experience.

The group of psalms with this heading all express the confidence and hope of a worshiping people, but more than any other they reveal the believing Israelite's social and devotional life. The emphasis on the family, prosperity of life, and brotherly love, all would be a natural part of the festive seasons when families participated together in the thanksgiving celebrations in Jerusalem.[10]

---

10. For more details, see my *Recalling the Hope of Glory* (Grand Rapids:

There were a number of festivals in Israel's calendar. Since their calendar was a lunar calendar, precise dates in our calendar cannot be given for each festival. I shall group them by seasons.

1. In the spring there was the feast of *Purîm,* celebrated on Adar 13. It was not a pilgrimage festival in the pre-exilic times; on Nisan 15 (March or April) there was *Pesaḥ,* Passover. It was is also called the Feast of Unleavened Bread in Exodus 12:14. Within the week there was *Bikkurîm,* Firstfruits. It was the first feast of firstfruits for the year; the first fruits of the barley harvest were to be offered the day after the Sabbath following Passover according to Leviticus 23:11.

2. In the early summer (Silvan 6, around June) there was the feast of *Shābuʿōt:* the Feast of Weeks, or Pentecost. It was a celebration of the harvest of wheat (see Exod. 23:16).

3. The rest of the festivals came in the autumn, roughly September or October. There was *Rōsh Hashānāh,* on Tishri 1, the New Year. This convocation was signaled by the blowing of trumpets and horns; it began two weeks of convocation in Jerusalem. Ten days later, Tishri 10, came *Yôm Kippûr,* the Day of Atonement, the holiest day of the year. Then there was *Succôth*, Booths, or Tabernacles, also called the Feast of Ingathering (meaning the harvest of summer fruits). This started on Tishri 15.

For all these feasts there were three pilgrimages, at Unleavened Bread in the spring, at Weeks in the early summer, and at Ingathering in the fall. Of course, the Israelites could go to Jerusalem any time they desired, or for a Sabbath celebration, or New Moon, or any of the lesser feasts; but the Law required them to appear for the three major festivals.

These festivals did not only provide the people with the

Kregel, 2006), 223–241 for seasonal celebrations, and 262–289 for the use of the psalms in these times of worship.

privilege of praising God for the various harvests and paying their tithes on them, but they preserved the history of the faith as well. With the celebration of Unleavened Bread as the spring festival, there was the re-enactment of the Passover at the Exodus. Each Israelite was to look on himself as if he had been in that congregation, and so the people followed the instructions for the Passover as carefully as possible. After all, it was a memorial to be preserved throughout every generation. The pilgrims would remain in Jerusalem for a week, for the Passover, Unleavened Bread, and the Firstfruits.

Then in the early summer they would make the pilgrimage to Jerusalem for Weeks. The Law told them to count fifty days from the morning after the Sabbath until the festival of Weeks. So Weeks fell Silvan 6. The feast was another harvest festival, a thanksgiving for the harvest of wheat to Israel; but it also commemorated the giving of the Law at Mount Sinai (which occurred at the same time as this festival). Not much is known of the contents of Israel's celebration of this feast. It included *tôdāh*, acknowledgment or praise for God's harvest, as well as holy convocations with the Hallel Psalms. Essentially the people would praise God for the harvest and give to him loaves of dedication from the grain.

Then, in the fall the Israelite would again make a pilgrimage to the holy city, staying for two weeks for New Year, *Yôm Kippûr*, and Booths (Tabernacles). The harvest at this time was summer crops and fruits, the end of the agricultural year. The festival corresponds to the autumnal equinox (Exod 34:22). So the fall pilgrimage had three high points: the New Year was a day of memorial, the Atonement was a day of purgation, and Booths was a celebration of harvest, hence Ingathering. The three marked the culmination of a successful year and a clean start to the next year. In time the last day of the Festival became prominent; it was known as "the great day of the feast," the great Hosanna. At that time the priests blew the trumpets, the Levites waved branches, and all the worshipers sang *Hallel* songs.

The festivals, then, are characterized by three factors:

1. rejoicing, which often included ceremonial meals and the prohibition of work;

2. the liturgy, which included the sacrifices and the psalms;

3. and special ceremonials of each type of festival attended.

The festivals would be a marvelous time of celebration for the Israelite family. Their attention would turn to Zion in all its glory; their pilgrimage to the holy city would be filled with expectation, especially as they prepared their hearts and minds with the Pilgrim Songs. They would indeed be glad when the people said, "Let us go to the House of the LORD."

The pilgrim songs, then, should be read in the light of these festivals. For example, Psalm 121 is a psalm of trust for the journey. Its message is that the pilgrim can rest assured that the LORD, the keeper of Israel, will keep him at all times on his journey to Jerusalem because he trusts in him.

Then, in Psalm 122 the pilgrim has arrived in Zion. After recalling his pilgrimage to Jerusalem and the splendor of this spiritual and civic center of the nation, the psalmist calls the pilgrims to pray for the peace and prosperity of Jerusalem, both for the sake of the godly and for God.

Songs of Zion would find their greatest use at the festivals as well. For example, in Psalm 84 the pilgrim proclaims the blessedness of the one who in faith makes a pilgrimage to Zion to offer up a petition to the LORD of hosts for Israel's king.

HALLEL PSALMS

Psalms 113–118 came to be known as the *Hallel* psalms, hymns of praise, which were to be sung at the three great Festivals in the spring, summer, and fall, as well as at the Festival of the Dedication and at the New Moons.[11] At a domestic celebration of

---

11. See L. Finkelstein, "The Origin of the Hallel (Pss. 113–118)," *Hebrew Union College Annual* 23 (1950): pp. 319–327. The group of psalms is also called the Egyptian *Hallel* (see 114:1). The designation of Great *Hallel* was also used, but there is no agreement as to what it means. It may refer to Psalm 136, or to Psalms 120–136, or Psalms 135 and 136.

the Passover, some of them would be sung before the meal and the rest after the meal.[12]

It is difficult to know when the custom of singing Psalms 113–118 at the festivals began. All indications are that it was pre-Christian, but that is about all that can be determined. It may have been operative before the final editing of the collection because these passages are together. The church naturally brought over Psalms 113, 114 and 118 as psalms to sing at the Easter period, not only because they saw the natural succession from Passover to Unleavened Bread to First Fruits as fulfilled in Jesus' death and resurrection, but also because of the explicit use of the *Hallel* by Jesus at the festival in conjunction with his teaching on the meaning of the text.

The themes of these psalms fit the celebrations at the festivals (as do other psalms in the Psalter). Psalm 113 is a psalm of praise for the LORD's greatness and grace. Anyone who knows of the incarnation could not miss the obvious parallels between the psalm and that Christian doctrine. According to the psalm, it is the nature of the LORD to come down in order to exalt the helpless and the weak. Psalm 114 celebrates the Exodus from Egypt, and so is altogether appropriate at Passover, or any other national festival. It declares how God delivered his people with miraculous intervention and calls for the earth to tremble at his presence. Psalm 115 was apparently written in a time of national humiliation. It is a prayer for the LORD to vindicate his honor by delivering his people. The psalm contrasts the powerless gods of the pagans, who drag down their worshipers to their level of impotence and senselessness, with the sovereign LORD who is omnipotent. Psalm 116 is a psalm that praises the LORD for answering a prayer for deliverance from imminent death; for this the psalmist promises lifelong praise. The righteous can look forward to a long, tranquil life because the LORD proved himself gracious. The psalmist had not lost faith in the great time of trouble, and so can now encourage others. Psalm 117 is a call for all peoples, Jews and Gentiles alike, to praise the LORD for his loyal love and truth. This short passage may have served

---

12. Psalm 118, at least, was probably the hymn sung by Jesus and his disciples in the upper room at their Passover supper (Matt. 26:30; Mk. 14:26).

as a doxology in use at the festivals. The apostle Paul used it in Romans 15:11 to show that the grace of God was extended to Gentiles. Finally, Psalm 118, perhaps the grandest of the *Hallel* psalms, is a praise for the LORD's deliverance of his people from the chastening of the exile. The praise dramatically culminates in a procession to the sanctuary.

ENTHRONEMENT PSALMS

There is a group of psalms that celebrate the reign of the LORD over all the earth. They have come to be known as enthronement psalms because they were interpreted as an integral part of a cultic approach to the psalms presented by Sigmund Mowinckel.[13] The theory generated a great amount of interest, and while it is no longer widely followed, its influence is still felt. The name that was given for these psalms is still present in the literature. It does at least identify the group of psalms with the emphasis on the exaltation of the LORD as king, but it is more likely that these psalms present an eschatological vision than record cultic acts.

The unifying feature of the enthronement psalms is not their form but their content and possible function. Central to the theme of each is the expression "the LORD reigns" (יְהוָה מָלַךְ, *YHWH mālak*; see Pss. 47:8; 93:1; 96:10; 97:1; 98:6; and 99:1). Mowinckel's view was that it referred to an annual festival in Israel that celebrated the LORD's kingship over the earth, the festival taking as

---

13. Mowinckel's work, *The Psalms in Israel's Worship,* serves more as a historical study now. In addition to the work of Mowinckel, the following sources will be helpful for those who wish to study further: D. J. A. Clines, "Psalm Research Since 1955: I. The Psalms and the Cult," *TB* (1969): pp. 105–125; "The Evidence for an Autumnal New Year in Pre-Exilic Israel Reconsidered," *JBL* 93 (1974): pp. 22–40; Keith R. Crim, *The Royal Psalms* (Richmond, VA: John Knox, 1972); J. H. Eaton, *Kingship and the Psalms* (Naperville: Alec R. Allenson, Inc., 1975); A. Gelston, "A Note on *YHWH malak*," *VT* 16 (1966): pp. 507–512; John Gray, "Canaanite Kingship in Theory and Practice," *VT* 2 (1952): pp. 193–220; "The Kingship of God in the Prophets and Psalms," *VT* 11 (1961): pp. 1–29; Edward Lipinski, "Yahweh Malak," *Bib* 44 (1963): pp. 405–460; Julian Morgenstern, "The Cultic Setting of the Enthronement Psalms," *HUCA* 35 (1964): pp. 1–42; and Helmer Ringgren, "Enthronement Festival or Covenant Renewal," *Bib Res* 7 (1962): pp. 45–48.

its central feature the cultic (representative) enthronement of the LORD. He supported this hypothesis (he called it a valid hypothesis) by arguing that the use of the perfect tense suggested that the LORD was just made king, or declared to be king, that there existed parallel customs and expressions in the other nations, and that there were references in post-biblical literature to the existence of such a festival. It was in studying the myths of other cultures that he saw parallels with expressions and passages in the psalms.

In the Canaanite Baal myth, the cardinal motifs were: the death of Baal, his restoration to life in triumph, the fixing of destinies, procession, and the enthronement that fixed fertility for another year. Baal acquired kingship by vanquishing the rebellious lord of the sea; he was enthroned in a palace especially built for him on the sacred mountain of the north. The myth may have been concerned with the autumn season that commenced the seasons of the rains that guaranteed the agricultural year. However differently scholars explained this myth, most proponents of the cultic approach saw some direct influence of it on Israel's festival in the autumn.[14] In some cultic ritual in Israel, the God of the Hebrews was thought to have ensured world order and supremacy by the primeval combat with Leviathan, and therefore, amidst great revelry, was enthroned king of the universe, inaugurating the season of the rains and ensuring fertility. This "myth," the theory suggests, was enacted each year at the autumnal festival (New Years) with the king acting the part of God; but due to the tendency to suppress anything of mythological nature, we are told, it all receded into the background of the Scriptures.[15]

The psalms that salute the LORD as king were claimed as cultic cries at the festival in which the LORD was ceremonially enthroned year after year. In the festival the King-God comes (Ps. 98:9) and makes himself known (Ps. 98:2). Since God's kingdom is founded on creation, the primeval conflict

---

14. See, for example, T. H. Gaster, *The Festivals of the Jewish Year: A Modern Interpretation and Guide* (New York: Sloane, 1953), p. 113.

15. A. Kapelrud, *The Ras Shamra Discoveries and the Old Testament* (Oxford: Basil Blackwell, 1965), pp. 65–79.

was also a part of the founding of his kingship (Ps. 93:3). After this establishment of supremacy, in a procession to the holy mount God ascends to his throne with a shout.[16] So Psalm 47 celebrates this with clapping, playing, singing, and dancing, as well as shouting that the LORD is king and God of the earth. This seemed logical; because if the LORD descended to defeat Israel's enemies, he would ascend in triumph. Such victories would have inspired the people's acclaim of his kingship and the expectation that someday he would likewise judge the whole world.

The main problem for the theory was that there is no substantial evidence of such a festival in the prose literature of the Bible, and there is no clear evidence in the psalms of expressions and ideas that only can be interpreted correctly if taken with such a festival. And disagreement over the nature of the festival argues against its being the central part of Israel's ritual. According to the Book of Deuteronomy (16:13–16), one of the feasts that Israel was to observe was Tabernacles ("booths"), also called Ingathering. This festival time was in the autumn; it included New Years, Atonement, and Booths. Very little ceremony is connected with these festivals (which cannot so easily be explained as pious suppression of pagan ideas). So as far as ceremonies were concerned, the Old Testament records nothing like what has been proposed.

There have been several modifications of this cultic view; most prominent are those of Weiser and Kraus that were discussed earlier. Although their proposals differ extensively, they both continue the idea that there was a significant festival in the autumn that is alluded to frequently in the Book of Psalms, but more recently scholars have almost completely rejected the cultic approach as the key to the whole collection.

Gerstenberger thought that the psalms were probably the

---

16. Mowinckel suggested that the presence of the LORD in the festal procession was symbolized by the ark, but the only evidence for the movement of the ark in procession comes from the transference of the ark to Jerusalem by David. The Old Testament bears witness that the ark was not to be treated lightly (see 1 Sam. 6:19–21; 2 Sam. 6:6–7). See Marten H. Woudstra, *The Ark of the Covenant from Conquest to Kingship* (Philadelphia: Presbyterian and Reformed, 1965), p. 122.

expression of pious believers over time.[17] And Greenberg said that the psalms were not exclusively connected to the cult but represent individual communion with God apart from the restraints of the temple ritual.[18] The focus on the psalms as Torah, introduced in the first psalm, meant that these were considered to be the word of the LORD for the development of individual piety. The individual psalms were collected and used in the worship of Israel, but they were not written for one cultic purpose. Goldingay concluded "it is a hazardous assumption that a psalm referring to a theme of Israel's faith (e.g., the covenant) must connect with a festival that celebrated that theme."[19] It is far better to deal with each psalm on its own merits to determine its message before suggesting the ways they were applied and adapted to the faith and worship of Israel.

However we explain the nature and use of the psalms in the collection, we are left with a group of psalms that announce "the LORD reigns," and celebrate his sovereignty over the world with epiphany language. One possible interpretation is to understand them as referring to the universal reign of God.[20] This would require taking the perfect tense as a gnomic perfect, a universal truth. A reading of Psalm 93 would harmonize well with this interpretation. Another possibility is that they refer to the LORD's historical reign over Israel. Here the acclamation would mean that the LORD demonstrated his sovereignty by defeating Israel's enemies. Possibly Psalm 99 could be seen in this light. Many commentators, including Delitzsch, Gunkel, Oesterley, Kraus, and Westermann among others, have seen these psalms as referring to eschatological events (or at least including such). Childs noted that the final form of the Psalter

---

17. E. Gerstenberger, "Psalms," in *Old Testament Form Criticism,* ed. by J. H. Hayes (San Antonio: Trinity University Press, 1974). He argues that the psalms' background lies in the worship of the post-exilic community. Any attempt to limit their use in worship to a particular time is without compelling evidence.

18. M. Greenberg, *Biblical Prose Prayer* (Berkeley: University of California Press, 1983).

19. J. Goldingay, *Psalms 1–41* (Grand Rapids: Baker, 2006), p. 54.

20. See Alva J. McClain, *The Greatness of the Kingdom* (Grand Rapids: Zondervan, 1959) pp. 22ff.

is eschatological in nature in that it looks forward to the future fulfillment of the covenant promises.[21] Similarly, in Isaiah 52:7 the clause "God reigns" clearly refers to the time in the future when the suffering servant will be exalted over the earth. The perfect tense in these psalms may be left as an English present tense and explained as the acclamation of the future, or it may be explained as a prophetic perfect, describing something that appears to have happened but will happen in the future. If there was an event that inspired the writing of one of these psalms, the psalmist used poetic language that exceeded the reality of the event, but would become literally true at the end of the age.

We know that Israel had some kind of celebration in the festival in the autumn. It very likely included the reading of the Torah, the re-enactment of the wilderness experience with the booths, singing of psalms and celebrating, and the renewal of the covenant (at least on the part of the individual's devotion).[22] Great victories would naturally be celebrated in any festival and such would be described in terms of divine intervention. In the process Israel depicted the final act of the LORD as analogous with his earlier acts of salvation, i.e., the deliverance from Egypt and epiphany at Sinai. The prophets and these enthronement psalms used the epiphany language from Sinai as a harbinger of the final days when the LORD will indeed come down and all the world will change.

So, for example, in Psalm 47 the psalmist calls upon all peoples of the earth to do homage to Israel's sovereign, holy monarch, the LORD, as he assumes his kingship over them after subduing them. And in Psalm 97, the psalmist exhorts the saints to hate evil and to rejoice in the LORD in the light of his vision of the awe-inspiring epiphany of the LORD when he will

---

21. Brevard S. Childs, *Introduction to the Old Testament as Scripture* (Philadelphia: Westminster Press, 1979).

22. In the study of individual psalms it will become evident that early psalms were used in different contexts and so their function took on a different significance. And given the great changes in the historical and religious circumstances of Israel, it is difficult to see how all the psalms could be given one setting. See Patrick D. Miller, *Interpreting the Psalms* (Philadelphia: Fortress, 1986).

judge his adversaries in righteousness. Similarly, in Psalm 98 the psalmist calls upon all the earth at the time the LORD establishes his kingdom to sing a new song to him because he has done wondrous things: he has saved Israel and is about to judge the earth in righteousness.

ROYAL PSALMS

There are a number of psalms that Gunkel classified as royal psalms, not because they share any single literary structure but because they share the common motif of the king. The role of the monarch was important in ancient Israel, as it was in all the ancient Near East, for the king had the power to direct the destiny of the nation for good or for evil. In many instances he was considered to be the representative of the nation. It is not surprising, then, to discover a number of psalms written for the most important events in the king's experience. We must be careful not to broaden the type to include any psalms with references to kingship imagery, or to psalms that have themes that are similar to the royal psalms. This group includes only those passages written for some momentous occasion in the life of the king, occasions such as his coronation, his wedding, the charter by which he would rule, or his greatest military campaigns in which the LORD gave the victory to his servant the king.

According to the traditions of ancient Israel, kingship was always a part of God's plan for his people, in spite of how it developed historically. The oracle to the patriarch Abraham includes kings in the promise of descendants (Gen. 17:16). Jacob's oracle on the destiny of the tribes specifies that the scepter would not depart from Judah until the one comes to whom it belongs (a passage to which the Targumist added the clarification "King Messiah" [Gen. 49:8–12]). Balaam, the pagan diviner, foresees Israel's future king from the steppes of Moab (Num. 24:7; 24:17–19). Hannah's song also refers to the LORD's king being victorious (1 Sam. 2:10). Even the Law included legislation for the king not to multiply wives or horses (Deut. 17:14–20). So one begins to understand from these passages as well as the historical narratives of Samuel that it was God's intention from the beginning that the administration of his theocracy would be through his chosen king.

This king, then, had to be installed by the LORD himself, and not come to power through palace intrigue or usurpation as many of the northern kings later did. In order for the king to rule legitimately he had to be elected or chosen by the LORD. To David God said, "I took you from the pasture and from following the flock to be ruler over my people Israel" (2 Sam. 7:8). Once the covenant was made with David (2 Sam. 7:5–16), every Davidic king was considered to be elected by God. Accordingly, the king was anointed by the LORD's prophet and referred to as the "anointed one" (מָשִׁיחַ, or māšîaḥ, popularly "messiah"). This act of anointing was the outward sign of the election. If the prophet of the LORD anointed a king, it was a sign of special relationship between God and his chosen administrator of the covenant. Often the anointing conferred power so that the monarch could rule effectively; that power came by the presence of God's Spirit on the king (see 1 Sam. 16:13–14). This power was the divine enablement for the administration of the covenant.

When kings ascended the throne in the ancient world, they assumed honorific titles that expressed their special relationship to God and the aspirations for their administration. While this custom was not widespread in Israel,[23] titles were used to designate the special standing of the individual (note especially the titles of the coming Messiah in Isaiah 9). In the last words of David there seem to be several designations used, although they are not all royal: "The oracle of David, the son of Jesse, the oracle of the man exalted by the Most High, the man anointed by the God of Jacob, Israel's singer of songs" (2 Sam. 23:1).

---

23. See the articles on David and Solomon by J. J. Stamm, "Der Name des Königs David," *VT Supplement* 7 (1960): pp. 165–183; and "Der Name des Königs Salomo," *ThZ* 16 (1960): pp. 285–297; the article on the throne-names of the Messiah in Isaiah 9 by H. Wildberger, "Die Thronenamen des Messias, Jes. 9, 5b," *TZ* 16 (1960): pp. 314–332, as well as in his commentary, *Isaiah 1–12* (Minneapolis: Augsburg Fortress, 1991); and the general article on the evidence for regnal names in Israel by A. M. Honeyman, "The Evidence for Regnal Names Among the Hebrews," *JBL* 67 (1948): pp. 13–25.

The greatest title for the king was "son." In the Davidic Covenant the LORD promised this title perpetually to David's seed:

> When your days are over and you rest with your fathers, I will raise up your offspring to succeed you, who will come from your own body, and I will establish his kingdom. He is the one who will build a house for my name, and I will establish the throne of his kingdom forever. I will be his father and *he will be my son*. When he does wrong, I will punish him with the rod of men, with floggings inflicted by men. But my love will never be taken away from him, as I took it away from Saul, whom I removed from before you. Your house and your kingdom will endure forever before me; your throne will be established forever (2 Sam. 7:12–16).

This title for the king as God's "son" was used in the coronation royal psalm, as well as in prophecies about the coming Messiah in Isaiah 9 and Daniel 7. The New Testament writers saw its fulfillment in the Lord Jesus as the Son of God as well as the son of David (Rom. 1:4).

For the king to be called God's "son" in ancient Israel, however, did not mean that he was divine. That should be clear from the fact that this king was chosen and blessed by the LORD God (Ps. 45:7) and designated as the son when he was crowned (Ps. 2:7). Moreover, this one who would bear the title would be disciplined by the LORD should he go astray, and the history of Israel bears this out. No, such a king was only called the firstborn (Ps. 89:28), "adopted" as the son for the sake of ruling over the theocracy as the heir of the kingdom (Ps. 2:8). He was not, as the pagan monarchs claimed for themselves, divine. The term "God" could be applied to the human king (Ps. 45:6), as well as to judges (Ps. 82:1) or other human administrators (Moses in Exod. 7:1), but only in the sense that the king was God's representative.[24] According to the teaching of the New Testament, the incarnation presented

---

24. For further discussion on the subject, see Ivan Engnell, *Studies in Divine Kingship in the Ancient Near East;* A. R. Johnson, *Sacral Kingship*

a higher meaning to the royal psalms, including the full meaning of the title for the promised king. The fact that the king could be disciplined by the LORD meant that he was under Torah—he had to obey the Law. Therefore, he was to be the "servant of the LORD," one of the highest titles to which a human should aspire, for it designates a person as truly devout and obedient. For the king to be the servant of the LORD was a perpetual reminder that the kingdom was a theocracy, administered through a human king who was subject to Torah and the prophetic word (cf. Ps. 18: 1; 89:4, 21: and 144: 10). The sad history of the nation reveals that while many of the kings could rule others effectively, they were not obedient servants (see 2 Sam. 12:7–10).

If the king was God's agent on earth, it meant that the peace and prosperity of the nation was effected by the LORD and not by the king himself (see Ps. 144:15). God's promise of a sure dynasty was secure, but participation in the promises to that dynasty demanded faith and obedience. If the king was a faithful servant of the LORD, he would be blessed by the LORD in his many enterprises.

Because the Davidic monarchy was central to the existence and well-being of the nation, it is not surprising that many psalms were written for major events in the life of God's designated "son." Moreover, since David, with whom the covenant was cut, was himself a psalmist, it is not surprising that several of these psalms were traditionally identified as Davidic. Whatever the occasion for their composition, the royal psalms would have been appropriate to any "messiah," i.e., any anointed king in Israel, and so were probably used on many occasions over the centuries. And then with the appearance of the Lord Jesus in the line of David, the apostles saw how these psalms applied to the Messiah; the royal psalms are frequently cited in the writings of the New Testament.

The main psalms classified as Royal Psalms are as follows:

---

in Ancient Israel; Sigmund Mowinckel, *He That Cometh;* and J. H. Eaton, *Kingship and the Psalms.*

ROYAL PSALMS	
Psalm 2	The Coronation of the Son and the Certainty of His Dominion
Psalm 18	The King's Song of Victory in Battle
Psalm 20	A Prayer for the King for Victory in Battle
Psalm 21	A Praise by the King for Victory in Battle
Psalm 45	The Wedding of the Victorious and Righteous King
Psalm 72	A Prayer for the Righteous and Prosperous Dominion of the King
Psalm 89	The Davidic Covenant Assured in Spite of Its Failure
Psalm 101	The Charter by Which the King Will Rule
Psalm 110	The Establishment of the Priestly Kingdom by Holy War
Psalm 144	The Establishment of Peace and Prosperity by the King's Victory

Other psalms may contain royal motifs, but these are the established royal psalms in which the office, character, or activity of the king is central.

WISDOM PSALMS

There are portions of the Old Testament that give attention to the importance of living one's life in accordance with the *Torah*, a practical wisdom that produces a pious and productive life. Wisdom literature in the Old Testament, as well as in the ancient Near East in general, recognizes an established order in the world that rewards virtue and industry while bringing justice to evil and sloth. Any thorough study of this genre would require a detailed examination of Proverbs, Ecclesiastes, Job and what has come to be called "wisdom psalms" (or "learned psalmography" as Mowinckel preferred to call them).[25]

Features of Wisdom Psalms

Kuntz listed seven distinctive features of psalmic wisdom, pointing out that no psalm that is classified as a wisdom psalm has all seven, nor is each device limited to wisdom literature.

1. The "better" saying

Frequent in Proverbs and Ecclesiastes, this occurs in only six in the Psalter: Psalms 37:16; 63:4; 84:11; 118:8,9; and 119:72. Psalm 37:16 stands clearly in a wisdom context.

2. The numerical saying[26]

Roth listed three passages in the Psalter: 1:6; 27:4; and 62:12–13a. Only the latter reference is an example of a graded numerical saying that is present in wisdom literature.

3. The admonition with and without motive

This feature is more widely attested in the psalmic literature than the first two. It is present to some extent in Psalms 32 and 49, and takes on a dominant role in Psalms 34 and 37 (where motive clauses are introduced with כִּי).

4. The admonitory address

In Proverbs the sages often addressed their students as sons (23 times); but in the psalms this is rare. Psalm 34:12 heads a strophe of sapiential admonitions with "Come, O sons, listen to me; the fear of the LORD I will teach you!" In

---

25. The article on wisdom literature by J. A. Emerton in *Tradition and Interpretation*, edited by G. W. Anderson (Oxford: Oxford University Press, 1980), will provide a good survey of the literature. Also most helpful is the article by J. Kenneth Kuntz, "The Canonical Wisdom Psalms of Ancient Israel—Their Rhetorical, Thematic, and Formal Dimensions," in *Rhetorical Criticism*, edited by Jared J. Jackson and Martin Kessler (Pittsburgh: Pickwick Press, 1974), pp. 186–222.
26. W. W. Roth, *Numerical Sayings in the Old Testament: A Form Critical Study* (Leiden: E. J. Brill, 1965).

other passages the writer calls for the attention of all people (Pss. 49:1; 78:1). The point is that the satisfactory teaching of wisdom depends on the attentive presence of willing listeners, sons and others.

5. The ʾashrê formula

This is an exclamatory sentence that begins with the "beatitude" (אַשְׁרֵי). It focuses on the concern of wisdom—who is fortunate? It is found in Psalms 1, 34, 112, 127, 128, and twice in 32. It is not found in wisdom Psalms 37, 49, and 133; but it is found in Psalms 40:5–6, 94:8–15, and 119:1–2 which are not wisdom psalms but have similar features. Other passages also use the word.

6. The rhetorical question

The sages used different types of rhetorical questions, as in the wisdom section of Psalm 94:9–11. Rhetorical questions are not often found in wisdom psalms; but see 34:13 and 49:6, as well as 25:8–14 which some classify as wisdom sections.

7. The Simile

Similes drawn from the world around them as explicit illustrations are common in wisdom literature. Psalm 1:3, 4 is perhaps the best known sample of this feature. See also Psalm 49:13; 37:2, 20; 32:9; 127:4; etc. The presence of similes does not make a poem wisdom literature. It is but one common feature found in wisdom literature.

Themes of Wisdom Psalms

Wisdom literature consistently includes certain motifs. There are four that can be found in the passages that are clearly psalmic wisdom.

1. The fear of the LORD and the veneration of Torah

The wise knew that the fear of the LORD was the beginning of knowledge, and that fear was gained from the Torah. Thus, wisdom literature places a heavy emphasis on the Torah. And the wise subordinate themselves to the divine will.

143

2. *The contrasting life styles of the righteous and the wicked*

The righteous and the wicked figure predominantly in the Bible. The wicked lives a godless life of self indulgence; this is the fool and the sinner. The righteous lives an untarnished, prosperous life in compliance with the fear of the LORD. Wisdom literature often contrasts features of these two life-styles; see Psalm 1 for the clearest example, but also Psalm 37.

3. *The reality and inevitability of retribution*

The problem that all wisdom literature grapples with is that of injustice in this life. How is it that the righteous one who lives in the fear and obedience of the LORD often suffers while the wicked prospers? Wisdom finds a solution for this tension with an understanding of retribution, either in this life or beyond. The contrasting fate of the pious and impious appears clearly in wisdom psalms such as Psalm 49 and Psalm 1. The presence of it in Psalm 73 has caused many to classify that passage as wisdom as well.

4. *Miscellaneous counsels pertaining to everyday conduct*

Wisdom texts give basic, practical advice, such as: be prudent in speech, desist from anger, be mindful of the company kept, live in harmony, integrity, generosity, trust in the Lord and not your own understanding, shun evil and do good.

Common Vocabulary

Scott has demonstrated that wisdom literature has a characteristic vocabulary: "The words of this are rarely peculiar to it, but their proportionate frequency is noticeable".[27] He gives a list of 77 words which are helpful in studying the wisdom material, 64 of which occur in the Psalter. Frequent use of certain words does not make the genre; however, when taken into consideration with the other features and motifs it is a helpful observation.

Five of the psalms (1, 5, 73, 92, and 139) use nine of the wisdom words, two (10, 107) use ten of them, three (19, 37, 49)

---

27. R. B. Y Scott, *The Way of Wisdom in the Old Testament* (New York: MacMillan, 1971), p. 121.

use eleven of them, two (25, 55) use twelve of them, three (32, 15, 94) use thirteen of them, and Psalm 119 uses 28 of them. In the 15 psalms that use nine or more of these words, several of the predominant features of wisdom literature are also present.

The classification of psalms as Wisdom Psalms is a difficult matter, as a survey of the literature will show. Kuntz concluded in his discussion that four psalms (1, 32, 37, and 49) may legitimately be called wisdom psalms, four psalms (25, 92, 94, and 107) contain clearly identifiable wisdom elements of varying lengths, and another four (19B, 73, 119, and 139) reflect some of the concerns of Israelite wisdom.[28] Other psalms that are classified as wisdom psalms on stylistic and thematic grounds contain relatively few wisdom words: 34, 112, 127, 128, and 133.

The expositor will have to weigh the evidence for any given psalm to determine whether or not there is sufficient evidence for that classification. It is important to remember, however, that no psalm will have all the devices, features, or vocabulary that is so common to wisdom literature.

---

28. Kuntz, "The Canonical Wisdom Psalms," pp. 186–222.

PSALMS IN WORSHIP

The psalms were essential to the worship of ancient Israel, and are to worship today as well. They were deposited in the sanctuary for the Levitical choirs to use in the services, or for individuals to use in whatever way was necessary or appropriate. The psalms themselves are filled with references to the sacrifices, the priests, the temple, and the festivals.[1] While the exposition of a psalm will focus on its message, it is often helpful to consider how it might have been used in worship, especially if there is evidence of liturgical use in the structure of the passage.

PSALMS IN ANCIENT WORSHIP

Many of the psalms were designated for use at specific services. Hayes writes:

> The primary worship services in ancient Israel were community affairs. Regular and routine services were held daily, on the sabbath, at the new moon (first day of the month), and at seasonal festivals. References to the daily sacrifices are noted in Exodus 29:38–46; Numbers 28:1–8; 1 Kings 18:36; and 2 Kings

---

1. For a more thorough discussion of the Psalter and Israel's worship, see my discussion in *Recalling the Hope of Glory* (Grand Rapids: Kregel, 2006), pp. 221–92.

147

16:15. Although the Old Testament itself does not refer to the singing of psalms in conjunction with daily sacrifices, we know from later Jewish tradition that the following psalms were sung during the daily services; Psalm 24 (Sunday); Psalm 48 (Monday); Psalm 82 (Tuesday); Psalm 94 (Wednesday); Psalm 81 (Thursday); Psalm 93 (Friday); and Psalm 92 (Saturday; see the title to Psalm 92). This selection of psalms for the daily services reflects the practice during the time of the second temple, but on the basis of this evidence it can be concluded that such a use of some psalms was quite ancient.[2]

We have already noted that many of the psalms were sung on the pilgrimages (pilgrim psalms), and at the high festivals (*hallel* psalms), and at times when people came to the sanctuary to pray or to praise. Oesterley noted that "inasmuch as all these types of utterances are addressed to a divine being, they are, in effect, the essential elements of which the later more formal and elaborated forms of divine worship were composed.[3] He discusses four types of psalmic literature from the very earliest period of Israel.

1. As an illustration of a petition, he uses Numbers 10:35. This was prayed in the presence of the ark in the belief that the LORD was there; thus the words were part of a divine service.

2. For a blessing (what he calls supplicatory utterance), he cites the priestly benediction of Numbers 6:24–26. This was clearly connected to the sanctuary as it was spoken when divine service was taking place or concluding.

3. For thanksgiving, he mentions the song of Hannah in 2 Samuel 1. Again, this poem was uttered in the sanctuary.

---

2. J. H. Hayes, *Understanding the Psalms* (Valley Forge: Judson, 1976), 16.
3. W. O. E. Oesterley, "Worship in the Old Testament," in *Liturgy and Worship,* edited by W. K. Lowther Clarke and Charles Harris (London: SPCK, 1933), p. 52.

4. And finally, with reference to praise he looks at Exodus 15 and the song of Moses. There is clearly an organized worship of praise as Miriam and the women responded antiphonally to the words of the song.

So these four pieces of early poetry represent different aspects of sanctuary worship. Oesterley then corresponded these to the types of psalms we find in the Psalter, prayers for individual spiritual needs, supplications and intercessions, psalms of thanksgiving, and songs of praise. He concludes by saying:

> The four types of psalms mentioned may without hesitation be pointed to as the earliest, so far as content is concerned, to have taken shape; but various other types came into existence in course of time; and in most cases, though probably not in all, they were sung in the Temple worship during the offering-up of sacrifices. The evidence for this is derived mainly from the Mishnah; and although this evidence is comparatively late, it must be recognized that, in view of the tenacious character of religious uses, much of it must reflect traditional custom . . . . We conjecture, therefore, that utterances of petition, supplication, and thanksgiving, which in course of time developed into psalms of these types, were originally used by an individual worshiper, and that later many of these were adapted to congregational use.[4]

The laments, which form a significant part of the petitions, whether of individuals or the people as a whole, would be most effectively poured out to God in the sanctuary. And as people gathered to pray, many of these psalms were used again and again as part of the liturgical structuring of the worship.

Included in the psalms are prophetic utterances, either in criticism of the worship or in prediction of judgment and redemption. Encouragement from prophets or priests often centered on the LORD's protection and blessing of the king; this meant that royal psalms were included in the liturgical collection of psalms. In time the prophetic element began to emphasize the sovereign reign of the LORD over all the earth. As part of the Temple

---

4. Ibid., pp. 52–59.

hymn book, these psalms would have inspired greater devotion and confidence in the faithful worshiper.

It is not difficult to see how the psalms in the collection were used by individuals or the congregation in worship, but their use was not limited to the sanctuary. They would be learned easily and recited or sung on the journeys to the holy city, or in places of separation from the sanctuary, or in meditations in the night. For the devout Israelite, the psalms were essential to the spiritual life, and when the psalms were brought into the worship in the church, the whole tradition of their use continued.

Notations in the Psalms

Since I have discussed the musical guilds and instruments in *Recalling the Hope of Glory,* it will not be necessary to repeat all that information here. Instead, I will restrict the discussion to the notations in the Psalms.

(1) "To the Chief Musician" (לַמְנַצֵּחַ) is found with 55 psalms. The word is a participle from the verb "to be preeminent" (נָצַח). There are many suggestions for the meaning of this word; the AV and RSV use "chief musician." If it refers to the choir director, then it would designate a psalm deposited in the temple for singing.

(2) "For the Sons of Koreh" (לִבְנֵי־קֹרַח). It is unlikely that the preposition in this case indicates authorship, since that would mean a clan wrote the psalms. Besides, Psalm 88 uses the title along with the note "Of Heman the Ezrahite." The heading probably indicates that the psalms that have this notation formed the music of this family of temple singers and may have originated from them.[5]

(3) For headings that list other personal names, the exegesis will have to determine whether authorship is meant or liturgical musical use. "Asaph," for example, was one of David's chief musicians (1 Chron. 6:38; 15:17; 16:5f; 2 Chron. 5:12). One of the psalms with this note describes the destruction of the temple

---

5. See D. Wanke, *Die Zionstheologie der Korachiten,* BZAW 97 (1966): pp. 23–31.

(see Ps. 74). If the name refers to that Asaph, it may be that "Of Asaph" has been shortened from "son of Asaph," or that the name became the name of a guild.

(4) "According to Jeduthun" (עַל־יְדוּתוּן) is found in Psalms 62 and 77 and in Psalm 39 (with לְ). According to 1 Chronicles 16:41 Jeduthun was one of David's chief musicians. The title in the psalms may refer to the family of singers or their kind of music. The preposition in the musical and melody indicators may be translated "set to" or "upon." The former is the most appropriate when voices and tunes are indicated.

(5) "[With] Stringed Instruments" (נְגִינֹת) refers to the musical accompaniment, excluding wind and percussion instruments. It goes with Psalms 4, 6, 54, 55, 67, 76, and 61 (in the singular).

(6) "Flutes" (נְחִילוֹת) occurs with Psalm 5 (אֶל־הַנְּחִילוֹת). It may refer to times of lamentations.[6]

(7) "*Ălāmôt*" (עֲלָמוֹת [עַל־]) is written with Psalm 46, along with "Of the Sons of Korah" and "A Song." The Greek version has "hidden things," assuming another root, but Jerome and Aquila have "maidens." The psalm may have been played upon lyres tuned to the voices of maidens.

(8) "Eighth" (הַשְּׁמִינִית [עַל־]) occurs with Psalms 6 and 12. With the preposition it probably means "set to the eight-stringed lyre."

(9) "*Gittîth*" (גִּתִּית) is found with Psalms 8, 81, and 84; with the preposition and article it is translated, "set to the *Gittith*." It is an obscure heading, but may mean "the Gittite (lyre)," or "for the wine press" (Greek), or "a vintage melody." Gath was a location, but the word means "winepress"—hence the uncertainty.

(10) "*Selah*" (סֶלָה) is the term most often queried by the modern reader. It is unclear. The form is an imperative, "lift up," and may

---

6. Sigmund Mowinckel, *The Psalms in Israel's Worship*. Translated by D. R. Ap-Thomas. Volume II (New York: Abingdon, 1967), p. 210).

denote places in the psalm where worshipers were to lift their voices (and so not a superscription). The Greek version used "pause" (διάψαλμα), an interlude or pause of some kind, marking places where something else was said or played. The Vulgate omits the word. Jewish traditions interpret it "forever." Mowinckel connects it to an Aramaic word *sl*' ("to turn, bend, pray") and suggests it marks the place where the people prostrated themselves in prayer.[7]

Finally, there are some headings in the psalms that appear to be ancient tunes to which the psalms were set (much like in modern hymnals).

(11) "[Set to] *The* Lilies'" (שׁוֹשַׁנִּים [עַל־]) is found in Psalms 45, 69, and 80, while in Psalm 60 "testimony" (עֵדוּת) is added to the word in the singular: "set to the lily of testimony." The flower is probably the anemone, a type of poppy. The title is uncertain; it may be a tune.

(12) "[Set to] '*māḥălat* '" (מָחֲלַת [עַל־]) heads Psalm 53, and in Psalm 88 *leʿannôt* (לְעַנּוֹת) follows it. These are very obscure. They could be tunes, or they could be liturgical indicators. Mowinckel suggests *leʿannôt* means "for penance."[8]

(13) For the heading "to the 'Hind of the Morning'," see the literature on Psalm 22. Likewise, see the comments on "to the 'Dove on Far Off Distances'" with Psalm 56. These also may be tunes, but some writers see ritual acts involved.

(14) "Do not destroy" (אַל־תַּשְׁחֵת) goes with Psalms 57, 58, 59, and 75. Mowinckel saw it as a ritual act[9] (II, 215), but Kraus said it was an allusion to singing (cf. Isa. 65:8).[10]

(15) "Upon *the* death of a son" (עַלְמוּת לַבֵּן) occurs with Psalm

---

7. Ibid., p. 211.
8. Ibid., p. 212.
9. Ibid., p. 215.
10. Hans-Joachim Kraus, *Theology of the Psalms.* Translated by Keith Crim. (Minneapolis: Augsburg, 1979).

9 and might be "for *the occasion of the* death of the son," unless it is a corruption of ʿal-ʿălāmôt.

The singing of the psalms in Israel's worship must have been highly organized and very impressive in view of these few references to tunes, instruments, and guilds.

The Israelites themselves would be actively engaged in the various parts of worshiping and singing. Clapping the hands was a part of their rejoicing (Ps. 47:1; 98:8; Isa. 55:12; and 2 Kings 11:12), but it must have been spontaneous and natural. The cultic dance was part of the celebration (Exod. 15:20–21; 2 Chron. 6:12–19; Pss. 87:7, 149:3, 150:4). Again, however, we are speaking of festivals, processions, and joyous celebrations in honor to God, but music always played an important part in worship. The very nature of the psalms as poetry, and no doubt the musical accompaniment, worked to impress the message in the memory of the people. Even today worshipers often know the lyrics of hymns much better than the text of Scripture. Whereas the Israelites' hymns and songs were inspired Scripture, modern music is not; therefore, the impression that music makes on the memory of the worshiper no longer is always positive.

THE INFLUENCE OF THE PSALMS ON CHRISTIAN WORSHIP

The early church used the psalms in worship. The Psalter had been the hymn book of the temple and in time came to be used in the synagogues as well, although at first those were places of study alone. By New Testament times the worship in the temple and synagogue was fully developed to include a regular and comprehensive use of the psalms. The influence of this hymn book on the life of the righteous would have been inescapable. Jesus would have participated in singing the psalms at all the festivals, even though they did not entirely apply to him. In fact, he was so well-versed in them that he used them throughout his life. The force of Satan's quotation of Psalm 91 in the temptation, for example, lay in the fact that a beloved psalm of trust was being presented for application. He uncovered the foreshadowing of his own experiences in the psalms and taught his disciples how such passages prepared the way for him (John. 13:18; 2:17; Luke

24:44). The *hallel* psalms were sung in conjunction with the Last Supper. A psalm filled his thoughts when he was hanging on the cross, and with a psalm he dismissed his spirit.

The influence of Jewish liturgy on early forms of Christian worship is also evident from the New Testament. The early Christian hymns (the *Magnificat*, the *Benedictus,* and the *Nunc Dimittis*) were patterned after the psalms. James and Paul endorsed the singing of the psalms as the natural expression of the spiritual life (Jas. 5:13; Eph. 5:19; Col. 3:16), and the mention of their use in worship in 1 Corinthians 14:26 shows that they had formed part of the liturgy from the very beginning.

The frequent quotations from and allusions to the psalms in the writings of the Apostolic Fathers demonstrate their centrality in worship, both in reading and singing. Tradition says that Ignatius of Antioch (ca. 100) introduced antiphonal singing of the psalms to the church. Tertullian and Jerome both attest to the common use of the psalms in Jewish and Gentile congregations.[11] Tertullian said that on the first day of the week after the reading of the Old Testament lessons "the hymns of David" were sung, and people sang the antiphons.[12] Over the centuries the psalms were used in the teaching of doctrine and recited in prayers; but they were also sung in private meditations and divine service. So the influence of the Psalter on the hymns and liturgy and devotion of the church has been truly great.

---

11. Tertullian, *Apology*, chapter 39; Jerome, *Letter*, 46:12.
12. See *Apostolic Constitutions*, ii. 57. For a more detailed study, see James H. Charlesworth, "Prolegomenon to a New Study of the Jewish Background of the Hymns and Prayers in the New Testament,"*Journal of Jewish Studies* 1-2 (1982): pp. 265–285. Charlesworth surveys the early Jewish hymns with a view to understanding portions of the New Testament. See also Eric Werner, *The Sacred Bridge* (New York: Columbia University Press, 1959); and William L. Holladay, *The Psalms Through Three Thousand Years* (Minneapolis: Fortress Press, 1993).

THEOLOGY
OF THE PSALMS

We use the psalms in our public worship, for prayers, praises, music, and liturgy, and in private devotional life for similar meditations; but there is another, neglected use of the psalms, which is the primary interest of this commentary, exposition.

Since the material of the exposition is the exegetically derived theology of the text, expositors must think theologically when reading the psalms. A general overview of the theological ideas in the collection will provide a framework for that step in the process of developing the message.

In fact, the foundation of any use of the Book of Psalms must be the theology of this collection of prayers and praises of Israel. For it to become the prayer book of the temple, it clearly had to have a consistent theology, a central theological message on which all the related ideas and motifs were based. It was the firm conviction of the faithful in Israel, and certainly the compilers and editors, that it did, and that central theme was the sovereign rule of the LORD God over his creation, not just Israel but the entire world. The careful study of the entire Book of Psalms will demonstrate that this is the underlying belief that informs the use of all the psalms, for prayer, praise, instruction, encouragement, and hope. Such a study would involve the exegetical analysis of each psalm and then the collating of the theological themes into a clear presentation. The following pages lay out a general survey of how this central theme appears in the different types of psalms. It is only intended as a guideline for expositors to use in addressing the theological themes that are found in the different types of psalms. As with so many surveys like this, it will oversimplify the issue because there is so much material here, but as a workable framework it should be helpful.

THE CENTRAL THEOLOGICAL THEME

While there is a good deal of debate over the center of biblical theology, or whether there even is a center, the presentation by Walther Eichrodt seems to work well and will be useful for the study of the Psalms.[1] He divides his discussion between the themes of the covenant God, the covenant people, and the instruments of the covenant. The basic development of this covenant is through the breaking in of the kingdom of God on earth. Thus, the rule of God over all creation becomes the prominent emphasis of the covenant. The covenant God is Yahweh, Israel's God, but also the God of the universe; so the entire creation is subject to God's rule. It is true that God rules over all creation and that all people are subject to his dominion, but the real focus of the establishment of God's rule is over a people who will enter into covenant with him. God's rule is the general description of the relationship between God and his creation. God extends his rule by sovereign grace and power, and people submit to his kingship by faith and submission to his law. This is a very basic way of getting at the central point of theology. The ideas cannot be narrowed more than this without changing the message, but they can be expanded with many clarifying details.

THE THEOLOGICAL MESSAGE
IN THE TYPES OF PSALMS

With these general considerations in mind, we may now trace how this theological center would fit the different kinds of psalms in the collection. And in the process we will see how the many theological doctrines and ideas are revealed.

---

1. Walther Eichrodt, *Theology of the Old Testament,* 2 vols., translated by J. A. Baker (Philadelphia: Westminster, 1961).

The Enthronement Psalms

Nowhere is the rule of the LORD celebrated more openly and convincingly than in the enthronement psalms. The expression, "the LORD reigns," the primary motif of this group of psalms, is the acknowledgment of the sovereignty of the LORD by the faithful, probably in response to some great event. These psalms are ultimately eschatological; the verb "reigns" may be taken as a prophetic perfect in view of the messages of these psalms and the language they use. Delitzsch referred to this group as eschatological Yahwistic psalms. They anticipate the future triumphant reign of the LORD over all the earth. Because the prophets foretold such a glorious future, often with similar expressions, the people probably understood that the reign of the LORD over all the earth would be fulfilled in the future. In view of the eschatological hope, the LORD could always be trusted by his covenant people in any circumstances (Pss. 106, 135, 136). The plan of God would reach its culmination in his sovereign reign over all creation.

The Royal Psalms

The rule of God over his creation was to be administered by a human king known as his "son," and so throughout the psalms there is an emphasis on the covenant God made with David and the way that God protected and blessed his chosen king. A number of psalms focus almost entirely on the monarchy. In fact, according to Psalm 2 the reign of the human monarch was so much a part of the sovereignty of God that to submit to the one was to submit to the other, and to rebel against the one was to rebel against the other. The royal psalms reveal the importance of the monarchy to God's program. Even when the monarchy came to an end, the psalmists still looked for the Davidic king to be restored. This group of psalms was considered to be so key to the meaning of the Psalter that they were apparently used as the organizing theme of the final editing.

These royal psalms also have an eschatological meaning. They are not direct prophecy (with the exception perhaps of Ps. 110), but typological (what Delitzsch called indirectly messianic psalms). They were applicable to the Israelite kings, but they find

157

their full meaning in the Messiah. Therefore, they are the most frequently used psalms in the teaching of the New Testament.

Thanksgiving Psalms

The enthronement psalms and the royal psalms clearly focus on the rule of God over all his creation, but how do the other types fit in this synthesis? The many declarative praise psalms are the responses of God's people to the manifestations of his rule. These psalms celebrate answers to prayer, victories, deliverance from enemies or dangers, and forgiveness for sin; but they often do it by declaring that the LORD saved them. The things for which they praise, however, are not the ultimate and total salvation, as is witnessed by the regular incorporation into the praise of prayers calling for complete and final deliverance from enemies, iniquities, or catastrophes. The praises attest to God's sovereign rule in the world (see Pss. 65, 67, 68, and 118); for them such intervention was part of the extension of God's rule (Pss. 40:4, 41:11–14, 92:16). For all such saving acts, the psalmists call for everyone to praise him for his demonstration of kingship (see Ps. 22:28–32). The psalms of confidence focus entirely on the sovereignty of the one who sits enthroned in the heavens.

Hymns

Hymns, or descriptive praise psalms, describe who God is and what he does; they normally praise his greatness and his grace (e.g., Ps. 113 says he is enthroned high above the earth, but he comes down to deliver people). There are many types of hymns; enthronement psalms, royal psalms, and Zion songs may include hymns. The common theme of hymns is that the LORD is over all things, evaluating, judging, saving, because he created all things (Ps. 33). His powerful word of creation also sustains and controls the universe (Ps. 29), and his dominion is over all nature (Pss. 19, 104, and 8).

Not only is he praiseworthy as the Creator and Ruler of the universe, but also of Israel. Israel is to praise her Maker and King (see 111:2–6, 114:1–8, 111:7–11, 149:7–9, 100: 1–5, 150:1–6), who sustains his people forever (33:1–5, 103:20–22, 117, 113,

146:3–10, 147:1–20). Here too, then, we have the theological foundation of God's sovereign rule over his creation.

Wisdom Psalms and Torah Psalms

Life does not always appear to be under his sovereign control. People are living in rebellion to God and seem to be prospering. Psalms that face the difficulty of living in the midst of the prosperity of the wicked, that is, the wisdom psalms, reaffirm the rule of the LORD in spite of temporary appearances. The rule of God does not always work to the immediate advantage of his people, but ultimately his justice will triumph. There will be divine retribution when the sovereign of the universe will make all things right.

In the meantime, the faithful are exhorted to live by his commandments. Since the nation of Israel was a theocracy, the Law of God was their binding law. They were to demonstrate their allegiance and gratitude to their heavenly king by keeping his commandments. Several psalms, Psalm 119 especially, concentrates on the merits of living by God's Law. Those who follow his precepts are living in submission to his rule; they assert their allegiance to his righteous cause, and confidently await his vindication.

Lament Psalms

In waiting for vindication the people of God have to deal with evil in every form—sin, sickness, famine, malicious enemies, war, and even deceitful friends. They lament these conditions; because, they reason, if God is truly the sovereign ruler of the whole earth, his faithful followers should not have to deal with these things, and so they pray for God to hear their lament and deliver them. In different ways they are praying for his kingdom to come, for they think that something appears to be very wrong with the LORD's sovereign rule.

Their prayers regularly appeal to God to deliver them from suffering, which is most often at the hands of the wicked enemies. These enemies are primarily enemies of God, but they afflict the people of God. To the psalmists, when God delivers them he will not only demonstrate his sovereignty, but also extend his rule. So they pray, "Be exalted, O God."

Whenever the psalmists found themselves in distressing states, they knew that the reputation of God was also at stake. This was made real to them when enemies taunted their faith because God had abandoned them. The faithful would diligently seek to discover the cause for this interruption of God's sovereign rule. If it was their own sin, confession was in order (e.g., penitential psalms like Pss. 6 an 32) as part of the prayer for relief; if it was undeserved suffering (e.g., Pss. 22, 44), justice was part of the prayer for deliverance (see the imprecations in the psalms). In either case, they knew in their prayers that they were appealing to the sovereign Lord of all creation and the judge of the whole earth.

Confidence and praise enhance the lament psalms. The people of God never lost sight of his lordship, then or in the future when he would put down all enemies. Their confidence was based on past saving acts of God (44:1–9), his delight in the righteous servants (12:7–8), his covenant with them (74:20), or most importantly, the reputation of the LORD who deserves to be trusted and praised and not ridiculed (74:18–21, 83:1–18).

Sometimes their confidence became a complete psalm of confidence in and of itself. They were convinced that he was ruling from on high; and those who trust in this Rock, Fortress, Shepherd, Tower, Refuge, or Keeper, will ultimately see his intervention on their behalf. He will vindicate their faith and demonstrate that he sits enthroned above the earth.

THE LIFE TO COME

We know from our perspective that the full realization of the promise of the LORD's dominion lies in the future, beyond death. The resurrection of Christ reveals how the promise of a universal kingdom of righteousness will be fulfilled in spite of death. The Israelites did not have this full revelation, but they knew that they did not cease to exist at death. Everyone in the ancient world knew that! Pious Israelites also believed that they would not be herded by death in *she'ōl* with the wicked, but they would have some kind of continued communion with God. Just how much they understood is too difficult to discern, but the fact that the New Testament uses portions of the Psalter to support the doctrines of resurrection and the life to come requires further consideration of the matter.

Israelites may have known that death was not annihilation or the end of personal existence, but to them it was the end of all that was known to them as life (Ps. 143:3). They lament that if they die and go to the grave they will not "see" the LORD in the land of the living and they cannot serve or praise him for his faithfulness (Pss. 6:5; 30:9; 88:4–5, 10–12). Any continuance of existence after death had no moral or religious element in it. Death was viewed simply as non-existence (Ps. 39:13). It brings no solution to the enigmas of the present life. It was in this life that the faithful wanted to see recompense and retribution. They knew there was a judgment after death; the whole world knew that! Yet the Israelites did not think that dying and going to heaven was the answer to their prayers. They wanted deliverance in this life so they could go and praise the LORD in the land of the living (Isa. 38). Kirkpatrick explains further:

> Nowhere in the Psalter do we find the hope of a Resurrection from the dead.[2] The prophets speak of a national, and finally of a personal resurrection (Hos. vi. 1 ff.; Is. xxvi. 19; Ezek. xxxvii. 1 ff.; Dan. xii. 2), and predict the final destruction of death (Is. xxv. 8). But just where we should have expected to find such a hope as the ground of consolation, it is conspicuously absent. Indeed it is set on one side as incredible (lxxxviii. 10). It is evident that there was as yet no revelation of a resurrection upon which men could rest; it was no article of the common religious belief to which the faithful naturally turned for comfort.
>
> But do we not find that strong souls, at least in rare moments of exultant faith and hope, broke through the veil, and anticipated, not indeed the resurrection of the body, but

---

2. It is true that the doctrine is not unambiguously stated in the Psalter, but there are hints that suggest they knew a little more than we might think. Some scholars assume the idea of resurrection came much later, and so any passage that seems to get close to the doctrine is assigned a later date. These passages will be discussed in the commentary.

translation through death into a true life of unending fellowship with God, like Enoch or Elijah?

Do not Pss. xvi, xvii, xlix, lxxiii, plainly speak of the hope of
the righteous in his death? The answer to his question is one of
the most difficult problems of the theology of the psalter. It can
only be satisfactorily treated in the detailed exposition of the
passages as they stand in their context. Some of the expressions
which appear at first sight to imply a sure hope of deliverance
from Sheol and of reception into the more immediate presence
of God (e.g., xlix. 15, lxxiii. 24) are used elsewhere of temporal
deliverance from death or protection from danger, and may
mean no more than this (ix. 13, xviii. 16, xxx. 3, lxxxci. 13, ciii.
4, cxxxviii. 7). Reading these passages in the light of fuller revelation we may easily assign to them a deeper and more precise
meaning than their original authors and hearers understood.
They adapt themselves so readily to Christian hope that we are
easily led to believe that it was there from the first.

Unquestionably these Psalms (xvi, xvii, xlix, lxxiii) do contain the germ and principle of the doctrine of eternal life. It
was present to the mind of the Spirit Who inspired their authors. The intimate fellowship with God of which they speak as
man's highest good and truest happiness could not, in view of
the nature and destiny of man and his relation to God, continue
to be regarded as limited to this life and liable to sudden and
final interruption. (See Matt. xxii. 31 ff.). It required but a step
forward to realize the truth of its permanence, but whether the
Psalmists took this step is doubtful. But even if they did, there
was still no clear and explicit revelation on which the doctrine
of a future life or of a resurrection could be based. It was but
a "postulate of faith," a splendid hope, a personal individual
conclusion.[3]

This is a very careful way of stating the case, but I think

---

3. A. F. Kirkpatrick, *The Book of Psalms* (Cambridge: Cambridge University
Press, 1914), pp. xciv–xcvi. He acknowledged with Delitzsch that there is
nothing that comes to light in the New Testament which does not already
exist in germ in the Psalms. Death and life were linked to God's wrath and
love in a way that made it easy for the New Testament to appropriate and
deepen the ideas in the light of fuller revelation.

some of the psalmists understood a good deal more than the average Israelite. And yet, we have to work with what they actually said in the poetry. Each of the passages in question will be dealt with in detail in the commentary.

NEW TESTAMENT FULFILLMENT

The central theme of the theology of the Psalms finds confirmation in the fulfillment in the New Testament, especially by the use of the psalms in conjunction with teaching about the establishment of the kingdom of God on earth. The use of Psalms 110, 45 and 2 in Hebrews points to the righteous reign of the Messiah to be instituted at his second coming to earth.

Many of the psalms do find fulfillment in the first advent of Christ in which he made entrance into the kingdom possible through his death. The evangelists found in the psalms the eloquent and appropriate words to highlight his suffering, opposition, death, and resurrection, without which of course, there could be no new covenant and no kingdom. Now that we have the full revelation in Christ, we can see the correlation between the promise and the fulfillment. Just as Israel celebrated God's righteous rule over creation by virtue of his past deliverance, yet looking in anticipation to his actual reign, so too the church anticipates that coming in glory to rule in absolute dominion. Just as Israel entered his kingdom by compliance with his provision of atonement and longed for the day that his righteous kingdom would redeem them from all their iniquities, so too the people of this age submit to the Son to escape the coming wrath, pray for his kingdom to come so that righteousness would triumph throughout the earth, trust in him and his word when his dominion seems ineffectual, and confidently praise him for his demonstrations of sovereignty in their times of distress, all of which are harbingers of that glorious day when the King shall come to redeem his people and rule the world.

One can see in reading through the psalms that there are many texts that are relevant for Christology. Psalms that are called "messianic" are not limited to the royal psalms; the designation applies to many psalms that may be partly or completely messianic.

Delitzsch provided a clear distinction in the types of messianic psalms, or messianic elements in the psalms.[4]

1. His first category was called "Typically Messianic Psalms." In this type, the subject of the psalm is in some way a type of Jesus Christ; the truths concerning the psalmist find ultimate fulfillment in him. For example, see Psalm 34:20.

2. The second category was "Typico-prophetically Messianic Psalms." Here the psalmist uses language to describe his present experience, but that language goes beyond his own experience, and becomes historically true only in the Lord Jesus Christ (e.g., Psalm 22).

3. The third was "Indirectly Messianic Psalms." These are the psalms which at the time of composition had reference to a contemporary king or to the house of David in general, but await their final fulfillment in the Lord Jesus Christ, the greater David (these are the royal psalms, such as Psalms 2, 45, and 72 and others).

4. Fourth, "Purely Prophetic Psalms." The psalm refers solely to the LORD Jesus Christ without reference to any other son of David. Psalm 110 is the only one that could fit in this category; even then, however, the psalm had to have had some meaning for the ancient congregation.

5. And the fifth, "Eschatologically Yahwistic Psalms." These psalms refer to the coming of the LORD and the consummation of his kingdom; they will find their ultimate fulfillment in the person of Christ the Lord (Psalms 96–99, the so-called enthronement psalms fit in this section).

Delitzsch's categories, with modifications, are helpful for trying to explain just how certain psalms are being used in the New Testament. We may simplify them a bit to establish

---

4. Franz Delitzsch, *Biblical Commentary on the Psalms*, trans. by Francis Bolton (Grand Rapdis: Eerdmans, reprint of the 1871 translation), I: pp. 68–71.

guidelines for the correlation of the testaments. Because the Psalms do not have much direct prophecy, it is a little more difficult to explain the New Testament usage. In fact, there are times when they use passages in ways that do not seem to be in the understanding of the psalmists.

Any use of the Hebrew Scriptures by later writers, especially the New Testament writers, is based on the presupposition that the literature of ancient Israel has far-reaching theological significance. It was not just written for them in their day; it was written for us as well. The biblical interpreters saw that the record of God's dealings through his people was constantly moving forward from promise to promise. This can easily be illustrated, but our Lord's use of Isaiah in speaking to his audience is a good example: "Well did Isaiah speak of you." Obviously, Isaiah spoke to his audience, but what he said is certainly meant for Jesus' audience as well, as also for ours.

The apostles saw that the Old Testament in general was the history of the promise which was being fulfilled through and in Christ. Even the advent of Christ brought the promise of a new fulfillment, another advent. Many passages were seen in a new and clearer light; even scriptures of non-prophetic substance seemed to carry a new significance in the light of the coming of Christ. All such interpretations of the Bible reveal an understanding of the process of the development and fulfillment of the promises of God.

It may be an oversimplification, but the following three categories will probably work with all the uses of the psalms in the New Testament.

Direct Prophecy

Prophecy is clearly displayed in linear history and provides an explicit statement of what shall be in the last days. In the Psalter directly prophetic material is greatly limited; it would include Psalm 110 most likely (although some commentators see the psalm as a coronation psalm and that would make it typology). It may also include the enthronement psalms if they are interpreted to reflect future events only; but if they were partially fulfilled by some historical event ("near fulfillment") and completely fulfilled at the end of the age ("far fulfillment)," then they too would be typology. Psalm 110 should be considered prophetic since its contents has no near fulfillment in the experience of a Davidic king.

Typology

There is hardly any hermeneutical principle applied more freely by Bible students than typology. If it is a hermeneutical principle, then we must be able to write some description of it and certain guidelines to follow. Lewalski said:

> Typology . . . [is] a mode of signification in which both type and antitype are historically real entities with independent meaning and validity, forming patterns of prefiguration, recapitulation, and fulfillment by reason of God's providential control of history. In precise terms, typology pertains to Old Testament events, personages, ceremonies, and objects seen to foreshadow and to be fulfilled, *forma perfectior*, in Christ and the New Dispensation.[5]

Typology and prophecy accomplish the same thing but from different means. Prophecy is explicitly stated in linear history, but typology looks back to the events and discerns that the New was already in the Old implicitly. Typology identifies the correspondences between type and antitype within the historical framework of God's revelation. Thus, it is based on the sovereignty of God over history and revelation, but it must be remembered that typology is a form of prophecy—indirect prophecy—because it is divinely intended. It is not merely an interpretation contrived by New Testament writers.

Typology must also be distinguished from archetypal symbols. A pure type has one fulfillment; an archetype has many. For example, Christ is the passover, according to Paul. There are no more "fulfillments" to come. Now that Christ has come, we can look back and see the correspondence and identify the old as a

---

5. Barbara Lewalski, *Protestant Poetics and the Seventeenth-century Religious Lyric* (Princeton, NJ: Princeton University Press, 1979), p. 111.

type. The old does not lose its meaning in the exposition of that passage in its context, but the divine intent for it is incomplete without the (now revealed) fulfillment. Cain, on the other hand, is an archetype. He is held up as the paradigm of hatred for a brother. Every individual who hates his brother is a murderer like Cain. Archetypal symbols and events seem to fit better in the next category.

To identify typology there should be some communication from a writer of Scripture that something in the text was a type. This is not to say that it must be called a "type" in the New Testament, or that the "fulfilled" formula must be present (such as, "this was said that the Scripture might be fulfilled . . ."). There may be specific literary allusions or references to the item(s) and a subsequent theological implication derived from them. The types do not lose their importance as part of revelation, after the greater antitype appears, by fading into mere shadows and schemes as the course of time extends beyond them; they become part of the eschatological proclamation while keeping their contextual significance.

Because typology and prophecy are so closely related, the New Testament writers could use the same formulae to introduce both. "That it might be fulfilled" or "spoke of the Christ" or any similar expression cannot be limited to the fulfillment of prophecy. Rather, it may be used also for a typological use of the Old Testament in which the fullest sense is developed.[6] The royal psalms are clearly typological. Because Jesus is a Davidic king, those psalms are applicable to him as well—but in a way that was never possible to the ancient kings. Psalm 22 is also classified as typology; the language of the psalm is lavish but becomes historically true in Jesus Christ. Many times the New Testament writers drew on this passage to show its ultimate meaning ended with Christ's death and exaltation. It might be applied to believers who suffer, but the full meaning applies only to Christ.

Delitzsch's other category, "Typically Messianic Psalms," does not seem to me to belong to the category of typology, even though the samples do find correspondence with Christ's

---

6. See S. Lewis Johnson, *The Old Testament in the New: An Argument for Biblical Inspiration* (Grand Rapids: Zondervan, 1980), pp. 66ff.

experience. Psalm 34:20, for example, seems to be applicable in a wider sense. So the third category covers passages like this.

Application

In many places the New Testament seems to make an application of the text by analogy; it is not prophecy and it is not typology, but a general use of appropriate texts. It is true, however, that when some of those passages are applied to Christ, they do take on a greater meaning and significance. For example, a passage that laments how a familiar friend betrayed the psalmist may be applied to the betrayal of Jesus. There is a similarity that makes the application work, but it is a general application of the text. Likewise, Peter applied passages from the imprecations of Psalms 69 and 109 to promote the necessity of replacing Judas. The lines were fitting for someone who brought a curse on himself by betraying Jesus. In the same analogous way Paul used the law prohibiting muzzling of an ox to argue for supporting ministers. In this category we see that verses or passages are applied based on analogy. The Jewish teachers did it; Jesus and the apostles did it; and when we make applications from passages in our expositions we often do the same thing.

These three categories—direct prophecy, typology, and application—may provide ways of thinking about the use of the Psalter in the New Testament. Each case will have to be studied on its own; but on the whole the New Testament writers knew that these inspired psalms were part of divine revelation, and Christ Jesus would be the complete and full revelation. They did not force a Christological fulfillment on every passage; but knowing that the theology of the Psalms, and the Old Testament as a whole, was laying the foundation for the coming king, they were able to apply many of them easily. When Christ suffered and died and rose again, the apostles began to look further into the passages and discovered they had more to say about the Messiah than they had previously understood. They also realized that the long-awaited deliverance of the people of God and the establishment of a righteous kingdom awaited the second coming.

EXPOSITION
OF THE PSALMS

Developing an exposition from a passage like a psalm can seem daunting, but if expositors follow the basic exegetical procedures it will come together nicely. The following discussion will briefly review the procedures to be taken and focus on some aspects that I think would be most helpful in this study. The discussion will follow a logical order, but in most cases expositors will find the steps overlapping because often when researching in one area material for another is discovered. Moreover, not every step will apply fully to every passage. Nevertheless, these are the basic things that expositors should be prepared to do.

PRELIMINARY OBSERVATION OF THE TEXT

In working with a psalm expositors will not have to determine the literary unit to be covered. The psalm is the unit. To start the preparation they should read the passage in several English translations to see where there are major differences that will have to be explained. Most importantly they should make a note of major textual difficulties that will need more attention, key words that will need to be studied, poetic devices and figures of speech that are not obvious, and variations in the translation of the tenses and other grammatical forms.

RESOLUTION OF CRITICAL MATTERS

The next step is to determine insofar as it is possible the precise and original form of the text by studying the textual critical problems. Here most expositors will have to rely on the more thorough commentaries for help. Then, other major critical issues will need to be considered, such as the composition and possible circumstances of the text.

THE STUDY OF WORDS

The most important words in a passage, theological words, rare words, words that are at the heart of the message, will have to be studied so that they can be easily explained. These may have been encountered already in sorting out textual difficulties, but now they will have to be studied using dictionaries, concordances, and word study books.

GRAMMATICAL AND SYNTACTICAL ANALYSIS

Poetic passages often are more challenging than simple prose, especially in view of the way the psalms use the perfect and imperfect tenses. Those who know Hebrew will need to review the categories of the grammar, at least to be able to understand the translations and commentaries. In studying the tenses, along with the normal range of uses for the perfect tense, the prophetic perfect should be reviewed. And for the imperfect tense, it may be helpful to review the imperfect with the *waw* consecutive (or preterite as it may be called) because in poetry it is occasionally used without the *waw*. Many of the modal uses of the imperfect tense will also appear.

A survey of the English translations should alert expositors to differences in the translations of the tenses. Frequently one version might use a simple future tense (an imperfect), and another might make it a prayer (a jussive). The expositor will have to study the context to decide which is more plausible.

ANALYSIS OF THE POETICS

In studying the psalms it will often be helpful to consider the literary type of psalm, if that type has a distinctive structure. Knowing this will help the expositor keep the different sections of the psalm separate and clear but also maintain the right tone for the message (praise or lament).

Then the significant figures of speech will have to be studied to determine the full meaning for their use. This will not come easily at first, but the more expositors work in the psalms the more they will get the feel of the literature. Many of the figures will be used frequently, making the study easier over time.

EXEGETICAL SYNTHESIS

It is important that expositors make outlines and summaries of the psalm; this will help them understand it and explain it easily. This too may seem to be a lot of work at first, but after a while it can be done faster. Essentially in this step expositors are putting into their own words what the verses and groups of verses are saying; this is what they will have to do in delivering the exposition any way. In doing an exegetical outline before changing it into an expository outline ensures that the exposition is true to the text and covers the whole passage. In the commentary I have prepared an exegetical outline for each psalm, and then in the commentary section I have changed the main points into an expository outline. These outlines are not the only ways that the passages can be divided and summarized, but they will help make the work of the expositors easier as they can use them in the process of developing their own ideas. What follows is the exegetical and expostional process in some detail in order to illustrate the method that I use with any passage in the Bible.

The synthesis of a passage will begin with an exegetical outline and then the formation an exegetical summary. Most expositors skip this step, but to me it is one of the most critical steps, even though it is an intermediate stage. You must outline a passage in order to

1. Be able to trace the argument of a passage,

2. Be able to show how the ideas change in their immediate contexts, and

3. Be able to put in your own words what the text is saying.

And then you must use an outline to help people to

1. Be able to follow your discussion,

2. Be able to see the divine design of the passage, and

3. Be able to summarize the sections in their own minds.

1. Form the Exegetical Outline

An exegetical outline is an outline that describes in your own words the contents of the passage. It is to be written in full sentences (= complete thoughts) and not topics. It is to be historical and descriptive in its wording, and it must interpret and not retain high figures. For this discussion I will use Psalm 2.

Step One: Summarize the Verses Line by Line

Write a brief summary statement for each line of poetry (which usually means each English verse) in your own words (this is excellent preparation for explaining the lines in a sermon). Do not retain the figures of speech in your wording unless it is a common and understood idiom, but give an interpretive meaning where possible. Do not restate if the parallelism does, but interpret the whole verse as a unit. Use complete sentences. Do not worry about final form at this stage, only the accuracy of interpretation. For Psalm 2 these summaries are workable:

1. The psalmist expresses amazement that the nations' leaders scheme a rebellion that cannot succeed.

2. The psalmist says that these earthly kings have decided to oppose the LORD and his anointed king.

3. The psalmist words their resolution to rebel against the authority of the LORD and his king.

4. The psalmist reveals that the LORD holds their ridiculous plan in contempt.

5. The psalmist predicts that one day the LORD, declaring judgment in anger, will terrify these rebels.

6. The psalmist quotes the LORD's declaration that he has installed his king upon the throne in Zion.

7. The psalmist quotes the king's resolve to recite the covenant statute that declares him to be the anointed king.

8. The psalmist quotes the king's affirmation that the LORD promised to give him all the nations as his possession when he asks for it.

9. The psalmist quotes the king's affirmation that the LORD instructed him to destroy the nations that rebel.

10. The psalmist exhorts the people in the nations to heed his advice.

11. The psalmist exhorts them to worship the LORD.

12. The psalmist exhorts the nations to do homage to the LORD's king because his judgment is coming soon.

Step Two: Group the Summaries

Study your line-summaries to see which of them can be grouped into natural units, either by structure of the literary form of the psalm (if such is discernible), or by subject matter. For this psalm I suggest that the contents of the verses indicate four sections of three verses each:

1–3	The first three verses describe the activities of the rebellious nations that wish to overthrow the LORD and his king.
4–6	The next three verses record the response of the LORD to their ridiculous plan.
7–9	The next three verses all discuss the resolution of the king who shows his rights and privileges as the LORD's chosen.
10–12	The last three verses all record the exhortations of the psalmist for these foolish nations to submit to the king and become true worshipers of the LORD.

Step Three: Summarize Each Group

Once you have settled on the divisions of the passage, write summaries for each group. These summaries should include the contents of the verses subordinated under them, but with less detail than the individual summaries. These group summaries will now become Roman numerals of the psalm, and the verse summaries (or other summaries of sub-sections) under them become sub-points. The following is my final, polished exegetical outline of Psalm 2. Realize, however, that it took some intermediate steps of condensing, editing, and rewriting to get to this point.

I. The psalmist reveals how the nations foolishly desire to rebel against the LORD and his anointed king (1–3).
  A. He is amazed at the tumultuous and vain resolve of the nations (1).
  B. He explains the resolve of the nations: they have united to end the authority of the LORD and his anointed king (2–3).
    1. Rulers sit in conclave together against the LORD (2).
    2. They resolve to break away from his authority (3).
II. The psalmist reveals the resolution of the LORD to set his king on Zion's throne (4–6).
  A. The sovereign LORD of heaven holds their feeble plan in contempt (4).

    B. The LORD will speak in his wrath against them to appoint his king (5–6).
      1. He will speak in his wrath and terrify them (5).
      2. He will announce the installation of his king in spite of them (6).

III. The psalmist reveals the affirmations of the king to show by right he rules (7–9).
    A. The king resolves to declare the statute of the covenant (7a).
    B. The king reiterates the promises of God in the covenant: coronation as a "son," inheritance of the earth, and sovereign dominion (7b–9).
      1. "Today" the LORD makes him king (7b).
      2. The LORD invites him to ask for his kingdom so that he may have dominion over the rebels (8–9).

IV. The psalmist exhorts the foolish nations to submit to the new king lest judgment come upon them quickly (10–12).
    A. He calls for the leaders of the nations to use wisdom (10).
    B. He instructs them to serve God in submission to the king lest they be judged quickly (11).
    C. He announces a blessing for those who trust in him (12).

One of the values of an exegetical outline like this is that you have clearly stated in your own words what each line of the text is saying, and that will make your exposition flow smoothly. You have also grouped sections and subordinated verses in the sections, so you can handle the text in parts at a time; those parts flow in a sequence that is the argument of the passage, so you can trace the development for people. If you have done this step, the homiletical outline will not only come easily, but it will be accurately outlining the text.

2. Writing the Exegetical Summary

What we want to do now is to write a one-sentence summary of the entire passage. If you do this, you will be able to show the unity and the organization of the psalm. The way to do this is to take the Roman numeral points you have written and put them together as a paragraph. Decide then which section of the passage will be the main idea, the central focus, or the climax (here I decided everything was leading up to the psalmist's exhortation to the nations, and so that will be my central clause or sentence–the other sections being subordinated).

First write the points together and then start to edit, condense, revise to a shorter format, turning some of the points into subordinate clauses to the main clause in your understanding.

Here are the sentences that you might write. The psalmist reveals how the nations foolishly desire to rebel against the LORD and his anointed king. The psalmist reveals the resolution of the LORD to set his king on Zion's throne. The psalmist reveals the affirmations of the king to show by what right he rules. The psalmist exhorts the foolish nations to submit to the king lest judgment come on them quickly.

It will take a little bit of editing to get it into a workable form, unless you are very good with writing and editing; but if you go through the process, you will be so involved with the ideas of this psalm that you will be able to think through it clearly. You are not yet writing a sermon idea, but an apt summary of the contents of this psalm. It should be brief enough to be a summary in one good sentence; but it should be precise enough to fit this psalm and this one only. My final polished sentence summary for Psalm 2 is as follows:

> The psalmist exhorts the pagan nations to abandon their ridiculous plans to rebel against the LORD and his anointed king and submit to the authority of this king whom God has ordained to possess the nations and end their rebellion.

There are other ways this could be summarized, of course; but this is how I decided to word it. It fits this passage only in the whole Bible; and it adequately covers the main parts of the passage. It puts the emphasis on the psalmist's advice to the foolish people. In that light we can see that the psalm is rather evangelistic!

3. Developing the Expository Outline

The exegetical outline is fairly easy to develop. It ensures that you can explain the text in your own words—but it cannot be your outline for the exposition. If it were, it would be a historical lesson (stating what happened back there) and not a message to your current audience, and it would be too hard for people to take in only hearing you say it. Having done an exegetical outline makes it rather easy to write an expositional outline and ensures that the message's outline will actually fit the passage.

Take the Roman numeral points and change them into shorter and more direct objective, propositional statements. They will no longer be historical and descriptive; they will be timeless and theological—but still fit the passage. The method to follow is to substitute, usually by abstracting ideas, to get to a general principle; the test to apply to see if it works is to determine if the principle you write fits the original audience as well as your modern audience. Psalm 2 yields this homiletic or expository outline:

   I. Folly: It is futile for humans to try to throw off God's authority (1–3).
  II. God's Plan: God's sovereign authority establishes his "Son's" rule (4–6).
III. Messiah's Claims: God's anointed king will rule the world with absolute authority (7–9).
 IV. Wisdom: It is wise for humans to find refuge from God's judgment by submitting to his Son (10–12).

The points are principles that cover the verses in those sections and are not historically descriptive statements now. The way the statements are worded would be clear and useful to the original audience as well as your audience today. They are timeless truths (which is why you have to try to tie Old and New Testaments together in forming the theology). If you worded the point to say "Christians need to . . . ," that would leave out the old audience; if you said "Israel was to . . . ," that excludes your current audience. You have to hit that mark for the principle in such a way that if you said it in either setting it would be an adequate summary of the point of the section and relevant to the listeners. In other words, you are taking your exegetical interpretation of the few verses and stating what God is saying practically and theologically through them. This step will take more thinking than writing.

4. Writing the Expository Idea

Now, the final step in the synthesis is to reduce the exegetical summary to a shorter statement in the same manner as was done with the outline. This will be a clear, theological statement, worded to fit the original context as well as the modern audience. It is the central theme of the psalm—and so of your message. It is the biblical theology of the passage that has been exegetically derived, condensed, and put into a rhetorically effective statement for homiletical purposes. You will not just expound on this statement; you will preach the psalm. The wording of this idea will keep your exposition on target and enable your audience to perceive the main theme of the message. Your message will explain the psalm to show how you got this outline and idea, and then make its relevant points based on these theological ideas. For Psalm 2 I have written:

It is wise to submit to the authority of the Messiah, because God has declared that he will rule the world.

There are many details and related ideas in the passage for each word or phrase in this sentence, to be sure, but this captures the main point of the psalm. The delivery of the lesson or sermon will have to bring enough material from the text itself to show how this idea, as well as the outline, was developed. The expository idea simply provides an easy-to-remember summary statement of the exposition of the psalm.

After this has been developed, you can develop the rest of the essentials for the message—what words you will explain, how much time you can give to background information, what illustrations you might add, and when you will tie in other Scripture. All of this has to be planned since time is limited; everything must be evaluated for its usefulness and effectiveness in the message. There are some things you would like to include, but due to the time, or the occasion for the message, you might have to curtail to cover other things that are more important to the message. You always gather more and learn more in the preparation than you can deliver in the exposition, especially in longer psalms.

THE THEOLOGY OF THE PASSAGE

The theology of the passage by now should be very clear, but it should be stated clearly, if it is not identical to the summary of the psalm. Organize the theological details of the passage so that they will be addressed in the presentation (what the passage says about God, his names, his nature, his acts, and what it says about the people, their names, natures, actions, and about the covenant).

Correlate the theological idea, as well as any minor points, to the theology of the whole Bible, especially the New Testament. This will involve noting how the New Testament may use the psalm, or how the New Testament addresses the same practical or theological issue. In this way people will see that the message in the psalm is still applicable even though the ritual and other circumstances have changed.

APPLICATION

Finally, the exposition will need to develop practical applications. Sometimes the psalms will do this for you, especially if they are didactic or instructive; other times you will have to draw analogies between the psalmist's situation and that of believers today. The application should be able to say on the basis of the exposition of the psalm what you want people to believe and what you want them to do.

There are many ways to preach or teach from the Book of Psalms. This, the exegetical exposition, is but one of them, but it is the one method that guarantees the entire psalm will be explained, correlated and applied in a clear, interesting, and meaningful way.

PSALM 1

The Life That Is Blessed

INTRODUCTION

Text and Textual Variants

1 Blessed is the one
   who does not walk in the counsel of the ungodly,
   nor stand in the path of sinners,
   nor sit in the seat of the scorners;
2 but whose delight is in the law of the LORD,
   and in his law he meditates day and night.
3 He will be like a tree planted by channels of water,
   that brings forth its fruit in its season,
      whose leaf does not wither;
   and whatever he does will prosper.[1]
4 Not so are the ungodly,[2]
   but *they* are like the chaff which the wind drives away.[3]

---

1. Greek may be translated "shall be prospered."
2. Greek repeats οὐχ οὕτως, "not so . . . not so."
3. Greek adds ἀπὸ προσώπου τῆς γῆς, "from the face of the earth."

5 Therefore the ungodly will not stand in the judgment,
    nor sinners in the congregation[4] of the righteous.
6 For the LORD knows the way of the righteous,
    but the way of the ungodly will perish.

Composition and Context

Psalm 1 sets the tone for much of the rest of the Psalter by contrasting the way of the righteous with the way of the ungodly
and sets the stage for the hostility of the ungodly. Along with
Psalm 2, it forms the introduction to the entire collection. Psalm
2, a royal psalm, lays out the connection between God's rule and
the human monarchy. Psalm 1 says nothing about the king, but
it focuses on the way of the righteous that is to be lived out in
accordance with the law of the LORD. Putting the two psalms
together we have the main themes of the book, the way the righteous are to live among the ungodly, and the salvation the righteous have in their divinely chosen king.[5] Psalm 1 then begins by
reminding the reader that those who order their lives by God's
word will find success in this life and in the life to come, but
those who reject God's word have no hope of escaping his judgment. The message of the psalm centers on the importance of
meditating on God's word (and so the psalm is often studied as
a *torah* psalm[6]).

The psalm is put together in a way that focuses attention
on the righteous life that is based on the law of the LORD.[7]
The first three verses lay out the untarnished (v. 3) and blessed
(v. 1) life of the believer who lives by God's word (v. 2). The

---

4. In place of בַּעֲדַת, "in the congregation," the Greek has ἐν βουλῇ, "in the
   counsel," the same word it used in verse one for Hebrew בַּעֲצַת.
5. See P. D. Miller, "The Ruler in Zion and the Hope of the Poor: Psalms
   9–10 in the Context of the Psalter," in *David and Zion, Biblical Studies
   in Honor of J. J. M. Roberts,* ed. by B. F. Batto and K. L. Roberts (Winona
   Lake: Eisenbrauns, 2004), pp. 187–198.
6. See J. L. Mays, "The Place of Torah Psalms in the Psalter," *JBL* 106
   (1987):3–12; but see also H. W. Wolff, "Psalm 1," *EvTh* 9 (1949, 50):385–394.
7. For a more detailed study of the poetical structure, see Sebastian Bullough,
   "The Question of Meter in Psalm i," *VT* 17 (1967):42–49; and Walter Vogels, "A Structural Analysis of Ps 1," *Bib* 60 (1979):410–416.

second part of the psalm provides a strong contrast ("Not so are the ungodly"); it portrays the life of the ungodly as worthless and therefore doomed in God's judgment. The last verse of the psalm provides a fitting conclusion: the way the righteous live is the way of salvation; the way the ungodly live is the way of judgment.

There is no indication of authorship or date for the psalm; the commentators offer a wide range of suggestions. Kraus, for one, concluded that a date in the first or second century before Christ was likely.[8] On the other hand, Perowne presented the traditional early date (Solomonic),[9] noting that the psalm had several themes of wisdom literature: it contrasted the righteous and the ungodly, emphasized the fear of the LORD and the love for the law, and concluded with the inevitability of reward for the righteous and judgment for the ungodly. One may observe that like wisdom literature in general Psalm 1 employs similes, has the formula "blessed is," and uses vocabulary common to the genre. As a wisdom psalm it extols the wisdom of living in accordance with the law of the LORD, but it is the emphasis on meditation in the word of the LORD that has prompted many modern scholars to choose a later post-exilic date for the psalm (see Introduction). Broyles suggested that the lack of a super-scription, especially in Book I which consistently uses super-scriptions, indicates that this psalm and the next were added to introduce the collection.[10] Whether they were added after all the psalms had been collected or not is hard to prove. In fact, settling on a date for the composition is equally hard to determine, but there is no compelling reason it should be post-exilic. An earlier psalm could have been selected to form part of the introduction to the collection.

---

8. He reasons that it was a time that the "congregation" was distinct from all Israel, that the study of the Law had become more common by then, and that the individual who was the truly fortunate person went against the trends of the worldly life (Hans-Joachim Kraus, *Psalms 1–59*, pp. 114–115). There is sufficient evidence in the Bible to identify these traits in pre-exilic Israel as well.

9. J. J. Stewart Perowne, *The Book of Psalms*, I:108.

10. Craig C. Broyles, *Psalms*, p. 42.

Exegetical Analysis

Summary

The psalmist describes the blessed individual who leads an untarnished and prosperous life in accord with God's word, and contrasts the worthless lives of the ungodly who will perish in the day of judgment.

Outline

I. The psalmist describes the blessed person who leads an untarnished and prosperous life in accord with the word of the LORD (1–3).
   A. He announces the blessedness of the untarnished life (1).
   B. He attributes this life to meditation in the Law of the LORD (2).
   C. He describes the prosperity of the righteous under the image of a fruitful tree (3).
II. By contrast, the psalmist describes the ungodly as worthless and without hope (4–5).
   A. He portrays the worthlessness of the ungodly under the image of chaff (4).
   B. He predicts the final separation of the ungodly from the righteous (5).
III. The psalmist concludes that the ungodly shall perish but that the LORD will save the righteous (6).

COMMENTARY IN EXPOSITORY FORM

I. The Way of the Righteous: Those who are blessed by God lead an untarnished and prosperous life in accordance with his word (1–3).

A. *The righteous lead an untarnished life (1).*

The first verse gives a summary description of the life of the righteous: it begins with an announcement of their spiritual state and then qualifies it with three clauses. Their state is that they are "blessed" (אַשְׁרֵי), a term that refers to the joyful spiritual condition of those who are right with God and the plea-sure and satisfaction that is derived from that. It is an abstract plural, stressing the fullness of joy; it may be paraphrased: "O the heavenly blessedness[es] of the person[11] who . . . ."[12]

Following this three relative clauses explain the blessed life. In the clauses there is a threefold trilogy of ascending intensity.[13] First, the three terms for the people of the world are "ungodly," "sinners," and then "scorners." The "ungodly" (רָשָׁע) here are unbelievers, people who have no part in the covenant and so remain guilty before God.[14] A translation "the

---

11. The text says "blessed *is* the man," but the word "man" was not intended to limit the application to males but to anyone trying to live a godly life.

12. The translation "happy" does not capture the sense very well; happiness can be a superficial feeling based on what happens. This word refers to that sense of joy and satisfaction that comes with knowing that one is right with God—in spite of what happens. See also W. Janzen, "'Ašrê in the Old Testament," *HTR* 58 (1965):215–226.

13. Andre Gunnel, "'Walk,' 'Stand,' and 'Sit' in Psalm i 1-2," *VT* 32 (1982):327. The words used in the verse are common to Proverbs, but reminiscent of Deuteronomy 6:7 as well; see G. W. Anderson, "A Note on Psalm i 1," *VT* 24 (1974):231–34 and S. Reif, "Ibn Ezra on Psalm i 1–2," *VT* 34 (1984):232–36.

14. The word for the "wicked" (רָשָׁע) is very common in the Book of Psalms, and while it is a good translation, it calls for some explanation at the outset. Modern translations prefer "wicked" to the old versions' "ungodly," but that may give the casual reader the impression that the passage is only referring to those unbelievers who are particularly evil and dangerous, and not calling the unbelieving relative or friend "the wicked."

 The word basically describes people who are not members of the cov-enant, not believers, and therefore ungodly. The main idea is that since they have not come to faith in the LORD and found forgiveness for their sins, they stand condemned as guilty and deserving the punishment of God. In some places the verb as well as the adjective requires a translation of "guilty." Those who stand condemned can only expect divine judgment. In Genesis 18:23 and 25, Abraham was concerned that the righteous might be destroyed with the people who deserved the judgment—the wicked.

 In the Bible the word "wicked" is certainly used to characterize people as doing wickedly: they might be guilty of any crime against the law of Israel (see Isa. 58:4; Prov. 10:2; 12:3; 16:12), or any wicked acts within the realm of ethical and moral activities (see Deut. 9:27; Jer. 14:20). They are declared guilty because their sins are against the laws of God. In ad-dition to describing violations of the law, the word often describes people who are attacking and trying to destroy the righteous, as evidenced by the prayers of the psalmists for protection from the wicked (e.g., Pss. 9:5–6;

wicked" gives the impression that they only do wicked things. This may be true at times, and in some contexts that describe their works, "wicked" would be a better translation. The word can also describe people who may seem to be kind and who may even be part of the congregation; they are just not godly. Next in intensity is the word "sinners" (חַטָּאִים), those who are either ignorantly or intentionally failing to obey God.[15] Finally, there are the "scorners" (לֵצִים), those who ridicule the righteous and try to destroy their integrity. The word probably focuses on things they say because the verb is used elsewhere

---

10:2; 17:13). In this sense it is used especially for the great wickedness of Pharaoh (Exod. 9:27), Babylon (Isa 14:5), and the Chaldeans (Hab. 1:4, 13), all of whom were bent on destroying God's people. One can easily identify with the plea of the psalmist who was surrounded by bloodthirsty men, "O that you would slay the wicked, O God" (Ps. 139:19).

The word certainly can describe people who are doing evil things, but it can also describe people who are basically unbelievers, just not godly. They have no reverence for God. The "ungodly" may be capable of truly wicked acts, but they may also seem to be pleasant and kind. They may even be members of the congregation (Ps. 50:16), whose presence in the worship service is therefore hypocritical—they have no intention of obeying God's word but are more comfortable associating with adulterers and thieves and are themselves malicious slanderers (among other things). If the text does not specify the wicked acts of the unbeliever, the sense of "ungodly" may be a more appropriate translation to ensure that people know the word is referring to all unbelievers. Some of these people may seem to us to be good people, but as far as God is concerned they are "wicked" because they have rejected their creator and chosen to live in violation of his laws and refuse his provision of salvation. They are guilty of sin before God and stand condemned (Ps. 1:6).

In the messianic prophecies we read how the Lord hates wickedness (Ps. 45:7) because he loves righteousness. He will root out all wickedness when he comes to reign (Isa. 11:4). With the expectation that the judgment of the Lord will fall on the ungodly/wicked, all that can be said is that there is no peace for the wicked (Isa. 57:21). It is no wonder that throughout Proverbs such wickedness is described as utter folly, since it leads to destruction, both in this life and the life to come.

15. The verb "sin" (חָטָא) means "to miss the mark, goal, or way" (s.v. Ps. 51:2). It can be used in secular contexts, such as the warning in Proverbs that if one hastens he may miss the way (19:2), or the passage in Judges of the stone slingers who do not miss (Judg. 20:16). In the religious sense it describes missing God's standard revealed in his Law, and so sinning against God.

with meanings of "interpret" or "translate" (Gen. 42:23). These people are vicious in their words, often using double meanings and cutting taunts; they are an abomination (Prov. 24:9). In the three descriptions of the unrighteous there is a growing intensity, signifying that what may start as a harmless bit of advice from an unbeliever may end up with a dangerously close connection to those who want to destroy the faith.

Similarly, the verbs also increase in force. The first is "walks" (הָלַךְ, an implied comparison that became an idiom), which signifies how one lives, whether morally and ethically or not; here it would refer to living according to the advice of the ungodly. Next is "stands" (עָמַד, another implied comparison), indicating a halting to consider the life style of the sinner. And finally there is "sits" (יָשַׁב), which would signify joining in collusion with the scorners and being identified with them (and so probably a metonymy of adjunct).[16] These verbs, "walks," "stands," and "sits," are all characteristic perfects that should be translated by the present tense. In this case they are negated: those who are right with God do not characteristically live like the various types of unbelievers.

Third, the nouns in the prepositional phrases correspond to this pattern of intensification. The verse starts with "counsel" (עֵצָה), a general word for advice that is concerned with the moral and ethical decisions in life.[17] Next is "way" (דֶּרֶךְ), an idiom (based on an implied comparison) that refers to the course of life, how one lives. And finally, there is "seat" (מוֹשָׁב), a figure that indicates the place of joining with the scorners and identifying with their activities (a metonymy of adjunct). In the Psalms the pious do not want to join the assemblies of the wicked (Ps. 26:4, 5).

---

16. This may be classified as a metonymy because unlike the figures of comparison there is a reality to the figure—one might actually sit down with the wicked in their assemblies. And that sitting would signify participation. Lot illustrates the progression presented in this psalm: he first pitched his tent next to Sodom, then he moved into the town, and then he actually came to act as a magistrate, sitting in the gate in the evil town, condoning some sins and condemning others.
17. The passage is not concerned with obtaining advice about mechanics or repair work but with issues of righteousness and integrity.

The point of this threefold intensification is to show that if people at first take their spiritual guidance from unbelievers instead of God, they will gradually begin living like the world and become more entangled in it.

B. The righteous love to meditate on God's word (2).

To be blessed and remain untarnished in the world, the faithful must live according to God's word. The word "law" (תּוֹרָה) can refer to instruction in general, or an individual teaching, or the commandments, or the books of the Law, or Scriptures as a whole.[18]

---

18. The word is usually related to a verb (יָרָה) that means "to show, point, direct." That verb in the *qal* stem was used for shooting arrows (Ps. 64:4), or rain shooting down (Hos. 6:3), unless that is another word entirely. In the *hiphil* stem the verb was used for pointing the way to Goshen (Gen. 46:28), God's pointing out to Moses a tree that would sweeten the bitter waters (Exod. 15:25), and the duty of the priests to teach the laws of God (Deut. 33:10). The Hebrews no doubt made some connection between the noun תּוֹרָה and the verb that meant "guide, instruct, teach."

The noun "law" (תּוֹרָה) would then refer to any instruction or authoritative direction. It could be used for any specific teaching or collection of teachings in general, such as the instruction in wisdom given to children by their parents (Prov. 1:8, 3:1, and 4:4). It was also used for traditional customs handed down to be followed (2 Sam. 7:19) and for the training of people in a skill, such as for the construction of the sanctuary (Exod. 35:34).

Most of the uses of the noun refer to teaching that comes from the holy books. It basically refers to divine revelation recorded in Scripture (Josh. 24:26), but how much of Scripture was included in a reference to the "law of the LORD" is difficult to say. In general it probably refers to the entire law code, that is, the books of the law that were available (and so probably in Ps. 19:7 as well as Ps. 1:2). It could refer to specific instructions in the law code, such as concerning unleavened bread (Exod 13:9), or to the heart of the code, the commandments and decisions (Exod. 24:12, which may refer to the contents of Exodus 20–23). Deuteronomy is also called the law of the LORD (Deut. 1:5), and depending on one's conclusions about the dating of the books of the law, these books of the law or their contents would have been available to the pre-exilic community. The word can refer to decisions that were made in judging civil cases (Exod. 18:16), instruction that came through the servants of the LORD (Isa. 30:9), collections of prophetic books (Isa. 42:21, 24), or the teachings about the ritual that the Levites were to

Wisdom literature does not always designate which is meant, but it would be hard to think of the word *tôrāh* without reference to the Pentateuch and other Scripture based on it. In general the psalmist is thinking of meditation on divine revelation, beginning with the Law.[19]

The verse begins with a figure to refer to this meditation in God's word: "his delight is in the Law of the LORD" (a metonymy of adjunct or cause). The parallel colon makes it clear that he meditates in the Law, but this first part tells us it is his delight. For believers it was a delight to study God's instructions; it was sweeter than honey and opened the way to a full and healthy life (Ps.19).

The verb in the second half of the verse is "meditates" (יֶהְגֶּה; s.v. Ps. 2:1). Because it is qualified by "night and day," a figure (merism) that means "all the time," the translation should be put in the present tense (a progressive or habitual imperfect). The spiritual discipline of meditation, according to the Psalter, begins with the memorization of divine instruction so that along the way by day, or on the bed at night, one could recall it and think about it. This hiding of God's word in the heart also requires gaining a full understanding of it. Then, one can speak to God about the word, turning its ideas and concerns into prayer. And finally, meditation concludes with self-exhortation—rebuking, exhorting, or encouraging—as the case might be ("why are you cast down, O my soul?"—the refrain in Pss. 42:5, 11 and 43:5). The "meditation" is fixed in the mind more by speaking or uttering the words, which is what the Hebrew term actually

---

be doing (Mal. 2:7). So any divine instruction from a single teaching to all of Scripture could be included in a reference to the "law," but the most likely understanding is that it would refer to the instructions of the Law code itself.

19. The reference does not necessarily mean that he possessed a copy of the Law, as believers are privileged to do today. He would have been taught by the priests and prophets on what the Law said; then he would remember it and meditate on it. He could have had personal access to the commandments or parts of the Law. Even after the exile individuals did not possess personal copies of the Scripture. A. A. Anderson says the word referred to the revelation of the will of God in general but originally probably referred to a written document (*The Book of Psalms*, I:59).

indicates (s.v. Ps. 2:1). Such meditation in the word prevents people from being caught up in the ideas of the world.

C. The righteous have success in this life (3).

With emblematic parallelism, the third verse gives a lovely picture of the success of the person who lives according to divine revelation. The emblem is in the first few clauses, beginning with the simile—"like a tree"—and including an elaboration on it; then the final clause states the intended reality.[20]

The simile of the tree represents a flourishing and fruitful life; the simile is here extended for clarification. First, it is planted (שָׁתוּל) by channels of water or irrigation ditches. If the tree represents the individual, then the water represents the word of God, for as the water makes the tree grow, the word causes the person to grow spiritually.[21] Similarly, Paul says that some have to water the seed that was sown, meaning teach the new believer so that there would be growth (1 Cor. 3:6).

Secondly, the tree produces (יִתֵּן) fruit in its season—not all the time, but when it is supposed to bear fruit. The verb, either the habitual or progressive imperfect, affirms that such a tree continually or regularly gives fruit in its season. If a tree is alive and being watered, it will show the proper growth; likewise, if true believers are in the word, they will produce righteousness (see Paul's discussion of the "fruit that the Spirit produces" in Gal. 5:22–23). Broyles explains "in its season" by cautioning that "while believers may be able to sustain spiritual life through times of adversity, they may be productive only at certain times, whose determination is beyond their control"[22].

Third, "its leaf does not wither." If the tree is carefully planted so that it can grow and is well-watered, it will not only live, but

---

20. For a detailed analysis of the image of the tree in relation to the individual who does the will of the LORD, the creator, see Meir Weiss, *The Bible from Within, The Method of Total Interpretation* (Jerusalem: The Magnes Press, 1984), pp. 135–63 ("Psalm 1:3–4").

21. Jerome F. D. Creach, "Like a Tree Planted by the Temple Stream: The Portrait of the Righteous in Psalm 1:3," *CBQ* 61 (1999):34–46.

22. Broyles, *Psalms,* p. 43.

also flourish. Likewise one would expect to find the spiritual life alive and flourishing if nourished by the word of the LORD.

Now the last clause leaves the emblem part of the parallelism and states the reality intended by it: "and everything he does will prosper" (or "flourish," יַצְלִיחַ; s.v. Ps. 45:4). This is not a blanket statement promising unlimited success; the context itself restricts the application. If the righteous meditate in God's word, they will live in obedience to it—and doing that is what will succeed.

II. The Way of the Ungodly: Those who are not believers produce nothing of value for God and have no future with God (4–5).

A. The life of the ungodly is worthless (4).

A strong contrast now shifts the focus of the psalm: "Not so are the ungodly!" The rest of the verse uses a simile to explain that the ungodly life is worthless—and this makes the warning to avoid the advice of the ungodly even more compelling. Even though unbelievers appear to be good people, they do not understand the faith and have no desire to please God or obey his word, and so they produce nothing of value for God. What could they say that would assist believers in doing the will of God?

The psalmist compares them to chaff, the worthless husks that have to be separated from the grain. Harvested wheat was crushed with a threshing sledge and then thrown into the air in a breezy location so that the little flakes of chaff could be blown away and the heavier grain fall to the ground. The figure shows that the ungodly are not only of no value, but also will eventually be removed. This imagery of winnowing at the harvest provided biblical writers with a vivid picture of judgment (e.g., Matt. 3:12).

One might protest that even unbelievers are worth something. On the one hand they may be charitable and kind, involved in community works, and even improve everyone's living conditions by their deeds. And on occasion God will even use what they do for his own purposes. On the other hand the witness of the Bible is clear: unless good works are done by faith and to the glory of God, they are worthless to God and therefore of no merit before him (see Psalm 127:1–2).

191

B. The ungodly will not survive the judgment (5).

Using the image of the chaff's being blown away, verse five declares that the ungodly will be separated from the righteous because the ungodly are not righteous (v. 4), that is, they do not live by faith in obedience to the word of God, promoting and producing righteousness, and they do not receive blessing as the people of God do; therefore, they will be removed. Since these folks have never come to faith, never repented of their sins, and never sought to please God, in the judgment they will not survive ("rise up," יָקֻמוּ; s.v. Ps. 3:1).

The psalm does not specify what judgment is meant. The word (מִשְׁפָּט; s.v. Ps. 9:4) can be used for any kind of judgment. One normally thinks of the final judgment when God will separate between the wheat and the chaff, the righteous and the unrighteous. The psalmist could have in mind a more immediate judgment from God, some event that might occur in the life of the nation that would be a divine punishment on unrepentant sinners.[23] Down through history in such times of judgment many righteous people also died in the wars, or the plagues, or other catastrophes. Because Psalm 1 announces the separation of the righteous and the wicked in the expected judgment, it seems best to understand it as the final judgment. Besides, final retribution is a major theme in wisdom literature (Pss. 49, 73), namely, that at the end of the age the righteous will stand before God in glory, but the ungodly will not.[24]

III. The Judgment: The righteous will be saved because the Lord knows them, but the ungodly will perish (6).

The final verse summarizes this separation in judgment, using the form of a causal clause. Its main point should be of great comfort to the faithful: the LORD knows them. This verb

---

23. For a discussion of this see John Goldingay, *Psalms 1-41*, pp. 87–8. He suggests that it is the righteous assembly who will judge, something like a jury that will determine the case of the wicked. He does allow that God would be judging through them.
24. See further E. R. Arbez, "A Study of Psalm 1," *CBQ* 7 (1945):398–404.

is a participle (יוֹדֵעַ), emphasizing the knowing as continuous or durative in nature. The idea is more than a mental awareness, what we call knowledge; Delitzsch said it was "a knowledge which was in living, intimate relationship to its subject and at the same time was inclined to it and bound to it by love" (s.v. Ps. 139:1).[25] While the study of the usage of the word provides a good general understanding of the meaning, the determining factor for its meaning here is the antithetical parallelism: "but the way of the ungodly will perish." In other words, "knows" is the opposite of "will perish." Thus it is a knowledge that saves. If the LORD knows them, they will not perish; if he does not know them, they will. And this is the language the New Testament says that Jesus will use in the coming judgment: "I do not know you" (Luke 13:27) and "I am the good shepherd. I know my own, and my own know me" (John 10:14).

In these last two verses the psalmist contrasts the word "righteous" (צַדִּיקִים) with its antonym, "ungodly" (or "wicked"). The basic meaning of "righteous" has to do with conforming to the standard; in religious passages that standard is divine revelation. The righteous are people who have entered into covenant with God by faith and seek to live according to his word (2).[26] The

---

25. Franz Delitzsch, *The Psalms*, I:87–88.
26. The word for the "righteous" (צַדִּיק) and its related verb and nouns occur frequently throughout the psalms. As a description of the people of God, the word emphasizes both their relationship with God through the covenant and their way of living in obedience to the covenant. One helpful way to summarize the meaning of this group of words is "to conform to the standard"; this idea is illustrated in the description of standardization of weights and measures in Deuteronomy 25:13–15. In the religious sense, the standard is God himself and his revealed will. The term "the righteous" came to describe people who had entered into a covenant with the LORD by faith. This is best illustrated with Abraham in Genesis 15:6, which says that he believed in the LORD and the LORD reckoned to him righteousness. Then when he prays for Sodom in chapter 18, he can distinguish between the righteous and the wicked. Believers can be called "the righteous" because they are justified (declared righteous) by the LORD.
   The terms also describe the way people are to live to please God. The activities of people living under the Law were to be right, i.e., to correspond to the will of God revealed to them. Here we find that righteousness is often linked with truthfulness, meaning what is dependable and trustworthy (Isa. 48:1; Jer. 4:2). In general it means to do what is right (Ps.

covenant that they have makes them the people of God—God knows them, and because God knows them, they shall never perish. They may do unrighteous things at times, but they know to find forgiveness because they want to do what is right.

In this contrast the emphasis is on the word "way." The LORD knows the "way of the righteous," but the "way of the ungodly" will perish. The word "way," as noted above, has become idiomatic for the course of action that people follow (how they live, their motives, what they produce). Thus, the ungodly and all they do will perish, but the righteous and the righteousness they produce will remain.

MESSAGE AND APPLICATION

By drawing a contrast between the righteous and the ungodly, the psalmist instructs believers not to live the way the world lives, not to take spiritual, moral, or ethical advice from unbelievers, and not to join them in their profane enterprises; rather, believers must study the word of God in order to live an untarnished and productive life for God, and that life will be evidence of a living faith that will see them through the judgment, when God judges the wicked.[27]

45:7; Prov. 11:6; 21:3). Along with this emphasis on personal righteousness there is also the use of the words for justice in the courts, decisions that are right (Prov. 16:12; Amos 5:7 and 6:12). The decisions are to be right, because the Judge of the whole world does right (Gen. 18:25). In fact, righteousness is one of the main descriptions of God in the Bible. He is just and right in everything he does because it is his nature; he loves justice and hates wickedness (Ps. 11:5–7).

There are a number of passages in which "righteousness" is used figuratively for what the righteousness produces. For example, Psalm 24:5 seems to use the word to mean "salvation." Likewise, if God reveals his righteousness in battle, it must refer to the proper outcome of the war (Ps. 98:2).

Briggs nicely captured the related ideas for this term: (1) God is the standard of righteousness; (2) people are called righteous because they are vindicated and justified by God; (3) people are known as the righteous because of their zeal for God and the righteousness of his Law; (4) and they are called righteous because of their conduct and character which is most often in line with the Law (C. A. Briggs and E. G. Briggs, *The Book of Psalms,* I:10).

27. It is not only the study of Scripture that is blessed by God—it is the careful and prayerful study of Scripture by believers with the intention of obeying

The central point of this psalm expressed in an expository statement would be something like this: *The righteous who live an untarnished and prosperous life in harmony with Scripture will be saved from the judgment of God on the ungodly.*

For believers, the application is obvious: they must spend time meditating on God's word so that they may live a distinct and productive spiritual life for God, and in the process find assurance that God knows them and will preserve them through the judgment. To unbelievers the message is urgent: they must come to faith in the Lord, because if they live their lives without faith in him or his word, not even their good deeds will count and they will not survive the judgment to come.

The New Testament also emphasizes these themes. Jesus prayed, "Sanctify them by the truth; your word is truth" (John 17:17). James stressed that by studying and doing the word of God people would be blessed in what they do (Jas. 1:22–25). But Paul reflected more of the message of this psalm when he wrote, "Do not be conformed to the pattern of this world, but be transformed by the renewing of your mind. Then you will be able to test and approve what God's will is—his good, pleasing and perfect will" (Rom. 12:2).

With all this in mind we see how the Psalm provides a fitting part of the introduction to the collection. Throughout the Psalter the reader will be confronted with the tension of living in a world that is not only alienated from God but antagonistic to him and his people. They must, therefore, find their direction and confidence in his word. And in so doing, they will also find their hope that someday the LORD will judge the world and vindicate them.

---

it. Kraus observed that the Pharisees with their utmost, rigorous obedience to the Law did not fulfill the picture this psalm presents (*Psalms 1-59*, p. 121). Today those who study the Bible without a living faith committed to obeying it fall far short of the description in this psalm. In fact, Kraus added that one could conclude that ultimately only Jesus Christ the righteous ever fulfilled the picture. With a living faith in the Lord, believers will find themselves more and more conforming to the descriptions of the righteous in the psalms.

PSALM 2

The Coronation of God's Son

INTRODUCTION [1]

Text and Textual Variants

1 Why do the nations rage,
   and the people plot a vain thing?
2 The kings of the earth take their stand,
   and the rulers take counsel together,
     against the LORD and against his anointed, *saying,*
3 "Let us break their bonds in pieces
   and cast away their cords from us."

4 He who sits enthroned in the heavens laughs;
   the Lord[2] holds them in derision.
5 Then he will speak to them in his wrath,
   and terrify them with his anger, *saying,*
6 "Yet I have set[3] my king
   on Zion, my holy hill."

---

1. See Robert Cole, "An Integrated Reading of Psalms 1 and 2," *JSOT* 98 (2002):75–88.
2. The word "Lord" is pointed with the vowels that normally go with the word when it represents the holy name: אֲדֹנָי. This was probably done to ensure that the identification of the Lord was correct. A large number of Masoretic manuscripts actually have here the four letters (*tetragrammaton*) of the holy name יהוה.
3. The Greek has a passive verb κατεστάθην βασιλεὺς, "I have been made king," meaning that the king and not the LORD is speaking. To harmonize with this, the Greek has "by him" to follow, and not "my king."

7 "I will declare the decree:[4]
   The LORD said to me,
      'You are my son;
      today I have begotten you.
8 Ask of me, and I will give
      the nations *for* your inheritance,
      and the ends of the earth *for* your possession.
9 You shall smash them[5] with an iron rod;
      you shall dash them to pieces like a potter's vessel.'"

10 Now therefore, be wise, O kings;
      be instructed, you judges of the earth.
11 Serve the LORD with fear
      and rejoice with trembling.
12 Kiss the son,[6] lest he be angry,

---

4. The Greek version understood this to be in construct, "the decree *of the* LORD," and then added another "LORD" to be the subject of the next verb. Thus: κυρίου Κύριος.

5. The Greek (and Syriac) has ποιμανεῖς, "you shall shepherd them," whereas the Hebrew text has תְּרֹעֵם, "you shall smash them." The Hebrew verb is רָעַע; but the translator of the Greek version saw תרעם in the manuscript and took it to be תִּרְעֵם, from רָעָה, "to shepherd." The word "shepherd" is used for kings and other leaders and would come to mind readily in this context; but if that common word was the original reading, it is difficult to explain why the Hebrew scribe would have replaced it with "smash," except to match the parallelism. The Masoretic reading fits the parallelism well and explains the origin of the variant reading of "shepherd." The verb "smash" focuses on establishing the reign; the Greek is more general for ruling. Both forms are at home in this kingship psalm, and that made it easier for the Greek reading of "rule" to be used in the New Testament. Neither New Testament usage is a direct quotation from the psalm (Rev. 2:27; 12:5), but both use the psalm to describe the complete reign of the Messiah over the world. The idea of rule fits the context of the psalm; but the Hebrew reading more specifically looks at the establishment of that reign.

6. The MT has "kiss the son" (נַשְּׁקוּ־בַר), using a word for "son" common to Aramaic and Phoenician but not Hebrew. In addressing leaders of other countries where Aramaic was spoken, using the Aramaic word made sense. However, this line caused the versions a good deal of difficulty. The Greek text has δράξασθε παιδείας, "accept correction"; the Aramaic "receive instruction," and the Latin *apprehendite disciplinam*. These translations assume a Hebrew בַר, meaning "piety, obedience." Jerome took it as an adverb: *Adorate pure* (also Aquila and Symmachus), "worship in purity." The Syriac

and you perish in the way,[7]
    for his wrath is quickly kindled.
Blessed are all those who take refuge in him.

Composition and Context

Psalm 2 is a royal psalm focusing on the coronation of the Davidic king in the holy city on Mount Zion.[8] It was included in the collection to be sung by the choirs at any appropriate time—certainly at coronations of kings, but also in times of national crises when people needed to be reminded that God had installed their king and the threats from the nations would fail.[9] There is no indication of authorship in the tradition of superscriptions, but since the psalm makes clear use of the Davidic covenant in 2 Samuel 7, it likely came from the time of the monarchy, and perhaps fairly early in that period. Along with Psalm 1, Psalm 2 forms an introduction to the collection. As a royal psalm it was placed here as part of the final structuring of the entire collection (see Introduction); when the final editing took place there was

---

retained "kiss the son," going against the Greek. Jerome in his *Apologia adv. Rufus* (lib i, 19) explained that he used "worship" because those who worship are wont to kiss the hand and bow the head. Either interpretation would fit the context, but since the psalm has already introduced the king as a "son," then "kiss the son" would harmonize with that theme.

    As would be expected, many suggestions have been made to resolve the difficulty of the line. The editors suggested some kind of reconstruction to read "with trembling kiss his feet." Goldingay preferred "submit sincerely" (*Psalms 1–41*, p. 93); and S. Olofsson explained the clause with בַּר to read "kiss the field" as a sign of homage ("The Crux Interpretum in Ps 2,12," *SJOT* 9 [1995]:185–199). If the expositor has the time to read all the proposals, there is a good deal of literature available in the commentaries and elsewhere. See, for one, A. A. Macintosh, "A Consideration of the Problems Presented by Psalm II. 11 and 12," *JTS NS* 27 (1976):1–14.

7. The Greek text adds δικαίας, "lest you perish from the *righteous* way."
8. See J. W. Watts, "Psalm 2 in the Context of Biblical Theology," *HBT* 12 (1990):73–97.
9. Kraus notes that it is not possible to reconstruct from the text an enthronement festival ritual with different speakers; the singer and speaker is the king himself (*Psalms 1–59*, p. 126). Rather, it is a composition that focuses on the king's claim to the throne, but it does incorporate speakers, real or imagined, to present the crisis and resolution.

no Davidic king, and so this introduction served as a reminder of God's plan. Thus at the outset of the book we have one psalm focusing on the way of the righteous, and another psalm focusing on the victory of the LORD's anointed king over the nations.[10] The psalm reflects a crisis as its original occasion, a crisis that probably occurred frequently in Israel's history. The coronation of a new king was a particularly vulnerable time, for the surrounding nations would have seen it as an opportunity to raid across the borders, capture cities, and in general, try to end Israelite control over them. Accordingly, one of the first tasks of a new king would have been to solidify the borders by defeating the enemies.

The poem is well-crafted, having four stanzas of three verses each. The first stanza reports the plan of the nations to rebel against the LORD and his anointed king; stanza two reveals the response of God to their ridiculous plan; stanza three recounts the king's claims to the throne in spite of opposition; and the last stanza records the sage advice to those foolish nations.[11]

The theology of the psalm portrays the LORD as the sovereign king of the universe who reigns from heaven. It is his prerogative to control nations (Isa. 40:15–17), establish borders (Deut. 32:8), and set up or remove kings (Dan. 2:21). It was he who put his king on the throne. No matter how well-planned or powerful the opposition was, it was doomed to fail if God was against it.

Because this royal psalm would have applied to every Davidic king, it ultimately applies to David's greatest son, Jesus Christ. The apostles saw that it was to be fulfilled in the coronation of the Messiah at his exaltation (Heb. 1:5) and then in the establishment of his reign on earth at his second coming (Rev. 2:27; 12:5); and since Messiah's reign will be eternal, the psalm would apply to no other king again.

---

10. Goldingay finds Psalms 1 and 2 somewhat inappropriate for an introduction to the collection of psalms; he observes that Psalm 1 fits well with the literature of Proverbs, and Psalm 2 would be at home in a prophetic book (*Psalms 1–41*, p. 94).

11. See further Pierre Auffret, *The Literary Structure of Psalm 2, JSOT* Supplement 3 (Sheffield: JSOT, 1977).

Exegetical Analysis

Summary

The psalmist exhorts the pagan leaders to abandon their rebellious plans against the LORD and his anointed king and submit to the authority of this king whom God has ordained to rule all the nations with crushing power.

Outline

  I. The psalmist reveals how the pagan leaders foolishly desire to rebel against the LORD and his anointed king (1–3).

  A. He is indignant at the tumultuous and vain resolves of the nations (1).

  B. He explains that the nations united to throw off the authority of the LORD and his anointed king (2–3).

 II. The psalmist reveals the resolution of the LORD to install his king (4–6).

  A. The sovereign God of heaven holds their feeble plan in contempt (4).

  B. The LORD will end their efforts by declaring his plan to install his king (5–6).

III. The psalmist reveals the decree of the anointed king to show by what right he rules (7–9).

  A. The king resolves to declare the statute of the covenant (7a).

  B. The king reiterates the divine promises of the covenant (7b–9).

   1. He is on this day crowned as God's chosen king (7b).

   2. He will receive from God dominion over all the rebellious people (8–9).

 IV. The psalmist exhorts the foolish nations to trust God and to submit to this enthroned "son" in order to escape destruction (10–12).

  A. He calls for the leaders to act prudently (10).

  B. He instructs them to serve God and submit to the king or be destroyed when God's wrath is poured out (11–12).

COMMENTARY IN EXPOSITORY FORM

I. Folly: It is futile for humans to try to throw off God's authority (1–3).

A. Rebellion against God is futile (1).

The first stanza focuses on the rebellious plot of the nations. It begins with a rhetorical question, "Why do the nations rage?" This is not an inquiry into the reason for their activity but an expression of amazement and even indignation at their rage. The verb "rage" (< רָגַשׁ) can be used to describe something like the raging of the sea, but here it refers to the tumultuous meeting of rebels to plan an attack,[12] a meeting going on at the time of the coronation (and so the verb is put in the present tense, a characteristic perfect). The parallel verb, "plot, devise" (< הָגָה, a progressive imperfect), clarifies this raging. The word is often used in a religious sense of meditating (1:2), but here it means that they were plotting a rebellion.[13]

The rebels are called "nations" and "peoples," terms that

---

12. רָגַשׁ may be an Aramaic word, which would be fitting because it refers to the nations, many of whom spoke Aramaic. It appears in the Aramaic section of Daniel to describe the way people came thronging in to accuse Daniel (6:6).

13. The verb הָגָה has the definitions "to moan, growl, muse, speak." There are some derivatives that carry similar meanings: הֶגֶה is a noun, "growling"; הָגוּת is a noun, "musing"; and הִגָּיוֹן is a noun, "meditation, musing," linked with sounding music (Ps. 92:4). In all the uses there seems to be the emphasis that something is said, or some sound made.

   The verb (and a noun) can be used for inarticulate sounds, such as the growl of a lion (Isa. 31:4), moaning (Isa. 16:7), or groaning in physical weakness and distress (Isa. 38:14). The *hiphil* verbal system uses the participle to describe the chirping and muttering of spiritists (Isa. 8:19).

   Another group of passages use the verb with the sense of uttering something (Pss. 35:28; 38:13; Job 27:4). This use is found with a different verbal stem in Isaiah 59:13 to refer to conceiving and uttering something.

   The verb also means "meditate, muse," perhaps uttering words under the breath or in fact speaking them out loud. This use may be found in Joshua 1:8, and Psalms 1:2; 63:6 and 77:12. Silent meditation is strengthened by actually speaking the words.

   There is also a category meaning "devise, imagine," that is closely related to the meaning of meditate. In Psalm 2:1 it could mean "devise" a

often refer to the tribes around Israel, such as Aramaeans, Ammonites, Moabites, Edomites, Phoenicians, and Philistines— all perennial enemies of Israel. These surrounding people were constantly fighting with Israel so that Israel's kings regularly had to drive them back into their territory.

What they plan is said to be "a vain thing" (an empty thing, רִיק).[14] This is an interpretive substitution by the writer for the actual object, which would have been something like a "strategy" that they were planning; but because what they were planning was futile, the psalmist put this description in the place of the expected object (so "vain thing" is a metonymy of adjunct).

This line was used by Peter in Acts 4:25–26 with a broader application. After the rejection and crucifixion of Jesus, Peter included the Jews who opposed Jesus with those nations that rage against God and his Messiah.

B. The futile effort pits mortals against deity (2–3).

Verse 2 clarifies that the leaders of this plot were the "kings of the earth" (מַלְכֵי־אֶרֶץ) and the "rulers" (רוֹזְנִים) of these peoples. The genitive "earth" limits their sphere of influence;[15] and this limitation will be put in the strongest light in the next section where the LORD is described as sitting enthroned "in the heavens."

The verbs in the first two parallel units of verse 2 have the same classifications as those in verse 1, except now the order of tenses is reversed—first the progressive imperfect is used for "take their stand" and then the characteristic perfect, "take counsel together." The verb "take a stand" (יִתְיַצְבוּ) has an antagonistic meaning with the preposition "against" following it; the parallel verb would then continue this negative connotation.

---

plan by thinking it through; but it could also mean talking about the plan, an idea that would certainly fit the context.

14. The addition of "vain" balances the meter, even though the two halves are not completely synonymous: there are parallel verbs (rage//plot) and parallel subjects (nations//people), but the pronoun "why" in the first colon was not matched, so there was room for the variant, "vain." The point of this decision not to parallel but to use "vain" puts the emphasis on the futility of their plan.

15. This is true whether it is an attributive genitive ("earthly kings") or locative genitive (["kings in the earth"]) or even a genitive of the thing possessed ("kings over the earth").

The idea of kings taking counsel together, or even taking their stand against someone, would be of some concern if it were not for the third unit of the verse, "against the LORD and against his anointed."[16] They may have thought they were merely fighting an Israelite king, but their plot was actually against the LORD and his anointed. This term "anointed" (מָשִׁיחַ), a passive adjective,[17] refers to the chosen king. The Anglicized pronunciation is "messiah" or when referring to the greatest and final one, "the Messiah." For the surrounding nations to attempt to throw off the authority of the anointed king would be to try to overthrow the plan of God.

The rebellious plot is put into words in verse three. Since these words form the content (real, or imagined) of their resolution, they are so represented in the translation: "*saying*, 'Let's break their bonds and cast their cords from us.'" The two cohortatives have the force of exhortation: "let's break" (נְנַתְּקָה) and "let's cast off" (נַשְׁלִיכָה). The objects of these two verbs are "bonds [chains]" and "ropes [fetters]." They were not actually tied up or chained in some prison (if they were they could not have been meeting to plan a rebellion). Rather, they saw their domination by the king in Jerusalem as bondage (so the words form an implied comparison). To them to be under Israelite control was *like* being in bonds and ropes; thus they came rushing together to plot their strategy of breaking free.

II. Divine Decree: God's sovereign authority establishes his king's rule (4–6).

A. *The LORD regards their plan as ludicrous (4).*

The psalm now makes a sudden shift from the plotting of the nations to the response of the LORD. The structure of this

---

16. The editors of BHS suggested deleting this second half of the verse ("against the LORD and his anointed") for metrical considerations: it would leave a neat synonymous parallelism. But the unbalanced line throws emphasis on the second half, the focus of their attack—against the LORD and his king.

17. The word translated into Greek is Χριστός, transcribed as "Christ," "the anointed [king]." The form in the Greek text is κατά τοῦ Χριστοῦ αὐτοῦ. See also J. Durham, "The King as 'Messiah' in the Psalms," *Review and Expositor* 81 (1984):425–36.

stanza parallels the first: verses 1 and 2 describe the actions of the earthly kings, verse 3 records their speech, verses 4 and 5 describe the response of the heavenly king, and then verse 6 gives his speech.

With bold figures the psalmist portrays the sovereign God's reaction to this ridiculous plan. In the first colon we have the general description "He who sits in the heavens laughs"; and in the second half the clarification that "the Lord mocks them" ("holds them in derision").

The designations of God here are significant. The substantival participle "[He who] sits" (יוֹשֵׁב, an anthropomorphism) means that he sits enthroned or reigns. Then the prepositional phrase "in the heavens" makes the description even more powerful; for in contrast to the limited earthly realm of the rebellious kings, the LORD reigns over them all in the heavens. The second designation is "Lord." This is not the holy name "Yahweh" (represented by LORD) but the title "Lord," even though the spelling was designed to assure the connection. The use of this title indicates that he is the sovereign master, and everyone else is a servant.

Now God is portrayed as if laughing at their plan and mocking it, just as humans would mock something ridiculous. The two verbs "laughs" (יִשְׂחָק) and "mocks"[18] (יִלְעַג) are also bold anthropomorphic expressions; they are used to enable us to understand how foolish this plan is. The point of the figure is that the plan was utterly ridiculous.

B. The LORD will end their rebellion by installing his king over them (5–6).

The announcement of God's plan to end their rebellion is introduced with the adverb "then" (אָז), which forms a transition to the future: "he will speak" (יְדַבֵּר) and "he will terrify them" (יְבַהֲלֵמוֹ; s.v. Ps. 83:16). The two verbs taken together cover the full action: the first colon gives the cause, "he will speak" (a metonymy of cause), and the second gives the effect, "he will terrify them" (a metonymy of effect). This balance is also evident in the

---

18. The tenses are put in the present tense (progressive imperfects) because the verse portrays God's response to action that is underway and because the adverb in the next line shifts to the future.

chiastic word order: speak + wrath // anger + terrify. This arrangement throws the emphasis upon the wrath of God because in the text the two words for it are placed back-to-back, while "speak" and "terrify" bracket the whole verse.

Both words "wrath" (אַף; s.v. Ps. 30:5) and "anger" (חָרוֹן; s.v. Ps. 37:1) have to do with heat, i.e., a burning anger and a heated rage. Here again the writer uses anthropomorphic language (idioms) to describe God's wrath in terms of flaring nostrils and burning rage.[19] The point is that the declaration from God will be angry condemnation, and they will be terrified.

But what exactly will he say to them? Unless the expositor thinks the decree is missing and needs to be supplied, verse 6 would provide the content of the divine speech. The psalmist was portraying the divine decision to install the Israelite king as condemnation of their plot. In other words, if people tried to throw off this king, and then God declared that he was putting this king on the throne, that would mean that God was against them and they would be terrified. Not only would they be defeated by the new king, they would be judged by God as well.[20] So what he will say to them is that he, the God in heaven, has chosen this king they oppose.

The speech begins with a strong contrast: "But as for Me." God is in effect saying, "they may do such and so, but as for me, I will do this . . . ." The verb that follows is the perfect tense "set, install" (נָסַכְתִּי). Since this is the coronation psalm, the tense might best be classified as an instantaneous perfect, meaning "Here and now I set my king."[21] This fits well with the king's designation "today" (v. 7).[22]

---

19. The classification with this figure does not mean that there is no attribute of anger for God. God is a person who has intellect, feelings, and will; but describing that anger with heat and rage in human terms is the figurative aspect.

20. This is why Peter's use of the psalm in Acts 4 is so poignant. He argued that if people (Jew or Gentile) opposed the Messiah—Jesus, they opposed the God who sent him. In short, they had become enemies of God who declared that Jesus Christ would reign forever.

21. It could also be taken as a very recent past, "I have [just now] set my king"; a perfect of resolve, "I have resolved to set me king"; or even a prophetic perfect, "I have set" meaning "I will set."

22. See J. H. Tigay, "Divine Creation of the King in Psalm 2:6," *Eretz-Israel* 27 (2003):246–51.

The announcement also states that the coronation is on Mount Zion, meaning the palace on the mountain (a metonymy of subject). Zion was a unique mountain, "set apart" for the worship and service of the LORD, which is why it is designated "holy." This designation made it even more explicit that God was behind this Israelite king.

III. The Claims of the King: As God's chosen king he will rule the world with absolute power (7–9).

A. The king will rule by divine decree (7).

In the third stanza we read how the king declares by what right he rules. His right to rule was based on the decree from the LORD, a reference most likely to the Davidic covenant that promised the king sovereignty over the nations and declared that the king would be a son to God and God would be a father to the king (2 Sam. 7:14). The verse begins with the cohortative (אֲסַפְּרָה), expressing the king's resolve to recite the decree (חֹק; s.v. Ps. 119:5).[23] The father-son language of the covenant was certainly figurative, for no human king, no one at all, was ever the literal, physical son of God. That would require procreation within the Godhead, an idea that may have been acceptable in pagan religions, but not to the Hebrews. At best the Davidic king might claim to be an adopted son with all the rights and privileges of sonship.[24] In this line "you are my son" (בְּנִי) is a pure metaphor. The statement makes a comparison between what a son is to a father and what the king is to God to describe the special relationship between them. The immediate significance of this special relationship concerns the inheritance of the kingdom, beginning on the coronation day.

This initial metaphor is extended in the parallel line, "today

---

23. See G. H. Jones, "The Decree of Yahweh," *VT* 15 (1965):336–44; and Helmer Ringgren, "Psalm 2 and *Belit's* Oracle for Ashurbanipal," in *The Word of the Lord Shall Go Forth* (Festschrift for David Noel Freedman), edited by C. L. Meyers and M. O'Connor (Winona Lake, IN: Eisenbrauns, 1983), pp. 91–95.

24. This would be in contrast to some of the kings of the ancient world who took the title and meant that they were born divine. See Gerald Cooke, "The Israelite King as Son of God," *ZAW* 73 (1960):202–25.

I have begotten you." This is also a figure of speech (an implied comparison), assuming a comparison between the coronation of the king and the idea of begetting a son. Since "today" the king is designated God's son, today is also his begetting, his coronation. He was already grown, even if a youth, but was being crowned as king, that is, the "today" on which he is "being begotten."

The psalm is quoted in the New Testament with reference to Jesus, the Messiah ("the Christ"), in Hebrews 1 with exactly the same sense that the psalm has in using this language about the coronation of the king.[25] After the writer of Hebrews told how the Son of God ascended to the right hand of the Majesty on High, he then quoted this psalm: "Today I have begotten you," along with the lines from the Davidic covenant. The psalm in its context of a coronation decree is therefore used properly for the exaltation and coronation of Jesus.

The use of the word "today" also helps in the classification of the tense of the verb "begotten." It may be interpreted as a very recent past, "I have [just now] begotten you." This fits very well with "today" and the declaration "You are my Son."

B. The king will establish dominion throughout the world (8–9).

The words of the decree continue, expressing the significance

---

25. The language of sonship is used for Jesus in a number of different contexts. For example, he is called the "only begotten Son" in John 1. The verb "begotten" in its literal sense refers to a child who shares the nature of the father (as opposed to words like "made" and "created"). To describe Jesus as "begotten" indicates that he has the nature of the Father, i.e., divine and eternal; and if he is eternal, then "begotten" refers to nature and not a beginning. The description is figurative. This is why the Nicene Creed clarifies the point: Jesus is "begotten not made." When Scripture uses "begotten" in that sense, the expression includes "only" ($\mu o \nu o \gamma \varepsilon \nu \acute{\eta} \sigma$, "the only begotten"); there is only one person who shares the divine nature of the Father, and that is Jesus Christ.

But "You are my son" in Psalm 2 is used specifically for the coronation of the anointed king. The expression was applied to every descendant of David who came to the throne. And so in the New Testament it is used precisely in that way for the coronation of the Messiah at his exaltation to glory; he is the eternal king.

of "sonship" as inheritance. As the sovereign King's "son," the anointed king will inherit the kingdom, including sovereignty over the very people who attempt to throw off his dominion. The sequence of the volitional moods shows the process: the imperative "ask," and the conjunction with the cohortative, "and then," or, "so that I may give." In this sequence the use of the cohortative adds the note of certainty that comes from the divine resolution to fulfill the promise to give him the kingdom.

The two parallel objects are "the nations" and "the ends of the earth." The latter expression is a metonymy of subject, referring to the people who live in the ends of the earth. The kingdom will extend through all the lands to the most remote regions. Each of these objects is also joined by a clarifying noun that functions adverbially: "the nations [for or as] your inheritance" and "the ends of the earth [for or as] your possession." In the text the two words in each pair are simply juxtaposed, and so a word like "for" is needed to make the adverbial connection clear.[26] When God gives his "son" the kingdom, these nations will be his "inheritance." Ultimately this will take place when the anointed king receives the kingdom.

When the king receives this dominion, he will first put down all rebellion (v. 10). The two verbs (imperfect tenses תְּרֹעֵם and תְּנַפְּצֵם) have been translated as specific futures in view of the context that promises future dominion. The two verbs seem to be well-matched in the parallelism and clear in the reference to establishing the dominion with power: "you will smash" and "you will dash them."[27]

The means by which the king will establish his reign is expressed in the two prepositional phrases. The first is "with an iron rod." The "rod" (שֵׁבֶט) most likely refers to the scepter of the king, which represented authority. Here, as a metonymy of adjunct, it signifies that he will rule with sovereign authority, but the word is modified with "iron" (a genitive of material), an indication of the strength of the dominion.

---

26. The poetry is an unbalanced 5 + 2 meter, with incomplete parallelism. After "ask of me and I will give," there is synonymous parallelism with the repeated object phrases, written in a chiasm: nations + inheritance / possession + ends of earth.
27. See also John Emerton, "The Translation of the Verbs in the Imperfect in Psalm ii.9," *JTS* 29 (1978):499–503.

The parallel figure is the simile "like a potter's vessel." This figure may be based on the Egyptian custom in which the name of each city under the king's dominion was written on a little votive jar and placed in the temple of his god. Then, if the people in a city rebelled, the pharaoh could smash that city's little jar in the presence of the deity.[28] Such a symbolic act would terrify the rebellious—not that the city had much of a chance of withstanding the pharaoh in the first place. The psalmist may be drawing on that imagery to stress how easily the king, with all the authority of heaven behind him, will crush the rebellion swiftly.

IV. Wisdom: It is wise for people to find refuge from God's wrath by submitting to his king (10–12).

A. People must act prudently (10).

In the last stanza the psalmist now draws his conclusions from this meditation on the coronation liturgy, and his attention focuses on giving advice to the disruptive kings and rulers who tried to rebel. Verse 10 is the general statement of warning to the rebels: "Be wise." The irony is that one expects kings and judges to possess wisdom already, but in this case they are woefully deficient.

The verb "be wise, act prudently" (הַשְׂכִּילוּ; s.v. Ps. 36:4) instructs the kings to make correct choices, choices that will lead to their success with God and not to their destruction. The main choice will be to submit to the LORD's chosen king, for that will bring life. The second verb is "receive instruction," or "be instructed" (הִוָּסְרוּ; s.v. Ps. 6:1); it has the idea of discipline, instruction, even child training, any of which carries a good deal of irony when addressed to the judges of the earth.

B. It is wise to become worshipers of the LORD (11).

Now the psalmist makes it clear that being wise means to

---

28. See the graphic depiction of this in Othmar Keel, *The Symbolism of the Biblical World: Ancient Near Eastern Iconography and the Book of Psalms* (New York: Seabury, 1978); see also A. Kleber, "Ps. 2:9 in the Light of an Ancient Oriental Ceremony," *CBQ* 5 (1943):63–67

become a true worshiper of the living God. Such a call to worship the LORD, that is Yahweh of biblical revelation, would be staggering, for these nations had their own deities.[29] The holy name is emphasized here, being the only word not paralleled.

The call for them to submit to the LORD is expressed in terms of serving. The verb "serve" (< עָבַד; s.v. Ps. 134:1) has the religious sense of worshiping God and obeying his commands. For these pagan leaders, to serve him would mean changing loyalties from their gods to the one true God, but it would also mean accepting God's king and serving him. This service was to be performed "with fear" (בְּיִרְאָה), a term that includes fear, reverence, and adoration. One who fears God is drawn to him in love, adoration, and amazement because of his power and glory, but because of his power and glory one also shrinks back in reverence and even fear. Evidence of fearing God includes obedience, worship, and service.[30]

---

29. What is prescribed here is the kind of response to the true God of heaven that one reads about with reference to Nebuchadnezzar in Daniel 4:34–35.

30. The combination of serving and rejoicing with "fear" may seem to be out of harmony, but an understanding of the word "fear" (יִרְאָה, related to the verb "to fear, be afraid," יָרֵא) will clarify its appropriateness here. One basic meaning of these words is the simple idea of "fear" or "dread," such as the terror of the mariners in the storm (Jon. 1:5), or the sinners in the garden (Gen. 3:10). There is no reverential element in such passages, only terror of the consequences. At times the word of the LORD seeks to allay such fears, as in the words to Abram after the battle, "Fear not" (Gen. 15:1).

The word can also be used in a positive sense to describe reverential awe for the LORD (Exod. 34:30; Lev. 19:14; Ps. 66:5). It can be used in this sense for honoring parents (Lev. 19:3) or other things, but it is mostly with reference to God, or the word of God. The devout worshiper is even referred to as a God-fearer, and leaders like the elders were supposed to fear God (Exod. 18:21; see also Josh. 22:25). The English word "revere" includes the ideas of regarding something as sacred or exalted, of holding something in deep and usually affectionate respect, or of venerating. The religious sense of our word as reverential awe does not eliminate the idea of fear, but it turns it into a positive devotion. Like the Israelites at the foot of the fiery mountain, the devout are drawn to the LORD in adoration and amazement because his power is glorious, but they also shrink back because the power is frightening. This same tension between adoration and fear occur with human responses to other things as well, such as dangerous animals, tornadoes, or natural wonders.

211

The second half of the verse intensifies what the first part has. "Rejoice" (גִּיל ; s.v. Ps. 13:6) means "to give a (cultic) shout of joy," and so this may very well be part of the religious service enjoined in the verse. That it is to be done "with trembling" (בִּרְעָדָה) ensures it will be appropriate for God's service. People could rejoice greatly in the sanctuary, but realizing that they were in the presence of the LORD God they would make sure that their celebration was honoring to him. So the balance between rejoicing and fearing captures the true sense of proportion for worship of the holy God.

C. Submission to the king is urgent (12).

The outward sign that people believe the warnings of God would be submission to his designated king. The call to submit to the king is actually a call to submit to God. The imperative "kiss [the] son" (נַשְּׁקוּ־בַר) has the Aramaic word for "son" probably because the psalmist was addressing pagan kings who would have likely spoken Aramaic. To "kiss [the] son" would be a symbolic act (a metonymy of adjunct): conquered and submissive kings would bow before the victor and give him homage in this way; but more is being enjoined here than a kiss—they are to give the homage that a kiss signifies.

The urgency of the call for submission is met by the warning that he may be angry. There is some question about the subject "he" of the verb "be angry" (יֶאֱנַף). The context might suggest that the "son" is the subject, but the terms for anger and wrath were used earlier in the psalm for the LORD. Moreover, this entire section, apart from the command to kiss the son, calls for submission to the LORD God. The better interpretation would be to take God as the understood subject of "lest he be angry." In either

---

God's presence is both attracting and frightening, which is why people can rejoice in his presence, but with reverential fear. The word includes both aspects; for the believer the aspect of reverence will be uppermost, but for the unbeliever who has every reason to fear God the aspect of fear in the word is primary.

Many passages will refer to the activities that result from a believer fearing the LORD: e.g., obedience to God's word and the avoidance of evil result from it (Ps. 34:11–14), as well as pure worship (Ps. 5:7) and praise that honors the LORD (Ps. 118:4).

case, though, the result would be the same—the king will put down their rebellion, but it will be God giving him the victory. To rebel against the one is to rebel against both, and to submit to one is to submit to both. This point is stressed frequently in the teachings of Jesus; for example, he said, "You believe in God, believe also in me" (John 14:1).

The psalm closes with a blessing for all who take refuge (חָסָה; s.v. Ps. 7:1) in him. The word is used figuratively (an implied comparison) throughout the psalms for trusting in the LORD for safety and security. Based on its usage the reference here is probably to trusting in the LORD, although it could be interpreted to mean taking refuge in the LORD's chosen king. Either way the meaning would ultimately be submitting to God. The expression supplies the balance to the negative warning: to rebel is to perish; to take refuge is to find blessing.

MESSAGE AND APPLICATION

The psalm is essentially prophetic. It applies first to any Davidic king who came to the throne, but ultimately to the King of Kings.[31] It is therefore not directly prophetic, but typologically so. The LORD's anointed who speaks in the middle of the psalm comes forward with the same power and glory with which the Messiah appears in the prophets.[32]

The final stanza clearly forms the instruction of the psalm; everything builds to this point in the passage. So the wording of

---

31. Of course, the psalm would find significant relevance at many times. Richard J. Clifford observed that there were three important contexts in history where the psalm would have spoken most powerfully: first, when there was a Davidic king on the throne the people needed to be reminded that God had chosen the king in spite of opposition; second, in the postexilic period where there was no king the people would have drawn on this psalm for hope that the monarchy would be restored to deliver them from their enemies; and third, in the Christian context the believers confessed the name of Jesus as the anointed King, God's Son (in a much greater way) and looked for his coming to judge the world (*Psalms 1–72* [Nashville: Abingdon Press, 2002], p. 46).
32. Delitzsch, *Psalms*, I:89.

the expository idea should capture this flow: *It is wise to submit to the authority of the Messiah because God has decreed that he will put down all rebellion and rule the world.* The wording captures the main point of the psalm and reflects or assumes the other parts adequately. The word "Messiah" fits the Old Testament context but is also applicable to Christ. The New Testament shows that the psalm will be fulfilled ultimately by the exalted Savior, Jesus the Messiah, the Son of God (Heb. 1:5; Rev. 19:15). Just as with the Israelite kings of the Old Testament, so today people want to throw off the authority of the true God and his anointed Son. The writer to the Hebrews reminds us of the point of this psalm, that Christ Jesus will come again to put down all rebellion and establish his kingdom.

The psalm's clear application is for people to believe the word of God and submit to the authority of his Son before he comes to judge the world and establish his reign. This application would not be for believers, for they have already submitted to Christ as their king and Lord. It is a warning for people in the world who foolishly try to throw off the authority of the LORD's anointed king, for by doing so they are actually rebelling against God. Many claim to worship the one true God, but they cannot do so and reject the Son of God, the Messiah.

For believers the message is one of great comfort. The antagonism in the world to God in general and to Christianity specifically will end. The outcome is not in question, even though it seems it is. Believers then can be strengthened in their faith in God's plan that Christ shall come to put down all wickedness and rule the world. Related to this point is a second application for believers: just as the psalmist exhorted people to submit to the Messiah, so too Christians should warn the world not to act foolishly but to submit to the Christ and escape the wrath to come.

PSALM 3

Confidence in the Face
of Adversity

INTRODUCTION [1]

Text and Textual Variants

A Psalm of David,
when he fled from the presence of Absalom his son.[2]

---

1. See for further material on this psalm John S. Kselman, "Psalm 3," *CBQ* 49 (1987):572–580; Christopher Schroeder, "Psalm 3," *Bib* 81 (2000):243–51.
2. The writing of the psalm was inspired by the praise and prayer of David the morning after his initial flight from the palace (see 2 Sam. 17:21–22). The record in 2 Samuel 15:12–17 also provides a literary link as it reports how Absalom's numbers "increased." Some suggest that because in the historical event David did not have the kind of confidence we find here, the psalm does not refer to a flight, and that the reference to the people in verse 8 makes this fit a national crisis instead—someone saw some literary connections between the event in David's life and the psalm and put them together (Goldingay, *Psalms 1–41*, p. 109). Kraus said that the application of the psalm to the event in David's life was simply erroneous because of the contents of the psalm itself; to him the ascription was evidence of early exegetical activity (*Psalms 1–59*, pp.138–9). But there is really nothing in the psalm that makes its writing by David impossible. It was a national crisis for the king and his supporters to be driven out of the royal city. The work would have been composed sometime after the event anyway when there was time to put it into its poetic form that made it applicable to many similar crises. As a piece of poetry it need not reflect all the details of the event, such as the confusion and haste of the flight (see the discussion in Perowne, *Psalms,* I:120–122).

215

1 O LORD, how many are my adversaries!
   Many are rising up against me.
2 Many are saying concerning me,
   'There is no deliverance for him in God.'[3] *Selah*
3 But you, O LORD, are a shield[4] about me,
   my glory, and the one who lifts up my head.
4 With my voice[5] I cried to the LORD,
   and he answered[6] me from his holy mountain. *Selah*
5 I lay down and slept;
   I awoke, because the LORD sustained me.
6 I shall not be afraid of myriads of people
   who set themselves against me on every side.
7 Arise, O LORD!
   Deliver me, O my God!
   For you have struck[7] all my enemies on the jaw;[8]
   you have broken the teeth of the wicked.
8 From the LORD comes deliverance.
   Your blessing is upon your people.

Composition and Context

It is fitting that the first lament psalm of the book is filled with confidence, because throughout the collection confidence and praise form significant parts of laments. This witnesses to the fact that the faith of the psalmists was steadfast in spite of the

---

3. The Greek clarifies by adding the pronoun: "in his God."
4. The Greek reads ἀντιλήμπτωρ μου, "my helper," instead of "shield."
5. The use of "voice" in this grammatical construction makes it clear that he cried aloud.
6. The versions by Aquila and Jerome translate this as a simple imperfect tense, prompting some commentators to revocalize the word to a simple conjunction instead of a *waw* consecutive (see Kraus, *Psalms 1–59*, p.137).
7. Another interpretation is to take these perfect tenses as precative perfects and translate them as imperatives as well. W. VanGemeren says that they must be interpreted as imperatives in this verse to harmonize with the preceding forms (*Expositor's Bible Commentary*, "Psalms," p. 105). However, the presence of "for" beginning the second half of the verse argues against this.
8. Instead of "jaw" the Greek has ματαίως, which would correspond to Hebrew חִנָּם, "gratuitously."

lamentable circumstances they faced; it was steadfast because they had come to know the LORD by experience as well as revelation. The psalm was attributed to David by the superscription. Most modern commentators have difficulty with this, because the confident tone of the psalmist seems to conflict with the account of David's fleeing from Absalom. But the first part of the psalm, the lament, does reflect the anxiety and deep concern of the psalmist in trouble, but that soon turned to confidence as he saw God's protection being extended to him. It is not impossible that the psalm comes from that event.

The prayer concerned the increasing number of adversaries who wished to destroy him and undermine his faith—a constant danger for the faithful in this world. Even though Psalm 3 is a lament, because of its great emphasis on confidence in the midst of opposition, it may be better described as a prayer song.[9]

Exegetical Analysis

Summary

In spite of innumerable adversaries who rise up against him and taunt his faith, the chosen servant of the LORD finds confidence in the LORD's immediate protection to pray for complete victory over those who set themselves against him.

Outline

I. The psalmist reports the increasing number of his adversaries who seek to destroy him and his faith, but finds confidence in God's glorious provisions for him (1–3).
  A. He cries out to the LORD because many rise up against him (1)
  B. He explains that they taunt his faith in an effort to destroy him (2).
  C. He expresses his confidence in God's protection and provision for him (3).

---

9. See further J. S. Kselman, "Psalm 3: A Structural and Literary Study," *CBQ* 49 (1987):572–80.

II. The psalmist renews his courage in the face of great
odds because God sustained him through the night in answer to his prayer (4–6).

    A. He praises God because his immediate prayer was an-
swered (4).

    B. He explains that God sustained him through the night
(5).

    C. He expresses his renewed confidence in the face of great
odds (6).

III. The psalmist anticipates complete victory for deliverance
(7–8).

    A. He petitions the LORD to deliver him (7a).

    B. He anticipates in his prayer that it will be a great deliv-
erance (7b).

    C. He acknowledges that the deliverance comes from the
LORD (8).

COMMENTARY IN EXPOSITORY FORM

I. As believers face increasing numbers of adversaries who taunt their faith, they may find confidence in God's plan for them (1–3).

A. Enemies of the faith continue to increase (1–2).

What will become a familiar note in the Psalter is sounded
here at the outset, namely, that there is an ever-increasing
number of people who would like to destroy the righteous and
their faith. Their opposition to the people of God may be subtle
at times, but at other times it may also be open and direct, far
more dangerous than scorning (v. 1).

In David's life an insurrection turned into a personal attack
on him and his faith, but his faith overcame the crisis. That
faith is first signaled by his immediate cry to God, "O LORD."
This turning to the LORD in the midst of a crisis is characteristic of a lament because it is how people pray in times of
trouble. The urgent address is then followed by four lines that
lay out the problem. The clauses emphasize the dilemma by
repetition, and build to a climax: "many are my adversaries,

many are rising against me, many are saying . . . , 'there is no deliverance for him in God.'"

The psalmist's initial amazement over the growing opposition is immediately expressed: "How many are my adversaries!" The stative verb (רַבּוּ) is translated as a predicate adjective: "many are," and this idea is continued with the repetition of the adjective "many" (רַבִּים) to emphasize the growing number of people rising up against him (the participle קָמִים stressing on-going action).[10] These "adversaries" (s.v. צָרַר, which has the

---

10. The verb קוּם means "to arise, stand up, stand." Words related to it are קוֹמָה, "height," קָמָה, "standing grain," קִים, "adversary, uprising," and מָקוֹם, "place." The Akkadian cognate *kumu* means "place."

There are several ways the word is used in the Old Testament. The first category is the simple meaning "arise." Samples are easy to find: it can mean rising up from a meal (Gen. 25:34), rising from lying down (Ruth 3:14), rising after kneeling (1 Sam. 24:43), and (not) rising after falling wounded (Ps. 18:38)."

Related to this idea are uses where the purpose of the rising is clear. In Judges 20:8 it indicates rising up to speak; in Psalm 27:12 false witnesses rising up against the psalmist; and in Psalm 3 the hostile sense of people rising up in rebellion, i.e., organizing an attack.

A second category uses the word "arise" in the sense of someone coming on the scene, such as a king, a prophet, a leader rising to power (e.g., Exod. 1:8).

A third group of uses emphasizes arising for action. This is the use in Judges 4:14. In Jonah 1:3 it has the sense of making a start on the journey. It is used in the Psalms in addressing the LORD in prayer: asking the LORD to "arise" is asking him to act on one's behalf, to get involved, in contrast to a period of inactivity (Ps. 3:7).

The word can also mean "stand," but the uses do not simply mean "stand"; e.g., in Leviticus 27:14 it signifies that a price stands, or is fixed. The meaning "stand" can indicate persisting in something, taking a stand (Isa. 32:8); maintaining oneself, as in standing firm (Josh. 7:12–13); and in terms of covenants, that which is established or confirmed, as in the kingdom (1 Sam. 24:21), or that one is ratified (Ruth 4:7).

The uses of the verb in the *hiphil* system simply add the causative element to add related categories of meanings. For the definition "to arise" we have the meaning "cause to arise, raise," such as setting up stones (Josh. 4:9), erecting a building (Exod. 26:30), or raising up judges (Judg. 2:16). In Psalm 113:7 it is used to tell how the LORD reverses fortunes—he raises the poor from the ash heap and causes them to sit with princes.

For the definition "to stand" we have the meaning "cause to stand." It can be used in the sense of establishing a covenant (Gen. 9:9, 11), or

sense of hemming in) continued to surround him even when he went to sleep for the night. And when he awoke, he knew that they were still there (v. 6).

But at the climax of these opening verses we read of their taunting challenge to his faith: "There is no deliverance[11] for him

---

carrying out an oath, a vow, or a covenant (1 Sam. 15:11). In Psalm 40:2 the word is used for God's making the psalmist secure—"he set my feet upon a rock."

11. The verb "save, deliver" (יָשַׁע) and its related nouns (תְּשׁוּעָה ,יְשׁוּעָה ,יֶשַׁע) occur frequently in the Book of Psalms: of the 354 uses of the root (apart from names), 136 are in Psalms. Translations differ on whether to translate the words with "save/salvation" or "deliver/deliverance" or "give victory/victory" or even "rescue." All are legitimate translations, but whatever translation is used in a given passage will have to be explained because of the different connotations. Using a translation "deliverance" or "victory" avoids confusion with the predominantly New Testament idea of spiritual salvation, i.e., regeneration; but there is a spiritual sense to the deliverance in many passages and it has to be included. "Salvation" works well, but it will have to be carefully explained.

Word books often give the etymological idea as "to be wide, spacious," in view of Arabic. This sounds good when one of the related terms is used in contrast to a word like "trouble," meaning a narrowing or a strait (צָרַר>). But there are difficulties with this connection, and so it should not be stressed in the exposition (s.v. ישׁע by F. Stolz, in *Theological Lexicon of the Old Testament,* ed. by Ernst Jenni and Claus Westermann, and tr. by Mark E. Biddle [Peabody, MA: Hendrickson, 1997], II:584).

As far as uses are concerned, most concern a physical deliverance, such as a military victory (e.g., Pss. 44:4; 21:1, 5). The charismatic judges who delivered Israel from their oppressors are called "saviors/deliverers" (e.g., Judg. 3:9). This salvation/deliverance may come from God through human agencies (Judg. 15:18; 1 Sam. 11:13), but sometimes the deliverance comes through a supernatural intervention alone (Exod. 15:2; 2 Kings 6:27). The deliverance is not always in a battle; it could be from some personal difficulty or time of trouble (Ps. 37:39), and it could be in legal situations where another person would rescue someone (Deut. 22:27).

There are a number of contexts where the words in this group have a spiritual sense. Psalm 51:14 uses the expression "God of my salvation" (i.e., God who saves me) in an appeal for forgiveness, but the reference is general and could refer to the many ways God has saved him. The psalmist also requests that the joy of his salvation may be restored (51:12), which may refer to the relationship he had through faith in the LORD. So God saves/delivers people from war, famine, sickness, legal difficulties, and

in God." The adversaries were wicked[12] people (v. 7) trying to kill him as part of their planned revolution. Since the enemies were opposing God's anointed (cf. Ps. 2) and since they had no prophetic sanction, no authority to remove him, they could not succeed. All they could do was declare in their arrogance that the psalmist had no hope of salvation from God. This attack on his faith was meant to be painful and discouraging. David had not lost faith in the LORD's salvation, as the prayer indicates (v. 7); he remained confident that "salvation was of the LORD" (v. 8).

In this point many Christian expositors have noted comparisons with Jesus. Most of the nation rejected him as their king, choosing rather to follow the murderous leaders who wanted to put him to death. And, if such opposition was true for the LORD's anointed, it will also be true of all who follow him. Therefore, in the face of such opposition, believers must turn to God in prayer, pouring out their lament as David did; but their prayers must exhibit genuine faith through expressions of confidence and words of praise.

B.Believers may find confidence by rehearsing God's glorious plan for their lives (3).

Because the adversaries were striking at his faith, the psalmist expressed his faith with the greatest confidence: "But

---

even death. Saving from sin is part of many deliverances because the deliverance is the result of divine forgiveness.

In the Psalms the urgent cry for the LORD to "save" is a frequent part of the petition in a lament (Ps. 6:4). It is because God's assistance or salvation has been made available for his people, especially for the poor and suffering (Ps. 18:27) who need it, or for the king (Ps. 20:6, 9) who will be the agent of it (Ps. 72:4), that the cry for salvation is a recurring theme. The witness to God's past interventions is usually found in the confessions of confidence where the people acknowledge that salvation belongs to the LORD, or that their God is a saving God (Pss. 18:48; 25:5).

See a more detailed study of this and related words in John F. A. Sawyer, *Semantics in Biblical Research, New Methods of Defining Hebrew Words for Salvation, Studies in Biblical Theology, Second series, 24* (London: SCM, 1972), pp. 60–88.

12. Here the word is better translated "wicked" rather than the general "ungodly," because they were malicious enemies.

you, O LORD" signals the change from lament to confidence. He found confidence in the fact that God's character and care for him contrasted sharply with their challenge.

The figures in this verse amplify the relationship God had established with him that gave him such confidence. The first is the (metaphor) "shield." God was the only defense that he had, but God was the only defense that he needed against the numerous adversaries. If God was his defense, who could harm him? The second image is "my glory." This word (כָּבוֹד; s.v. Ps. 19:1) is commonly used to describe God as the most important person in existence, a fact that is often manifested by accompanying phenomena (called the "glory of the LORD"); but here it may refer to the glory and honor that David had been given when the LORD chose him and gave him the kingdom (so it would be a metonymy of effect). David may have been driven from his palace; but his glory was still intact, for God had bestowed honor and power on him as the chosen king (NIV has "you bestowed glory on me").[13] The third figure is the "lifter up of my head" (מֵרִים רֹאשִׁי; s.v. Ps. 46:10). The image is one of honorable exaltation. God "lifts up the head" of the dejected one and exalts him above others.[14] David may have felt dejected and afraid when he fled, but as he reflected on his relationship with God, he became confident that he would be restored to the position of leadership over the people of God. God is the one who would exalt him (so the expression is a metonymy of adjunct or effect). God had not done all he did for the king to let him die in an insurrection. The king knew that he would return to the royal city with head held high.

II. Facing an uncertain future, God's people may build their confidence as they experience God's present protection through answered prayer (4–6).

---

13. VanGemeren argued for the interpretation of "my glory" as a designation of God, "my glorious One." It would then signify the LORD's rule over his kingdom (*Expository Bible Commentary*, "Psalms," p. 102).

14. In Genesis 40:13 Pharaoh "lifted up the head" of the cup-bearer, restoring him to his position. The text also uses the expression to form an unpleasant play on the image, for the baker was also lifted up, i.e., hung.

Confidence in the Face of Adversity

A. God answers the prayers of his people and sustains them in times of trouble (4–5).

In this section the psalmist praises God for answering his prayer by sustaining him through the night. In the first three verses David had addressed God directly, now he speaks about the LORD to others; in the first verses he had described the present, growing danger, now he describes his present deliverance in the past tense.[15] He will still pray for complete deliverance from his enemies (v. 7), but here he praises God for answering his prayer. How can this contrast be explained?

One interpretation would take the lines to be speaking of his faith in general terms; accordingly, the verbs would be translated with the present tense: "I cry out . . . he answers." Then the prayer at the end of the psalm would be a continuation of such a prayer life.

But it makes more sense in this type of psalm to translate the verbs in these verses with the past tense, so that the verses report how God answered his prayer and sustained him through the night. But since he had only been sustained through the night, he would still pray for complete deliverance. The first verb (אֶקְרָא) could be interpreted as a simple imperfect tense, but it is followed by "and he answered," a preterite (imperfect) with the waw consecutive (וַיַּעֲנֵנִי). While this form could be given an English present tense to harmonize with a present tense translation of the first verb ("I cry . . . and he answers"), it could also be given its more common past tense translation. The first verb could then be taken as a preterite as well—without the waw consecutive: "I cried . . . and he answered."[16] The next verse supports this interpretation because it elaborates on the report using the past tense: "I lay down" is a perfect tense (שָׁכַבְתִּי), indicating the completed action; it is followed by another preterite (imperfect) with waw consecutive, "and I slept" (וָאִישָׁנָה); then

---

15. The versions are inconsistent in their translation of the tenses here. We have to note what part of the psalm this is in, and what the forms are, to make the translation. Here David is reporting what happened.

16. Here the fact that the first verb comes at the end of the colon ("with my voice / to the LORD / I cried") would explain why the waw consecutive would not be present on the form.

223

there is another perfect tense expressing the definite past, "I woke up" (הֱקִיצוֹתִי). Finally, the verb "sustain" could also be taken as a preterite without the *waw* consecutive, "he sustained me" (יִסְמְכֵנִי; s.v. Ps. 51:12), although it would not disrupt the flow of the verse to take this last verb as a habitual imperfect: I made it through the night because the LORD (always) sustains me.[17] In this view, then, the two verses are a report of what happened, not a general expression of faith.

There are a couple of ways to explain this report of answered prayer. The verses could be the anticipatory wording of a vow to praise God. In other words, in the midst of his prayer, the psalmist rehearsed the praise that he would give when he was finally delivered. This is why it would be in the past tense; it would be a report of what God did (or was about to do). Such vows were common in lament psalms, although they more often come at the end of the psalm.

The verses could also be David's immediate praise for God's protection in the crisis. The praise would have been given spontaneously as he awoke and realized that God had answered his prayer for deliverance by sustaining him through the night. God was truly his shield; but he still was faced with adversaries, and so he prayed that God would utterly destroy them. In other words, the immediate deliverance became a sign of the complete deliverance desired (it is what Westermann calls an oracle of salvation). This explanation seems more natural in the flow of the psalm. In either case verses 4–6 form a section of confidence in the midst of a prayer for deliverance, and whether this was intended to be a vow of praise or not, it was part of what he would say when he stood in the sanctuary once again.

B. God's protective care inspires greater confidence to face the increasing opposition (6).

The psalmist's being sustained through the night prompted greater confidence; he declared, "I shall not fear the tens of thousands who set themselves (שָׁתוּ) against me on every hand."

---

17. A. A. Anderson said that the imperfect tense here may imply God's care has been and will continue to be unceasing (*Psalms,* I:74).

His focus on the character of God and his experience of protection through answered prayer strengthened him to face the enemies, no matter what the odds might be.[18] All the time that he was praying, and sleeping, the adversaries were taking their stand all around him, readying themselves for a final attack. Because God was on his side, David would not be afraid of them.

III.Petition: God's people may anticipate complete deliverance when they pray to the LORD (7–8).

The petition section of the psalm begins with verse seven. It follows the normal pattern of lament psalms: "Arise . . . deliver . . . ." The call for the LORD to arise (an anthropomorphism, almost like calling for God to spring into action) is a call for immediate and swift intervention by the LORD. The choice of the word "arise" (קוּמָה) also balances the lament: many were "rising" (קָמִים) up against him, and so he prays that God would "arise" on his behalf. It is a *talionic* prayer: when God arises, i.e., begins to act, the uprising, i.e., rebellion, will fall.

The second imperative specifically asks for deliverance, "save/deliver me" (הוֹשִׁיעֵנִי), the very thing that they claimed God would not do for him. This deliverance would be the effect of God's rising up: therefore, the petition uses a metonymy of cause (God's rising up) with a connected metonymy of effect (delivering him).

The request is clear and direct; it is also a prayer of faith. The petitioner expected a great deliverance. This expectation is expressed in the causal clause in which the verbs are written in

---

18. The word used is מֶרְבְבוֹת; it can mean "multitudes, myriads, ten thousands, great numbers" in general. In this verse the psalmist is not saying there are tens of thousands around him; he is saying he will not be afraid of myriads of people who set themselves against him. It is a hyperbolic statement, and somewhat hypothetical. To argue that this psalm does not fit the threat by Absalom because there were not ten thousand people there misses the point of the language (Kraus, *Psalms 1–59*, pp. 137–8). Besides, if the psalm is placed in a later period, such as the Maccabean period, because of this, following Kraus' thinking, then the same problem exists— finding a time when tens of thousands were surrounding the psalmist, or even surrounding the people of God if this were taken as a national psalm.

the perfect tense (הִכִּיתָ, "you struck," from נָכָה; and שִׁבַּרְתָּ, "you smashed," from שָׁבַר). These could be interpreted as "present perfects," meaning "you have struck" my enemies in the past, and so I know you can do it now. But lament psalms often express confidence with such past tense forms with reference to the future (often called the perfect of confidence, which is akin to the prophetic perfect). In other words, the psalmist is so confident of the outcome that he writes it as if it had happened already. The meaning, then, is that he expected the deliverance to be a crushing blow on his enemies. The verse could be translated with a future tense for clarification of the certainty, or left as a past tense to fit the way the psalmist expressed his absolute confidence (to be explained by the expositor).[19]

The bold images do not mean that God would personally and literally smash the enemies on the jaw or break their teeth. Rather, they mean that he would enable the king and his loyal subjects to do it ("you will [cause us to] smash"—a metonymy of cause). Breaking teeth and smashing jaws would very likely be part of a military combat. The point is that the psalmist was confident that a great deliverance was coming because God would enable them to strike the enemies decisively.

IV. Praise: God's people must acknowledge that deliverance is from the LORD alone (8).

The final verse expresses the lesson of the psalm in the form of the praise proper, which, because the psalmist was still praying for victory, must be either part of the confidence in his prayer, or the vow of praise. Since laments often end with such vows, the verse probably expresses the theme of the praise that he wanted to and would be obliged to give when back in the sanctuary: "Deliverance/salvation comes from (or, belongs to) the LORD; your blessing is upon your people." Here is the third use of the related words for "deliverance"—they had said there was no deliverance for him in God, he prayed for God to deliver

---

19. A few commentators have suggested imperative translations for the perfect tenses here, but the note of confidence in the final section of the psalm is more fitting to the type of psalm.

him, and he will soon be able to declare that deliverance is from God. The blessing, a gift and an enablement from God, would be the victory that comes from God. The adversaries may have taunted his faith by saying that God would not save him, but he was confident that God would prove them wrong. And when in the sanctuary, his very presence there among the people of God would be witness to the truth.

MESSAGE AND APPLICATION

Because his faith was in the LORD, the one who protected him, gave him a glorious reign, and would exalt him once again to his throne, the king was not filled with despair. Rather, in the most trying circumstances he cried out to the LORD, and then lay down and slept, knowing that the LORD would sustain him. God's protection of him through the night further built his confidence that God would ultimately deliver him. Psalm 3 is therefore the confident prayer of a true believer who found his adversaries increasing in number and resolve, but who was not afraid of them because the LORD was on his side. This is a prayer that was dominated by confidence and praise.

The psalm presents us with a basic truth of the faith; for exposition the central idea may be worded as follows: *When opposed by many adversaries, the faithful may pray with confidence for deliverance because the Lord's plan for them cannot be thwarted by the world.* The exposition of this psalm will show that the key to such confidence comes from a personal knowledge of God's character and care for his people, and a personal experience of answered prayer. Paul reiterated the point: "If God is for us, who can be against us? (Rom. 8:31). Indeed, nothing will separate us from the love of God in Christ Jesus our Savior. To make this truth a source of confidence in prayer, believers must focus on God's character and on his calling for them to serve him in a world that is opposed to the faith; and to confirm and strengthen this confidence they must have regular and recent answers to prayer.

PSALM 4

Safe and Secure
in God's Love in spite
of False Accusations

INTRODUCTION

Text and Textual Variants

To the Chief Musician. With Stringed Instruments.
A Psalm of David.

1 When I call, answer me,[1] O God of my righteousness!
—you *who* have given me relief [2] *when I was* in distress.
Be gracious to me and hear my prayer!

---

1. The Hebrew verb is the *qal* imperative, but the Greek text has εἰσήχουσέν μου, "[the God of my righteousness] has heard me," reading it as a perfect tense.
2. The verb (literally "you made room") is a perfect tense; the clause could be a relative clause without the relative pronoun. The Greek has a finite verb, "you have made room for me." The editors of BHS propose reading it as an imperative (הַרְחִיבָה) to harmonize with the verse, but an imperative meaning could be given without changing the text. Because the word occurs in the context of volitives, the verb could be interpreted as a precative perfect and translated as an imperative; hence, NIV has "give me relief from my distress."

229

2 You important people,[3] how long *will* my honor *suffer* shame?[4]
  How long will you love empty words, will you seek after a
  lie? *Selah*

3 But know that the LORD has set apart[5] the godly[6] for
  himself;
  the LORD will hear when I call to him.

4 Tremble,[7] and do not sin;
  ponder in your own hearts on your beds, and be still.
  Selah

5 Offer right sacrifices,[8]
  and trust in the LORD.

6 Many are saying, "Who can show us *something* good?
  Lift up the light of your face upon us,[9] O LORD!"

---

3. Literally, "sons of man" (אִישׁ); but since that does not communicate much, perhaps the intended meaning of "sons of a man" could be reflected in a paraphrase referring to some who are important (Ps. 49:2).

4. Literally, "How long is my honor (my glory) for shame." The Greek text has "How long will you be slow of heart?" (βαρυκάρδιοι, "slow of heart," would reflect כָּבְדֵי לֵב).

5. Some follow the proposal to alter the text slightly to read "Yahweh has made wonderful his love to me" after Psalm 31:21 (הִפְלָא instead of הִפְלָה). This change would require changing חָסִיד לִי to חֶסֶד לִי, "love to me." The Greek and Jerome follow פלא and have "done wondrous things." But the word in the MT is the by-form פלה meaning that God has separated the godly for himself (as in Targum). The fundamental idea in the line is separation. A. A. Anderson concludes that in either reading the point is that God has marked out the godly for a different treatment (*Psalms*, I: 78).

6. The word "godly" is a passive form, חָסִיד, indicating one who is the object of divine love–the beloved. But it can also have an active sense to it, for the godly in turn shows mercy, and so "loyal one." For a study of this word see Ps. 23:6.

7. The Greek text has ὀργίζεσθε, "be angry," which is arguably in the range of the emotions of the Hebrew word, but not a very close translation. The NIV followed the Greek in its translation. Ephesians 4:26 cites the Greek at this point: "In your anger do not sin" (NIV).

8. Literally, "sacrifices of righteousness"; see also John S. Kselman, "A Note on Psalm 4:5," *Biblica* 68 (1987):103–5.

9. The Hebrew has "Lift up" נְסָה. One manuscript has נשא. The MT seems to have a variant form for "lift up." The Greek text has ἐσημειώθη and renders the line as "The light of your face was made a sign to us." The editors propose נָסְעָה to read "the light of your face, O Yahweh, has departed from us" (J. H. Eaton, "Hard Sayings: Psalm 4.6–7," *Theology* 67 (1964):355–57;

7 You have put joy in my heart
    more than[10] when their grain and their wine abound.
8 In peace I will both lie down and sleep;
    for you alone, O LORD, cause me to dwell in safety.

Composition and Context

This psalm may be generally classified as a lament psalm, an evening prayer; but because it is so filled with confidence, it is close to being a psalm of confidence. Its motifs reflect the prayer song, Psalm 3, in a number of ways, which is probably why it was placed after it. For example, in Psalm 3 David said that he lay down and slept, and in Psalm 4 he says that he will lie down in peace and sleep; in Psalm 3 David is filled with confidence in the presence of many who were challenging his faith, and here he has that same confidence even though many are disheartened; and whereas Psalm 3 was a praise and prayer in the morning, this psalm is an evening prayer. Perowne, seeing the similarities between Psalms 3 and 4, suggested that the interval of time between the two may have been the time between the morning and evening of the same day.[11]

There is nothing in Psalm 4 that demands it be connected to the crisis of David's flight from Absalom. In fact the evidence of this psalm suggests a different crisis, one in which false accusations were made against the psalmist.[12] Others take the psalm very differently, such as seeing it as essentially an issue of praying to the right God for agricultural produce. Broyles suggests that the psalm was not a private prayer but a liturgy that was intended for others to hear, the others being worshipers of false deities, or if followers of the LORD, people who were

---

Kraus, *Psalms 1–59*, p. 31), or, "the light of your presence, O Yahweh, has fled from us" (Anderson, I:80; see also NEB). However, NIV translates it as "Let the light of your face shine upon us."

10. The translation "more than" reflects the comparative *min*, מֵאֵת

11. For example, Psalm 3 reports how the psalmist lay down and slept, and Psalm 4 records his decision to lie down (Perowne, *Psalms*, I:125). Such connecting words are used commonly throughout the Psalter to link passages in some kind of an orderly arrangement.

12. Anderson, *Psalms*, I:76.

not sure of what deity they should appeal to for produce.[13] Of course, that the psalm could have been cast in that form and used for that purpose does not nullify an original composition by an individual.

Exegetical Analysis

Summary

Having cried out to God for help, the psalmist warns his enemies not to sin against God by wronging him because God has set him apart in protective care, a fact that gladdens his heart at a time when many were disheartened.

Outline

I. Petition: The psalmist calls to God who gives him relief in distress (1).

II. Exhortation: The psalmist earnestly warns his enemies not to wrong him, but to turn to trust in the God who has lovingly set him apart (2–5).

    A. He asks how long they will try to turn his glory to shame by seeking after lies (2).

    B. He affirms that the LORD has set him apart and meets his needs (3).

    C. He warns the wicked not to sin but to trust and worship the LORD (4–5).

III. Expression of Trust: The psalmist joyfully expresses his peace and security in God at a time when many were disheartened (6–8).

    A. He calls for God's favor when many were looking for evidence of God's provisions (6).

    B. He exults in the joy God has given him, a joy that is greater than the joy of a harvest (7).

---

13. C. C. Broyles, *Psalms,* p. 52. While there is some warrant for interpreting the psalm this way, as we shall see in the exposition, the interpretation is not obvious from a careful reading of the psalm and therefore not very convincing. Moreover, a psalm that was originally an independent psalm would have become liturgical when deposited with the chief musician for sanctuary use.

C. He is confident of peace and security in the LORD (8).

COMMENTARY IN EXPOSITORY FORM

I. God can give relief to his people when they are in distress (1)

The psalm begins with a brief prayer in which the petitioner also expressed his confidence based on God's dealings with him in the past. The prayer is simply "Answer me" (עֲנֵנִי) in this distress. In the word order of the text it is preceded by "when I call." The emphasis is on his calling out to God, and God is addressed as "God of my righteousness." The word "righteousness" could be taken as an attributive genitive, "my righteous God" (as NIV); but it may rather emphasize the righteousness given to David, meaning that God maintained or vindicated David's righteous cause against those who opposed him—"God of my right." The expression is relational; the righteous God champions the rights of his people.

The second clause of verse one seems to be a relative clause without the pronoun (which is not unique here), although the NIV has classified the verb as a precative perfect and made it a part of the prayer: "give me relief."[14] If the perfect tense (הִרְחַבְתָּ) is translated as a present perfect it would be rendered, "you [who] have made room for me in my distress" (or if a characteristic perfect, "you [who] make room for me in my distress"). So in addition to basing his plea on God's righteousness for him, he recalls how the LORD has set him free from distress before. "Distress" means a tight place or bind (צַר); a related idea is used for enemies who harass and hem people in.

The psalmist completes the petition in the last part of the verse, asking God to be gracious to him and hear his prayer. It

---

14. The NIV and others have interpreted this form as a precative perfect and therefore equivalent to an imperative. There is some evidence for such a category, but sure cases are rare. The text here makes very good sense as a relative clause referring to God's past dealings with David. An imperative might make the verse harmonious, but it is not necessary.

is an appeal for unmerited favor.[15] And the appeal is specifically for God to hear (שְׁמַע), i.e., respond favorably to the prayer (s.v. Ps. 45:10).

II. The proven confidence of the people of God should be a warning to those who try to disgrace their faith (2–5).

A. They may be confident God will answer their prayers in spite of false claims (2–3).

The psalmist turns to address his enemies, whether they

---

15. חָנֵּנִי, "be gracious to me," is the imperative of חָנַן. The verb and its related forms are often translated in terms of "grace, favor, mercy," but the fundamental meaning in them all concerns favorable treatment that is undeserved. The adverb חִנָּם illustrates this point, for it means "gratuitously, free, for nothing, for no reason" (see Job 2:3; Gen. 29:15). The common noun is חֵן, "grace," which also expresses unexpected or undeserved favor (see Ruth 2:10; Gen. 6:8).

The petition for grace is used for the forgiveness of sins in Psalm 51:1. It can also be used for other appeals, such as delivering the people from their troubles (Ps. 31:9). In such prayers the related noun תְּחִנָּה, "supplication (for grace)" may also be used. Throughout the psalms the petition for God to be gracious is linked to the appeal for God to hear (see also 27:7; 30:10 as well as here in 4:1). It is like obtaining an audience with a gracious sovereign—in his good grace he will grant the petition, although there may be no reason binding him to do so.

The word can also refer to God's bestowing favor in tangible ways. In Genesis 33:5 it refers to God's gracious provision of children for the patriarch. It can also be used for human kindness, such as showing favor to the needy, meaning giving them help (Prov. 14:31). Also, Job asks his friends to show him some pity (Job 19:21). And the high priestly benediction, referred to in this fourth psalm, announces the LORD's grace on the people to protect and bless them (Num. 6:25; see also Ps. 67:1).

The adjective חַנּוּן is used often in a designation of the character of God (see Exod. 34:6; Exod. 22:27). It is the nature of the LORD to be gracious, meaning to show forgiveness and to provide good gifts to people who do not deserve them. The implication of the words for grace is that the recipients not only do not deserve the benefit, but that they deserve the opposite.

In the Greek version the noun is commonly translated χάρις, but the verb is rendered ἐλεέω. For further information, see D. R. Ap-Thomas, "Some Aspects of the Root ḤNN in the Old Testament," *JSS* 2 (1957):128–48.

could hear his warning or not. He calls them "sons of (an individual) man" (בְּנֵי אִישׁ), which may indicate that they are men of high degree, perhaps distinguished and influential people (see Pss. 49:2; 62:9). The warning to them is expressed in the form of a rhetorical question. The first part reads "How long [will] my honor [suffer] to shame?" This could refer to David's personal honor, his estate as a king (see 3:4); but it could be used in reference to anyone's dignity or honor, and not just a king's. Their opposition to him had attempted to turn it "into shame" (לִכְלִמָּה). The question is lamenting the fact that they were trying to ruin him, but the interrogative "how long" also implies there is a limit to this treatment by them.

The second half of the verse is also a rhetorical question, criticizing them for loving vanity and lies. These expressions probably refer to false accusations that were designed to bring disgrace to David (see Ps. 31:18). The interrogative "how long" applies to this part as well, but the clause simply reads "will you love empty [words]," "empty" (רִיק) probably referring to words since the next clause says "will you seek after a lie (כָזָב)."[16] The verbs are imperfect tenses, expressing the simple future in the questions; but the wording of these questions implies that what they were doing would suddenly come to an end.

These rhetorical questions are based on the psalmist's confidence that the LORD will answer his prayer and deliver him from them. His "but know" (וּדְעוּ; s.v. Ps. 139:1) strikes the note of confidence and calls for them to realize the facts of the case. They should know that the LORD has separated the godly for himself. The "godly" is literally the "beloved" (חָסִיד; s.v. Ps. 23:6), one who has entered into covenant with the LORD by divine love, i.e., one who has received and also practices this loyal love. The point of the line is that God has marked out (הִפְלָה) the godly for himself and will not abandon them to the wicked. So David declares that he is one whom God loves, whom God has

---

16. It is possible that "empty" and "lie" could be referring to false gods that they loved, and to whom they prayed for rain and produce from the fields if verses 6 and 7 are to be connected here in that sense; but if that were the intended meaning it is rather obscure. It is simpler to say that these terms refer to their words which were slanderous, false accusations, because they were trying to discredit the faithful.

marvelously chosen for himself. To try to discredit him is to deny God's love for him.

Because he belongs to God, God will hear his prayer when he calls to him (3b). This confident statement picks up the motifs in verse one, "when I call" and "hear my prayer."

B. They may confidently warn their antagonists to abandon their sins and put their trust in the LORD (4–5)

The psalmist continues his direct address to his adversaries by calling for repentance and faith. He instructs them, "Tremble and do not sin." The word "tremble" (רִגְזוּ) can refer to any strong emotion—anger, fear, disquietude; but it essentially means to tremble in fear and dismay, here in response to God's goodness to his people in spite of the attempts of the slanderers to discredit them. The Greek text's "be angry" found its way into Ephesians 4:26 (which is not a direct quote). In the Psalm, David was calling for his enemies to be shaken to the core so that they would stop sinning (the construction וְאַל־תֶּחֱטָאוּ is a negated jussive calling for immediate compliance).

What they were to do was to think carefully about their sins and let that quiet, sober reflection cause them to change their ways. "Ponder" is literally "say" (אִמְרוּ), but here it has the connotation of meditating or thinking during the night hours—just think! He tells them to consider these things in their hearts and be still (וְדֹמּוּ).[17] The silence or stillness could refer to the time that they would be contemplating; but it more likely refers to the result of their meditation, that is, that they would cease trying to shame the godly with falsehood.[18]

That this was the intended purpose of the meditation is clear from verse 5 which instructs them to offer sacrifices to the LORD. The first colon of verse 5 (offer sacrifices) is actually the

---

17. M. Dahood argues for a translation of "weep" (with an emphatic *waw*) based on a cognate root *dmm,* but the translation of the line in this context does not make as much sense as "be silent" in their false accusations (*Psalms,* I:24).

18. See additionally M. L. Barré, "Hearts, Beds and Repentance in Psalm 4:5 and Hosea 7:14," *Bib* 76 (1995):53–62.

result of the second colon (trust in the LORD). The psalmist's instruction to trust (וּבְטְחוּ) in the LORD is wise advice, since the LORD protects those who belong to him and will oppose those who do not.[19] If they trust in the LORD they will become part of those who are dear to God. And the evidence of their faith will be

---

19. The verb "trust" is here בָּטַח. It may be given an array of translations: "trust, be confident, be reliant, feel safe." BDB suggested a link to the Arabic with a meaning of throwing oneself down on the ground, meaning complete dependency; but this seems to be a developed sense and not obviously present in biblical Hebrew. The basic idea of the word seems to be the assured reliance upon someone or something with an emphasis on the security of that trust. One related noun, בֶּטַח, has the idea of "safety, security"—it is used in this sense in the eighth verse of this psalm. And the noun מִבְטָח means "confidence" but always refers to the object of the confidence. These words can describe secure circumstances or a secure frame of mind.

The idea of placing confidence in someone or something, whether properly or not, is clear in the uses. In Proverbs 31:11 the husband trusts his wife, meaning that he entrusts all the affairs of the household to her care because she is fully capable. A neighbor lives in security next to another (Prov. 3:29); there has to be a trust or confidence that it is safe and secure. Sometimes this kind of trust turns to complacency (Isa. 32:9–11). Or it may simply be misplaced trust for security, such as trusting in fortified cities (Jer. 5:17), or ill-gotten gain (Pss. 62:10; Jer. 48:7), or in mankind (Jer. 17:5), even a close friend who might betray (Ps. 41:9). The words may be used for trusting or placing confidence in false gods, but because they are impotent that trust has no security and the people will be put to shame (Isa. 42:17). And the one who trusts in his own heart is a fool (Prov. 28:26). Nevertheless, in all cases the trust carries a feeling of confidence that one is in a place of safety and security. Only a careful study of the object of this trust will determine if it is truly safe and secure. Ultimately, only trust in Yahweh will bring these desired results (Prov. 3:5).

And so בָּטַח is found frequently in prayers and songs of Israel's worship: the idea stressed is that one can place confidence only in the LORD. In the Psalter the statement "I/we trust in the LORD" is a frequent expression of faith, often strengthened with the pronoun (Ps. 56:4, 11, etc.). Placing confidence by faith in the LORD brings God's loyal love as opposed to the sorrows of the wicked (Ps. 32:10); happiness (Prov. 16:20); and also safety and security (Ps. 125:1–2). In general, those who put their trust in the LORD are truly blessed (Ps. 40:4). They will live obediently and faithfully because they fear the LORD (Ps. 115:11). And as God's faithful believers, they will dwell securely in the land (Lev. 25:18). And in Psalm 4:8 the psalmist is confident that he can lie down and sleep in peace because the LORD has caused him to dwell in safety (or

in true worship: "Sacrifice right sacrifices" (the cognate accusative places an emphasis on making sacrifices). But the sacrifices had to be right—"sacrifices of righteousness." This suggests that they may have been making sacrifices, but not the right ones, either not to the right God, or not with righteous conduct behind their ritual. Righteous sacrifices (if this is an attributive genitive) means that they will be sacrifices that God will accept (see Ps. 51:19). The verse instructs them to offer in the right spirit and with wholehearted trust in the LORD, not from hearts bent on destroying other people.

III. The faithful find greater joy in God's provision of peace and security than the joy at the time of harvest (6–8).

In words that reflect the taunting challenge of the ungodly in Psalm 3, this psalm says that "many" are saying, "Who can show us [something] good?"[20] These people now are possibly friends or companions, people who were disheartened by the circumstances. But there is no compelling reason to say this; they still could be the same antagonists that the psalmist has been dealing with in the psalm. In either case, their challenge is for someone to show them something good, some evidence of divine favor. This could refer to produce from the ground,[21] but "good" is certainly not limited to that (s.v. Ps. 34:8). The challenge may be to any sign of divine favor.

Yet the psalmist has an abiding faith. He recalls the blessing of the priests at the sanctuary, which said, "The LORD bless you and keep you; the LORD make his face shine upon you and be gracious to you; the LORD lift up his face toward you and give you peace" (Num. 6:24–26). This is one of four psalms that

---

security). The confident feeling of security, then, has the connotation of being unconcerned.

20. Dahood here argues that *ṭôb* means "rain" (Deut. 28:12; Jer. 17:6), making this a prayer for rain: "Who will show us rain?" (*Psalms,* I:24). The general idea in reference to God's blessings may be plausible, but the translation does not have to be changed this way.

21. C. Broyles says that "good things" meant produce, based on Pss. 34:10, 12; 104:28; and 85:11–13 (*Psalms,* p. 54).

refers to that blessing.[22] Here the petitioner turns the words of the blessing into a prayer, "Lift up the light of your face upon us, O LORD." The light of God's face (an anthropomorphic expression) refers to divine favor for deliverance (cf. Ps. 31:16), so this is a prayer that his favor be given to them.

Verse 7 provides confidence for this prayer for divine favor with a remembrance of God's gracious dealings in the past: "You have put joy in my heart, more than when their grain and their new wine abound." The verb is a perfect tense, referring to what God has done in the past. The reference to "their" grain and wine may be a reference to his enemies—perhaps indicating that they have resources, but he does not; but he has spiritual joy, and they do not. Or it may simply be a comparison, for rejoicing at the harvest was an occasion of great joy. He was affirming that God had given him greater gladness than that which comes with full granaries and vats.

The joy that the psalmist had in his heart over knowing how God cared for him in the past and would deliver him from his current crisis enabled him both[23] to lie down quietly at night and sleep in peace (this peace that he enjoyed is also a reference to the high priestly blessing). His confidence was only in the LORD: "You alone, O LORD, cause me to dwell in safety." The expression "in safety" (לָבֶטַח) recalls his advice to the enemies to "trust" (בִּטְחוּ) in the LORD. Trusting in the LORD is the only place of safety in this troubled world; and those who would cause trouble for the godly must know that the LORD is on the side of his beloved.

MESSAGE AND APPLICATION

Psalm 4 is a prayer for help, but the prayer is dominated by the psalmist's confidence in the LORD's loving care of the beloved

---

22. The psalm has been taken to be an interpretive transformation of Aaron's blessing (see Michael A. Fishbane, *Biblical Interpretation in Ancient Israel* [Oxford: Oxford University Press, 1985], 331).

23. The word יַחְדָּו means "together" or in this passage "both." Dahood suggested on the basis of a Ugaritic cognate verb that it should be translated here "his face" (*Psalms*, I:27), but the word denotes the combination of the things mentioned. Here the psalmist anticipates lying down and at once falling asleep (Delitzsch, *Psalms*, I:118).

and in the prospect of peace and security. So the message should focus on that confidence against the backdrop of the distress caused by the antagonists. The expository idea could therefore be worded: *The righteous can rejoice in God's protecting grace that brings them peace and security in the face of distressing attempts to disgrace them.* The lies of the enemies of the faith are a constant harassment to the righteous, but the righteous know that God will vindicate them in spite of it.

The occasion for conflict in the psalm could have been the need for a harvest, the antagonists trying to undermine the faith of the psalmist and the people in general looking for some evidence of God's provision. The psalmist's allusion to the high priestly blessing would fit with the time of a harvest festival as well, although it was given on many occasions. On the whole the evidence for that association is sketchy; the meaning of the psalm seems to have a much wider application. Whatever the situation might be, believers must endure the false accusations about them and their faith; but they have the assurance from God of his protective care and provision of peace and security. In the New Testament, Jesus likewise encouraged the faithful by saying, "Blessed are you when people insult you and falsely say all kinds of evil against you because of me. Rejoice and be glad, because great is your reward in heaven, for in the same way they persecuted the prophets who were before you" (Matt. 5:11–12). And few people have experienced this more than the apostle Paul. In writing to the Corinthians he could affirm that his joy knew no bounds, even though he had been wronged and harassed at every turn (2 Cor. 7:2–5). Only a proven faith can overcome such antagonism from the world.

PSALM 5

Deliverance from Dangerous Deception

INTRODUCTION

Text and Textual Variants

To the Chief Musician. For flutes.[1]
A Psalm of David.

1 Give ear to my words, O LORD;
   consider my sighing.
2 Pay attention to the voice of my cry for help,
      my King and my God,
   for unto you I pray.
3 In the morning, O LORD, you will hear my voice,
      in the morning I shall lay *my request* before you
         and wait in expectation.
4 For you are not a God who takes pleasure in wickedness;
      evil cannot dwell with you.[2]

---

1. The word נְחִילוֹת refers to musical instruments, probably made of a hollow reed. The Greek has taken it from נָחַל which has to do with possessions and inheritance: "concerning her that inherits," ὑπὲρ τῆς κληρονομούσης. Aquila (Symmachus, Jerome) have κληροδοσιῶν, assuming נַחֲלֹה.
2. The suffix on the verb provides the accusative of persons with whom the dwelling occurs; see also Pss. 62:5, 68:19, and 120:5.

5 The arrogant[3] cannot stand in your presence;[4]
  you hate all doers of iniquity.
6 You destroy those[5] who tell lies;
  bloodthirsty and deceitful men the LORD abhors.
7 But I by the abundance of your loyal love shall come into
    your house;
  I shall bow down toward your holy temple in reverence.
8 O LORD, lead me in your righteousness
    because of those watching for me;
  make straight[6] your way[7] before me
9 For there is nothing trustworthy in their[8] mouth;
  their heart *is filled* with destruction.[9]
  Their throat is an open grave;
  with their tongue they speak deceit.
10 Declare them guilty,[10] O God!
  Let them fall because of[11] their intrigues.

---

3. The participle הֹלְלִים is related to הָלַל, but there are homonyms. If it is linked to the common word "praise," then it might have the idea of arrogant and noisy boasting (A. A. Anderson, *Psalms,* I:83). If it is connected to the word "mad," then it might mean "foolish" or wild" (Goldingay suggests "wild men"; *Psalms 1–41,* p. 125). See additionally Perowne, *Psalms,* I:136.
4. Literally, "before your sight (eyes)."
5. The Greek adds "all"—"all those."
6. The Q*ʳe'* would be הַיְשַׁר which is what the majority of the manuscripts and the Targum have (see the *hiphil* also in Prov. 4:25; Isa. 45:2); the K*ᵉthiv* would be הוֹשַׁר.
7. The MT reads "your way before me," but some would change it to "my way before you." And some Hebrew and Greek manuscripts, as well as the Vulgate, make this a plural, reading דְּרָכֶי
8. The Hebrew text has the singular suffix on the word, בְּפִיהוּ. The editors propose reading this as בְּפִימוֹ with a plural suffix to harmonize with the parallel line. This would follow the Greek, Syriac, Targum and Jerome; one Hebrew manuscript has בְּפִיהֶם.
9. The word הַוּוֹת refers to destruction that is worked through wickedness. A related meaning is "desire," suggesting that the destruction is purposed and prepared—it is malicious destruction (see further Perowne, I:136).
10. The verb אָשַׁם means "to be guilty"; only here is the *hiphil,* meaning "declare guilty, condemn."
11. The preposition may express the means by which they fall, or the condition in which they fall, as in the New Testament's "you shall die in your sins" (John 8:21, 24).

> Banish them for their many sins,
>   for they have rebelled against you.[12]
> 11 But let all who take refuge in you be glad;
>   forever let them shout for joy.
> And spread your protection over them
>   that those who love your name may rejoice in you.
> 12 For you bless the righteous, O LORD;
>   you surround them[13] with your favor as with a shield.

Composition and Context

Psalm 5 is a morning prayer like Psalm 4. Only in this case the psalmist faced a different threat—people were lying maliciously about him.[14] His consolation was that he was not separated from the sanctuary but was still able to enter the sanctuary and bow before God in the holy place. His prayer for help, then, is based on the strong conviction that God is bound to defend the righteous because he is a righteous God; and yet, when contrasting himself with the wicked, he does not list his righteous acts but declares that God's loyal love has made him acceptable to God.[15] Thus, as a devout believer he can appeal to his divine king for protection.[16] So the psalmist focuses on the fact that he is accepted into the sanctuary, but the wicked are not because God hates wickedness. No setting is provided by the psalmist, and so we are left to the internal evidence to suggest possible occasions for the writing. Tradition assigned it to David, but that has been challenged by critics.

---

12. The Greek version adds, "O LORD" reading "because they embittered you, O LORD.
13. The form is תַּעְטְרֶנּוּ. The editors propose reading the *piel* of this verb instead of the *qal* because of the double accusative. In the sentence the second accusative is put first and the prepositional phrase before that even though it is in apposition to the second accusative. The suffix on the verb is "him," meaning "them"; it can also be read as "us" (the form is the same), and so the Greek has "us"—"you crowned us."
14. See also G. W. Anderson, "Enemies and Evildoers in the Book of Psalms," *BJRL* 48 (1965):18–29.
15. See also J. W. McKay, "Psalms of Vigil," *ZAW* 91 (1979):229–47.
16. Kidner says that the whole psalm expresses the spirit of the cry in verse two, "My King and my God" (D. Kidner, *Psalms 1–72*, p. 57).

243

Broyles suggests that the psalm was a liturgy with the "I" sections in verses 1–3 and 7–8, the contrast between the works of the wicked described in verses 4–6 and 9–10, and the qualification of the righteous described in verses 11–12. He proposes that it might have formed the pilgrim's response to the gate liturgies, preserved in Psalms 15 and 24, that list the qualifications of those who could enter, and this psalm described the characteristics of those who could not.[17] Such a use of the psalm is certainly possible, but it does not exclude the likelihood that there was an individual occasion for the original writing.[18]

The psalm may be divided into three sections: an appeal to be heard, an expression of confidence, and a prayer. The first three verses form the appeal to God to hear the morning prayer. This is followed by a section of confidence in which he declares his acceptance by the righteous God, a God who hates wickedness and those who persist in it (vv. 4–7). Because of this relationship with God, he prays for continued divine guidance, judgment on the wicked, and protection for all who love the Lord (vv. 8–12).

Exegetical Analysis

Summary

Pleading with God to respond to his urgent cries, the psalmist affirms his assurance of being accepted by God who hates iniquity and separates himself from all of it, and then prays for divine guidance and for the destruction of the wicked, all in anticipation of the great joy it will bring to those who trust the LORD.

---

17. Broyles, pp. 58 and 61.
18. Kraus raises the possibility that the psalm was a prayer formulary and that it may be assumed that such formularies were composed by the temple priesthood. This, he says, meant that a detailed description of the petitioner was to be rejected (*Psalms 1–59*, p. 153). He accepts Beyerlin's conclusion that there was nothing in the text that precluded a provenance from the era of the pre–exilic Zion temple. He eliminates the idea of Davidic authorship because of the mention of "temple" in the psalm (pp. 153–4). Most critics have assumed that the psalm was post–exilic, written for the temple cult by some priest or Levite.

Outline

I. The psalmist asks God to hear his heartfelt sigh and earnest cry in his morning prayer (1–3).
 A. He calls on the LORD to listen to his sighing words (1).
 B. He prays for his God and King to respond to his cry for help (2).
 C. He expects God to hear him in the morning when he prays and watches (3).
II. In contrast to the wicked whom God hates and removes, the psalmist affirms his acceptance into the sanctuary by the love of God (4–7).
 A. He describes God's hatred of iniquity (4–6).
  1. God takes no pleasure in iniquity and separates it from himself (4).
  2. God hates the foolish workers of iniquity and banishes them (5).
  3. The LORD destroys deceitful, bloodthirsty men (6).
 B. He affirms his acceptance into the sanctuary by the love of God (7).
III. In view of the threat from the arrogant, the psalmist prays for guidance and for the condemnation of the malicious enemies, and confidently anticipates the joy of the believers whom the LORD protects (8–12).
 A. He asks for divine guidance in the way of righteousness because of his enemies (8).
 B. He prays for the condemnation of those who are deceitful and destructive (9–10).
  1. The wicked, like an open grave, are deceitful and destructive (9).
  2. His prayer is that the wicked be condemned by their own intrigues and banished in their rebellious acts (10).
 C. He anticipates the joy of the believers whom the LORD protects (11–12).
  1. They will rejoice because God will defend those who take refuge in him (11).
  2. God will bless the righteous by protecting them like a shield (12).

COMMENTARY IN EXPOSITORY FORM

I. The righteous may confidently entreat their God and King to hear their cries as they earnestly watch and pray (1–3).

A. *Their prayer is to their sovereign Lord (1–2).*

The first two verses form a strong appeal for God to hear the prayer; the psalmist asks God to "give ear"[19] to his words, "consider" his sighing,[20] and "pay attention" to his cry for help.[21] The piling up of appeals strengthens the urgency of the petition. More importantly, the appeal is addressed to his King and God; for the psalmist there is no one else he can turn to for help, and so he states "for unto you I pray."[22]

---

19. "Give ear" (הַאֲזִינָה) is common in poetry; it means to listen closely.
20. The word הָגִיג can be translated "meditation" or "sighing" (s.v. Ps. 2:1). This word occurs only here and in Psalm 39:4. It describes a scarcely audible utterance (such as when Hannah was praying and misunderstood).
21. In contrast to his barely audible utterances, his cry for help is loud, as "Pay attention (הַקְשִׁיבָה, "regard") to the voice of my cry (שַׁוְעִי)" indicates.
22. There are many words for prayer: שָׁאַל, "to ask"; הִתְחַנֵּן, "to seek favor"; חָלָה, "entreat favor (mollify, appease)"; שִׂיחַ, "lament, pour out a lament"; עָתַר, "to entreat"; קָרָא, זָעַק/צָעַק, "to cry out, call"; and צָוַע, "to cry out of distress." Here we have the basic word "to pray," הִתְפַּלֵּל, the *hithpael* of the verb פָּלַל. תְּפִלָּה is its related noun, "prayer."

    פָּלַל means "to intervene, interpose, mediate." In the *piel* verbal system the meanings of "mediate" and arbitrate" appear, but there are not many references (see Ezek. 16:32; Ps. 106:30). There is a noun פָּלִיל that means "judge" or "umpire"; as well as a a few more words with the same sense or judging or giving a decision.

    In the *hithpael* stem it has the meaning "to pray." The connection between the two systems may be explained as seeking mediation or arbitration for oneself or someone else. The two appear in a word play in 1 Samuel 2:25: "If a man sins against another man, God will arbitrate (*piel*); but if a man sins against the LORD, who will pray (*hithpael*) for him?"

    If the prayer concerns a need of the one praying, then a translation "pray" is appropriate (1 Samuel 1:27 where Hannah's prayer was for a child or Jonah 2:2 where the prayer is for deliverance from the fish). If the prayer is on behalf of someone else, it may be translated "intercede" (Genesis 20:7, 17, where Abraham intercedes for the king and his household; Numbers 21:7 where Moses prays that the snakes would be taken

In addressing the LORD as his King and his God, the psalmist is acknowledging that the LORD is the supreme judge and administrator of all his affairs, and because his King is the LORD God in heaven, he is al so sovereign over the whol e earth. "King" is appropriate as a title for God (see Ps. 68:24), because the "government" is a theocracy. If this psalm was in fact written by the king, then the earthly king is appealing to the divine King for help—the monarchy was under the theocracy.

Verse 3 indicates the psalmist's expectation: "In the morning, O LORD, you will hear my voice; in the morning I shall lay *my request* before you and wait in expectation." The verbs have been given a future nuance[23] because the context suggests that he anticipates the answer in the morning when he prays. The verb "I shall lay out before you" (אֶעֱרָךְ־לְךָ) has no direct object. It may be taken to refer to laying out in order the petitions; however, the verb is not used elsewhere for prayer. It is used in the Law for laying wood on the altar in preparation for the sacrifice (e.g., Lev. 6:5, and Num. 28:4); it may, then, be given an object of "sacrifice," indicating that he was planning to go to the sanctuary and lay out his sacrifice, presumably to accompany his prayer. Anderson suggested a different object still, also to be supplied: a defense or legal case.[24] In this way it would refer to his appeal, his case, that he would be laying out before the LORD. Whether the translation supplies "request" or "sacrifice" or "case," the idea is that he planned to appeal to the LORD formally in the morning. And since the psalm will affirm that he was welcome in

---

away from the people). The prayer is almost always made to the LORD, but in a few passages it is used for praying to idols (Isa. 44:17; 45:20).

The noun תְּפִלָּה has the same basic meanings as the verb. It also shows up in a reference to the temple as the "house of prayer" (Isa. 56:7). It is used a number of times in headings for the psalms, perhaps indicating that those prayers would now become liturgical prayers (17:1; 86:1; 90:1; 102:1; 142:1; as well as Hab. 3:1). In general it refers to the Davidic psalms in the collection as the "prayers of David" (Ps. 72:20).

23. Anderson suggested that תְּשָׁמַע be here given a sense equal to the imperative, an injunction nuance, to continue the appeals to God (*Psalms,* I:81). For the word שָׁמַע, s.v. Ps. 45:10.

24. Ibid., 81.

the sanctuary, we may assume that he was planning to go there to pray.

And after the morning prayer he will then watch for the answer. The verb "I will wait in expectation" (וַאֲצַפֶּה from צָפַה, "wait") can be used with the sense of waiting for revelation (see Hab. 2:1). The petitioner here will keep vigil, waiting for an answer to his prayer, like a watchman (the participle is used this way in Isa. 21:5; Mi. 7:4). This is the Old Testament background for watching and praying.

II. The righteous may pray with confidence because the Lord who has accepted them hates and removes wickedness (4–7).

A. The God they pray to hates wickedness (4–6).

The point that the psalmist makes in the next four verses is that he may be confident in his prayer for deliverance from the wicked because God has accepted him into his sanctuary, but hates and banishes wickedness from his presence. In other words, here is a righteous man praying to a righteous God for protection from the unrighteous. If God indeed punishes evildoers, then he can pray confidently for him to do that now and spare the righteous from their wickedness.

In describing the character of the wicked, he bases his thoughts on God: "For you are not a God who takes pleasure in wickedness; evil[25] cannot dwell with you."[26] There is not any part of the way of wickedness that God tolerates. In fact when he says that "evil cannot dwell with you" (יְגֻרְךָ, a potential imperfect from גּוּר), he means evil cannot even lodge temporarily in God's presence (גּוּר meaning "sojourn, dwell temporarily"). It cannot be God's guest, for that would entitle evil to God's care and protection. Evil is not welcome in God's house.

---

25. The Greek and Jerome interpreted this to mean "an evil man."
26. The word "wickedness" רֶשַׁע refers to the deeds of the wicked, or the ungodly. They therefore would be understood to be criminal acts that God condemns (s.v. Ps. 1:1). The word "evil" רַע can refer to any kind of evil, but it usually carries with it the implications of disaster or catastrophe—anything that causes pain or harm to life (s.v. Ps. 10:15).

In fact, the arrogant cannot even stand in God's presence (v. 5). The "arrogant" people are vain boasters, arrogant fools (הֹלְלִים; s.v. Ps. 33:1). Because they exalt themselves independently of God and therefore over God, they cannot take up any place (יִתְיַצְּבוּ) in his presence. This verb could be taken to refer to "standing" in the judgment (as in Ps. 1:5–6), or to a decision in court, or to the court in the service of the king; however, it could refer to standing before the LORD (as in Ps. 2:2; here "in your sight"). Where the LORD makes his presence known, these fools cannot stand their ground or retain their position.

The reason that they cannot hold their arrogant position in God's presence is that God hates all "doers of iniquity" (פֹּעֲלֵי אָוֶן; for "iniquity," s.v. Ps. 28:3). This is not simply a reference to people who sin; the participle describes people whose characteristic activity is that of doing iniquity (cf. Matt. 7:23). If God "hates" them, it means that he rejects them completely because they are incompatible with his holy and righteous nature. These ideas are amplified in verse 6, which parallels the order of verse 5:[27] "You destroy those who tell lies" (דֹּבְרֵי כָזָב). The evil that the psalmist was confronted with took the form of lying. "Lying" (כָּזָב) is paralleled with deceit (מִרְמָה).[28] Their deceit is malicious because they are "bloodthirsty," literally "men of bloods," the plural use of "blood,"

---

27. Verse 5 states that the arrogant cannot stand in God's presence and then gives as the reason that God hates doers of wickedness; verse 6 states that God will destroy the liars and then gives the reason that God abhors bloodthirsty and deceitful people.

28. The word "deceit" (מִרְמָה) is related to the verb רָמָה, which in the *piel* system means "to deceive, betray." It is cognate to רְמִיָּה and תַּרְמִית, words for "deceitfulness" and "treachery." The basic meaning appears to be common to all these related words.

There are a number of uses that illustrate the meaning. The term מִרְמָה is used for the deal proposed by Levi and Simeon to deceive the Shechemites into thinking they were making a covenant (Gen. 34:13). Similarly, the Gibeonites deceived Joshua into thinking they had come from a far country by dressing up in old clothes and carrying old products (Josh. 9:22). Another good illustration is in 1 Samuel 28:8–12 where Saul deceived the witch of Endor.

The word is regularly linked to what is said; but it can also be used for actions and things, such as "dishonest" scales (Prov. 11:1; Amos 8:5). David used the word in the sense of betrayal in 1 Chronicles 12:17. In Proverbs "guile" or "deceit" is the mark of the fool, not the wise. The one who has no

indicating that they shed blood. Their deception was treacherous; their lying was dangerous—the psalmist's life was in danger. The only hopeful thing the psalmist can say here is that God abhors these people. The verb "abhors" (יְתָעֵב) is related to the well-known noun "abomination" (תּוֹעֵבָה; s.v. Ps. 14:1), which describes that which is totally abhorrent to God—off-limits, taboo; so if the psalmist was being endangered by people God abhorred, he could feel more confident in his prayer.

B. The righteous have been accepted into God's sanctuary (7).

To make the point that God was for him, the psalmist does not record his righteous acts in contrast to their wicked deeds; rather, he simply declares that he has been accepted by God's love, a love which is open to anyone who trusts in the LORD. The contrast is formed emphatically: "But as for me" (וַאֲנִי), and then immediately points to the reason for his being accepted: "by the abundance of your loyal love" (בְּרֹב חַסְדְּךָ).[29] He has by faith entered into covenant with the LORD, and because of the LORD's loyal love for his people, he has access into the sanctuary ("your house" // "your holy temple," where the evil–doers cannot stand). In this the psalmist distinguishes himself from the wicked.

Some commentators have pointed to the mention of the "house" of the LORD and the "temple" as evidence that the psalm could not have been written by David, for Solomon built the temple, but both words were applied to the sanctuary at Shiloh before David came on the scene. The word "house" was used this way in Joshua 6:24 and 2 Samuel 12:20 to refer to the tabernacle at Shiloh; it links the idea of an earthly sanctuary to God's presence for the worshiper (see its use even for the location

---

guile is blessed, meaning that he confesses his sins openly to God and does not deceive himself into thinking they were not sins (Ps. 32:2).

29. The word חֶסֶד means "loyal love." It is a covenant word; it describes the faithful love that God has for those who are members of the covenant. It also is used for the expected loyal love that members of the covenant have for the LORD and for other believers. It is often translated "lovingkind-ness," but it stresses more of the faithfulness of that love. See the more detailed word study with Psalm 23:6.

of Jacob's vision of the "ladder" in Genesis 28:15). The word for "temple" (הֵיכָל) is a little more difficult, for it is nowhere used for the portable shrine of the tabernacle. However, it too was used for the temporary location of the sanctuary at Shiloh, probably referring to the building that was part of the sanctuary (see 1 Sam. 1:9; 3:3). It may simply be used here as well for the place that the ark was located before Jerusalem was chosen.[30] The point that the psalmist is making is that as a true believer he is welcome into the sanctuary of the LORD to worship and in this case to pray. He is only accepted because of God's loyal love. He will therefore not enter in arrogance or self–sufficiency but with reverence and humility—he will bow down (אֶשְׁתַּחֲוֶה)[31] toward the holy temple in fear. So he mixes his confidence over free access into God's presence with awe and humility.

III. Because they belong to the God who hates wickedness, the righteous may anticipate a joyful deliverance from God as they pray for divine guidance for themselves and judgment for the enemies (8–12).

A. Because of the threat of destruction and deceit the righteous must pray for divine guidance (8–9).

---

30. Kraus says that Davidic authorship (a view he dismissed as being held by fundamentalists) came to grief with the mention of "house" and "temple" (pp. 153–4). But the use of these terms is not without parallel in the Old Testament; see further on this issue Perowne, *Psalms*, I:133. Besides, it is not impossible that an original psalm was altered slightly (updated) for use in the later temple.

31. This verb is listed in the older dictionaries, such as BDB, under a root שָׁחָה, explaining the spelling as metathesis. It may rather be a *hishtaphel* form from a root חָוָה, the stem prefixes giving the causative and reflexive ideas: "bow oneself down" to the ground, perhaps as sinking to the knees and then putting the forehead to the ground, as in coiling up. In most places it is simply translated "worship," but it means "bow down" (the interpretation taking the word as a metonymy of adjunct, a posture that goes with worship or obeisance). It can be used of people bowing to a monarch as well. For a full discussion, see John A. Emerton, "The Etymology of *Hištaḥāwāh*," *OTS* 20 (1977):41–55.

The psalmist now prays for the LORD to lead him in his righteousness; it is a perceived necessity. The verb "lead me" (נְחֵנִי) is used in Psalm 23:3 of the divine shepherd, and of the LORD in Psalm 31:3. The guidance he desires is centered in the righteousness of God (צִדְקָתֶךָ; s.v. Ps. 1:5). In the Bible this righteousness is identified with God's character, for he is righteous; but it also refers to the righteousness that he gives to those who believe (see Gen. 15:6 and Rom. 3:21, 22, 25). Here it probably means the righteousness in life that he requires (cf. Prov. 8:20; 12:28); the psalmist needs such divine guidance because he is dealing with deceivers.

The parallel colon in the verse asks for God to "make straight" his way. This imperative (< יָשַׁר; s.v. Ps. 67:4) is a request that the direction be free from hindrances and temptations, that the way be straight and plain. The figure of God's "way" (the idiom based on an implied comparison) refers to a life of moral purity as well as a life of safety.

The reason for the petitions of this verse is "because of my enemies" (שׁוֹרְרִי). These are they who lie in wait, watching for the right chance to act;[32] their intentions mean that the righteous need divine guidance and protection.

The next verse, a quatrain, lists the characteristics of these enemies. First, there is nothing trustworthy in their mouth (that is, in what they say, "mouth" being a metonymy of cause). The word "trustworthy" (נְכוֹנָה, from כּוּן; s.v. Ps. 93:1) means that nothing they say is firm or settled—it cannot be counted on or trusted. Second, their heart is destruction (הַוּוֹת), that is, their desired plan ("heart" being a metonymy of subject) is to destroy the righteous in one way or another, no matter what they say. Third, what they say will ruin people. Their "throat" means their speech (a metonymy of cause); and the metaphor "open grave" means that what they say leaves death and ruined lives in their wake. That the grave is open speaks of the swiftness of the destruction and the efficiency of getting rid of those destroyed (as in the efficiency of battle with no time for decent burial; see

---

32. The verb שׁוּר means "behold, regard." The participle is used for those "watchers" with evil intent (see Jer. 5:26; Job 33:27), people waiting for just the right moment to act (see Pss. 27:11, 54:7, 59:11, and 92:11).

Jer. 5:16). The word "throat" was probably chosen over "lips" or "mouth" to make a significant parallel with the open grave, and "grave" (קֶבֶר) in 9b forms a word play with "heart" (קֶרֶב, literally "midst") in 9a. Finally, the fourth description is that with their tongue they speak deceit (יַחֲלִיקוּן, from חָלַק). The verb has the idea of smoothing something over to conceal it (see Ps. 36:3 and Prov. 29:5; it is used of words in Ps. 55:22). It certainly is the equivalent of lying, but it is done in such a way as to give the false impression of trustworthiness or truthfulness. Then in the unfolding of the event, the true intent is revealed, and it is malicious. It takes divine guidance to avoid the snares of such crafty and dangerous enemies.

B. Because the wicked have rebelled against God, the righteous may pray for deliverance at their expense (10).

To the psalmist, the easiest way to deal with this perpetual danger was for God to judge them—and they deserved judgment, because they had rebelled (<מָרַר) against God. The request may sound harsh to New Testament believers who are asked to pray for their enemies. But this prayer is well within the will of God, for the psalmist was not asking God to do something that he was not going to do anyway, eventually. David's prayer was that the judgment planned for the wicked begin sooner than later. After all, the king was the leader of the people of God and had to watch out for their spiritual welfare. Similarly, in the New Testament when believers pray for deliverance from wicked attacks, it may be brought about by God's removal of the wicked.

So the prayer begins with, "Declare them guilty." The verb (הַאֲשִׁימֵם) is the causative stem (only here) of the verb "to be guilty" (אָשֵׁם; s.v. Ps. 34:22). The verb is used in Leviticus for the person guilty of sin who has to bring a "reparation offering" (an אָשָׁם, also translated as "trespass offering") to accompany the confession and remove the guilt. If there was no repentance and no offering of this sacrifice, then the person remained guilty, i.e., barred from the sanctuary of God. And that is this prayer: the psalmist wants God to pronounce judgment on them because they are so malicious and destructive. That would mean that they would fall in their sin, i.e., be ruined by some misfortune either caused by their intrigues (מֹעֵצוֹת), or simply ruined in their schemes. Even before such judgment they would be banished for their sins (הַדִּיחֵמוֹ from נָדַח, "to thrust away, banish") so that they would be outcasts, rejected and neglected. And so the petition is for that too. Yet this prayer is not merely a personal vendetta; the wicked are the psalmist's enemies because they were first God's enemies—thus "against you" in the text (see Ps. 139:19–22).

C. Because the Lord protects those who trust in him, the righteous expect everlasting joy (11–12).

The other side of his prayer for God to deal with the wicked is the prayer for the protection of the righteous. The request is made in a way that expresses the expectation that the righteous will sing for joy forever. "All who take refuge in you" (כָּל־חוֹסֵי בָךְ; for חָסָה s.v. Ps. 7:1) refers to believers in the LORD, those who accepted his loyal love (v. 7). The prayer is that these will "rejoice" (יִשְׂמְחוּ; s.v. Ps. 48:11) and "shout for joy" (give a ringing cry, יְרַנֵּנוּ; s.v. Ps. 33:1). These two verbs could be taken either as imperfects or jussives, and the various translations have both. Since the section is a prayer and since the next verse will subordinate the rejoicing to the deliverance, they should probably be taken as jussives. In either case they are figurative (metonymies of effect), the praise being the effect of the deliverance.

The prayer for the righteous is that God would spread his protection over them (תָּסֵךְ, the "injunction" use of the form from סָכַךְ, literally "screen" or "cover" in this stem), so that those who love his name, meaning devoted members of the covenant, might rejoice (<עָלַץ). The name of the LORD refers to his character, i.e., the LORD himself (so "name" is a metonymy of subject); s.v. Ps. 20:1.

The prayer for the LORD to cover his people is based on the fact that the LORD "blesses" them (the nuance of the verb being either habitual imperfect or possibly a future).[33] This blessing is

---

33. The word "bless" in this passage is בָּרַךְ; the related noun "blessing" is בְּרָכָה. These words are not to be confused with the homonym, "kneel down," and

explained in the parallel colon as divine protection: "like a shield *with your* favor you surround them." The shield (צִנָּה) would be a large shield for the whole body (see 1 Sam. 17:7), harmonizing with the verb (עָטַר), "to surround." The simile, drawing on military terms (see also Ps. 91:4), emphasizes the often-expressed idea that God protects his people. God's favor (רָצוֹן; s.v. Ps. 30:5), meaning the favorable dealings God has for his people (a metonymy of cause then), forms a protective shield around them so that the malicious designs of the wicked deceivers will not ruin the people of God. And this favor, according to Psalm 30:5, lasts a lifetime.

---

its noun "knee," בֶּרֶךְ, even though older dictionaries lumped the two roots together. The verb is used primarily in the *piel* verbal system, but it does occur in the *qal* passive participle in the form of praise, בָּרוּךְ יהוה, "blessed [be] the LORD," and related expressions.

The basic meaning of the verb "bless" is "to enrich" in some way, physically, materially, or spiritually; and the noun "blessing" can even mean a "gift" (Gen. 33:11). The enrichment that comes from the LORD often included the divine enablement to achieve the blessing, such as the initial blessing for Adam and Eve to be fruitful and multiply. Such declarations of divine blessing often fell to the theocratic administrators who spoke for God, such as the High Priest who announced the blessing on the people (Num. 6:22–27; see also Gen. 14:19 for Melchizedek; and Deut. 33:1 for Moses). In many cases the expressed desire for the LORD's blessing on someone serves as a favorable greeting on arrival or departure (Gen. 24:60).

The blessing from the LORD on people would bring any number of benefits to those blessed, such as children, victory, fruitful crops in the field, rain, privileges of the priesthood, peace, and the like. But the LORD also blessed things, such as the Sabbath Day (Gen. 2:3), which apparently enriched that day as a special time.

When people blessed the LORD, the meaning was essentially "praise." In what way can people enrich the LORD? He is blessed forever above all that is imaginable, but in offering praise, one enriches the reputation of the LORD in the mind of the congregation. It is here that the expression "Blessed be the LORD" finds its specific meaning. Morever, giving praise to the LORD is giving a gift to him, and so "bless" does fit well.

For further information, see A. Murtonen, "The Use and Meaning of the Words L^ebarek and B^erakah in the Old Testament," *VT* 9 (1959): 166–68; and especially Claus Westermann, *Blessing in the Bible and the Life of the Church,* tr. by Keith Crim (Philadelphia: Fortress, 1968).

MESSAGE AND APPLICATION

The occasion for the psalm describes a situation that most believers will find themselves in at some time or another and therefore provides a very useful prayer for protection. The central article of faith here is that the righteous are the beneficiaries of the love of God—they are accepted into his presence and therefore his protection. Therefore, when the wicked try to destroy them maliciously, they know that their divine king hates and deposes such wickedness. Here, then, is the basis of their confidence. The expository idea may be worded this way to capture the point: *The righteous may pray with confidence for deliverance from deceitful and malicious attacks because their God hates wickedness.*

In the New Testament Jesus announced a blessing on those who would suffer such reproach and malice for his name's sake, reminding believers that the wicked hated him first (Matt. 5:11–12). And while he did instruct his followers to pray for their enemies (Matt. 5:44), he also taught them to pray not to be lead into temptation but to be delivered from the evil one (Matt. 6:13). And when believers pray for God's will to be done, they are turning such matters over to God to deal with in his way.

PSALM 6

A Prayer for Deliverance from Severe Chastening

INTRODUCTION [1]

Text and Textual Variants

To the Chief Musician.
With Stringed Instruments; Set to the Eight-stringed Lute.
A Psalm of David.

1 O LORD, reprove me not in your anger,
   chasten me not in your wrath.
2 Be gracious to me, O LORD, for I am languishing;
   heal me, O LORD,[2] for my bones are distressed;
3 and I[3] have become greatly distressed.
   But you, O LORD—how long . . . ?
4 Turn, O LORD; deliver my life;[4]
   save me because of your loyal love.

---

1. See Robert Althann, "Atonement and Reconciliation in Psalms 3, 6, and 83," *JNSL* 25 (1999):75–82.
2. A few of the Hebrew and Greek manuscripts do not have this second occurrence of the name.
3. Hebrew וְנַפְשִׁי, "and my soul/life"; s.v. Ps. 11:5
4. Hebrew נַפְשִׁי, "my soul/life."

5 For in death there is no remembrance of you;[5]
    in the grave[6] who can give praise to you?
6 I am weary with my moaning;
    throughout the night I flood my bed with tears,
    with my weeping I drench my couch.
7 My eye wastes away because of grief;
    it grows weak because of all my enemies.
8 Depart from me, all you workers of evil!
    for the LORD has heard the sound of my weeping.
9 The LORD has heard my supplication;
    The LORD accepts my prayer.
10 All my enemies will be put to shame and greatly troubled;[7]
    they will again be put to shame suddenly.

Composition and Context

That Psalm 6 has many of the features of a lament psalm in which the singer laments his illness with its intense suffering and distress is obvious from a reading of the text; that it is a penitential psalm as well is clear from the beginning cry that God not chasten in anger. The psalmist does not explain why he is being chastened—there is no mention of his sin, no penitence, and no confession (and so some question calling it a penitential psalm). He is more troubled that the chastening may be with God's anger because it is already intense. His lament, however, soon gives way to confident prayer, which prompts him to warn his enemies to depart because when the chastening is over God will deal with them for their eagerness to destroy him.

The psalm can be analyzed in different ways. It appears to include four strophes (vv. 1–3, 4–5, 6–7, and 8–10), the first three using both laments and petitions, and the fourth introducing an abrupt change in which the psalmist displays a

---

5. The Greek ὁ μνημονεύων σου, "no man remembers you," apparently reads זֹכְרֶךָ instead of זִכְרֶךָ. Kraus says this was the original reading in view of the presence of אִין in the line (*Psalms,* pp. 159, 160).
6. Hebrew שְׁאוֹל.
7. The verbs in this verse have been interpreted as volitives in the Greek translation: "Let all my enemies be put to shame . . . ."

defiant faith. The last part is so different it has brought on theories that it originally was a separate composition, but the exegesis will show how closely it is linked to the rest of the psalm. The first three strophes can be united in the first major point, and the fourth can stand as a separate point to show the contrast.

There is no reason why the psalm could not have come from the life of David, even though it is impossible to identify an experience in his life that would be the setting.[8] The language of intense suffering fits formulations and concepts that were used frequently during the Israelite period and cannot be limited to the time of Jeremiah or thereafter.[9] The lack of a specific reference is just as well because the underlying experience is not unique to the psalmist, whether David or someone else. God does chasten people for sin, and God does use other people as part of the chastening process. For a king, this may have involved personal enemies or national enemies with their armies (see 2 Sam. 24:13). When God is through using the natural animosity of enemies as part of the discipline, he then judges them for their eagerness to destroy his people (see Hab. 2).

Like the other psalms in the collection, this one was deposited in the sanctuary for people to appropriate when they found themselves in similar situations. So whatever the original occasion of the psalm may have been, its use by the faithful became more important. And when the Church appointed certain psalms to be used in services on particular days, Psalm 6 became one of the penitential psalms to be sung during Lent. By using this prayer in their own prayers, the saints down through the

---

8. A. A. Anderson acknowledges that there was no compelling reasons why the psalm could not be early, but concludes a post-exilic date is more likely because of the psalm's dependence on other later psalms and Jeremiah (*Psalms,* I:87). But the dates of similar psalms are also debated, and the idea of dependence on Jeremiah is not convincing (see J. Coppens, "Les Psaumes 6 et 41 dependent-ils au livre de Jeremie," *HUCA* 32 [1961]:217–226).

9. Kraus, *Psallms 1–59,* p. 161. Kraus makes the point in response to the theories that say the psalm drew upon Jeremiah. He concludes it is impossible to date the psalm, but he accepts a pre-exilic composition.

ages have learned how they should pray, and with what confidence they may pray, when they find themselves severely ill and deeply troubled because of God's chastening.[10]

Exegetical Analysis

Summary

The penitent believer pleads with the LORD for relief from intense chastening for sin inflicted on him by his enemies, and finding assurance that his prayer has been heard, warns his persecutors to leave before God destroys them.

Outline

I. The psalmist prays for relief from his enemies who have inflicted great suffering on him in God's chastening (1–7).
   A. David offers a prayer and a lament that the LORD's chastening not be with such anger (1–3).
      1. He asks the LORD not to chasten him in anger (1).
      2. He appeals to the LORD for relief because he is at his end (2).
      3. He laments that the LORD delays his deliverance (3).
   B. David pleads with the LORD to deliver him, basing his petition on God's love for him and his desire to praise God (4-5):
      1. He asks the LORD to deliver him because of his loyal love (4).
      2. He asks the LORD to rescue him because of his desire to praise (5).
   C. David laments his extreme suffering for its severity and its prolonged distress (6-7).
II. The psalmist warns his enemies to turn away from him because he is assured that the LORD has heard his prayer and will put them to shame (8-10).
   A. David warns them to leave because the LORD has heard his prayer (8).

---

10. See additionally P. Miller, "Trouble and Woe: Interpreting the Biblical Laments," *Int* 37 (1983):32–45.

B. David warns them that the LORD is about to deliver him (9).

C. David warns them that they will be utterly defeated (10).

COMMENTARY IN EXPOSITORY FORM

I. The chastened believer can only appeal to God for deliverance from the anguish and pain of chastening (1–7).

A. They pray for relief from the chastening (1–3).

As indicated in the outline, the first half of the psalm can be subdivided into three parts: the introductory cry (vv. 1–3), the petition (vv. 4–5), and the full lament (vv. 6–7). The psalm begins, then, with an urgent appeal for relief in chastening, and its word order is striking:[11] "O LORD, not in your anger reprove me, and not in your wrath chasten me." By making this negative petition the psalmist is acknowledging that his suffering was God's chastening of him; thus, it is an implied confession of sin.[12] The prayer is that the chastening not be with God's fierce anger; the emphasis on "anger" (אַף; s.v. Ps. 30:5) and "wrath" (חֵמָה)[13] in the poetic structure cannot be missed. The anger of his enemies did not concern him as much as the anger of God, that is, that the divine chastening might come with the severity of divine wrath.

The two parallel jussives, "reprove" (תּוֹכִיחֵנִי from יָכַח; s.v. Ps. 38:1) and "chasten" (תְיַסְּרֵנִי from יָסַר), both are used in Scripture for corrective and disciplinary actions taken in relationships, such

---

11. The emphasis can be seen in the parallel lines following:

יְהוָה אַל־בְּאַפְּךָ תוֹכִיחֵנִי
וְאַל־בַּחֲמָתְךָ תְיַסְּרֵנִי

12. Broyles argues that there is no confession of sin in this psalm, and therefore cautions the expositor against imposing the idea that all such sufferings have a moral cause (*Psalms*, p. 63). But there seems enough in this first verse to support the conclusion that the psalmist saw such a connection in his case.

13. The synonym חֵמָה (s.v. יָחַם) like the other words for anger has the idea of heat, i.e., a burning rage.

as in the training of a son by a father.[14] For example, Proverbs 19:18 instructs the father: "Discipline (<יַסֵּר) your son while there is hope." The point is that there was still hope for behavioral change, but it required forceful measures. Such terms are likewise appropriate to describe divine discipline. Proverbs 3:11 says, "For whom the LORD loves he reproves (<יוֹכִיחַ)." These corrective acts would include both the verbal rebuke or instruction and some disciplinary action designed to correct error and rebelliousness.

---

14. The word "chasten" is יָסַר, and its noun "chastening" is מוּסָר. The basic meaning is "to chastise"; and this chastisement could be either verbal (the most frequent use) or corporal. The term includes an emphasis on teaching. Frequently in the Bible this word is linked with יָכַח, which emphasizes more of the rebuke or reproof.

Of the several categories of meaning one is the positive meaning of "instruct (vb), instruction (n)." For example, in 1 Chronicles 15:22 Chenaniah instructed (<יָסַר) others about songs because he had understanding. David in Psalm 16:7 says that his heart instructed him at night, probably meaning the word he had memorized God used to form his planning. In Psalm 50:17, the wicked are rebuked for hating instruction—they know the word, but they go on sinning. In these contexts the words in parallel lines are frequently verbs of teaching.

A second group of passages show the meaning "admonish, correct." Proverbs 9:7 uses the word in this sense when speaking about correcting a scoffer. In the verse the parallel line uses מוֹכִיחַ, (<יָכַח, "to reprove, rebuke"), "the one who reproves" a wicked person. This is the parallel word in Psalm 6:1 as well. The noun מוּסָר occurs frequently with the meaning "correction." It may be translated as "instruction" in some versions, but the parallelism with "rebuke" indicates it means correction: "My son, do not despise the LORD's discipline/correction, and do not resent his rebuke" (Prov. 1:8; 4:1; 13:1).

The chastening could be verbal, as is clear from Proverbs, but it can also be corporal. Isaiah 53:5 says the "chastisement" that brought us peace was upon him." The NIV translates it as "punishment." It is probably this sense that is intended in Psalm 6 where the prayer is that the chastening and the rebuke be not with anger. Likewise, Proverbs 15:10 warns, "Correction awaits him who leaves the path; he who hates reproof (< יָכַח) will die."

Another group of texts require the idea of "discipline." Sometimes when one of the words is used the effect is intended, and so we find at times translations using "discipline" or "edification." The effect of instruction, admonition, and correction is discipline, moral and spiritual primarily. Deuteronomy 11:2 says that the works of the LORD in the wilderness had a disciplinary effect on the people. To acquire discipline, people have to submit to the correction and admonition when it comes (Prov. 23:12).

Discipline and correction may or may not be a corrective measure for sin; but when these verbs are here joined with the repeated mention of God's wrath and the vivid description of intense suffering, the most plausible conclusion is that he has sinned.

After this initial appeal that God's discipline not be severe, the psalmist asks the LORD to be gracious to him (v. 2). The basic meaning of this verb (חָנֵּנִי from חָנַן; s.v. Ps. 4:1) is to "be gracious, show favor, be merciful"; and in almost every use the favor is undeserved. In fact, the one seeking divine favor usually deserves just the opposite. By asking God to be merciful, David acknowledges that he deserves chastening but desires grace. The parallel verb is "heal me" (רְפָאֵנִי; s.v. Ps. 30:2); such healing would be the effect of God's being gracious to him (so a metonymy). From the description of his illness and weakness in this psalm, he certainly needed healing; but this word (רָפָא) is not limited to a physical healing. It may also be used for spiritual healing (as in "I am your healer" in Exod. 15:26), and for uplifting low spirits, as in one who has been dealt a harsh blow.[15] The healing in this psalm most likely goes beyond physical healing.

The causal clauses in the verse reveal the urgent need for divine relief. In the first colon the psalmist prays for mercy because he is "languishing"; this adjective (אֻמְלָל) refers to a withered or weakened condition, physically or emotionally. Then, secondly, he prays for healing because his bones are troubled (נִבְהֲלוּ; s.v. Ps. 83:15). "Bones" may refer to the whole physical structure of a person, but the word often means the spirit within the boney structure, the center of his painful distress (so a metonymy of subject). Everything within him is deeply troubled, the verb capturing the emotional and spiritual distress in the psalmist's spirit.[16] This colon in the psalms, then, forms a powerful parallel to the first part of the verse that focuses on his weakened physical condition. In short, he is both physically and emotionally weak and distressed.

Verse three brings the lamentable condition to a focus: repeating

---

15. See S. Mowinckel, *The Psalms in Israel's Worship*, II:15–16.

16. This verb (בָּהַל) has a wide range of applications: it is used to describe terror as in the day of battle (Judg. 20:4), or from a vision (Dan. 4:2), or over sudden death (Lev. 26:16), or because of divine activity (Ps. 90:7; and Ps. 2:5).

the fact that he is terrified he cries to God, "But you, O Lord, how long . . . ?" The verse began with "I,"[17] but the beginning of the second colon, "but you," contrasts with it sharply. It is in effect saying, "as for me, I am terrified; but as for you, O LORD, how long?" This question is unfinished. The sentence is simply broken off because of the extreme frustration and stress (the figure is aposiopesis, a sudden silence). One might suspect that he was going to say something like, "How long, O LORD, will you allow me to continue in this condition?" But he could only utter "How long . . . ?"

So the psalmist was weak, terrified, and anxious; his suffering at the hands of his enemies had wreaked havoc with his health and well-being. What made it so frustrating was that the LORD was silent and apparently willing to let him languish in pain and depression. He knew his suffering was divine discipline, so all he could do was appeal for a gracious deliverance.

B. They must base their appeal on God's faithful love and the praise that will be given to him (4–5).

This principle may be derived from the next two verses which provide the petition proper. The psalmist's prayer is based on the loyal love of the LORD and motivated by the desire to praise the LORD. In verse 4 he pleads with the LORD to turn (שׁוּבָה) and deliver (חַלְּצָה) him ("my life") again. The use of "turn" or "return" may be interpreted in the light of God's apparent turning away from him. The emphasis, though, is most certainly on the request for deliverance: "Return (שׁוּבָה) . . . deliver (חַלְּצָה) . . . save me (הוֹשִׁיעֵנִי)." The last verb, parallel to "deliver," is "save" (יְשַׁע; s.v. Ps. 3:2); it can be used for both spiritual and physical salvation. These imperatives indicate the plea is for an immediate rescue from the suffering of God's chastening.

The basis for this appeal is clearly stated: "because of[18] your loyal love (חֶסֶד)." "Loyal love" is the covenant word; it expresses

---

17. A literal translation might have "and my soul is terrified," which is certainly possible. But the word נֶפֶשׁ refers to the whole person, body and soul (that is, a soul in a body). With the pronominal suffix, "my soul," the form often indicates simply "I," or "I, myself." See further Anderson, *Psalms,* I:88, 266.

18. The prepositional form לְמַעַן means "on account of" or "for the sake of."

God's unwavering faithfulness to his covenant promises to his people (Exod. 34:7, 8; Deut. 7:9; 1 Sam. 20:8).[19] The loyal love of the LORD is the reason he should be delivered, not simply because he has a covenant that is characterized by God's faithful love to his people, but because the covenant promises of the LORD's loyal love would fall into disrepute if he did not demonstrate them by delivering the sufferer. David has no other basis on which to make his appeal than God's faithful love—but he needs no other. God's faithful covenant love is sufficient; that is why it is at the heart of all his dealings with his people, even when they are sinful and need discipline.

Next is the motivation for the LORD to answer the prayer—the praise that will be offered. The righteous know full well that God answers prayers so that people will give glory to God through public praise.[20] According to Psalm 111:4, God made all

---

19. The word חֶסֶד is often translated "lovingkindness," but it is more specific. It is a covenant term and describes the faithful and loving keeping of covenant promises (s.v., Ps. 23:6).

20. The verb "praise" is the *hiphil* verbal meaning of יָדָה; its related noun is תּוֹדָה. These words are used throughout the psalms for public acknowledgment or praise. Although most versions have retained the translations "give thanks" and "thanksgiving," this word says much more. Giving thanks, even though honoring to God, can be a private and quiet act; in giving thanks the object of the praise is not always elevated in the hearing of the people. Biblical praise represented by these words would normally occur as a public acknowledgment of who God is and what he had done; it would be offered in the sanctuary along with the peace offering, or, as it would be called, "the sacrifice of praise" (Ps. 50:14–15).

There are several categories of meaning that are instructive for understanding the term. In the *qal* verbal system it has a basic meaning of "throw, cast" (assuming the word is related). It is used for shooting arrows in Jeremiah 50:14 and for throwing stones in Lamentations 3:53. The connection of these uses to praise is unclear, and so not much should be made of them.

The basic meaning of the verb in the *hiphil* verbal system is "to praise" or to "acknowledge" the LORD. Psalm 111:1 uses it to announce public praise in the assembly. Psalm 122:4 explains that the primary statute commanding Israel to go to Jerusalem was to offer praise. And Psalm 105:1 says, "O give thanks/praise to Yahweh, proclaim his name; make known his deed among the people." The praise or acknowledgment of the people could be written down, as the psalms of declarative praise attest, and set to music (1 Chron. 16:4–10; Neh. 12:46).

his wonderful works a memorial. In other words, his great deeds, especially his saving acts, were to be kept alive in the memory of the people by the constant praise of the faithful. In line with this the psalmist reasons that if God does not deliver him, he will die, and God will not receive any praise from him. People will not hear how God delivered him because he would not be there to participate in the festivals where praises were offered (Ps. 122:4). When he says "there is no remembrance of you in death," he is using the word "remembrance" (זֵכֶר) as an equivalent to "praise," which occurs in the parallel line. To remember God's saving acts is to praise God for them, to keep them in the memory of the congregation.[21] But to forget God is to fail to acknowledge his provisions for life (Deut. 8:10–14).

Another category that concerns the noun primarily, but sometimes the verb, is that of making the sacrifice of praise—the תּוֹדָה This is instructed as one type of peace offering in Leviticus 7. 2 Chronicles 30:22 tells how they ate the peace offering and praised the LORD. Psalm 54:6 unites the sacrifice and the praise. The meal would be communal, provided by the person praising (see the similar motifs in Hebrews 13:15–16).

A final category is "confess" or "acknowledge" sin. This is the meaning of the *hithpael* verbal system primarily (Lev. 16:21) but also the *hiphil* (Ps. 32:5). The fact that the same verb can mean "confess sin" and "praise" God is good reason to offer the translation of "acknowledge." To confess sin requires an acknowledgment of God's grace, and to praise God correctly requires an acknowledgment of sin and need.

There are many other words for praise in the Old Testament, but this one seems most closely connected to the ritual of the sanctuary as a public acknowledgment of the wonderful works of the LORD. It will serve to edify and encourage others to trust. But, as this psalmist says, if he dies he cannot tell of God's faithfulness.

21. The verb זָכַר, "remember," can mean simply a mental recollection, but it often has an emphasis on acting on the basis of what is remembered (such as in a prayer, "LORD, remember me"). We find this, for example, in Genesis 8:1 which says "And God remembered Noah." This means that God now began to act on Noah's behalf to rescue him from the flood. Likewise the noun אַזְכָּרָה, "memorial," has the same import. Portions of the sacrifices were offered as a "memorial," intended to remind God of the worshiper's devotion, and to remind the worshiper of God's grace and of the stipulations of the covenant. It made the ritual a covenant renewal service (as in the New Testament's, "Do this in remembrance of me").

The noun זֵכֶר, "memorial, remembrance," came to signify what was being remembered. We find this, for example, as a substitute for the divine

The rhetorical question that follows makes this point clear: "In *sheol*,[22] who can praise you?" If he died he could not praise God for faithful love, gracious intervention, or answering his

---

name; in Exodus 3:15 the word "my memorial" (זִכְרִי) is parallel to "my name." The words refer to the nature of the LORD that is to be preserved by creed and praise.

It is in the *hiphil* verbal system of the word that we find the connection with "praise." It can mean "cause (people) to remember" the LORD (Isa. 43:26; Ps. 71:16) through what is said, but it can also be an internal causative with the sense of keeping something in the memory, pondering or meditating (Ps. 20:7). This word clarifies how praise has the important function of preserving in the memory the acts of the LORD and the expected acts of devotion and service of the worshiper. See Brevard S. Childs, *Memory and Tradition* (Naperville, IL: Alec R. Allenson, 1962), pp. 1–8.

22. There have been numerous suggestions for the etymology of שְׁאוֹל, but none have proved convincing. Our understanding of the word comes from its biblical usage. One category of meaning is "the grave." In Genesis 37:35 Jacob laments the death of his son by anticipating going down to the grave in sorrow. Ezekiel 32:27 uses the noun for the place where the bodies of dead soldiers are placed.

A second category is "death." This is a closely related usage, close enough that some passages would fit well in either the first group or this. In Proverbs 5:5 the word is parallel to "death" in warning of the dangers of the adulterous woman whose "feet go down to death." Psalm 18:5 also has these parallel terms: "The cords of death (שְׁאוֹל) coiled around me, the snares of death confronted me." The word is also paralleled with "dust," which could mean the grave or death (Job 17:16).

The word can also be used for "extreme danger," danger that is life-threatening. In Psalm 30:3 the psalmist declares that God brought him up from שְׁאוֹל. He did not die, so "grave" and "death" are ruled out. He was as good as dead, though (see also Jon. 2:2).

Finally, there is the category of "hell" or "hades"—the realm of the departed spirits, the shades (Job 11:8; Isa. 14:11). Numbers 16:30–33 may have this meaning in mind when Korah's men were swallowed up. Psalm 49:14 is a clearer example, for it is the place where death shepherds the inhabitants. It is a place where people are cut off from fellowship with God (Ps. 88:5). It is clear from some of the passages that this is a horrible place for the spirits of the ungodly. It is also clear that the righteous do not go here. In all the passages that speak of the righteous going to שְׁאוֹל, the meaning is either death, the grave, or danger. In fact, when the horrible place is described, the contrast is usually that the righteous will have a more glorious prospect. For further discussion see Alexander Heidel, *The Gilgamesh Epic and Old Testament Parallels,* chapter 3, "Death and the Afterlife" (Chicago: University of Chicago Press, 1946), pp. 137–223.

prayer, for being in the realm of death would indicate just the opposite. A. A. Anderson notes that the gravity of the situation was a constant reminder to the psalmist that he was beginning to experience already something of the *sheol* condition.[23] David words this point as a rhetorical question to motivate God to answer: if God desires that he praise him for his faithful love, then God would have to show him that faithful love by delivering him. Such a motivation for God to act was not crass bargaining—it was simply acknowledging what the outcome of the answered prayer would be, namely, that God would be glorified and the faith of the people strengthened.

C. They may pour out their grief to the LORD (6–7).

The next two verses form the lament, and it is intense. God desires that his people do this so that he will have compassion on them. The psalmist first describes his weariness that has come with his weeping and groaning under the distress. The verb "I am weary" (יָגַעְתִּי) expresses the effect of his suffering and groaning over a long period of time. It can describe a physical exhaustion that often results from intensive activities (cf. Isa. 57:10, where it refers to the exhausting quest for false gods); but it can also refer to a mental or emotional aspect to the weariness, such as being tired of certain words and attitudes (e.g., when the people wearied the LORD with their words in Mal. 2:17). In this case the psalmist's weariness is a combination of both the physical and the emotional, brought on by his distress that was the constant concern of his weeping and groaning.[24] The physical suffering may have been due to the attacks of his enemies, but the internal groaning and weeping were compounded by God's prolonged silence that was part of the divine discipline.

The psalmist follows this with hyperbolic descriptions of weeping that heighten the intensity of his distress. Without

---

23. Anderson, *Psalms,* I:89. Broyles adds that the inability to praise God left people feeling near death; not to praise was a form of death to the Hebrews (*Psalms,* p. 65).

24. The text uses the preposition בְּ. with these words; it may be understood to indicate the condition or the cause, and in this case possibly both. Thus, he is weary in groaning and because of it.

this obvious exaggeration the reader might not fully appreciate the distress. The psalmist says that he causes his bed to swim all night and drenches his couch with his tears. The two verbs, "cause to swim" (אַשְׂחֶה, from שָׂחָה) and "dissolve" (אַמְסֶה, from מָסָה, "melt, dissolve") express the ongoing activity (and so may be classified as progressive imperfects). The point is that he spends his nights in great agony and incessant weeping—it felt like he was soaking his bed with his tears.

In verse seven he takes the description of his grief one step further: "my eye wastes away because of grief, it grows weak because of all my enemies." The verbs (עָשְׁשָׁה and עָתְקָה) express what has been happening and what is still true (now perfect tenses, with the nuance of characteristic perfect). The "eye" serves as an excellent measure of his grief, weakness, and weeping; it represents his general condition (so perhaps a synecdoche, meaning that his whole body was wasting away). The first verb is used in Psalm 31:10 where it describes a wasting away that was the result of a long period of trouble, a life spent in sorrow. Even today the condition of the eye is a good measure of the person's general health and stability. The parallel colon says that his eye has become weak because of the enemies—if the eye looks weak, it is that he seems to have aged under the duress. There is no life or vitality in his eyes because he is totally worn out.

There is no doubt that the adversaries are the cause of this woeful condition, even though the psalmist knew it was part of God's chastening. The thought that the adversaries were the instruments of this suffering seems to give David a burst of confidence that his God would not surrender him to these people who were out to destroy him. After all, God's discipline is temporary but his favor lasts a lifetime (cf. Ps. 30:5).

II. The confessing believers can anticipate deliverance from the chastening affliction of adversaries (8–10)

A.They can be confident that God hears their prayers (8–9)

The psalmist turns immediately away from the lament over his suffering at the hand of his enemies to warn those very enemies that they are now in mortal danger: "Depart from me all you workers of iniquity!"[25] This abrupt change in audience (an apostrophe) signals a striking change of mood that is so characteristic of lament psalms. The psalmist is now convinced that the LORD has answered his prayer to end the chastening, and that means that the LORD was about to end the power of those evil enemies who were willingly afflicting him. And this is right; after all, they are "doers of iniquity."[26] These wicked enemies were trying to destroy the psalmist by their iniquitous acts, which may have included slander, cursing, false accusations, or various other sins of word and deed that "iniquity" (אָוֶן) describes (s.v. Ps. 28:3). Whoever they were and whatever they were doing, they are here instructed to depart while they can.

The reason for this warning is that the psalmist is convinced that the LORD has heard (the present perfect) his weeping, the weeping that accompanied the agonizing prayer (so a metonymy of adjunct). Then, in verse nine, he reiterates his point that the LORD has heard[27] (present perfect) his supplication and accepts[28] (progressive imperfect) his prayer to deliver him from his enemies and restore his physical and emotional health.

B. They can be confident that God will punish their oppressors (10)

The psalm concludes with the confident expectation that all the enemies will be put to shame (יֵבֹשׁוּ; s.v. Ps. 31:1) and greatly troubled (וְיִבָּהֲלוּ; s.v. Ps. 83:15). They were the reason that he

---

25. Note the reference to this line in Matthew 7:23 and Luke 13:27.
26. The participle (פֹּעֲלֵי) stresses the nature of the enemies as doers or practitioners of iniquity. It is not that they are simply doing something evil—this is what they characteristically do.
27. The verb שָׁמַע, "to hear," usually means to respond to, that is, answer the prayer. In different texts the construction "listen to the voice of" means "obey." If psalmists prayed for God to hear their prayer, they meant that they wanted God to respond favorably to their prayer, to do something (s.v. Ps. 45:10).
28. The verb "receives" (יִקָּח) could be taken as a progressive imperfect, meaning that the LORD is receiving the prayer, or it could be a simple future, meaning that the LORD has heard and will receive it.

was terrified; now they will be terrified because God will destroy them. And God will punish them because even though they were used by God, they acted by their will and in their own wickedness to try to destroy the servant of the LORD. The word "put to shame" expresses the sense of confusion, embarrassment, and dismay when matters turn out contrary to what one expected; it is often used for chaotic defeat (s.v. Ps. 31:1). The two verbs are figures of speech (metonymies of adjunct or effect), expressing the effect of the sudden reversal of fortunes and defeat they will experience.

The last colon says "they will return (turn) and be put to shame suddenly." The verb "they will return" (יָשֻׁבוּ from שׁוּב; s.v. Ps. 126:1) is somewhat difficult. It could be saying that they will turn away from the psalmist;[29] but it probably functions adverbially (as a verbal hendiadys) with the rendering "they will again be put to shame." The main point of the verse is clear enough though—they will be destroyed "quickly."[30]

MESSAGE AND APPLICATION

This psalm, then, is an urgent prayer for deliverance from the painful affliction and anxiety caused by bloodthirsty adversaries. What makes the psalm unique is that the intense suffering seems also to be divine chastening for sin. Not all physical suffering or affliction at the hands of enemies is chastening for sin. However, when devout believers find themselves in such trying situations, they naturally will do some soul searching to see if they are in fact being chastened (see Ps. 44). If no obvious sin can be uncovered, then the believer may consider other explanations for suffering. Now in David's case in Psalm 6 it appears to be divine correction, and David is doing what any penitent believer must do—pray for relief from the chastening, which in effect is an acknowledgment of the sin.

A general expository idea may be worded as follows: *When*

---

29. The verb is שׁוּב, though, as used earlier when he wanted the LORD to return to him, and not סוּר as used in his warning "depart."
30. The word "suddenly" or "quickly" is רֶגַע, "in a twinkling."

271

God chastens his people with the rod of their adversaries, the truly penitent may pray for relief because of God's faithful love.

The Book of Hebrews spends a good amount of time explaining how the Lord chastens those whom he loves (12:4–11). The discussion focuses on divine discipline in general that is designed to bring about holiness, but it includes correction. So the message of the psalm is applicable to believers in the Old Testament and in the New. Since the divine chastening is done in love, then the believers can appeal to God for relief on the basis of his divine love for them.

PSALM 7

An Appeal of the Innocent before the Righteous Judge

INTRODUCTION[1]

Text and Textual Variants

A *shiggaion*[2] of David,
which he sang to the LORD
concerning the deeds of Cush, a Benjamite.

1 O LORD my God, in you I have taken refuge;
    save me from all who pursue[3] me, and deliver me,
2 lest they[4] tear me[5] apart like a lion,
    ripping me to pieces,[6] and there is no deliverer.

---

1. R. R. Hutton, "Cush the Benjaminite and Psalm Midrash," *HAR* 10 (1986):123–37; J. Leveen, "The Textual Problems of Psalm 7," *VT* 16 (1966):439–445; G. J. Thierry, "Remarks on Various Passages of the Psalms," *OTS* 13 (1963):77–82.
2. Perhaps this means a poem with irregular meter. The Greek translation simply has ψαλμός.
3. The word רָדַף can mean "pursue" or "persecute." The Greek translation chose τῶν διωκόντων, probably "persecute."
4. Hebrew has a singular form יִטְרֹף. The Greek has "lest at any time he seize (μήποτε ἁρπάσῃ) my soul as a lion."
5. Hebrew is נַפְשִׁי; s.v. Ps. 11:5.
6. The difficulty comes with the word פֹּרֵק, whether it goes with the first half of the verse or the second (as in the Greek and the Syriac). The word means "tear off, tear away"; it can have the sense of ripping away, breaking off, or removing, and in a few cases it can have the sense of rescuing. The latter is the meaning understood in the Greek version which harmonizes the word with the last part of the verse: "while there is none to rescue me, nor to save"

273

3 O LORD my God, if I have done this;
 if there is iniquity on my hands,
4 if I have repaid evil to him who was at peace with me—
 rather, I rescued[7] *him who is* my adversary without a
  cause,—
5 then let the enemy pursue[8] after me[9] and overtake *me*;
 let him trample my life to the ground
 and make my glory lie down in the dust. *Selah*

6 Arise, LORD, in your anger;
 rise up against the rage[10] of my enemies.
And awake for me justice[11] *that* you have commanded.[12]

(μὴ ὄντος λυτρουμένου μηδὲ σῴζοντος). In this case one might have expected אֵין פֹּרֵק in the text. But the way the text is constructed supports the linking of the word with the first half of the verse: "ripping me to pieces."

7. The meaning of וָאֲחַלְּצָה in this line is unclear. It could be interpreted to mean "and if I have spoiled (robbed) him who is my enemy without a cause," making it another supposition he is denying and parallel to 4a (see the NIV). It could also be translated as a parenthesis: "yes (rather) I have delivered him who is my enemy without a cause." This line would then be antithetical to the two preceding lines. The first reading harmonizes well with the context and continues the protasis neatly. But it has the problem of the usage of the *piel* which means "deliver" and not "spoil." In support of it is the fact that there is a derived noun which means what is stripped off, i.e., plunder (occurring twice). The second interpretation may be a better reading because it is an abrupt change and therefore more difficult. The Greek version has instead of these, "may I then perish empty by means of my enemies."

8. Greek again has "persecute."

9. Hebrew is נַפְשִׁי

10. The Greek has ὑψώθητι ἐν τοῖς πέρασι τῶν ἐχθρῶν μου, "Be exalted in the utmost boundaries of my enemies," possibly "deaths" of my enemies.

11. Greek has "Awake, Lord my God, according to the decree which you commanded." "Unto me" (אֵלִי) in the MT was taken to be "my God" (אֱלֹהַי), and several modern versions follow that reading (NIV), as does Goldingay (*Psalms 1–41*, p. 103). It makes a nice parallel expression: "Arise, O LORD" // "awake, my God" (although the Greek has "Lord, my God"). But how probable would it be for the scribe to change "my God" to "unto me." While the words are close in form, the meaning is very different. The variant "my God" is a simplification that is unwarranted, however.

12. The MT has the perfect tense, possibly translated "you have commanded" (צִוִּיתָ), referring to the "justice." This is a more complicated reading of the line, but not impossible. Kraus suggests that perhaps we ought to read the

7 Let the assembled peoples gather around you,
  and over them[13] return on high.[14]
8 The LORD judges the peoples.
  Vindicate me, LORD, according to my righteousness,
  and according to my integrity, *be it done* to me.[15]
9 Let the evil of the wicked come to an end
  and establish[16] the righteous;
For an examiner[17] of the hearts and minds
  is the righteous[18] God.

10 My shield is of God,[19]
   who saves the upright in heart.
11 God is a righteous judge,
   a God who is angry every day.[20]

---

imperative, צַוֵּה (*Psalms 1–59*, p. 167). It is possible to read the form in the text as a "precative perfect," translating it as "command" without actually changing the text. This would certainly make a smoother reading of the line if the change to "my God" is also accepted: "Awake, my God; decree justice."

13. Hebrew has "over it." The Greek ὑπὲρ ταύτης for עָלֶיהָ may mean "for this cause."

14. Because this line does not seem to make much sense at first glance (turn back, turn away, return?), commentators suggest an emendation. Kraus, for example, suggests שֵׁבָה, "sit as king, be enthroned," instead of שׁוּבָה, "return" (p. 167). For support passages like Numbers 10:36 and Psalm 116:7 show a similar interchange. But there is no manuscript support for the change, and the idea of the LORD's returning on high is not impossible.

15. The MT simply has עָלָי which would mean "unto me." It could be taken with an understood jussive, "*Let it be done* unto me," or it may simply be "my integrity *which is* within me." The Greek text has "according to my innocence *that is* in me (ἐπ' ἐμοί). Some translations interpret the word to refer to God "Most High" (see NIV)

16. The Greek translates the imperfect וּתְכוֹנֵן as κατευθυνεῖς, "and then you shall direct."

17. The sentence literally reads, "And an examiner of the hearts and minds kidneys] is the righteous God."

18. The Greek has "righteous" connected to the next verse.

19. The Hebrew has עַל אֱלֹהִים, which could be rendered "of God" or "upon God." Some take it to be a description of God and translate "Most High God." The Greek text reads differently: "My help (βοήθειά) is righteous, from God who saves the upright in heart."

20. The verse in the Greek version reads: "God is a righteous judge, and strong and patient, not inflicting vengeance every day."

12 If he does not turn,[21]
    he will sharpen his sword;
    he has bent his bow and prepared it.
13 And for him he has prepared *his* deadly weapons;
    he makes his arrows fiery *arrows*.[22]

14 Lo, he travails with evil—
    he has conceived trouble and brought forth falsehood.
15 He has dug a pit and has scooped it out;
    and he falls into the pit he makes.
16 His trouble shall return on his own head;
    and his violence shall come down on his own pate.

17 I will praise the LORD according to his righteousness;
    and I will sing praises to the name of the LORD Most
      High.

Composition and Context

This psalm is more than a prayer for deliverance from enemies; it is a prayer for vindication from the righteous judge of the world—a righteous judge must vindicate the righteous. In praying for deliverance from his enemies, the psalmist solemnly affirms his innocence and appeals to the righteous judge to vindicate him by destroying the wicked. It is a psalm for which "Will not the judge of the earth do right?" could serve as the motto.[23] He appeals to the righteous judge to deliver his righteous people. Broyles suggests that the psalm has a liturgical origin; this he says is

---

21. The verb is simply יָשׁוּב; it could be taken to mean "if [God] does not relent" from his anger, or it could be taken to mean "if [a sinner] does not turn." The Greek text interpreted this way, translating it, "if you will not repent/turn" (ἐπιστραφῆτε). See further A. A. MacIntosh, "A Consideration of Psalm vii.12f.," *JTS* 33 (1982):481–90.
22. The MT reads literally "his arrows for flames (לְדֹלְקִים) he makes." The word דָּלַק means "burn hotly," or "hotly pursue," and so the participle here is literally "for burning ones." Greek interprets the participial use as follows: "he has completed his arrows for those being burnt" (καιομένοις).
23. Perowne, *Psalms,* I:141.

implied primarily by the use of the ritual oath in the protestation of innocence and the change from prayer to testimony.[24]

The superscription refers to David's experience with Cush, a Benjamite, one of Saul's tribal kinsmen. This is the only reference to such an event. The name "Cush" could refer to an individual or to a group in the tribe. If the song came from the time when David was being hunted by Saul's men (1 Sam. 22:8; 24:9; 26:19), Cush may have been one of Saul's men who took a strong part in opposing David with bitter words. Apart from this we do not know for certain what the occasion of the psalm was. There is no reason it could not have originated in the time of David's flight from the men of Saul. The psalm fits the style of other Davidic psalms, and parts of this psalm fit the events recorded in 1 Samuel 24 and 26 (e.g., Ps. 7:3, 4 and 1 Sam. 24:11[12] as well as verse 17). Whatever the origin of the psalm, once it was put into poetical form and adapted for sanctuary use, it was available to be put to a much wider application by people in similar situations. As with all such compositions, the message of the psalm is clear in and of itself.[25]

Exegetical Analysis

Summary

In praying for deliverance from his slanderous enemies, the righteous psalmist solemnly protests his innocence and appeals to the righteous Judge of the earth to vindicate him by destroying the wicked in their own planned malice.

Outline

I. The psalmist confidently prays for deliverance from his slanderous enemies (1–2).

---

24. Broyles, *Psalms*, p. 66. See further W. H. Bellinger, "Psalms of the Falsely Accused: A Reassessment," *SBL Seminar Papers* 25 (1986):463–69; and G. Kwakkel, "'According to My Righteousness': Upright Behavior as Grounds for Deliverance in Psalms 7, 17, 18, 26, and 44," *OTS* 46 (Leiden: E. J. Brill, 2002).
25. Kraus suggests that the setting was the Jerusalem Temple courts; but he also notes the archaic elements of the psalm and suggests the psalm be dated early (*Psalms 1–59*, p. 169).

A. He expresses confidence in God for refuge (1).

B. He prays for deliverance lest he be utterly destroyed by them (2).

II. The psalmist, protesting his innocence before God, appeals to the righteous judge of the earth to manifest his righteousness by vindicating his cause (3–9).

A. He solemnly protests his innocence (3–5).

1. There is no iniquity in his hand (3).

2. He has not rewarded evil to a friend, nor plundered an enemy (4).

3. He solemnizes the oath by announcing that if he has done these, then let the enemies destroy him (5).

B. He appeals to the righteous judge of the earth to vindicate his cause (6–9).

1. The LORD should display his righteous judgment before the congregation (6–7).

2. The sovereign judge should establish his integrity (8–9).

III. The psalmist confidently describes God's dealings with the wicked in direct punishment and in indirect entrapment by their own devices, all of which displays the righteousness of the LORD (10–17).

A. He is confident that God will save the upright of heart (10).

B. He describes the direct judgment of God on the wicked who will not turn (11–13).

1. The righteous judge is angry every day (11).

2. The angry judge will unleash his judgments (12–13).

C. He portrays how God destroys the wicked with their own schemes (14–16).

1. The wicked falls into the pit of his own wickedness (14–15)

2. The violence he planned will return on his own life (16).

IV. The psalmist vows to praise the LORD most high for the righteousness that he will manifest when he vindicates him (17).

COMMENTARY IN EXPOSITORY FORM

I. Those who trust in the Lord God may appeal to him for deliverance in times of imminent danger (1–2).

The psalmist confidently prays for deliverance from his enemies who were about to tear him to pieces like a lion (cf. 10:9; 17:12; 22:13, 21; 35:17; 57:4; 58:6). He knows that if God does not rescue him, no one can; so he begins the brief appeal with a clear affirmation of his faith, stating that the LORD is his God in whom he has taken refuge (a present perfect nuance of חָסִיתִי). The figure of taking refuge (an implied comparison with the idea of seeking shelter) is common in the psalms; it means he has put his trust in the LORD for protection and safety.[26]

His request is straightforward: "save me" (הוֹשִׁיעֵנִי; s.v. Ps. 3:2). The verb may be translated "save me" or "deliver me"; it can refer to any number of things, including here deliverance from people who pursue him. The parallel verb on the line simply means "deliver me" (הַצִּילֵנִי; s.v. Ps. 22:20); it may have the connotation of being snatched or plucked from danger.

The psalmist wants to be delivered from all his pursuers (מִכָּל־רֹדְפַי), who, the next verse explains, desire to tear him to pieces like a lion. There is a shift in verse 2 to a singular verb, "lest he tear me to pieces (פֶּן־יִטְרֹף), perhaps indicating that one of his enemies is prominent, or perhaps indicating that the many are represented as the enemy. In either case the fear is that the

---

26. The verb חָסָה means "to take refuge, seek refuge, hide." It has the literal sense of searching for a secure or protected place, such as in the shadow of a tree (Judg. 9:15) or Zion (Isa. 14:32). Most often it is used for seeking refuge in God (Pss. 2:11; 5:11; 7:1; 11:1; 16:1; etc.), although it can be used also for taking refuge in false gods as well (Deut. 32:37). Sometimes it adds the zoomorphism of "wings" to paint a full picture: people can take refuge under the shadow of his wings (see Pss. 36:7; 91:4)–or under the wings of another human (Ruth 2:12). In the Book of Psalms the word is used in a formula to express confidence in Yahweh's protection.

The related noun (מַחְסֶה) is a "shelter" or "refuge." It too can have the literal meaning, such as a shelter in a storm (Isa. 4:6; 25:4). It also serves as a metaphor for divine protection; e.g., God is a hiding place (Ps. 91:1). This verse identifies the people with the experience of prior generations of worshipers.

enemies will destroy him violently, as the comparison with a lion indicates. This simile is qualified further in the second colon of the verse: "ripping me to pieces" (פֹּרֵק), and there is no deliverer (מַצִּיל).

II. In appealing to the righteous judge to vindicate them, the righteous must be innocent (3–9).

A. The righteous should protest their innocence (3–5).

In order to legitimize his appeal for vindication, the psalmist solemnly affirms that there is no iniquity in his hands.[27] If there were sin, then the appeal for vindication would be hypocritical. These verses are framed in expressions that would normally be used in oaths: "If I have done this, if there is iniquity on my hands, if I have repaid evil to him who was at peace with me . . . then let the enemy pursue after me and overtake me." In view of his prayer for vindication, these lines must be taken as a solemn assertion of his innocence. He is saying that he has not done these things and is willing to stake his life on it.

The charge that he is denying is clarified in verse 4. His enemy has apparently brought a slanderous charge that he had "repaid evil" (רָע s.v. Ps. 10:15) to one who was at peace with him (שׁוֹלְמִי; s.v. Ps. 38:3). Not only does his oath continue in this verse in protest to the charge, but he interrupts the flow with a point to the contrary—in fact, "I delivered *him who is* my adversary without a cause." His actions give the lie to the charge. This seems to be the preferable reading of the line, although the other interpretation makes good sense as well, that is, he continues the conditional clause format with "if I have robbed."

His protestation of innocence is compelling because he invokes death by his enemy's hand if he is guilty (v. 5). He picks up on the theme of the enemy's pursuit, saying, "Let the enemy pursue me and overtake me, and let him trample my life to the ground." The result of this trampling would be that they make him lie down in the dust. In reference to himself, he uses "my

---

27. "Hands" is a metonymy of cause, meaning that he has not done anything iniquitous.

glory" (כְּבוֹדִי), focusing on his intrinsic value and not just his life.[28] For his enemy to make his glory sleep or lie down (יַשְׁכֵּן) in the dust means that he would kill him (cf. Dan. 12:2). The use of "dust" (a metonymy of adjunct for the grave) signals an ignominious death. The language of "sleeping" does not indicate an unconscious existence in death—it is figurative because the dead person appears to lie down in sleep. The petitioner is so sure of his innocence that he puts it in an oath, that if he is guilty of the charge his enemies should kill him; but in saying this he clearly knows that he is innocent and has no intention of seeing them victorious over him.

B. The righteous may appeal for vindication (6–9).

Because he is innocent of the charges, the psalmist is free to appeal for divine vindication, and this is the thrust of the message in the next four verses. First, in verse 6, David calls for the LORD to come to his aid. He uses bold imperatives: "arise (קוּמָה; s.v. Ps. 3:1) . . . rise up (הִנָּשֵׂא; s.v. Ps. 24:7) . . . and awake" (וְעוּרָה). These very human appeals (anthropomorphisms) are meant to prompt God to act quickly on his behalf. His appeal was for God to rise in his anger against the rage of these enemies. The use of "awake" in the verse suggests that so far God had been inattentive to him. Now the appeal is for God to rise to the occasion and administer justice. This justice will involve judgment on the enemy, which could be judgment in general, or a specific judgment that is the focus of the next two verses. As noted earlier, there are two possible ways to read the last few words of the verse. They could be taken as an independent clause: "command justice." Or they could be read with "justice" as the object of the verb "awake," followed by a relative clause: "awake for me *the* justice *that* you have commanded." In this interpretation, the psalmist is praying for God to bring justice into action, a justice

---

28. "Glory" means himself, his soul, but emphasizes the noblest part of a person (see Ps. 4:2, 16:9, 30:12); it is his character and his good reputation together (s.v. Ps. 19:1). See also John W. McKay, "My Glory—A Mantle of Praise," *SJT* 31 (1978):167–72.

that God decreed for him. Either way the verse is a call for divine justice.

According to the request of verse 7, the psalmist wants a clear, deliberate vindication with all the assembled peoples to witness it.[29] The second colon in the verse is a little difficult to interpret; it literally reads: "and over it return on high" (וְעָלֶיהָ לַמָּרוֹם שׁוּבָה). It is as if God should come to earth, gather witnesses, and return to his judgment throne over them; the verb "return" would call for God to resume his activity of judging, which it seemed for a while he had abandoned.[30] If this interpretation seems too forced, then the alternative is to change the text and have it read "rule over them from on high"; but since the context is a call for divine justice which seems not to be operating at the time of praying, "return" is not impossible.

With verse 8 the petition is clear and direct. It begins with the affirmation that the LORD judges (יָדִין; s.v. Ps. 140:12) peoples/nations.[31] The verb has the sense of ruling or ministering justice, and since the LORD does this throughout the world, the psalmist requests that he judge him now (שָׁפְטֵנִי), i.e., vindicate him (s.v. Ps. 9:4). His appeal is that the vindication be according to his righteousness and his integrity.[32] In other words, he is

---

29. See further J. H. Tigay, "Psalm 7:5 and Ancient Near Eastern Treaties," *JBL* 89 (1970):178–86; and R. L. Hubbard, "Dynamistic and Legal Processes in Psalm 7," *ZAW* 94 (1982):268–79.
30. Perowne, *Psalms,* I:145–6.
31. It is also possible to read the verb as a jussive here: "May the LORD judge."
32. The word for "my integrity" here is תֻּמִּי, from the noun תֹּם which means "completeness, integrity." It is used in Genesis 20:5 and 6, for the king's protestation of innocence over the patriarch's wife. The word is related to the verb תָּמַם, "to be complete, finished." It has this literal sense in many places, such as completing writing (Deut. 31:24), or building the temple (1 Kings 6:22); and it can refer to things coming to an end, such as a year (Gen. 47:18). The derived adjective תָּם means "complete, wholesome, sound"; e.g., Jacob was balanced (even–tempered) or civilized because he lived in tents, or the Shulamite had perfect beauty (Song 5:2). If it refers to a life coming to an end, it often has the negative sense of "being finished," i.e., destroyed.

But the word has an application of meaning in the spiritual realm; it can mean "be complete, sound," or "unimpaired ethically" (see Ps. 19:13). More frequently do we find the adjective תְּמִים with the sense of "whole, sound, innocent," or "having integrity." This adjective mostly modifies

pleading for a decision that would reveal that he has been acting with righteousness and integrity, in spite of the false accusations made against him.

He also asks that the righteous and omniscient judge would end the evil of the wicked and make the righteous secure (or, "and establish [וּתְכוֹנֵן; s.v. Ps. 93:1] the righteous"; v. 9). Understandably, the prayer of the righteous is often for God to set things right on earth. The basis for this appeal is the penetrating knowledge of God: "for the examiner of hearts and minds is a righteous God." Although the line is a bit cryptic and could be given different translations, the point remains clear—the God who examines (בֹּחֵן; s.v. Ps. 139:23) human hearts is a righteous God. People who are righteous, therefore, have nothing to fear from divine scrutiny.

III. By observing how God foils the wicked, the righteous may renew their confidence in the righteousness of God (10–17).

A. Their defense rests on God who saves the upright (10).

Verse 10 records a personal word of application: God is a shield who saves the upright. The line is a little difficult grammatically: it literally reads, "my shield [is] upon God," meaning "my shield [rests] upon God," or possibly "my shield [is] of God." "Shield" is a figure for protection or defense (an

---

cultic offerings, with the additional qualification that the offering was to be without blemish. Someone who has integrity, who is called blameless, enjoys an untroubled relationship with the LORD and is welcome in the sanctuary. Also, God makes the way perfect (Ps. 18:32), his law is perfect (Ps. 19:7), and people like Noah (Gen. 6:9) and Job (1:8; 2:3) are perfect. Abraham was told to be perfect (Gen. 17:1).

When a psalmist claims to be blameless or perfect, it means that he is in the proper spiritual condition to commune with God in his sanctuary. He is sound, complete, and morally unimpaired. He may have sinned, but he knew how to deal with sin according to the law. On the whole, because he is a faithful believer, he acts with integrity—he is whole. The claim may be made in general for his way of life; or it may be in reference to a specific charge brought against him to which he responds with a claim of innocence.

implied comparison). The line is somewhat cryptic, but it can be interpreted as it stands without reading "upon" as a title for God ("my shield is most high [עַל] God").[33] The second part adds to the psalmist's sense of safety—this God saves (מוֹשִׁיעַ; s.v. Ps. 3:2) the upright in heart. In short, he is a just God who protects and delivers the righteous.

B. God is a righteous judge who is ready to judge the unrepentant (11–13).

David next describes how God, in saving the upright in heart, brings direct judgment on the wicked. First, judgment is inevitable for the wicked because God is a righteous judge, the only righteous judge (cf. 9:8), and therefore he is angry every day (for "angry," זֹעֵם, see Nah. 1:2, 6). Obedient believers can take comfort, then, in the fact that the wickedness in the world does not go unnoticed; but they also must be advised that vengeance belongs to the LORD—he will repay in his own time (cf. Deut. 32:35; Rom. 12:19; Heb. 10:30).

Second, the anger of the LORD will be turned into judgment if the wicked person does not turn from his evil ways (v. 12). Like a warrior God prepares his deadly weapons for the wicked (12–13). Sword, bow (v. 12), weapons of death (deadly weapons), and fiery arrows[34] (v. 13) often provide the imagery for God's decree of judgment that will destroy the wicked, whatever form of judgment that might take, whether there was some immediate intervention or whether the psalmist and his supporters would be enabled to destroy the enemies with such weapons.[35]

---

33. If this interpretation is accepted, then the figure "shield" is a straight metaphor.
34. The description may refer to arrows wrapped with some flammable material. See also Ephesians 6:16.
35. The figures are probably best taken as implied comparisons, comparing God's judgment on the wicked to a military attack. The images would naturally suggest themselves if David was being pursued by military men and God was about to turn their devices back on them. It is possible that these figures could be metonymies of cause, the passage attributing the use of

C. God will turn the plans of the wicked back on them (14–16).

Now the psalmist focuses on how the LORD will execute judgment on the wicked. First, he uses the imagery of conceiving and bringing forth (implied comparisons) to describe what the wicked will actually produce. The first verb is an imperfect, "he travails" (יְחַבֶּל) to set forth the general principle: "he travails with evil."[36] Then he uses two perfect tenses, "he has conceived" (הָרָה) and "he has brought forth" (יָלַד), to elaborate on the first clause: he has conceived trouble (עָמָל) and brought forth falsehood (שָׁקֶר). Those who begin to develop a plan to cause trouble against the righteous will find that it will not produce its intended results. Rather, the evil scheme will be turned back on the plotter, as verse 15 vividly portrays with a comparison to digging a trap: he has dug a pit (בּוֹר) and scooped it out, but has fallen into the pit (שַׁחַת) that he prepares (יִפְעָל) as a trap for the righteous—perhaps falling into it while preparing it as the imperfect tense might suggest (see Ps. 9:15; 35:8; 57:6; and Prov. 26:27).[37] This is retribution from God, for his trouble and violence will come down on his head (see 1 Sam. 25:39; see for another example how the gallows that Haman had built for Mordecai in the Book of Esther became his place of execution).

IV. The righteous may rightly resolve to sing praises to the LORD most high according to his righteousness (17).

The psalm ends with David's vow to acknowledge (אוֹדֶה; s.v. Ps. 6:5) and sing praises (וַאֲזַמְּרָה; s.v. Ps. 33:2) to the LORD most high according to his righteousness. The first verb, usually translated "give thanks," refers to a public praise, an acknowledgment of all that the LORD has done. The second verb, the

---

the weapons to God but meaning that he would cause armies to defeat the enemies.

36. NIV takes the verb as representative of a type of person: "He who is pregnant with evil and conceives trouble gives birth to disillusionment."

37. On the other hand, the line could be read "he has fallen (preterite) into the pit he has dug (preterite meaning for the imperfect).

verb that is related to the common word "psalm," means to sing praises to musical accompaniment. This verse could be joined to the last section as a note of confidence, but it is strong enough to stand alone as a vow to praise. As the righteous anticipate how the LORD will vindicate them by destroying the wicked in their own evil plots, their petition should be replaced with anticipatory praise. It is anticipatory because in this psalm the vindication is still a petition—God's righteous judgment is yet to be manifested in the psalmist's experience. Even though he was slandered and attacked, David wholeheartedly trusts in his righteous LORD, the Most High (עֶלְיוֹן here) for vindication.

MESSAGE AND APPLICATION

The psalm is essentially about how the LORD vindicates the righteous when they are attacked and falsely accused by malicious enemies. The exposition of this psalm could be summarized as follows: *The people of God who walk in their integrity may pray with confidence for the LORD to vindicate them by turning the malicious schemes of the wicked back on the wicked themselves.* The application for believers is to be sure to walk in integrity, leaving no reason for the ungodly to accuse them in an effort to destroy them. As they live righteously and from time to time face such malicious attacks, they can pray with confidence for the righteous judge of all the earth to vindicate them and destroy the threat. This he will do, if not immediately, in time to come, for he is a righteous judge who will ultimately vindicate the righteous. At times sinners are even now caught in their own sins (Jas. 1:15) and are blind to their course of action (1 John 2:11). In the future the LORD will come in great glory to judge the wicked (Matt. 25:31–46).

The ideas of this prayer are relevant today in numerous experiences, whether believers find themselves in court or simply the object of false accusations. Their confidence, after all, is in a righteous judge, who will vindicate the righteous at the expense of the wicked.

PSALM 8

Glory Condescending to Mankind

INTRODUCTION [1]

Text and Textual Variants

For the Chief Musician. According to the *gittith*. [2]
A Psalm of David.

1 O LORD, our Lord, [3] how majestic [4] is your name in all the
   earth!
You have set [5] your glory above the heavens.

---

1. Among the numerous articles on this psalm, the following may be helpful
   for an overview: B. S. Childs, "Psalm 8 in the Context of the Christian
   Canon," *Int* 23 (1969):20–31; Donald R. Glenn, "Psalm 8 and Hebrews 2:
   A Case Study in Biblical Hermeneutics and Biblical Theology," in *Walvoord: A Tribute,* edited by Donald K. Campbell (Chicago: Moody Press,
   1982), pp. 39–52; Michael Goulder, "Psalm 8 and the Son of Man," *NTS* 48
   (2002):18–29.
2. The form is a feminine adjective from the word "Gath," (גַּת), "wine-press,"
   which is also the Philistine city. This word may be the name of an instrument that was named after the name of the city, or a melody. The title is
   also in Psalms 81 and 84. The Greek has ληνῶν, "wine–presses."
3. The MT has יְהוָה אֲדֹנֵינוּ and the Greek has Κύριε ὁ Κύριος ἡμῶν.
4. Greek θαυμαστὸν, "wonderful."
5. The MT has אֲשֶׁר תְּנָה, the relative pronoun followed by an imperative,
   "who—give." The imperative is problematic. It would have a translation
   of "which [glory of yours] do set (above the heavens)," but the point seems

287

2 From the mouth of children and infants you have
    established strength[6]
  because of your adversaries,
    to stop[7] the enemy and the avenger.

3 When I see your heavens, the work of your fingers,
    the moon and *the* stars which you have set in place–
4 what is man, that you are mindful of him,
    and the son of man, that you visit him?
5 Yet you made him[8] a little lower than God,[9]
  and crowned him with glory and honor.

---

to be that the glory is already there to be observed. Delitszch takes it to be an infinitive construct based on a parallel construction in Gen. 46:3 and translated as "you, the setting of whose glory is above the heavens" (*Psalms,* I:150). This suggestion has not been widely accepted. Others following the Syriac and Targum conclude the form is a corruption of the perfect tense, נְתַתָּה. It would then be: "you have set your glory above the heavens." The Greek text interprets it as a passive: "your magnificence was exalted ($\dot{\epsilon}\pi\acute{\eta}\varrho\vartheta\eta$) above the heavens." See also Mark S. Smith, "Psalm 8:2b–3," *CBQ* 59 (1997):637–41.

6. For "strength," עֹז, the Greek has $\alpha\tilde{\iota}\nu o\nu$, "praise."
7. Greek: $\varkappa\alpha\tau\alpha\lambda\tilde{\upsilon}\sigma\alpha\iota$, "put down."
8. In this line the verb is the preterite with the *waw* consecutive, referring to the original act of creation. The verbs in 5b and 6a are imperfect tenses, and the verb in 6b is a perfect tense. The forms that appear to be simple imperfects may be taken as preterites without the *waw*, making all the verbs in verses 5 and 6 past tenses (Greek). Otherwise, there would be a reference to creation in 5a and 6b, but the idea of the imperfects in 5b and 6a might speak of what man is in the present.
9. The translation of אֱלֹהִים is uncertain here. It could be translated "God, gods, supernatural beings," "heavenly beings," or "angels" as the Greek text has it ($\dot{\alpha}\gamma\gamma\dot{\epsilon}\lambda o\upsilon\varsigma$). The difficulty is compounded by the fact that the Greek version is quoted in Hebrews 2:6–9, notably verse 7, to assert that Jesus was made a little lower than the angels. The psalm is stressing the point that man in his greatness is less than divine, but the Book of Hebrews is using the verse to stress the humiliation of Christ. The wording of the Greek version was obviously more appropriate for the writer of Hebrews, but the main point of the psalm is basically retained, i.e., that the first man was lower than God, and so the second Adam was similarly clothed with human nature, to fulfill all that man had never fulfilled. For a detailed study, see Donald R. Glenn, "Psalm 8 and Hebrews 2: A Case Study in Biblical Hermeneutics and Biblical Theology."

6 You made him to have dominion over the works of your
    hands;
  you put all things under his feet;
7 sheep and oxen, all of them,
    and also *the* beasts of the field,
8 *the* birds in *the* sky, and the fish in the sea,
    that pass[10] through the paths of the seas.

9 O LORD, our Lord,
  how majestic is your name in all the earth!

Composition and Context

The praise of God for creation is a recurring theme in the Book
of Psalms (see for example psalms such as 19, 29, and 104).
Although Psalm 8 focuses on aspects of creation, it does not
praise nature, but the God who formed it—in fact, as Tate points
out, this is the only psalm in the collection that is addressed entirely to God.[11] Accordingly, the admiration of nature by believers
is an acknowledgment of the glory of God. The contemplation
of the heavens leads to praise; and in the contemplation of the
heavens, one senses the insignificance of a human. The praise
that comes from such contemplation necessarily focuses on the
divine plan of the creator to make mankind great, and even to
make mankind able to offer praise and adoration to the creator.
Since this hymn is a lyric echo of Genesis 1, it is not surprising to
see how the emphasis on the creation of mankind as the climax
of all creation has been carried over to this psalm of praise.

There is a significant structure to the psalm that is obvious
to the casual reader: the entire psalm is bracketed by the refrain
of praise in verses 1a and 9, and in between these verses there
are two considerations, the glory of God (1b, 2) and the celebration of mankind (3–8). Brueggemann notes that at the center
of the psalm is the affirmation of human power and authority;
but he stresses that the center (v. 5) and the boundaries (vv. 1a

---

10. The participle is singular (עֹבֵר) and is in apposition to "the fish of the sea."
11. Marvin E. Tate, "An Exposition of Psalm 8," in *Perspectives in Religious
    Studies* 28 (2001):343–59.

PSALM 8

and 9) must be read together, for either taken alone will miss the point. He says, "Human power is always bounded and surrounded by divine praise. *Doxology* gives *dominion* its context and legitimacy."[12] God intended for humans to have such power and authority, but without praise to God humans only pervert and abuse that power.

The psalm is not a messianic psalm. It speaks of the present, that is, that God by his grace has made mankind to rule over all creation. Humans are not divine, according to the psalm, but have been invested with greatness and its responsibilities. In the New Testament the psalm is applied on a higher level, reflecting a typological interpretation. The writer to the Hebrews reminds the reader that all things are not yet under such dominion (Heb. 2:6–9). However, the fulfillment of the divine plan will be realized because the Son of God became man, a little lower than the angels, and he will eventually put all things under his dominion (1 Cor. 15:27).

Exegetical Analysis

Summary

The psalmist marvels that the glorious Lord of heaven whose name is excellent in every way should even give thought to a human let alone exalt him and give him dominion over all creation.

Outline

   I. Introductory refrain: The psalmist extols the excellency of the nature of the LORD (1a).
  II. The psalmist praises the LORD's greatness in confounding the enemy with children and his grace in giving humans dominion over creation (1b–8).
    A. It is marvelous that this majestic LORD should use "children" to confound the mighty (1b–2).

---

12. Walter Brueggemann, *The Message of the Psalms, A Theological Commentary* (Minneapolis: Augsburg, 1984), pp. 37–38.

1. The majesty of the LORD is displayed in the heavens (1b).
2. The LORD uses the words of children to silence the enemy (2).

B. It is marvelous that this majestic LORD who created the universe should regard humans enough to entrust his dominion to them (3–8).
1. The work of creation is God's finger work (3).
2. God endowed man with glory and entrusted him with dominion (4–8).
a. It is amazing that God even thinks of a mere mortal (4).
b. It is marvelous that God granted mortals glory and dominion over creation (5–8).

III. Concluding refrain: The psalmist extols the excellency of the nature of the LORD (9).

COMMENTARY IN EXPOSITORY FORM

I. The LORD's Majesty: People must praise the majesty of the creator (1a).

The psalm begins with a direct address to the LORD, and this will be sustained through the entire psalm. The holy name (יהוה, "Yahweh") is used first, rendered here in English as usual with "LORD." And then in apposition to it is the plural "our Lord" (אֲדֹנֵינוּ), i.e., our sovereign master or king.[13] This clearly expresses the foundational meaning of the psalm, and indeed, of Scripture, that Israel's God is the sovereign creator.

The exclamation is the praise: "how majestic is your name in all the earth!" The "name" is the nature of the LORD, here probably emphasizing his sovereignty over all his creation (for "name" s.v. Ps. 20:7). His nature is "majestic" (אַדִּיר, "lofty, high,

---

13. The use of "our Lord" normally signifies that he is sovereign (see W. VanGemeren, *Psalms*, p. 138). But the form is the plural of the word and so is designed to stress the association with deity; it would suggest the sense of "our divine Lord," as opposed to all other lords.

noble, splendid") in all the earth.[14] The point is not that all people in the earth know the LORD or acknowledge his power and his glory, but rather that the faithful know and acknowledge that he is the mighty sovereign over all.

II. The LORD's Power and Grace: People must acknowledge the power and the grace of the creator (1b–8).

A. The LORD uses weak things to confound the mighty (1b–2).

The center of the psalm is divided into two unequal parts, with the first focusing on the glory of the LORD. Verse 1b is very difficult due to the textual problem; but if the form is taken to be a corruption of the perfect tense, it then declares that God has set his glory above the heavens. The fact that his glory is above the heavens explains why his name is majestic in all the earth. The word "glory" (כָּבוֹד; s.v. Ps. 19:1) emphasizes the essence, the very person of God as majestic—he is the most important person in existence. But the "glory of the LORD" may also refer

---

14. The word "majestic" (אַדִּיר) is not a very common word in the Bible, but it certainly is significant. The basic ideas it includes are usually given as "wide, great, high, powerful, noble." There is a related word אַדֶּרֶת which means "glory" or "cloak." If "cloak" is connected to this root, then it must be that the idea of "majestic" described the garment and became the designation for it. The word is used for Elijah's cloak (1 Kings 19:13, 19).

אַדִּיר describes people and things as wide, lofty, or powerful. For example, the sea is majestic, but not as majestic as the LORD (Ps. 93:4); a great tree is powerful and splendid (Ezek. 17:23); kings are majestic with all their pomp and power (Ps. 136:18); other leaders are also magnificent in the same ways (Judg. 5:13, 25); and according to Psalm 16:3 the righteous people on the earth—they are the noble ones. They may not have the power and the influence of kings, but of all people on earth they are magnificent.

Ultimately, though, it is Yahweh who is magnificent because of his power and his glory (Ps. 8:2). He is the mighty God who is victorious in battle (Exod. 15:6), and whose shrine alone brings terror to the enemies of his people (1 Sam. 4:8). But his majesty—his greatness and his power—is demonstrated by his dominion over his creation (Ps. 93:4) and by his brilliant presence (Ps. 76:4).

to phenomena of nature that witnesses to his power and majesty. The psalm is declaring that this God, whose majesty and power the heavens reflect, has glorified himself in all the earth and in mankind in particular.[15] More specifically to the content of the psalm, it is the glory of God to form a frail man from the dust of the ground and then entrust dominion over the earth to him. Such power, such authority, is unique to the LORD who is indeed "our Lord."

The psalm then focuses on a specific aspect of the sovereign power of God in verse 2. The specific meaning of this verse is uncertain, as the variety of interpretations attest; but the general idea seems to be that God works through things that appear to be weak and insufficient. What comes from the mouths of children would be words; but they could be expressions of a child's faith, expressions of praise for God's creation or salvation, or even cries for help.[16] Some such words by a child who appears to be insignificant will be attended to by God in his plan to establish strength to silence the wicked, especially if the cries are out of pain or terror.[17] God can take what seems to be merely desperate cries and fulfill the need by destroying whatever threatens danger to the weak and innocent, or by guarding the weak from the wicked. In other words, some individuals may appear weak and vulnerable, but they have access to divine power—this is the way that God has ordered creation.[18]

God has chosen to use the weak things to confound the mighty. He does not need to use powerful people or eloquent speakers

---

15. Delitzsch, *Psalms,* I:149–150.
16. The psalm speaks of actual children, and so when children in the temple began saying, "Hosanna to the Son of David, " Jesus reminded the critics of this passage (Matt. 21:16).
17. Kraus, *Psalms 1–59,* pp. 181–182.
18. In picturing this, Broyles suggests that the cries of children are heard by parents who are strong, so the strength resides in the cry of one who has access to one who embodies strength (*Psalms,* p. 71). Goldingay says that the cries of suffering children came up to God and made God determined to set up barriers that stop opposition powers from overcoming his purpose (*Psalms 1–41,* p. 161). The cries of children may be out of pain or fear, as the infants in Matthew 2:16–18, or the lad in Genesis 21:16, 17. See further Barbara Pitkin, "Psalm 8:1–2," *Int* 55 (2001):177–80; and Thomas L. Thompson, "From the Mouth of Babes, Strength," *SJOT* 16 (2002):226–45.

to silence the adversaries; rather, a simple cry for help will be heard by God and will overcome the world. This is the design of God to stop the enemy and the avenger (the infinitive "to stop" is לְהַשְׁבִּית, "to cause to cease" [from שָׁבַת; s.v. Ps. 46:9]). Here, then, in God's glorious creation, and under his sovereign majesty, the enemies of God exist and pose a threat to the righteous, especially the vulnerable. But God will bring the wicked to their end; and that victory will be a triumph of faith, no matter how small and simple the acknowledgment of God's power may be.

B. The LORD graces mankind with dominion (3–8).

The second and larger part of the body of this composition concerns the care and design that God has for mere mortals. This amazing observation is similar to the first, although now the psalm does not speak of God's using what children say to establish strength, but of God's entrusting humans with dominion over all creation. It begins in verses 3 and 4 with an observation. When the psalmist looks at (אֶרְאֶה) God's creation, the first feeling is a sense of being overwhelmed—people are just a tiny part of God's creation. The psalmist sees all of creation as God's finger work, the work of the divine craftsman. The fact that the text mentions only the moon and the stars may indicate that the psalmist was observing the night sky. Even if that is the case, the conclusion is still overwhelming—God is so majestic and powerful that he could create all of these things by a powerful decree.

Why, though, should such a God occupy himself with mere mortals? This is the wording of the questions of verse 4, but they are rhetorical questions, expressing amazement and wonder: "What is man that you are mindful of him, and the son of man, that you visit him?" The choice of the words for "man" underscores the point of insignificance. To heighten the amazement, "man" is here designated the simple human, the mortal (אֱנוֹשׁ); and in the parallel line he is the earthy man ("the son of man," בֶּן־אָדָם). The descriptions are of humans, people in general, and not of males as opposed to females; they portray humans as frail and insignificant, especially when placed in the context of the expansive universe.

The questions use two verbs that are very clear in their significance. The first is the verb "you are mindful of him" (תִּזְכְּרֶנּוּ, from זָכַר; s.v. Ps. 6:5). The word is "to remember"; and it usually signifies acting on what is called to mind. The psalmist is amazed that the majestic God of creation thinks of him in such a way as to do things for him, to meet his needs. And the parallel verb makes the point even stronger. The traditional translation is "you visit him" (תִּפְקְדֶנּוּ, from the verb פָּקַד), but modern translations prefer "care for" or the like. The word "visit" usually indicates divine intervention that changes the destiny of people.[19] No matter how frail or insignificant people may seem, God

---

19. The verb "visit" is פָּקַד. The dictionaries list the basic meanings as "attend to, visit, muster, entrust," which indicates the wide range of uses in the Bible. There are a number of related forms for this verb, and these also show the range of meanings: פְּקֻדָּה is "visitation," such as "punishment" (Hos. 9:7) and "prison" (Jer. 52:11); but it can also be "storage" (Isa. 15:7), "overseeing" (1 Chron. 26:30), and "mustering" fighters (2 Chron. 17:14). This range of meanings parallels the verb. Among the rest of the related derivatives for the noun there is פָּקִיד, an "overseer" and פִּקּוּד, a "precept," something to be obeyed (Ps. 19:8).

For the verb we find the same range: The first use is "attend to" (which is probably the category for Psalm 8 because it means "pay attention to, care for." Another example is Zechariah 11:16 which prophesies the shepherd that will attend to those who are in need.

The second use is "visit," some kind of direct intervention by God for blessing or cursing. Genesis 21:1 says that the LORD visited Sarah and she had a child. Ruth 1:6 says the LORD visited his people and gave them rain. Genesis 50:24, 25 announces "God will surely visit you," meaning intervene to deliver from bondage. But the intervention can be punishment as well: Exodus 32:34 says that the LORD would visit their sin, meaning punish them for it. In 1 Samuel 15:2 God visited the Amalekites, i.e., destroyed them. In Job 7:17–18 the morning visits by the LORD were for testing.

Four other uses of the verb may be listed briefly here: the third is "to number" troops or people (Num. 1:3); the fourth is "to appoint" someone for a task or position (2 Chron. 36:23); the fifth is "to entrust" those who are appointed (Gen. 39:4); and the sixth is "to muster" (Isa. 13:4).

The common theme running through all the uses is the attention given to someone or some activity, and when that attention is from God the effect is to determine the destiny of the one visited. The intervention has a purpose beyond taking care of someone. See on this word Gunnel André, *Determining the Destiny, PQD in the Old Testament* (Lund, Sweden: CWK Gleerup, 1980).

intervenes in their lives to set in motion the plan he has for them.

In verses 5 and 6 we have a description of just what God intended for mere mortals. First, the clarification is made that humans are not divine or supernatural beings. The text affirms that the LORD made man "a little lower than God." The word "God" in this verse (אֱלֹהִים) has caused a good deal of debate. The word was translated as "angels" in the Greek version, but the word by itself is not normally used of angels. In modern translations it has been rendered "divine beings" or "supernatural beings" or "heavenly beings." These appear to be another way of saying "angels." Since verse 6 refers to Genesis 1:26, to the "image of God" specifically, it may be best to leave "God" as the translation. The Creator made man less than divine.[20]

Even though God made man lower than divine, he crowned him with glory and honor. The words "glory and honor" (כָּבוֹד, s.v. Ps. 19:1; and הָדָר, s.v. Ps. 96:6) are words that usually refer to the divine majesty; the first stresses dignity and importance, and the second the external splendor. God in his grace has "crowned"[21] mankind with these, the verb being carefully chosen to anticipate the dominion given to mankind in verse 6 (there is an implied comparison being made with crowning a king and the bestowing of the qualities of majesty. This is another way of saying humans are made as the image of God.

The creation of humans and crowning them with glory and honor had a purpose, to make them have dominion over the works of God. Here we have a different word than is found in Genesis; here it is a word that stresses mastery and rulership (תַּמְשִׁילֵהוּ, the hiphil from מָשַׁל; s.v. Ps. 66:7). The second colon in verse 7 that declares God has put all things under his feet retains the idea of

---

20. Goldingay says that the Creator made him fall short of God by a little (*Psalms 1–41*, p. 159).

21. This translation takes the verb as a preterite, parallel to the first verb of the verse, referring to the act of creation. Another option would be to take this verb as a progressive imperfect, meaning that God still crowns mankind with glory and honor. But beginning verse 6 there is another imperfect form, which clearly refers to the creation; and it is paralleled by a perfect tense ("you have put"). So it is best to take all the verbs in these two verses as referring to what God did in creating mankind.

dominion in Genesis ("subdue it and have dominion," וְכִבְשֻׁהָ וּרְדוּ, in Genesis 1:28). In short, by God's creation every human was given the commission and the capacity to rule over life on this planet. The rest of the psalm delineates this dominion, the territory and the subjects—sheep, oxen, all of them, and cattle in the fields, birds in the sky, and fish in the sea, whatever passes through the paths of the sea. These are the works of God's hand that were put under the dominion of mankind.

In the New Testament the apostles point out that because of the presence of sin, mankind has not ruled over God's creation as intended. Creation is not in submission, but in chaos. The message in the New Testament explains how this plan will be fulfilled. By the incarnation, the Son of God took on mortal flesh and was made a little lower than the angels (the New Testament using the wording of the Greek translation). He never ceased being divine, but he did empty himself to become the second Adam. Even though all dominion and authority has been given to him, we do not yet see all things put under his feet. That will happen at the end of the age. Paul emphasizes that he will not simply put created life under his feet. He will subdue things visible and invisible, and the last enemy that he will subdue will be death. Those who trust in the Lord will share in that dominion, for they will reign with him (Rev. 5:11). Then the human race will fulfill its destiny, in and through the new Adam.

III.The Lord's Majesty: People must praise the majesty of the creator (9).

The first verse of the psalm is now repeated to close the psalm, and even though the psalm has focused on the glory and dignity of mankind's dominion over the earth, the ending of the psalm reminds us that praise is to be given to the LORD. The fact that we have been given the capacity and the privilege to reign over the earth—the fact that we were even created, is by God's grace and goodness. Like the shepherds in the field at the birth of the Savior, gazing into the heavens and hearing the host of angels, we too must always sing "Glory to God in the Highest."

MESSAGE AND APPLICATION

The psalm certainly inspires the reader to praise the majesty of the Lord God, and the substance of the praise of this psalm is distinct. The message of the passage can therefore serve as the substance of the praise, but it will also inspire theological reflection on the teachings included here. It portrays God as the majestic Lord of all creation, who delights in using things that are weak to confound the mighty when the things that are weak call out to him, either in prayer, or in praise, acknowledging his majestic nature.

There are a number of ways that the message of this psalm could be expressed in an exposition. One that is workable is: *God has chosen to display his majesty by enabling weak and vulnerable mortals to play a part in carrying out his plan for creation.* This could be extended to specify that he uses the cries of the weak and vulnerable to display his strength on their behalf and that he uses mere mortals to have dominion over creation. The exposition itself will explain this. The point that the Book of Hebrews makes is that whatever dominion humans have over the creation today is not what God had intended in creation. Through the incarnation of the Lord the plan of creation will be fulfilled, so Christians reading this psalm will offer even greater praise to God for his amazing plan to perfect creation through the Son. The psalm will still bring comfort in its teaching that God's power can be accessed through the simplest cries for help, and the psalm will still bring believers amazement that God should choose to use humans to rule over creation. Believers will need to discover the capacities that have been given to them and how to use them correctly to do the will of God in this world. The psalm is a reminder that we are here on earth with divinely ordained responsibilities. These ideas will be better understood in the light of the incarnation; for by being born into the human race and suffering as a human, Jesus was able to demonstrate the power of God to overcome the world. In his second coming he will display that power in his glorious reign. Then as the redeemed reign with him they will realize their full potential.

PSALM 9

Confident Praise for Vindication

INTRODUCTION

Text and Textual Variants

For the Chief Musician. Set to 'The Death of a Son.'[1]
A Psalm of David.

א 1 I will acknowledge the LORD[2] with my whole heart;
         I will tell of all your wonderful works.
    2 I will rejoice and exult in you;
         I will sing to your name, O Most High.

---

1. The expression is difficult because of the undivided form עַלְמוּת). The traditional rendering is "set to 'the death of a son'," probably referring to a
musical tune of that name. But even this translation has given rise to a
good deal of speculation, including suggestions that it refers to the death
of Goliath (see *ben* in 1 Chron. 15:18), or Absalom. The Greek has "concerning the secrets (ὑπὲρ τῶν κρυφίων) of the son" (reflecting עֲלָמוֹת). Symmachus has "eternal things." Many commentators believe that the MT
reading is improbable. Briggs, for example, thinks it is corrupted from the
form עֲלָמוֹת, "young girls" (the heading that appears in Ps. 46:1, e.g.); he
suggests the idea of a maidenlike voice of a youth (*Psalms,* I:lxxvii).
2. Because the next three cola are directly addressed to the LORD, some
commentators (see e.g., Kraus, p. 190) suggest that "LORD" in this line
should be a vocative, the verb be understood with a suffix, and the line
read to agree with the Greek ("I will give thanks to/acknowledge you, O
Lord").

ב 3 When my enemies turn back;[3]
    they stumble[4] and perish at your presence.
  4 For you have maintained my right and my cause;
    you sat down on the throne, a righteous judge.[5]
ג 5 You have rebuked the nations, you have destroyed the
    wicked;[6]
    their name you have blotted out for ever and ever.
  6 The enemy is finished—they are in perpetual ruins;[7]
    and the cities which you have rooted out—
    the very memory of them has perished.[8]

ה 7 But the LORD sits *as king* forever;
    he has prepared his throne for judgment.
  8 And he will judge the world in righteousness;
    he will minister justice to the peoples in uprightness.
ו 9 That so the LORD will be a high tower to those who are
    crushed;
    a high tower in times of trouble.
 10 And those who know your name shall put their trust in
    you,
    because you have not forsaken those who seek you, O
    LORD.

---

3. The sentence has also been translated "because"; the form is בְּשׁוּב, the infinitive construct with the preposition, probably serving as a temporal clause.
4. The Greek renders this "be feeble" (ἀσθενήσουσιν).
5. Greek has "one who judges righteousness."
6. The Greek has "and the ungodly one has perished" (ἀπώλετο, which would suggest וְאָבַד).
7. The Greek translation has this line "the swords (αἱ ῥομφαῖαι) of the enemy have failed utterly." The Hebrew text has חֳרָבוֹת, "ruins" (s.v., חָרְבָּה); "swords" would be חֲרָבוֹת (s.v., חֶרֶב). In the text the word is not in construct with "the enemies," but rather is adjectival.
8. The line in the MT reads: "perished / their memory / they." The pronoun "they" surely takes up the suffix on "their memory." This final pronoun "they" (הֵמָּה) has to begin the next line if the alphabetic arrangement is to be followed throughout, but it does not make any sense in that position. The editors suggest reading it as הֹמֶה instead, more in line with the Greek text's μετ᾽ ἤχους, literally "with a noise." Kraus suggests reading the word at the beginning of verse 7 (to keep the alphabetical arrangement) and translating it as "Impassioned, the LORD sits . . . " (pp. 188, 190).

ז **11** Sing praises to the LORD, who dwells in Zion;
    declare his doings[9] among the peoples.
  12 For he who requires blood remembers them;
    he does not forget the cry of the afflicted.[10]

ח **13** Have mercy on me,[11] O LORD;
    see my affliction *which I suffer* from those who hate
      me,
      you who lifts me up from the gates of death,
  14 so that I may tell all your praise;
    in the gates of the daughter of Zion
      I will exult in your saving help.

ט **15** The nations have sunk down in the pit[12] that they made;
    in the net which they hid their *own* foot is captured.
  16 The LORD has made himself known, he has executed
    judgment:
      In the work of his own hands is the wicked snared.[13]
      Higgaion.[14] *Selah*
י **17** The wicked shall return to the grave,
    even all the nations that forget God.
כ **18** For the poor shall not be forgotten forever;
    nor the hope of the afflicted perish eternally.

  19 Arise, O LORD, let not mortal man be strong;
    let the nations be judged in your sight.

---

9. Goldingay suggests that the word עֲלִילוֹתָיו should have a meaning something like "extraordinary things," since the usage of the word suggests something arbitrary or wanton (*Psalms 1–41*, p. 163). BDB simply lists the meaning as "deeds" when used of God.
10. The reading with the most support is Q*e*re', reconstructed as עֲנָוִים (K*e*thiv is עֲנִיִּים). See the discussion with verse 12.
11. The MT has חָנְנֵי but most manuscripts have חָנֵּנִי. A couple of versions (Aquila, Jerome) have a past tense instead of an imperative, "The Lord was gracious to me" (חֲנָנַנִי).
12. Greek, "destruction" (διαφθορᾷ).
13. Reading נוֹקֵשׁ with the versions instead of MT's נוֹקֵשׁ.
14. Higgaion is probably a musical notation but may mean "meditation."

20 Put them in fear,[15] O LORD;
    let the nations know that they are but mortal men.
        Selah

Composition and Context

This psalm is a psalm of thanksgiving to God for punishing the
wicked oppressors and defending the oppressed; but it turns
into a prayer for the righteous judge of the whole earth to once
again vindicate the oppressed. The tone of the song is victorious
and hopeful; and so various suggestions of times of victory have
been suggested as the occasion for the writing–such as after the
Philistine or Syro–Ammonite wars. But numerous other occasions could qualify just as well. The shift between singular and
plural forms raises the question of whether this was a personal
crisis or a national crisis. And the motif of the psalmist's recollection of God's acts in the past have been taken by some to support
a date in the time of the second temple.[16] However, there is not
enough evidence to identify the setting or occasion for the psalm.

Psalms 9 and 10 bear the marks of being one psalm originally
that was divided into two in the Hebrew tradition.[17] The following
observations can be made: Psalm 10 has no superscription, which
is rare in the Book I collection of Psalms; (2) the two psalms

---

15. The Greek text has understood מוֹרָא, "fear," to be מוֹרֶה, "teacher, lawgiver"
     (νομοθέτην). It would read: "O Lord, appoint a teacher/lawgiver over
     them." This understanding would give a negative sense to the normal use
     of "teacher." The idea of fear in a section on judgment makes the most
     sense. Goldingay argues for a more specific sense, not the feeling of fear,
     but of something fearful (*Psalms 1–41,* p. 164).
16. This alone is not the only reason for dating the psalm later. The didactic na-
     ture of the passage, the themes of God as judge and king of the whole world,
     and the problems addressed in the psalm are said to fit the post-exilic pe-
     riod. Broyles thinks that Psalms 9 and 10 are post–exilic because of the
     formulaic phrases and acrostic arrangement, which he says give evidence
     that a once liturgical psalm has become literature and therefore post–ex-
     ilic (*Psalms,* p. 74). Kraus notes, however, that the acrostic structure was
     popular in the sixth century B.C. (*Psalms 1–59,* p. 194). Many of the themes
     and expressions are not limited to the later Old Testament period.
17. See among others Robert Gordis, "Psalm 9–10," *JQR* 48 (1957):104–122.

together form the alphabetical arrangement (although it is uneven and cannot be restored precisely); (3) there are phrases and expressions that are unique to these two psalms[18] (although this would not necessarily show there was one psalm, just possibly one author); (4) both psalms end with a prayer against mortal man and anticipate judgment; and (5) in the Masoretic Text Psalm 9 ends with "*selah*," which otherwise is written internally and not at the end of a psalm. Although they may have originally formed one psalm, there is good reason why they were divided—psalm 9 is mostly thanksgiving, with a confident hope for triumph, and psalm 10 is all prayer, concerned with violence and wickedness.

When taken together the two psalms exhibit a structural pattern:[19] Psalm 9 begins with a statement of faith and praise to God for his past acts (9:1–12), and is followed by a plea to God (9:13–14); there is then another statement of faith with further praise to God for past acts (9:15–18), which is followed by another plea to God (9:19–10:2). Then in Psalm 10 there is a lament over the present circumstances (10:3–11), followed by a plea to God (10:12–13); there is finally a statement of faith and praise for God's past acts (10:16–18).

Even though these two psalms may have originally formed one psalm, this commentary will deal with the psalms separately as they now stand in the Hebrew (and English) texts. However, because most expositors may not have the luxury of expounding each psalm separately, at the end of the discussion of Psalm 10 I shall present an expository outline and unifying idea for an exposition that would cover both passages in one exposition.

Exegetical Analysis

Summary

Having praised the LORD for displaying his righteousness in judging the wicked nations, and for being a true and eternal

---

18. For a few examples: The expression "in times of trouble" is found in 9:10 and 10:1; the "crushed" are in 9:9 and 10:18; "mortal" (frail man, mortal man, אֱנוֹשׁ) man is in 8:19, 20; 10:18; and "forgotten" and "afflicted" is in 9:13, 19, and 10:12.
19. See further Goldingay, *Psalms 1–41*, pp. 167–8.

judge in whom the afflicted may trust, the psalmist prays that God will finally judge the wicked and give him further reason to praise for helping the afflicted.

Outline

I. Praise: The writer praises the LORD, the true and eternal judge, the hope of the afflicted, for displaying his righteousness (1–10).
   A. He will acknowledge the LORD wholeheartedly and sing joyfully to his name (1–2).
   B. The LORD displayed his righteousness by destroying the wicked enemies of the afflicted (3–6).
      1. The sovereign and righteous judge has established the psalmist's just cause by defeating his enemies (3–4).
      2. The LORD God has brought wicked nations to an end (5–6).
   C. The sovereign and eternal LORD will judge the world and bring justice to the oppressed who trust in him (7–10).
      1. The sovereign and eternal LORD has prepared for judgment (7).
      2. He will judge the world and minister justice (8).
      3. He will do this to provide safety for the oppressed who seek him (9–10).
   D. He exhorts the people to sing and praise the God who has not forgotten the afflicted (11–12).
II. Prayer: The writer prays that God who destroyed the wicked in the past will once again come to the aid of the afflicted (13–20).
   A. He calls on God to respond to his affliction so that he may publicly tell of his saving help (13–14).
   B. He tells how God has judged the wicked so that the afflicted should not lose hope (15–18).
      1. The LORD has revealed his justice by catching the wicked in their own devices (15–16).
      2. The LORD sends the wicked who forget him the unseen world because he remembers the hope of the afflicted (17–18).

C. He calls on God to judge the nations so that they will realize that they are mere mortals and be in fear (19–20).

COMMENTARY IN EXPOSITORY FORM

I. The sovereign and eternal judge of the whole world is worthy of our praise (1–10).

A. *Those who trust in him must resolve to praise him (1–2).*

The psalm opens with a strong resolution to give praise to
the LORD. Each colon includes a cohortative, each beginning
with the letter *'aleph* in the alphabetic arrangement, thanks to
the nature of the inflected forms. The repetition adds to the point
that the praise will be wholehearted.

The content of the praise will be the name of the LORD, that
is, his divine nature revealed in all his wonderful works. And the
"wonders" that he has done reveal that he is the Most High God,
for there is none like him.

B. *He has demonstrated his righteousness by destroying the wicked (3–6).*

The immediate occasion for the praise is that the LORD has
apparently just won some victory for the psalmist. The clause
of verse three could be read as a temporal or causative clause;
in either case it provides the basis for the praise. The enemies
are turned back (בְשׁוּב אָחוֹר) so that they no longer can oppress.
The reason is that they stumble and perish at the presence of
the LORD (the two verbs, יִכָּשְׁלוּ and יֹאבְדוּ, are progressive imperfects, describing what is going on). The figure of stumbling
(perhaps a metonymy) uses an aspect of their defeat, one that is
fitting for the battlefield.

The significance of this divine intervention is that the LORD
has vindicated the psalmist (v. 4) by administering or maintaining (עָשָׂה) his righteous cause. The text literally says "my
right and my cause" (מִשְׁפָּטִי וְדִינִי); but since these are synonyms,

they are probably to be taken together (as a hendiadys), "my righteous cause." By dealing out justice on the psalmist's behalf, God sat down "a righteous judge." This last expression is adverbial—"*as* a righteous judge"; he has taken his throne by setting things right, punishment for the wicked and vindication for the righteous.[20]

The psalm focuses for the next couple of verses on how decisively God has judged the wicked. Verse five uses three decisive verbs: "you have rebuked," "you have destroyed," and "you have blotted out." The three verbs are present perfects, emphasizing the

---

20. The words for judgment in this passage are common throughout the Old Testament, the verb שָׁפַט ("to judge") occurring some 144 times, and the noun מִשְׁפָּט ("judgment") occurring 422 times. The words have such a wide range of uses that it is difficult to express a basic idea; but G. Liedke offers a helpful summary by saying it is an action that restores the disturbed order of a (legal) community ("שָׁפַט, *špṭ*, **to judge**," in *Theological Lexicon of the Old Testament*, ed. by Jenni and Westermann, III:1392–1399).

The words refer to a decision, basically, often between individuals. Here the use of the noun מִשְׁפָּט, especially the plural, applies most clearly to the legal sphere. "Decisions" form a basic section of the law, beginning with Exodus 21:1. They are actually verdicts in cases, and so casuistic laws. The verbal idea then has to do with making a decision. The decision might be to condemn the guilty party, and so judgment in that case will involve punishment (e.g., 1 Sam. 3:13). If the judgment comes from the LORD and not simply judges, it carries with it absolute authority and justice (Gen. 18:25; Ps. 50:6).

The judgment or decision may also vindicate the innocent ("the one who bears the consequences of the violation of the law), so the oppressed will cry for vindication, pleading "make justice for me" (Ps. 7:8). In these passages the English gloss "judge" is misleading—better, "vindicate me" or "declare me right." In this sense the judge is a deliverer, and this applies to human judges (see Isa. 1:17; 1 Sam. 24:16) as well as the LORD.

The expression "to judge Israel" has overtones of ruling: it refers to the constant activity of preserving peace in the community by punishing oppressors and violators and championing the needs of the poor and afflicted. It essentially means to govern, both in making decisions and carrying them out (1 Sam. 8:5; and Ps. 67:4 for the LORD). This would be the sense of the participial use, "the judges" (הַשֹּׁפְטִים; see Judg. 2:16–19; Ruth 1:1).

Divine judgment often is part of the proclamation of eschatological salvation and judgment (Isa. 2:4; 51:5, and especially 11:3 which describes how Messiah will make judgments when he reigns).

act and the continuing results.[21] "Rebuke" (גָּעַר; s.v. Ps. 76:6)refers to the divine decree of judgment (so a metonymy of cause) that stops the wicked in their tracks; "destroy" (אָבַּד) simply means he caused them to perish; and "blot out" (מָחָה) emphasizes that they are completely removed from the scene, as the generation of the flood was also blotted out (Gen. 6:7; the verb is an implied comparison). What has been "blotted out" is their "name"—their evil nature and powerful oppression.[22]

The sixth verse turns its attention on their state as a result of divine judgment. "The enemy is finished" (תַּמּוּ; s.v. Ps. 7:8), completely cut off, meaning that they are in ruins forever. Even the memory of their cities has perished because God rooted them out. The last clause is somewhat cryptic: "perished / their memory / they." Their memory" (זִכְרָם) is comparable to "their name."[23] This is certainly emphasized in the way that the line is written: "their memory, even they themselves"; "their memory" is the figure (a metonymy of adjunct), and "they" clarifies the meaning—they themselves have perished.[24]

C. He is a refuge to the afflicted because he will judge the wicked (7–10).

Because of his great judgments on the wicked enemies, especially what was referred to in this psalm, the LORD has shown himself to be the righteous judge of the whole earth. Verse 7 declares that "he sits" (יֵשֵׁב, a habitual imperfect) enthroned forever (the expression is also anthropomorphic). His past acts

---

21. Kidner suggests that the verbs be taken as prophetic perfects in verses 5 and 6; but this is not necessary since the psalmist will turn to the future in verse 7, (Psalms 1–72, p. 69).

22. The traditional translation and its familiar meaning does not convey what the verb means, for the idea of "blotting" has come to mean removing excess ink with a blotter, and not actually removing or effacing the writing.

23. There is a difficulty with the syntax. The "enemy" is singular, but the suffix on "memory" is plural, "their memory." The simplest solution is to take "the enemy" as a collective to harmonize with the plurals in the line.

24. It has been suggested that this pronoun (הֵמָּה) was written at the beginning of the next line to provide the letter (ה) for the alphabetical sequence of the psalm. Otherwise, this letter of the alphabet is not present.

demonstrate his sovereignty, but they are only a prelude to what is yet to come. He will yet judge because he is the sovereign judge and because wickedness still exists. Therefore, he has prepared his throne for judgment (the verb כּוֹנֵן is a present perfect; s.v. Ps. 93:1). The throne is the symbol of his sovereign reign, and everything is set for him to judge the world. This is the point of verse 8. The verbs are here in the future tense, pointing to a future divine intervention in which the whole world will see the rule of righteousness. He will judge the world in righteousness! And in the process he will minister justice (יָדִין; s.v. Ps. 140:2) to the peoples in uprightness. Because the judgment will be fair and just, the wicked will be destroyed and the righteous vindicated, once again, finally.

The next two verses (9 and 10) explain the effect of this coming judgment. First, it will occur so that the LORD may be the protection for those who are oppressed. What the line is saying is that by virtue of his just rule he will be (become, or prove to be) a high tower, a place of refuge and security (a metaphor), for those who are crushed. This next figure (an implied comparison) says that the oppressed are "crushed" (דָּךְ) like fine powder, meaning utterly destroyed. "In times of trouble"[25] they have had no ability to resist the powerful wicked oppressors, and no place to go for safety—until the LORD became their place of refuge by faith.

Moreover, those who know the name of the LORD will place their trust in him, realizing that he does not forsake those who seek him. So those who may be crushed but believe in the LORD find him to be a high tower. They know the name of the LORD, meaning that they understand who the LORD is and experience by faith his promise of protection and provision. In times of trouble they trust in the LORD because he has not forsaken (עָזַב; s.v. Ps. 103:2) those who seek him (literally, "your seekers" [דֹּרְשֶׁיךָ], the participle stressing their character as people who seek the LORD). The choice of the verb "he has not forsaken" is an understatement; it means that he will gloriously deliver them. It is chosen because in the time of trouble it may have

---

25. "In times of trouble" links this psalm with the next. The expression (בַּצָּרָה from the root צָרַר) refers to the state of being destitute or diminished.

seemed like the LORD had abandoned them; but those who know him know that is not true, and so they continue to make him their refuge, waiting for the great deliverance yet to come.

D. Those who trust in him should praise him because he has not forgotten them (11–12)

"Sing" is repeated from verse 1, but now as an imperative, calling for the faithful to sing praises "to the LORD *who* dwells (יֹשֵׁב) in Zion" (it is the LORD who dwells in Zion because the participle is singular). God's dwelling among his people (the figure meaning his presence with them) ensures their protection. The psalmist calls for the faithful to declare his actions ("his doings," עֲלִילוֹתָיו) among the peoples. The theme of their praise is the theme of this psalm, that the sovereign judge has not forgotten the cry of the afflicted. The description of the righteous judge as one "who requires blood" (דֹּרֵשׁ דָּמִים) affirms that God will demand punishment for bloodthirsty oppressors (Ezek. 33:6, 8; Gen. 9:5). It is his character to call to account and demand satisfaction for such crimes. The good news for the afflicted who trust in the LORD is that they are del ivered f romoppr ession. The "afflicted"[26]

---

26. There are two important words that are related to the verb עָנָה, which is defined as "to be bowed down, afflicted." They are עָנָו and עָנִי, both defined as "poor, afflicted, humble." In this passage the second word is the *K^ethiv* and first is the *Q^ere'*, considered to be the correction of the other. Some clarification is in order.

    A brief survey of the verb connected to these words is helpful. It occurs most often in the *piel* verbal system with a number of illustrative uses. It can mean "humble, afflict, mistreat," as in the treatment of Hagar by Sarai (Gen. 16:6), or the affliction of a nation in war or bondage (Gen. 15:13), which could be part of divine testing of discipline (Deut. 8:2–3). It is also used for the rape of Dinah (Gen. 34:2), and it can be used to describe the spiritual preparation for special rituals, a preparation that was described as afflicting oneself (Lev. 16:29; 23:29), usually interpreted to mean deprivation of comforts and luxuries in order to live humbly and simply. It was a way of showing complete dependence on the LORD for all things spiritual and physical.

    The distinctions between the two words in question here is not always clear in a passage. The word עָנִי may look at the external condition, and so describe someone who is bowed down, i.e., oppressed and afflicted. This can be seen in most of its uses. For example, it describes the poor and weak

are those who are persecuted and oppressed, crushed by wicked tyrants. The psalm certainly has an application for people living in the world under tyrannical governments or at the mercy of terrorists. The two verbs used here are figurative—"he remembers" and "he has not forgotten" (they may be classified as metonymies of cause, although the meanings of the verbs include the effects); they indicate that God acts on what he remembers, he acts on behalf of his people. Every act of deliverance is cause for praise, and every act of deliverance is a preview of the final deliverance to come, which is cause for greater praise.

II. The judge of the whole world will again judge the wicked and fulfill the hopes and prayers of the oppressed (13–20).

A. *The faithful pray to the LORD to respond to their affliction (13–14).*

The nature of the psalm now turns from a song of victory to an earnest prayer for God's gracious intervention ("be merciful to me," חָנְנֵי; s.v. Ps. 4:1), specifically that God would "see" his affliction. The language is anthropomorphic: by asking God to look he is asking God to have compassion and remove his affliction,

---

as oppressed by the rich and powerful (Isa. 3:14), and it describes poor, weak afflicted Israel afflicted by other nations (Isa. 51:21; 54:11). It can also describe the poor without reference to oppression (those who glean, Lev. 19:10), or the humble king (Zech. 9:9). The noun עֱנִי means "affliction" (e.g., Ps. 44:24) or "poverty" (e.g., Prov. 31:5).

The other word, עָנָו, has the same uses, but also at times focuses more on the inner spirit, and so has the sense of humble, gentle, or meek. Moses, for example, is said to be meek (Num. 12:3). This is similar to the humble king in Zechariah 9:9 above. The feminine noun עֲנָוה means humility or meekness; it is used for the conquering king who champions it (Ps. 45:4). It is not a term of weakness, then, but of humility; it does not describe someone who is afflicted and oppressed, but someone who does not think too highly of himself.

There is a good deal of overlap between the words, making a contextual analysis essential for the proper emphasis. The common idea in the uses is that the one so described is in need of help, whether it is because of oppression or poverty, or the challenge of leading the nation.

and it is an affliction that he suffers at the hands of those who hate him.

Yet his prayer is confident, not desperate. He describes the LORD as the one "who lifts me up (מְרוֹמְמִי; s.v. Ps. 46:10) from the gates of death." The entrance to death is described as if it has gates (so an implied comparison)—but God is the one who prevents his people from going through them at the hands of the wicked.

The purpose (לְמַעַן) of his salvation is so that the redeemed can praise him in the gates of the daughter of Zion.[27] The faithful are prevented from going through the gates of death prematurely so that they can stand in the gates of the city to praise the LORD for salvation ("gates" in this case are literal gates; but the expression means in the plaza or area of the gates, and so it is a metonymy of subject). There the righteous will tell God's praises ("your praises" is unusual, but must mean the praises that are due to you," the suffix being a genitive of worth or perhaps objective genitive); there the righteous will exult (perhaps a cultic shout of praise [אָגִילָה from גִּיל; s.v. Ps. 13:6]) in his salvation ("your salvation" means "the salvation you bring," the suffix being a subjective genitive).

B. They may be confident that the LORD will again judge the wicked (15–18).

In the next couple of verses the tenses of the verbs are perfect tenses, but then in verses 17 and 18 the forms are imperfect tenses. It seems most likely that the verbs in verses 15 and 16 should be taken as referring to the future as well, and so classified as prophetic perfects. Otherwise, the psalm would make an abrupt change from the petition of verse 13 to a report of deliverance. Verse 15 introduces a section of confidence, an expectation of the future defeat of the wicked that will parallel what he had experienced before.

---

27. The figure is an implied comparison; Zion is the mountain on which the holy city is located, and so it is as if the mountain has produced the city and its sanctuary—it sprang up on the mountain (perhaps "daughter" is used because cities are feminine nouns).

The justice meted out on the wicked will be talionic. The nations have sunk (will sink) in the pit they made, and their foot is captured (will be captured) in the net they made. The pit (שַׁחַת) and the net (רֶשֶׁת) are figures (implied comparisons) for the plans the wicked made to destroy the innocent victims. God is able to turn their own devices back on them so that they will perish by their own hands. Again the classic example of this is Haman in the Book of Esther, who was hung on the gallows he prepared for Mordecai.

Through this reversal the LORD has made himself known.[28] By executing ("he has made") justice in this way God will reveal himself as one who sets things right—he destroys the wicked by their own devices and rescues the righteous from those devices. The sum of the matter is that the wicked is snared (נוֹקֵשׁ in MT is the *qal* participle of נָקַשׁ) in the work of his hands ("hands" being a metonymy of cause). In other words, he destroys himself by trying to destroy others. This is divine justice at work.

The equity of divine judgment is the focus of verses 17 and 18. The nations that forget God will enter *Sheol*, but the afflicted will not be forgotten by God. The first verb in verse 17 (יָשׁוּבוּ) could be a simple future, "the wicked will return," or an obligatory imperfect, "the wicked must return." There may be an allusion here to Genesis 3:19, which declared that sinful humans were taken from the dust and would return to the dust, meaning death. In this line, though, "dust" is not used. They return to *Sheol* (שְׁאוֹל), a word that can refer to death, or the grave, or to the realm of the departed spirits, often called Hades (for the discussion, s.v. Ps. 6:5). The Bible certainly teaches that the wicked, all those who forget God, will go to Hades. But it is hard to know if that is the intended meaning in this psalm. The passage at the least describes their sudden judgment and removal from the land of the living. Death is their destiny and their future state, however it is to be defined. The contrast with the righteous who do not perish (v. 18) indicates that more is meant than the death of the wicked. The point is that when God intervenes finally there will be a parting of the ways—the afflicted who trust in

---

28. The form is נוֹדַע, perhaps "is known" rather than "has made himself known."

the LORD will never perish, and the nations that forget God will return to *Sheol*, the realm of the dead.

The poor shall not be forgotten forever. It may seem at times that they are forgotten, but the Scripture makes it clear that God will vindicate them. It is said that their hope shall not perish. What they expect, what they desire, what they pray for, what keeps them going, will not perish. It will be fully realized.

C. They should pray for God's judgment so that the oppressors will be brought down (19–20).

The last two verses are the prayer of the psalmist for divine intervention. This prayer is instructive: he prays, and so should all who suffer under tyranny and terror at the hands of the wicked likewise pray for vindication. The prayer sounds bold: "Arise, O LORD," the imperative (קוּמָה; s.v. Ps. 3:1) calling for God to begin to act as judge and not let these tyrants remain strong. The request refers to "mortal" or "frail" men (אֱנוֹשׁ)–mere men! God should not let them be strong (אַל־יָעֹז; s.v. Ps. 29:1). In their great acts of tyranny and terror they seem to have strength; but when they will be judged they will be seen for what they are.

The prayer continues that the LORD would put them in fear (מוֹרָה is the spelling here). They have spent their lives forcing those they oppressed to live in fear of them; but if the LORD judges them, then they will know what it means to live in fear. The fear the LORD will impose on them will be of a much greater magnitude. Morever, the world will know that they are but mortal, ordinary frail human beings. Thus it is with all tyrants and terrorists when they are stripped of their power and their supporting henchmen. The world is left wondering how they could have done so much damage to other people.

MESSAGE AND APPLICATION

The psalm in many ways focuses on God's sovereign rule over the affairs of men. The psalmist thinks of his own experience of vindication when God judged the wicked, and from there he looks forward to what it all prefigures, a great and final judgment to come (Kidner, *Psalms 1–72*, p. 69). The LORD is the champion of the weak and afflicted who trust in him, and he will one day bring justice into the world by putting the oppressors in their place. Their place will be *Sheol*, their native element.

The message of the psalm is timeless. It may be worded as follows: *Because God has demonstrated that he is the righteous judge of the world, believers may trust in him now for protection from the wicked and confidently pray for final vindication in the judgment to come.*

There are two ways this psalm may be directed. One is that people hearing this psalm may have to acknowledge that they are part of those who are being prayed against in this psalm— they may have a share in the oppression of others, either on a small scale or by being part of powerful nations (see further Goldingay, *Psalms 1–41,* p. 184). Passages such as this should inspire believers to relieve the suffering and the affliction of others when they have the opportunity to do so.

The other way this psalm may be directed is the straight-forward meaning of the text. Any individual believers who are oppressed by wickedness in high or low places will find strength and comfort from this psalm to pray for relief and vindication. They will certainly understand the plight of others who have been afflicted, and join in their ancient prayer, "How long, Sovereign Lord, holy and true, until you judge the inhabitants of the earth and avenge our blood?" (Rev. 6:10).

PSALM 10

The Oppression of the Helpless

INTRODUCTION

Text and Textual Variants

ל 1 Why do you stand far off,[1] O LORD?
Why do you hide[2] *yourself* in times of trouble?

2 In his pride[3] the wicked hotly pursues the afflicted;
they will be taken[4] in the devices they have conceived.
3 For the wicked boasts of[5] his heart's desire;
and he blesses the robber,[6] he reviles the LORD.

---

1. Hebrew בְּרָחוֹק.
2. For "you conceal," the Hebrew is תַּעְלִים; the editors suggest reading it תֵּעָלֵם since "yourself" is understood. The Greek translation has "overlook [us] (ὑπερορᾷς) in times of need, in affliction?"
3. Literally, "In *the* pride of *the* wicked."
4. The verb could also be taken as a jussive, "Let them be taken," if the subject is taken to be the wicked.
5. Hebrew "boasts of" (הִלֵּל עַל) poses a problem for interpretation. The meaning is probably that they boast according to their heart's desire, meaning, they follow the prompting of their heart (Perowne, *Psalms,* 1:168). The Greek has "Because the sinner praises himself" or "is praised" (ἐπαινεῖται). Kraus concludes that in any case the preposition עַל needs to be deleted (*Psalms 1–59,* p. 191).
6. There are two difficulties here: the meaning of the word "bless" and the syntactical connection of "robber" (בֹצֵעַ), or "greedy" as NIV has it. One interpretation would read, "the robber curses and despises the LORD";

315

4 The wicked in his arrogance,[7] *says,*
    'He will not call it to account.'
    'There is no God' *is the sum of* all his devices.[8]
5 His ways are prosperous[9] at all times;
    your decisions are far above out of his sight.
    As for all his adversaries, he sneers[10] at them.
6 He says in his heart, 'I cannot be moved;
    from generation to generation I shall not have
       misfortune.[11]
פ 7 His mouth is full of false swearing,[12] deceit, and
    oppression;
    under his tongue is trouble and iniquity.

---

but the word "bless" (בֵּרֵךְ) does not have this meaning. Another view that takes the robber as the subject would read, "the robber blesses and [yet] despises the LORD." The Greek also takes the word as the subject but translates the line as "the unjust one blesses himself" (ἐνευλογεῖται). It is preferable to take the robber as the object and make the line parallel with the preceding: "he blesses the robber, he despises the LORD."

7. The Hebrew line is כְּגֹבַהּ אַפּוֹ, "according to the exaltedness of his face." This is the pride of his appearance, or the arrogant look he has, such as a scornful look. The Greek text reads this line as follows: "The sinner has provoked the LORD according to the full extent of his wrath."

8. The Greek text has "God is not before him" for the line.

9. The Hebrew (יָחִילוּ) means "strong, sure, prosperous" (see also חַיִל). The Greek translation confuses the word with the root "profane" (חָלַל) and translates it with βεβηλοῦνται: "(his ways) are being defiled."

10. The verb is "puffs," יָפִיחַ; puffing at them would signify scorn and contempt, sneering at them. It may taken to mean that he only has to blow at them and they wither. Perhaps this idea is behind the Greek "gains mastery (κατακυριεύσει) over them."

11. The line is difficult due to the pronoun אֲשֶׁר. It literally reads "from generation to generation which not in misfortune" (אֲשֶׁר לֹא־בְרָע). It must mean something like "from generation to generation which [I shall have] no misfortune," or be free of misfortune. The Aramaic has "I shall not be moved from doing evil." The Greek text omits the relative and has ἄνευ κακοῦ, "I shall not be moved [remaining] without evil from generation to generation."

12. The word for "false–swearing," often rendered "cursing," אָלָה, is put at the end of the previous line of text so that the first word of this line can begin with the letter פ (פִּיהוּ) to carry the acrostic forward. Goldingay leaves it as part of the previous line and renders it "[I shall never be in adversity] he swore" (*Psalms 1–41,* p. 180).

8 He sits in the hiding places by the villages;[13]
    in the secret *places* he slays the innocent.[14]

ע   His eyes[15] watch in secret[16] for the helpless.

9 He hides in the secret place, as a lion in its cover;
    he hides to catch the afflicted;
        he catches the afflicted, drawing them off in his
        net.

10 So the crushed[17] sinks down;
    the helpless[18] falls under his strength.[19]

11 He says in his heart, 'God has forgotten;
    he hid his face; he never saw it.'

ק 12 Arise, O LORD! O God, lift up your hand!
    Do not forget the afflicted.

13 Why has the wicked reviled God,

---

13. Hebrew חֲצֵרִים was read by the Greek translator as עֲשֵׁרִים, "rich," πλουσίων.

14. The Greek reads the verse as "he lies in wait with rich men in secret places in order to slay the innocent (ἀθῷον).

15. This line begins a new line in the text to bring the letter ע (עֵינָיו) to the front.

16. Hebrew is יִצְפֹּנוּ from צָפַן, "to hide, treasure." The editors suggest יִצְפִּיו (from צָפָה, "to spy out") in closer connection with the Greek version's ἀποβλέπουσιν and its reading of the line as "his eyes focus on the poor." Kraus has it, "on the lookout" (*Psalms 1–59,* p. 189).

17. For the form in the text (וְדָכָה) the *Qᵉre'* יִדְכֶּה would be translated "he is crushed." Goldingay suggests an alternate construction could be as follows: "The helpless is crushed, sinks, and falls . . ." (*Psalms 1–41,* p. 181). Kraus suggests "he is knocked down" (יִדְכֵּא), adding that some have suggested adding "the righteous" as the subject of the verb, giving a צ to fill out the acrostic; but that is unnecessary, given the unevenness of the acrostic (*Psalms 1–59,* p. 191). Now, if the letters of the text are pointed וְדָכֶה the word might be read as an adjectival "the crushed one." This would make a better parallelism with the second colon.

18. The form חֵלְכָּאִים is difficult. It seems to be the word חֶלְכָה, the א not being part of the root word. The MT pointing makes it חַיִל, "army, company," and with the plural, perhaps "the army/host of the disheartened" (חֵיל כָּאִים), but a root חָלַךְ, "weakness," may be behind the form, based on its existence in other languages and the translation of the versions (the Greek has τῶν πενήτων, "the poor").

19. The form עֲצוּמָיו is plural and so has been translated by some to mean "his strong ones," perhaps referring to the young of the "lion," but it probably should be taken as an abstract plural, "strength."

and said in his heart, 'You[20] will not call it to account'?

ר 14 You do see (for you[21]) trouble and grief;
    you consider it to take it into your hand;[22]
The helpless leaves it to you,
    you have been the helper of the orphan.

שׁ 15 Break the arm of the wicked and the evil man;[23]
    Call him to account[24] *for* his wickedness until you find
      none.

16 The LORD is king[25] for ever and ever;
    the nations will perish[26] out of his land.

ת 17 The desire of the afflicted you have heard, O LORD;
    you establish their heart,
    you pay attention with your ear,

18 to defend the orphan and the broken person,
    so that mortal man of the earth may terrify no more.[27]

---

20. Greek and Syriac have the third person form of the verb to harmonize with the pervious line.

21. The editors consider "for you" a dittography and would simply read: "you (do) see trouble and grief." It may be that "for you" came first, but when the verb was placed first (for the acrostic) this became superfluous.

22. The Hebrew is simply לָתֵת בְּ, "to give/take in(to) . . . ." Attempts to make the expression similar to the engraving in the hands found in Isaiah 49:16 are forced. The verse simply says that God will take care of it, and the next line harmonizes with that ("the helpless leaves it to you").

23. This division goes with the sense of the line but against the accents of the MT which would put "and the evil man" with the second colon.

24. The Greek has ζητηθήσεται which would indicate a reading of יִדְרֹשׁ, "his sin will be sought." Likewise, the other verb in the line was also taken as a passive, εὐρεθῇ, indicating a reading as יִמָּצֵא, "[not] be found."

25. The Greek reads this as a verb, "shall reign" (βασιλεύσει).

26. This translation takes the perfect tense as a prophetic perfect. The Greek reads "you nations shall perish (ἀπολεῖσθε). The verb could be a past tense if it is referring to historical interventions.

27. The line has been interpreted in two different ways, depending on the placing of מִן הָאָרֶץ, "from the earth." One way is to join the prepositional phrase with לַעֲרֹץ and read the line as "terrify men out of the land." This would mean that they were driving people away. The difficulty is that אֱנוֹשׁ, "man," is not what would be used of the sufferers, but of the tyrants; one would have expected "the afflicted" if it referred to the sufferers. The second way is to connect the phrase with "man," and read the line as "so that mortal man of the earth may terrify no more." The word for "man" is

Composition and Context

Psalm 10 begins with a sudden cry to God in lament. It may be that this distinct focus is what prompted the division of the psalm into two psalms. Psalm 10 may have a lengthy lamentation, but it is not all lamentation. It is an interesting blend of lament over the oppression of the wicked and triumphant jubilation at the prospect of divine judgment. Kraus suggests that the whole psalm may at first have been an individual song of thanksgiving that received didactic extension. The extension took the form of hymnic expressions, laments and pleading for help in the light of Godforsakenness.[28] The result is an artistic composition with linking motifs throughout what are now the two psalms. The composition is a prayer for God to destroy the wicked with their scorn and insolence, especially since they boast over their successful but wicked activities, or when not immediately overtaken, act as if God does not demand punishment for their acts, if he exists at all. In the lamentation section (10:1–10), the psalm provides an extensive description of the wicked in their prosperity (v. 5), security (v. 6), insolence (vv. 4, 11), deceit (v. 7), and violence (vv. 8–10). Then the lamentation gives way to hymnic praise and confidence in God's vindication of the faithful. In spite of all the disorder in the world dominated by the wicked, the LORD is still the king (10:16). This expression of his sovereignty is a continuation of the confident depiction of the LORD as the Most High God (9:2) and the judge of the world (9:4, 8, 16, 19; 10:5, 18). The psalmist affirms that the LORD dwells among his people and does hear and does answer their cries. The wicked may not yet be driven out, but the expectation is that they soon shall be, and their judgment will be the vindication of the faithful. The issues expressed in the psalm may come from an ancient culture, but they are timeless. Their difficulties, and their faith solutions will be appreciated by the modern believers who also face oppression and ruin at the hands

---

chosen to pour contempt on the proud plunderers. They are mere men of the earth (in contrast to the God of heaven).

28. Kraus, *Psalms 1–59*, pp. 198–199.

of greedy, powerful people, or who have to live with the constant threat of terrorism.

As it stands in its final, fixed form, the psalm falls into three sections. The first is a description of the evildoer who for the present succeeds in his evil devices and threatens to destroy innocent people (vv. 1–11). The second section is a prayer for the LORD to help the helpless who are overpowered by such people (vv. 12–15). The final section is the triumphant acknowledgment that the LORD is king, and he will judge the wicked oppressors and vindicate the afflicted who trust in him (vv. 16–18).

Exegetical Analysis

Summary

After describing the frightening power of the wicked in their impiety towards God and their violence against the helpless, the psalmist appeals to the LORD, the sovereign King, to deliver the oppressed by destroying the wicked.

Outline

   I. The psalmist offers a frightening description of the wicked in his insolence towards God and his violent oppression of the helpless (1–11).
     A. He laments God's lack of help in his time of need (1).
     B. He describes the nature of the wicked oppressor (2–7).
        1. In pride the wicked afflicts the weak and despises God (2–3).
        2. In self–confidence the wicked is sure there is no God to require justice (4–5).
        3. In his heart the wicked is convinced he cannot be stopped (6).
        4. In his mouth the wicked speaks only deceit and cursing (7).
     C. He portrays the powerful attacks of the wicked against the afflicted (8–11).
        1. The wicked sits lurking in secret places to catch the afflicted (8–9).

2. The wicked crushes the helpless (10).
3. The wicked is sure God has forgotten him and will never see it (11).

II. The psalmist petitions God to vindicate the faithful by destroying the oppressor (12–15).
   A. First appeal: God should act soon to rescue the afflicted (12).
   B. The reason: The wicked should not be allowed to despise God any longer (13).
   C. The motivation: The afflicted trust in God who has seen their affliction (14).
   D. Second appeal: God should destroy the oppressor and remove the evil (15).

III. The psalmist proclaims his confidence that the LORD, the heavenly king, will answer his prayer to destroy the wicked and vindicate the faithful (16–18).
   A. The proclamation: Because the LORD is king forever, the nations perish (16).
   B. The confidence: The LORD has heard the prayer to vindicate the oppressed and remove the terror of the wicked, who are merely mortal (17–18).

EXPOSITION IN COMMENTARY FORM

I. The faithful must live in a world that is terrorized by impious and violent oppressors (1–11).

A. There are times that God seems far off (1).

The psalm begins with an immediate lamentation of God's hiddenness. The immediate trouble is one thing, but God's failure to intervene is a greater problem to the psalmist. The first verse is in the form of a rhetorical question: "Why, O LORD, do you stand far off? // Why do you hide in times of trouble?" Such questions are used occasionally in lament psalms (e.g., 13:1; 22:1–2). They form the cry of a faithful believer to the LORD, the covenant God. They express the sense that God has distanced himself. The covenant God should not be standing far off or hiding himself. These bold figures (anthropomorphisms) signify the LORD's failure to intervene, as if he has distanced himself from the afflicted believer, or hidden in time of distress (צָרָה). However, such questions are designed to prompt God to draw near and pay attention (cf. Ps. 22:11, "Do not be far off from me, for trouble is near, and there is no one to help").

B. There are times when the oppression of wicked people becomes unbearable (2–11).

Now the psalm will focus on the problem: powerful wicked people are trying to destroy innocent and helpless people in order to get what they want. While the word "wicked" can refer to the "ungodly" in general, here it refers to them in their worst activities. The word is singular, but is collective of wicked people, as are the words for the innocent and the afflicted. These wicked people are malicious, blasphemous, and ruthless; they are insolent and impious, practicing atheists, but perhaps not convinced ones[29]. On the human level, whatever these people plan to do would easily destroy the helpless people of the land.

1. They are insolent and self-confident in their malicious plans (2–7). In this first main section the psalm provides a long depiction of the arrogance and impiety of the wicked oppressors in their planned attacks. Their pride is mentioned first (בְּגַאֲוַת): it is through pride the wicked inflict suffering on the afflicted. The text says that the wicked hotly pursues (יִדְלַק) the afflicted; the verb has the idea of "burn" and so intensifies the suffering that is endured by the afflicted. As Perowne says it is as if they put their victim in the fiery furnace of affliction.[30] Having stated this general idea of affliction, the psalmist adds that "they" (now a plural verb) are taken in the devices or schemes (מְזִמּוֹת)[31] that they have imagined or conceived (חָשָׁבוּ; s.v. Ps. 32:2). The subject of the verb (יִתָּפְשׂוּ), "they," is either

---

29. Kidner, *Psalms 1–72,* p. 71.

30. Perowne, *Psalms,* I: 165

31. The word for their devices (מְזִמָּה) is a common word for "purpose, device, plan'; it is related to the verb זָמַם that means "to purpose, devise, consider." The word itself is neutral–the purposes can be for good or for evil, depending on who is devising them; but the most common uses concern

the afflicted or the wicked. If the latter is the case, the verse would anticipate the destruction of the wicked—their schemes actually entangle them instead of the afflicted.[32] If the subject of the verb is the afflicted, which makes more sense in the context, then it is a continuation of the lament, indicating that the afflicted are taken in the devices of wicked people.

Next the arrogance of the wicked is demonstrated by what they appreciate and what they despise (v. 3). We first are told

---

wicked schemes, and the wicked acts that are planned, making them premeditated crimes. There are four areas of usage to consider:

The first category is positive, but not very common. The verb has the meaning of "consider, have discretion," and the noun, "discretion." Proverbs 31:16 says "the woman considers a field and buys it." Proverbs 1:4 says the purpose of the book is to give to the young person knowledge and discretion/purpose—purposive knowledge (the ability to act or judge on one's own or to make the right choice).

The second category is more common; it has the meanings "plan, purpose, devise." When used of humans, the verb and the nouns all have the meaning of plan or purpose, usually in bad sense. It appears in Genesis 11:6 for the generation at Babel whose enterprise was with an evil purpose. In the psalms it frequently describes wicked plots or schemes of evil people (Pss. 10:2; 10:4; 21:11). The passages often parallel the word with חָשַׁב, "to think, plan," strengthening the emphasis on planning.

Sometimes the noun מְזִמָּה is used for the wicked acts that are planned (this category would have grown up by metonymy). Proverbs 12:2 speaks of a man of evil devices; he obviously had to be doing something for others to know about his plans. Psalm 37:7 provides the bridge, telling people not to fear when the wicked carry out their schemes. Psalm 139:20 uses it for people who take the LORD's name in vain: "they speak of you with wicked intent." We also find the related word זִמָּה used for premeditated acts of wickedness, such as murder in Hosea 6:9. But it is also used for all the major sins, adultery, incest, idolatry and the like—all of them being planned and therefore premeditated crimes.

Finally, by talionic justice the words in this group are often used for the plans or purposes of God, most often in punishing people for their planned wickedness (see Jer. 23:20; 30:24; 51:11; Zech. 1:6). In the last passage the people acknowledged that the LORD had done to them (the captivity) just as he had planned, and in Zechariah 8:15 the verb describes how the LORD plans to do good things for his people.

32. A. A. Anderson takes the verb as a jussive: "Let them be caught . . . ." He bases this on the use of the plural verbs to refer to the collective noun, "the wicked" (*Psalms 1–72*, p. 114).

that he boasts (הָלַל; s.v. Ps. 33:1) according to the desires of his heart. This probably means that his desires, his evil schemes, are the boast—he praises his heart's desire. Whatever the wicked desire, they achieve and so boast about it. The verb is a characteristic perfect, as are the verbs "bless" and "revile" to follow; these express characteristic actions of the wicked, true in the past and present, but will not be true in the future.

Then, to demonstrate their misguided appreciation of things that are evil, the text says that the wicked man "blesses the robber (בֹּצֵעַ)." The robber need not be a highwayman, or a thief who breaks in and steals; he could be a greedy business person who is clever and ruthless, someone who might ruin the investments of others and yet walk away with a fortune. Wicked people have nothing but praise for the one who can take advantage of the hapless in order to be successful—it is the world they understand. If the wicked blesses the criminal, then he must of necessity revile the LORD who prohibits such activities. The word (נָאֵץ) can mean "despise, contemn, revile"; in contrast to "bless" it should mean revile. To "revile" goes beyond speaking evil of someone; it assumes a hatred and contempt. Of course, the irony is that people should bless the LORD and revile the robber.

In verse 4 the psalm describes insolence and impiety. The text literally says, "The wicked, according to the exaltedness of his face (כְּגֹבַהּ אַפּוֹ), says. . . ."[33] This is pride, the haughty look, the arrogant expression. His very appearance shows a scornful insolence. Such an arrogant person is convinced that God "does not require it" (בַּל־יִדְרֹשׁ), probably meaning that God does not call him to account for his crimes (see by contrast v. 13). In fact, the last line clarifies that he is a practicing atheist: "There is no God [is] all his devices." Everything the wicked schemes is characterized by the idea that there is no God to bring him to justice.

The course of life that he follows is sure; it appears strong and prosperous—as far as the world measures such things (the verb יָחִילוּ is related

---

33. The second word can, of course, be translated "anger", but "the exaltedness of his anger" would have to be paraphrased to mean that (in the opinion of the wicked) even when the LORD's anger is high he still does not demand anything from the wicked (see A. A. Anderson, *Psalms 1–72*, p. 114). In this context it is simpler to take the words to refer to the scornful proud expression on the face of the wicked.

to חַיִל, "strength, power"; s.v. Ps. 49:6). There seems to be no weak point, no wavering in his schemes and conduct. In fact, in his opinion, the decisions (מִשְׁפָּטִים; s.v. Ps. 9:4) of God are far above him, way out of his sight. In other words, God's decisions, even if there is a God, are unrelated to him and ineffective, so the will of God is not even considered in his decisions. One may contrast the way of the righteous, for the ways and the thoughts of God are ever before them (18:22, 23); but for the wicked, because there is no one preventing his evil schemes, he scorns all his adversaries. The verb is "puffs, blows"; it is a figure, perhaps a metonymy of adjunct, signifying disgust, contempt, or scorn, as in Malachi 1:13 where the evil priests likewise "sniff" at the ritual in contempt. He is so sure of himself, and so sure there will be no divine intervention, that he has no regard for anyone.

In fact, according to verse 6 he does not think he can be moved (בַּל־אֶמּוֹט; s.v. Ps. 62:2), that is, shaken from his course of action; and with this sense of security, he believes[34] that he will never have to face adversity or misfortune, not now, not in generations to come. Such a person is clearly blinded in his own pride and self-confidence by the immediate circumstances.

With such arrogance, such impiety, such malice against people, this wicked person reveals his character every time he opens his mouth. His mouth is full of cursing (אָלָה), possibly reckless, false swearing in this context (see 59:12–13; Hos. 4:20), deceit (מִרְמוֹת; s.v. Ps. 5:7), especially in any ventures he engages in, and injury or oppression (תֹּךְ, from תָּכָךְ).[35] Under his tongue (meaning either speech ready to be expressed or speech that is characterized by deceit) are things that can only bring trouble (עָמָל) and iniquity (אָוֶן; s.v. Ps. 28:3). The warning to people should be clear even in this part of the psalm. If an individual despises and denies God, denies any accountability for his deeds, boasts about triumphs at the expense of weaker people, then people would be warned to avoid any business dealings or social contacts with such a one.

---

34. If the word אָלָה is taken with this sentence and not with the next, and if it is taken to be a verb "he swears," the same as "he says," then the meaning would be that he vows never to face misfortune (see also Briggs, *Psalms,* I:86).

35. If "cursing" is removed from this verse, then that leaves a neater couplet of "deceit and injury" paralleled by "trouble and iniquity."

2. Their attacks are secretive and sudden (8–11). Now the psalmist turns to describe how the wicked attack the helpless. It is portrayed as an ambush. Verse 8 says the wicked sits in a hiding place by the village. This word "village" refers to an unenclosed area, making it vulnerable to any attack. What exactly the hiding place (מַאֲרָב) might be is unclear; it seems to describe any place of advantage from where the helpless and hapless person might be attacked by someone who lies in waiting. This is not an open confrontation but a secret attack. The text says that he watches secretly, as if treasuring the prospect, waiting for the right moment to slay him. The victim is called an innocent person (נָקִי; s.v. Ps. 19:13) and a weak or helpless person (חֵלְכָה), sometimes translated "hapless." and unsuspecting. The text says the intent is to slay the innocent person. This could be taken literally, of course, as people familiar with acts of terror are well aware. But it more likely refers to ruining the victim in the broader sense. One thinks of people who might seem to follow the letter of the law in their judicial proceedings, but pervert justice in the process, as in the judicial murder of Naboth over his vineyard (1 Kings 21). In this case there actually was a slaying of an innocent man, but it was made to look like a proper legal decision and all designed to satisfy the greed of Ahab for Naboth's property.

The lurking motif continues in verse 9. Now the wicked is compared to a lion in his lair, perhaps in his cover, waiting to catch the prey; he hides, or lurks (יֶאֱרֹב), to catch the afflicted, and he catches him "by drawing him in his net"(the infinitive describes how he catches them—drawing them in [בְּמָשְׁכוֹ]). Now the figure changes to that of a hunter with a net (an implied comparison); the wicked scheme secretly sprung on the victim is like a net, and the clever ploy will draw the innocent into it so that he is caught.[36] The result is the destruction of the helpless (v. 10). The verse describes the afflicted, first as "crushed" and then as "helpless." The first word is textually difficult. It could be read as a verb, "he is crushed," which might have "the helpless" as the subject: "the helpless is crushed and sinks down and falls . . . ." Or it could be subordinated to the next verb meaning

---

36. Recall that in 9:15 their feet are eventually caught in the net they have hidden.

"being crushed he sinks down and falls." The other reading could be explained as an adjective: "The crushed one sinks down . . . ." This would form a clean parallelism with the second colon.

The other word is also problematic. It (חֵלְכָה) occurs twice in the singular and once in the plural in this psalm. The word is likely related to a noun for "weakness," and so here means "helpless" or even "hapless." The afflicted person who is weak is no match for the planned attacks from the wicked, and so the imagery of the verbs reports the outcome: he sinks down and falls because of the strength of the enemy. The wicked are simply overpowering. In fact, the word for "strength" is written in the plural as an abstract plural to emphasize the idea. The weak and afflicted are simply overwhelmed. This is the psalmist's portrayal of the attack of the wicked.

The psalmist is not finished. He points out that the arrogant destroyer remains convinced he will get away with it. Verse 11 repeats the theme of verse 4, but with additional force. He says in his heart that "God has forgotten."[37] This suggests that he allows for the existence of a God, but not a God who intervenes in human affairs. To say God "has forgotten" means that he did not act on it.[38] He adds that God "hid his face" and "never saw it" (both anthropomorphisms), i.e., that God has withheld his favor from the afflicted and did not pay attention to the need. His thinking is that if there is a God he either could not or would not intervene.

It is not hard for the modern reader to think in terms of a wicked person, a powerful and ruthless person, or even a terrorist, who hides in secrecy to find innocent and helpless victims to ruin, for his own advantage or cause, and then boasts of the deeds among his friends and sympathizers and mocks God in the process. There is a sense of futility among the afflicted, for no matter how vigilant they might be, they are helpless against such attacks. But they have a sure recourse–God in heaven.

---

37. Recall that in 9:12 the psalmist says that the LORD does not forget the cry of the afflicted.

38. Likewise, to say that God remembers something means that he acts on what he remembers; or to say he remembers our sins no more means that he will not remember them against us. But God, being God, knows everything equally well.

II. The faithful can pray for God to help his people (12–15).

A. *They may pray for a sudden and powerful deliverance (12)*

With verse 12 we have an abrupt break in the tone of the psalm—a change from lamentation over the domination of the wicked to a prayer for God to come to the aid of his people. It is a cry for help and for vengeance. Recalling Psalm 9, Broyles says that this petition calls for God to re-enact his deeds that had earlier elicited praise.[39] The prayer starts boldly, "Arise, O LORD, lift up your hand! Do not forget the afflicted." Calling for God to arise (קוּמָה) is a way of calling for God to begin to act now (s.v. Ps. 3:1). It is a very human idea to call for God to arise, and it is a bold idea because it calls for God to cease his apparent indifference and inactivity. The appeal for God to lift his hand is a call for divine intervention. In fact, the act of lifting the hand could be interpreted as a divine act of hostility against the wicked.[40] The request that God not forget is a reversal of the false assumption of the arrogant and an appeal based on the confidence that God does not forget the afflicted (9:12). It is actually a call for God to remember, i.e., to act on behalf of his afflicted people. The afflicted are people who trust in the LORD and cry out to him for help; and the oppressors are wicked unbelievers who despise God and love violence. To the psalmist it was obvious what God should do, now, and not later.[41]

B. *They may base their appeal on the honor of God (13).*

The appeal is based on God's honor, which has been challenged by the blasphemies of the wicked. Why has the wicked person reviled God? Why should that be allowed to go unanswered? Why should the wicked be allowed to think that God will not call his sin into account? The psalmist's reason for God to intervene concerns the reproach of God's honor which is brought

---

39. Broyles, *Psalms,* p. 78
40. This idea may be illustrated from 2 Samuel 20:21 where we read how Sheba lifted up his hand against King David.
41. Recall that it is the LORD who remembers and who avenges (Ps. 9:12).

on by the insolence of the wicked in his apparently successful schemes. When God rescues his people, he will also rescue his reputation.

C. They may be sure that God does see and does intervene for his people (14).

In verse 14 the psalmist acknowledges that God is aware of the problem and is about to rescue them. The line reads, "You do see trouble and grief, // you consider *it* to take it into your hand."[42] The psalmist is making a strong protest against the words of the wicked. The wicked did not think God saw their wicked deeds, but the psalmist affirms that he did, for he always sees what people are doing (he is aware, and he is involved; see Pss. 33:13; 80:15). In this line the psalmist includes past interventions— "you have done this before, and it needs to be done again." And so, the helpless person leaves it to the LORD, who has been a helper to the orphan, perhaps the most vulnerable person, the one with the fewest resources. The word "helper" (עוֹזֵר) often describes God; it means that he is able to do for people what they cannot do for themselves (s.v. Ps. 46:1).

D. They may pray for God to destroy the wicked (15).

The prayer is repeated but now with far bolder images. The first petition is to "break the arm" of the wicked. The line should probably follow the sense rather than the accents and join "and the evil man" with this object: "Break the arm of the wicked and the evil man."[43] This likely includes a figure of speech, for

---

42. The first verb may be classified as a gnomic perfect since God always sees the affliction of the affliction, a fact the psalmist now acknowledges. The second verb may be parallel and so taken as a habitual imperfect, but a case can also be made for taking it as I future: because you see "you will show regard" by taking the matter in hand.

43. The word "evil" (רַע) is another major word for sin, and while it overlaps with רָשָׁע, it has a distinct meaning. There are several related words: a noun רֹעַ meaning "badness, evil"; the adjective רַע meaning "bad, evil"; a noun רַע and a feminine noun רָעָה meaning "evil, distress, misery"; and a denominative verb רָעַע "to be bad, evil." All of these words are used as a general

a literal meaning would not stop the wicked from planning and carrying out their evil schemes. The idea of breaking the arm means to break their power (cf. Ps. 44:3). The prayer is for God to destroy their ability to attack (a metonymy of cause, the arm being used in carrying out the schemes).

In the second colon the psalmist prays for God to seek out wickedness until no more can be found, i.e., wipe out wickedness completely. In this verse "seek out" would have more of the idea of "avenge" or "requite" (9:12), although "call to account" (as in 10:13) covers that. The point of the line is that the wickedness disappear. If God seeks it out and destroys it, then it will no longer be found. This may not seem like an appropriate prayer for New Testament believers; nevertheless, if believers pray for the LORD to come quickly, they are calling for him to come and judge the world and remove wickedness entirely.

III. The faithful can be confident that the LORD will vindicate them when he judges the wicked (16–18).

A. The faithful proclaim the sovereignty of the LORD (16).

Closing in hymnic style, the psalmist expresses his absolute confidence in the sovereignty of God in terms of divine kingship (a common theme in the psalms; e.g., 29:10; 47:7; 93:1). He

---

description of sin, but the passages where it is not specifically describing sin have the idea of "hurt" or "pain." The adjective can describe any number of things that are unpleasant, give pain, or cause misery—evil days (Gen. 47:9), evil report (Gen. 37:2), painful discipline (Prov. 15:10), bad water (2 Kings 2:19), bitter figs (Jer. 24:2), a sad heart (Prov. 25:20), and the verb likewise can refer to something displeasing (Jon. 4:1), or being sad (Deut. 15:10), or living in adversity and toil (Exod. 5:19) and the like. What is "evil" is unpleasant and either harmful to one's health and well-being, or simply not conducive to it. In this sense it is the opposite of "good," which describes things that promote, preserve, and enhance life and the enjoyment of it (e.g., Laban was not permitted to help or harm Jacob according to Genesis 31:52). "Feet that are quick to run to evil" (Prov. 6:18) certainly signifies eagerness to do harm. The numerous uses of the words for "evil" that describe hurt and unpleasantness in general indicate that when it refers to sin it has the connotation of causing pain and misfortune to other people.

proclaims that the LORD is king for ever and ever, in contrast to the temporary wickedness of people who are in the earth. The point is that this present evil age is temporary and limited, but the LORD's reign is eternal and universal.

The impact of this point is that the nations will perish out of his land (16b).[44] The verb is the perfect tense (אָבְדוּ), which may be taken as a prophetic perfect to refer to what will happen.[45] The Greek translation simply translated it as a future. In light of the fact that the psalm is a prayer for divine vindication, the future realization of this clause must be in the writer's mind.

B. The faithful may be confident that God will end all such terrifying wickedness (17–18).

In line with this is the last section of the psalm in which the writer expresses his confidence that God has heard the desire of the afflicted[46]—and their desire is that God will break the arm of the wicked and bring to naught the terror they cause. The verb is the perfect tense, perhaps expressing his confidence that God has heard the prayer of the afflicted. The next two verbs of the verse are imperfects, "you establish" and "you hearken." These imperfects may be classified as progressive imperfects, describing what God is now doing as a result of having heard— he is encouraging them and paying attention to their cries.

The desire of the afflicted is expressed more fully and finally in verse 18: "to defend (lit. to judge) the orphan and the broken person so that a mortal man of the earth may terrify no more."[47] The verb "judge" carries the sense of vindicate, for the orphan and the oppressed are the most vulnerable victims of the wicked oppression. If God destroys the wicked, the innocent victims will not only be rescued but vindicated in their faith in the LORD. The wicked in this verse are described as mere mortals (אֱנוֹשׁ may have the connotation of frail weak—no matter how strong someone might be,

---

44. Recall that in 9:7 the nations were rebuked.
45. It is also possible to take the verb as referring to what has happened down through the history of God's program of salvation.
46. Recall that in 9:18 we have the "hope of the afflicted."
47. The construction uses a verbal hendiadys, "may no longer add to terrify."

he is still from the earth, an earthly mortal). These are the tyrants of the world (see 9:10) who exalted themselves above everything godly, who thought they were invincible, who scorned the ability of God to demand anything of them. By calling them mortals of the earth, the psalmist pours contempt on them, indicating they are just mortal. In the final analysis, it is a case of mortal men versus the eternal king, earthly tyrants versus the God of heaven.

MESSAGE AND APPLICATION

If this Psalm 10 is developed as an exposition on its own, the beginning emphasis would certainly be on the lamentable plight of the afflicted faithful who have to endure the wicked oppression of ruthless and powerful people. In spite of the oppression and terror that this can bring, the faithful still pray with confidence to God to destroy the wicked and rescue the faithful, knowing that he will do that very thing because he is the eternal king and divine judge. We may provisionally summarize the idea of Psalm 10 by saying, *Even though wicked and powerful people terrify, oppress and even destroy the weak, the afflicted people of God may pray with confidence for divine justice because the LORD is the eternal and righteous King.* The focus would be on prayer as the only and best recourse of the righteous in a wicked world. That is the best recourse since the LORD is the eternal king of glory and the righteous judge of the whole earth.

If Psalms 9 and 10 were to be developed as one expository message, the message would have to be very well organized to cover all the basic ideas and deal with specific issues. In working up an expository outline, the main ideas of each psalm would become the major points, and the major points in each psalm would then be the subpoints.

I. Because God has demonstrated his righteousness by judging the wicked, believers may praise him for his protection now and trust him for vindication in the future (Ps. 9).

　A. God is to be praised because he has demonstrated his righteousness by protecting his people and destroying the wicked (9:1–12).

B. God is to be trusted because he will judge the wicked and fulfill the hope of the affliction who take refuge in him (9:13–20).

II. Because wicked and powerful men have oppressed and destroyed the weak, believers may pray with confidence for divine justice, knowing that God is the eternal king and righteous judge (Psalm 10).
   A. God's people must live in a world that is terrorized and oppressed by wicked and impious people (10:1–11).
   B. God's people may pray for deliverance with confidence because the LORD does not forget his people (10:12–15).
   C. God's people may expect vindication when the LORD, the eternal king, destroys the wicked from the earth (10:16–18).

Then, for this whole message, a homiletical idea may be developed that captures the essence of the passage. It will have to be broad enough to cover the two psalms but short enough to be understood in an exposition. *The afflicted people of God triumphantly overcome the tyranny of the wicked because God has demonstrated his loving care for them in the past, hears their cries for help in the present, and will vindicate them in the future when he comes to judge the wicked.* The call would be for believers to rejoice in his past protection and his promise of future vindication, trust him fully during times of oppression and danger, pray earnestly for his promised deliverance through the judgment on the wicked, and build confidence in him as the Most High God, righteous judge, and eternal king.

In the New Testament the Lord Jesus Christ is declared to be the Son of the Most High, the coming king, and the judge of the whole world. When he returns in glory, he will judge the wicked and vindicate the righteous in order to establish an eternal kingdom of righteousness and peace in which he is both worshiped and glorified. For that the saints of all ages have watched and prayed. In the meantime, in a world that could easily terrify them, and often manages to afflict them and even destroy them, the faithful praise God for every evidence of his care and deliverance and pray for his continued present to be manifested in acts of deliverance.

PSALM 11

Holding Fast to the Faith

INTRODUCTION[1]

Text and Textual Variants

1 For the Chief Musician. Of David.

In the LORD I have taken refuge.
   How can you say to me,[2]
      "Flee[3] like a bird to your mountain;[4]
2 For look, the wicked bend their bow;
   they set their arrow[5] on the string
      to shoot in the darkness at the upright of heart.
3 If the foundations are being destroyed,[6]
   what can the righteous do?"

---

1. Isaiah Sonne, "Psalm 11," *JBL* 68 (1949):241–245; J. Morgenstern "Psalm 11," *JBL* 69 (1950):221–31.
2. Literally, "to my soul."
3. The form נוּדִי is a *K^ethiv–Q^ere'* reading. *K* is the masculine plural imperative; *Q* is the feminine singular for grammatical agreement. *Q* is supported by most of the manuscripts, the Greek, Syriac, Targum, and Aquila. The English translation is not changed.
4. For "your mountain" (הַרְכֶם) the Greek version has ἐπὶ τὰ ὄρη ὡς, "to the mountains like," apparently reading הַר כְּמוֹ (or הָרִים כְּ).
5. Greek has βέλη, "arrows" (reading חִצִּים) instead of MT חִצָּם, "their arrow."
6. The Greek reads ἃ κατηρτίσω καθεῖλον, "they have pulled down that which you framed," probably reading הַשָּׁתוֹת יֶהֱרְסוּן.

4 The LORD is in his holy temple;
   the LORD, in the heavens is his throne.
   His eyes examine,[7]
     his eyelids try the sons of man;
5 The LORD examines the righteous,
     but the wicked and the one who loves violence
       his soul hates.
6 May he rain traps[8] on the wicked, fire and burning sulfur
     and a scorching hot wind will be the portion of their cup.
7 For the LORD is righteous; he loves righteousness;
     the upright[9] will see his face.

Composition and Context

One can only speculate on what situation might have been the
occasion for the writing of this psalm. Of the various suggestions Bellinger's idea that the psalm is originally concerned
with seeking asylum but then finds a wider application is

---

7. The Greek adds εἰς τὸν πένητα, "[look] upon the poor."

8. The Hebrew word פַּחִים means "traps," such as "bird traps." It would refer
   to any kind of traps, and here would be a general term leading into the
   words for fire and burning sulfur. W. VanGemeren concludes that the word
   "snares" followed by "fire" is meaningless (*Psalms*, p. 164). Most modern
   commentaries change the text from the noun פַּח in the plural to the noun
   פֶּחָם, "coal." But the only version that would support this is Symmachus. All
   the other manuscripts and versions have "traps" (παγίδας). The suggestion requires the last two letters be reversed, and the form should be read
   as פַּחֲמֵי , "coals of [fire]." This change obviously makes very good sense in
   the verse. However, if the original text had "coals of," it is hard to explain
   why a scribe would change it to "traps," a word that does not harmonize
   with the other words (unless he accidentally reversed the letters). But if
   the original was "traps," one could explain a scribal interest in changing it
   to "coals," just as the modern versions have done. The solution may lie in
   reading the words separately (see commentary).

9. The line is a little difficult in that "the upright" is singular, and must be interpreted as a collective (which is unusual for this word). The Greek reads,
   "his face beholds uprightness" (εὐθύτητα, reading יֹשֶׁר instead of יָשָׁר, "the
   upright"). Broyles suggests that in addition to this Greek rendering it could
   also be translated "his face will see the upright one," as well as the MT's
   "the upright (ones) will see his face" (cf. Ps. 17:15; *Psalms*, p. 81).

plausible.[10] He sees the arrangement of the psalm following in three parts, a lament, an expression of trust, and thanksgiving, although the thanksgiving is somewhat subdued. If David wrote the psalm there are several occasions that would fit the idea of seeking safety, some event in his conflict with Saul or Absalom perhaps.

The psalm has nine lines of poetry, the first four presenting the temptation to flee in view of the danger, and the last five the psalmist's confident faith expressed in answer to the temptation. The temptation to flee from the enemies forms a crisis of faith. The psalmist asks, "How can you say to me, 'Flee like a bird to your mountain'." He is quoting others, but the question is where the quotation ends. If it includes verses 2 and 3, the temptation would be that he is to flee because the enemies will uproot the foundations of society, and he, the righteous, would be helpless. On the other hand, if the psalmist is speaking in verse 3, he would be answering them by saying that without the foundations he could do nothing, the foundations referring to his faith in the LORD. Both of these ideas are possible, but the first seems more probable. They ask what the righteous can do if the foundations are destroyed, and David responds that they can take refuge in the LORD. So then, beginning with verse 4 there is a definite change of tone to that of noted assurance which enforces this confident answer.

Exegetical Analysis

Summary

Resisting the temptation to flee at a time when the destruction of lawful authority seems imminent, the psalmist holds fast to his faith in the LORD who loves righteousness and will ultimately destroy the wicked.

Outline

I. The psalmist resists the temptation to flee when the destruction of lawful authority seems imminent (1–3).

---

10. W. H. Bellinger, "The Interpretation of Psalm 11," *Ev Q* 56 (1984):95–101.

A. David is surprised by the temptation since he trusts in the LORD (1a).
B. David reports the temptation he has received to flee from the danger of the wicked (1b–3).
   1. He should flee like a bird (1a).
   2. He should flee because the wicked attempt to destroy the upright (2).
   3. He should flee because the safety of the saint is hopeless in view of the imminent chaos (3).
II. The psalmist reiterates his firm faith in the LORD who examines all people and will ultimately destroy the wicked because he loves righteousness (4–7).
A. David contrasts the problem on earth with the sovereign authority of the LORD in heaven (4a).
B. David contrasts the attacks of the wicked with their ultimate judgment (4b–6).
   1. God thoroughly investigates the righteous (4b–5a).
   2. God will thoroughly judge the wicked whom he hates (5b–6).
C. David explains that the righteous who trust in him will ultimately triumph because the LORD loves righteousness (7).

COMMENTARY IN EXPOSITORY FORM

I. God's people hold fast to their faith in the LORD when the social order is threatened (1–3).

A. The faithful take refuge in the LORD (1).

The psalmist begins with a strong expression of faith: "In the LORD I have taken refuge." The verb "take refuge" (חָסָה; s.v. Ps. 7:1) means to turn aside or away from something to seek shelter or protection; there is therefore an implied comparison between the physical act of taking refuge and the spiritual act of trusting the LORD for protection. The present perfect nuance of the verb stresses that the psalmist's trust has continued throughout life.

This affirmation of faith provides the main response to the temptation to flee for safety, for the psalmist asks how they could suggest such a thing. There is no indication of who is telling him to flee, but since they speak about the wicked attacking the upright, one may conclude that these are well-wishers, people who have his best interests at heart. David's reply is in the form of a rhetorical question (erotesis) to express his amazement and rejection of their proposal—how can they suggest that he flee when he has taken refuge in the LORD?

The verb "flee" (נוּד) means "move to and fro, wander aimlessly, retreat, flee, fly away." Cognate meanings include Aramaic, "to shrink from," and later Arabic, "run away." The precise idea is clarified by the comparison (simile) to a bird—fly away to the mountain where it is safer, but the psalmist clearly thought that such a frightened flight was incompatible with his faith.

B. The faithful hold fast to their faith when law and order are threatened by anarchists (2–3).

The reason for the temptation is that the wicked were attacking the upright and destroying the foundations of society. The enemies are simply described as "the wicked" (רָשָׁע), a word that often means "the ungodly" in general, with the sense that they are guilty before God. Here they show their worst side, and so a translation "wicked" is appropriate (s.v. Ps. 1:1). Here it is put in the singular (and the nouns following likewise), but it refers to the group of attackers.

In their attack "they bend their bow and set their arrow on the string." These are descriptions of their preparation to shoot. Bending the bow, literally treading on the bow (יִדְרְכוּן), may refer to stepping on one end to bend the bow to put the string on each end. The nuance of the verb would be a progressive imperfect, for the action was going on at the time of speaking. The parallel verb "they set" (a *polel* כּוֹנְנוּ; s.v. Ps. 93:1) would then be a characteristic perfect, stating that they were now making ready their arrows on the string as they had before. The verbs convey a sense of extreme urgency because the enemies were preparing to attack. The purpose of their preparation is expressed with the infinitive clause "to shoot (לִירוֹת, from יָרָה) in the darkness at the upright of heart." David was clearly one of the devout believers, upright in heart because he trusted and served the LORD. If he fled, there would be little reason for the wicked to shoot at him. Fleeing would not be compatible with his faith in the LORD.

The verbs may very well be literal, indicating that a military attack was underway. It is also possible that the language is figurative, comparing shooting arrows to destructive speech (and so an implied comparison). Arrows can be used for bitter words (see Ps. 64:3) The condition of darkness might lend support to such an attack, since shooting arrows in the dark may pose a difficulty (unless "darkness" is figurative and means "secrecy"). The word "darkness" (אֹפֶל) appears only in poetry; it is related to a verb that means "disappear, depart, set (of the sun setting)." The term is used in Isaiah 29:18 for spiritual darkness and in Job 10:22 for darkness and gloom (of the underworld). Here the word is probably descriptive of the secrecy of the attack, but it is less likely that verbal attacks would have been sufficient reason for him to flee for safety to the mountain than an actual physical attack.

In verse 3 an additional reason is added for the advice to flee: "If the foundations are being destroyed, what can the righteous do?" The word "foundations" (הַשָּׁתוֹת, related to the verb שִׁית, "to put, set") is figurative for the established customs, laws, and ways of life in the land (so an implied comparison; see also Isa. 19:10). It refers to the stays of society, the things upon which the culture is built (like a foundation).[11] These were apparently in danger of being "thrown down" (הָרַס, a term used in Prov. 24:31 for throwing down stones of a wall). The appeal is that in the face of such anarchy, what can[12] the righteous do? The question is rhetorical (erotesis), meant to suggest that the righteous could do nothing to stop the destruction of law and order.

---

11. Perowne notes that the foundations or pillars of society could refer to principal persons in society, magistrates and leaders, or to the principles of law and order that were now being subverted (*Psalms,* p. 173).
12. The perfect tense in this line has a very rare nuance of potential perfect, "what can they do?"

II. The faith of God's people is in the sovereign authority of the LORD who loves righteousness and hates wickedness (4–7)

A. *The sovereign LORD examines everyone on earth (4).*

In the second half of the psalm David gives the divine alternative. Why should the righteous trust in the LORD? The first reason is that the holy LORD reigns from heaven over the affairs on earth. Verse 4 affirms that the LORD is in his holy temple and then clarifies that his throne is in the heavens. Describing the LORD's temple as holy (s.v. Ps. 22:3) sets it apart from anything earthly, physical, or profane—it is the heavenly temple. And the location of his throne (a metonymy for his kingship) in the heavens confirms his sovereignty over all the affairs of mankind. If one is concerned over the coming anarchy and how it might shake the foundations of society, then the only hope is faith in the sovereign and holy LORD who reigns from heaven, and that reign is unshakable. The confidence expressed in this half-verse is comparable to that described in Isaiah 6, for at a time when the king died, the prophet saw the LORD, the king, in his holy heaven, surrounded by angels who continually cried out, "Holy, holy, holy." The point is that the faithful fix their confidence on the heavenly sovereign and his plans, and not on earthly, human institutions anyway.

The second reason that the righteous should trust the LORD is his examination of the affairs of all people (4b). David states this point beautifully: "His eyes behold, his eyelids try, the sons of men." Speaking in human terms (anthropomorphisms), he describes God's close examination of people. The use of "eyes" is understandable, but "eyelids" is a little more difficult. It probably refers to the squinting that takes place in focusing closely on an object, the eyelids becoming involved with the eyes. Of course, God always knows what people are doing, but this verse states it in human terms of careful and close scrutiny to make the point. The two verbs stress the examination: the first, "behold" (חָזָה), means "to gaze, look intently, behold"; here it refers to divine investigation, meaning the full awareness by God of every detail of human life. The second verb, "examine" (בָּחַן; s.v. Ps. 139:23), conveys the idea of testing or trying something. The words together show that the knowledge of God is an evaluating knowledge, and because this is always true of God's knowledge, the verbs should be classified as habitual imperfects. David knew that the LORD was not only aware of all his actions but was also testing them; therefore, he wanted to make sure that he was operating by faith and not fear.

B. The sovereign LORD deals righteously with the righteous and the wicked (5–6).

In the next two verses the psalmist draws out the implications of God's penetrating knowledge of the affairs of people. He first focuses on the righteous (5a), and then on the wicked (5b–6). Concerning the righteous, he simply reiterates that God examines them. In this context, therefore, the LORD may have been testing David's faith with the threat of anarchy and persecution, for in the Bible they are often God's way of proving the faith of the believers.

The contrast is with the way God deals with the wicked (the text uses a strong disjunctive *waw:* "But the wicked"), which forms another reason for David's standing firm in his faith. With the wicked there is no proving or testing (that action applies where the LORD wants to develop a stronger faith in believers); here there is only repudiation and a warning of judgment. The objects of divine wrath are "the wicked and the one who loves violence."[13] The word "violence" (חָמָס; s.v. Ps. 58:2) refers to a variety of acts of violence, ranging from social injustices to injurious language. The wicked are people who ultimately promote such violence; they might call it something else—shrewd business dealings, social reformation, or even ethnic cleansing—but if it destroys people in the process, it is wicked violence. The psalmist declares that the LORD hates violence with all his being (literally, "his soul hates").[14] The verb "hates" (שָׂנְאָה; s.v.

---

13. The two words may be taken together as a *hendiadys:* "the wicked one who loves violence" rather than "the wicked" and "the lover of violence."

14. Throughout the Psalter we have this word נֶפֶשׁ, which has traditionally been translated "soul." For a helpful treatment of the word see Hans Walter Wolff, *Anthropology of the Old Testament* (Philadelphia: Fortress Press, 1974), pp. 10–25. The word has a number of different meanings

Ps. 139:21) a gnomic perfect here to express a universal truth, indicates that not only does God find their violence detestable,

---

that must be considered in the exposition of individual passages. "Soul" is not very often the proper translation. This can be seen from the outset in Genesis 2:7 where the body and the breath of life together constitute a living נֶפֶשׁ. It refers to the whole living being, body and spirit. Man does not have a נֶפֶשׁ—he is a נֶפֶשׁ. The word refers to the whole person, the body with all its physical and psychical appetites, but the contexts will determine the precise emphasis. Wolff lists and discusses the following meanings: The first is "throat." It can be used in passages to describe the organ that takes in food (Ps. 107:5, 9); or it can use the meaning figuratively for the underworld that opens its throat (Isa. 5:14). It can also emphasize the craving of the appetite or throat (Prov. 10:3), a thirsty throat (Prov. 25:25), or breathing (Job 11:20).

A second meaning close to this is "neck." Psalm 105:18 says it is put in iron along with the feet. In Jeremiah 4:10 a sword was at their necks, and in 1 Samuel 28:9 a noose can be put around it.

The third category is "desire." This captures what Wolff calls the view of needy man—he longs for things or desires things, good or bad. Proverbs 13:2 describes the נֶפֶשׁ of the treacherous as violence; it means their desire. Proverbs 16:26 says that the worker's desire for food is what keeps him working. It often used for the desire of things other than food, such as the land (Jer. 24:4) or a woman (Gen. 34:2).

Fourth is the meaning "soul." Here the word is used for the seat and action of other spiritual experiences and emotions. In this sense the נֶפֶשׁ can be afflicted (Ps. 31:7), be miserable (Isa. 53:11), bitter (1 Sam. 1:10) troubled in illness (2 Kings 4:27), or a host of other feelings as well (such as love, hate, grief, joy). For someone to love or hate with the whole soul means with the whole innermost being. So in Psalm 103:1 the psalmist calls on himself, and everything within him, to praise: "Bless the LORD, O my soul."

Fifth is the meaning "life." If the word describes the organ of vital needs within the body which have to be satisfied to keep on living, then it can mean the whole life itself. Psalm 30:3 uses it this way as the psalmist says God brought up his life from *sheol*. Leviticus 17:11 says it clearly: "the life (נֶפֶשׁ) of the flesh is in the blood." And it forms the expression in the law, "a life for a life" (Exod. 21:23ff.). In Job 2:4 the tempter says that all a man has he will give for his life, but the life is the whole person. If the "life" departs, the person stops breathing and the life vanishes, for the breath that was given to the body by God made the man a living נֶפֶשׁ.

Finally, it can be used as a pronoun. Often we find "my soul" in the text meaning "me." Genesis 12:13 has Abram saying "that my נֶפֶשׁ may live," meaning "that I may live." In the psalms it may be parallel to the pronoun: "God helps me, the LORD alone upholds my נֶפֶשׁ/me" (Ps. 54:4).

but he also rejects it, for to hate something is essentially to reject it, and to love something is to choose it.[15] Things that the LORD hates will be punished in the end because they are sinful and destructive.[16]

Verse six portrays the result of divine displeasure—judgment. The certain judgment of God is here expressed in the form of a wish or a prayer, "Upon the wicked may he rain" (יַמְטֵר is the *hiphil* jussive).[17] The psalmist uses an ordinary word for "rain" (here in the causative, "cause it to rain") to express divine judgment that will fall on the wicked (an implied comparison, for there will be no actual rain); he does this to portray the destruction of the wicked in a way that will be clearly seen as supernatural.

The first object of the verb does not harmonize with the others. The word in the Hebrew text means "snares," any kind of traps, such as bird traps. Perhaps the psalmist used this word to express the irony of it: he was tempted to flee like a bird, but God would soon send snares—bird traps—to catch them in their wickedness. When judgment falls, it is the wicked who will flee to the mountains for safety (see Matt. 24:16), but they will find no escape.

The line continues with several other words for the judgment that God will send: "fire, burning sulfur, and a scorching wind"—these will be the portion of their cup. The symbolism of the cup in the Bible is used for one's lot in life; it could be a cup of blessing (Pss. 23:5; 16:5)), or a cup of judgment, fury, and terror (Isa. 51:17). What is in store for the wicked is fire and brimstone and a scorching wind. The scorching wind (possibly the burning breath, as in Isa. 11:4) means a raging and burning heat, a figure for divine judgment. These descriptions may very well reflect an actual fiery judgment (and so a metonymy of either effect or adjunct) if the psalmist has in mind something like the divine

---

15. Thus one reads in Malachi how the LORD loved Jacob and hated Esau (1:1–6). It has to do with one line of the seed of Isaac being chosen and the other not chosen.

16. Proverbs 6:16–19 lists seven things that the LORD hates.

17. Prayer often takes a sure word from God and turns it into a request, such as praying for his kingdom to come. Here the psalmist knows that judgment will come on the wicked, and so by faith he prays for that.

judgment that was poured out on Sodom (perhaps caused by volcanic activity that spewed the fire upwards to rain down on the city, or perhaps some other means by which God poured out a consuming judgment on the wicked). Whether the psalmist was thinking of it or not, the passage anticipates the great judgment that will occur at the end of the age (Zech 14:12–15). If he had in mind a more immediate fulfillment as well, then we may not know exactly what form this divine judgment might have taken at the time. The words apply very well to the ultimate divine judgment on the wicked at the end of the age, so this is the outcome of the LORD's hating wickedness.

C. The sovereign LORD loves righteousness and will cause the righteous to triumph (7)

In the last verse the reason for the judgment is looked at from the other side: "The LORD is righteous, he loves righteousness."[18]

---

18. This psalm speaks of the LORD's judgment on those who love violence (v. 5) because he loves righteousness (v. 7). The word for "love" (אָהֵב) occurs in Scripture in a wide array of uses. Most often it describes the love of humans, but the objects vary. The love could be for other people, such as a son (Gen. 22:2) or a wife (Gen. 24:67) or of a master (Exod. 21:5), all signifying deep affection and commitment.

The object of the love could also be food (Gen. 27:4), drink (Prov. 21:17), or sleep (Prov. 20:13), which show more of a choice based on enjoyment than commitment. The love can also be for knowledge and righteousness and wisdom (Prov. 8:17, 21, and throughout the book). The devout love the Lord (Ps. 5:11), Jerusalem (Ps. 122:6) and its courts and activities.

The object of the love could also be misplaced: it can be carnal desire based only on physical attraction (2 Sam. 13:1, 4), or it can be used as here for the love of folly (Ps. 11:5), and of course idolatry and false gods (Hos. 4:18).

"Love" becomes an important covenant word. Even in the political relationships of the countries of the ancient Near East we find this use. Hiram of Tyre, for example, loves David, meaning probably that they had a political relationship primarily (1 Kings 5:15). "Love" was also used in Israel to express loyalty to the king (1 Sam. 18:16). When the people of Israel were commanded to love the LORD their God (Deut. 5:10; 6:5), they were being called to a commitment to keep the covenant based on their love and devotion to the LORD. That love would also be shown through faithful acts to neighbors and foreigners (Lev. 19:18). These uses emphasize an act of

Because the LORD is righteous, wickedness cannot stand; because the LORD loves righteousness, he hates wickedness. For actions to be called "righteous" they must conform to God's standard, for he alone is truly righteous. Whatever does not measure up to this standard is sin. Thus, the promise of judgment is the immediate effect from the wickedness of the race, but the primary cause is God's righteous nature.

The psalm concludes with a promise of great triumph for those who are upright: "they shall behold his face." In one sense this line could simply mean that the righteous would see God's favor in defending and delivering them, for the "face" of God is used figuratively for divine favor (Num. 6:22–27; Ps. 30:7; 31:16). The psalmist may very well have more in mind than this; he may here be expressing the hope of the believers of all ages that someday they will see God (see Ps. 17:15; Job 19:26). That would be the greatest victory for the righteous, especially in contrast to the lot of the wicked.

MESSAGE AND APPLICATION

The central message of this psalm could be worded this way: *Faced with the breakdown of law and order with attacks from the wicked, the righteous must stand firm in their faith in the sovereign God who reigns and judges from above.* The psalm describes anarchy, wickedness in high places, and attacks on the righteous in this description of godless society. It is not all bleak; the righteous know that God is sovereign, that he loves the righteous, and that he will eventually set things right. God reigns

---

the will to live as a faithful community. Likewise, Jesus told his disciples and us that if we loved him we would keep his commands (John 14:15).

Covenant love is the proper response to the love of God for his people. Malachi reminded his audience that God loved Jacob but hated Esau. This means that the LORD chose Israel and made a covenant with them so that they would be a holy nation, but he did not make a covenant with the Edomites. Because the LORD is righteous, he loves righteousness and hates evil (Ps. 11:7; 33:5). His anointed king likewise loves righteousness and hates wickedness (Ps. 45:7). Accordingly, those who love the LORD are expected to demonstrate their covenant loyalty by hating evil (Ps. 97:10).

from heaven; it is his kingdom. He may allow evil to exist for a short while, but in the end he will destroy it.

But in the meantime the wicked have to be endured. There are times when one is tempted to flee, but if that is done out of fear and not by faith, it is wrong. The believer must live by faith, and that includes knowing when to leave and when to stay. By staying one can champion righteousness in the midst of a corrupt society, even though there will be malicious attacks and persecution. The believer must not give in to a corrupt environment, and if by remaining faithful the believer suffers for it, at least the suffering will be for righteousness's sake.

If believers are absolutely convinced that the sovereign God reigns from heaven and that some day he will destroy the wicked, then they may be courageous in the face of antagonists. Jesus warns his disciples that he is sending them as sheep among wolves (Matt. 10:16–20; cf. Acts 20:29), but he tells them that they should stand firm in the faith and not fear those who only have power over the body (Matt. 10:28), but fear the LORD who has power over body and soul. The servants of the LORD faced with such life-threatening opposition must respond with faith, faith that the LORD is ruling over the affairs of humans and will provide wisdom to decide what is the best way to respond to any given situation. For example, the apostle Paul endures much suffering in his service of the LORD as he stands up for the faith, but for the sake of continued service he also finds it wise to escape over the wall in a basket (see 2 Cor. 11:24–33).

PSALM 12

Truth in a World of Deception

INTRODUCTION

Text and Textual Variants

To the Chief Musician. Upon the Octave.
A Psalm of David.

1 Save,[1] O LORD, for the godly one has ceased,
   for the faithful[2] have vanished[3] from among the
       population.[4]
2 Everyone speaks lies, each one with[5] his neighbor;
   they speak with flattering lips and a double heart.
3 May the LORD cut off all flattering lips,
   the tongue that speaks great boasts,
4 those who say, "With our tongue we will do heroic things;[6]
   our lips are with us, who is LORD over us?"

---

1. Greek adds "me" (me).
2. The word is אֱמוּנִים and refers to people who are faithful, who can be trusted to keep their word. It is parallel to "the godly" and so refers to "the faithful," not "truths" (Greek has αἱ ἀλήθειαι).
3. The verb פַּסּוּ does not occur elsewhere; some suggest סָפוּ as with Psalm 73:19. The Greek has "is diminished" or "became scarce" (ὠλιγώθησαν).
4. The Hebrew rendered literally says, "the sons [children] of man," which may give a different impression.
5. The Hebrew has אֶת; the Greek makes it a bit smoother with "to" (πρὸς).
6. The Hebrew לִלְשֹׁנֵנוּ we may read "over our tongue (we are powerful)," or "as to our tongue (we are powerful)." The Greek version takes this as the accusative (as if reading simply לְשֹׁנֵנוּ): "we will magnify our tongue" (τὴν γλῶσσαν ἡμῶν).

349

5 On account of the violence[7] against the poor
   because of the groaning of the poor,
"Now I will arise," says the LORD,
   "I will set him in the safety for which he longs."[8]

6 The words of the LORD are pure words,
   like silver refined in a furnace in the earth,[9]
   purified seven times.
7 You, O LORD, will keep them,[10]
   you will preserve us from this generation forever.
8 The wicked walk to and fro on every side
   as worthlessness is exalted[11] among the population.[12]

---

7. The Greek translates this as "misery" (possibly looking at the effect of the violence).

8. The last two words simply say "he longs [pants] for it [safety]" (יָפִיחַ לוֹ). The Greek has something like "I will speak [to them] of it openly" (παρρησιάσομαι ἐν αὐτῷ). Symmachus has ἐμφανείς. Goldingay suggests a reading for the line: "I will take my stand as deliverance, he witnesses to him." He means by "deliverance" "deliverer." And he takes the verb from a second root פוּח, "witness" (*Psalms 1–41,* p. 195). This translation is not very compelling as a solution to a difficult line. See further Patrick D. Miller, "*Yapiah* in Psalm xii 6," *VT* 29 (1979):495–501; and J. G. Janzen, "Another Look at Psalm xii 6," *VT* 54 (2004):157–64.

9. The term עֲלִיל is a furnace for smelting, but the difficulty is with the next expression, לָאָרֶץ, which is often translated "of earth," meaning the material of the furnace. That would be unusual for the Hebrew expression, so a translation "belonging to" (fixed in or upon) the earth is more likely (see Perowne, *Psalms,* I:179).

10. The Hebrew suffix is ם- , "them"; but the Greek has "us" (ἡμᾶς), probably by harmony with the next line. The suffix there is נוּ-, either "him" or more likely in this passage "us."

11. The verb זָלַל means "weak, slack, languid," and so this word refers to what is contemptible or vile. The clause reads "according to the exaltation of worthlessness" (כְּרֻם זֻלּוּת). The Greek text has something very different: "according to your exalted state you have greatly regarded the sons of men" (κατὰ τὸ ὕψος σου ἐπολυώρησας τοὺς υἱοὺς τῶν ἀνθρώπων). The editors propose כְּרָמָה זֻלּוֹת. Other suggestions emend the text to read things like "constellations" (*mazzalot*) as objects of worship (see W. E. March, "A Note on the Text of Psalm xii 9," *VT* 21 [1971]:610–12), or "vineyard with spoils" (P. Wernberg–Moller, "Two Difficult Passages in the Old Testament," *ZAW* 69 [1957]:69–73).

12. Hebrew: "the sons of man."

Composition and Context

It would be difficult to single out any specific time that would be the occasion of this psalm. It says the majority of the people had chosen deceit, slander, and false flattery over honesty, and in the process mistreated the poor. Kraus, following Jorg Jeremias, suggests a late pre-exilic time based on similarities with Habakkuk 1 and other passages.[13] If the psalm is Davidic, however, it may indicate that the king had to endure more deceit and dishonesty in his court than most people could imagine, especially from those who despised him. The psalmist was surrounded by so many who spoke lies, having double hearts, saying one thing and meaning another, it seemed that all the faithful people had vanished. Whatever the exact situation, the psalm indicates that there was a smaller number of people who were faithful to God—and they longed for deliverance from the corruption of the time. In this the psalm is timeless: the world today is still filled with liars and false flatterers so that the righteous do not know who they can trust. The psalm affirms that only God's word can be trusted.

The psalm begins with a cry to God for help, followed by an outpouring of the lament that describes the rampant dishonesty (1–4). This is followed by a declaration from God to remedy the situation on behalf of those who are vulnerable (5). The rest of the psalm records the confidence the psalmist has in the pure word of God and how that word from God promises deliverance for those who suffer when vileness is exalted in the land. These last verses are essentially praise for the LORD's words and express confidence in the promise of deliverance. All the elements of a lament are present, except the closing vow; but the psalm does not follow the normal pattern of a lament psalm. Kraus says it is a prayer song in which an oracle has been incorporated.[14]

All commentators agree that this oracle (v. 5) is the focal point of the entire psalm. A. A. Anderson suggests that in the psalm's cultic use the oracle may have been said by a priest or

---

13. Kraus, *Psalms 1–59,* p. 208
14. Ibid., p. 207.

a cultic prophet, and the rest of the psalm repeated by the con-gregation.[15] A prophet may have participated in the service by declaring this message of salvation, but in the original setting it would have been revealed to the prophet–psalmist, otherwise it would have no authority.

Exegetical Analysis

Summary

In the midst of a culture that oppresses the poor with lies, false flattery, and arrogance, the psalmist expresses confidence in the pure word of God which assures him that the LORD will protect those who look to him for safety.

Outline

I. The psalmist prays for deliverance from arrogant liars and deceivers at a time when integrity seems to have disappeared (1–4).
   A. The psalmist prays to the LORD for deliverance in a completely corrupt culture (1).
   B. The psalmist laments over the lies and flatteries he hears around him (2).
   C. The psalmist prays that the LORD will destroy these ar-rogant and impious people (3, 4).
II. The LORD speaks: He assures the psalmist that he will deliver the poor who trust him for deliverance from oppression (5).
III. The psalmist expresses confidence in the untarnished word of God in the midst of a wicked world that exalts worthlessness (6–8).
   A. The psalmist describes the LORD's words as pure words (6).
   B. The psalmist expresses confidence that the LORD will preserve the poor as he promised (7).

---

15. Anderson, *Psalms 1–72*, p. 126.

C. The psalmist acknowledges the presence of the wicked round about him (8).

COMMENTARY IN EXPOSITORY FORM

I. The righteous can only turn to God for deliverance when deception and fraud replace faithfulness in the land (1–4).

A. *Their prayer is most urgent when faithfulness vanishes from the land (1).*

The psalm begins with the urgent cry, the imperative "save" (הוֹשִׁיעָה from יָשַׁע, s.v. Ps. 3:2). It is the common word for "save" with the sense of deliver, set free, liberate. The reason for this petition is that the godly have ceased (the present perfect nuance of the verb גָּמַר), that is, they are no longer present. And parallel to this is the explanation that "the faithful" have vanished. The use of the word "faithful" (passive participle of אָמַן) is instructive, for it has the clear idea of being reliable or trustworthy; the word is related to the word "truth" (אֱמֶת; s.v. Ps. 15:2). People who are reliable, who can be trusted in what they say or do, appear to have vanished (פַּסּוּ, a word that occurs only here, but that occurs in a cognate language with the meaning "blot out, do away with"). Living in a land where faithfulness and godliness have all but vanished and duplicity and fraud are rampant would have been oppressive and dangerous. No wonder the psalmist cried out to God.

B. *Their prayer is most urgent when deception and duplicity are prevalent (2).*

The second verse is the other side of the lament in verse one: the faithful may have all but vanished, but liars and frauds have not—they seem to have taken over. The psalmist's first observation is that everyone[16] speaks lies to his neighbor. The nuance of

---

16. The verb is the third person form, "they speak," but the noun is singular and so to be taken as "everyone."

the verb indicates that this is characteristic of people. Even with their neighbors they cannot speak the truth. "Lies" is a word often translated "vain" or "vanity" (שָׁוְא, as in the ten commandments [Exod. 20]), but it also has the sense of a false purpose, or deception (as evidenced by its use to describe false gods; Jon. 2:9; s.v. Ps. 127:1). Conversations were at best worthless, and at worst dishonest. In short, conversation had no good purpose.

The second half of the verse adds that they speak with flattering lips. Literally, this means they speak with smoothness. They say the right things that people want to hear. Their flattering (i.e., their smooth talk) lips come from a double heart (literally, "with a heart and a heart"). Hebrew uses the repetition here to express two different kinds of things (such as "a weight and a weight," meaning two different kinds of weights [Deut. 25:13]). So the expression (בְּלֵב וָלֵב), "with a heart and a heart," means two different intentions (a double–dealing heart).[17] What they said sounded flattering; but they were of another heart, intending something totally different, and so their words were deceptive. The false flattery might have been well-intentioned, or it might have been malicious. In David's case it might have been court flattery, but even such flattery is dishonest.

C. The urgent prayer is for God to destroy arrogance and deception (3–4).

The psalmist began the psalm with a cry for the LORD to deliver from the arrogant liars. The LORD will do this by removing the problem, the arrogant liars. Now he prays that the LORD will cut them off (יַכְרֵת). The verb form, a jussive, could simply express the desire of the psalmist, but in this section of the psalm it seems more likely that it is a part of the petition. He is praying for God to cut them off. The exact meaning of the verb "cut off" is not always easy to determine. Excision as a punishment in the Law could refer to excommunication from the community, physical death carried out by the community, or destruction by divine intervention. It is unlikely here that David simply wants

---

17. *Gesenius' Hebrew Grammar*, ed. by E. Kautsch, trans. by A. E. Cowley (Oxford: Oxford University Press, 1910), par. 123f.

them removed from the community; his prayer is more urgent and his appeal is for justice in the land. The particular liars he describes in this verse are not simply people who are flattering one another harmlessly. They are arrogant boasters who deflect any challenge to their hubris. They were a threat to society, and David asks God to destroy them

In this section "flattering lips" is repeated but now joined with "the tongue that speaks great things" (simply גְּדֹלוֹת). In view of the following lines, one would have to say that these great things they were saying were not magnanimous; they were not announcing great initiatives to help the poor and needy. No, they were boasting of their own ambitions and plans, while at the same time smoothing things over for the people to hear. It was all very deceptive. Their boast is expressed more fully in verse 4: "With our tongue[18] we shall do heroic things, our lips are with us, who is lord over us?" Here we learn that they were unwilling to submit to any authority; in fact, they denied that there was anyone who could have authority over them, and so they say ("tongue" being a metonymy of cause) great things. The verb (גָּבַר) basically means "to be strong, to be mighty" (s.v. Ps. 45:3), but in this form (a *hiphil* imperfect) it means that they will do great things. The expression "with reference to our tongue we give great strength" means that they had control over what they said, and the freedom to say anything they wanted (like a media controlled for propaganda). Delitzsch says that if any authority were to assert itself over them, their mouth would put it down and their tongue would thrash it into submission.[19] They firmly believed that their lips belonged to them, that they had the right to say what they wanted, and answer to no one. When such arrogance is joined with deception, there is no limit to the destruction that can follow.

II. The word from the LORD promises to deliver those who seek safety from such tyranny (5).

Until now David has been speaking to God; but now, as

---

18. The expression "with our tongue" (לִלְשׁוֹנֵנוּ) is difficult in view of the preposition. It could be taken to mean "over our tongue we have power," meaning that they could say what they liked. Or, it could mean "with reference to our tongue we have power." This second use seems to make the most sense.
19. Delitzsch, *Psalms,* I:195.

Perowne says, "David, instead of expressing his own feeling of confidence that God will answer him, seems as it were to hear God speaking."[20] The sentence begins with the reason for the promise of divine intervention: "Because of (מִן in a causal sense) the violence of the poor," meaning, the violence against the poor ("poor" or "afflicted" being the objective genitive; s.v. Ps. 9:12); and parallel to this is the statement: "because of the groaning of the needy" ("needy" now being the subjective genitive—they were doing the groaning). Putting the synonymous parallelism together we learn that tyrants were doing violence to the poor, and the poor were groaning, and God responded because of it all.

"Now" expresses the decisive turning point in God's dealings with his people, from forbearance to deliverance. The verb "I will arise" expresses the beginning of the divine action (s.v. Ps. 3:1). And that intervention was to set the people in safety who "long for it." This expression poses some difficulty, for which there are many proposals. The line literally says, "I will set [him] in safety he pants for it" (יָפִיחַ לוֹ, the *hiphil* imperfect of פּוּחַ, "to breathe out"). The last clause is written without a relative pronoun, but it clarifies either the object "safety" or it restricts the indirect object of the verb "set" in the first part.[21] It means the people who desire God's intervention for relief from the tyranny and deception of others.

III. The words of God are faithful and true, the only source of comfort in a world that exalts vileness (6–8).

In the last three verses David expresses his confidence in the words of the LORD. It is not a subjective feeling that he has about God's words; it is a fact that his words have been proven to be pure. In a world where it is difficult to believe what anyone says, friends or enemies, it is a comfort to know God's word is completely trustworthy, especially as it promises deliverance for the people of God.

---

20. Perowne, *Psalms,* I:177.
21. Perowne says it should either be taken as "for which (meaning the safety) he pants," or "that he may recover breath," the לוֹ being used in a reflexive sense (Ibid., I:179).

The declaration is that the words of God are pure words. "Pure" (טָהוֹר) is a term that is more at home in the ceremonial laws of Israel; it conveys the idea or being ceremonially clean, without flaws or defects of any sort (s.v. Ps. 51:10). God's word is clear, direct, true and reliable. To make his point David uses the image of refining ore in a furnace in the earth. In the process impurities would be removed from the metal being refined. It might take several attempts before all the impurities were removed. David is making a comparison with that process here: it is as if the word of God had been put through such a process to remove all impurities, such as misleading or deceptive statements, and that process was done to perfection—hence, seven times, the number of completion and perfection. Obviously the word of God was never at a stage where there were impurities in it. David is simply emphasizing how perfect the word of God is. It can be trusted completely in everything it says. It is the only word that can be so trusted.

Because God's word is pure, what that word has promised is certain. Thus, verse 7 reiterates the psalmist's expectation that God will preserve them from their particular generation. "Generation" (דּוֹר) can describe the general character of a group of people who share the spirit of the age (e.g., "a generation of vipers"). It does not here simply describe those who lived at a certain time, but those who shared the spirit of the time, which in this case was arrogance and deception.[22] How long will God preserve his people? Forever.[23] He does not say that God will immediately remove the problem, but God will preserve his people through it.[24] As VanGemeren says,

---

22. Briggs, *Psalms,* I: 97.
23. Dahood takes "forever" as a title for the LORD, and translates it "O Eternal One" (*Psalms,* I:72).
24. The verb שָׁמַר is commonly used with reference to God's protective care; it has the general meanings of "observe, keep, preserve." Verbal forms could be used for a number of things, from devotion, i.e., meticulously observing religion practices (Jon. 2:9), to retaining someone in custody (Gen. 37:11), to night watchmen (Ps. 130:6). Related nouns illustrate these ideas: מִשְׁמָר is a "prison"; מִשְׁמֶרֶת is a "guard, watch"; אַשְׁמֹרֶת is "watch," referring to a period of time (Judg. 7:19), and שְׁמֻרָה is an "eye-lid."

   The first category of meaning is "observe" (with the eye). Here the use of the participle for night watchmen would apply (Ps. 130:6). Watching is often connected with the idea of waiting (Jer. 20:10).

   A second and closely related category has the meaning of "preserve" by observing, i.e., keeping laws and customs. Here we find expressions

"God's guarding his people is a reality even when the wicked walk around like kings.[25]

Verse nine is a stark reminder that the ungodly are everywhere. This is only to be expected when a society exalts worthlessness. The word rendered "worthlessness" (זֻלּוּת, from זָלַל) is a difficult word to define; its cognates support the idea that it describes that which is contemptible and vile, morally as well as socially, characterized by shameful excess as well as worthlessness (cf. Jer. 15:19; Prov. 23:20; Deut. 21:20).[26] In any age, one need only look at what a society holds up as important, fascinating, or exemplary; and if it is vile and worthless, then one can see why the righteous need to pray, trust in the word of God, and live by it. That word promises God will destroy all such arrogance and dishonesty; but until then, he promises to set his people in safety.

---

about keeping a covenant (Ezek. 17:14). This usage may include the ideas of meticulous keeping of laws, vows, and holy days (see Deut. 5:12; 23:24; Jer. 35:18; Gen. 18:19; Neh. 13:14). Meticulously observing religious practices would be part of this idea (Jon. 2:9). It was also used for keeping something in memory (Gen. 37:11) or storing up food (Gen. 41:35).

A third category means "protect." This meaning may be expressed with a translation "guard" or "protect," but the objects are very different. It is used for the cherubim guarding the way to the tree of life (Gen. 3:24); the LORD guarding a city (Ps. 127:1); and Amasa, we are told, not on guard (the *niphal*) against Joab's sword (2 Sam. 20:10). The guarding or protecting could have the connotation of restraining something, such as an ox from harming others (Exod. 21:36), or the mouth from harming others (Prov. 22:23). In a spiritual context, Malachi warns the people to "take heed," watch themselves, so that they do not deal treacherously (Mal. 2:15, 16).

This idea of "protect" ("keep" or "guard") is used for the LORD's protection of his people as well (see the priestly benediction in Num. 6:24). The LORD is known as "the keeper of Israel," the result of which is protection from harm (Ps. 121). God may do this by assigning angels to guard his people (Ps. 91:11); or he himself may protect his people from all dangers, as he did through the wilderness years (Josh. 24:17). People may lock their doors and windows, but ultimately their safety comes from the watchful care of the LORD. If God protects his people from evil enemies, he may do it by destroying the enemies or by enabling his people to overcome them.

25. VanGemeren, *Psalms*, p. 169.
26. See Perowne, *Psalms,* p. 179.

MESSAGE AND APPLICATION

The expository idea drawn from this passage could be written like this: *In a world that lives by deception and tyranny, God's words are the only true words.* It would be easy to relate the message of this psalm to the world today; deception, false flattery, fraud, propaganda, and double talk dominate. Dishonesty functions on all levels, but it becomes malicious when people in positions of power or authority use it to destroy the weak. Who can people trust? What can they read that is true, that is nothing but the truth? The word of God. Kraus appropriately concludes, "The psalm shows how all things depend on God's word and how reliable and helpful this word actually is."[27]

God's word is pure. It is truth (John 17:17). What it reports is completely accurate; what it teaches is proper and right; what it promises is sure. People may not always like what the Bible says, but it tells the truth. They therefore can build their lives on it. This is the obvious application from this passage. If God's word is perfect and true, then God's people must read it, learn it, trust it, live by it, and share it with others who need to hear the truth.

---

27. Kraus, *Psalms 1–59,* p. 211.

PSALM 13

The Cry of the Afflicted

INTRODUCTION

Text and Textual Variants

For the Chief Musician. A Psalm of David.

1 How long, O LORD—? Will you forget me forever?
    How long will you hide your face from me?
2 How long must I take counsel[1] within myself[2]
    and have sorrow in my heart all the day?[3]
    How long shall my enemy be exalted over me?
3 Consider and answer me,[4] O LORD my God;
    light up my eyes, lest I sleep *the sleep of* death,[5]

---

1. Because "counsel" is primarily an intellectual activity and not associated with the intense feelings of the soul, editors and commentators propose repointing the word (עֵצוֹת) to עַצְבָת or עַצְבוֹת, meaning "troubles" or "grievances." W. VanGemeren suggests a reading "anguish, pain" (*Psalms*, p. 171). There is no manuscript support for this; the versions all agree with the MT. This is merely an attempt to form a closer parallelism with the next line. NIV translates it "thoughts": "How long must I wrestle with my thoughts?"
2. Hebrew בְּנַפְשִׁי is often translated "in my soul"; s.v. Ps. 11:5.
3. Some Greek manuscripts add "and night" (καὶ νυκτός).
4. The editors propose repointing the word to read עָנְיִי, "my affliction," in place of עֲנֵנִי.
5. The text has "lest I sleep the death." The kind of sleep is here indicated by the accusative.

361

4 lest my enemy says, "I have prevailed over him,"[6]
　lest my oppressors rejoice when I am shaken.

5 But as for me, I have trusted in your loyal love;
　my heart shall rejoice in your salvation.
6 I will sing to the LORD,
　because he has dealt bountifully with me.[7]

Composition and Context

Psalm 13 is clearly a lament psalm. It begins with the introductory cry and lament (1–2) with its focus on the enemies (2b), his suffering (2a), and God's apparent absence (1). There then follows the petition for God to hear (3a) and deliver (3b), with motivations for God to act (3–4). Finally there is the expression of confidence in God's loyal love, and the vow to praise the LORD for what is about to happen (5–6). The changes in tone in the development of this little psalm are amazing. Delitzsch notes that the composition begins with a deep sigh, followed by a gentle prayer, and concluded with great joy.[8]

　There is no information in the psalm or in the account of the life of David that would tell us what event this psalm reflects. There would have been many occasions when David, or any other believer, was surrounded by enemies and felt exhausted and abandoned, but cried out to God in prayer nevertheless. The fact that it was deposited in the sanctuary for the Levitical choirs to sing indicates that it was written for the purpose of encouraging other afflicted believers who felt abandoned by God and at their wits' end, and not simply to remind people of an event in the psalmist's life. There were many who needed encouragement for they too found themselves crying to God, "How long, O LORD?"

---

6. The Hebrew has יְכָלְתִּיו; the Greek has "I have prevailed against him (perhaps reading יְכֹלְתִּי לוֹ; ἴσχυσα πρὸς αὐτόν). Goldingay suggests the root כָּלָה: "I have put an end to him" (*Psalms 1–41*, p. 203).
7. Greek adds another line: "and I will sing psalms to the name of the LORD Most High."
8. Delitzsch, *Psalms*, I:199.

Exegetical Analysis

Summary

Even though the psalmist finds no immediate deliverance from his affliction at the hands of enemies, he is confident that his prayer for deliverance will be answered and he will offer songs of praise because it is based on faith in God's loyal love.

Outline

I. From his affliction at the hands of enemies, David cries to God not to abandon him any longer but to deliver him so that his enemies would not triumph over him (1–4).
  A. The psalmist laments that God has abandoned him in his distress (1–2).
   1. He feels forgotten and abandoned by God (1).
   2. He tries to resolve his grief every day but with no success (2a).
   3. His enemy is exalted over him (2b).
  B. The psalmist petitions God to deliver him lest he die and his enemies rejoice (3–4).
   1. He petitions God to look, answer, and save him (3a).
   2. He petitions God to save so that he will not die (3b).
   3. He petitions God to save so that his enemies will not have occasion to rejoice (4).
II. Because he has trusted in God's loyal love, David anticipates deliverance and vows to sing praises to God for it (6).
  A. The psalmist expresses with confidence his faith in God's loyal love (6a).
  B. The psalmist anticipates with confidence rejoicing in God's deliverance (6b).
  C. The psalmist vows to sing praises for God's bountiful dealings with him (6c).

COMMENTARY IN EXPOSITORY FORM

I. Oppressed believers who feel abandoned by God may pour out their complaints to God (1–2).

For the expository arrangement it may be simpler to divide

the first part of the psalm, the psalmist's address to God (1–4), into the lament and petition sections. This will allow the expositor to focus completely on the unique ideas in each section. Verses 1 and 2 form the lament.

A. When believers feel abandoned by God they should pray (1).

The distinctive feature of this psalm is "How long?" (עַד־אָנָה, "until when?").The expression receives emphasis in the psalm by its position in each sentence and by its repetition. Four times in this lament section is it used, making it clear that the psalmist had been oppressed for some time by his enemies, and for some time God has not responded to his prayer.[9] The expression "How long, O LORD? is a rhetorical question, intended to lament the fact that God has not delivered him. The sentence is incomplete; it is broken off before finishing the idea of how long until God delivers him. Breaking off a sentence is a way of expressing extreme emotions (the figure is called aposiopesis). God knows precisely what the afflicted mean when they cry out, "How long, O LORD . . . ?"[10]

This incomplete lament is followed by a clarifying clause, another rhetorical question "Will you forget me forever?" It seemed to the psalmist that God had completely forgotten him. The verb "forget" (תִּשְׁכָּחֵנִי, an imperfect indicating the future) has more to do with not answering the prayer than a loss of mental recollection (it is anthropomorphic; s.v. Ps. 103:2). When God "remembers" someone, it means that he acts on their behalf in accord with what he "remembers"; when God forgets someone, it means

---

9. The *Midrash* on the Psalms (1:176) notes four corresponding uses of "How long?" by the Lord: "How long will you–not keep my commands?" (Exod. 16:28); "How long will this people despise me?" and "How long will they not believe in me?" (Num. 14:11); and "How long will their congregation murmur against me?" (Num. 11:27). The suffering psalmist may have been aware of God's parallel question. Perhaps in lamenting how long the LORD did not respond to them they were reminded of their failure to repond to him (see Zech. 7:13).

10. A. F. Kirkpatrick says, "Feeling, not logic, shapes the sentence, combining two questions into a self–contradictory expression (*Book of Psalms,* p. 64).

that he does not come to their aid. The absence of divine help is elsewhere expressed by the ideas of forgetting, or of turning away the face (see Ps. 9:13, 19; 10:11, 12). The point is that God seems to have abandoned him, and the adverb "forever" (נֶצַח) indicates that the psalmist wondered if this would ever change. In this sentence the adverb may be translated to indicate that the abandonment would continue:"How long will you *continue* to forget me?"

The parallel line adds to the intensity of the lament: "How long will you hide (תַּסְתִּיר) your face from me?" Hiding the face is a figure (an anthropomorphism) to signify the withholding of favor (see Ps. 30:7 as opposed to Ps. 31:16 and especially Num. 6:25 where the LORD's face shining on people signifies that he is gracious to them). God has not only "forgotten" him, but he also has withheld favor from him.

B. When believers are at their wits' end, they should pray earnestly (2).

The third use of "How long? expresses the psalmist's personal frustration and grief. "How long must I take counsel within myself?" refers to his numerous but futile attempts to resolve the situation. The verb (אָשִׁית), meaning "set, place, establish," has as its object "counsel" (עֵצוֹת), yielding the translation "take counsel." In this line the verb has the "obligatory" nuance: "How long must I take counsel?" The counsel or planning he is doing within himself refers to ideas he has had to get out of the difficulty, but since he is still crying out to the LORD, his plans have been unsuccessful.

The parallel colon expresses the frustration of not being able to resolve the difficulty: he has sorrow in his heart all the time. The line has no specific connection to the preceding line; it simply reads "sorrow in my heart daily." It could be taken as an independent clause with the verb supplied ("and have sorrow . . ."); or it could be taken adverbially ("having sorrow . . ."). In either case part of his lament is that he endures this "inner sorrow" or "grief" (יָגוֹן) because of the oppression. The description is not one of physical pain, but emotional and spiritual—he was filled with a sadness that almost immobilized him. This was daily (יוֹמָם); there was no letup. Plan after plan failed and gave way to more grief.

C. When believers see the enemy exalted they pray more earnestly (3).

The fourth lament explains the immediate cause of his affliction—the enemy was being exalted over him. The verb "be exalted" (יָרוּם; s.v. Ps. 46:10) means "be raised" to a position of power and dignity and therefore arrogantly assume superiority over him. There is no indication who the enemy might be, although the context could be describing an insurrection in which there is a very troubling power struggle. The enemy is clearly wicked. The enemy of David is therefore an enemy of the LORD as well, or rather, the enemy of the LORD has become David's enemy (see Ps. 139:19–24). Given the lament "how long?" it is clear that his enemy was currently exercising domination over him, and if the LORD continued to ignore him, that domination would lead to his death and disaster for the faithful. The lesson from this is that the exaltation of the wicked over believers is a call to prayer.

II. Oppressed believers pray to God to prevent the troubling situation from getting worse (3–4).

We now come to the petition section of the psalm. While these verses record the psalmist's appeal to God, they are exemplary and instructive for all believers in life-threatening situations. What is most instructive here, though, is that the petition includes motivation for God to act, reasons why the prayer should be answered.

The prayer is first expressed plainly in typical lament-psalm style: "look" and "answer."[11] The first imperative, variously translated "look" or "consider" (הַבִּיטָה from נָבַט), means "to gaze intently" at or into something. It is a bold figure here (an anthropomorphism) calling for God to look closely at his dilemma. God does not have to look closely at the problem; he knows it

---

11. Meir Weiss demonstrates how the petition follows the lament, explaining the repeated "How long" questions. The structure follows the order of "you," "I," and "they": first is "How long O LORD" (you), then "How long shall I" (I), and then "how long will my enemy" (they). The petition then follows the same order: "Look, answer" (you), "lest I sleep" (I), and "lest my enemy say" (they). See "The Literary Work in Its Entirety, Psalm 13," in *The Bible from Within,* pp. 298–314, especially 303.

all. Used in conjunction with the expressions about God's having forgotten him and having hidden his face, the request to look closely seems natural. The second imperative is straight to the point, "answer me" (עֲנֵנִי). The imperatives are prayers, of course; their use in prayers underscores the urgency of the request, calling for immediate action. This urgent request was addressed directly to "Yahweh, my God." "Yahweh" is the personal and covenant name of God; so David was appealing to God on the basis of his relationship to him by covenant, using his personal name.

The second part of the petition also uses an imperative, but the word is figurative: "Light up my eyes" (הָאִירָה עֵינַי). The word in this (hiphil) stem can mean "give light, cause to shine, light up, or lighten." In some passages it has the sense of giving light through instruction, that is, illuminating someone, but that does not seem to be the case here. The situation here is much like that recorded in the story of Jonathan, who was failing quickly in his vitality until he ate and his eyes were enlightened (1 Sam. 14:27–29). Similarly, here the word means to revive the physical strength and moral energy (see also Prov. 29:13; Ezek. 9:8). How would God light up his eyes? By causing his face to shine upon him, meaning to show him favor and answer his prayer.

Next, the psalmist motivates God to answer his prayer with two reasons. The first is that if God does not answer his prayer, he will die—literally "lest I should sleep, the death" meaning "lest I should sleep the [sleep of] death" (פֶּן־אִישַׁן הַמָּוֶת). The particle "lest" introduces a negative purpose; it expresses the motive of the action in the preceding clause. The fear is that he should sleep, but it is not an ordinary sleep; it is a sleep that will be characterized by or result in death.[12] As Hengstenberg says, "The psalmist represents himself as a dying man, as one already half gone, who soon will be wholly overwhelmed with the darkness of death, if the LORD does not give him new power of life."[13]

The second motivation he gives concerns what his enemy and those who harass him would say if he was not delivered from

---

12. The word "death" serves as an internal object. The word sets forth the final effect of the action, or what will flow from it as a consequence. The sleep becomes death.

13. Hengstenberg, *Commentary on the Psalms*, I:201.

them. The enemy would say, "I have prevailed over him." In other words, he would claim the victory once and for all (the verb is a present perfect). If his enemy prevailed over him, then also those who were on his enemy's side oppressing him ("those who harass me," or simply "my oppressors," צָרַי) would rejoice when he was overthrown. Their joy would almost be a cultic cry (גִּיל; see below) and the occasion for their rejoicing would be his removal (the verb אָמוֹט means "be shaken, moved, removed, overthrown" from his place; s.v. Ps. 62:2).

The point is that David is a faithful believer in the LORD. The triumph of his enemies over him would be hailed by them as a triumph over David and his faith. David's appeal is that if God did not want them to rejoice, perhaps in a cultic setting, then he would have to answer the prayer.

III. Oppressed believers who have trusted in God's loyal love pray to God with confidence (5–6)

The final two verses have a completely different tone to them. Up to this point the psalmist's words have been urgent and anxious, the cry of an afflicted soul. Now his words are confident of God's deliverance—and of his own praise for that deliverance. This section shows that believers like the psalmist can also pray with confidence in the love of God.

A. Trusting in God's loyal love brings confidence in prayer (5).

The fifth verse begins with a strong adversative: "But as for me" (וַאֲנִי). He has been expressing his concern for what his oppressors were doing; now he declares what he does and will do. And what he will do—rejoice in God's deliverance—is due to the fact that he trusts in God's loyal love. The word order puts the "loyal love" first: "But as for me, in your loyal love I have trusted." This loyal love (חֶסֶד; s.v. Ps. 23:6) is the LORD's faithful covenant love for his people. In a world that is filled with oppressors and opposition, there is no better source of confidence—there is no other source of confidence. His expression of confidence uses the word "trust" (בָּטַחְתִּי, a present perfect nuance: I have trusted and continue to trust; s.v. Ps. 4:5), emphasizing that he has a faith that is holding fast to God for security.

B. Because of God's loyal love believers will praise him for victory (6).

Because of that secure trust in God's loyal love, the psalmist will "rejoice" (וְגִיל) in God's deliverance. This is the same word used for his fear that oppressors might "rejoice." Because of God's faithful love, the rejoicing will be over God's deliverance, not the defeat of God's people.[14] The term "deliverance" can also be translated "salvation" in a context like this. It does not refer to what

---

14. The word for "rejoice, shout for joy" (גִּיל), used twice in this psalm, refers to an enthusiastic praise, i.e., to shout exultingly, even to tremble with excitement. The related noun means "a jubilant shouting" (for the heavenly Jerusalem; see Isa. 65:18). The following categories illustrate its meaning in different contexts. First, it is used for jubilation for victory in war. Here in Psalm 13 the psalmist prays that the LORD will not let the enemies rejoice over him; this has the same sense of celebration in a victory. One illustration of the enemies rejoicing concerns the Babylonians (Hab. 1:15). On the positive side, the word has this sense of great jubilation in the Messianic passage that predicts the end of war forever (Isa. 9:3b). On a personal level, Proverbs 24:17 warns people not to rejoice when their enemy stumbles; this would be another celebration of victory.

    Second, it is used for domestic celebration. This rejoicing occurs a few times in Proverbs where parents rejoice over a wise child (23:24–25). It also celebrates marriage (Song, 1:4a). Unfortunately, the word also describes the celebration of those who delight in evil (Proverbs 2:11, 14).

    Third, it is used for cultic shouts in worship (mostly in the worship of Yahweh but also in idolatrous settings). It signifies a fervent shout or jubilation, an enthusiastic cultic celebration. The true worshipers know the joyful sound and "rejoice" all day (Ps. 89:15b, 16). David exhorts the people to "rejoice" and shout for joy (the parallel רָנַן referring to the ringing cry). Joel exhorts Israel to "rejoice" in view of the great things God has done (2:21). The word probably has this sense in Psalm 2:11, even though it is joined with "fear." If the word "rejoice" refers to an exuberant cultic shout for joy, the addition of "with trembling" would ensure that it did not get out of hand. All of these passages would have their setting, ultimately at least, in sanctuary worship. So when the text uses this word for "rejoice," it refers to expressing joy energetically, perhaps even without words—perhaps a yell, a shout, or a roar from the congregation. If God gloriously delivers his people, their response should be an enthusiastic one.

people today might call spiritual salvation; it is a spiritual and physical salvation that refers to God's saving him from the enemy who would destroy him (s.v. Ps. 3:2).

Because he is confident that his heart will rejoice over that, he vows ("I will sing") to praise the LORD with his song. The final clause of the psalm is a causal clause, providing the anticipated reason he will sing. It uses a simple perfect tense (גָּמַל), "he has dealt bountifully." This is what he will say when he sings to the LORD. In the vow it might be helpful to read this as a future perfect: "I will sing to the LORD because he shall have dealt bountifully with me." He anticipates God's bounty and so promises to praise.[15]

MESSAGE AND APPLICATION

The main message of this little psalm is clear enough; it can be captured in an expository idea like this: *In times of dangerous opposition when God seems to have abandoned his people, believers must press their appeal more urgently and with greater confidence in his loyal love.* The psalm captures the double problem of wicked enemies set on destroying the righteous and of God's abandonment of those in trouble. The psalm captures the intensity and urgency of the psalmist who appeals to God on the basis of his faithful covenant love. Likewise New Testament believers know that nothing will separate them from the love of God in Christ Jesus (Rom. 8), and so they pray without ceasing and with greater urgency in times of dangerous opposition, sometimes even including the heart wrenching cry, "How long O LORD?" Broyles observes that expressing a complaint need not indicate a lack of trust; nor does trust make complaint unnecessary.[16] This is because believers pour out their complaint to him, trusting that they shall praise him.

---

15. Weiss explains that the use of the perfect tense here shows that he does not speak of the future, but of the past, as of an event that has already taken place—he is certain that his petition has been accepted (*The Bible from Within*, p. 313).
16. Broyles, *Psalms*, p. 87.

PSALM 14

The Folly and the Future of the Fool

INTRODUCTION[1]

Text and Textual Variants

To the Chief Musician. Of David.

1 The fool says in his heart,
   "There is no God."
   They corrupt, they make their deeds abominable;
   there is no one who does good.[2]

2 The LORD looks down from heaven
   on mankind,[3]
   to see if there are any who understand,
   any who seek after God.
3 They have all turned aside;
   together they have become corrupt;
   there is none who does good,
   not even one.[4]

---

1. See Robert A. Bennett, "Wisdom Motifs in Psalm 14 = 53," *BASOR* 220 (1975):15–21.
2. Greek adds "not even one" as in verse 3."
3. Hebrew: "the sons [children] of man"
4. Romans 3:13–18 includes a series of quotations from different parts of the Old Testament to fill out the description of the wicked. In some Greek

4 Have they no knowledge,[5] all the doers of iniquity,
   who devour my people *as* they devour bread
      and who do not call upon the LORD?

5 There they are in terrifying dread,[6]
   for God is with the generation of the righteous.
6 You would put to shame the plans of the afflicted,[7]
   but the LORD is their[8] refuge.

7 Oh, that[9] salvation for Israel would come out of Zion!
   When the LORD restores the fortunes[10] of his people
   Jacob will rejoice, and Israel will be glad.

Composition and Context

Psalm 14 is a powerful description of the godless world in which

---

manuscripts, the Vulgate, and a few other sources these quotations are
added to the psalm after verse 3, but they are not added to Psalm 53. It
appears that the quotations were added later to those versions from Christian sources, although it is possible that Paul drew upon a collection of
descriptions already in existence. The addition is: "Their throat is an open
grave; with their tongues they use deceit; the poison of vipers is under
their lips; their mouth is full of cursing and bitterness; their feet are swift
to shed blood; destruction and misery are in their ways, and the way of
peace they do not know; there is no fear of God before their eyes."

5. The Greek version has οὐχὶ γνώσονται (along with Symmachus, Jerome
   and the Targum), a future tense, "Will they not know" (reading יֵדְעוּ instead of יָדְעוּ).
6. Greek adds to "There were they alarmed with fear" the clause "where
   there was no fear" after Psalm 53:6.
7. Kraus says that the context requires the meaning "plans against the
   weak," an objective genitive (Kraus, *Psalms 1–59*. p. 218), but Goldingay
   prefers to read "by the plans of the weak may you be put to shame" (*Psalms
   1–41*. p. 211).
8. The text has the singular form, but the idea is collective.
9. Hebrew "Who will give" (מִי יִתֵּן), expressing the optative. The Greek renders the idiom literally, "Who will give" (τίς δώσει), perhaps assuming that
   the reader would be familiar with the Hebrew idiomatic expression.
10. "Fortunes" is שְׁבוּת which forms a cognate accusative with the verb שׁוּב.
    The word is not related to the verb שָׁבָה, "to take captive," so a translation
    of "restore the captivity" is not correct. See John M. Bracke, "*šûb šebût*: A
    Reappraisal," *ZAW* 97 (1985):233–44.

372

the righteous must live and which poses a constant threat to them. Other psalms describe the evil acts of the wicked or a group of enemies, but this one speaks about all of mankind. And, as Kirkpatrick points out, this "deep and universal corruption of mankind is traced to its source in their failure to seek God."[11] Because of this and because the righteous are the target of their destructive ways, the description of the depravity in this psalm refers to unbelievers who persist in living as if there were no God. Because there is a God, their chosen way can only be described as utter folly.

The psalm cannot be easily classified according to the standard types that we have. It has some features that would be found in lament psalms, especially the communal lament; but it does not have a proper petition. It has some affinity with wisdom psalms, notably expressions dealing with the fool and with wisdom and knowledge. Here too it does not have enough of the features to be classified as a wisdom psalm. It also concludes with some elements that fit prophetic liturgical style. The psalm, then, seems to be a unique composition that draws on many features of different types of psalms.

In view of this it should be noted that Psalm 53 seems to be another version of Psalm 14, or an adaptation of Psalm 14 for a different purpose, in the so-called Elohistic section of the collection (Pss. 42–83). The reason for this duplication will be a little clearer when Psalm 53 is studied. Both psalms are said to be Davidic, and they are almost identical. A. A. Anderson suggests that their existence in each section of the book points to the independent existence of both the first collection (Pss. 3–41) and the second.[12] Even if that is the case, one would have to conclude that the two psalms were intended for slightly different purposes and perhaps at different times in the life of the psalmist.[13] Psalm 14 seems to focus on comfort for the faithful, but Psalm 53 offers more of a warning to the wicked. It is possible that Psalm

---

11. Kirkpatrick, *Psalms*, p. 65.
12. Anderson, *Psalms 1–72*, p. 130.
13. The differences between the psalms will be discussed more fully under Psalm 53.

53 was edited to make the changes in order to introduce a fresh historical reference.[14]

Exegetical Analysis

Summary

After describing the Godless and dangerous corruption of mankind, the psalmist declares that God will completely destroy the wicked, a prospect that inspires him to long for the establishment of the LORD's reign on earth.

Outline

I. The psalmist describes the LORD's appraisal of the Godless human race: they are totally corrupt and very dangerous (1–3).
   A. Summary: They are practical atheists and completely corrupt (1).
   B. Description: He reports the LORD's appraisal of mankind (2–3):
      1. The LORD searches for any who might be wise (2).
      2. The LORD concludes that the entire race has turned from good to evil (3).
II. The psalmist reveals the coming destruction on the corrupt race (4–6).
   A. Those who persecute the righteous are willfully ignorant (4).
   B. The ungodly will find themselves in terrifying dread in the future (5).
   C. The wicked will be put to shame (6).
III. The psalmist longs for the coming of the great day of salvation when the people of God will rejoice over the restitution of all things (7).

---

14. Kirkpatrick, *Psalms,* p. 66.

COMMENTARY IN EXPOSITORY FORM

I. The human race has foolishly denied God and followed its own perverse and corrupting way (1–3).

A. *Their folly is that they have denied God (1a).*

The Book of Psalms began with a contrast between the ungodly and the righteous, a contrast that will continually appear throughout the Psalms. The focus of this psalm is on the ungodly, but in a way that reveals what it means to be trying to live independently of God. What the psalm says is that the vast majority of the human race must be classed as fools; they try to deny that God exists, and because they do that, their way is completely corrupt and corrupting. It is one of the strongest passages in the Bible about the complete depravity of the human race, and yet in the world there is the other group as well, the righteous. They are people who by the grace of God have entered into covenant with him through faith and have been declared righteous. These are the people of God, and their very existence troubles the ungodly so that they are often persecuted by them. The psalm announces triumphantly that there is coming a day that it will all end, much to the shame of the foolish race and to the everlasting joy of the people of God.

The psalm therefore begins with the declaration that "The fool says in his heart, 'There is no God!'" This revelation sets a striking and troubling beginning to the psalm; and yet, for those who believe in God it is a reminder that it is utter folly to deny him. The word "fool" (נָבָל)[15] has no article, and so is not a reference to a particular person but to every individual in the class "fool." This is indicated by the fact that the following descriptions of the fool use the plural form of the verbs.

The chief characteristic of the fool is the heart-felt decision to

---

15. The word is related in the dictionaries to a verb meaning "to be senseless, foolish." נָבָל does not occur a great deal in the psalms; its meaning, and that of its related words, seems to be on the religious and moral insensitivity rather than a defective intellect. Basically, the fool lacks wisdom, not intelligence. The fool can be described as churlish, impious, and morally dense.

live a godless life, as if there were no God.[16] Accordingly, wisdom literature reminded the people that "the fear of the LORD is the beginning of knowledge, but fools (אֱוִילִים) despise wisdom and instruction" (Prov. 1:7). The negative particle (אֵין, "there is no") may indicate that the fools denies the existence of God absolutely, but more likely it shows that the fool denies the existence of God relative to the speaker, at least in this context. As such the person would be a practical atheist, living as if there were no God. After all, the fool says this in his heart; it is a conclusion based on the will and not the intellect. The fool is one who chooses never to think of a God as being involved with his daily affairs.

B. Their nature is that they are completely corrupt (1b–3).

What proceeds from the heart of a fool is moral perversion, according to the next few verses. The first declaration is that fools "corrupt" (הִשְׁחִיתוּ from שָׁחַת).[17] It would be difficult to find a

---

16. Goldingay says this is not a statement of theoretical atheism but a declaration that God can be discounted from everyday life (*Psalms 1–41*, p. 213). His translation of the word as "scoundrel" does not fit, however.

17. The verb "corrupt" (שָׁחַת) in this (*hiphil*) verbal stem could also be taken as an internal causative use, meaning they corrupt themselves or are corrupt; but it is more likely a normal causative used to say they corrupt [the deeds]. The word is a very strong one; it means to ruin suddenly, spoil, corrupt.

We find passages that refer to destruction in warfare (2 Sam. 11:1). The (*hiphil*) participle becomes at times a technical military term for the "slayer" (1 Sam. 13:17; 14:15; 2 Sam. 24:16). Marauding bands also could "ruin" the crop (Judg. 6:4).

It can also refer to ruining things within the community, such as ruining the covenant with Levi by corrupt teaching (Mal. 2:9), or marring an inheritance by marrying a Moabitess (Ruth 4:6). It is even used for wasting seed (Gen. 38:9). It is possible to ruin someone's life by careless words (Prov. 11:9). On the moral and spiritual level, the word describes the corruption of Israel when they made the golden calf (Exod. 32:7).

Sinfulness is described as corruption and perversion with this word. It was the assessment of the LORD that the human race had become corrupt morally and needed to be removed (Gen. 6:12; this is much the same theme that Ps. 14:1 has). Isaiah described the wicked, hypocritical people of his

stronger word to use, for this verb means "ruin, devastate, corrupt." It was used of the complete corruption of the human race prior to the flood (Gen. 6:11–12) and of the LORD's destroying Sodom and Gomorrah (Gen 13:10). Here it refers to moral and spiritual corruption; but the word reminds the reader that the corruption is as bad as it could be, so bad it would warrant the type of severe judgment God has used in the past. The verb shares the direct object with the next verb, literally "they make abominable" (הִתְעִיבוּ from תָּעַב, "to act abominably") so that the line reads: "they corrupt, they make abominable, [their] wanton deeds" (עֲלִילָה).[18] Even their wanton deeds they make corrupt and abominable to God and man.[19] The one who tries to ignore

---

day as having "acted corruptly" (Isa. 1:4). And, the Israelites' diseased and defiled animals they tried to offer to God are called "ruined" or corrupted (Mal. 1:14).

The word is therefore used of God's judgment on the corrupt human race (Gen. 9:11, 15; Exod. 8:20). It is used in Genesis 13:10 and 19:13 for the complete "ruin" of Sodom and Gomorrah (and see the intercession in Gen. 18:28). In Egypt if the people did not put blood on the doorposts, the angel of "destruction" would enter (Exod. 12:23).

Related to this theme of judgment is the prophecy in Isaiah 52:14 that describes the suffering servant as "disfigured").

18. The singular form is probably a poetic abbreviated form of עֲלִילוֹתָם, "their wanton deeds."

19. The verb "make abominable" (<תָּעַב) is the denominative verb related to the noun "abomination" (תּוֹעֵבָה). This word may be understood by its uses and by its synonyms. In general, it describes something that is incompatible with God and his order of life; it describes things that are dangerous, grotesque, out of place, and repulsive. It is hard to find a translation that works for all uses.

There are places where the emphasis is simply that things do not fit (somewhat of a neutral use). For example, the Egyptians thought it an abomination to eat with Semites (Gen. 43:32). Similarly, the law grew up in Israel that warned the people about eating any abominable food (Deut. 14:3). Certain types of people or conditions just do not fit together (such as the righteous and the wicked, Prov. 29:27; fools and turning from evil, Prov. 13:19; or kings and wrong-doers, Prov. 16:12).

Naturally, then, things that are totally incompatible with the divine nature are designated as abominations. In the social world, dishonest weights are taboo (Prov. 11:11; 20:10), as are evil judges (Prov. 17:15) and liars (Prov. 12:22).

377

God cannot simply live a life of self indulgence; even that will be made perverse and corrupt.

The last clause of the verse simply reports, "There is no one doing good" (no "doer of good"). This is the divine evaluation of the people who deny God, the fools. Not one of them is engaged in doing things that are good. Here we have a hard saying, for surely one could argue that atheists and unbelievers do some things that are good in society; but in God's sight they are not good because the deeds are not done to the glory of God. They are completely without merit.[20] The statement, "There is no one doing good" is the heart of the doctrine of complete depravity.

In verse two the psalmist records the divine search for any among the unbelieving world who might be seeking God or attempting to please God. The search is in vain, for there are none. The text literally says, "The LORD from heaven bows down (הִשְׁקִיף)[21] to see. . . ." The statement that the LORD leans down to look from heaven on mankind is figurative (anthropomorphic), because divine omniscience does not need to have a closer look. The expression calls to mind the anticipation of the great judgments at Babel and Sodom when the LORD also came down to see what the people were doing (Gen. 11:5; Gen. 18:21). The use of the expression is designed to communicate how thorough God's knowledge is of sinful mankind and how inexcusable their sins are.

The LORD is looking for someone who "understands and seeks

False worship is an abomination to the LORD (Isa. 1:13); lies, deceit, discord, and murder are also abominations (Prov. 6:16–19); idolatry and despicably pagan practices are also abominations (Ezek. 5:9; 11:7; Deut. 7:25; 17:1). Pagan cultic practices like prostitution (Deut. 23:19) and sexual rites (Deut. 22:11) are likewise taboo.

In these passages we find parallel verbs that provide color to the word "abomination"; for example: "reject" (מָאַס), "hate" (שָׂנֵא), and "abhor as cultically unclean" (שָׁקַץ), as well as other words for "harmful adulteration, taboo, unclean, abhorrent, shameful" and the like. What is described as "abominable" is therefore not only incompatible with the divine nature, but is so bad that it is repulsive. In Psalm 14 the pagans have even made their wanton deeds abominable.

20. The Bible elsewhere makes it clear that even their acts of righteousness are to be considered as filthy things.
21. The nuance of the form is probably a gnomic perfect, for it describes God's constant awareness of the sinful race, part of divine omniscience.

God." It is worth noting that the psalm uses the personal name of God, Yahweh, because of its connection to the covenant and the covenant people. If unbelievers understood who this God is, they would avail themselves of his provision of forgiveness and righteousness, as the latter part of the psalm makes clear that others have. So the divine quest is for any who might understand and seek God. These two words are participles; the first (מַשְׂכִּיל from שָׂכַל; s.v. Ps. 36:4) describes someone who has wisdom or prudence, someone who makes wise choices because of proper understanding and knowledge, someone who recognizes the sovereignty of God and tries to live by divine providence at least. The word is antithetical to "fool," and so looking for wisdom among fools will lead to the conclusion that there are none who act wisely. The search in effect confirms the previous observations about the human race. Connected to this is the other object of the search, to see if there is anyone "seeking (דֹרֵשׁ) after God." To seek God would be to investigate, to inquire, to search out. It would mean that the person realized that there is a God and that he must be found. The search would include praying to God and learning of God.

The result of God's investigation is utter futility (v. 3). All humankind has turned away (the present perfect of סוּר) from God completely and therefore remains separated from him. Moreover, they are all completely corrupted (the *niphal* of אָלַח, a term that elsewhere describes milk that has turned sour). The conclusion of this search reiterates the thesis of the psalm, "there is none doing good." This is stressed even more with "not even one solitary individual." The point being made here was reiterated by Paul in Romans 3, i.e., the human race apart from God is universally corrupted and depraved. Even divine omniscience fails (so to speak) to find any exception to this sad thesis.

II. The perverse human race persecutes the righteous not knowing that they will be thrown into terror and shame (4–6).

The subject so far has concerned the foolish human race that denies God and lives in defiance of his laws. The first verse set the limits for the descriptions to follow, for the psalmist was not talking about the righteous. While that was implied in the first three verses, it is more clearly presented in the next three verses, which will speak of the righteous who must live in the midst of people who reject the LORD, live in rebellion against him, and do not even understand the truth.

A. The ignorant workers of iniquity persecute the righteous (4).

The wording of verse 4 indicates that the LORD himself is expressing astonishment at the folly of the wicked. The language is anthropomorphic, for God is presented as finding it hard to believe the depth of the depravity of these "practitioners of iniquity," that is, people who are given over completely to doing iniquity.

The LORD expresses his amazement with a rhetorical question: "Have they no knowledge?" They are so spiritually blind that they do not know what they do. Because of their lack of spiritual understanding, they may not even think of their activities as iniquitous; it is when the Spirit of God breaks through to convict them of sin that they realize the enormous guilt they carry. Psalm 36 describes the wicked person as smoothing over his sins so that he does not see them; for if he did, he would hate them (v. 4).

What they were doing is (1) devouring the people of God and (2) not calling upon the LORD.[22] The first clause uses the image of devouring (an implied comparison) to portray their destruction of the righteous. The analogy with "eating bread" is meant to say that they devour God's people as if it were as natural as eating bread.[23] Spiritual blindness has lead to a calloused indifference to the lives of righteous people.

The final description of the godless society is that people do not call upon the name of the LORD. On the surface this seems

---

22. The two attributive clauses clearly explain their ignorance and provide the reason for God's astonishment. The knowledge they lack is both intellectual and experiential, as the beginning of the psalm makes clear—they say in their heart there is no God. This, they think, gives them the freedom to destroy the righteous.

23. Micah uses the same imagery, saying that the wicked tear the skin and flesh off God's people, and eat their flesh and break their bones, chopping them up like meat in a cooking pot (3:1–3). Such graphic language can only mean that they were guilty of violent and destructive attacks on the people of God.

to mean "to pray," but the expression may include more of the organized worship of Israel, especially the central activity of the worship which would be making proclamation of the person and works of the LORD. People could only live this wickedly if they completely refused to think about the LORD, let alone proclaim his nature. Calling on the name of the LORD would require spiritual understanding, repentance, and faith.

B. The wicked will soon be thrown into great terror and shame (5–6).

If they had any understanding of the nature of God, they would know that he is a righteous judge and that they will be judged for their sins. The transition to this theme of judgment is signaled by "there" (שָׁם). It probably refers to a spot where the scene described will be localized, perhaps it means that in the place that the wicked attack the righteous God would judge them. That has happened on occasion, but not enough to form a general principle. After all, the psalm has been describing a universal class of people (all unbelievers) with complete moral abandonment and will next describe a universal judgment on them all. So "there" may also have the sense of time. To make this clear the translation "then" might be used. The judgment envisioned is that introduced in passages like Psalm 2 and Psalm 110 that tell of the sudden wrath to come when the LORD's anointed will come to destroy the wicked with sudden terror (see also Matt. 24:30).

The intensity of the terror to come is stressed by the cognate accusative ("they will be terrified with a great terror"). It is a description of sudden horror when people will find out that they have been foolish, but it will be too late. They will then see that the God they have been denying will come to vindicate the people whom they have been devouring. This is the righteous[24] generation,[25] the people that God has

---

24. The "righteous" are the covenant people, the true believers in the LORD (s.v. Ps. 1:5). By faith they have been declared to be righteous; and by their faithfulness they live in conformity to the will of God, that is, their lives conform to the standard. In this psalm, and frequently in Proverbs, the righteous are contrasted with fools.

25. The word "generation" is used to describe the nature of the class rather than a period of time (as in a generation of evil–doers). See also Frank

been with all along; and while it may seem at times that they were unprotected, the wicked will discover that God never let things get out of hand. He will deal with the wicked even more harshly for the way that they treated his people. There have been times in the history of Israel that God has intervened and delivered his people from those bent on destroying them (such as in the Book of Esther), and the psalmist may have had that kind of deliverance in mind; but the fullest meaning of these words will come at the end of the age when the persecution of the people will be the most severe. It will be a time of tribulation unparalleled in the history of the race, and only the coming of the LORD in judgment will bring it to an end.

The folly of the fools is presented in a different way in verse 6. They would put to shame the plans of the afflicted, only to find out that the LORD is their refuge. In the flow of these verses, the psalm seems to be saying that faced with a warning of judgment for their sins, these fools do not repent but turn with great rage to humiliate the afflicted, that is, the righteous that they have been afflicting with persecution ("put to shame" is often used in military settings for utterly destroying and humiliating the enemy; s.v. Ps. 31:1). Psalm 53:5 will add that those who want to shame the righteous will themselves be shamed.[26]

III. The righteous long for the great day of deliverance to come (7).

The psalm is completed now by the prayer of the psalmist, a longing for the deliverance and restoration to come from the LORD. The source of the salvation is Zion, a figure meaning the place where the LORD dwells among his people (a metonymy of subject). The psalmist believed that the LORD truly was in the midst of his people, but he longed for that presence to manifest

---

J. Neuberg, "An Unrecognized Meaning of Hebrew *dor*," *JNES* 9 (1950):215–17;

26. The structure of verses 5 and 6 provide the proper perspective with the contrasts:

"There they are in great terror / because God is with the generation of the righteous //

You would put to shame the plans of the afflicted / but Yahweh is his refuge."

itself by delivering the people from the oppressive presence of the wicked.

When the LORD delivers his people, he will restore their fortunes (שׁוּב שְׁבוּת). The clause, especially with a translation "restore captivity," might suggest that the passage was written in the time of the exile. This is a common view, but the expression does not mean "captivity." Its reference is far more general, referring to the restoration of fortunes after some time of misery (see Job 42:10; Amos 9:14; Hosea 6:11, both pre-exilic passages). If one concluded that this verse refers to the restoration from the captivity, it might be a liturgical addition to an existing psalm.[27] Since the expression is used elsewhere to mean restoration of fortunes, any number of settings is possible. The righteous generation in this psalm are also called the afflicted, and so some misfortune needed to be reversed. The psalm may have had a significant application for the people in the exile, or even in the Diaspora, but it could have been written at some earlier period given the fact that the doers of iniquity are not limited to one period of time. This verse is not a compelling argument against Davidic authorship.

The psalmist anticipates that when the LORD restores the fortunes of his people, when he intervenes to make all things right, then the people of Israel will rejoice. For a time they are afflicted and appear to be humiliated by the world, but in times to come they will celebrate the LORD's victory over the world.

As with all the prayers for deliverance from the presence and power of the pagan world, the ultimate answer will come when the LORD appears to judge the world. That will be the great day of deliverance, the final restoration, and a time of endless rejoicing.

MESSAGE AND APPLICATION

The impact of reading Psalm 14 is staggering: there is none righteous, no not one. The whole race has become corrupt and dangerous because it chooses to live in defiance of God. If people ignore God, or the idea of a God, then they naturally ignore

---

27. Perowne, *Psalms,* I:185.

God's distinctions between good and evil. It is foolish to pervert life and become loathsome to God, for God will judge the wicked and bring relief and restoration to the righteous.

The exposition of this passage will include the powerful revelation of the godless world that is antagonistic to the faith, but it will have to emphasize the folly of that lifestyle in view of the certain judgment of God. What enables the righteous to endure in this world is the anticipation of a coming day of judgment that will bring them relief and joy. A summary expository idea that unites these ideas might be worded this way: *The righteous may have to live in a godless and corrupt world that seeks to destroy them, but there is coming a glorious day of reckoning when God will destroy the wicked and deliver his people.* It is this anticipation of a glorious deliverance when the saints will be filled with joy that inspires believers to live faithfully in this fallen world. For Jesus it was the joy that was set before him that he endured the cross and scorned its shame (Heb. 12:2). For the apostle Paul it was the hope of glory that kept him going in spite of severe persecution (2 Cor. 4). Believers are called to hold fast to their integrity, knowing that the world is passing away. The psalm is also a warning for believers not to get caught up in a world system that is atheistic and corrupt.

Qualifications of Worshipers

INTRODUCTION[1]

Text and Textual Variants

A Psalm of David.

1 O LORD, who may abide in your tent?[2]
   Who may dwell in your holy mountain?
2 The one who walks blamelessly, and does righteousness,
   and speaks truth in his heart;
3 who does not slander[3] with his tongue,
   nor does evil to his friend,
     nor takes up a reproach against his neighbor;
4 in whose eyes a vile person is despised,
   but who honors those who fear the LORD;
     who swears to his own hurt[4] and changes not;
5 who does not give his money at interest,

---

1. See Michael Barré, "Recovering the Literary Structure of Psalm xv," *VT* 34 (1984):207–211; Patrick D. Miller, "Poetic Ambiguity and Balance in Psalm xv," *VT* 29 (1979):416–24.
2. Many manuscripts have the word in the plural, reading בְּאָהֳלֶיךָ "in your tents," perhaps harmonizing with the common word "tabernacle" which is plural.
3. The Greek text has ἐδόλωσεν, "spoken craftily."
4. For Hebrew לְהָרַע the Greek has τῷ πλησίον αὐτοῦ, i.e. "to his neighbor," reading רֵעַ as "neighbor" and not the verb "do evil." Symmacus has ἑταῖρος

nor take a bribe against the innocent.
The one who does these things shall never be moved.

Composition and Context

Psalm 15 may be classified as a liturgy at the gate, because it
asks the question of who may enter the sanctuary to commune
with the LORD and then provides the response to the question. The question may have been posed by the worshiper who
wanted to be with God in the sanctuary; and the answer may
have come from a fellow pilgrim, or more likely, from a Levitical
gate-keeper, who had the task of reminding worshipers of the requirements for entering the holy place. There is no evidence that
this psalm was a script that was followed closely at the entrance
to the sanctuary, although its substance may have come from
a common list of qualifications for entrance; it is more likely a
liturgical psalm designed to remind people of the standard of
holiness in the presence of God.[5]

The psalm lists ten characteristics of the one who would
be permitted to enter the sanctuary and fellowship with the
LORD. There were no doubt other characteristics of qualified
worshipers, but this list may have been chosen to parallel the
ten commandments, the standard of righteousness.[6] The believing worshiper would not normally violate the ten commandments, but the same cannot be said for the things on this list.
Hearing these things recited at the gate the Israelite would
have been reminded that he had failed to live righteously, and

---

εἶναι. Goldingay following the *midrash* opts for "to bring calamity" (*Psalms
1–41,* p. 218).

5. Goldingay, *Psalms 1–41,* p. 219; he also raises the questions about the
speakers, whether it is for the ministers who dwell in the sanctuary, or for
the king, or the common person. It seems to me that if this is the standard
of being in the presence of God, it would apply to everyone. Kraus says,
"Whoever enters the realm of God's presence is interrogated regarding his
everyday manner of behavior and is called to account" (*Psalms 1–59,* p.
231).

6. Kidner says the portrait is not an exhaustive catalog; other features
emerge in passages like Psalm 24, Isaiah 33, and later the Beatitudes
(*Psalms 1–72,* p. 81).

by hearing these things he would have been reminded that he needed to bring a sacrifice and make confession if he was going to be granted access into the sacred precincts. Psalms like this one set the standard for communion with God: if people wanted to be welcomed into the presence of the LORD they had to measure up to the standard of the LORD. If they came thinking they had nothing to confess, a psalm like this would reveal things to be considered.

Exegetical Analysis

Summary

By listing ten characteristics of righteousness the psalmist reminds worshipers of the qualifications for entering the sanctuary to commune with the LORD.

Outline

    I. Question: The worshipers ask who may enter into the presence of the LORD and fellowship with him (1).

   II. Answer: The Levitical gate-keeper delineates the righteous characteristics of those who may abide in the LORD's presence (2–5).

      A. He describes those who are acceptable to God (2–5a).

         1. Their personal conduct is blameless (2a).

         2. Their whole life is characterized by doing righteous acts (2b).

         3. They speak the truth sincerely (2c).

         4. They do not slander (3a).

         5. They do not cause others pain (3b).

         6. They do not bring reproach on others (3c).

         7. They distinguish between vile people and righteous people (4a).

         8. They hold to the sanctity of the oath (4b).

         9. They do not lend their money with interest (5a).

        10. They cannot be bribed (5b).

      B. He concludes that the worshiper who does all of this will be secure in the presence of the LORD (5c).

COMMENTARY IN EXPOSITORY FORM

I. The people of God must examine their lives when they enter the presence of the LORD for worship (1).

The psalm poses a question that must be asked by all worshipers as they prepare to commune with the holy, living God. Who may enter his presence to do this?[7] The question comes close to being a rhetorical question, affirming that no one is good enough to commune with God; but since the rest of the psalm answers the question it is more than rhetorical. The answer will reveal that few, if any, would meet the standard of righteousness that God has established in his word.

The verse uses two parallel verbs: "who may abide" (גּוּר)[8], and "who may dwell" (שָׁכַן). Both are imperfect tenses with the nuance of "permission." And the location for this desired dwelling is the tent-sanctuary (the temple not yet being built in David's day) because the word "tent" would refer to the portable shrine the nation brought from the desert, and the "holy mountain" would refers to the place in Jerusalem where the ark of the covenant would rest.[9] These two words, "tent" and "mountain," are figurative (metonymies of subject), because the psalmist is referring to the presence of the LORD. The tent was where the LORD dwelt in the holy precinct, and Mount Zion was the hill on which it came to be located. Of course, no ordinary worshiper could live permanently in the sacred precincts; only the priests and Levites, because that was their place of service, would have their dwellings close by. These verbs, then, refer to the Israelite's participation in worship, and so verbs of temporary dwelling were used, sojourning and settling down for a short time. The worshiper could stay all day in the sanctuary, but usually only

---

7. See further Pierre Auffret, "YHWH, qui sejournera en ta tente?" *VT* 50 (2000):143–151.

8. The verb was traditionally translated as "sojourn." It means to stay or dwell in a place temporarily. It also is applied to aliens or strangers settling in the land without natural rights.

9. If David did write this psalm, it would have to have been written after the LORD chose Zion for his resting place and had the ark moved there.

stayed for the festivals, sacrifices, and prayers. But even that could be described as temporarily dwelling with the LORD.

II. The people of God must be perfectly righteous in order to enter the holy place to commune with the LORD (2–5).

The rest of the psalm will answer these questions with ten characteristics of those who may spend time in the sanctuary worshiping the LORD. There were, of course, many more qualifications that could have been added here, but ten was enough to make the point that to fellowship with God one must be perfect. The LORD was, and still is, looking for people who have sanctified him in their hearts and are living blameless lives before him.

A. *Those who may commune with the LORD must be completely righteous (2–5b).*

1. Their personal conduct must be blameless (2a). The first three descriptions of the acceptable worshiper are given immediately in verse 2. The verbal forms that are used are participles; in the substantival use of these participles the stress is on the characteristic nature of what is being described. The form is singular, but it applies to all worshipers. The first is that the manner of life is blameless: "who walks blamelessly" (הוֹלֵךְ תָּמִים). The verb "walk," of course, is idiomatic for living or following a course of actions. The key word here, however, is the modifier "blamelessly" (תָּמִים; s.v. Ps. 7:8). This word has a wide range of meanings, including perfect, unimpaired, innocent, having integrity, complete, sound, even-tempered, and flawless (without blemish, as of animals). Translations such as "flawlessly," "soundly," or "blamelessly" may work well, for this line sets the tone for the whole psalm. The standard is high; the standard is God. Jesus also said, "You, therefore, must be perfect, as your heavenly Father is perfect"(Matt. 5:48). This first line would have been sufficient to cause most pilgrim worshipers to realize they needed to make confession and offer the appropriate sacrifices.

2. Their life must be characterized by doing righteous acts (2b). The second description is "the one who does (פֹּעֵל) righteousness" or acts of righteousness. According to Revelation, believers are supposed to be adorning themselves with righteous acts (Rev. 19:8). The word "righteousness" (צֶדֶק) as discussed earlier (s.v. Ps. 1:5) refers to what is morally and ethically right according to the standard of God. This line therefore says that the person who is acceptable to God is one who does the will of God, one who conforms to the standard of God that is revealed in his law. As this psalm will show, that would include the heart attitude along with the external compliance with the commands.

3. They must speak the truth sincerely (2c). The third description is "one who speaks truth from the heart." The word "truth" (אֱמֶת) refers to what is reliable and dependable.[10] What is said must be right; it must correspond to reality. If it is a promise or a

---

10. The word for "truth" (אֱמֶת) is related to the verb אָמֵן and its various other derivatives. A survey of the usage of these words will not only help clarify the word "truth," but it will be valuable for the other words when they appear in the psalms. The dictionaries usually define the verb as "confirm, support, be firm, steady, trustworthy." The verb does not occur often in the *qal* verbal systems, but the participle is used for "foster-mother" (Ruth 4:16) and guardian or trustee (Est. 2:7). The relationship of a trustee to the idea of trustworthy, dependable, is obvious.

In the *niphal* system the verb carries the ideas of "steadfast, secure," e.g., it describes a lasting river (Isa. 33:16), or the moon as a lasting witness (Ps. 89:37). The house of David was to be "established" (2 Sam. 7:16), and the priesthood would have a "sure" house (1 Sam. 2:35). The *niphal* also is used for that which is "faithful, reliable." God says he would raise up a "faithful" priest (1 Sam. 2:35). Nehemiah uses it to describe "faithful" people in charge of the storehouses (13:13). Of course, God is "faithful" (Deut. 7:9). Psalm 111:7 says his works are "truth and justice" (dependably just), and his precepts are "sure." The prayer of Solomon asks that the promises be fulfilled, i.e., that God would be faithful to the promises (2 Chron. 1:9).

The *hiphil* is a little less obvious; it means "believe." This could be explained as a declarative use, i.e., considering something reliable or sure, and acting on it. Its common translation is simply "believe." It could refer to various things: the queen of Sheba did not "believe" what she had heard (1 Kings 10:6–7); Gedaliah did not believe the report about the threat on his life (Jer. 40:13–14); Moses was afraid people would not believe him (Exod. 4:8); and Achish came around to believe David (1 Sam. 27:12). Most importantly it refers to believing in God (the elders in Exod. 4:31; the men

report, it must be reliable. This line takes the standard to a higher level: truth must be spoken from the heart. The heart is considered the center of the will, the place of decisions and intentions (a metonymy of subject). This added description requires the sincerity of the speaker and the accuracy of what is spoken. There can be no guile, no hidden agenda, no half-truths. The truth that is spoken must be sincere; it must be the intent of the heart. Paul reminds believers to let their "yes" be "yes," and their "no" be "no"; they are to commend themselves to the conscience of others.

4. They must not slander (3a). The fourth qualification concerns slander.[11] The text puts this as "does not foot (לֹא־רָגַל) on his tongue," meaning, this one does not go about slandering. Incidental slander is bad enough; but to be actively spreading it all around is worse. Slandering refers to spreading damaging gossip that is usually untrue or unverified; it will destroy or bring great harm to the person slandered. Proverbs deals with this sin at great length.

5. They do not cause others pain (3b). Next is "does not do evil to his friend." The word "evil" (רָעָה), of course, refers to whatever harms life, or causes pain (s.v. Ps. 10:15). The righteous will do nothing that causes pain or misery to anyone. It may be that to help a friend it will be necessary to offer painful

---

of Nineveh in Jon. 3:5; and Abram in Gen. 15:6 who for his faith was credited with righteousness).

The common idea in the verbal uses seems to be reliable, dependable–something that can be counted on. A number of related words have this emphasis as well: the noun "master craftsman," אָמֵן (Prov. 8:30), a participle-noun "door-posts," אֹמְנוֹת (2 Kings 18:16), the word "amen, truly," אָמֵן (Neh. 5:13; Ps. 106:48), a noun "faithfulness, firmness," אֱמוּנָה (Exod. 17:12 for making Moses' hands steady; Hab. 2:4 for the righteous living by his faith), and a number of other related words that appear less frequently.

The most common derivative is the noun "truth, firmness, faithfulness." What is true is reliable; it can be trusted, depended on, believed. The word can be used for "truth" in general or faithfulness. The word often shows up in a hendiadys: "truth and peace," for example, would mean a "lasting peace" or a "reliable peace" (Isa. 39:8; Jer. 14:13); likewise "loyal love and truth" would mean "faithful love." So then, if people speak truth what they say is reliable and dependable.

11. The form changes now to a perfect tense; because it is continuing what the participles stress, this form may be classified as a "characteristic" perfect.

criticism." ("faithful are the wounds of a friend" [Prov. 27:6]), but this passage is not referring to anything with such a noble end. The righteous person has the good of a neighbor in mind—"Love your neighbor" (Lev. 19:18); and a neighbor is anyone nearby or anyone encountered who needs anything (as Jesus' parable of the Good Samaritan clarified in Luke 10:25–37).

6. *They must not bring reproach to others (3c).* A reproach (חֶרְפָּה) is a cutting taunt, scorn, sharp criticism or personal attack (s.v. Ps. 22:6). It refers to what is said. It is very easy to scorn another person, especially when things go badly for them; but the LORD prohibits this. The righteous will not incite this kind of ridicule nor indulge in it. The righteous will promote those who are nearby and praise them because they are good neighbors. James reminded the early church to control their tongues so that blessing and cursing do not come from the same speech (Jas. 3:9–11).

7. *They must distinguish between vile people and righteous people (4a).* The text says, "In whose eyes a vile person is despised; but who honors those who fear the LORD." This qualification has to do with spiritual discernment. The first colon uses two passive participles with the phrase "in his eyes": "despised / in his eyes / worthless" (נִבְזֶה בְּעֵינָיו נִמְאָס). There is some question of the arrangement of these words in the translation, but in the context of the psalm it makes most sense to understand the line to say that the worthless person is to be despised (in contrast to the verb "honor" in the next colon). The participle "worthless" (נִמְאָס) is from a verb that means "rejected, reprobate, worthless." The first participle in the verse (נִבְזֶה) is then the predicate: "[is] despised." This verb means "to despise, treat lightly, treat with contempt" (s.v. Ps. 22:6). In the eyes of the righteous, the reprobate is despised. This is contrary to popular culture in which people tend to idolize many who are vile and worthless. John reminds believers not to love the world or the things that are in the world, for they are passing away (1 John 2:15–17).

The second colon provides the contrast: "who honors those who fear the LORD." The verb is now the imperfect tense (יְכַבֵּד; s.v. Ps. 19:1) with either the habitual or progressive imperfect nuance for the qualification. The verb can mean "praise," as in giving glory to God, as well as "treat with honor" or "give respect," as in the decalogue with regard to parents. Those whom the righteous honor and respect should be the God-fearers, people who believe in the LORD and out of piety and reverence seek to worship and serve him. Therefore, those who are righteous must have true spiritual discernment to determine who is worthy of honor; they must look beyond the flow of popularity to see who are truly devout (for these are the noble ones in the earth [Ps. 16:3]; and they should be honored [1 Pet. 2:17]).

8. They must hold to the sanctity of an oath (4b). The eighth characteristic is that the righteous may swear but will not go back on their oath even if it is painful (נִשְׁבַּע לְהָרַע, "he swears to [his own] pain"; for שָׁבַע s.v. Ps. 63:11). Here the psalmist is dealing with faithfulness, keeping one's word, even if it proves costly or inconvenient. The righteous must not change their mind to avoid an unexpected painful outcome; they must keep their word even if it means they suffer loss of some kind. In fact, to take an oath and not keep it would be to take the name of the LORD in vain. It would be better not to take the oath in the first place if possible. Accordingly, many today have tried to heed the warning in the New Testament not to swear an oath (but they do take marriage and baptismal vows and they do pledge tithes and offerings). With or without oaths the Bible instructs the people of God to keep their word.

9. They must not lend their money with interest (5a). Verse five deals first with lending money. The righteous do not put out their money with interest (literally, "with a bite" [בְּנֶשֶׁךְ]). This may not refer to a business transaction in which one would borrow for acquisitions and investments, though it may always restrict the use of interest to burden a person so that he is dependent and humiliated for some time. The line certainly applies to helping people in need[12]; if there are some who need financial help, those who are able to help them should do so without taking further advantage of them by charging interest. The righteous person must give to those in need. This should be without thought of

---

12. This verse harmonizes with the prohibition of trading on someone else's misfortune (see Deut. 23:20 and Lev. 25:35–38). People were not even to sell food at a profit to the needy. The Bible in general was ruling against extortion and was promoting generosity.

gaining interest or perhaps even of repayment. The principle could be extended to say that giving financial help to someone in need must not be done in a way that will expect tribute and respect from the person; that too is putting a bite on the needy.

10. They must not take a bribe (5b). The last qualification says the righteous do not take a bribe (see 1 Kings 15:19; Isa. 45:13). Justice had to be preserved in the land, and to take a bribe against the innocent would be to pervert the course of justice. No one could do that and expect to be welcomed into the sanctuary to fellowship with the righteous judge of the whole earth. The idea of taking a bribe can be extended to any perversion of justice for some unjust gain. Showing partiality to the rich, or failing to be a witness in court, are essentially the same sin, especially if there is something to be gained. Sins like this disqualify a person from worship. Both Malachi and James warn of a subtle application of this, that of showing favoritism to people, especially the wealthy (Mal. 2:11; Jas. 2:1–10).

B. Those who live blamelessly and righteously will be safe and secure in the LORD (5c).

The meditation now draws a conclusion. Those who live this way, down to these kinds of details, will not only abide with the LORD but also will be secure. The verb "to be moved, shaken" (מוט in the passive; s.v. Ps. 62:2) with the negative adverb refers to the spiritual security of the devout, and not a mere physical stability (so an implied comparison). The righteous will not be shaken in their faith if they live this way, for they will abide in the presence of the LORD and go from strength to strength. So then, this summary of the whole psalm completes the answer to the question by saying that such people will not be moved from the dwelling place of the LORD (v. 1).

MESSAGE AND APPLICATION

The Israelite would have quickly learned what it would take to be pleasing to God so as to find acceptance in his sanctuary—perfection! That is what God's holy presence demands. A list like this would make worshipers realize that they needed to confess their failure to live up to the standard and to bring the appropriate offerings to find forgiveness and atonement. In time, with spiritual growth, worshipers would come closer and closer to measuring up to God's standard, for these requirements are doable, even though they seem impossible. Given the nature of human life, the reminder of God's requirements would uncover other things that needed to be confessed and removed before complete communion with God could be enjoyed.

The standard in the New Testament is not lower than this; it is perfection as well. Jesus said, "Be perfect, for your Father in heaven is perfect" (Matt. 5:48). The writer to the Hebrews instructed, "Follow after holiness, without which no one shall see the LORD" (Heb. 12:14). So we may word an expository idea for this psalm that applies to worshipers of all ages: *In order to have communion with the LORD, we must live blameless and righteous lives (and if we have not, we must confess our sins before attempting to have fellowship with him).*

When people initially come to faith in the LORD, it is because they acknowledge that they are not righteous enough to enter into the kingdom but that God has made provision for them through the blood of the atonement and the provision of the Spirit. Then, throughout life as they struggle to live by faith, whenever they seek to enter the sanctuary to have communion with the LORD, they are also reminded by his word that unless they are perfect they must find forgiveness before they can have fellowship with the living God. Accordingly, liturgies like Psalm 15 serve to remind believers of the qualifications for worshipers. The emphasis on obedience for fellowship was confirmed by the LORD. Jesus, who said, "If you keep my commandments you shall abide in my love" (John 15:10).

PSALM 16

The LORD's Everlasting Provision and Protection

INTRODUCTION[1]

Text and Textual Variants

A Contemplative Poem[2] of David.

1 Protect me, O God,
  for in you I have taken refuge.
2 *O my soul,* you have said[3] unto the LORD,
  You are my Lord,
  I have no good thing beyond you.[4]
3 As for the saints who are in the land,[5]

---

1. See H. W. Boers, "Psalm 16 and the Historical Origin of the Christian Faith," *ZNW* 60 (1969):105–110; and Walter C. Kaiser, "The Promise to David in Psalm 16," *JETS* 23 (1980):219–29.
2. Hebrew is מִכְתָּם
3. For the second person form in the MT, "you have said," the Greek, Syriac, and Jerome have a first person, "I said," making the addition of something like "O my soul" unnecessary. That is the sense of the line, but the more difficult Hebrew reading is probably the correct reading.
4. The MT has טוֹבָתִי בַּל־עָלֶיךָ, giving the line a difficult reading of "my good —not beyond you." The Greek has οὐ χρείαν ἔχεις, "you have no need of my goodness," or "good things." Symmachus has οὐκ ἔστιν ἄνευ σου. The editors propose בִּלְעָדֶךָ
5. The MT includes "they" at the end of the first colon, leading some to interpret it to say "As for the saints, they are in the earth, and the excellent in whom is all my delight" (literally, "excellent of all my delight in them").

397

They are the noble ones in whom is all my[6] delight.

4 Their sorrows will be multiplied,
　　they that obtain another *god;*[7]
　their drink–offerings of blood will I not pour out,[8]
　　nor take their names upon my lips.

5 The LORD is the portion of my inheritance and my cup,
　　you maintain my lot.[9]
6 *The* lines have fallen to me in pleasant places;
　　surely *my* heritage is good for me.[10]

7 I shall bless the LORD, who has given my counsel;
　　surely, my heart[11] instructs me in the night seasons.
8 I have set the LORD always before me;
　　because he is at my right hand I shall not be moved;
9 Therefore my heart is glad and my glory[12] rejoices;
　　surely my flesh also shall rest in safety.[13]
10 For you will not abandon me[14] to the grave;

Modern translations join it to the second colon as the subject and delete the conjunction that is present—וְאַדִּירֵי. For this word the Greek has a verb ἐθαυμάστωσεν, perhaps reading יַאְדִּיר, "he has magnified."

6. The Greek text has a 3msg pronoun, "his delight." The whole verse then reads: "He has magnified all his pleasure in them" [meaning "the saints" of verse 3a].

7. The translation follows BDB in tentatively assigning this verb to מָהַר III, "to obtain by paying a purchase price," hence, making payment to another. The Hebrew אַחֵר מָהָרוּ seems at first glance to read "they hasten after [another god]"; the Greek text reads verse four "(Their weaknesses have been multiplied;) afterward they hasted." Briggs suggests it reads "who hurry backwards," meaning apostates (p. 119).

8. The Greek reads this line as "I will not assemble with their blood offering meetings."

9. The Greek adds ἐμοι and reads this line as: "You are he who restores my inheritance to me."

10. Greek and Syriac read "my heritage."

11. MT has "kidneys."

12. Instead of "my glory" the Greek has ἡ γλῶσσά μου, "my tongue."

13. MT has לָבֶטַח, but the Greek has ἐλπίδι, in "hope."

14. Hebrew נַפְשִׁי.

you will not permit your holy one to see the pit.[15]
11 You will[16] cause me to know the path of life;
   with your presence is fullness of joy ;
In your right hand there are pleasures for evermore.

Composition and Context

It is essential for believers to keep uppermost in their minds the goodness of God, not only as it pertains to this life, but to the next as well. This is important because there are difficult times when believers otherwise might question the Lord's integrity and doubt his goodness, and consequently lose confidence in his word. Without a firm conviction of the goodness of God, guilty fears take over, insecurities run away with people, prayer becomes hoping against hope, and praise, if it exists at all, has a hollow ring to it. What is needed is a constant awareness of the goodness and grace of God—he is not capricious; he is not going to give up on his people because they are struggling to do his will; and neither is he going to guide his people through this life only to abandon them when they die. No, he loves the saints with an everlasting love, and it pleases him to do things for them.

Psalm 16 affords a wonderful opportunity for all believers to focus on this theme. The psalm is not in the form of a typical lament. It has features of a prayer song. But it is most likely a psalm of trust, or as Broyles clarifies, a confession of faith and loyalty

---

15. This translation follows most of the modern versions. The Hebrew word שַׁחַת (from שׁוּח which means "sink down, dig") is properly "pit," which forms a good parallel with "sheol." The translation "corruption" would be connected to the verb שָׁחַת, "to ruin." The word שַׁחַת only occurs 23 times, and of those uses only eight passages would allow the meaning "corruption," but only Psalm 55:24 and Job 17:4 would be convincing. Even in Job 17:14 the parallelism includes the word "worm," suggesting that "grave" could be parallel to "worm" too. But if the noun is from the verb "to ruin," a meaning "destruction" would be more likely, as in Job 33:18, 22, 30. The Greek text translated the word with διαφθοράν which means "destruction." The idea of the line is being abandoned to the grave where the body would be gradually destroyed, but the word in the text seems to be related to "to sink down," and not "to destroy."
16. The Greek renders this "have made known to me."

to the LORD.[17] The first part is the prayer for protection—God is able to protect his people (1–4); then there is a section of praise for the provision of God—God provides everything for his people (5–8); and the psalm concludes with an expression of confidence in the preservation of God—God will never, ever, abandon his people (9–11).

It is attributed to David, but few today would say he wrote it.[18] If he did not write it, then the apostle's argument in the New Testament makes little sense, for he goes out of his way to draw attention to the fact that David was dead and so the intended meaning of the psalm could not fit him (Acts 13:35–6). Among modern commentators there is a wide range of ideas for the occasion and authorship of the psalm. Different writers suggest that the psalm was written by a king, a priest, or an individual worshiper at the covenant festival. A number of commentators place the psalm in the early post-exilic period, but others argue for a pre-exilic date based on various references in the passage, such as the renunciation of foreign gods and the bestowal of land.[19] The New Testament writers, of course, saw the psalm as messianic and accepted the ascription of the work to David.

Exegetical Analysis

Summary

Because he is absolutely loyal to the LORD, and because he has come to know and trust in the LORD's goodness to him

---

17. Broyles, Psalms, p. 96
18. Kraus says that the difficulties of the psalm make any attempt at dating impossible; he thinks it is post-exilic, but allows that a pre-exilic date cannot be ruled out (*Psalms 1–59*, p. 235). A. A. Anderson observes certain motifs, such as the renunciation of foreign gods, and indicates it could be pre-exilic (*Psalms 1–72*, p. 146). Some have argued that because idolatry was not a major problem in the days of David, the psalm was not likely written by him; but there is nothing in this psalm that suggests that idolatry had become a national issue. The psalmist was simply avowing his allegiance to the LORD and no other god. Apart from this, the language of the psalm with its figures and expressions is certainly harmonious with other Davidic psalms, and the New Testament confirms that David wrote the psalm, as we shall see later.
19. See A. A. Anderson, *Psalms 1–72*, pp. 140–141.

throughout his life, the psalmist is confident that the LORD will not abandon him even in death.

Outline

 I. The psalmist prays for the LORD's protection, affirming that he has remained absolutely loyal to him (1–4).
   A. He petitions the LORD to keep him because he has taken refuge in him (1).
   B. He reviews his life of faith in the LORD (2–8).
     1. He announces his faith in the LORD alone, explaining that God is concerned with his well-being (2).
     2. He acclaims the saints with whom he has identified and denounces idolaters whom he avoids (3–4).
 II. The psalmist praises the LORD for his goodness and his guidance throughout his life (5–7).
   A. He describes the LORD as his portion in life, his pleasant inheritance (5–6).
   B. He acknowledges that the LORD has counseled him in his life during meditations in the word (7).
III. ("Therefore") As a result of the goodness of God throughout his life, the psalmist is assured that the LORD will never forsake him, not even in death, but will guide him into everlasting joy (8–11).
   A. He is confident that the LORD, whom he has set before him, will always keep him safe and secure (8–9).
   B. He believes that God would not permit his holy one to see the pit (10).
   C. He concludes that in spite of the present difficulties, he will find fullness of joy and pleasures from God (11).

COMMENTARY IN EXPOSITORY FORM

I. Prayer: God is able to protect those who trust in him wholeheartedly (1–4).

The first section is a prayer, but one in which David confesses his faith and affirms his loyalty to God. This is not just a prayer of desperation—it is a prayer coming from a faithful servant of the LORD and as such represents the way that devout believers of all times pray.

The request is for the LORD's protection: "Protect me (שָׁמְרֵנִי, s.v. Ps. 12:7) O God." As the psalm unfolds it becomes clear that David was in a life-threatening crisis—he was faced with the prospect of death at the hands of his enemies! He wanted to escape death and so he cried out to the LORD.

This, then, is all there is to the actual prayer in this psalm, because his thoughts quickly turn to focus on his faith in the LORD, his praise for the LORD's bounty, and his confidence in the LORD's preservation of the saints. The transition from the prayer to his faith is expressed in a causal clause: "for I have taken refuge in you." The verb (חָסִיתִי) is fitting for someone seeking protection in a dangerous situation (it is used for finding shelter as a bird [57:1; 61:4; 91:4], or taking refuge in a cave [Deut. 32:37], or finding safety with a shield [Ps. 144:2]; s.v., Ps.7:1). In his time of crisis, David knew where to find sanctuary—the LORD through prayer.

B. True believers confess their faith in God (2).

The first part of verse two restates his faith: "You are my Lord." By affirming that he is a loyal believer in the LORD, a committed member of the covenant, David is providing God reason enough to answer his prayer. His point is that he is totally dependent on the LORD his God and confident that the LORD will take care of him. In fact, he acknowledges that it is God who provides for his well-being—he can count on that.

The verse is a little difficult; it literally says, "my good is not beyond you (or, apart from you)" (טוֹבָתִי בַּל-עָלֶיךָ). "My good" is more specifically understood as "my welfare," meaning "my care and happiness" in general (it is used in Job 22:21 for Job's restoration and in Gen. 50:20 for God's care and exaltation of Joseph). By stating that his good is not beyond God, he means that it is God alone who provides for his well-being, all of it; and as a result there is no limit to that goodness.[20] There is nothing God cannot

---

20. The word בַּל is normally used with adjectives and adverbs, not prepositional phrases (only here and Prov. 23:7). The preposition עַל in this

provide; and there is nothing anyone else can provide that God has not provided.

C. True believers avow their loyalty to God (3–4).

Now the psalmist will show his loyalty to God to strengthen his appeal. First, he identifies with the saints (3), and second, he dissociates from false worship, religious apostates or idolatry (4).

Verse 3 says, "As for the saints (or, "Of the saints") who are in the land, they are the noble ones in whom is all my delight (or, noble ones of—my delight in them)." This line too has some unusual constructions, beginning with the preposition on the first word. It could be taken to link this line with the preceding, giving the sense of: "I have no good beyond you, belonging [as I do] to the saints, and the noble in whom . . . ."[21] Or, it could begin a new line, simply referring to the saints. The word "saints" is literally "holy ones" (קְדוֹשִׁים); it refers to the righteous Israelites, the worshiping community. Then the word "noble ones" (אַדִּירֵי, s.v. Ps. 8:1) describes them as splendid, majestic, or high ranking (as kings; Ps. 136:18).[22] It is with this group of people that the psalmist identifies himself—and more than that, it is in them that he delights. They may be the minority in the land, but they are the truly noble people. They may not always be easy to deal with, but their devotion to the LORD and the LORD's care of them makes them worthy of his admiration. These are fellow members of the covenant; these are they with whom he rightly desires to associate.

But there are others with whom he will not associate—those who have followed a false religion, whether they defected from the true faith to follow idolatry or were simply idolaters from the start. The line is cryptic; the text seems to say "who after another

---

passage means "beyond, in excess of" (as in Num. 3:46; Deut. 25:3; and Isa. 8:7). His welfare does not lie outside of the LORD.

21. Perowne, *Psalms*, I:199. The preposition לְ is used to introduce a new subject; the preposition plus the substantive may function as a *casus pendens* (GKC 143e [although Gesenius thought Ps. 16:4 doubtful]).

22. The word is in construct but has no noun after it. The following clause is used as the genitive: "noble ones of—all my delight is in them." The word "all" (כָּל) is hyperbolic; he means they are his chief delight.

hasten (אַחֵר מָהָרוּ)." This has been taken to mean "after another *god* they hasten," the designation "god" being understood;[23] and a variation of this interpretation is to take it to mean "they hurry backwards," referring clearly to apostates. The problem with the translation "hasten/hurry" is that the verb is in the *qal* stem; and if it is from the root that means "hasten, hurry, it should be in the *piel* stem. So it is likely that this is another verb altogether; and the verb that makes the most sense here is a homonym meaning "obtain by paying a purchase price." This would mean that some kind of offering, perhaps a financial investment, would have been made to false religions to show devotion. It could even have the sense of "barter for another (god)." In sum, he is talking about people who have gone away from God and acquired another deity to follow. His point is that those who do so "increase their sorrows (עַצְּבוֹתָם)." He is making a general observation—their choice brings sorrows, the word being general enough to include physical adversity and emotional pain and anxiety in the days to come, and great anguish in the judgment. There was a high cost for being involved in idol worship far beyond offerings and sacrifices. Those who defected exchanged the true God for false gods at the cost of their own spiritual and physical well-being, for they relinquished the grace and goodness of the one true God. Accordingly, David would continue to distance himself from them, for he knew that it was the prayer of the faithful that was effectual.

Thus he explains that he does not do what they do in their false religion. He does not pour out libations to the false gods. If he did so, it would be an appeal to their power, dignity, and value, and he cannot do that. He affirms that he will not even speak their names.[24] Even to utter their names would be considered an act of homage—Baal meaning "Lord," and Molech "King," for names meant the nature or reality of the one named, and the epithets described those gods as sovereigns. By not uttering their names, David did not recognize the divinity or power of any "god" other than Yahweh. In a time of serious trouble, David

---

23. In contexts about false worship, the word "another" is used 63 times with the word "God." Only here and in Isaiah 42:8 is "God" left out.
24. The reference here could be to the names of the apostates or idolaters, but it is more likely to be the names of the gods who are receiving the libations.

was able to support his petition for protection by denying that he had any relationship with false deities and their devotees; he was absolutely loyal to Yahweh.

II. Praise: God provides good gifts, guidance, and protection for his people (5–7).

The psalmist's declaration that the LORD is his God and the source of all good things for him prompts him to think further on the matter, and so without again referring to the crisis at hand, he breaks forth into praise.

A. God provides a pleasant and satisfying life (5).

In verse 5 David praises the LORD because he is his personal possession, his source of provisions, and the guardian of his destiny. He begins with two metaphors. The first is "the portion of my heritage (מְנָת־חֶלְקִי)," or, "my allotted heritage." The source of this metaphor is probably in passages about tribal allotments (Judg. 19:9), and especially in reference to the Levites who received no allotment (Num. 18:20–24). When the land was divided up among the tribes, every tribe received an allotment—except the Levites. They received none. God was to be their portion. The comparison with allotted land was that it was a possession that would be a source of supplies for life. If God is the believers' portion, it means that he is their possession and the constant source of supplies for life. When people put their trust in the LORD, he gives them himself and therefore all the provisions in life they could need.

The second metaphor is "cup"—"and [you are] my cup (וְכוֹסִי)." In the Bible the cup was a symbol of one's destiny. It represents one's portion in life, what one is given to drink as it were; so everyone has been given a cup. For the wicked it refers to judgment, a cup of staggering, or a cup of fire and brimstone (Ps. 11:6); but for the righteous the cup is a cup of blessing (Ps. 23:5). This passage is declaring that the believers' lot in life is good—it is the LORD. He is their provision and their destiny. All that the saints have or are is ordained by the LORD, but David elaborates on this further.

405

Whatever the LORD was to him, whatever the LORD gave to him, was made secure by the LORD himself. It is God who holds it (תוֹמִיךְ)—he grasps it, maintains it, makes it secure with his special care.

And all that David can do at this point is marvel at God's goodness to him. Still using the idea of the allotted inheritance, he observes that "the lines have fallen to me in pleasant places." The word for "lines" (חֲבָלִים) could refer to the cords used for measuring, or to the portion measured. Since it is plural, the first option makes the best sense. And the expression "to fall to someone as something" is an expression used for the granting of the allotment of land; so the figure is an implied comparison: just as one would go out to survey the allotment of land that was inherited to see how good it was, so the psalmist is saying that what he has in God, what he has received from God, is satisfying and pleasurable—the more he sees of it the more he is convinced it is the finest possession anyone could have.

The comparison of his life from the LORD with "pleasant places" (נָעֵם > נְעִמִים) in a land refers to both material and spiritual blessings. The emphasis on pleasing or pleasure with the use of this word would certainly refer to all the good gifts that come from God in this life, but knowing that those gifts are evidence of God's delight in and love for him makes it all a spiritual matter as well.

B. God provides moral guidance and instruction (6–7).

Not only does David acknowledge what the LORD gives him by his presence, he praises him for his guidance through life. He begins this section with "I shall bless the LORD." This common word (בָּרַךְ, s.v. Ps. 5:12) is used for the public praise of God's people that makes his nature and his works known throughout the world. Their praise will add to the glory of the LORD as it is perceived by people. Here David simply breaks into praise!

The subject matter of this praise is the LORD's "counsel" (from יָעַץ) and "discipline" (from יָסַר, s.v. Ps. 6:1)—how the LORD directs him in various courses of action, and how the LORD admonishes and corrects him. In line with this latter idea the psalmist uses the word "my kidneys" (כִּלְיוֹתָי), though "my heart" is often used for the translation.[25] He means the mind with the use of his conscience; but how does the LORD do this? The clue comes from the use of the plural word "night seasons." Elsewhere we find that night for the psalmist is the time of prayer and meditation on God's word. David is probably substituting the word "nights" for these activities during the nights (so a metonymy of subject). He is saying that the instruction from God comes through meditation and prayer in God's word as it was received through his mind and conscience.[26]

When people come to faith in the LORD, they surrender their lives to him; but they find that he gives himself to them as their God and Savior. Thus, they receive one who delights to give them good gifts and proper guidance throughout their lives.

III. Confidence: God's protective care endures forever (8–11).

A. God will protect his people (8–9).

Now we come to the third part of the psalm, the confidence for the future. First, the psalmist prays to God for protection, affirming his loyalty and devotion. This prompts him to praise God for the benevolent care and guidance he receives from God. And thinking of that he has become confident for the future— all of which strengthens his prayer in this crisis. David feels secure in the LORD because he reflects on the way that the LORD has taken care of him and on his life of faithful trust in the LORD.

Verse 8 begins the confidence; in fact, it epitomizes the

---

25. The visceral organs were used for the spiritual capacities, and so we classify them as metonymies of subject. The heart and the liver are the most frequently used, but the kidneys often refer to the conscience.
26. What access the psalmist had to portions of holy Scripture is impossible to say. As a king he could have had people reading to him or reciting for him from the law, or he could have memorized lines or even passages, enough to reflect on in the night.

confident message of the entire psalm. Here David takes the principles of verses 2 through 7 and applies them to the crisis in verses 9 through 11. He first declares his faith: "I have *set*[27] the LORD before me always."[28] This refers to his constant contemplation on God—he is ever mindful of the LORD, giving priority to him in all his thoughts and actions. This is the great influence in his life, no doubt coming from the prayers and meditations on his bed at night. To fail to have the LORD ever in his thoughts would be a lapse in devotion and would open the door to trouble.

Because of God's presence there is protection. He uses another anthropomorphic expression: "He is at my right side." The right side is idiomatic for the place of strength, support, and honor. Warriors would carry their shields on their left arms and fight with their right hand. This also left them vulnerable to attack on the unprotected side (Job 30:12; Ps. 91:7), but David has protection there. He knows that if the LORD is on his right side then the LORD is his strength and his shield; no adversary can harm him. He is not saying that he will never face adversity if the LORD is present in his life, but he is saying that divine protection brings him the confidence that he is secure.

For this there can only be a joyful response, an outbreak of spontaneous praise. His heart rejoices and his spirit ("glory," כָּבוֹד here; s.v. Ps. 19:1)[29] exults (וַיָּגֶל is the preterite from גִּיל, "shout exultantly," s.v. Ps. 13:6). He is filled with joy because of the security in the LORD. Even in his frail, human "flesh," he feels safe and can lie down (יִשְׁכֹּן) in security (בֶּטַח, s.v. Ps. 4:5).

---

27. The verb שִׁוִּיתִי is *piel*; the meaning "account as suitable" is not in this stem. The meaning should be "set."

28. The line uses an anthropomorphism to say that God is confined to an area when he is not; and a synecdoche, "me," to mean "my thoughts." The expression is similar to the Proverb: "in all your ways acknowledge (know) him" (3:6), that is, see God in everything.

29. The word "glory," being related to "liver," was used for the spirit, the place of the innermost feelings and choices. The word describes the whole person in a way that gives him dignity and a sense of personal worth to God. See also John W. McKay, "My Glory—A Mantle of Praise," *SJT* 31 (1978):167–72.

B. God will never abandon his people—not even to the power of death (10–11).

Now David affirms the basis for this confidence in the protection and preservation of the LORD.[30] He confidently asserts, "You will not abandon me to the grave" (שְׁאוֹל; s.v. Ps. 6:5). God will never abandon him, not even to the power of the grave.[31] "You will not abandon" (לֹא תַעֲזֹב) is a strong expression; it means forsake, leave, or abandon. David may have felt abandoned at times (see Psalm 22;1, "My God, my God, why have you forsaken me?"[32]); and he knew that he was going to die eventually (Ps. 89:48; see also Pss. 49:16; 55:16; 86:13), but his concern was that the LORD not abandon him to death, not now, and certainly not permanently.[33] He found comfort in the fact that in the final analysis God was not going to abandon him to the grave (here *she'ol* means the grave, for it is parallel to the "pit," and parallel to the "grave" in Ps. 6:5). David knew, as all the saints have known, that God did not establish a covenant with him and provide for him and guide him throughout his life, only to abandon him at the moment of his greatest need, death.

This expression is paralleled with "You will not permit your holy one to see the pit." A good part of this confidence came from his relationship with the LORD, which is expressed here by

---

30. See J. J. Kilgallen, "The Use of Psalm 16:8–11 in Peter's Pentecost Speech," *ExpT* 113 (2001):47–50; and G. V. Trull, "Views on Peter's Use of Psalm 16:8–11 in Acts 2:25–32," and "An Exegesis of Psalm 16:10," *BibSac* 161 (2004):194–204, and 304–321.

31. Delitzsch says that it is impossible for the faithful to fall into the hands of death (*Psalms,* I:228)

32. The typological fulfillment of Psalm 22 would say that because the Lord was abandoned in our place, we who believe in him will never be abandoned.

33. Speaking of the viewpoint of the author, Kraus says the psalm does not deal with resurrection or even immortality, but with the rescue from acute mortal danger (*Psalms 1–59,* p. 240). That is true to a point, but the psalmist seems to have thought his relation with the LORD would not end with death. Later Kraus expands the idea and says that some of these assertions by the psalm singers provided the early Christians with the language and categorical conceptions in which the ultimate could be expressed: the resurrection from death (p. 242).

referring to himself as a "holy one" (חָסִיד), or more precisely, one who is beloved of the LORD, a member of the covenant. The critical word in this colon is "the pit" (שַׁחַת), often translated "corruption" (in line with the Greek translation) as mentioned in the translation notes. The word refers to the grave; and calling it a pit may suggest something like a dungeon in *sheol*, i.e., an inescapable region of death.[34] The pit, i.e., the grave, is where the body decays, and so by referring to the pit David probably understood it with all its implications, as the place of death and decay. The verb in this half of the verse is even stronger than the first: God would not abandon him to the grave, but God would not allow his beloved to see the pit. He may have meant that at the time he was praying for preservation he would not see the pit—he would not die yet. Or, he may have meant that he would not see all that the pit signified. This may be why the Greek version understood the word to mean "corruption." In any case, his words are extravagant for his own experience, and yet their general meaning expresses the confidence that all believers have—God will not abandon them to the grave where they would decay.

In fact, David concludes the psalm by saying that the LORD would make him know the path of life. He would experience the way of life, the course of one truly alive, who has joy and pleasure in fellowship with God. This life, then, is union with the living God. And out of this path of life springs the idea of immortality.[35] The psalmist could not imagine that such a relationship with God would end at the grave. How his relationship with the LORD would overcome the grave may not have been clear to him,[36] but he knew that he would find the fullness of joy in God's presence and pleasure at his right hand forever.[37]

---

34. See Briggs, p. 119.

35. Perowne, *Psalms*, I:195.

36. Life after death was commonly believed throughout the world in every religion. But individual bodily resurrection was not well known. The words of David lead naturally into that belief, but how much of it he understood is hard to say. See also Norman A. Logan, "The Old Testament and a Future Life," *SJT* 6 (1953):165–172.

37. A. A. Anderson says that the word נֶצַח need not suggest eternity but can mean as long as life lasts (Psalms 1–72, p. 146). This is true for the word in general; the context must decide which of the meanings best applies (cf.

David would die, as all believers before him had, but he knew that the covenant promises would not end there, that unbroken fellowship with the LORD extended beyond this life, that God would never allow death to be the end of the covenant.

The words of this psalm represent an amazingly strong faith. And yet, the psalmist's choice of words leaves the impression that the meaning of the psalm was not fully exhausted in his immediate experience. In short, the full and precise meaning of the verse goes beyond his own experience; the words are so powerful they seem to be saying more.[38] This is the point that the apostles made in their preaching: David died; his tomb was proof of that; and his body that had been in the tomb for a thousand years had no doubt seen the decay of the grave; but Jesus rose from the dead because God did not let him see corruption (Acts 13:35–37). For the apostles the solution was made clear for all time when Jesus Christ rose from the dead, demonstrating how the promises would be fulfilled in spite of death. The language of Psalm 16 was excessive for the author's understanding but became literally true for Jesus Christ. In fact, Peter declares that David said these things about Christ (Acts 2:25–28). In other words, the New Testament writers bring this passage forward, knowing what the Spirit of God had intended when David wrote it. The apostles make it clear that these words could only apply to David in the general sense of a future resurrection, for his body had been in the grave for a thousand years; but they apply it to the Lord in the precise and fullest sense, for by the resurrection he did not see the effects of being in the grave that were true of every human being. Because Jesus' resurrection from the dead was the first fruit all who sleep in death (1 Cor. 15:20), it

---

Ps. 13:2): enduring, perpetuity, everlastingness, or forever. The psalmist may have thought in terms of perpetuity, but the word certainly signifies much more when taken in the context of all Scripture.

38. Kirkpatrick says "The doctrine of a future life is however involved in the Psalmist's faith. He grounds his hope of deliverance on his relation to Jehovah; and such a relation could not be interrupted by death (Matt. 22:32). But this truth could only be apprehended gradually and through long struggles, and only fully realized when Christ 'annulled death, and brought life and incorruption to light through the Gospel' (2 Tim. 1:10)." (*Psalms*, p. 78).

guaranteed that David, and all of the saints, would be raised from the dead. Therefore, God has not abandoned David—or any saints to the grave—but will yet raise him triumphantly.

The point is therefore that God will not abandon his faithful servants to the grave. God is greater than death; and if God is able to preserve his servants from premature death, he is also able to deliver them out of death. God will not let the covenant promises die in the grave, and the saints may take confidence in this very thing, believing the words of our Lord Christ, "I am the resurrection and the life; he that believes in me, though he were dead, yet shall he live; and whosoever lives and believes in me shall never die" (John 11:25). The death of Christ brings us redemption; and the resurrection of Christ guarantees everlasting joy and pleasure in his presence forever.

MESSAGE AND APPLICATION

Those who believe in Jesus Christ now have a greater knowledge of and confidence in the words of Psalm 16. The expository idea could be worded in this way: *God's protective care of his saints does not end in death but continues in everlasting life beyond the grave.* The exposition can lay down the truth that God does not abandon his saints to the grave, and then clarify from Scripture that the message of this psalm anticipates the full revelation of the doctrine of resurrection.

Therefore, believers need to build a strong faith in the faithfulness and goodness of God, fully assured that God's love and care for them extends beyond the grave—it lasts forever! Paul says to the Philippians: "Being confident of this very thing, that he who began a good work in you will perfect it (carry it on to completion) until the day of Christ Jesus" (1:6). God does not redeem his people, guide them through life, provide for them, and protect them along the way only to let it all come to an end in the grave. No, he will raise them from corruption to incorruption, to a glorious new estate in his presence forever.

As the saints face the trials and troubles of life, they must be absolutely sure of the goodness of God who remains faithful to his people, even in spite of their failures. They may build this kind of confidence as the psalmist did: by studying God's word with a new interest and purpose, by meditating on his goodness and guidance in the night seasons, by focusing on his grace and glory that he shares with his saints whom he loves eternally, by cultivating a life of obedience inspired by setting him always before them, by determining to remain loyal to him in the face of competing religious ideas, and by praising him more for all his care and guidance. Then they will be able to pray with confidence, knowing that nothing, absolutely nothing, neither death nor life, nor any power, will be able to separate them from the love of God that is in Christ Jesus (Rom. 8:38–39).

PSALM 17

Vindication and Protection for the Righteous

INTRODUCTION

Text and Textual Variants[1]

A Prayer of David.

1 Hear *my* righteous cause,[2] O LORD; give attention to my
    cry;
  listen to my prayer, *which is* not *uttered* by deceitful lips.
2 Let my vindication come from your presence;
  let your[3] eyes see what is right.
3 You have tested my heart, you have visited me in the night,
    you have tried me, and you find nothing;
  I have purposed[4] that my mouth will not transgress.

---

1. See Jacob Leveen, "The Textual Problems of Psalm xvii," *VT* 11
   (1961):48–54.
2. The text simply has צֶדֶק "righteousness"; the Greek has the pronominal
   suffix, reading "my righteousness." The verb "hear" and the parallel expressions concerning his cry and his prayer suggest that "righteousness"
   mean something like a righteous cause or plea. Less likely is a vocative, "O
   righteous one."
3. The Greek text has "my eyes."
4. The word is זַמֹּתִי. The form appears to be the perfect tense from זָמַם, "I
   have purposed," but with an irregular accentuation. The spelling does not
   fit as a noun with a suffix ("my thoughts, purposes"); but it may be taken
   as an infinitive (following the pattern of III *he'* verbs) with a suffix. Related to this issue is the question of how it is connected syntactically to
   the context. If it is connected to the clause before it (ignoring the accented

4 As for the works[5] of man, by the word of your lips
I have kept from the ways of the violent.
5 I have held fast[6] my steps to your paths,
my steps have not been moved.

6 As for me, I call upon you, for you will answer me, O God;
incline your ear unto me, *and* hear my prayer.[7]
7 Show the wonder of[8] your loyal love,
you who saves those who take refuge *in you,*
from those who are rising up against your right hand.
8 Keep me as the apple of the eye;
hide me in the shadow of your wings
9 from the wicked who assail me,
my deadly[9] enemies who surround me.
10 In their strength[10] they have enclosed themselves;

---

dichotomy), then the verse would be rendered "and you find no evil purpose of mine (i.e., in me); neither does my mouth transgress." But because
the form is the spelling of the perfect tense, and the major accent marks
it off from the preceding, it makes better sense to take it as the verb and
connect it to the next line, reading the two lines as "and you find nothing.
I have purposed that my mouth will not transgress" (as in NIV and ESV).
In this case the statement "you find nothing" must be explained to mean
"find nothing wrong." While there is little difference between the readings
for the overall meaning of the passage, the preferred reading would affirm
that God's examination does not find anything wrong, and express that the
psalmist's determination was to avoid transgressing with his lips.

5. The word for "works" is literally "doings" is לִפְעֻלּוֹת. The preposition is a לְ
of general reference, "with regard to," although it could also express time
or condition. The Syriac reads, "Nor have the works of man passed over my
mouth in discourse of my lips."

6. תָּמֹךְ is the infinitive absolute in place of the finite verb. It could also be
used as a gerund, "By holding fast . . . I have kept . . . ." See Ps. 35:15, 16.

7. Literally, "my word" or "my speech."

8. הַפְלֵה is "set apart, separate" with reference to something marvelously
unique (and so similar to הַפְלֵא); see Psalm 31:22 and Isaiah 28:29.

9. The MT uses "soul" (נֶפֶשׁ) in an unusual way, the expression reading "my
enemies up to my life," or "my deadly enemies." It could be interpreted to
mean "against my life" or "in greed." The Greek translation made "soul/
life" the object: "my enemies have surrounded my soul."

10. This is an interpretive translation of "their fat," which does not immediately communicate. But "fat" can be used for the prosperity and strength
of the greedy, self-sufficient person. The text simply says "their fat they

with their mouth they speak proudly.
11 They have now surrounded us[11] *in* our steps;[12]
   they set their eyes to cast *us*[13] down to the ground—
12 their[14] likeness[15] is that of a lion that is greedy of his prey,
   and as a young lion lurking in his lair.
13 Arise, O LORD. Confront him. Cast him down.
   Deliver my life from the wicked by the sword,
14 from men by your hand, O LORD, from men of the world,
   whose portion is in this life—
and whose belly you fill with what you stored up *for them,*[16]
   they are satisfied with sons,
      and they leave their substance to their children.[17]
15 As for me, in righteousness I shall see your face;
   I will be satisfied when I awake *with* your image.

---

close." The editors of *BHS* propose a conjectural reading of "the fat of their heart" (חֵלֶב לִבָּמוֹ) instead of "their fat" (חֶלְבָּמוֹ).

11. The *Qᵉre'* reading is "us." But many prefer the *Kᵉthiv* reading of "me" within the context.

12. The text has a double object with "our *steps*, now they have surround *us*." Consequently, some do not translate "us," only "our steps." But "our steps" (אֲשֻׁרֵינוּ) has proven difficult itself. The Greek version translates it with ἐκβάλλοντές με reading the verse with two verbs: "they have cast me out and compassed me round about." The form is frequently emended to יְשָׁרוּנִי, "they have tracked down" (as with the NIV; see M. Cohen, " 'AŠŪRĒNŪ 'ATTÁ SᵉBĀBÛNÎ (Q. SᵉBABÛNÛ) (PSAUME XVII IIA)," *VT* 41 [1991]:137–44).

13. The suffix in the first part of the verse does double duty and so is added here to make the reading smooth.

14. The text has "his likeness," but the singular must be distributive since the enemies are plural throughout.

15. "His likeness" *is* דְּמִינוֹ, which is usually rendered simply as "He is like." The Greek version translated it as ὑπέλαβόν με, "they laid wait for me."

16. The *Qᵉre'* is צְפוּנֶךָ, the passive participle with a suffix, "what you treasured, stored up"; and the *Kᵉthiv* is the noun צָפִין, meaning something that is stored up. So there is little difference in meaning between the two readings.

17. The Greek text offers a general interpretive translation of the verse: "from the enemies of your hand, O LORD, destroy them from the earth, scatter them in their life, though their belly has been filled with your hidden (treasure), they have been satisfied with sons and have left the remnant to their infants."

Composition and Content

In this psalm David is convinced of his own integrity while he was surrounded by enemies whose portion was in this life only. He prays to be protected from the evil world that oppresses him and to be delivered from the oppressors, a deliverance that would be his vindication. His prayer is filled with confidence which finds its greatest expression in his anticipation of seeing God's favor demonstrated on earth and of enjoying a glorious future in the presence of the LORD. The situation is not clearly explained, only hinted at in the text. Thus, it is not convincing to argue as some do that he was lying in the sanctuary to find protection while he awaited the LORD's determination of his innocence.[18] The allusions to the setting and circumstances are too ambiguous.

The psalm is similar in many ways to Psalm 16, but there are major differences. In Psalm 16 David is aware of danger in the background, but his faith encourages him not to fear. In Psalm 17, however, the danger is pressing in on him, so help from the LORD is urgently needed. In Psalm 16 David is convinced that God who had given him so much would not abandon him to death. In Psalm 17 he anticipates a glorious future in the presence of the LORD.

The structure of the psalm is clear: in verses 1 and 2 a petition is presented to the LORD, and in verses 3–5 it is followed by a profession of innocence. Then, in verses 6–12 another petition is made for God to display the wonders of his love by protecting the psalmist from the wicked; it includes a lamentation over the nature of the wicked. Finally, in verses 13–15 there is another

---

18. See Kraus, *Psalms 1–59*, p. 245. Broyles (*Psalms*, p. 99) links this passage to others, such as Psalm 26, to show that a judgment that separated the righteous from the wicked is presupposed in the process of entering the sanctuary (e.g., 5:11; 36:7; 73:28). He explains that the seekers of refuge had to establish that they were righteous, and this usually included the avoidance of deceitful speech (as in 17:1 as well as 5:6; 24:4; 36:3; 52:4). No doubt there was liturgy at the gate preceding participation in worship; but that does not necessarily lead to the conclusion from this psalm that the psalmist was in the sanctuary waiting to hear the verdict about his integrity.

appeal for God's deliverance from the worldly wicked, which includes an expectation of divine favor. There is not enough evidence to classify Psalm 17 as a lament; it may be called a prayer song that is marked by repeated petitions,[19] or more specifically an innocent person's prayer for protection.[20] The situation addressed in the psalm concerns accusers and persecutors, making his plea of innocence necessary, his prayer for deliverance urgent, and his expectation of a glorious future meaningful.

Exegetical Analysis

Summary

Conscious of his own uprightness but surrounded by enemies whose portion is in this life only, the psalmist prays to be kept from the evil world oppressing him, confident that he will see the abundant favor of the LORD.

Outline

I. The psalmist confidently appeals that his cause is right and his life upright (1–5).
  A. He petitions God to hear that his cause is just (1–2).
    1. There is no hypocrisy in his cause (1).
    2. The vindication must come from God himself (2).
  B. He declares his righteousness in thought and deed (3–5).
    1. God's examination of his heart finds nothing wrong (3).
    2. He has kept himself away from the destroyer (4).
    3. He has held fast to God's ways (5).
II. The psalmist prays to be kept from the evil of wicked people because they are full of vicious pride (6–12).
  A. He prays to be kept from the oppression of the world (6–8).
    1. The prayer is made on the basis of loyal love because the LORD saves those who take refuge in him (6–7).

---

19. Kraus, *Psalms 1–59*, p. 245.
20. Craigie, *Psalms*, p. 161.

    2. The prayer is that he be protected in the center of
       God's watchful care (8).
  B. He motivates God in the prayer by lamenting the nature
     of the wicked (9–12).
    1. They are his deadly enemies who would destroy him (9).
    2. They have become powerful and speak proudly (10).
    3. They are ruthless and relentless in their persecution
      (11–12)
III. The psalmist, confident that he will see a glorious future
   by the grace of God, prays to be delivered from the present
   persecution by worldly people (13–15).
  A. He prays to be delivered from the worldly people who are
     persecuting him to destroy him (13–14).
    1. He prays that the LORD might deliver him (13).
    2. The LORD should deliver him from men of this world
      who live only for the things of this world that God
      provides (14).
  B. He expresses his confidence that he will see a glorious
     future by the grace of God (15).
    1. He will witness the LORD's gracious response to his
      prayer.
    2. He will be satisfied with the LORD's likeness when he
      awakes.

EXPOSITION IN COMMENTARY FORM

I. Believers may confidently pray for divine vindication when their life is right with God (1–5)

A. Their appeal is for God to hear that their cause is just (1–2).

At the outset of the psalm David asks God to hear his plea to vindicate him. Three imperatives are used in verse 1: "hear" (שִׁמְעָה; s.v Ps. 45:10), "regard, give attention" (הַקְשִׁיבָה), and "listen, give ear to" (הַאֲזִינָה). This threefold plea strikes a note of urgency, and the urgency is for his vindication in the face of severe opposition. The first colon simply says "Hear righteousness (צֶדֶק; s.v. Ps. 1:5), O LORD." Several suggestions have been made for the interpretation of "righteousness," such as taking it to modify "the LORD," "O righteous LORD," or taking it as "[hear] a righteous man."[21] It probably serves as the object, with a suffix implied (used in the Greek), "my righteousness." This could mean "my righteous *cause*,"[22] or "my righteous *plea*" (NIV). The parallelism with the second clause, "give attention to my cry" (רִנָּתִי; s.v. Ps. 33:1) would be clearer then. His prayer was that God listen to his just cause.

The prayer does not come from a dishonest man. This is a righteous cause of a righteous man. The text simply says, "with no lips of deceit" (מִרְמָה; s.v. Ps. 5:7),[23] meaning that the prayer was not uttered with deception. When he speaks of his righteous cause, he speaks the truth. Of course, it would do no good at all to try to lie to God; the psalmist is simply underscoring his integrity.

In the second verse the psalmist makes it clear that he wants his vindication to come from God alone. The word order stresses this point: "From your presence / my vindication / let it come forth" (v. 2a), and "your eyes / let them see what is right" (v. 2b). Nothing short of divine vindication would make things right. The key words in this verse are "my vindication," literally, "my judgment" (מִשְׁפָּטִי; s.v. Ps. 9:4), and "equity," or, "what is right" (מֵישָׁרִים; s.v. Ps. 67:4). "My judgment" could also be translated "my decision" because he was asking for God to declare his case favorably—he wanted a decision that would vindicate him. The parallel word is "equity," a term that refers to what is right, fitting, or appropriate. The appeal is that if God heard his case, he would see that what he is doing is right (the language is of course anthropomorphic, for God knows all things). Then God would vindicate him. Subsequent believers who likewise pray for God's vindication from time to time must be able to claim such integrity in thought and deed.

---

21. Goldingay suggests taking it adverbially, "Listen faithfully" (*Psalms 1–41*, p. 238). But there is not much support for this, or a translation "faithfully."
22. Broyles, *Psalms*, p. 99
23. "Lips" is a metonymy of cause, meaning what he says; and "deceit" could be either an attributive genitive, "deceitful lips," or objective, "lips [speaking] deceit."

B. *Their prayer is made with a declaration of integrity (3–5).*

To strengthen his claim, the psalmist boldly declares his integrity. He has continued to hold fast to the faith, to walk with the LORD as it were—as God himself knows. Three verbs (perfect tenses) are used to express how thoroughly God knows him: you have tested (בְּחַנְתִּי; s.v. Ps. 139:23), you have visited (פָּקַדְתָּ, s.v. Ps. 8:4), and you have tried me (צְרַפְתַּנִי). All these verbs may be taken as present perfects to emphasize not only the action but also the continuing effects.[24] The words are commonly used for spiritual testing and examining, sometimes by means of the application of God's word, and sometimes by God's putting the individual in difficult circumstance to test that person's faith. The first statement emphasizes the test is of the heart, i.e., God examines his thoughts and decisions and not just the actions. The second one says that God attends to him (visits him), and this attention is in part at night. The clause could refer to his staying in the holy precincts until judged innocent, but it is more likely that it simply refers to his lying on his bed and in quiet thought contemplating his life in the light of the word of the LORD (see Pss. 4:4, 6:6, 16:7). It would be in such meditations that God would instruct him in the way that he should go. The attention given here (in this visit) includes an intense scrutiny, as the last verb of the series emphasizes. And the psalmist's conclusion of the matter is "you find[25] nothing." He is innocent before God.

Moreover, the psalmist says that he has made it his intention (זַמֹּתִי)[26] not to transgress in what he says ("my mouth will not transgress, "mouth" being a metonymy of cause). This could

---

24. The verbs could also be given a present tense translation: "you examine . . . you do not find." The NIV takes them as concessive clauses and supplies "Though": ". . . though you test me, you will find nothing." Dahood would read them as precative perfects, equal to the preceding imperatives (*Psalms,* I:94).

25. The tense now changes to the imperfect, allowing for the present tense translation, or even the future, "you will not find," which would fit the translation of the perfect tenses as present.

26. The verb זָמַם means "to consider, purpose, devise" (s.v. Ps. 10:2): "I have purposed."

refer to any transgression through speech, but specifically in this context it first applies to his claim of integrity, his claim to be in the right, to be innocent. What he says about his actions is true.[27]

In verses 4 and 5 he declares his righteousness in his activities. With regard to the works of man, he asserts that he has watched (שָׁמַרְתִּי; s.v. Ps. 12:7), meaning tried to avoid, or kept from, the ways of the violent or destructive person (פָּרִיץ).[28] How has he done this? "By the word of your lips." The word spoken by the LORD (lips being a metonymy of cause), i.e., the word of the LORD, has been the only way for him to maintain his integrity (the word could have been an oracle to him, or the word written for use in the sanctuary). It keeps him from the ways of the wicked, meaning either their way of living (in which case if he joins them he would have no integrity) or the destructive effects of their activities (which would cause him seemingly endless problems). And God's word also keeps him "holding fast" to God's ways.[29] The following word, "my steps, my goings" (אֲשֻׁרַי), could be either the subject or the object: "my steps have held fast to your paths," or, "I have held fast my steps to your path." In either case, his conduct, his course of actions, followed precisely from the ways of God. Accordingly, his activities in life have not moved from the ways God—he has not slipped or wavered at all. His integrity, his righteousness, is due to his living out the revealed will of God every step of the way. And because he is righteous, he could appeal to God with confidence to vindicate him.

II. Believers may confidently pray to be kept from evil because of the nature of evil people (6–11)

A. *Their prayer is for protection from oppressors (6–9).*

The psalm now returns to prayer, voicing a separate but

---

27. Delitzsch suggests that this might also mean that if he had entertained an evil thought it would not pass his lips (*Psalms*, I:235–6).

28. Goldingay makes this to be a specific type of reference: "I have kept watch for the ways of the robber" (*Psalms 1–41*, p. 240).

29. The verb תָּמַךְ means "hold, seize, grasp." It is used in Proverbs for holding fast or keeping the words of wisdom (4:4). And in Psalm 16:5 it was used for the LORD's holding secure the psalmist's lot in life.

related concern. David's petition is a righteous petition, because he is a righteous man among evil and dangerous people. He has remained faithful because he listens to God's words; now he wants God to hear his word. Verse 6 introduces the prayer in liturgical fashion. The first verb is a perfect tense, preceded by an emphatic use of the pronoun (אֲנִי־קְרָאתִיךָ). Because the verse includes the imperatives of the prayer, it makes the best sense to take the perfect tense as an instantaneous perfect and translate it with the present tense: "As for me, I call upon you." The second clause uses the imperfect, expressing his confidence: "for you will answer me." After this liturgical introduction, two clauses form the basic request; the first calls for God to incline his ear (an anthropomorphic expression), meaning, listen very closely. And the second pleads for a response "hear my prayer" (literally, "my speech" [אִמְרָתִי; s.v. Ps. 119:11]).

It is not a prayer for God to listen, but to act (as the verb "hear" implies), and act dramatically—"Show the wonder of your loyal love (חֶסֶד, s.v. Ps. 23:6)." The verb (הַפְלֵה) means "separate" with the sense of setting it apart as unique.[30] For God to make his loyal love distinct means to demonstrate it in a new and extraordinary manner. "Love" in this context must mean what the love would do (and so it is a metonymy of cause). This is clear from the epithet that is used to express how the love should be demonstrated: "You who saves/delivers (מוֹשִׁיעַ, s.v. Ps. 3:2) those who take refuge (חוֹסִים) in you." His salvation of his people would be the outworking of his loyal love for those who put their faith in him. The verb "take refuge" (חָסָה, s.v. Ps. 7:1), a common figure for trusting in the LORD, stresses the idea of seeking shelter (and so is an implied comparison).

Many commentators note here the use of several terms that are also found in Exodus 15, indicating a possible allusion. Just as the LORD had delivered his covenant people Israel from the oppressing Egyptians by wonderful acts, so will he deliver this Israelite from his enemies.

The need for taking refuge indicates that the psalmist is presently under attack. And the following line clarifies the point: the

---

30. It has been associated by some interpreters with the verb meaning "make wonderful" because the uniqueness would be supernatural (= הפלא).

LORD saves his people "from those who are rising up against your right hand."[31] The participle "rising up," literally "lifting themselves up" (מִתְקוֹמְמִים; s.v. Ps. 3:1), carries the sense of active opposition against the LORD and his powerful plan (see 27:12; Mic. 7:6). By delivering those who take refuge in him, the LORD would also be confounding their planned opposition to him.

The request for a display of God's extraordinary love is followed by the prayer for protection (vv. 8–9). The two images used in verse 8 are found elsewhere in the Bible. The first is (a simile): "Keep me (שָׁמְרֵנִי; s.v. Ps. 12:7) as the apple of your eye" (cf. Deut. 32:10, Zech. 2:8). The expression "the apple of the eye" is a reference to the pupil and the tiny image in it of what the eye sees. In Hebrew it is "the little man (אִישׁוֹן) of the eye." The request is that God's protective care should never let him out of his sight (an anthropomorphic way of speaking). The other image also refers to protective care; it is a comparison with the "shadow of your wings" (see Deut. 32:11; Pss. 36:7, 57:1, and 61:4; this figure, a zoomorphism, is also used by Jesus in Matthew 23:37). Because it is an image of loving care and safety, "hide me" (תַּסְתִּירֵנִי, an imperfect of injunction) is an appropriate verb.

The focus of the protection is expressed in the continuation of the prayer in verse 9: "from the wicked who assail me, my deadly enemies who surround me." Wicked people are gathering against him to destroy him. The first description of them is found in the verb "assail" (שַׁדּוּנִי, the perfect tense of שָׁדַד), which means "devastate, lay waste, deal violently with." The next description flows from this—literally "my enemies with/in/up to the life" (אֹיְבַי בְּנֶפֶשׁ), they are "deadly enemies." This expression has been given various translations, but all with the same point that the enemies want to end his life.[32] They assail him and surround

---

31. The Greek text joins this line with the next verse, "keep me . . . from those who rise up . . . ." NIV also rearranges the lines to get "you who save by your right hand those who take refuge in you from their foes." The only change of meaning here is that "by your right hand" becomes the means of deliverance instead of the point of the opposition "against your right hand."

32. Goldingay offers an interpretive translation of "life/soul"; he has it, "enemies surround me with longing," i.e., desiring his life and possessions (27:12; 35:25; *Psalms 1–41*, pp. 241–2).

him with the intent to destroy his life. Only God can protect him from such attacks.

B. *Their prayer is urgent because of the power of the enemies (10–12).*

The next three verses comprise something of a brief lament about the wicked and their plans. The description already begins in the last section, especially verse 9. But in this section the description focuses more on their nature and their wicked plans. First, their nature is calloused and arrogant (v. 10). The first expression is cryptic: "their fat they close up." The proposed reading in *BHS* ("they close off the fat of their hearts") focuses the attention on their hearts that are closed to the people they hurt, i.e., they are indifferent or calloused. Goldingay suggests the same without the proposed change in the text, arguing that the fat surrounds the place where the heart is, the midriff.[33] ESV translates this line with a free interpretation: "They close their hearts to pity." This interpretation is workable, but the fact that the text does not mention "heart" is a drawback. The image of fat often refers to the best portion, the healthy part, or prosperity and success. The image is figurative here for the wicked; it may describe them as those who prosper in the world and become strong in their rebellion against the LORD (compare Deut. 32:10–15; see also Ps. 119:70), or it may be using fatness to describe their rebellious spirit against God (see Deut. 32:15; Isa. 6:10).[34] These people in their strength and their greed were rebellious against God and therefore indifferent to others.

They may have been closed to God and to those in need, but they had not kept their mouths shut. They took the liberty to speak arrogant things with their mouths, proud things that justify their deeds in defiance of God, and so they are both indifferent and arrogant.

Second, their planned actions are cruel and destructive (v. 11). "They have now surrounded us *in* our steps." Perowne

---

33. Goldingay, *Psalms 1–41*, p. 242.
34. Anderson, *Psalms 1–72*, p. 150.

paraphrases "our steps" with "whithersoever we go," [35] which captures the idea that "our steps" would refer to going different places (the implied comparison has become idiomatic in the Bible). The psalmist finds that wherever his steps lead the enemies materialize to surround him, and the evil intent of their presence is seen in their eyes: they set their eyes to cast us to the ground (setting their eyes being a metonymy of adjunct, their facial expression with its determined gaze fits the intended action). Their "eyes" betray them to be malicious, intent on destroying him, but the psalmist believes that God will keep him as the apple of his eye.

Third, the fierceness of their attack is recorded in the next verse that compares them to strong lions (the singular form is probably distributive, referring to each of them). The use of "his likeness" at the beginning of the verse underscores the simile of the lion, and the parallelism heightens the danger: the enemy is like a lion hungry for prey, like a young lion, full of energy, sitting in its hiding place ready to attack. The danger the psalmist faces is therefore a planned and powerful attack intent on destroying him. The world has not changed in its opposition to the righteous and their cause.

III.Believers may pray with confidence as they anticipate a glorious future (13–15).

A. They pray for God to destroy the wicked whose only care is for this life (13–14).

The psalm returns to petition once again, asking God to act now ("arise") to destroy the wicked. The series of imperatives in verse 13—"arise (קוּמָה; s.v. Ps. 3:1), confront (קַדְּמָה), cast down (הַכְרִיעֵהוּ), deliver (פַּלְּטָה; s.v. Ps. 37:20)"—stresses the urgency of the appeal. After the initial imperative for God to begin immediately to act, the next two imperatives call for the destruction of the enemy, and the last the corresponding rescue of the psalmist's life. This rescue would come by the

---

35. Perowne, *Psalms*, I:204.

LORD's sword, a figure for military victory.[36] The prayer is for deliverance from worldly men, so the petition continues into verse 14 (although the NIV repeats the verb from verse 13 to make verse 14 a separate appeal).

Verse 14 has a number of difficulties and judging from the variety of explanations in the commentaries, there is no easy solution. The first half of the verse reads literally "from men (מְמְתִים) by your hand, O LORD, from men of the world (מֵחֶלֶד), their portion [is] in life ('whose portion is in this life"). The word for "men" (מְתִים) simply means mortals or human beings, perhaps suggesting their wretchedness (see Isa. 41:14).[37] Broyles thinks that the lines have been corrupted, and he suggests that instead of "men" we read "putting them to death" (מְמִיתָם), and instead of "world" we read "make an end of" (< חָדֵל). He translates this as "putting them to death by your hand, putting them to death; make an end of their portion in life."[38] The reconstruction is interesting but not convincing. The lines simply describe the enemies as men of this world who see this life as their portion— they live for the moment because they are worldly.

The second half of verse 14 is more difficult. The text reads, "and with your treasure (i.e., צְפוּנְךָ, what you have stored up) you fill their belly; they are satisfied *with* sons, and they leave their substance to their children." There are two ways that this half-verse can be taken. (1) It may be interpreted as a continuation of the first half of verse 14, meaning that it is a continued description of the wicked, worldly man, who lives only for this life. What was stored up for the wicked could either refer to the punishment that God was saving for them, or to the basic provisions of life that come by way of common grace (people might live only for this life; but they seldom acknowledge that everything in this life is from God). In line

---

36. If the psalmist has in mind the victory would be military by the Israelites, then "your sword" would be a metonymy of cause, for the LORD would use them to gain the victory (or he could use other armies as well). If the deliverance came through some divine intervention apart from the Israelites' participation, "sword" would be an implied comparison, perhaps comparing the word of the LORD to a sword.

37. Goldingay, *Psalms 1–41*, p. 243.

38. Broyles, *Psalms*, p. 101.

with the first option, the verbs could be taken in the sense of the psalmist's desire or appeal: fill their belly with (the punishment) you have stored for them, and may even their sons be sated with it.[39]

(2) Or, verse 14b may begin a new section with a description of the righteous, now referred to as the "treasured ones" of God. The verse would then say that God provides for the needs of the righteous, blesses them with children, and ensures the future of their families. This would form a contrast, then, with the men of the world in verse 14a. The NIV follows this view, making a major break in the middle of the verse and translating these lines as "you still the hunger of those you cherish; their sons have plenty, and you store up wealth for their children." The critical issue in the interpretation concerns the meaning of "your treasure" or more specifically "what was stored up by you." For a number of reasons it seems more likely that the reference is to what the LORD has in store for the wicked than a reference to the righteous as the people God cherishes. First, there is the strong contrast beginning in verse 15, "as for me," indicating that verse 15 begins the contrast with the wicked in verse 14. Second, the reference to "their" in 14b does not appear to have changed in any clear way from the use of "their" in verse 14a. And finally, in 14b "your treasure" ("what you have treasured") is a singular form and contrasts with the plural "their."[40] So the verse is saying that the LORD fills their belly with what he has stored for them, either punishment, or things in life from common grace in spite of their rebellion against him.[41] Since their interest is only in the things of this life, they are satisfied with children, and when they are gone they leave what is left to their heirs. Their satisfaction is in what is temporal and temporary.

---

39. Anderson, *Psalms 1–72*, p. 152)

40. See further the elaboration of these reasons in W. VanGemeren, "Psalms," p. 200. Broyles follows this second view, but makes the verbs volitional: "may you fill their belly with what you have stored up, may their sons be sated and deposit the remainder to their children" (p. 101).

41. The ESV translates "belly" as "womb" and takes it as a reference to God giving them children. This is probably an attempt to make the line fit the next more directly.

B. They are confident of seeing the LORD (15).

The righteous, on the other hand, will be satisfied with much more, as the final verse of the psalm affirms. If the last verse was difficult syntactically and grammatically, this verse is difficult theologically. The translation is straightforward: "I [as for me] in righteousness (בְּצֶדֶק) shall see (אֶחֱזֶה) your face, I will be satisfied when I awake *with* your likeness (תְּמוּנָתֶךָ)." The psalm ends then where it began, with the psalmist claiming to be righteous; and this righteousness will carry him through life, for he expects a glorious future in which he will be satisfied with God's presence. The wicked, on the other hand, who are satisfied with the life in this world, have no future with God. God will destroy them and deliver his people.

Seeing the face of the LORD seems to be in tension with verses like Exodus 33:20 that say no one can see God. To avoid this conflict the Greek text interpreted the line to say, "I shall appear in righteousness before your face, I shall be satisfied when your glory appears." But the verb is clearly "I shall see" (an active verb, not a *niphal*). Since the "face" of the LORD is associated with divine favor (compare the blessing of Num. 6:22–27), seeing his face would mean witnessing his divine favor. The expression is similar to what we find describing the experience of worship in the sanctuary, such as is expressed in Psalm 63:2. Seeing God's power and glory in the sanctuary meant seeing evidence of his favor (so the expression would be metonymical), namely his power and his glory as it was revealed through the praises of the people. The psalmist's expectation was the answer to his prayer, that the LORD in his favor would deliver him from the enemies. In that deliverance he would see God. There is no compelling reason in this part of the verse to say that the psalmist was anticipating death and would therefore see the face of God afterwards. Rather, this expectation is part of the contrast between the destruction of the wicked, who live their lives without God, and his life, which would continue in God's grace.

However, the idea is made more complex by the parallel colon. It says, "I will be satisfied when I awake with your likeness." The verb "I will be satisfied" (אֶשְׂבְּעָה) stresses the certain expectation of being satisfied. The form could also be interpreted as a request, "Let me be satisfied," a prayer for the future expectation to be realized. In either case, the satisfaction will come when he awakes "with" or "in" God's likeness (תְּמוּנָתֶךָ). The NIV has added the idea of seeing from the context to form a more perfect parallel, "*with seeing* your likeness." That is certainly a possible interpretation, but the expression "when I awake" complicates the verse. It could mean when he awakes from sleep, but that would carry little force here. The word "awake" can mean awake from death in the Old Testament (see 2 Kings 4:31; Job 14:12; Jer. 51:39; Isa. 26:19). Dahood actually translates it "At the resurrection," which is a possible interpretation.[42] Most commentators do not want to see a reference to resurrection or afterlife in this psalm, either because they do not think the doctrine was known, or because they do not think it fits the argument of the psalm.[43]

There is no reason why the psalmist could not extend his confidence in the LORD's immediate deliverance to include his ultimate vindication beyond death (whether he thought in terms of resurrection or simply a future existence beyond death in the presence of God). Accordingly, as VanGemeren says, the psalmist by inspiration was looking for a greater experience with God that can only be part of the post-resurrection world.[44] A present vindication would bring temporary satisfaction, but a future and final deliverance would bring complete satisfaction in the presence of God. This idea would add an additional contrast, then, to the description of the wicked as people of this world, whose portion is in this life. The fact that the understanding of resurrection may not have been widespread at the time does not mean that the psalm could not make a brief reference to a future life (as in Psalm 16). The truth of Scripture is that ultimate vindication comes in the life to come; and the language of this psalm harmonizes with the future revelation of glorification, i.e., that in the life to come the righteous will be like him. Whether the psalmist intends or understands this is impossible to say, but in

---

42. Dahood, *Psalms*, I:99.
43. Goldingay argues that the emphasis here is for God to act now, and a glimpse of the afterlife would undermine the point of the psalm (*Psalms 1–41*, p. 245).
44. VanGemeren, *Psalms*, p. 200.

light of the full revelation of Scripture, this psalm can be read now in a wider context.

MESSAGE AND APPLICATION

The psalm, then, is a confident prayer for God to vindicate the righteous by bringing the opposition and arrogance of the wicked to an end. The psalmist was confident in his prayer because he knew that he was righteous before God, and he knew that God had a glorious future in store for him. The message may be worded this way: *Those who live godly lives may confidently pray for vindication and protection from the wicked, their confidence coming from the knowledge that they are right with God and that they will enjoy a glorious future with God.*

The important emphasis in this psalm is that those praying can claim to be righteous—tested and examined by God, and yet righteous. Because of this they can pray with confidence for God to vindicate them by destroying the wicked and ending their antagonism. The New Testament will confirm that the prayers of the righteous are effectual, but especially a prayer for vindication (e.g., Rev. 6:10, and also Matt. 6:10). The opposition comes from worldly people, whose satisfaction comes from this life alone. Their life, and their satisfaction will come to an end when the LORD arises to deliver his people, now, and in the age to come (Rev. 22:20). The psalmist fully expected to witness God's favor in his immediate deliverance—he expected to awake to a glorious future and be satisfied with the likeness of God.[45] Just what he expected is not totally clear, but the righteous have come to expect this glorious future will extend to the life to come. The words of this psalm anticipate the New Testament words, promising ultimate vindication for the righteous, "We shall be like him, for we shall see him as he is" (1 John 3:2).

---

45. Jaki says, "This is one of those cryptic phrases in the Old Testament that indicate a faintly visible belief in a life after death which is immensely superior to a shadowy existence in Sheol" (*Praying the Psalms*, p. 60).

PSALM 18

A Royal Thanksgiving for Divine Intervention in Battle

INTRODUCTION

Text and Textual Variants

To the Chief Musician. A Psalm of David, the Servant of the LORD, who addressed the words of this song to the LORD on the day that the LORD rescued him from all his enemies, and from the hand of Saul; he said:

1 I love you, O LORD, my strength.
2 The LORD is my rock and my fortress and my deliverer,
   my God, my rock, in whom I take refuge,
my shield and the horn of my salvation, my stronghold.
3 I call upon the LORD, *who is worthy* to be praised,
   and I am saved from my enemies.

4 The cords of death encompassed me;
   the torrents of destruction assailed me;
5 the cords of the grave entangled me;
   the snares of death confronted me.

6 In my distress I called upon the LORD;
   to my God I cried for help.[1]

---

1. Some manuscripts confused this form אֲשַׁוֵּעַ, "I cried," with the form אִוָּשֵׁעַ, "I am saved." The parallel poem in 2 Samuel 22:7 simply repeated the verb אֶקְרָא, "I called."

From his temple[2] he heard my voice
    and my cry to him reached his ears.
7 Then the earth reeled and rocked;
    the foundations also of the mountains trembled
      and quaked, because he was angry.
8 Smoke went up from his nostrils
    and devouring fire from his mouth;
glowing coals flamed forth from him.
9 He bowed the heavens and came down;
    thick darkness was under his feet.
10 He rode on a cherub and flew;
    he came swiftly on the wings of the wind.
11 He made darkness his covering,
    his canopy around him,
      thick clouds dark with water.
12 Out of the brightness before him
    hailstones and coals of fire broke through his clouds.
13 The LORD also thundered in the heavens,
    and the Most High uttered his voice, hailstones and coals
      of fire.[3]
14 And he sent out his arrows and scattered them;
    he flashed forth lightning and routed them.
15 Then the channels of the sea were visible
    and the foundations of the world were laid bare
at your rebuke, O LORD,
    at the blast of the breath of your nostrils.

16 He sent from on high; he took me,
    he drew me out of many waters.
17 He rescued me from my strong enemy[4]
    and from those who hated me,
      for they were too mighty for me.

---

2. Greek has "holy temple."
3. It is possible that this phrase, "hailstones and coals of fire," was copied inadvertently from verse 12 where it actually fits.
4. The Hebrew text has the singular form, "my enemy." But the Greek and Syriac and many modern versions have the plural form to harmonize the two cola of the verse. If the form had been the plural, it would be hard to explain why it was changed to a singular and created the difficulty.

18 They confronted me in the day of my calamity,
  but the LORD was my support.
19 He brought me out into a broad place;
  he rescued me, because he delighted in me.
20 The LORD dealt with me according to my righteousness;[5]
  according to the cleanness of my hands he rewarded me.
21 For I have kept the ways of the LORD
  and have not acted wickedly before my God.
22 For all his rules were before me,
  and his statutes I did not put away from me.
23 I was blameless before him,
  and I kept myself from iniquity.
24 So the LORD has rewarded me according to my
    righteousness,
  according to the cleanness of my hands in his sight.
25 With the loyal you show yourself loyal;
  with the blameless man you show yourself blameless.
26 with the purified you show yourself pure;
  and with the crooked you make yourself tortuous.
27 For you save a humble people,
  but the haughty eyes you bring down.[6]
28 For it is you who light my lamp;
  the LORD my God lightens my darkness.
29 For by you I can run against a troop,[7]
  and by my God I can leap over a wall.
30 This God—his way is perfect;
  the word of the LORD is proven *true*;
he is a shield for all those who take refuge in him.

31 For who is God, but the LORD?
  And who is a rock, except our God?—
32 the God who equips me with strength
  and makes my way blameless.
33 He makes my feet like the feet of a deer

---

5. Here and in verse 24 the text uses צֶדֶק, but some manuscripts and the parallel psalm in 2 Samuel use the other word צְדָקָה.
6. The Greek took the line to mean "you humble the eyes of the proud."
7. The Greek has "I shall be delivered from a troop."

and sets me secure on the[8] heights.
34 He trains my hands for war,
    so that my arms can bend a bow of bronze.
35 You give me your saving shield,
    and your right hand sustains me,[9]
    and your graciousness[10] makes me great.
36 You broaden the path beneath me
    so that my ankles do not turn.

37 I pursued my enemies and overtook them,
    and did not turn back till they were consumed.
38 I thrust them through so that they were not able to rise;
    they fell under my feet.
39 For you equipped me with strength for the battle;
    you made those who rise against me sink under me.
40 You made my enemies turn their backs to me,
    and those who hated me I destroyed.[11]
41 They cried for help, but there was none to save;
    they cried to the LORD, but he did not answer them.
42 I beat them fine as dust before the wind;
    I cast them out like the mire of the streets.
43 You delivered me from conflicts with the people;
    you made me the head of the nations,
    people whom I had not known served me.
44 As soon as they heard of me they obeyed me;

---

8. MT has "my heights."
9. This colon is not in the poem in 2 Samuel.
10. The Hebrew text has "your meekness (or lowliness)" (עַנְוָתְךָ). The use of this word for the LORD is unusual, but it can be explained in terms of the LORD's stooping down to help him (NIV), meaning his gracious intervention. The word would be a metonymy of adjunct then. I used the intended meaning in the translation instead of the literal rendering for clarification. On the other hand, there are different readings for the word. The Greek (with some variations) translated this as "discipline" (παιδεία)—your discipline has upheld me. That would reflect a Hebrew *piel*, עִנּוֹתְךָ. M. Dahood suggests the root '–n–w, "to conquer," and translates it as "your triumph" (*Psalms*, I:116). More plausible is the suggestion of "your answering" (עֲנֹתְךָ), which is found in the parallel poem of 2 Samuel 22:36; it would form a contrast with verse 41. This could also signify "your hearing, your oracle, your encouragement" (Kraus, *Psalms 1–59*, p. 255).
11. The verb has a pronominal suffix: "those who hated me I destroyed them."

> foreigners cringe before me.
> **45** Foreigners lost heart
> and came trembling out of their fortresses.[12]
>
> **46** The LORD lives, and blessed be my rock,
> and exalted be the God of my salvation—
> **47** the God who gave me vengeance
> and subdued peoples under me,
> **48** who delivered me from my enemies;
> yes, you exalted me above those who rose against me;
> you rescued me from the man of violence.
> **49** For this I will acknowledge you, O LORD, among the
> nations,
> and sing praises to your name.
> **50** *He brings* great victories to his king,
> and shows loyal love to his anointed,
> to David and his offspring forever.

Composition and Context[13]

This rich and rather complex psalm may be classified as a royal thanksgiving psalm. It is a royal psalm because it focuses on the experiences of the king, and it is a thanksgiving because of the contents and the structure. The psalmist begins with a summary praise of what the LORD means to him (1–3) and then turns to report his great suffering and miraculous deliverance (4–19). This is followed by a didactic section in which he attributes the deliverance to the LORD (20–30). Then, in a lengthy tribute, the psalmist reports the blessings he has received from the LORD in his military experiences (31–45). The psalm closes with a doxology (46–51).

The fact that the psalm is also recorded in 2 Samuel 22, albeit with variations, witnesses to the unity of the composition.

---

12. The Greek version interprets the images more specifically, saying the foreigners "lied to me . . . grew old (i.e., withered) and limped from their paths."

13. See F. M. Cross, Jr., and D. N. Freedman, "A Royal Song of Thanksgiving: II Samuel 22 = Psalm 18," *JBL* 72 (1953):15–34; and J. Kenneth Kuntz, "Psalm 18: A Rhetorical–Critical Analysis," *JSOT* 26 (1983):3–31.

It appears that it may have been edited or altered slightly when deposited in the sanctuary for liturgical use. At first glance its location in 2 Samuel suggests it was written near the end of David's military career, but the superscription of the psalm links it to the end of the wars with Saul. It may have been placed later in 2 Samuel as a summary of his lifetime of wars. The psalm appears to refer to one significant battle in which God supernaturally intervened, but it also provides a summary of God's interventions to enable David to have victory over many enemies and so cannot completely be limited to one event. The psalm reveals the writer to be both a warrior and a king, and the language and images fit the experiences of David.[14] Even though few would accept the psalm as Davidic, everything about it fits his life better than any other. Most commentators simply dismiss Davidic authorship out of hand. Goldingay appears to entertain its possibility, but he prefers a time during the Persian period when someone wrote the psalm in honor of David. One of the difficulties about the psalm for him concerns the psalmist's claims of personal integrity; he contrasts this with the life of David, saying, "given his wickedness it is hardly proper for David to speak of his integrity in such unequivocal terms."[15] He thinks it would be more likely for someone else to write about David and focus only on the positive aspects of his life. This, of course, in no way solves the problem he raised.

A better explanation of this apparent tension comes from an understanding of the claims of innocence within this context. David was claiming that he had been a true Israelite, faithful to the covenant and the covenant God, not that he was sinless. There is a similar claim to innocence in Psalm 44, a national lament over a military defeat. In it the people claimed they had been faithful to the covenant God and had not sinned to bring about their disaster—they had not followed other gods, they had not rebelled against the LORD, and yet they were being slaughtered all over the battlefield. They had not sinned in such a way as to deserve such a humiliating defeat. So what David was claiming was

---

14. For just one example Kidner notes the mention of fighting on foot (vv. 29, 33) as opposed to the use of chariots after his time (*Psalms 1–72*, p. 90).
15. Goldingay, *Psalms 1–41*, p. 254

loyalty and faithfulness to God as the king and military leader of God's people. Because he had been faithful in this, God had shown himself faithful to his covenant promises to Israel and its king.

Similarly, in Psalm 17 there is such a claim of loyalty and faithfulness to God. Because the psalmist is righteous, he is confident in asking God to vindicate him (see also Ps. 26). The fact is that those who truly believe in the LORD and walk in his ways are called the righteous, the faithful, the holy ones—not because they are sinless, but because they are faithful to the covenant.[16] The psalmist was not claiming to be sinless; no one could ever make that claim. To be blameless means that one is free from sin or forgiven for sin.

Psalm 18 also has connections with Psalm 19.[17] For example, Psalm 19 will focus on the God of heaven (vv. 1–6), reminding the reader of the epiphany language of Psalm 18:9, 13, and 16; Psalm 19 will draw attention to the perfect word of the LORD (vv. 7–11), recalling Psalm 18:30; and Psalm 19 will call for the continual pursuit of a life of integrity (vv. 12–14), a central point in both Psalms 17 (vv. 3–5) and 18 (v. 20).

Exegetical Analysis

Summary

Having reviewed all that the LORD means to him, the psalmist reports his perilous suffering and the LORD's miraculous deliverance, explaining this and all his victories by his faith and Almighty God, and then he rejoices in the mercies shown to him, concluding with a doxology.

Outline

I. The psalmist declares his love for the LORD who time and time again protects and delivers him from his enemies (1–3).

---

16. The question of how the faithful deal with sin will be addressed in the exposition of Psalm 51.
17. VanGemeren, *Psalms*, pp. 201–02.

A. He expresses his love for the LORD who gives him
   strength (1).
B. He describes the LORD as one who has proved to be his
   protector and deliverer (2).
C. He calls on the LORD and is saved from his enemies (3).
II. The psalmist details how the LORD has supernaturally
   delivered him from his anguish and peril by using all the
   forces of nature, explaining such amazing intervention in
   terms of faith in the LORD (4–30).
   A. He records the great, supernatural deliverance he has
      received (4–19).
      1. Report of the Dilemma: He was headed for the grave
         at the hands of the wicked (4–5).
      2. Report of the Deliverance: The LORD supernaturally
         intervened to deliver him from death (6–19).
         a. Summary Report: The LORD answered his cry for
            help from his distress (6).
         b. Poetic Description: The LORD responded from
            heaven and supernaturally destroyed the enemies
            (7–15).
         c. Conclusion: The LORD reached down and rescued
            him from the enemies because he was pleased with
            him (16–19).
   B. He explains the deliverance in terms of his faithfulness
      to God and God's faithfulness to him (20–30).
      1. He affirms that has remained faithful to God by living
         in accordance with the ways of the LORD (20–24).
         a. God dealt favorably with him because of his righ-
            teousness (20).
         b. God's ways and decisions have guided him in life
            (21–23).
         c. God rewarded him for his righteousness (24).
      2. He declares that the way of the LORD is perfect,
         because he is faithful to those who are righteous and
         delivers those who are humble (25–30).
         a. God deals with people as they live according to his
            ways (25–26)
         b. God enables those who humbly trust in him to gain
            the victory because his way is perfect (27–30).

III. The psalmist acknowledges that the LORD, the living God, has demonstrated his loyal love to the king by enabling him to triumph over all his enemies (31–50).

A. He rejoices over the many blessings God has given to him (31–45).

1. Introduction: God is his Rock (31).
2. God strengthens him and trains him for battle (32–34).
3. God gave him victory over his enemies (35–45).

B. He acknowledges the living God who has demonstrated his loyal love to him by enabling him to triumph over the nations (46–50).

1. He calls for blessings for his rock, the LORD who lives (46).
2. He praises God who works vengeance on his enemies by subjugating them (47–48).
3. He vows to acknowledge God's loyal love to his anointed king in giving him magnificent victories over his enemies (49–50).

COMMENTARY IN EXPOSITORY FORM

I. Devoted love is due to God, who protects and delivers his people whenever they call upon him (1–3).

A. The faithful love the LORD (1).

Looking back on a life filled with divine intervention in times of danger, the psalmist begins with a declaration: "I love you, O LORD, my strength." The verb used here is unusual (אֶרְחָמְךָ); this is the only place this form and this meaning occur.[18] It describes a deep feeling of compassion and tender affection (s.v. Ps. 51:1). It usually refers to the LORD's tender compassion for his people, but

---

18. Anderson refers to exegetical reconstructions of the form, such as the attempt to change it to "I exalt you" (אֲרֹמִמְךָ; see A. A. Anderson, *Psalms 1–72*, p. 154). Goldingay diminishes the idea of intimacy and chooses that of dedication; he translates it, "I dedicate myself to you" (*Psalm 1–41*, p. 256).

here the psalmist used it to express his deep affectionate for the LORD. The expression "my strength" (חִזְקִי; s.v. Ps. 27:14) is in apposition to "the LORD," further describing him as the one who gives strength to his servants ("strength" is then a metonymy of cause). David saw the strength of God in the way he was enabled again and again to gain victory after victory—and referring to God as his strength surely brought to mind a lifetime of experiences. These experiences he now refers to with a series of figures.

B. The faithful describe the LORD in terms of his saving acts (2).

Verse 2 focuses on the character of God with a series of figures of speech (see similar listings in Pss. 31 and 71). The images are drawn from both military settings and geographical locations. Kidner says that in listing these descriptions David was reliving his escapes and victories.[19] The first description, "my rock" (סַלְעִי), is a geographical metaphor; it refers to a natural place of protection, a rocky crag that serves as a defense.[20] Another word for "rock" is used later in the verse: "my rock (צוּרִי) in whom I take refuge" (see Pss. 40:17 = 70:5). By these metaphors he was saying that God was his place of safety and security.

There are also four military metaphors in the verse. The first is "my strong fortress" (מְצוּדָתִי; see 1 Sam. 22:4). This word was applied to the huge rocky plateau in the desert called Masada, a formidable place of refuge; whether David was ever there or not is impossible to know, but it does provide a good illustration of a natural desert fortress (use a geographical location for a military fortress). A parallel term is the last one in the verse, "my stronghold" or "my high tower" (מִשְׂגַּבִּי, from שָׂגַב, meaning "to be high, unassailable"). Such a stronghold might be isolated high

---

19. Most commentators would say that since the author of the psalm was not David, it is unlikely that the imagery is taken from specific places David visited (A. A. Anderson, *Psalms 1–72*, pp. 154–155).

20. Kidner, *Psalm 1–72*. p. 91. In 1 Samuel 23:28 the word was used in a commemorative naming. The armies of David and Saul were moving along either side of a rocky ridge, but Saul was suddenly called away. As a result of this providential deliverance, the place was called סֶלַע הַמַּחְלְקוֹת or "Rock of Divisions" ("escapes").

up in the rocks (see Isa. 33:16) or built high. A third military metaphor, "shield" (see Ps. 3:3; Gen. 15:1), signifies God as the one who protects his people, especially in the midst of the battle. Finally, he is called "the horn of my salvation" (or, "my saving horn"). The image of the "horn" is drawn from the animal world; it signifies power, and is therefore used for kings (cf. Ps. 132:17; Dan. 7:7, 8).[21] By this image God is described as his saving power, the one who delivers him in battle. The remaining description of the LORD is not a metaphor like the others; it simply declares that the LORD is "my deliverer" (מְפַלְטִי; s.v. Ps. 37:20), "the one who delivers me." All the images in the verse serve to illustrate the many ways and times that the LORD delivered him from danger—because he took refuge in him (s.v. Ps. 7:1).

C. The LORD delivers his people when they pray (3).

Verse 3 provides a summary explanation: the psalmist calls on the LORD and is saved from his enemies. All of the LORD's past acts of deliverance and protection prompt the inescapable conclusion: he is to be praised. Who better to call on in trouble than one worthy of praise, for that means he has a history of answering prayers? And so the verse includes the description of the LORD as "praised" (מְהֻלָּל). Because this word is placed first in the verse and does not appear to be clearly connected, the translation has to clarify the syntax. This may be done rather easily: "I call upon the LORD *who* is praised." NIV has "*who is worthy to be* praised."[22]

The verbs of verse 3 could be taken in one or two different ways. If they (imperfects) refer to many situations, then they should be given a present tense translation (habitual or

---

21. It could be a reference to the horns on the altar, which would then signify asylum in the sanctuary, but this psalm is about the divine enablement of the king to win battles. The horn could also be the animal horn used in battle to marshal the armies.

22. Kraus suggests changing it to מְחֻלָּל, "pierced through," meaning when he was pierced through he cried to the LORD (*Psalms 1–59*, p. 255). A. A. Anderson suggests מֵהֹלְל, "from the boastful" (*Psalms 1–72*, p. 155). The Greek translation is closer to the word in the MT: "With praises (αἰνῶν) I will call upon the LORD."

progressive imperfects): "I call out . . . I am saved" (the *niphal* imperfect of יָשַׁע; s.v. Ps. 3:2). The first could be made subordinate as a temporal clause, "Whenever I cry out . . . I am saved (or: shall be saved)." Goldingay wants to take them as past tenses (as in verse 6), and start the summary report with verse 4 instead of verse 6: "I called . . . I was delivered,"[23] but the verse fits better as a general statement of the principle based on his experiences.

II. God has a history of using supernatural means to deliver those who put their faith in him (4–30).

A. The faithful retain the memory of God's supernatural acts of deliverance (4–19).

1. Report of the Dilemma: Death seemed certain (4–5).

In highly poetic language the psalmist reports how he was almost dead at the hands of his enemies. He uses four parallel expressions to stress the point that he was being entangled and pulled down to the grave;[24] he focuses on "the cords of death" (חֶבְלֵי־מָוֶת), "the torrents of destruction" (נַחֲלֵי בְלִיַּעַל), "the cords of the grave" (חֶבְלֵי שְׁאוֹל), and "the snares of death" (מוֹקְשֵׁי מָוֶת). The figures of "cords" and "snares" are implied comparisons, indicating the captivating power of death; it is as if ropes were wrapped around him pulling him down to death. There may also be an allusion here to the idea of chaos as a force, for in the pagan Canaanite world "death" was deified as a god named *Mot* ("Death"), and the river (current, *Nahar*) and the sea (*Yam*), symbols of chaos in antiquity, were also made deities. The reference to "torrents of destruction" may be an allusion to that understanding of chaos, especially in view of this particular word

---

23. Goldingay, *Psalms 1–41*, p. 258.
24. The verbs in the two verses are simple past tenses because this section begins the narrative report. Three of the verbs are perfect tenses, but one is the prefixed conjugation יְבַעֲתוּנִי, which in light of the parallelism in the verse should be taken as a preterite/imperfect without the *waw* consecutive.

for "destruction" (בְּלִיַּעַל) with its connotations for pagan beliefs.[25] In the parallel psalm (2 Sam. 22:5) the first clause does not have "cords of death," but "waves/breakers of death," making the

---

25. The term *bᵉliyaʿal* (בְּלִיַּעַל) describes, primarily, an act of wickedness that results in the breakdown of the established social order. It could easily be translated "worthless(ness), useless(ness), wicked(ness)" or "unprofitable." A less frequent meaning is "destruction" or "ruin." The etymology of the word is uncertain. It is most likely a combination of the negative prefix *bᵉli* (בְּלִי) and a noun *yaʿal* (יַעַל), "without worth"; but there are other possible explanations as well.

The first few categories of meaning have the ideas of "wickedness, worthlessness," describing acts of wickedness that lead to the dissolution of this order. The first category shows specific violations of the Law. For example, it describes a person who does not care about the poor (Deut. 15:19), but the violations are usually more vile than this. The wicked men of Gibeah are called "men of *bᵉliyaʿal*" (Judg. 19:22); they raped and abused a woman all night (20:13), which act is described as lewd and disgraceful (20:6). The expression "sons of *bᵉliyaʿal*" is used for the two men who lied under oath that Naboth cursed God and the king (1 Kings 21). A slanderer in Proverbs 16:27 is also described this way.

A second category simply describes refractions of the laws of society so that the idea of worthlessness is also present. Nabal is called a "son of *bᵉliyaʿal*" for his general hostility to civilized behavior (1 Sam. 25:17). In Psalm 101:3 the king vows never to set a worthless wicked thing before his eyes.

A third category is for cultic abuses. Eli's sons were called "sons of *bᵉliyaʿal*" because they did not wait for the ritual. They took their portion first, and they also engaged in cultic sexual intercourse (1 Sam. 2:12).

A fourth group concerns infractions against the monarchy. For example, the riff-raff that supported Jeroboam I in the newly formed northern kingdom are also described with this expression (2 Chron. 13:7).

The other major area concerns the meanings of "destruction" or "ruin." In Psalm 41:8 when the psalmist was ill, enemies and false friends took advantage of him by pouring *bᵉliyaʿal* on him. This must mean some kind of physical peril; it may refer to a "deadly injury." The same kind of use appears here in Psalm 18:5 (//2 Sam. 22:5) where it refers to physical ruin. Because it is parallel to "death" and "*sheʾol*," some have thought it to be a reference to the underworld. But "streams of the underworld" is not as useful as "streams of [bringing] destruction."

In a personal sense, *bᵉliyaʿal* can mean "the destroyer." This occurs in Nahum 1:15 (2:1), and possibly in Job 34:18 (according to KBL). This reference may be the basis for *bᵉliyaʿal* being taken to refer to Satan in Rabbinic literature, the pseudepigrapha, and 2 Corinthians 6:15, and to Antichrist in later literature.

connection to the torrents stronger. A violent death might seem to the psalmist to be part of the chaos of this life, a chaos that dominated life in the pagan mentality. It might even have seemed to him that the deified forces of paganism would triumph if he met such an overwhelming death, but the LORD delivered him supernaturally from such a chaotic death, a death that seemed to have power over life. God would not surrender his servant to such an untimely death, and certainly not to any evil powers of death and hell, real or imagined.[26]

2. Report of the Deliverance: The LORD intervened supernaturally (6–19).

In this section there is a summary statement of the answer to the prayer (6), a description of God's supernatural intervention (7–15), and then a report of the rescue (16–19). The summary statement simply reports that he cried out to the LORD in his distress and the LORD heard his cry. The verbs in 6a appear to be imperfects, similar to the expressions in verse 3. "I called" is the same form translated "I call" in the previous verse (אֶקְרָא); but there it was a general statement, and here it is a summary report and so treated as a past tense (a preterite without the *waw* consecutive). The second verb likewise appears to be an imperfect, but it must also be translated as a past tense, "I cried for help" (אֲשַׁוֵּעַ). The next verb is "he heard" in 6b; it too appears to be an imperfect tense (יִשְׁמַע), but in this report is a past tense. Interestingly, in the parallel poem in 2 Samuel this form is clarified to be a definite past (preterite with *waw* consecutive in 22:7, וַיִּשְׁמַע). God answered the prayer from his temple, which in view of all the heavenly images to follow, most likely refers to the heavenly sanctuary.

In verses 7–15 we have the description of a supernatural intervention. The use of the first person verbs and suffixes disappear from this section, and rightly so because it is all about the LORD.

---

26. Such references to pagan ideas are not signs of simple Israelite borrowing, for the religious systems were so diverse. It is much more likely that they were used polemically against pagan ideas. The writer used expressions and images common in the culture in order to defuse them of any deification or power in the presence of the living God.

It uses the language of epiphany in which all the forces and elements of nature are involved in the LORD's presence to deliver. The language draws on the phenomena at Sinai when the LORD made his presence known among his people. As then, so in subsequent miraculous interventions, all the phenomena of nature envelops God in his appearance.[27] And even though the phenomena veil the LORD from plain sight, they are so compounded and so dazzling that they cannot be mistaken for ordinary events—when God comes in power to rescue his people, all nature is moved at his coming. There are two ways to explain this language. If in the experience of the psalmist there had actually been an earthquake, perhaps some volcanic activity, dark and ominous clouds, hailstones and lightning and thunder, then the descriptions would be metonymies of adjunct, phenomena that accompanied the reality of his presence and communicated various ideas. If on the other hand the phenomena did not occur literally and the psalmist was simply using the language of epiphany to describe the awesome power of the LORD who intervened on his behalf, then the figures would be implied comparisons. It seems most likely that there was an array of natural phenomena in the heavens and on the earth that were clearly a sign of divine intervention.[28]

First is the earthquake (v. 7). Earthquakes seem to be the common starting point for theophanies (Judg. 5:4ff.; Deut. 33:2f.; Ps. 97:2ff.; Isa. 30:27ff.). Because rebellious forces were on the earth, the earth quaked in anticipation of the LORD's wrath. The earth reeled and rocked at his quake, and the very foundations of the mountains trembled because he was angry.[29]

---

27. Kraus, *Psalms 1–59*, p. 260.
28. One good example of this is the battle that Deborah and Barak fought against Sisera the Canaanite (Judg. 4–5). The song of Deborah uses a lot of imagery from the forces of nature; it seems to be a poetic record of the event, but the chapter before records the historical event: a heavy thunderstorm mired the enemy chariots in the mud and enabled the Israelites to defeat the Canaanites. There was a timely phenomenon in the weather that was God's provision for the Israelites' victory; the song describes that phenomenon in the language of epiphany.
29. The parallel verse in 2 Samuel says "the foundations of the heavens." This is probably equivalent to saying the mountains, because of the idea that the mountains held up heaven (see Job 26:11).

Smoke and fire and glowing coals flamed from his nostrils (v. 8).[30] These are symbols of divine wrath being breathed out. The language of a volcanic eruption is reminiscent of the end of Sodom. Verse 9 adds the imagery of thick darkness under his feet. The dark clouds hovered over the area, and above them was his presence, veiled by the darkness. His movement was swift and decisive (v. 10), for he rode on the cherub and came swiftly on the wings of the wind. In the midst of the storm, beyond the dense, dark clouds, the LORD rode in victory. His chariots were the angels (Ps. 68:33), here identified as the powerful and terrifying composite angelic creature called a "cherub." The dense clouds seemed to bear him up, but it was in reality the angelic chariotry (Ezek. 1). His swift flight across the heavens was like riding on the wings of the wind (see Ps. 104:3–4). Here there may be another allusion to pagan religions, for in Canaan Baal was known as "the rider of the cloud"—it was part of his description as lord of heaven and earth. That description was simply part of a mythological text; this description in the Bible is of the very presence of the LORD of armies. The victory over such forces that were deified in Canaan was what made it clear that the biblical account was true.

The darkness in the dense clouds became his canopy. Apparently the phenomenon of a dark thunderstorm appeared to be a covering for his glorious presence (v. 11), but ahead of the clouds was a dazzling brilliance that preceded him as he went (v. 12; see Deut. 33:2; Hab. 3:4). From this dark cloud cover came hailstones and coals of fire, the imagery of the thunderstorm and the volcanic eruption being joined together as evidence of his swift judgment. All of this precedes the terrifying thunder, which signifies the mighty voice of the Most High God (see Ps. 29; see also Rev. 19:6). Baal also was said to thunder when he was about to bring the rains; but this passage is different in that it does far more than accompany rain that would then be explained as coming from a deity—it accompanies the LORD's actual intervention in battle to give his people victory over the

30. The word "nostrils" could also be translated "anger," but since the verse also uses "mouth" this change is unnecessary. The image of smoke from the nostrils is the image of anger anyway.

pagan enemies. Out of this storm God sends down bolts of lightning like arrows (see also Ps. 77:17; 144:6; and Hab. 3:9–11) to scatter the enemy.

Finally the language turns to a description of the foundations of the land without the presence of the chaotic waters.[31] What is terrifying and chaotic in nature and deified by the pagans is all under the power of God to be used for the destruction of evil forces. In this there is a similarity to creation in which the LORD controls the waters by his powerful commands so that the dry land appears. Here we read that as a result of the blast of his rebuke through this fierce storm the channels of the sea[32] are seen, and the foundations of the world are laid bare. This brings to an end the description of the theophany, the manifestation of the divine presence in the phenomena of nature.

Then verses 16–19 record the thanksgiving for the actual rescue. This section picks up where verse 6 ends, and the first person forms reappear. The LORD hears his prayer and intervenes from heaven. He rescues him from his enemies, which is like being rescued from many waters (a reference to the torrents of verse 4, an implied comparison). The word for "rescue" is "draw out" (מָשָׁה); it was used in Exodus 2:10 for Moses' being drawn out of the water. There may be an allusion to that event which was the initial deliverance of Israel from the nations symbolized first by rescuing the leader from the water.[33] It is also possible that it alludes to the waters of the netherworld,

---

31. Kraus, *Psalms 1–59*, p. 260. There may be another allusion here to pagan mythology, for in Canaan the abode of the high god El is located at the source of the two rivers in the midst of the two channels (*'apq*) of the two oceans (Anderson, *Psalms 1–72*, p. 159). This would emphasize further that the LORD not only destroyed the enemies of Israel but in the process uncovered and controlled the powers of chaos.

32. The psalm reads "channels of water," but the parallel in 2 Samuel 22:16 says "sea." Anderson suggests that the initial *mem* of *mayim* ("water") should be added to the preceding word (*'apike*, "channels of") as a *mem* enclitic, and the resultant meaning would then be almost the same as that in Samuel (*Psalms 1–72*, pp. 158–9). There does not seem to be a compelling reason to harmonize the texts this way.

33. In Exodus 2 Moses was drawn out of the water and named to commemorate the event ("I have drawn him out"), but in Exodus 14 Moses rescued the Israelites by drawing them out of the sea.

or the chaos, which symbolized powers that were hostile to the LORD.[34] Scripture elsewhere uses the language of a flood of water simply to describe the armies of invaders (Isa. 8:6–8), and that would fit this section of the psalm very well. Verse 17 clearly states the dilemma: his enemies,[35] those who hate him, are too strong for him. They no doubt are national foes who were defeated on the battlefield, but the expression may also include forces of darkness driving the enemies. Then verses 18 and 19 clearly state the deliverance: when the enemies confront him in the day of his calamity, the LORD brings him out into a broad place. The LORD rescues him because he delights in him (v. 19b). This report of deliverance emphasizes the reversals in the psalmist's experience: instead of being in a place of disaster the LORD provides a solid support for him (v. 18); in the place of distress, a narrowness or strait, the LORD gives him room (v. 19), and even though his enemies hate him, God is pleased with him (v. 19).

B. The faithful praise the LORD for his faithfulness to those who are loyal to him (20–30).

1. They affirm their integrity (20–24).

Verses 20 through 30 provide the explanation for the LORD's supernatural deliverance—it is the faithfulness of the LORD to those who are faithful to him. In the first section (vv. 20–24), the psalmist asserts his faithfulness to the LORD, and then in the second part (vv. 25–30) he declares God's faithfulness to his people. The first part is testimony; the second is instruction.

Verses 20 and 24 form an *inclusio* for the first section, for they say essentially the same thing with a minor variation in verse 24: God rewarded him for his righteousness. These verses

---

34. See Anderson, *Psalms 1–72*, p. 159.

35. The word for "enemy" in the text is singular, whereas "those who hate" me is plural. Many commentators simply change the word to the plural to make the better parallelism, but the singular could be a collective noun. Or, the first colon might have one main enemy in mind, and the second colon expand the report to include all who hate him. In sum, there are other ways to explain the singular form than changing the text.

may at first seem like arrogant boasting, but that is not the case since they form part of the praise for God's faithfulness. They simply affirm that because God deals with people as he sees their heart to be towards him,[36] the people of God may explain divine intervention through prayer as divine reward for righteousness; and so beginning in verse 20 the psalmist says that God deals with him on account of his righteousness and rewards him because of his clean hands (a metonymy of cause, indicating that what he has done has been done in righteousness). The first verb is often translated "reward" because of the context, but it means "deal with" (וַיִּגְמָל); the second verb (שׁוּב) means "return" and has the idea of recompense in this verse. God reciprocates the righteousness of his people. By "righteousness" (צֶדֶק, s.v. Ps. 1:5), the psalmist means that he has faithfully lived in accordance with God's law. Verse 21 also says that his hands were pure (כְּבֹר יָדַי, "according to the purity of my hands," hands being the metonymy of cause for what he does).

The language of this section is reminiscent of that which was used in the entry liturgy of the sanctuary. To find acceptance by God, worshipers would have to be able to attest that they were righteous, pure, and blameless (see Pss. 15 and 24). Here the psalmist knows that God has approved him—because of the supernatural intervention on his behalf—and so these are affirmations of that fact. Similarly, in Psalm 118:19–21 the worshiper could enter the gates of righteousness because God had delivered him and become his salvation.

The specific details of the affirmation concern his obedience to the law of the LORD, specifically the ways of the LORD (the section is similar to Ps. 17:1–5). According to verse 21 he not only kept the ways of the LORD but also did not act wickedly; and according to verse 23 he kept himself from iniquity. By keeping God's ways and by keeping himself from iniquity, he means he has maintained his integrity (תָּמִים, s.v. Ps. 7:8). Moreover, he keeps God's decisions (rules; s.v. Ps. 9:4) before him in all his activities and has not put them away.[37] This is not

---

36. Perowne, *Psalms*, I:213.
37. The text has the *hiphil* form of the verb, אָסִיר, so that the clause reads, "I have not put away his statutes." The poem in 2 Samuel has it slightly

pride, because the LORD has delivered him, and the LORD delivers the humble. This is simply claiming that God accepts him as righteous in that he delivers him.

2. They acknowledge that the LORD gives them the victory (27–30).

Victory comes from God alone. In the first two verses we read how God deals with people in accordance with their compliance to his will—with the faithful he shows himself faithful; with the blameless he shows himself blameless; with the purified he shows himself pure; and with the crooked he makes himself seem tortuous (vv. 25–26). In the first expression we have the word "the faithful" (חָסִיד, s.v. Ps. 23:6), often translated "the merciful" here. This is a common description of the faithful people of God in the Psalter (see Pss. 16:10; 30:4 etc.); it describes those who are loyal to the covenant that God has made with them (see Ps. 50:5). So to those who are loyal to the covenant, God will show himself loyal as well, meaning, he will demonstrate his faithful love to his own (see Ps. 17:7). Likewise, in the second expression, with the blameless (תָּמִים) God shows himself blameless, meaning that God's dealing with people who maintain their integrity will be in faithfulness and righteousness—no one could find fault with it. The third expression concerns purity. The description of the people as "purified" (נְבָר, the *niphal* from בָּרַר, "the purified one" or "the one who purifies himself"),[38] refers to a moral purification. Describing believers as the "purified" would include the cleansing of sin through divine forgiveness, but in this context which stresses faithfulness, it would refer to remaining pure by living a righteous life. To the pure God deals in purity, openness, and perfection as he administers kindness and justice.

With the last colon of verse 26 there is a change to note that

---

different, using the *qal* of the verb, אָסוּר, making the line read "I have not turned away from his statutes."

38. Some commentators follow the suggestion of G. R. Driver and render the word "boorish" (from Syriac, "rude, simple); so "with the boorish God shows himself boorish." This would make a closer parallel to verse 26b and therefore provide the entire 26th verse as a contrast to 25 (see A. A. Anderson, *Psalms 1–72,* p. 161).

God also deals in kind with the wicked. They are here described as "twisted, perverse" (עִקֵּשׁ; see Prov. 2:15; 28:6). With them, God shows himself perverse, devious (תִּתְפַּתָּל). This idea may at first seem troubling, but it simply says that God deals with the perverse in kind—he can match them in their capacities, twisting their wickedness around to come back upon them.[39] God gives them up to follow their own perverse ways until they bring destruction on themselves (see Lev. 26:43; Rom. 1:28).[40] To the perverse God may appear to be perverse because he does not deal with them as he does with the righteous, and they might complain that God is not gracious and loving after all.

After laying down the principle by which God deals with people, the psalmist next describes how God gives the victory to the humble who take refuge in him (vv. 27–30). These lines should be taken as general principles as well, although they undoubtedly have reference to specific events. The main point is in verse 27: God saves the humble, but brings down the proud. The word "humble" (עָנִי, s.v. Ps. 9:12) can mean the afflicted, poor, or humble. Here it is in contrast to the proud, and therefore stresses humility, the awareness of needing help. Accordingly, the king is victorious in battle because he champions those whom God champions. God brings down (שָׁפֵל) the proud, the "haughty eyes" (עֵינַיִם רָמוֹת). The arrogant think they have no need of God, and as a result they disregard the value or the needs of others. This arrogant attitude, expressed by their eyes, is one of the things the LORD hates (Prov. 6:16). Their gaze may be high, but God brings them low.

In the next two verses the psalmist uses several figures.

---

39. The psalm breaks the pattern of the last three cola by not repeating the description word (here "perverse") to the action of God. Instead it changes the verb, even though the sense is the same (see them in parallelism in Deut. 32:5 and Prov. 8:8). The word used for God's dealings with them has the idea of twisting or crookedness (פָּתַל). It is the word used in Genesis 30:8 to describe the struggle over the right to be the mother of Jacob's children, and using this word the child Naphtali was named. In fact, Kidner suggests that the Jacob-Laban cycle serves as a good illustration of the point the psalm is making, namely, that God used the deviousness of Laban to turn the tables on Jacob (*Psalms 1–72*, p. 94).
40. Perowne, *Psalms*, I:214.

The first is light—God lights his lamp (v. 28).[41] The lamp is a figure (an implied comparison) meaning prosperity, continuation of life, and divine guidance. Lighting the lamp would indicate God gives life (whereas quenching a light would mean extinguishing a life; see 2 Sam. 21:17). Even in the darkness God is the source of life. The darkness here is also a figure (an implied comparison) for times and circumstances that are life-threatening.

The next expression concerns overcoming barriers by the power of the LORD. Verse 29 says, "By you I can run against a troop" (a synecdoche, referring to all kinds of conflicts in warfare).[42] The second half of the verse may also refer to some aspect of war, although the idea is not readily clear: "I can leap over a wall" (perhaps escaping; see 1 Sam. 23:2).

Verse 30 provides the summary conclusion of this section, affirming that the way of the LORD is perfect (תָּמִים again). It also serves as a transition to the next section which will delineate the divine perfections (vv. 31–36). "This God" (הָאֵל) focuses the reader's attention on all that has been said of God. Everything that he does is blameless, perfect. Moreover, his word (אִמְרָה) has been proven (צְרוּפָה, as if refined in a fire [see Ps. 12:6]). The psalmist knows that God's word is true and therefore trustworthy, because he has been a shield (a metaphor for protection) to those who acknowledge their need and take refuge in him.

III. God is worthy to receive praise and glory in all the world because of who he is and what he does for his people and their king (31–50).

A. The righteous rejoice over God's blessings (31–45).

---

41. The parallel poem in 2 Samuel 22:29 simply says, "You are my lamp."

42. There is a possibility that the line could be translated differently. The verb "I run" is אָרֻץ, usually taken from רוּץ, "to run." The form could also be taken from a root רָצַץ, meaning "to crush" (see Goldingay, *Psalms 1–41*, p. 271, n. 39); but the translation "run" is correct—it is what the parallel poem in Samuel has written fully, אָרוּץ.

1. They must acknowledge his perfections and provisions (31–36).

This praise sets the pattern for the saints to follow. It begins with a hymn-like confession of faith, affirming that Yahweh alone is God. The verse uses rhetorical questions to make the point: "Who is God but Yahweh?" meaning there is no god besides Yahweh. "Who is a rock, except our God?" meaning our God alone is the source of all strength and security (the metaphor of the rock is treated more fully in Deuteronomy 32:4, 15, and 18). The point is that no other deity can be trusted, and no other deity should receive praise that is due to the LORD.

In verses 32–36 the psalmist explains in detail what this means to him. Some versions translate the verbal forms in this section as past tenses, forming a thanksgiving report of what the LORD has done. The variety of verbal forms used suggests that these should be taken as general descriptions of what the LORD does, which would obviously include what the LORD has done. Verses 32, 33, and 34 each begin with an active participle ("who equips me," "makes" and "trains"); verse 32b uses a preterite ("makes/gives"), verse 33b uses an imperfect ("sets me secure"), and verse 34b changes the subject, but uses a perfect tense: "so that my arms can bend a bow of bronze."

First, the psalmist declares that God makes him strong (v. 32). The line reads "The God who equips me with strength," using the participle of "gird, surround" (הַמְאַזְּרֵנִי).[43] Girding with strength (חַיִל) means making strong (the figure referring to equipping for war). The verse is similar to Isaiah 45:5 which has the same sequence of ideas: the only true God, Yahweh, is the one who strengthened Cyrus for his task. Here the psalm adds that if God gives him strength he also makes his way perfect, probably meaning safe and without difficulties. He does this because his way is perfect (v. 30).

Second, in verses 33 and 34 the psalmist describes this enablement by means of specific activities. The first is based on a comparison with deer (a simile), perhaps ibex, that are sure-footed on the rocky ledges and cliffs. God makes him sure-footed—he

---

43. The poem in 2 Samuel has here "my strong refuge" (מָעוּזִּי).

enables him to stand on the heights. The point is the agility he needed to scale the cliffs and seize mountain strongholds. Then, in verse 34 he moves from legs to hands and arms. God trains (teaches, מְלַמֵּד) his hands for war so that he is able to bend[44] a bow of bronze. The description of the bow as bronze if taken to mean a bow made out of bronze would be hyperbole. It may rather refer to a wooden bow strengthened with bronze, or perhaps a strong bow used to shoot arrows made with bronze tips. The point is that he is able to use such heavy-duty weapons because God gives him the ability and the strength to do so.

Then, in the next two verses (vv. 35–36) the psalmist changes from the third person (about God) to the second person (addressing God directly). He acknowledges that God protects him and sustains him and makes him great. The verbs of verse 35 are imperfects, except the first one has the *waw* consecutive, but they all may be given the present tense translation. The protection God gives is described as "the shield of your deliverance," or "your delivering shield." He may be attributing his own shield in this way, or simply comparing God's protection to a shield (see Gen. 15:1). Then he acknowledges that the power (i.e., the right hand) of God sustains him. Finally he affirms that God's "meekness," that is, his kind and gracious dealings with him, make him great. In view of all of this the psalmist asserts that God broadens (an imperfect tense) his path so that his ankles do not twist (the perfect tense with *waw* on the negative). The figures used say that God makes his way flat and broad, so it is an easy walk; it refers to all his activities, but primarily his military activities.

2. They must acknowledge that he has given them the victory (37–45).

This section provides a report of what God enabled the psalmist to do on the battlefield. The verbs for the most part are prefixed conjugations (i.e., imperfects) but require a past tense translation (so they may be given a preterite classification). In

---

44. The form וְנִחֲתָה is the *piel* perfect of נָחַת, "press down, bend"; it refers to either bending the bow to string it, or bending it in the process of shooting. The verse begins with the participle, "he trains," and concludes with this form in sequence.

several places the parallel poem in 2 Samuel includes the *waw* consecutive on the form, confirming the past tense translation. The section reads as if David was bragging about his military exploits; but the psalm has made it very clear that God enabled him to do this, and so this is a delineation of the divine enablement.

The general statement is in verse 37, which states that he chased his enemies and overtook[45] them, adding that he was relentless in his pursuit until they were finished (כִּלּוֹתָם). To this he adds that he thrust them through so that they were not able to rise[46]—they fell[47] under his feet, meaning they were killed, not doing homage. The reason for this victory was that God equipped (girded) him with strength and made the enemies sink under him. In fact, God gave their backs to him (v. 40). This could mean that they fled before him, or more likely to this context that says he destroyed them that he placed his foot on their backs as they groveled before him (see Josh. 10:24).

In verse 41 he explains that their cries to God were not heard: "They cried for help,[48] but there was no one to deliver (no deliverer, מוֹשִׁיעַ). The parallel colon adds "(they cried) to the LORD," but it uses the preposition "concerning, against, unto" (עַל). Most translate it "unto" (as if it were אֶל, which is what 2 Samuel has), but this preposition would normally signify the content of the prayer; so it may be that they were crying out about the way God was dealing with them. At any rate, there was no deliverance. On the contrary, the psalmist reports that God enabled him to beat them down like dust (simile) and cast them out like the mire (simile).[49] The comparison of his defeated enemies with dust and mire depicts them as worthless rubbish.

---

45. The poem in Samuel 22:38 has "destroyed" (< שָׁדַד).
46. 2 Samuel 22:39 has a different arrangement of this colon: it begins with a different verb, "I consumed them" (וָאֲכַלֵּם), then says "I struck them down" (with a waw consecutive for past tense), and ends with "they did not rise/ were not able to rise" (simply יְקוּמוּן). MT has the verb "to be able" before the infinitive "to rise."
47. The poem in 2 Samuel 22:39 uses the form with the *waw* consecutive.
48. The verb "cried for help" is יְשַׁוְּעוּ; 2 Samuel 22:42 has יִשְׁעוּ, "they looked."
49. MT has "cast out / empty out" (אֲרִיקֵם < ריק). The line in 2 Samuel 22:43 has "I stamped them and crushed them" (אֲדִקֵּם אֶרְקָעֵם) to form a closer parallel with the first colon.

The next three verses speak of his conquest of the nations. He begins by saying that God delivered[50] him from conflicts with the people (v. 43a). "Conflicts" is from a word (רִיב) that often refers to a legal complaint, but here it may refer to the battles (hence the plural construct) with people.[51] God not only delivered him, but made[52] him the head of nations—people whom he had not known now were his servants. On this point he dwells for two more verses, noting how these foreigners came cowering[53] to him when they heard of him, and explaining that they had lost heart (withered) and so came trembling[54] out of their fortresses. God subdued the nations around him so powerfully that they lost the will to fight and gladly submitted to the king.

B. The righteous proclaim to the world that the LORD lives and extends the reign of his anointed king over the nations (46–50).

1. The LORD lives and is to be exalted with praise (46).

The last section of the psalm is filled with praise to the LORD; it forms a fitting conclusion to a psalm that has acknowledged the LORD's saving acts from beginning to end. This doxology begins with the acclamation, "Yahweh lives" (חַי יהוה). It is an affirmation not only of the existence of the LORD, but of his power revealed through his acts—the evidence that he lives. And this distinguishes him from the pagan gods, who are mute and impotent (Ps. 115:3, 5 etc).[55] But because the LORD lives, he is worthy of praise: "Blessed

---

50. 2 Samuel 22:44 uses the *waw* consecutive here, indicating the past tense again.

51. Instead of מְרִיבֵי, "from the battles of/with," some commentators suggest reading מֵרִבְבוֹת, "from the multitudes of" (see Ps. 3:6; Kraus, *Psalms 1–59*, pp. 255–6)

52. For MT's "place, put" (< שִׂית) the poem in 2 Samuel 22:44 has "kept" (< שָׁמַר)

53. The form in the MT is יְכַחֲשׁוּ, but in 2 Samuel 22:45 it is יִתְכַּחֲשׁוּ. Instead of "cower," a translation of "grow lean" meaning "wither" has been put forward (J. H. Eaton, "Some Questions of Philology and Exegesis in the Psalms," *JTS* 19 [1968]:603–9).

54. MT is וְיַחְרְגוּ, but 2 Samuel 22:46 has וְיַחְגְּרוּ, "limped."

55. Other interpretations of this expression are untenable, such as taking it as a wish formula, "Long life to the LORD" or "May Yahweh live" (Dahood,

(בָּרוּךְ, s.v. Ps. 5:12) be my rock, exalted (יָרוּם) be the God of my salvation (God who saves me)."

2. God works vengeance on his enemies (47–48).

That this salvation is at the expense of the enemies is the point of the next two verses. Vengeance belongs to the LORD, according to Deuteronomy 32:35; but there are times when God's vengeance is executed by his people. This passage refers to such a time, as David says that God gives him vengeance over his enemies.[56] It is

---

Psalms, p. 118), which Kidner rightly calls naive (*Genesis 1–72*, p. 96). And, the suggestion that this is drawn from the dying-rising god mythology of the ancient world is without support. Even Anderson's comment that the formula is of Canaanite origin is without evidence; he does say it now refers to the unchanging vitality and power of the LORD in contrast to pagan deities (pp. 165–6).

56. The verb נָקַם means "to avenge, take vengeance." The word occurs in several of the cognate languages; in Arabic the usage was expanded over the years to include "be hostile, full of rancor, vindictiveness, have spite, be resentful" (Wehr, p. 1168). Biblical Hebrew usage is more focused; it is used to describe action taken to correct an imbalance based on a wrong committed. In a case or two the meaning is vindictive retaliation, but the normal use is with a non-pejorative sense.

The word is used in what may be called "non-legal" passages, meaning they are not part of the law, although they address cultural justice. In Genesis 4:15 the LORD promised to avenge Cain sevenfold if anyone killed him. The promised action was preventative. In Judges we read how Samson took revenge on the Philistines for the loss of his wife (15:7) and his sight (16:28). By destroying the culprits he was correcting the imbalance that was caused by their actions against him. On a grander scale, the Bible also says that God corrects the imbalance of justice by taking vengeance on nations that brought harm to Israel (Ezek. 24:8; 25:12, 15). Sometimes this was done by the LORD giving Israel's armies success.

The word is used in strictly legal contexts as well. In Exodus 21:20–21 it occurs with regulations about the killing of a slave. If the killing was intentional, the law required the slave be compensated for with the life of the owner. The purpose was to protect the slave, not simply get even for his death. Here the word shows the balance or payment incurred in a legal sense. On the national scale, God warned Israel that if they violated the covenant he would execute vengeance. The vengeance would come through pestilence or defeat in battle; it would correct the imbalance of their violation of the covenant. Likewise, in Isaiah 1:24 the LORD states that Israel will receive just punishment for their disobedience as the LORD takes revenge

accomplished by God's subduing people under him and delivering him from enemies who are rising up against him. The enemies are referred to as men of violence (חָמָס; s.v. Ps. 58:2)—they not only rise up against the king but bring about disorder and chaos in the world. God enables the king to subdue them under his authority (compare this point in Psalm 2).

3. God demonstrates his loyal love to the king (49–50).

The royal psalmist declares that he will publicly praise the LORD among the nations. The cohortatives used in verse 49, "I will acknowledge" (אוֹדְךָ, s.v. Ps. 6:5) and "I will sing praises" (אֲזַמֵּרָה; s.v. Ps. 33:2) are terms used in psalms of thanksgiving. They indicate the psalmist's acknowledgment will be in public worship for all to hear and share, but the public declaration will be intended for the benefit of the nations who need to hear that it was the living God who subdued them under this king. That is emphasized by the last part of the praise (v. 50), which says literally: "[to the LORD] who makes great the victories of his king and acts with loyal love for his anointed, to David and to his seed forever." The victories the king desires are made into great (מַגְדִּל) victories by the LORD. And all of this is the LORD's working out of his faithful covenant love (חֶסֶד, s.v. Ps. 23:6) to the royal family. The faithful love of God will not come to an end with this ruling king, but is guaranteed to the seed of David forever.

God, the Divine Warrior, chose his anointed king to establish his kingdom over the nations as well as Israel. Every successful king who came to the throne in Jerusalem had occasion to make this psalm his own as God enabled him to rule. Of all the kings, it fits David most closely, for he established a united monarchy and subdued all the surrounding tribes and nations; but since the acclamation refers to David's "seed" (a collective singular,

---

In Leviticus 19:18 the people are commanded not to take vengeance or bear a grudge. The meaning here probably is more vindictiveness than correcting an imbalance.

The meaning of the word overlaps with other terms, such as שָׁפַט, "judge, vindicate"; and רִיב, "bring a legal dispute" to settle the strife. The most frequently used Greek rendering is ἐκδικέω, which is used for vengeance and vindication

such as is explained in Gal. 3:16), the passage finds fulfillment in subsequent monarchies and ultimately belongs to Jesus the Messiah as part of the fulfillment of the promises of the New Covenant. Paul quotes from this psalm in Romans 15:8–12 along with three other passages to show that Christ came for Gentiles as well as Jews and that his kingdom will be universal and everlasting. The New Testament teaches that when he comes again he will put down all his enemies and redeem his people from the world.

MESSAGE AND APPLICATION

Psalm 18 is a long, detailed thanksgiving for the LORD's great acts of deliverance; it is the kind of thanksgiving one would expect from someone looking back over a lifetime of experiences in which the LORD answered his prayers time and time again. Now finally at rest from conflicts and crises, the psalmist can at length express his love and gratitude for the LORD, his rock and his deliverer. From the words of his thanksgiving the saints of all ages can learn much.

The world in which the believer lives is a wicked and dangerous world, opposed to God and all who follow his ways; but this should not immobilize people in fear. God enables the believer to overcome the world by faith and to proclaim to the nations that God will subdue them and give them to his anointed king as subjects. If they refuse and rebel, they will be put to shame.

The psalm, like so many others in the collection, is concerned with warfare. War is, of course, an evil part of the human experience, but the Israelite experience demonstrates that at times it was necessary if the people of God were to survive. God not only used their warfare, but he enabled them to achieve victory. The question always has to be asked whether the war was just and necessary, or was it a violation of God's will. Both types are found in Scripture, and this is a question that every age has to face. However, God enabled David to establish the kingdom by defeating all the enemies of Israel; but God did not allow David to build the temple because of the bloodshed, even though necessary. The church today functions on a different level, for it is not a nation in a single location. Our warfare today is a spiritual warfare, against unseen forces and powers, requiring spiritual weapons and methods (Eph. 6:10–18). Violent and bloody warfare in the name of God that is on the news so often today is not holy war, for the kingdom of God in Christ is to be extended by the gospel, calling people to repentance and faith. In this the enemy will be engaged, and conflict will arise. Spiritual warfare requires every bit as much faith and courage as Israel's conflicts; and it has the same goal as their warfare, to defend the covenant community while extending the kingdom of God in the world. The warfare of God's anointed king awaits the second coming; Paul reminds us that the Father has put everything in subjection to Christ, and he will subdue all his enemies (1 Cor. 15:22–28). John saw the vision of the time when the kingdoms of the world becomes Christ's kingdom, and thanks and praise will be given in heaven and on earth because it will be the time to judge, the time to reward the faithful and destroy those who destroy the earth (Rev. 11:15–18). The Christian is in a climate of warfare, but the outcome is certain—all nations will submit to the anointed king. In the meantime the believer can live faithfully, confident that the LORD delivers his people.

Because of the reality of divine protection and deliverance and the prospect of final victory in the future, the faithful owe their love and their gratitude to the LORD. If nothing else this psalm is a reminder to all believers that they owe everlasting praise to the LORD their God. That praise should include the rehearsing of God's history of answering prayers and delivering his people, not just in the history of the faith but in the lifetime of the believer. Out of those experiences there should be a few marvelous experiences in which God's supernatural intervention is most obvious. Believers therefore should be able to describe God and his works in expressions and epithets that fit their experiences, explain their successes and accomplishments in theological terms, and make their praise public and edifying, not just for the immediate hearers, but for the world to hear: He is the living God, and he will have an everlasting kingdom of righteousness.

However, the psalm has didactic elements as well that must be heeded. It reminds believers that God delivers those who trust him fully, who pray to him in the time of distress, and who are like him in the way they live (to the faithful he is faithful, to the blameless he is blameless, and to the pure he is pure). The LORD responds to his needy people when they pray, but he resists the proud and abases them. Humility, obedience, and faith are essential for those who call on the LORD in times of need.

There is much to include in an exposition of a psalm like this, and so the material will have to be carefully arranged and precisely explained. A summary expository idea will capture the main thrust of the psalm and keep the exposition tied to the message of the passage. It could be worded as follows: *The living God is to be praised because he intervenes supernaturally to destroy the forces of evil and give his people victory; and in the process he even subjugates people to the dominion of his anointed king in accordance with his loyal love to the covenant.* Every saving act is another step in the direction of the fulfillment of the promises, but the final victory awaits the appearance of the king.

PSALM 19

The Design of Divine Revelation

INTRODUCTION

Text and Textual Variants[1]

To the Chief Musician. A Psalm of David.

1 The heavens are telling the glory of God
   and the firmament declares the work of his hands;
2 day unto day utters speech,
   and night unto night proclaims knowledge;
3 there is no speech and there are no words,
   their voice is not heard;[2]
4 their line[3] has gone out through all the earth,

---

1. In general, see J. v. d. Ploeg, "Psalm XIX and Some of Is Problems," *Jaarsbericht v. h. Vooraziatisch–Egyptisch Genootschap 'Ex Oriente Lux,'* 17 (1963):193–201;

2. The clause may be subordinated as a relative clause to the preceding; the Greek has: ὧν οὐχὶ ἀκούονται αἱ φωναὶ αὐτῶν, "in which their voices are not heard." Delitzsch follows this interpretation, translating it "whose voice is unheard (inaudible)." The point would be it is a discourse that is everywhere audible in the kind of words that everyone on earth can understand (as Rom. 1:19; Psalms, I:282–3).

3. The MT has the word for a measuring "line," קָו, with a suffix (קַוָּם). The idea of a plumb-line does not fit this context, but the word may be understood as a line of text, as in "line upon line" in Isaiah 28:10, 13. The Greek translation (Symmachus and the Syriac) has "voice" or "sound," φθόγγος; and Jerome has *sonus*. Either the translator of the Greek text had trouble with

---

465

and their words to the end of the world.
For the sun[4] he has set a tent in them,
5 which,[5] like a bridegroom coming out of his chamber,
   it rejoices like a strong man to run its course;
6 its rising is from the end of the heavens,
   and its circuit to the *other* end of them.
And there is nothing hidden from its heat.
7 The law of the LORD is perfect, restoring the life;
   the testimony of the LORD is sure, making wise the
      simple;
8 the statutes of the LORD are right, making the heart
      rejoice;
   the commandment of the LORD is pure, enlightening the
      eyes;
9 the fear[6] of the LORD is clean, enduring forever;
   the decisions of the LORD are true, they are righteous[7]
      altogether.
10 More to be desired are they than gold, yea, than much fine
      gold;
   sweeter also than honey and the droppings of the
      honeycomb.
11 Moreover by them your servant is warned;[8]

---

the idea of "line" and assumed the form should be the same as the word in
the previous line, קוֹלָם, or a scribe copying the Hebrew text omitted the ל
and introduced the confusion. The NIV follows the Greek and emends the
text to read "their voice."

4. The Greek has "*In* the sun he has set *his* tabernacle, and he comes forth as
   a bridegroom. . . ."
5. MT has וְהוּא.
6. The "fear" of the LORD does not seem to fit the sequence of words for the
   Law. Kraus says that "fear" could be retained, but suggests אִמְרַת, "word
   of," in line with Psalm 119:38 instead (*Psalms 1–59*, p. 268), but the change
   is not necessary and without support. The versions all read "the fear of."
   The word "fear" refers to the Law, not to the outward aspect of law but
   its effect on the heart (a metonymy of effect). Similarly, God is called the
   "Fear of Isaac" (Gen. 31:42).
7. The Greek has δεδικαιωμένα, "justified": "the judgments of the LORD are
   true and justified altogether."
8. The Greek has "your servant keeps (φυλάσσει) to them, and in keeping
   them there is great reward."

and in keeping them *there* is great reward.
12 *As for* errors—who can discern *them*?
 Clear me of secret *faults*.
13 Keep back your servant also from presumptuous[9] *sins*;
 let them not rule over me.[10]
Then I shall be blameless,
 and I shall be innocent of great transgression.
14 Let the words of my mouth and the meditation of my heart
 be acceptable in your sight,
O LORD, my rock,[11] and my redeemer.

Composition and Context[12]

Psalm 19 is a classic presentation of divine revelation and its intended effects. The psalm falls into three distinct parts, the contemplation of divine revelation in nature, the reflection on the value and benefits of written revelation in the word of the LORD, and a prayer for cleansing and preservation from sin— the designed effect of all revelation.

Because the first two sections are so very different, both in content and in style,[13] many commentators conclude that they

---

9. The word זֵדִים is properly "presumptive people" or "wicked people" (s.v. Ps. 119:69). Kraus suggests זָדוֹן, "presumption, defiance" would make a better contrast with the inadvertent errors; still, he translates it "the wicked" (*Psalms 1–59*, p. 268). But the word as it stands in the MT can be given the sense, "presumptuous sins." Presumptuous sins that are repeated enslave the sinner, and so the additional idea of "let them not rule over me" is appropriate (Delitzsch, *Psalms*, I:289). The Greek translation has "strangers" (ἀλλοτρίων), likely thinking of זָרִים.
10. The Greek translation subordinates this line to the next: "If they [the strangers] do not gain dominion over me, then I shall be blameless . . . ."
11. The Greek interprets the figure "my rock" as "my helper" (βοηθέ μου). Many translations today use "strength," but that does not fully express the meaning of "rock."
12. See additionally Walter Harrelson, "Psalm 19," in *Worship and the Hebrew Bible,* Festschrift for John T. Willis, ed. by M. Patrick Graham et al, *JSOT Supplement* 284 (1999):142–147; Julian Morgenstern, "Psalm 8 and 19A," *HUCA* 19 (1945–1946):491–523; A. H. Van Zyl, "Psalm 19," *Biblical Essays 1966* (1967):142–158.
13. For example, concerning poetic style verses 1–6 are characterized by a trimeter with longer lines, whereas verses 7–11 fit a pentameter measure

467

were originally individual compositions. Briggs,[14] Morgenstern,[15] and others assume the first part (19A) was originally non-Israelite, an old hymn to the sun god *Shamash/Shemesh* identified as El, and not to Yahweh. Others do not go quite so far, suggesting only it was an old hymn to the creator that the writer of 19B used as an introduction to his work.[16] There is some similarity in expressions and ideas between verses 1–6 and extrabiblical references to the sun god, but the similarities are better explained as deliberate polemics rather than selective adaptation. In setting forth his belief that Yahweh is the creator as well as the lawgiver, the psalmist used expressions that attributed certain aspects to the sun god in order to undermine pagan belief and set forth the truth that the sun (that the pagans worshiped) was created by Yahweh. The fact that this sun god was also the god of justice adds to the polemic, for the psalm will go on to say that law came from the LORD who made the sun. The hymnist had no intention of giving credence to a pagan god of justice and law when writing a hymn to Yahweh as the creator of the universe and the giver of the law. It is possible, however, that this psalmist used an old hymn to the creator to introduce the praise of Yahweh for the law; but this does not mean the hymn had to be of Canaanite origin, and neither does it require part A

---

with shorter lines. See H. Leo Eddleman, "Word Pictures of the Word: An Exposition of Psalm 19," *Review and Expositor* 49 (1952):413–24.

14. Briggs says that Psalm 19A was originally composed in honor of "Shemesh" (Hebrew word for "sun" [שֶׁמֶשׁ], but in other languages probably vocalized differently, perhaps "Shamash" or "Shamshu"), but was adapted to the worship of Yahweh. For example, he suggests that it originally read "Shemesh has set up his tent," but the Hebrew scribe changed it with the preposition to say God set up a tent for the sun (*Psalms*, I:166).

15. Morgenstern argues that because the first part does not mention Yahweh, it must have originally been a hymn to the god El (p. 515).

16. A. A. Anderson, for example, says the writer used fragments of an older, pre-exilic hymn as the introduction to his work. He does not rule out the suggestion of others that it was of non-Israelite origin, but he suggests it may have been part of a New Year festival in Israel (*Psalms 1–72*, p. 167). Kraus similarly suggests that the psalm was composed of two cultic hymns used at the autumn festival, allowing that the first part came from sun god worship (*Psalms 1–59*, pp. 269–70).

to be so much older than part B. It might simply mean that 19A was an earlier polemical composition.

The two parts belong together because the sun imagery gives unity to the whole composition:[17] if the sun is the most glorious gift of the creator for physical life, the word of Yahweh is the most glorious gift for the spiritual life; and if the sun dominates life and illumines everything under it, the word dominates every aspect of the spiritual life—and the physical life as well—all the time. There is no physical life without the sun; there is no spiritual life without the word. There is a perfect complementarity between the two parts, showing that their connection was well designed.[18] All speculation on the origins of the psalm apart, the themes that Yahweh is the creator of the universe (and therefore certainly the sun) and the source of all law and justice had always been believed in Israel. Without these basic beliefs the covenant would never have been made at Sinai.

A close examination of Psalm 19 leads to a better explanation for the differences between the sections and to the conclusion that it was a single composition, i.e., that the author of part B was responsible for the inclusion of part A, and probably wrote it as well. The psalm begins with the praise of the creator, who is referred to as "God" (אל), not because the reference was to some Canaanite god, but because the emphasis is on the sovereign power of the creator (as in Genesis 1). The second part focuses on the word of Yahweh; it uses all the major terms for the stipulations of the covenant to call attention to the mercy and love of God. Because of these clear references to the covenant, the covenant name Yahweh is used seven times. If the first part tells of the glory of God, the second part tells of

---

17. Jonathan T. Glass, "Some Observations on Psalm 19," in *The Listening Heart,* Festschrift for Roland E. Murphy, ed. by Kenneth G. Hoglund, et al, *JSOT Supplement* 58 (1987):147–159; and N. Sarna, "Psalm XIX and the Near Eastern Sun–God Literature," *Fourth World Congress of Jewish Studies* 1 (1967):171–175

18. Broyles says that God (the Revealer) made this complementarity known to the editor, but not to the author (*Psalms,* p. 108). He does not explain this rather unusual statement, nor does he offer any support for it; he assumes the writer of the second part could not have joined the first part to his work, let alone have written it.

his will; if the first part emphasizes that all creation is dominated by the sun, the second part affirms that all life is dominated by God's word. The abrupt change from the first section
to the second is due to the change in subject matter; in fact, the
sudden change gives more force to the contrast—the revelation
of God in his word is far greater than the revelation of God in
nature.[19] The parts of this psalm belong together; they form a
unified composition.[20]

Moreover, there is no compelling evidence to date the composition in the post-exilic period; on the contrary, there is good
reason to date it earlier. For example, Psalm 19 has a number
of ties to Psalm 18, both in its poetry and subject matter.[21] Some
of the important common themes in the two passages are God's
dominion over creation, the psalmist's desire to be found blameless in his sight, and the description of the LORD as the rock.
One may at least say that these and other details in the two
passages probably led the final compiler of the psalms to place
Psalm 19 after Psalm 18 in the collection of Davidic psalms.
Now if Psalm 18 can be placed in the earlier Davidic period
in view of the parallel passage in 2 Samuel 22, the recognized
links with Psalm 18 might suggest an earlier date for Psalm 19
as well. Moreover, long before the exile the contents of the Law
were made known to the people, at least in the prophetic messages or teachings.

---

19. Goldingay allows that part A refers to general revelation and part B to spe-
    cific revelation, but he then sets about to qualify what he means by this.
    He says that the second part "does not offer a revelation of further truths
    that could not be known from nature, such as the truths about God's pur-
    pose expressed in the story of Israel that came to a climax in Jesus" (p.
    298). He allows that part B talks about the nature of God's instructions,
    but suggests that the teachings and morals in Israel were similar to those
    of other countries. It is not clear what is behind this discussion (perhaps
    his concern about people who in his opinion seem to worship the Bible [p.
    299]), but the comments are confusing.
20. M. Fishbane notes another thematic link between the sections: in the first
    part the cosmos speaks, in the second part the LORD speaks, and in the
    third the psalmist speaks (*Text and Texture*, p. 86).
21. James R. Durlesser, "A Rhetorical Critical Study of Psalms 19, 42, and 43,"
    Studia Biblica et Theologica 10 (1980):179–97.

Exegetical Analysis

Summary

Moved by the observation that the heavens, under the dominating influence of the sun, declare the splendor of God's handiwork, the psalmist asserts that the dominating influence on life is the efficacious law of the LORD, which prompts him to pray for cleansing and preservation so that his life will be acceptable before the LORD.

Outline

I. Natural revelation: The psalmist observes that the heavens, under the dominating influence of the sun, declare the splendor of God's work (1–6).
  A. He reports the proclamation of the parts of creation in the heavens (1–4a).
    1. Summary statement: The heavens declare the glory of God's work (1).
    2. Description: The heavens declare his glory continually and universally, without human words (2–4).
  B. He focuses on the sun, which dominates the creation (4b–6).
    1. The sun has a night-place in the heavens prepared by God (4c).
    2. The sun dominates the creation when it runs its course (5–6).
II. Specific Revelation: The psalmist describes the powerful, life-changing word of the LORD (7–11).
  A. He enumerates the nature and effect of the word (7–9).
    1. The perfect, sure word of the LORD transforms people (7).
    2. The pure, direct word of the LORD inspires and enlightens people (8).
    3. The awe-inspiring decisions of the word of the LORD are just (9).
  B. He discloses the value and benefit of the word of the LORD (10–11).

1. The teachings of the word of the LORD are enjoyable and desirable (10).
2. The teachings of the word of the LORD guide him into a life that is pleasing to God (11).

III. Response to Revelation: The psalmist prays for complete cleansing so that he may live a blameless, acceptable life (12–14).
   A. He prays for complete clearance from hidden faults (12).
   B. He prays for preservation from presumptuous sins so that he may be blameless (13).
   C. He prays that his words and thoughts would be acceptable before the LORD who strengthens and redeems him (14).

COMMENTARY IN EXPOSITORY FORM

I. Natural Revelation: The heavens under the dominating influence of the sun constantly reveal the glory of God (1–6).

A. All creation is a clear witness to the glory of God (1–4a).

The first few verses of the psalm describe God's wordless revelation in the universe: creation clearly reveals the glory of God. For many the observation of the sun, moon, stars and planets is a scientific study; for others it might serve the purposes of divination, but the believer will be filled with praise and adoration for such a God who created all things. In fact, the poetry of this psalm is so elegant and the theme so lofty that it has inspired some of the greatest musical praise in the history of the faith.

The first verse introduces the revelation with a summary statement: "The heavens are telling the glory of God, and the firmament declares the work of his hand."[22] The verse begins with "the heavens," which is probably meant to indicate everything

---

22. The line in the text is a chiasm: (A) The heavens / (B) are telling / (C) the glory of God // (C') the work of / his hands / (B') declares / (A') the firmament.

in the heavens (a metonymy of subject)—primarily the sun, moon, clouds, stars, and planets.[23] Parallel to this is the word "firmament" (רָקִיעַ), the "expanse" of space beyond the immediate skies. In Genesis 1:8 the "firmament" is called "heavens," and so the words can refer to the same thing. All the heavenly hosts "are telling" (מְסַפְּרִים) the glory of God, the participles of the verse ("telling" and "declaring" [מַגִּיד]) emphasizing the ongoing revelation. Here we have personifications to indicate that these parts of creation are actually revealing something about God. The word "telling" (סָפַר) has an additional connotation: it is consistently used in the Psalter for the laudatory declaration of God's deeds in a worship setting.[24] It is as if all the contents of the heavens are glorifying God in his heavenly sanctuary—just by their actual existence. The parallel verb (נָגַד) usually refers to the disclosure of something that was not known. Thus, the firmament, also meaning everything in the heavens, reveals the work of God's hands, i.e., that there is a creator who has made everything. The language is figurative (anthropomorphic), for God did not make things with hands. He called everything into existence by decree (Gen. 1:3; Ps. 33:6–9), but the expression "the work of his hands" communicates on a human level that he made everything (see also Ps. 8:1, 3; Rom. 1:20; Acts 14:17).

At the heart of the verse is the theological description of what the heavens declare—"the glory of God." The title used for God (אֵל) signifies the sovereignty and power of the creator and supreme being in the universe. The term "glory" (כָּבוֹד) is a little more difficult for people to understand.[25] It retains the basic idea

---

23. "Heaven" or "heavens" (שָׁמַיִם) could refer to the sky where the birds fly, or to the visible universe, or to the presence of God. From an earthly perspective it appears that the stars and the planets are "in" the heavens, but only in the second sense of the term (the language is phenomenal).

24. S.v., ספר in NIDOTTE, III:282, by A. R. Pete Diamond.

25. The word "glory" (כָּבוֹד) is related to the verb "be heavy" (כָּבֵד), which by extension means "important." In its literal sense the word describes anything that is heavy, such as a man (1 Sam. 4:18) or a rock (Isa. 32:29); but it can also be used figuratively to describe blindness (eyes that are heavy; Gen. 48:10), or unbelief (a heavy or hardened heart; Exod. 9:7). The related meaning of "important" arises because what has weight is perceived as important (as in our expression of throwing one's weight around). So things and people are said to be important, such as the temple (Hag. 2:3),

of the verb with a metaphorical development of heaviness to its meaning of "importance." To speak of God's glory is to speak of his intrinsic value, what gives him his importance. Anyone looking at the universe and understanding that God created all this by his powerful word could come to no other conclusion than that he is the most important person in existence—ever—no one else could even come close. In this verse we read that everything that exists in the heavens reveals the work of a creator and that all creation tells us that there is no one as important as he.

The personification continues in verse 2 with day and night continually making God known, pouring forth speech (יַבִּיעַ אֹמֶר)

---

or robes (Exod. 28:2), or even a forest (Isa. 10:18). The apostle Paul plays on the meaning of the word when he speaks of the eternal weight of glory (2 Cor. 4:17).

In a derived verbal stem the word comes to mean "to treat as important, to honor," such as honoring parents (Exod. 20:12), or the sabbath (Isa. 58:13), or most importantly, honoring God (Ps. 50:15). If people honor God, they will show it by obeying his commands (Mal. 1:6).

The word "glory" is used for the soul on occasion, meaning the real person, the essential life (Ps. 30:12). A related noun is "liver," which is also used figuratively for the heart of the human life—it was the heaviest and considered the most important organ. The use of "glory" for the essential person is what gives that person "importance." Everyone has this "glory", this inner glory or importance, but the LORD has a quality of it superior to everyone else (see further E. Jacob, *The Theology of the Old Testament*, tr. by A. W. Heathcote and P. J. Allcock [New York: Harper & Row, 1958], p. 88).

The noun "glory" came to be used for the trappings that reflect the importance or greatness of someone. For example, Joseph told his brothers to tell their father of his glory (NIV "honor"; Gen. 45:13). When this meaning is applied to the LORD, as in "the glory of the LORD," it refers to all the manifestations of his powerful presence, such as the work of creation here in Psalm 19. It could also refer to the brilliant, luminous cloud at the sea and in the wilderness (Exod. 14:19–20, 24). Moses saw all that, but still wanted to see God's glory (Exod. 33:18). He wanted to see past the phenomena to the real person (here the Greek version translated "glory" as "yourself").

When the Bible uses the word "glory" or "glorious" with reference to the LORD, it is basically saying that he is the most important or preeminent person in existence. And when the Bible refers to the glory of God, it is usually referring to all the evidence of God's preeminence and greatness, whether creation as here, or salvation, or a manifestation of his presence.

and proclaiming knowledge (יְחַוֶּה־דָּעַת). "Day" and "night" refer to everything visible in the heavens during the day and during the night (so metonymies of subject); and the use of both day and night (a merism), as well as the repetition, "day unto day," and "night unto night," emphasize that the testimony is continuous and never failing, that the message goes out all the time. The very existence of the parts of creation continuously and characteristically speak to us and proclaim knowledge (habitual imperfects). The communication is irrepressible, as the verb translated "utters" (נָבַע) underscores. It is used for the bubbling up and overflowing of a river or a pool of water, but here it has the more frequent, figurative meaning of the outpouring or overflowing of praise, wisdom, and knowledge. What is ever pouring forth constantly is the evidence of the majesty and power of God. The knowledge the heavens proclaim concerns the nature of God: the act of creating everything by his own will and through his own command reveals his power; the vast expanse of the universe and all its complexities reveals his infinity and sovereignty; the perfect functioning of all aspects of creation reveals his wisdom; and the beauty of all creation reveals the beauty of God.

Natural revelation may not communicate with specific words, but its message is clear nonetheless. In fact verse 3 makes the point that there is no speech (אֹמֶר, the very word he has just used to say "day to day utters speech"), and there are no words (דְּבָרִים) to this revelation, not literally anyway, and their voice (קוֹלָם) is not heard. The suggested reading of "where their voice is unheard" fits this point well. The heavenly witnesses may seem to be silent, but their testimony is heard continuously.

Verse 4 adds the extent of this revelation: it goes throughout the inhabited world. Verse 4 begins with an unusual expression, "their line" (קַוָּם). The main use of this word is for a "measuring line," but that is not the point in this verse. This is why ancient versions and modern commentaries alike preferred reading it as a corruption of "their voice," a word first introduced at the end of verse 3. Such a change would fit the context well and make a better parallel with "their words" in 4b; but these are the very reasons why a scribe would have changed the difficult word "line" to a clear word. Besides, "their line" is not impossible in the verse, for the term can also refer to a line of text, as is found in Isaiah 28:10, 13.[26] It is as if the heavenly revelation continues as a line of text throughout the whole earth, the "words" reaching to the end of the inhabited world (תֵּבֵל; "earth" and "world" are metonymies of subject, meaning the people in those areas who are to receive the revelation). Wherever people live on this planet, natural revelation communicates the truth to them that there is a sovereign Creator.

B. The sun on its vigorous and powerful course dominates the heavenly proclamation (4b–6).

In the middle of verse 4 there is a change of focus from the whole creation to the dominating part of creation as we see it— the sun (שֶׁמֶשׁ). During the day the sun is so bright it is impossible to see the stars and planets in the heavens; and the sun is so powerful that it changes the weather from night to day, warms the earth so people can live, and causes everything to grow on the earth for the benefit of mankind. The poetry refers to the sun's night-place in the heavens as a tent God made for it. Thus, the psalmist continues with personification (employing some pagan descriptions of the god), representing the sun as a vigorous bridegroom: at night he goes into his tent, and darkness falls; in the morning he comes out of his chamber filled with happiness and enthusiasm and runs his course for the day. This course is from one end of the heavens where the sun rises to the other end where it sets; under its dominant presence nothing is hidden from its light or heat. By observation anyone can see that the sun is the dominant part of our universe (the language is written from our perspective on earth), but with further understanding we can observe how light, heat, and energy come from the sun, giving life to this planet. This too reveals the knowledge and understanding of the creator, for he so ordered the universe that the sun and the earth are in the exact relationship for the right time to sustain life of the earth.

---

26. The passage was traditionally translated "line upon line (צַו לָצָו), line upon line, precept upon precept (קַו לָקָו), precept upon precept" (NIV: "do and do // rule on rule"). The point is that קַו refers to text.

But there is more to this section than a poetic description of the appearance and importance of the sun in God's creation. In the ancient world the pagans worshiped the sun god, called either *Shamash* or *Shamshu* (or *Shapshu*). The Babylonian god Shamash is even called "bridegroom," probably in reference to the myth of the sun god either resting in the arms of his beloved (the sea) at night or in marriage.[27] It appears that the Hebrew writer was drawing on some of the expressions from the pagan world to form a polemic. The sun may be compared to a mighty man rising in the morning from a bridal chamber; but contrary to pagan myth it is still the sun, and the language is poetic. The sun is just part of God's creation.

Moreover, the sun god in Mesopotamia was also considered to be the upholder of justice and righteousness. For example, on the stele that has Hammurabi's law code, Shamash is portrayed as either giving the law to the king or guiding him in writing it (see J. Pritchard, *ANET,* p. *163;* and *ANEP,* plate 246). The psalmist will counter this and attribute law to Yahweh instead. The first two parts of the psalm deliberately counter pagan ideas for the purpose of undermining them and replacing them with the truth. Creation is not to be worshiped; it is a witness to the Creator who is to be worshiped. Creation does not give the law or champion justice, but Yahweh, the God of creation does.

II. Specific Revelation: The word of the LORD is most desirable because it not only reveals God's will but also transforms the lives of people (7–11).

A. The word of the LORD reveals God's will and transforms the lives of people (7–9).

In verse 7 there is an abrupt change in language, style, and content. The attention shifts from the splendor of God's creation to the value of the word of the LORD. Natural revelation declares a good deal about the power and majesty of God, but it cannot communicate the details specific revelation reveals. All the heavenly hosts and especially the sun have a great impact on

---

27. A. A. Anderson, *Psalms 1–72,* pp. 169–70. Kraus, *Psalms 1–59,* pp. 272–3.

life on this planet, but they cannot match the impact of specific revelation. Lives are transformed and enriched as people follow the instructions and principles of the word of the LORD. The material in verses 7–11 comes close to wisdom or *torah* ("law") literature with its emphasis on Scripture. The first part, verses 7–9, extols different aspects of the word of the LORD and describes the effect of each on the believer. The second part, verses 10–11, proclaims how desirable and beneficial the teachings of Scripture are for the believer.

There are six aspects of the word of the LORD that are extolled.[28] The first is the general heading, "the law of the LORD" (תּוֹרַת יהוה, s.v. Ps. 1:2). This word translated "law" can refer to an individual teaching, the law given at Sinai, all the books of the law in general, or all of Scripture. Here it seems to refer to the law given at Sinai, but it can easily be applied to any biblical revelation. With the shift to specific revelation the covenant name "Yahweh" is now used instead of "God." Natural revelation can tell us about a sovereign, powerful God who created all things; specific revelation can tell us about the personal, covenant God Yahweh who revealed his will and his plans to his people. This law, David says, is perfect" (תְּמִימָה, s.v. Ps. 7:8). It is flawless. It is without error. There is no misleading or unnecessary instruction. It is sound, consistent, unimpaired, and genuine. In other words, the law of the LORD has divine integrity, and its effect on people is that it restores life ("restoring the life" is מְשִׁיבַת נָפֶשׁ)—it brings the person back (< שׁוּב, "to return"; s.v. Ps. 126:1; for נֶפֶשׁ s.v. Ps. 11:5). No matter what spiritual condition people might be in, or what physical location or event might have brought about their waywardness, the law of the LORD shows them how they may be restored to a right relation with God. Many people hear the word "law" and think only of rules with condemnations; but the law also included all the ritual of the sacrifices—God's gracious provision for forgiveness and restoration.

The second topic listed (v. 7b) is "the testimony (עֵדוּת; s.v. Ps. 119:2) of the LORD." The word may be translated "covenant" or "testimony"; it is a general reference to the laws and

---

28. For a more detailed discussion of the various terms used for the word of the LORD in the Psalter, see the introduction to Psalm 119.

commandments that make up the covenant God made with Israel. This testimony is "sure" (נֶאֱמָנָה, from אָמַן, s.v. Ps. 15:2). This means that it is reliable or trustworthy, and the effect is that it makes wise the simple. The "simple" (פֶּתִי) is the naive person, often young, who has had no training and is therefore without knowledge or discipline, and who wanders into all kinds of danger (see, for example, Prov. 1:4; 8:5; 9:4, 16; 14:15, 18; and 19:25). The simpleton desperately needs wisdom, which is the skill to live a life that is disciplined and productive, bringing honor to the community, the family, and to God.[29] By entering into the covenant with the LORD and living according to its stipulations, the simple may become wise; but without Scripture, there can be no godly wisdom.

The third topic is "the statutes of the LORD" (פִּקּוּדֵי יהוה, v. 8a). The verb (פָּקַד, s.v. Ps. 8:4) means "appoint" among other

---

29. "Making wise" is the (*hiphil*) participle of the verb "to be wise" (חָכַם). Related words are the noun "wisdom" (חָכְמָה) and the adjective "wise" (חָכָם). The basic meaning of the word can be seen in the non-theological uses of the group. Common to these uses is the idea of a practical skill (for the noun) or act skillfully (for the verb). For example, the noun is used in Exodus 31:6 and 35:10 for the skill given to the people who were to build the tabernacle. Likewise in Isaiah 3:3 it refers to the artificer. Psalm 107:27 uses it to describe the sailors' skills in the midst of a storm. It is used for administrative skills (Gen. 41:33) as well, which is certainly the concern of Solomon's prayer (1 Kings 3:12). Finally, it is used of the Messiah's administrative skills as he is given the Spirit of wisdom and understanding (Isa. 11:2). In all these the basic idea of "skill" or "practical ability" is present: it is a skill that is prepared to produce successful results.

Wisdom is also one of the attributes of God. What wisdom, what skill and knowledge, to be able to create and sustain everything (Job 28:12–20; Prov. 8:22–31). The apostle Paul can only marvel at God's wisdom when he considers the sweep of history (Rom. 11:33).

The words for wisdom also mean ethical and religious activities. The basic idea of skill also applies here as well. Wisdom literature is designed to teach people how to live their lives skillfully in moral and spiritual matters so that in the final analysis they produce something honoring to God and useful for the community. This will involve knowledge, discipline, and understanding as well. God has prepared people with the capacity to gain wisdom (Prov. 2:6–7; Job 38:36), and therefore desires wisdom from his people (Ps. 51:6). Wisdom needs to be acquired and cultivated (Prov. 4:7), and the emphasis of the wisdom literature in the Bible is that it cannot be acquired apart from the fear of the LORD and meditation in his word.

things; it often has an emphasis on changing someone's position or destiny. The LORD's statutes are like divine appointments to higher service with additional responsibilities and duties. They are "upright" (יְשָׁרִים; s.v. Ps. 67:4); they are exactly right, appropriately clear and direct. The effect of these statutes, should one receive them and live on this level, is that they cause the heart to rejoice (מְשַׂמְּחֵי־לֵב; s.v. Ps. 48:11). Living out the plan of God revealed in the covenant will bring joy. A sense of sadness and insecurity come from the realization one is living in rebellion to God's law.

Next is "the commandment of the LORD" (מִצְוַת יהוה). The singular use of "commandment" is a reference to the entire law with all its commandments and provisions (see Deut. 8:1). This covenant program is "pure" (בָּרָה), without any imperfection or pollution (like pure gold); and because God's command is pure, it "enlightens the eyes" (מְאִירַת עֵינָיִם)—it gives people spiritual understanding and guides them in the right choices ("eyes" representing more than ordinary sight). Spiritual perception is essential for survival in a corrupt world.

The fifth topic (v. 9) does not seem to fit the pattern: "The fear of the LORD (יִרְאַת יהוה) is clean" (טְהוֹרָה). Since all the other topics are terms for the law of God, the intended meaning here must be the law as well. The psalmist has put the effect of the law, fear, for the law (the figure is therefore a metonymy). The law properly understood and received will prompt reverential awe in the believer (s.v., Ps. 2:11). The law, which prompts such fear, is said to be clean (טָהוֹר), a term that is at home in the Levitical ritual of the sanctuary (s.v. Ps. 51:10). Its antonym, "unclean," described anything that was contaminated or corrupted through defilement in the world outside the sanctuary and was therefore not permitted in the presence of God. "Clean" in Psalm 19 would describe the law that produced reverential awe as being acceptable in the presence of God because it was not polluted or perverted in any way; and the effect is that it lasts forever (more specifically, it stands forever [עוֹמֶדֶת לָעַד]). God's holy word will endure forever because it is truth. Heaven and earth will pass away, but not the word of the LORD (see also Matt. 24:35).

Finally, we have "the decisions of the LORD" (מִשְׁפְּטֵי־יהוה). The word "decisions" may be translated as "judgments" (s.v. Ps. 9:4), but in this context it probably refers to the rulings in the law that decided cases (the so-called מִשְׁפָּטִים, Exodus 21–23, for example). Because "truth" is related to the words "faithful" and "reliable" (אֱמֶת, s.v. Ps. 15:2), truth is that which corresponds to reality and is therefore reliable. In deciding a legal case, the purpose is to get to the truth. All God's decisions will do just that, and so the conclusion is that "they are righteous altogether" (צָדְקוּ יַחְדָּו). Since righteousness describes that which corresponds to the standard (s.v. Ps. 1:6), all of God's decisions or judgments are right. This is to be expected because he is righteous and loves righteousness (Pss. 11, 45). Only in the decisions of God will anyone ever find true justice.

B. The word of the LORD is desirable and enjoyable because it enables people to be pleasing to the LORD (10–11).

After this survey of the value and effect of the word of the LORD in the lives of people, the psalmist announces his delight in and benefit from the word of the LORD. For believers the laws of God were not a burden; they were desirable (הַנֶּחֱמָדִים). Such a desire usually leads to acquiring what is desired (Gen. 3:6 for desiring something off-limits; Ps. 39:12 for treasured things, wealth). The psalmist knew that the laws of the LORD were more to be desired than fine gold, and they were sweeter than honey from the honeycomb. God's word is sweet in the enrichment and satisfaction of life that it brings to the faithful believer, and its sweetness increases its desirability day by day.

As David reflected on the enjoyment the word of the LORD gave him in life, he also reflected on its impact in his life (v. 11). First, he, God's servant, is warned (נִזְהָר) by them (see for example the use of this word in Ezekiel 33:7 for warning the wicked). One need only read the Book of Proverbs to see how the application of the law of the LORD provided warning after warning for the choices one makes in life. The law not only told people what they should not do, but also warned them of the consequences if they violated the law. On the other hand, by keeping the laws of God there was "reward" (עֵקֶב basically means "results," but in this context it must mean good results). The laws of God were sweet and desirable—they prevented people from ruining their lives and the lives of those around them, and they promised a good outcome for abiding by the law (see the lists of blessings and curses in Leviticus 26). Based on the first part of this psalm, one may conclude that this is so because the sovereign Creator knows what is best for his creation.

III. Response to Divine Revelation: The proper response to divine revelation is the confession of sin and the desire to be accepted by God (12–14).[30]

After rehearsing natural revelation, the revelation that all the heavenly host provides about the majesty and glory of God, and after delineating the different aspects of the word of the LORD, the specific revelation that transforms and enhances the lives of believers, David responds with an acknowledgment of his waywardness and a prayer for cleansing from sins and preservation from sinfulness so that he might lead a life that is acceptable to God. In this all who believe in divine revelation must share this concluding prayer.

A. Believers must pray for cleansing from hidden faults (12).

Verse 12 begins with a rhetorical question, "Errors—who can discern *them*?" The point he is making is that no one can discern them. The type of sins he is talking about are "sins of ignorance" (שְׁגִיאוֹת).[31] The term can describe waywardness in general, but in the cultic laws it describes sins that were unintentional, hidden, or inadvertent. That they were sins of ignorance is evidenced by the fact that Leviticus prescribed the sin offering for these sins when the guilty found out about them or was made aware of them (4:28). The word could refer to any sin that was committed

---

30. This point could be more fully explained as: *Having contemplated the glory of God through natural revelation and the will of God through special revelation, believers pray for cleansing and preservation from sin so that they might be acceptable to the LORD* (12–14).

31. Jacob Milgrom, "The Cultic שגגה and Its Influence in Psalms and Job," *JQR* 58 (1967–68):115–125.

out of ignorance of the law, or any sin that was committed inadvertently, or any sin that was rationalized. These are clearly not the premeditated violations of the Law; but even though they may have been committed unwittingly, they were nevertheless sins. David knows he cannot detect them, and so he prays for God to clear him of secret or hidden (< סָתַר) sins. The verb "clear me" (נַקֵּנִי) is from the verb "acquit"; he wants to be declared innocent or free of any sins that are hidden to him at the moment.[32] If he meditated on the Law he would discover them; his prayer is that they be removed so that he would be free.

B. Believers must pray for preservation from presumptuous sins (13).

He also prays for God to preserve him (< חָשַׂךְ, "withhold him, hold him back") from presumptions sins (מִזֵּדִים). The verb (זִיד) means "boil over," but also "be arrogant, act presumptuously" (in the sense of overstepping boundaries). The reference is to

---

32. The verb נָקָה means "to be innocent." The adjective נָקִי means "guiltless, innocent." The etymology may suggest the idea "empty out" and therefore "be free" or "released." In Deuteronomy 24:5 the word is used of the newlywed who is "removed" from military obligations. It is also used in Genesis 44:10 to mean "leave free" instead of becoming a slave, but the usual idea of the verb means "remain unpunished" or "be free, acquitted."

The adjective "innocent" often signifies vulnerability, as the innocent could be a victim of bribery (Ps. 15:5) or in danger of being killed by a gang (Prov. 1:11). Shedding innocent blood was particularly heinous, bringing bloodguilt on the one responsible (Deut. 19:10), whether it was shedding blood of an ordinary person, or an innocent child in child sacrifice (2 Kings 21:16).

In legal contexts the emphasis of the verb is on freedom from obligations, punishment, or guilt. The court decides if someone goes "unpunished" (Exod. 21; Num. 5:31). And the idea of "leave unpunished" always occurs in prayers calling on God to "pronounce innocent" or to clear one of guilt (Ps. 19:13). If punishment was to be enacted, then the law said the guilty were not to go unpunished (Exod. 20:7, meaning the guilty would not be cleared).

There is also a cultic sense for the declaration of innocence (Ps. 73:13). The qualified worshiper was to have "clean hands" (Ps. 24:4); here the word is both cultic and ethical—the worshiper was supposed to be free of guilt, innocent, in life's activities.

pre-meditated sins, sins of the high hand (Num. 15:27–31). He does not want to act with presumption as the presumptuous do. The one guilty of presumptuous sin was a willful sinner; the presumption came in the idea that he could sin knowingly and wilfully against God. David's prayer is that such arrogant sins not have dominion over him—they are that powerful.

If the psalmist was cleared of secret sins and prevented from presumptuous sins then he would be blameless and innocent of great transgression. The word for "blameless" (אֵיתָם, the first person form of the verb, normally אָתַם) is related to the ordinary form of "blameless" (תָּמִים). Of its many applications the word describes animals without blemish that could be brought into the sanctuary. In a similar sense David is saying that when he is free of sin, he will be blameless before God and therefore welcome in his presence. The other word, "innocent" (נִקֵּיתִי) is the word "free, clear, acquitted"—he will be acquitted of great transgression. What the psalm means by "great transgression" is hard to say. The word "transgression" is more specifically a rebellious act (as illustrated by the word's use in military uprisings; s.v. Ps. 51:1). In the ancient world the "great sin" often referred to adultery, but the use of the expression in this psalm is probably not that specific. He wants to be free of any serious sin.

Thus it is the case with all the people of God, that when they are cleansed of secret sins, and protected from committing presumptuous sins, they are blameless and innocent in the eyes of God; but it takes a constant vigil to maintain such spiritual integrity.

C. Believers must always pray that their words and thoughts be acceptable to the LORD (14).

The concluding prayer is one of the best known prayers from the Psalter. The prayer is that the words and meditations be[33] acceptable[34] to the LORD; it follows the pattern of the formula

---

33. The verb יִהְיוּ is a jussive, "let [them] be."
34. לְרָצוֹן would translate literally "[let them be] for acceptance" (s.v. Ps. 30:5). It is usually rendered "let them be acceptable." The verb רָצָה is another word that is used in the Levitical ritual with reference to the pleasing nature of acceptable sacrifices. The psalmist was well aware of the

used for dedication (see Ps. 104:34; 119:108). The psalmist has dwelt on the words of natural revelation that reflect the glory of God and the words of special revelation that come from God and guide and direct his life in obedience to God; now he prays that his words to God would also be acceptable to God.[35] But the concern is not for words only, but meditations as well. Delitzsch says, "Prayer is a sacrifice offered by the inner man. The heart meditates and fashions it; and the mouth presents it, by uttering that which is put into the form of words."[36] In the good sense, "meditations" (הָגָה > הֶגְיוֹן) would refer to the prayerful analysis and application of divine revelation (Ps. 1:2), but in the bad sense the word can also be used for any contemplation or imagining against God (see Ps. 2:1). Here the prayer is that everything he says and everything he thinks be acceptable to God—and this would eliminate improper meditations.

The LORD is addressed in this prayer as "my rock and my redeemer." The figure of the rock was used in Psalm 18:2 in the context of describing the sovereign God of creation as the one who delivers and protects from the enemies. Modern versions tend to translate it as "my strength" alone; but the significance of the figure is broader than that because it represents God as the solid foundation of his life, his place of security and safety, and his strength.

The epithet "my redeemer" (וְגֹאֲלִי) is also multifaceted.[37] On

---

unacceptability of sinful people to God. His prayer to be acceptable would assume forgiveness and preservation from sin.

35. Recall how the prophet Isaiah confessed that he was a man of unclean lips when he saw the vision of the angels who sang praises to God continuously (Isa. 6:1–3).

36. Delitzsch, *Psalms,* I:289.

37. This verb "redeem" (גָּאַל) is connected to the customs of the near relative and in general has the idea of performing the right and office of a relation via the Law. All of the activities of the kinsman are concerned with protecting the family, and so a definition of "protect" as an interpretation of "redeem" is appropriate.

The underlying meaning concerns a relative, some family member, who will act to redeem, protect, or restore property, liberty, life, and if necessary posterity to a family member. The kinsman would protect property by buying back land that a relative had to relinquish (Lev. 25:25–34; and Ruth 4:6). The kinsman would secure the liberty of a relative who may have found it necessary to sell himself into service to pay off debts

the human level the word refers to the kinsman redeemer who protects and provides for the family, as in paying off debts or marrying a widow; but on the divine level the word refers to God's protection and deliverance of his covenant people, usually requiring his taking vengeance on the enemies. Calling God his redeemer means God is his loyal protector, the one who will make things right. The combination of "my rock" and "my redeemer" provides a powerful summary of the nature and provision of God.

(Lev.25:35, 39, 47–54). The kinsman would also avenge the death of a relative if the guilty person left the city of refuge and went about freely (Num. 35:19–24), and the kinsman would also provide an heir for a deceased relative (Deut. 25:5–10; Ruth 4:5, 10) if he was willing and able to do so.

These duties were considered so important for the welfare of the family and the nation that most of them were considered the duty of the king who had to champion the poor and the needy (Ps. 72:12–14).

With God as the subject the word is used for the deliverance of Israel from bondage or exile. The first instance was God's promise to Israel in Egypt (Exod. 6:6). The exodus is also referred to as a redemption in Psalm 74:2 and Isaiah 51:10, but the word is used more frequently for redeeming Israel from the Babylonian captivity (Isa. 48:20; Mic. 4:10). The prophets also use the word to describe the glorious future restoration of Israel (Isa. 52:9).

As the divine kinsman redeemer who set his people free, the LORD also took vengeance on those who harmed his people. Isaiah 47:4 states that because the LORD was Israel's redeemer Babylon would be destroyed. And in Isaiah 63:4 the "year of my redemption" is parallel with the "day of vengeance."

The word is also used for deliverance from all evil (Gen. 48:16), from destruction (Ps. 103:4), and from death (Hos.13:14). In this regard we also have the statement by Job, "I know that my redeemer lives" (19:25). Job knew he was about to die; but he knew that someone, the LORD, his redeemer, would make things right after all. This usage combines the meanings of rescue and revenge.

Finally, the word can be used for redemption from sins. Isaiah 44:22 uses the verb redeem to explain the removal of sins. This may refer to the deliverance from exile, but that deliverance included blotting out the sins of the people.

When God is described as the redeemer, the emphasis will be on his ability and willingness to deliver his people from bondage, distress, imminent death, and sins. Because Israel was not strong enough to do this, God had to do it (Jer. 31:11). His redemption is based on love and pity (Isa. 63:9) and is accomplished through judgment on the oppressors. After all, the people belong to him

MESSAGE AND APPLICATION

Psalm 19 stands out as a reminder of God's revelation in nature and in his word, but the value of that revelation would be lost if it did not lead to greater spiritual reflection and commitment. Certainly believers can join in the praise of the Creator and marvel at the power of the word, but that is not the main thrust of this psalm. All revelation demands a response, and so the climax of this psalm is reached in the psalmist's response. Accordingly, we may word the central expository idea to focus on this so that the exposition will not come up short: *The careful contemplation of the revelation of the LORD in creation and scripture will inspire greater adoration and renewed spiritual commitment in the believer.*

The exposition will, of course, connect the different strands to the teachings of the New Testament. Natural revelation is the starting point for Paul's letter to the church at Rome, and in the book Paul cites Psalm 19:18 to make the point that Israel cannot say they never heard the word (Rom. 10:18). The revelation of God has been constant: natural revelation displays his power and majesty, but the word of the LORD reveals his will. According to Paul the Law is holy, righteous and good (Rom. 8:12); it reveals the will of God, but most importantly it reveals sin (Rom 8:13). Because it is God-breathed, Scripture is able to make people wise and is profitable for instruction in righteousness (2 Tim 3:15, 16). Divine revelation leads people to praise God, to confess their sins, and to renew their commitment to obey.

Christians will also attest that with the coming of Christ revelation is complete. We have far more than the psalmist ever had, and yet the nature and effect of divine revelation is the same—except that Christ has the pre-eminence in all things. He is the Creator, and so the heavens declare the glory of Christ (John 1:1–10; Col. 1:15–20); and he is the Word, the complete revelation of God, and so faith in him brings life and joy and spiritual understanding (John 1:1–18; Heb. 1:1–3). As we learn of him through the Word, our secret sins and rebellious acts will be uncovered so that we might find forgiveness and gain the spiritual strength to resist great sin (1 John 1:7).

PSALM 20

Confidence in the Name of the LORD

INTRODUCTION

Text and Textual Variants

For the chief musician. A Psalm of David.

1 May the LORD answer you in the day of distress,
   may the name of the God of Jacob set you on high;
2 may he send you help from the sanctuary,
   and sustain you from Zion;
3 may he remember all your offerings,[1]
   and accept[2] your whole burnt offering;
4 may he grant you according to your heart's desire,
   and fulfill all your counsel.
5 We will shout for joy because of your salvation,
   and in the name of our God we will wave our banners![3]
May the LORD fulfill all your petitions.

---

1. The form in the MT is a plural written defectively: מִנְחֹתֶךָ. A few manuscripts write it fully: מִנְחוֹתֶיךָ. The Greek text and Jerome have the singular,
   equal to מִנְחָתְךָ, which the form in the text without the *yod* would suggest
   to the translators.
2. The MT has יְדַשְּׁנֶה, "declare fat," meaning "accept." Commentators suggest
   emending the text; e.g., Kraus endorses the suggestion that the word be
   read as יִדְרְשֶׁנָּה, "may he ask about." This would assume ר dropped from the
   word (*Psalms 1–59*, p. 277). The emendation is unnecessary.
3. The MT uses דֶּגֶל, "banner," for the expression נִדְגֹּל, "we will wave our banners." The Greek version has the form μεγαλυνθησόμεθα, perhaps "we

6 Now I know that the LORD has saved his anointed!
  He will answer him from his holy heaven
    with the saving mighty deeds of his right hand.
7 Some in chariots, and some in horses,
    but as for us, we will keep our confidence
    in the name of the LORD our God;
8 They are bowed down and fallen,
    but we have risen and stood firm!⁴
9 O LORD, save the king.
    May he answer us when we call.⁵

Composition and Context

The theme of Psalm 20 is confidence in praying. The passage records an intercessory prayer of the people for the king,⁶ who was
himself praying for deliverance in battle. The people all have a
confidence that is expressed with certainty—and this is what is
so instructive for believers today.

Psalm 20 is also classified as a royal psalm, that is, a psalm
in which the king is in the foreground. This one is about prayer
before going to war, the prayer of the people for their king who
is praying, and then the confidence of the king that his prayer
has been answered. The individual who speaks is most likely the
king himself, although some commentators think it could be an

---

shall magnify (glory)," perhaps reading נַגְדִּיל. It will use this same verb to
translate "we will make mention/keep our confidence" in verse 7.

4. The verbs in this verse are prophetic perfects; they are to be interpreted as
a future certainty.

5. This translation reflects the metrical and logical division of the line. The
accents in the MT would have it read, "Save O LORD, Let the king answer
us when we call." The verb "may he answer us," יַעֲנֵנוּ is read by the Greek
translation as if וַעֲנֵנוּ, "and hear us (καὶ ἐπάκουσον ἡμῶν) in whatever day
we call upon you."

6. Goldingay does not take this as intercessory prayer. He says that it is
a blessing for the king in which the blesser is empowered by God to say
the blessing of God over him (*Psalms 1–41,* p. 309). The interpretation is
forced; it may reflect a modern use of the psalm. Moreover, Psalm 21 appears to be the praise offered for the answer to this prayer in Psalm 20.

individual who addresses the king.[7] There is no reason why the king could not be David himself, as the superscription claims; but the psalm would find repeated use by later kings once it was deposited in the sanctuary. The psalm's focus on the "name of the LORD" does not require a late date when the concept was thought to be more highly developed. The "name of the LORD" was used in biblical texts well before the seventh century.[8] In addition to this, we may note that the royal psalms are often typological of the greater king, Jesus the Messiah in the New Testament, but there are limits to the correspondence between the royal psalmist and Jesus. For example, in the New Testament believers do not pray that their king will be successful in battle when he comes again, but they do pray for his coming in power and glory to judge the world and redeem his people.

Not only is Psalm 20 a confident prayer for the king's victory in battle, it is a liturgical psalm as there is a change of speakers. One may imagine that after the original incident for which the prayers were offered, David recalled the events and wrote the prayer and its accompanying praise in the form of liturgical poetry to be used in the future in similar situations. Such a powerful psalm undoubtedly found much use in the battle days down through Israel's history, and perhaps even in times of personal struggles by believers.

The psalm lends itself to a possible reconstruction of the dramatic situation: Once again it was time for the king to lead his armies into battle. The burden of the day weighed heavily upon him, for although he could remember great past victories, he knew that this struggle would be disastrous without divine intervention. The enemies had boasted of their horses and fierce war chariots, but his strategy was limited to foot soldiers—and faith in the LORD. He had relied on the LORD in battle ever

---

7. Broyles says that the king at no point is a speaker in Psalms 20 or 21 (p. 110), but it is probable that the congregation is praying for their king who is also praying (vv. 1–5). Therefore, it is likely that the king is the speaker in the second part of the psalm, expressing his confidence.

8. See the discussion in Kraus, *Psalms 1–59,* p. 279. Some scholars, of course, have tried to make the composition late pre-exilic, in harmony with their understanding of the theology of the Deuteronomist.

since that memorable day when he faced Goliath "in the name of the LORD." This would be no exception.

Before the battle David came to the sanctuary to pray. He had brought the burnt offering and the meal offering for the memorial. When the animal was sacrificed it was placed on the altar; and while the smoke ascended as a pleasing aroma to the LORD, David stood at the corner of the altar petitioning God for victory. While he was praying the congregation gathered in the courtyard to intercede for him. Their words clearly displayed the great expectation with which they prayed—an expectation that praises the LORD before the victory is won! What they prayed has been preserved in verses 1–4 and their confidence in verse 5.

An undetermined period of silence followed, a silence in which the Spirit of God could speak to the heart of David and assure him that his prayer was heard and that victory was assured. Then, the king emerged with his triumphant declaration that God answered his prayer—indeed, had already delivered him (vv. 6–8).

Fully trusting in the name of the LORD, he led his armies out to the battle with the surging cries of the people echoing in his ears. Their words reiterated their confident prayer for victory for their king (v. 9).

Such great trust in the face of overwhelming odds is exemplary. To discover how such confidence can be developed, one must carefully study the strong affirmation of faith on the part of the king in relation to the confident intercession of the people. Both the people and the king have this kind of faith, but it will be the king's words that reveal how it is possible. Then in Psalm 21 we have the report of the outcome of the battle, the victory that came by faith in the LORD.

Exegetical Analysis

Summary

In response to the intercessory prayer of the people for their monarch who is praying for victory, the king expresses his confidence that the LORD in whom he trusts will give them an overwhelming victory.

Outline

I. The psalmist records the intercessory prayer and praise
of the assembled worshipers who desire that the LORD
answer the king's prayer for help in the battle (1–5).
   A. The assembled worshipers pray for their king (1–4).
      1. They ask God to answer his requests (1).
      2. They ask God to send help from the sanctuary (2).
      3. They ask God to accept his sacrifices (3).
      4. They ask God to fulfill his heart's desire (4).
   B. The assembled worshipers voice their confidence that
   God will answer his prayers (5a).
   C. The assembled worshipers reiterate their prayer (5b).
II. The royal psalmist announces the assurance that he has
received that because he trusts in the name of the LORD he
shall have an overwhelming victory (6–8).
   A. He is convinced that the LORD will save him, the
   LORD's anointed (6).
   B. He explains his assurance by his faith in the name of the
   LORD alone (7).
   C. He anticipates an overwhelming victory (8).
III. The assembled worshipers cry out together that the LORD
fulfill his promise of deliverance (9).

COMMENTARY IN EXPOSITORY FORM

I. Believers may have confidence when they intercede for those who lead them in righteous causes (1–5).

A. *Supportive intercession for the faithful is encouraging and edifying (1–4).*

The first four verses record the intercession of the people
(and so all the verbs will be jussives). These lines of poetry ac-
centuate four aspects of their intercession, and in the process
reveal four aspects of the faith of the king.

First, it is a prayer for God's power in the time of trouble
(v. 1). They pray that God would answer David's prayer: "May

Yahweh[9] answer you in the day of distress, may the name of the God of Jacob set you on high." In this parallelism, the second clause specifies the desired answer to their prayer. The prayer is specifically that God would deliver him in battle. "Set you on high" (שָׂגַב) has a military connotation; its use provides an implied comparison: just as someone might place something inaccessibly high, so should God make the king safe and secure in battle, out of the reach, so to speak, of his enemies.

The contrast between this desired protection and the distress must not be missed. "Trouble" (צָרָה) is literally a "strait, a narrowness." It describes a situation in which the adversaries would surround and pressure the Israelites. One might say that Israel was in a tight spot, a bind, so God should place their leader safely out of their reach.

From such trouble only the mighty God was able to deliver. The personal name of God, Yahweh, is used in the first half, and is paralleled by "the name of the God of Jacob." This allusion to Jacob recalls the patriarch's vow: "I will make there [Bethel] an altar unto God, who answered me in the day of distress" (Gen. 35:3). The answer of "the God of Jacob" became proverbial for powerful, divine intervention, and so now the people looked for a similar deliverance in the day of their distress. Here the reference is to the "name" (שֵׁם) of the God of Jacob. On the surface the "name" of God might simply be assumed to mean the name "Yahweh," but this does not seem to be the intended meaning in this psalm, or in places where "the name of Yahweh" is the expression. How can the "name" set the king in safety? A brief discussion of how "the name of Yahweh" is used will benefit this study.[10] Of the many passages that could be used, perhaps none

---

9. I will use the actual holy name in the discussion of this psalm because it is important to the exposition of the psalm as a whole.

10. The word "name" (שֵׁם) is very common in the Old Testament (770 times in the singular and 84 times in the plural). It occurs three times in this psalm alone. Opinions on the etymology differ, but the basic idea of the word seems to be a distinguishing mark or name.

Apart from the common use of the word to refer to a name without any further emphasis, the word is frequently used with the meaning "reputation," as in the case of the promise to make a name for Abram (Gen. 12:2). Likewise, wisdom literature extols the value of a good name (Prov. 22:1).

The nuance of reputation overlaps with the meaning of character description, especially when referring to God (as in Isa. 9:5–6; and Exod. 34:5ff.). From this comes the nuance of "fame." To make a name for oneself would be to seek fame (Gen. 11:4). The connotation of fame may be clarified by the parallel use of זֵכֶר, "memorial," meaning "name" (Exod. 3:15).

Many passages show the relationship of these ideas. E.g., the removal a "name" results in cutting off of remembrance (Deut. 9:14). Unknown and dishonorable outcasts are "sons of no name" (Job. 30:8). Conversely, having a name is equivalent to remembrance, or social immortality (Isa. 56:5; Zeph. 3:19).

Israelite naming customs conveyed this same significance. In the beginning when Adam called names for the animals, he was probably describing them. When parents named their children, they used words or verbal expressions to describe the child or the circumstances of the birth.

The name came to be identified with an essential part of the person's nature. This is why someone could act in the name of another (1 Sam. 25:9). It does not mean that people subconsciously lived up to the meaning of their names, but that their name was identical to their existence. In Israel to die childless meant the name dies (2 Sam. 18:11), so the *levirate* custom grew up to preserve the name of the deceased (Deut. 25:5–6). Because the name was so identified with the person, we read how the name can be cut off, destroyed, blotted out, covered over, sinned against, or established. The name might be considered to be powerful, but only because the person so named was powerful.

If the name of a person is connected to that person's power or importance, then the "name of the LORD" is understandably the predominant force in the Old Testament. In fact, the "name of the LORD" is often considered a designation of his actual presence. We read how the "name of the LORD" acts (Ps. 20:2), or that the LORD put his name in the sanctuary (Deut. 12:5). The psalms link the "name of the LORD" with his attributes: righteousness (89:15), faithfulness (89:24), salvation (96:2), holiness (99:3), goodness (100:4), mercy (109:21), love (119:55), truth (138:2) and glory (148:13). To fight, or be sent, or pray "in the name of the LORD" meant to do so by faith in his power and authority. Finally, since the "name of the LORD" is associated with his presence at the ark, it is connected with worship: it can be praised (Joel 2:26), loved (Ps. 5:11), declared (Ps. 22:22), feared (Mal. 4:2), waited on (Ps. 52:9), or walked in (Jer. 34:16). It can also be blasphemed (Isa. 52:5), polluted (Jer. 34:16), or profaned (Ezek. 36:21ff.). The "name of the LORD" stands for the LORD himself, his essential nature revealed as an active force in the lives of the people. Thus, the expression "the name of the LORD" could be explained as a metonymy of subject, because the expression refers to the nature of the LORD. See my article on שֵׁם, "Name" in *The New International Dictionary of Old Testament Theology and Exegesis,* edited by W. VanGemeren.

is more to the point than Exodus 34:5–7, a passage in which Yahweh himself proclaimed "the name of Yahweh":

> And Yahweh descended in the cloud and stood with him there and proclaimed the name of Yahweh [וַיִּקְרָא בְשֵׁם יהוה].[11] And Yahweh passed by before him and made proclamation: "Yahweh, Yahweh, a God merciful and gracious, slow to anger, abundant in loyal love and truth, keeping loyal love for thousands, forgiving iniquity, transgression and sin, and that will be no means clear the guilty, visiting the iniquity of the fathers upon the children, and upon the children's children, upon the third and fourth generations."

The content of the proclamation is a list of the divine attributes. Similarly, the messianic prophecy in Isaiah 9:6 says: "His name shall be called 'Wonderful, Counselor, the Mighty God, the Everlasting Father, the Prince of Peace.'" Here too the "name" is identical to the attributes or nature. The "name of God" represented to Israel all that God was known to be, his nature and his reputation, revealed in his acts. The congregation was therefore making their appeal to a God whose reputation of delivering his people from distress was a great part of their shared experience. They based their prayer on the "name"; and this called to mind the nature of God and thereby encouraged even greater confidence.

Second, it is a prayer for help from God (v. 2). The faithful subjects' next request is for help from the sanctuary on Zion. The two parallel lines again form a unified idea, for the sanctuary came to be situated on Mount Zion and represented God's dwelling among his people. By referring to that dwelling place as the source of help, they mean that Yahweh himself was the source.

Exactly how God would send "help" to the king is not specified, but the term "help" (עֶזְרְךָ, "your help," the genitive "your" meaning help for you; for the word see Ps. 46:1) has the meaning of doing for someone what that person cannot do for himself or

---

11. This could be translated "and he made proclamation of Yahweh by name (= nature)."

herself. It is used to explain victory in military conflicts in which
God gave the victory. Samuel, for example, set up a stone named
"Ebenezer" ("stone of help") after defeating the Philistines,
saying, "Thus far has the LORD helped us" (1 Sam. 7:12). Psalm
46:1 praises God as "an ever present help in trouble" because of
his power over the nations. The congregation knew that military
victory required and was assured by the LORD's "help." It was
not that God would simply lend support to David's efforts–it was
that without divine intervention David would fail completely.
And the parallel verb "sustain" (< סָעַד) adds the emphasis that
the help be preserved.

Third, it is a prayer to honor devout faithfulness (v. 3). The
righteous now appeal to the LORD to answer their king's worshipful petition: "May he remember all your offerings, and accept your whole burnt offering." They readily invoke God to help
the king because he was faithfully bringing the offering and the
sacrifice—an act of devout worship by a faithful believer. He was
a righteous man who was making a righteous petition to God
with tributes of worship. All this made it compelling to intercede
for him.

In this verse there are two elements—the blood sacrifice
(עוֹלָה, Lev. 1) and the accompanying gift offering (מִנְחָה, Lev. 2).
The "whole burnt offering," the blood sacrifice, represented the
worshiper's total submission to God and his complete acceptance
by God on the basis of the atoning sacrifice.[12] The entire animal
was burnt on the altar and its smoke ascended to heaven as
a sweet aroma. The congregation's prayer was that God accept
this sacrifice offered in faith by David. The verb "accept" (דָּשֵׁן
in the *piel*) literally means "to find [or make] fat."[13] The fat was
symbolic of the best, and so if God found the sacrifice "fat," it

---

12. You may gain a more complete understanding of the essence of each kind
of sacrifice in my book *Recalling the Hope of Glory* (Grand Rapids: Kregel,
2006), pp. 198–204.

13. The verb דָּשֵׁן in the basic stem means "to be fat, grow fat." Most of its uses
are in the *piel* and *pual* systems with a causative meaning of "make fat." It
has several related meanings in the texts, though. In Psalm 23:5 it has the
sense of anointing, which is symbolic of festivity and joy in the presence
of the LORD. Here it means "find a sacrifice fat" or "make it fat," meaning
find it acceptable. It can also mean to take away the fatty ashes from

meant that he would be pleased that it was the best and accept it.

It was understood by the Israelites that the faith (and faithfulness) of the person making the sacrifice determined whether or not the sacrifice was accepted. It was not simply that the faithful would bring a good animal, but rather that they would offer it in faith. With God, obedience is preferred above empty ritual (1 Sam. 15:22; Ps. 40:7). The LORD, who knows the hearts of the people, would reject the sacrifice of the unbeliever and the hypocrite (Isa. 1:10–15; Jer. 6:20), but accept the sacrifice of the true worshiper (Isa. 56:7). If the individual's life was marred by sin, sacrificial worship should first take the form of a broken spirit (Ps. 51:16–17), which would find expression in confession. In ancient Israel, as in Christianity today, it was the inner condition of the heart and not the outward form of religion that determined true, acceptable worship. If David's heart was right before the LORD, his sacrifice would be accepted.

Accompanying this sacrifice was the "offering." Not only was David basing his appeal on the atoning blood of the sacrifice, but he was also declaring his dedication to God with this offering (the מִנְחָה), for this gift or tribute, usually a meal or fruit offering, spoke of commitment. The part of this tribute gift that was burned was a called a "memorial" (אַזְכָּרָה in Lev. 2:2); it was intended to bring to God's memory the one for whom it was made. It is in this same sphere that one reads of the prayers of Cornelius ascending to God as a memorial of his faith (Acts. 10:4)—God would receive such prayers and commitments and act on them.

Accordingly, it was their prayer that on the battlefield the LORD "remember" (יִזְכֹּר) and reward his faith and dedication. The verb "to remember" (s.v. Ps. 6:5) means much more than

---

the altar (Num 4:13). It also has the meaning of being prosperous (Prov. 11:25).

The noun is דֶּשֶׁן "fatness" or "fat ashes." It is used for the ashes mixed with the fat in the ritual (Lev. 1:16); it can be used to signify abundance, luxuriance, or fertility (see Judg 9:9; Isa. 55:2; and Ps. 36:8).

The adjective דָּשֵׁן means "fat." It is parallel to "oil" in Isaiah 30:22, representing the abundant produce of the ground, and in Psalm 22:29 it refers to healthy, vigorous people—"the fat ones of the earth."

call to mind; it means to begin to act in accordance with what is remembered (as in "Lord, remember me"). It usually means to act according to the divine promises. In this psalm the people wanted God to respond to David's faith and keep the promises made to him by covenant (cf. Ps. 132).

Fourth, it is a prayer for the fulfillment of the king's counsel (v. 4). The final line of the intercession submits the plans of the king to the power of God: "May he grant you your heart's desire, and fulfill all your counsel." The second half explains that the heart's desire of David was his counsel, a term used elsewhere for battle strategy (see 2 Kings 18:20). Edmund Jacobs says that the heart is where ideas are transformed into projects which end in actions.[14] This description of heart fits well with the emphasis in the verse on David's war plans (see Ps. 21:2, the praise for the answer to this prayer). Here, then, faith and works join together. Because the king is a devout worshiper, his plans will harmonize with the divine plan (see Prov. 16:3).Although there was going to be a confident employment of the means given, the battle plans and the carrying out of the same, the psalmist's true confidence rested entirely upon God.

B. Supportive intercession is powerful if prayed with confidence (5).

Now there is a strong change in the tone of the psalm. Having made their intercession for the king, the worshipers next voice their great expectation of victory (v. 5): they will shout for joy at the deliverance of their king. The verb translated "shout for joy" (רָנַן; s.v Ps. 33:1)[15] is used often in military contexts, such as in 1 Samuel 4:5 when the people gave a "ringing cry" over the victorious return of the ark. It is a loud, shrill, vibrating shriek of victory, not a calm word of thanksgiving.

The reason for this exuberant rejoicing is the anticipated

---

14. *The Theology of the Old Testament*, p. 165
15. The form in the text is the cohortative נְרַנְּנָה. While it could be interpreted as a cohortative of request, continuing the prayers of the people, the change to the first person and the following imperfect tense indicate it is a cohortative of resolve, "we will shout for joy."

victory of the king. The noun used is the common term for "salvation" or "deliverance" (יְשׁוּעָה, s.v. Ps. 3:2). The noun, and especially its related verbal forms, stress almost exclusively divine intervention or the activities of divinely appointed agents. This intervention could refer to victory in battle (1 Sam. 17:47), deliverance from bondage (Exod. 14:30) or from oppressors (Judg. 2:16), either in a victory on the battlefield or through ensuring peace. In this psalm it is a military victory they expect.

The congregation's thoughts carry them to the triumphant return when they will wave their banners in the name of their God (the verb now is the simple imperfect נִדְגֹּל for the future expectation). Such jubilation will be a testimony to the effectual faithfulness and power of that name that they trust, the nature of their God demonstrated in his saving acts. They will share in the praise, for they have shared the burden by interceding for David.

Finally, the people reiterate their prayer in summary form (v. 5b): "May Yahweh fulfill all your petitions." Because the king's petitions would be in the best interests of the nation and in conformity to the will of God, the people would faithfully support them all.

These first five verses of the psalm provide a better understanding of what lay behind David's proclamation of faith in verse 6. Here was a man who admitted his need of God and in faith petitioned him for help, who understood God's stipulations for true worship and faithfully observed them, and who recognized the inadequacy of his own strategy and by faith submitted it to God. And this was the faith of this congregation as well. Here is a faith that can praise God before the answer actually comes.

II. The righteous find greater confidence in praying by meditating on the nature of God (6–8).

The second major section of the psalm (vv. 6–8) focuses attention on the great confidence expressed by an individual, most likely David, the spiritual leader of these people. This is signaled by a shift to the first person, "Now I know." It is the king who prayed for help in the battle, and it is the king who, having found great confidence, thus electrified his people with his declaration. For the reader, these verses provide instruction for the kind of faith necessary for effectual prayer.

A. *The prayer of faith can anticipate the answer with confidence (6, 8)*

Now the king declares the certainty of the answer, and this certainty is the most striking aspect of this verse. "I know" (יָדַעְתִּי) expresses the certainty. This verb usually signifies an experiential knowledge, but in this case the experience is about to be realized. One may observe that true faith in the LORD is usually expressed in such strong expressions of confidence. "Now I know" is affirmation, not hope. It is comparable to Paul's, "I know whom I have believed" (2 Tim. 1:12). It is as if the psalmist had experienced the great deliverance already.

And what he knew by faith was the certainty of the victory that God would grant. Referring to himself in the third person as he frequently does, David says, "Now I know that Yahweh saved his anointed; he will answer him from his holy heaven with the saving deeds of his right hand." He knew by faith that the battle had been won. His expression "saved" (הוֹשִׁיעַ, translated in some versions in the English present tense "saves") may be taken as a prophetic perfect (or as some explain it in the Psalter, a perfect of confidence). It shows that by faith he realized the final fulfillment and viewed the future as completed. He was now convinced of that victory for which the congregation prayed.

The expression displays another aspect of David's confidence: it was not "somehow" but "triumphantly!" He was convinced that the deliverance would be accomplished in an overwhelming display of power. He affirmed this in two ways. One is the expansion of the thought expressed by the intercession: whereas the people prayed that help would come from the sanctuary, the king was sure that it would come from heaven. The dwelling place on Mount Zion represented God's presence and suggested his condescension, but in the heavens was his throne (Ps. 11:4). The other way that he presented this picture was by his description "with the saving mighty deeds of his right hand" (literally: בִּגְבֻרוֹת יֵשַׁע יְמִינוֹ, "with mighty[16] deeds of salvation of his right hand"). David's faith enabled him to expect an awesome display

---

16. For this word, s.v. Ps. 45:3.

of the power of God in answer to his prayer so that the deliverance would be demonstrably God's.

We may look ahead to verse 8 to see this confidence amplified: true faith in God vividly anticipates the outcome. The psalmist advances from prayer to praise and from praise to confident expectation—almost prophecy—when he portrays the outcome of the battle as if it had already taken place. He describes the completed conquest by saying, "They have bowed down and fallen, but we have arisen and stand firm" (the verbs would be prophetic perfects here as well). These actions are metonymical of the outcome in which David's army would be victorious and the enemies defeated. Here, then, the magnitude of his faith visualizes the outcome.

B. The certainty of faith is based on the nature of the LORD (7)

Verse 7 is the key to the confidence of the king, of the people interceding for him, and of all believers. The verse is constructed by a contrast (antithetical parallelism) between the armies of the enemies and Israel's armies: "Some in chariots, and some in horses, but as for us, we will keep our confidence in the name of Yahweh our God." There is no verb in the first half of the verse; the verb in the second half serves both halves, strengthening the contrast between the different objects of faith. One may observe from this verse that true confidence is based on a proper concept of the proper object of faith—not military strength but divine power (see Ps. 33:17).

The first half of the verse deals with the improper object of faith—human resources. The self-confident enemies had their reliance on their resources, horses and chariots. Their invincible chariots were of iron and equipped with weapons that could easily annihilate an army. Yet, biblical history includes incidents in which the weak things have confounded the mighty. On one such occasion David defeated Hedadezer, king of Zobah, who had many chariots and horsemen (1 Chron. 18:4), and on another day he defeated a Syrian army that fought in chariots (1 Chron. 19:18). Perhaps this psalm is behind one of these incidents. At any rate, the Scriptures make it clear that those who trust in human methods and devices alone will soon realize their folly.

The proper object of faith is not military machinery—people can have no sure confidence in weapons.

The proper object of faith is "the name of Yahweh." What the war machines were to the nations, the "name of Yahweh" was to Israel. As long as the Israelites trusted the LORD for their battles, they were victorious; but when they in unbelief multiplied horses and engaged in alliances and treaties for their security, abandoning God as the object of their faith and even embracing foreign gods, they fell to their pagan enemies.

The verb translated here as "keep confidence," or by others as "be confident, make mention" or "have confidence in" or "trust," is a form of the verb "to remember" (נַזְכִּיר from זָכַר). Earlier in the psalm this verb was used by the congregation to bring David's offering to the memory of God so that God would remember David. Now the psalmist avows that he and his fellow believers continually keep God in mind as their object of faith. In fact, in the sentence "in the name of our God" is put first for emphasis. The verb in this verse (a *hiphil* form) takes on the significance of keeping something in the memory, that is, an inner meditation that issues forth into confident praise (sometimes translated "ponder, meditate").[17] While the psalmist prayed for help, and when he went out in confidence to the battle, he did so with ever-increasing confidence gained by meditating on, pondering, keeping in remembrance, the "name of the Yahweh."

We have already seen that the "name of Yahweh" refers to the revealed nature of God, his divine attributes revealed in divine acts. David went to battle, trusting in God's power, faithfulness, loyal love, and righteousness, to name but a few. David knew all about the abilities and perfections of the LORD from his understanding of the LORD's past dealings with his people, as well as from the rich experiences in his own life. When he was faced with an obstacle which was distressing, he would pray. He was a mature believer who knew Yahweh and had many spiritual experiences with him, so much of the time of his prayer would be spent

---

17. The *hiphil* may be classified as an inner causative, meaning that one reminds oneself, keeps it in mind, ponders, or meditates on something. In essence this means confidence in, trust in, or even making boast in something.

pondering and meditating on the glorious, incomparable attributes of God which he knew to be real. There was no doubt in his mind after such a marvelous and holy meditation that God was fully able to answer the prayer. With all the confidence that meditation would supply, he would go to fight in the "name of Yahweh" and return to praise the "name of Yahweh." It is no wonder that the prayers and praises of Israel are filled with attributes of God!

Here, then, is the source of David's (and the congregation's) confident faith. The "name of Yahweh," that is, his demonstrated attributes, filled their thoughts and inspired their praise.

III. Believers should nonetheless continue their intercession until the victory is attained (9).

In the final verse the psalmist records how the people persevered in their intercession, calling on the LORD to demonstrate that victory of which they were so confident: "O LORD, save the king; may he answer us when we call."[18] The use of the terms "answer," "day" [idiom: "when"], and "save" in this verse reflects the beginning of the psalm, providing a nice recapitulation of the prayer and thereby unifying the psalm (words related to יָשַׁע occur four times). But the point of this last verse, even though the text is difficult, is that the people keep on praying with confidence as the king goes out to the battle.

MESSAGE AND APPLICATION

In this psalm we have demonstrated the confidence of intercession and supplication in a prayer for deliverance in battle. The Psalter includes many other prayers that turned to praise before the answer actually came—it is one of the features of the prayers of Israel. This psalm, however, provides insight into the basis for such confidence. Evidently, while the psalmists prayed,

---

18. The line is difficult; MT reads: יהוה הוֹשִׁיעָה הַמֶּלֶךְ יַעֲנֵנוּ, "O Yahweh, save; may the king answer us (when we call)." But if the division is made after הַמֶּלֶךְ, then the sentence can be read: "O Yahweh, save the king; may he answer us when we call."

they meditated on the revealed nature of the LORD, and in the process became convinced that their prayer had been heard.[19] On the basis of that, the psalmists could begin to praise.

But to many modern Christians, such faith is unproven, for they read with unannounced disbelief the words of Jesus: "Truly I say to you, whoever says to this mountain, 'Be taken up and cast into the sea,' and does not doubt in his heart but believes what he says is going to happen, it shall be granted to him. Therefore I say to you, all things for which you pray and ask, believe that you have received them, and they shall be granted to you" (Mark 11:23–24).

All of the royal psalms are typological of Jesus Christ in one sense or another—he is the fulfillment of them, for he is the greatest Davidic king. When we study the life of the Lord on earth, it becomes apparent that he was the man of faith pre-eminently; consequently, he was fully able to teach people how to pray and to set the pattern for effective faith. If we wish to see the message of Psalm 20 lived out, we need only look to the prayer life of Jesus.

As we reflect on the required faith of which Jesus spoke and see it so vividly illustrated in this psalm, many ideas come to mind that could be stressed in an exposition, but the main idea of the psalm should be emphasized. For by it the psalm is unified and set apart from other songs, and from it we can learn to develop greater faith: *Assurance that prayer has been answered—true faith—is developed and strengthened by meditation on the attributes of the LORD.* If people are ignorant of God's revealed attributes and perfections, that is, if they have never realized his power in their lives, in a time of distress the problem may be presented to the Lord in prayer, but there will be very little confidence in the prayer. The necessary procedure to develop greater confidence in praying is to discover what God has done and is capable of doing so that in the time of trial the "name

---

19. See Claus Westermann, *The Praise of God in the Psalms,* pp. 65 and 70. Westermann calls this an "oracle of salvation"; such an oracle could be a word from a prophet, a change in circumstances, or a growing inner conviction—something to let the one praying know that God was about to answer.

of the LORD" will fill our thoughts and strengthen our faith. In line with this, Jesus says, "If you ask anything in my name, that will I do" (John 14:14). Far from being a formula for quick results, this expression "in my name" should be our expression of utter dependence on him whose nature, whose history, whose abilities, we have come to know.

PSALM 21

The Triumph of the LORD's Anointed

INTRODUCTION

Text and Textual Variants

To the chief musician. A Psalm of David.

1 O LORD, in your strength the king rejoices;
    and in your deliverance, how[1] greatly he exults![2]
2 You have given him the desire of his heart,
    and the request of his lips you have not refused;
3 For you came[3] to meet him with rich blessings,
    you put on his head a golden crown.
4 Life he asked from you—you gave[4] it to him,
    length of days for ever and ever.
5 Great is his glory in your deliverance,
    honor and majesty you lay upon him;
6 For you place on him eternal[5] blessings;
    you make him glad with joy with your presence;

---

1. The Greek text, the Syriac and Jerome do not have "how." This was apparently to simplify the text.
2. The *K^ethiv* reading is יָגֵיל and the *Q^ere'* is יָגֵל.
3. The verbs are prefixed conjugations and taken here to be preterites; they are often taken as imperfects and given an English present tense translation.
4. Greek and Syriac have a conjunction, "and you gave."
5. The Greek text has εἰς αἰῶνα αἰῶνος, perhaps influenced by verse 4: "For you will give him a blessing forever and ever."

7 For the king trusts in the LORD,
    and through the loyal love of the Most High
        he shall not be shaken.
8 Your hand will reach after[6] all your enemies,
    your right hand will find out those[7] that hate you;
9 You will make them like a furnace of fire
    in the time of your appearing;
  The LORD, in his wrath, will swallow[8] them,
    and a fire will devour them.
10 You will destroy their fruit from the earth,
    and their seed from the sons of men;
11 Although[9] they intend evil against you;
    and plan a treacherous plan,[10]
        they cannot prevail;
12 For you will make them turn their backs,[11]
    on your strings you will make ready *your arrows*
        against their face.[12]

13 Be exalted, O LORD, in your strength;
  we will sing and praise your might.

---

6. The Hebrew text has the verb "find." The first occurrence has the preposition and so would mean "reach after, aim at" (see Isa. 10:10); the second has אֵת and would mean "find out, attain." The Greek version translates it (and subsequent forms) as a volitive, and puts it in the passive voice: "Let your hand be found."
7. The Greek and Targum have "all," which would reflect a reading of לְכָל.
8. The Greek translation has the verb συνταράξει, "trouble (them)," for MT's יְבַלְּעֵם, "swallow them." This could have been an unintentional confusion with בָּהַל (see Ps. 2:5) or an attempt to interpret the figure.
9. The particle כִּי could be interpreted as a causal "for," giving the reason for their destruction, but the concessive interpretation is more forceful to the message.
10. The MT and the Greek version have the singular noun (מְזִמָּה), but some Greek manuscripts, Symmachus, the Targum and the Vulgate read a plural.
11. MT reads "you will make them shoulder."
12. The Greek version has "in your remnants (ἐν τοῖς περιλοίποις σου) you will prepare their face." The MT has "with your strings (בְּמֵיתָרֶיךָ) you will make ready [your bow] against their face." The word מֵיתָר is a "cord" or "string," but the related verb יָתַר means "remain, leave over." The Greek translation may have been etymologizing.

Composition and Context

In this royal psalm of praise the king rejoices greatly in the LORD who has given him the victory in battle because he trusts in the LORD. The victory, the desire of the king's heart, was a direct answer to prayer, probably the prayer of Psalm 20 as some of the connections suggest.

A more precise classification of the psalm is difficult. The first seven verses are clearly thanksgiving for the answer to prayer, but verses 8–12 seem to anticipate a future battle. A. A. Anderson concludes that this section could either be an oracle addressed to the king or a section of confidence addressed to the LORD. He further suggests the psalm might be a liturgical composition for something like a coronation.[13] It might seem unusual for the king to praise the LORD for a recent victory and have the people anticipate greater victories to come, but in the world of ancient Israel it would not have been so unusual. The psalm is liturgical nonetheless, although not as clearly as Psalm 20. It could have been used over the course of time for any victory of a king in battle.

The psalm opens the thanksgiving section with the declaration that the king rejoices in the LORD. Then verses 2–6 explain why he is able to rejoice: God has answered his prayers, in fact he has anticipated his needs, and exalted him on the battlefield. By protecting the king in the battle, God has extended his life and given him glory and majesty and blessing as well. Because God has blessed him, he will be a blessing to the people. In this section the psalmist's reasons for praise move from the specific to the general.

The king then states clearly why God has answered his prayer and blessed him so gloriously: he trusts in the LORD and the LORD treats him with loyal love (v. 7). This verse is the key to the psalm and therefore forms the transition to the next section. Not only does his trust in the LORD supply the reason why he was blessed so greatly, but it also provides the basis for his assurance in future conflicts. Verse 7 then brings out the basic message that the king has learned by this experience: because of the loyal love of the LORD, those who trust in him shall never

---

13. Anderson, *Psalms 1–72*, p. 179.

be moved. Because this is a royal psalm prepared for use in the sanctuary, future kings who share his faith can also expect deliverance and therefore find reason to praise as well—even making use of this psalm of praise.

In the second part, verses 8–13, the congregation or a representative of the congregation addresses the king with a message of assurance. They announce the confident anticipation of a victorious future—just as the congregation in Psalm 20 anticipated praising and banner waving when the king was victorious. Here the message is that the king will never be shaken but will destroy those who plot against him. Through it all the people will sing and praise God for his great strength. This word "strength" or "might" (עֹז, s.v. Ps. 29:1) seems to be one of the distinctive words of the poem; the passage opens with "O LORD, in your might" and closes with "Be exalted, O LORD, in your might."

Psalm 21 is probably the complement of Psalm 20 because of the repetition of ideas. At least it fits as a complementary thanksgiving to the prayer (and so was placed next to it in the collection). In Psalm 20, David was going into battle, trusting the LORD, with the people interceding for him by praying, "May the LORD grant you the desire of your heart." Here, he praises the LORD, saying, "You have given him the desire of his heart." In his praise the king acknowledges that the battle was won by the LORD whose powerful help was indispensable. Because the king was God's chosen servant, and because he went to battle in the name of the LORD, the battle was not his alone, and the victory was not his either. The only possible response of those who have experienced such a deliverance as this psalm depicts is to exalt the LORD in praise. Thus, Psalm 21 may be taken as the praise for the answer to the prayer in Psalm 20.

Exegetical Analysis

Summary

The psalmist rejoices in the strength of the LORD, who has responded to his faith with an overwhelming victory, and finds added encouragement from the faithful who anticipate God's future victory.

Outline

I. Praise: The king rejoices in the strength of the LORD who has given him the victory in battle because he trusted in him (1–7).
   A. He rejoices greatly in the victory he has been given (1).
   B. He rejoices because the LORD has wonderfully answered his prayer for victory (2–6).
      1. God gave him the desire of his heart (2).
      2. God gave him good things, including the crown (3).
      3. God granted him life through it all (4).
      4. God wonderfully blessed him so that his glorying is great (5–6).
   C. He realizes that God demonstrated his loyal love to him in this victory because he trusts in him (7).
II. Confidence: Because the king trusts in the LORD, the people anticipate that not only will he remain secure, but he shall also defeat future enemies (8–12).
   A. They anticipate the tremendous defeat their king shall inflict on his enemies (8–10).
      1. He will find those who hate him (8).
      2. He will defeat them thoroughly as the LORD destroys them in wrath (9).
      3. He will end their posterity and their memory from the earth (10).
   B. They explain why the enemies will be overthrown by their king (11–12).
      1. They intended evil against him through their devices (11).
      2. They cannot perform their schemes because their king will triumph (12).
III. Prayer: The people pray that the LORD will be exalted so that they might praise his might (13).

COMMENTARY IN EXPOSITORY FORM

I. Every demonstration of the power of God demands praise (1–7).

511

A. Announcement of Praise: God is to be praised for his great acts of deliverance (1).

The first verse sets the tone for the entire psalm—it is a time of great rejoicing. The verse announces that the king rejoices in the might of the LORD. The king is probably the speaker, referring to himself in the third person (as in 20:6); but his words are addressed to the LORD directly. He announces that he rejoices (יִשְׂמַח; s.v. Ps. 48:11) in the LORD's might and exults (יָגֵל, s.v. Ps. 13:6) in his deliverance. These verbs could be taken as future tenses, expressing what the king was going to do; but since the psalm is the praise, they are better translated with the English present tense (progressive imperfects). The verse is actually a summary introduction: the king rejoices—and what he rejoices about will be recorded next. The rejoicing is greatly intensified in the second half of the verse, not only by the choice of a word that describes cultic celebration (וְגִיל), but also by the addition of the adverb "greatly" (מְאֹד). The clause also makes use of the interrogative particle (מַה־) as an exclamation: "How greatly he exults!"[14]

The two parts of this verse parallel the focus of the praise: "might" (עֹז; s.v. Ps. 29:1) and "deliverance" or "victory" יְשׁוּעָה), s.v. Ps. 3:2). The words are common figures of speech: the first is a metonymy of cause, and the second a metonymy of effect, meaning that God's might is the cause of the victory, and the victory is the effect of that might. The two words describe the whole event; without the victory the might would not have been witnessed. The word "might" can be used for all levels of might; but when it describes God's might, it is supernatural (such as over creation; see Ps. 29:1, 11). The "deliverance" referred to here is the victory; but it is nothing short of salvation (one of the common translations of the word), not salvation from sin, but salvation from certain death in the battle.

B. Content of the Praise: By his power God delivers and blesses his people who pray to him (2–6).

In the next few verses the psalmist provides the details

---

14. The use of the particle with the verb (מַה־יָגֵל) for the exclamation is the reason the short form of the conjugation is used.

of this deliverance—the reason for the praise. In verse 2 the tenses change to the perfect tense (נָתַתָּה) to report the answer to the prayer, but since the benefits of that answer remain, a present perfect is the best translation: "you have given," and then stated negatively, "you have not refused." The deliverance that David had desired in his heart he also requested with his lips (Ps. 20:4). The word "desire" (תַּאֲוָה) means a thing desired; it is a strong word, even used in the commandment prohibiting coveting (Exod. 20:17). And the parallel word "request"[15] expresses not only the desire but the need, for he was poor in strength and so prayed for God to manifest his divine strength.

In verse 3 the psalmist explains how God did this: God anticipated his need and blessed him with good things. The verbs now are prefixed conjugations;[16] and while they could express the continuous actions on the part of God as he answers prayers and cares for his people, it is more likely in this context that they refer to what God did (and so may be classified as preterites). First, God "came to meet him" (תְּקַדְּמֶנּוּ). This verb could also be interpreted to mean that God "came before him," meaning that God anticipated the prayer and went before him. Either idea fits the context. The purpose of the divine intervention was to meet him"[with] blessings of good," or, "good blessings."[17] "Blessings" are good gifts, enrichments, and so the expression is pleonastic; the idea is emphatic—rich blessings (s.v. Ps. 5:12; and for "good," s.v. Ps. 34:8). Then, secondly, God put a golden crown on his head. This could be his own crown that was a symbol of his honor from God, or it could refer to something like the crown of the king of the Ammonites captured by David (2 Sam. 12:30). If the latter is the case, then the coming to meet

---

15. אֶרֶשֶׁת occurs only here; it may be related to רוּשׁ "to be poor, in need," and so the noun would mean a need or request.

16. In poetry the form is frequently used without the *waw* consecutive to express the past tense: "You came to meet him . . . you put a golden crown on his head." Briggs, although taking a slightly different interpretation, explains the tenses similarly: "This causal clause, with imperfects between perfects, changes the tense as well as the construction, in order to go back to the inauguration of the king which it vividly describes" (*Psalms*, p. 184).

17. "Blessings" is an adverbial accusative, and "good" is an attributive genitive.

him would refer to the provision of victory in the battle (and so a metonymy of cause).[18]

The psalmist gets to the heart of the matter in the next verse (4): "He asked life from you—you gave it to him." The second colon expands the idea of "life" to "length of days for ever and ever"— no end in sight. It was because of the battle that the psalmist asked for his life, meaning protection in the battle from death; but God went far beyond that. David says that God prolonged his life beyond what he could have imagined. For the psalmist, "forever and ever" is hyperbolic language, and yet, in the full revelation of God the words take on their fullest meaning (s.v. Ps. 61:5). A prayer for deliverance from death will have an immediate answer, but as we now know it will also have a greater answer in that the LORD will also deliver his people from death to eternal life. If this psalm has a typological element here, as most of the royal psalms do, then the deliverance from death for the King of Kings would certainly be eternal.

The deliverance in battle was the immediate evidence that God bestowed great glory on the king. Verse 5 is an expression of praise for God's blessings: "Great is his glory in your deliverance; honor and majesty you lay upon him." "Glory" is usually used as a divine attribute or perfection, but here, as in Psalm 3, it is used of the king's honor in representing the divine glory as the king (for the meaning of the word, s.v. Ps. 19:1). It was through the deliverance, the victory on the battlefield, that God displayed the glory of David; and the second line enhances this point, adding that God gave him honor (הוֹד) and majesty (הָדָר; s.v. Ps. 96:6). The first word means "majesty, vigor, splendor"; and the second word is "ornament, splendor, honor." The two are so close that they could be referring to one thing (so a hendiadys), "majestic honor." The verb "lay" (תְּשַׁוֶּה, from שָׁוָה) basically means "set" or "place." With the preposition (עַל) it is used of divine investiture (see Ps. 89:21). David's glory was great because God bestowed majestic honor upon him; and by delivering him in battle, God revealed how David reflected God's glory to the people.

---

18. It is possible that the expression is figurative, comparing bestowing victory on him to putting a crown on his head.

The reason for this glory and honor is that God gave him eternal blessings[19] and made him glad with his presence (v. 6). In the sequence of ideas he has now come full circle to the beginning of the psalm in referring to the rejoicing of the king. He started with the rejoicing over the deliverance (v. 1) which was an answer to prayer (v. 2) and a demonstration of divine blessings and exaltation (v. 3); then he reiterated the answer to prayer (v. 4), the exaltation (v. 5), and now the blessings and the joy (v. 6). The verb "you made him glad" (תְּחַדֵּהוּ, from חָדָה) means "to cheer, make joyful" (see Exod. 18:9). The Arabic cognate was used for cheering beasts of burden with a song and urging them to a quicker pace. Here, "You make him glad with joy"; the last two words (אֶת־פָּנֶיךָ) explains how— the preposition "with" (אֶת) indicates that it is the face of the LORD, that is, the divine presence, that makes David glad. The image of the face signifies the divine presence showing favor by intervening in his life and thereby giving him reason to rejoice.

C. Principle: God demonstrates his loyal love to those who trust in him (7)

The LORD answered the psalmist's prayer and blessed him because he was trusting in the LORD. The verse begins with a causal clause; and the verb in it is a participle (בֹּטֵחַ), stressing continual or durative action. The verb means "rely on" or "be confident, secure"; its related nouns mean "quietness, security, safety, confidence" (s.v. Ps. 4:5). David had confidence in the LORD; his confidence gave him a sense of safety and security. His trust was in the LORD, but more specifically according to the second colon, "in the loyal love of the Most High" (בְּחֶסֶד עֶלְיוֹן). His faith was in the supreme God, the God who is higher than all, but the God who also established a covenant with him in love (s.v. Ps. 23:6). He trusted that the sovereign God would maintain that love for him. As a result of this trust, he was secure.

---

19. The text has כִּי־תְשִׁיתֵהוּ בְרָכוֹת לָעַד, literally, "for you make him blessings for ever." It probably means that God made him full of blessings, for himself and for others (see Perowne, *Psalms*, I:234).

The verb "shall not be shaken" (בַּל־יִמּוֹט) comes from a verb that means "totter, shake, move" (s.v. Ps. 62:2); the meaning is here applied to David's position as king and leader of the armies—he could not be overthrown. His kingdom was secure because his relation with the LORD was also sure. The principle expressed here would apply to all who trust in the LORD, whether subsequent kings or individuals: security comes through faith, but it is made possible by the love of God.

II. Such demonstrations of divine deliverance guarantee the ultimate victory for the people of God (8–12).

A. God will destroy the wicked (8–10).

In the second part the psalm anticipates the future defeat of the king's enemies. Perowne says that the writer "could not but augur a glorious future from a glorious past."[20] This section is an outgrowth of the first strophe and is actually a practical application of the past experience. That experience helped build the psalmist's confidence, for this section is not a hoping against hope, but a full expectation that what God had begun to do to the wicked would someday be completed.

There is a shift now in speakers, for these words are addressed to the king. Someone speaking for the congregation offered the words of encouragement for the future, and the psalmist recorded them in his poem.[21] They first affirm that the king will "find" (תִּמְצָא) all those who hate him and try to destroy him (v. 8). The verb "to find" has the meaning here "to come upon, light upon, plunder." The formal subjects in the two cola are "hand" and "right hand" (metonymies for the powerful action of the king). The picture in the verse suggests a hand reaching into a nest, an evil nest in this case, to plunder it. This expectation is certain because the king is loyal to God and the enemies are wicked men who are hostile to him and want to see

---

20. Perowne, *Psalms*, I:23.
21. It is also possible to interpret these lines as being addressed to God and not the king, anticipating that he will destroy his enemies. In a sense, both are true, for if David destroys his enemies, it will be God who does it.

him slip and fall, but God will enable the king to find them out and destroy them.

The destruction is vividly described in the next verse (9). The king will make them like a furnace (תַּנּוּר, a portable stove) of fire, the point of the simile being that they, like the contents of a furnace (so a metonymy as well) will be utterly consumed (see Mal. 3:19; Isa. 31:9; Gen. 19:28). It may well be that fire would be part of the attack on them that would destroy them, as in many ancient battles. This anticipated victory would be at the time of the king's appearing (literally, "at the time of your face"), meaning when he shows up for the battle.

The second half of the verse clarifies that it would be the LORD who would swallow them up in his wrath.[22] The image used here is bold (an implied comparison), comparing the defeat of the wicked with swallowing them. This verb forms a close match to the idea that "a fire will devour them." It means that the LORD in his wrath will completely destroy them in the battle so that they will be gone. The fire that will devour them could be a literal conflagration that will come upon the enemies in their cities and towns as they are destroyed by the king, but it could also be taken as a figure of the burning anger of the LORD that will consume the wicked.

The anticipation is of a final defeat of the enemies of the king. According to verse 10 they and their descendants will be destroyed from the face of the earth. The idioms of "fruit" and "seed" refer to their posterity who will be removed in judgment. There will be no continuation of the wicked from generation to generation, for they all will be removed. The language used here is extravagant, for the psalmist certainly was referring to the total defeat of his immediate enemies. But in the typological sense of the psalm the extravagant language will be literally and historically fulfilled when the Messiah destroys all the wicked in the final judgment (see also Psalm 2).

---

22. By the Masoretic accents "Yahweh" starts the second half and is therefore the subject of the verb. If the name is taken with the first colon, then it would be a vocative, clarifying that "you" of verse 9 is the LORD.

B. God will destroy the wicked because they intend to destroy the righteous (11–12).

The psalm now elaborates on their destruction. It first clarifies that this will happen even though they intended (stretched out, extended [נָטָה]) evil against the king, God's personal representative on earth. They did this by planning (< חָשַׁב, s.v. Ps. 32:2; and compare Ps. 2:1) a treachery (מְזִמָּה, a deceitful or treacherous plan; s.v. Ps. 10:2—but it was a plan that could not succeed (a "vain thing" in Ps. 2:1). The two verbs, perfect tenses, are found in concessive clauses leading up to the affirmation that they cannot prevail.[23]

The reason that they cannot prevail is supplied in verse 12: "For you will make them turn their backs." David will make them all shoulder (literally)—they will be beaten in the battle and have to turn and run away. All that will be seen will be their backs. This will take place when Israel's army makes their arrows ready on their bows directly against their faces. The line is cryptic but clear enough: "on your strings you will make ready [your arrows] against their faces." The words "your arrows" must be supplied as the usage elsewhere indicates (see Pss. 7:4; 11:2). The king will utterly defeat them and put them to flight.

The battle is to be another evidence of divine intervention. It is the king who will conquer with fire and shoot arrows, but it is clearly the LORD who will do this through the king and his armies (Pss. 18:14; 97:3–5). This is what gives the assurance of victory—the LORD who will fight for his people.

III. God is to be praised for his mighty power (13)

The psalm closes with a call for the LORD to be exalted (רוּמָה; s.v. Ps. 46:10), meaning, to show himself victorious in battle over the king's enemies. It is a call for God to manifest his power (גְּבוּרָה; s.v. Ps. 45:3) so that the people will again to be able to sing and praise. They will acclaim him to be the source of all strength; they will sing continually of his great deeds. Therefore,

---

23. The clauses could also be taken as causal clauses, "for," supplying the reason for the destruction

518

the psalm ends on the same note it began—praising the LORD because of his display of might on behalf of those who trust in him.

MESSAGE AND APPLICATION

Psalm 21 displays one of the strongest expressions of security in the LORD in the face of enemies; it is a security that causes great joy and rejoicing. There are many ways that this psalm could be developed in an exposition, but the clear subject would be the security of believers—those who put their trust in the LORD, like the king, find security. Nothing is able to move or shake the saints because of the power of the LORD manifested through his loyal love for his people. This confidence in God's promise of victory over the wicked applies today as well as in the age to come. We could provisionally develop an expository idea along these lines: *Those who put their trust in the LORD will rejoice when God gives them the victory over the world (both now in individual conflicts and in the future in the final victory).* This confidence is built up through regular prayer and praise; as prayers are answered the praise of the LORD becomes more convincing.

Since this psalm is a royal psalm, it also has an application for David's greater son, Jesus the Messiah. He asked for life and restoration to glory when facing his enemies (John 17), and he received them through the resurrection and exaltation. He has been crowned in glory and blessed forever. As the perfect human he trusted in God with a faith that could not be shaken; as the divine Son he is fully able to defeat all wickedness, which he will do when he comes again as our glorious king. His coming victory over the world is the victory that all believers anticipate with joy.

PSALM 22

Afflicted by the Wicked, Abandoned by God— A Cry of Despair

INTRODUCTION

Text and Textual Variants

To the Chief Musician. Set to "The Hind of the Morning."[1]
A Psalm of David.

1 My God, my God,[2] why have you forsaken me?
   Why are you far from helping me *and* the words of my
      roaring![3]
2 O my God, I cry out by day, but you do not answer,
   and in the night season, and there is no silence to me.

---

1. This is likely a melody used for the psalm. The Greek text renders it "concerning the morning aid." Many have tried to make something more significant out of it. Martin Luther, for example, took it to refer to Christ, hunted through the night and killed at dawn. Delitzsch said it represented the dawn of redemption after the night of anguish. Even Jewish scholars saw something symbolic here: the "Hind" was a name for the *Shekainah* (the LORD) on the day of redemption; and the *Midrash* of Canticles (2:8) saw here a reference to the lamb offered at dawn as the morning sacrifice, or the dawn itself as a hind leaping—which seems too happy for a psalm like this. None of these could be proven, of course; but they represent the belief that nothing in a psalm like this could be without deeper meaning.
2. The Greek has "O God, my God." Then it continues with "attend to me" (πρόσχες μοι).
3. The Greek has "the account of my transgressions (οἱ λόγοι τῶν παραπτωμάτων μου) is far from my salvation."

521

3 But you are holy,[4]
    you who are enthroned in the praises of Israel.
4 In you our ancestors trusted,
    they trusted, and you rescued them;
5 To you they cried out, and were delivered,
    in you they trusted—and were not put to shame.

6 But I am a worm, and no man,
    a reproach of men, and despised by people.
7 All who see me laugh me to scorn,
    they shoot out *their lip*, they shake their heads, *saying,*
8 "Cast yourself[5] on the LORD! Let him rescue him,
    let him deliver him, if he delights in him."

9 But you *are the one* who took me out of the womb,
    making me trust[6] on my mother's breasts.
10 Upon you I was cast from the womb;
    from my mother's belly you are my God.

11 Do not be far off from me, for trouble is near,
    for there is none to help.
12 Many bulls have surrounded me,
    mighty *bulls* of Bashan have encircled me;
13 They open wide their mouth upon me
    as a raging and roaring lion.
14 Like water I am poured out,

---

4. The Greek renders this line, "But you, the praise of Israel, dwell in a sanctuary/among saints" (σὺ δὲ ἐν ἁγίοις (ἁγίῳ) κατοικεῖς, ὁ ἔπαινος τοῦ Ἰσραήλ). A few manuscripts, Syriac and Jerome, have the singular "praise." It was apparently easier for the Greek version to think of the LORD's dwelling in the sanctuary than in the praises of Israel, and so קדוֹשׁ was thought to be קֹדֶשׁ.

5. The Greek (Syriac and Jerome, followed by Matt. 27:43) took the word גל to be a perfect tense (גָּל), working without vowels of course, for it has ἤλπισεν, "he hoped (trusted) in the Lord"; but Matthew has "he trusts in God," πέποιθεν ἐπὶ τόν θεόν. The textual evidence supports the imperative form in the MT, because it does not fit the normal pattern and a scribe would easily assume it to be the perfect tense. The imperative in the Hebrew is a harsher taunt, calling on the sufferer to trust in the LORD

6. The Greek has a noun instead of a participle, "my hope" (ἡ ἐλπίς μου).

and all my bones are out of joint;
my heart has become like wax,
   it melts within my body.

15 My strength[7] is dried up like a potsherd,
   and my tongue cleaves to my jaws—
and you are laying me in the dust of death!

16 For dogs[8] have completely surrounded me,
   the assembly of evil-doers has enclosed me;
they pierced my hands and my feet.[9]

---

7. The word does not give a precise parallel and so is usually emended to חִכִּי, the palate or roof of the mouth. The word "strength" could be metonymical for the dryness of the mouth.

8. The Greek text adds "many."

9. The Hebrew text at this point has כָּאֲרִי, which makes no sense in the sentence: "Like a lion (*ka'ari*) my hands and my feet." All the ancient versions, and the early Jewish sources as well, have a verb instead of "like a lion." Some of the Masoretic manuscripts also have verbs, either כָּאֲרוּ or כָּרוּ, plural forms of the perfect tense. The difference in the current Hebrew text and the Hebrew that was behind the versions would essentially be the last letter, a ' (*yod*) if it is "lion" and a ו (*waw*) if it is the plural verb. And since the *yod* and the *waw* are similar, it would have been easy to make the change.

So on the one side ("like a lion") we have the standard Masoretic reading in the Hebrew Bible, but on the other side (a verb) we have two manuscripts in the Masoretic Hebrew tradition that do not go with the reading of "like a lion" (Kennicott ms 39 has the *yod* changed to a *waw*, and DeRossi ms 337 has a *K*^e*thiv–Q*^e*re'* reading, attesting to both forms). Three later Hebrew manuscripts have the scribal emendation to the verb *k–r–w* (no '*aleph*), and the ancient Greek, Arabic, Syriac, and Latin versions have verb forms. They read something like "they pierced, they dug, they bored through" (Greek has ὤρυξαν). The later Greek revisions have different verbs, but still verbs nonetheless: Aquila has ἐπέδησαν and Symmachus ὡς ζητοῦντες, "they bound" or something similar. The Midrash has a verb, but with the translation of "conjure."

There is a further development of this issue within the Hebrew tradition. In the notes on the page (*Masorah finalis*) the medieval editor of the manuscript Jacob ben Chaim had a comment that there was a *K*^e*thiv–Q*^e*re'* reading at this point, that while "like a lion" was in the text, something else was to be read in its place. The evidence for ben Chaim was found on a Jewish manuscript called "*'ochlah v*^e *'ochlah*," which was a list of words in the Hebrew Bible that occur in two places with different meanings. The

17 I can count[10] all my bones;
    they stare, they look at me;
18 They divide my garments among them,
    and for my clothing they cast lots.

19 But you, O LORD, do not be far off;[11]
    O my strength, hasten to help me.
20 Deliver my life from the sword,
    my dearest possession from the power of the dog;
21 Save me from the mouth of the lion;
    from the horns of the wild ox—you have answered me![12]

22 I will declare your name to my brethren;
    in the assembly I will praise you.
23 You who fear the LORD, praise him!
    All you descendants of Jacob, honor him!

---

word *ka'ari*, "like a lion" was on that list; in the other place where it occurred it meant "like a lion," and so could not mean that here.

A protestant scholar of the 1800s, Hupfeld, insisted that Ben Chaim had inserted that note under the influence of his Christian friends. C. D. Ginsberg addresses this issue (in *Introduction to the Massoretico-Critical Edition of the Hebrew Bible* [New York: KTAV, 1966], p. 969), stating that Hupfeld's accusation was inexcusable because the manuscript list to which ben Chaim referred was in the library at the University of Halle where Hupfeld taught, and he did not check to see if it was there. Ginsberg follows the reading in the Targum, which has both: "like a lion" and "they tore, pierced."

All the external evidence, the manuscripts and versions, supports the presence of a verb in the verse, probably with the meaning "they pierced." The text, then, was changed to avoid the reading in favor of "like a lion." The image in the psalmist's mind was probably of dogs nipping at the hands and feet and puncturing them. Similarly, the idea that Messiah would be pierced is found in Zechariah 12:10 (and see Isaiah 53:5).

10. Greek has "they count (ἐξηρίθμησα) all my bones."
11. The Greek has "do not put my help far away."
12. The form in the MT is a perfect tense. Many translations make it an imperative, a precative perfect, to fit the verse; but the psalmist is certain of his prayer being heard, so here the verb closes the lament and forms a transition (Kraus, *Psalms 1–59*, p. 292). Greek does not have a verb: "and from the horns of the wild oxen my lowliness" (τὴν ταπείνωσίν μου).

Revere him,[13] all you descendants of Israel!
24 For he has not despised nor abhorred
    the affliction of the afflicted;[14]
  Nor has he hidden his face from him;
    but when he cried to him,[15] he heard!
25 From you comes my praise in the great assembly;
    before those who fear you I will pay my vows.
26 The poor will eat and be satisfied;
    those who seek the LORD will praise him—
  Let your hearts[16] live forever!
27 All the ends of the earth will remember and turn to the
    LORD,
    and all the families of the nations will bow down before
    him,
28 For dominion belongs to the LORD,
    and he rules over the nations.
29 All the prosperous ones of the earth will feast and worship;
    all who go down to the dust will kneel before him—
    even the one who cannot stay alive.[17]

---

13. Greek has φοβηθήτωσαν, "let (all the descendants of Israel) revere."
14. The Greek translation reads "the supplication (τῇ δεήσει) of the poor/afflicted." The reading can be explained by confusion of letters, leading the translator to think of צְעָקַת, a "cry" or "supplication of," instead of עֱנוּת, "the affliction of." The word before, שִׁקַּץ, "abhorred," ends with a צ; that letter in regular form might have been copied a second time, beginning this word. The letter ע comes next. Then perhaps the נ and ו were tightly together and thought to be ק (ם). The final ת would have been the ending on either word. This can account for how the Greek might have seen the word. Both interpretations make good sense in the context; but the Greek ("supplication") can be easily explained as a secondary reading, whereas the Hebrew ("affliction") cannot.
15. Greek changes the pronouns: ". . . turned away his face from me, when I cried. . . ."
16. Greek has "their hearts (αἱ καρδίαι αὐτῶν) shall live for ever."
17. The line is fraught with textual difficulties. The MT has נַפְשׁוֹ לֹא חִיָּה, possibly "his life he cannot keep alive," meaning anyone who cannot keep himself alive. The Greek has καὶ ἡ ψυχή μου αὐτῷ ζῇ, rendered "my soul lives for him." The Greek text has different pronouns, "my" instead of "his," which may be confusion due to a slight change in the writing of the Hebrew character; but it understands the verb in the more simple translation of "lives," not indicating a *piel* form ("causes to live" or "preserves alive"). The negative לֹא in the Hebrew text was understood to be the pronoun with

30 A posterity[18] will serve him;
    future generations will be told about the Lord.[19]
31 They will come and proclaim his righteousness
    to a people yet unborn—
        that he has done it![20]

Composition and Context

Psalm 22 is one of the most magnificent psalms in the entire collection, not only because it is a passionate portrayal of the problem of the suffering of the righteous compounded by the frustration of unanswered prayer, but also because it is a picture of the suffering of our Lord Jesus Christ. Christians cannot read this psalm without remembering how Jesus appropriated it to his own sufferings on the cross, and so the passage must be read on both levels to gain all that the Spirit of God intended when he spoke through the psalmist. It has to be read first in the suffering psalmist's experience as an urgent prayer to be delivered from enemies who were methodically putting him to death; then it may be read on the higher level to see how the psalm was applied to the greater sufferings of Jesus. That the words of the psalm find their greatest meaning in the suffering of Jesus in no way minimizes the suffering of the psalmist or the thanksgiving and praise that resulted from his being delivered from death. In both settings the suffering in the psalm describes a death by execution at the hands of taunting enemies—its seriousness cannot be minimized. In both cases the lament is intensified because God seems not to hear the cry of the sufferer, but is apparently laying him in the grave.[21]

---

the preposition, לוֹ, "to him." The difficulties in the line call for much more study than can be done here, but it seems that the Greek translation was trying to make sense out of a difficult line.

18. Greek has "my seed (τὸ σπέρμα μου) shall serve him."
19. Greek has "the generation that is coming will be announced to the Lord."
20. Greek B has subordinated this last clause and rendered it "[. . . the people that shall be born], whom the Lord has made" (ὃν ἐποίησεν ὁ Κύριος). Others: ὅτι ἐποίησεν ὁ Κύριος, "because the Lord acted, or because the Lord did it."
21. There is an amazing amount of literature on this psalm; a few key articles should be mentioned for further study and additional resources on

Because of the nature of the suffering the ascription of the psalm to David has been challenged. We know of no time in the life of David that even comes close to the event that is described here; if it came from his experiences, the language of the psalm must be poetic and somewhat hyperbolic in places. It may be difficult to connect such a specific and significant event to David's life; but it is not impossible that it came from that time, for we do not know all that he experienced. However, commentaries suggest other occasions because of this. Perowne, for example, suggests that the most likely author would be some suffering Israelite in the Babylonian exile.[22] But would that be an attempted execution? We still would not know of any specific event. Others have suggested it came from Hezekiah (see 2 Chron. 32:23), but this would not solve the problem either. Jeremiah is a frequent candidate (see Jer. 37:11ff.),[23] or even Esther facing death at the hands of Haman. None of these are too compelling.

One approach would be to say the psalm was direct prophecy and its meaning fits only the fulfillment; but the psalm is not direct prophecy, even though it includes some predictive or anticipatory elements in it. Neither is the psalm clearly messianic, since it never refers to the anointed king. By all assessments the psalmist was describing a time when his enemies attempted to put him to death, a time of intense sufferings that left him almost dead; but the LORD did eventually hear his prayer and deliver him so that he was able to praise the LORD in the congregation. Whether it should be called prophetic or messianic may be debated, but what is certain is that Jesus appropriated this psalm to himself in his greatest sufferings, and thereafter the evangelists and apostles

---

some of the details in the text: Richard D. Patterson, "Psalm 22," *JETS* 47 (2004):213–33; John H. Reumann, "Psalm 22 at the Cross: Lament and Thanksgiving for Jesus Christ," *Int* 28 (1974):39–58; and H. D. Lange, "The Relation between Psalm and the Passion Narrative," *CTM* 43 (1972):610–21.

22. Perowne, *Psalms,* I:236.

23. Jaki simply connects it with Jeremiah and relies on tradition for some of his reasoning, such as the idea that Jeremiah was literally laid in the dust of death, but his bones stuck out so much from his emaciated body that they could be counted (Stanley L. Jaki, *Praying the Psalms* [Grand Rapids: Wm. B. Eerdmans, 2001], p. 67).

saw the connections between the psalm and his passion. We are safe in calling it typological; the psalmist may not have known how the psalm would be fulfilled, but God did. Since typology does not nullify the original intent and meaning of a passage, we are also free to use this psalm as an inspiration for our perseverance in praying even when God seems not to be there.

The psalm is for the most part an extended lament psalm, but where the vow of praise would normally be we have the main features of a declarative praise psalm. This may indicate that the praise section was an actual praise rather than a vow to be fulfilled. This would mean that while praying David received some indication that his prayer was answered, some "oracle of salvation" such as the retreat of his enemies or some divine intervention,"[24] and as a result proceeded to offer the praise without returning to the lament or the petition again.

Exegetical Analysis

Summary

Apparently forsaken by God, the God of the fathers and the God of his youth, and surrounded by scornful enemies who were killing him, the suffering psalmist laments his desperate plight, petitions God to deliver him from death, and suddenly, when confident that God finally heard his prayer, praises God for not abandoning him[25] and predicts that believers in all ages will join him in praising God for this great salvation.

---

24. In a lament psalm the praise is often a "vow of praise," but here the change from lament to praise is so dramatic that something had to have happened to change the way the psalmist thought—either he heard through a prophet the prayer was heard, or he had the inner conviction that it was heard, or something changed in the circumstances (Claus Westermann, *Praise of God in the Psalms,* called it an "oracle of salvation").

25. I worded this statement to reflect what the psalm has, an actual praise section for the answer to the prayer. If the psalm had ended with a vow of praise I would have worded it more in line with his anticipation of offering praise to God.

Outline

I. Extended Introductory Cry: David, apparently forsaken by the Lord and scorned by his enemies, remains confident that the God of his fathers and of his youth will not abandon him (1–10).
  A. Cycle One: Apparently forsaken by the Lord, David is convinced that the God of his fathers will deliver him (1–5).
    1. Complaint: The LORD seems to have forsaken him because he does not answer his desperate cries (1–2).
    2. Confidence: The history of the faith is filled with answers to prayer (3–5).
  B. Cycle Two: Scorned by men, David is still convinced that the God he has come to trust will not forsake him now (6–10).
    1. Complaint: Men have forsaken him and mock his faith (6–8).
    2. Confidence: He has trusted the Lord all through his life (9–10).
II. Lament Proper: David laments his imminent death at the hands of inhuman and insensitive enemies (11–18).
  A. Introductory petition: David calls on God to come to his aid because there is no one to help (11).
  B. Lament: David describes his enemies who torture him and the severity of his suffering (12–18).
    1. Cycle One:
      a. "They": His enemies are insensitive, inhumane, powerful, and ready to destroy him (12–13).
      b. "I": He is at the brink of death (14–15a).
      c. "You": The LORD is apparently laying him in the grave (15b).
    2. Cycle Two:
      a. "They": His enemies are trying to end his life and look on him triumphantly (16–17).
      b. "I": He is weakened, in despair, and robbed of his last possession (18).
III. Petition Proper: David prays that the LORD would hasten to deliver him from death at the hands of his ruthless

enemies—and finds confidence that God has answered his prayer (19–21).

IV. Declarative Praise: David resolves to praise the LORD in the assembly for his great deliverance, encouraging others to join him in praising God and anticipating that future generations will turn to God because of his deliverance from death (21–31).

A. He praises God for deliverance from death and assures the congregation that God hears his afflicted people (22–26).

1. He will praise God in the assembly (22).
2. He invites others to praise God with him because God has answered the prayer (23–24).
3. He encourages others not to lose heart in praying (25–26).

B. He anticipates that the world and future generations will turn to the LORD in worship when they hear that he delivers from death (27–31).

1. He predicts that the world will worship the King (27–28).
2. He predicts that all kinds of people will praise the LORD for his deliverance from death (29).
3. He predicts that future generations will praise the LORD for his great deliverance (30–31).

COMMENTARY IN EXPOSITORY FORM

I. Introductory Cry: Those who have a proven faith in the LORD pray with increasing confidence even when everything seems to be against them (1–10).

The psalm begins with an extended introductory cry of ten verses. In it we have two cycles of complaint and confidence, showing how the psalmist drew upon his knowledge of God in this time of great distress.

A. Complaint: There are times in which God seems to have abandoned his people (1–2).

In the first line David sets the tone for the verses to

follow—God appears to have abandoned him. "My God, my God" (אֵלִי אֵלִי) is the familiar beginning of the psalm. Here is the painful irony for the believer: "my God" should not be abandoning me. The repetition of the words with the same sense (epizeuxis) projects a depth of feeling and pathos that few other expressions could provide. Putting the lamentation in the form of a rhetorical question (erotesis), "Why have you forsaken me?" expresses in a powerful way the great alienation that he felt. He did not want to know why God had not responded—he was lamenting the fact that God appeared to be abandoning him. He wanted God to respond to his cry.

For those who know the Gospels these words are very familiar. It is this rhetorical question that Jesus appropriated on the cross (Matt. 27:46), expressing in Aramaic (לָמָה שְׁבַקְתַּנִי) the Hebrew clause (לָמָה עֲזַבְתָּנִי). We have to look at the line on two different levels. For David to be abandoned by God simply meant that his prayer would be left unanswered and he would die, but for Jesus to be abandoned to death by the Father in heaven meant that his death would accomplish our redemption. Or, to put it more precisely, because the Father "abandoned" him who died in our place, he will never abandon us who have come to faith in him.

The second half of the verse forms a loosely synonymous parallel. It could be translated, "[Why are you] far from helping me and the words of my roaring?" (which would continue the rhetorical question), or "your helping me is far from the words of my roaring." In either case the point is that there is no help in sight, and the prayer has taken the form of a desperate roaring (שַׁאֲגָתִי, "my roaring," a cry of great distress; see Psalm 32:3 and Job 3:24).

The second verse repeats the main points. It tells how he had been crying out continually ("day" and "night" form a merism), but there was no answer and there was no "silence." This word "silence" or "cessation" (דּוּמִיָּה) could be parallel to "you do not answer" and mean "there is no release," or it could be parallel to the crying and rendered "and [I] am not silent." The latter seems to be more to the point of the verse. He cries to the LORD continually, but the LORD does not answer his constant pleas.

B. Confidence: When God appears to be silent, the faithful should recall how he answered prayers before (3–5).

The psalmist found confidence in the fact that God is a God who answers prayer. His initial expression seems at first to be abstract, but it is right to the point: "But you are holy, sitting enthroned in the praises of Israel." The term "holy" (קָדוֹשׁ) means set apart, unique, distinct.[26] All the other attributes of God are

---

26. This word "holy" (קָדוֹשׁ) is one of the most important words in Old Testament theology. This is the adjective; there is also a verb "to be, become holy, set apart," a noun קֹדֶשׁ, "sacredness, apartness," a noun מִקְדָּשׁ, "sacred place," a noun קֶדֶשׁ, "sanctuary," and also two forms קָדֵשׁ and קְדֵשָׁה which mean "cult prostitute" (simply meaning separated from normal marital life for a specific purpose in the pagan temples). These last words illustrate that the common idea of this word group is not holy in the sense of righteous, but simply set apart, different, distinct.

In the Bible this is one of the primary attributes of God. He is the holy one (Isa. 57:15); there is no one like him (Isa. 45:5, 11–13, 19); he is incomparably holy (Isa. 6:3). This means that he is set apart from all other; he is unique. There is no one like him in heaven or on earth. In discussing this attribute of God, we need to survey all the other attributes in order to clarify in what way God is different, e.g., God is eternal, and no one else is. Or, God is omniscient, and no one else is. God is righteous, and while we may have moments of righteousness, we are not like him— he is different. God is all powerful, and we are not. This is probably how Psalm 22 is using the adjective. To say God is holy in the midst of a lament about unanswered prayer means that God is not indifferent or impotent like the pagan gods—he is different; he has power; and he has a history of answering prayers.

Places are set apart, or holy. Mount Zion is holy in Jerusalem (Ps. 2:6) because the place was set apart for the sanctuary. It was a holy mountain because God was there. And things connected to the sanctuary had to be sanctified, such as the utensils, the altar, and the tent (Exod. 29:37; 30:29). In fact, the antonym of "holy" is "profane, common, ordinary" (< חָלַל); in English the etymological explanation of "profane" is "outside the temple."

Times are set apart or holy. God sanctified the sabbath day (Gen. 2:3), meaning that he set it apart for his own purposes. Nothing common or ordinary could be done on the holy day.

People are set apart or sanctified. God established Israel to be a holy nation (Exod. 19:6), a people set apart for the service of the LORD, but religious leaders such as priests were expected to be set apart to service, and in their activities to sanctify the LORD in the eyes of the people

needed to clarify in what ways he is distinct. For example, he is powerful, but we are not; we are weak, and the false gods are completely impotent. God is not like us, or them; he is distinct, that is, "holy." Likewise, he is faithful, sovereign, righteous, and the like—all showing that he is set apart from every being—he is "holy." The point is that he is distinct from the pagan gods because he is alive, he answers prayers, he saves his people, and he can therefore be trusted even though at any moment he may seem not to answer. In the context, then, this attribute of God's holiness is appropriate for building confidence. The rest of the verse builds on this general description for the immediate need: God is so faithful in answering prayers that his people are constantly praising him in the sanctuary. To express this the psalmist describes God as one who sits enthroned in their praises (a metonymy of adjunct, "praises" meaning the sanctuary where the praises are given). The praises are so numerous that God is said to sit enthroned on them. God was obviously answering prayers.

Verses 4 and 5 explain this by noting that God has a history of answering the prayers of his people. This is emphasized by the word order, "In you they trusted" and "To you they cried" (the verbs being indefinite past), and with the repeated reports of their deliverance. These do not refer to any one time, but to the whole history of the faith. All who truly know the LORD can appreciate this fact of history for their own encouragement as well.

Interestingly, the psalmist ends the section with an understatement, "they were not put to shame" (v. 5). This figure (tapeinosis) was intended to convey the opposite, that the ancestors were gloriously delivered (and not put to shame), but the use of this understatement serves to make a transition back to the present—the ancestors were not put to shame as it seems he is, for if God does not answer his prayer he will be put to shame (metonymy of effect—"put to shame" would be the effect of his death).

(Lev. 10:3). People had to see that this worship was set apart from everything earthy and pagan. Ordinary people would sanctify themselves for all kinds of service, in the sanctuary or elsewhere (e.g., Josh. 7:13). The simple law of Leviticus was "Be holy, because I the LORD your God am holy" (19:1).

C. Complaint: When God seems to be silent the wicked may mock the faith (6–8).

In this second cycle the psalmist laments his suffering at the taunting of his enemies.[27] "I am a worm," he begins, "and no man." With the metaphor "worm" he is saying that (in their eyes) he is worthless because no one cares if he lives or dies. He is not regarded as a valuable human by his enemies; they consider him to be a worthless pest.

He adds that he is a "reproach of [by] men, despised of [by] the people." In both phrases the genitives are agents—people were reproaching and taunting. A "reproach" (חֶרְפָּה) is a cutting taunt, an insult or ridicule intended to hurt or destroy people—or their faith.[28] The participle "despised" (בְּזוּי) indicates that he was held in contempt—he was being looked down upon and

---

27. For some interesting comparisons with this verse, see some of the descriptions of the suffering servant in Isaiah (41:14; 49:7; 53:3; 50:6 and 52:14).
28. The word חָרַף means 'to reproach." The word has cognates that have the idea of "sharpen," suggesting that the Hebrew verb means "to say sharp things." The noun that is related to the verb is חֶרְפָּה, "a reproach" or "cutting taunt." In all the categories listed this is the basic meaning.

   There are several clear examples where the word, either verb or noun, describes the taunt of an enemy: Goliath taunting the Israelite camp (1 Sam. 17:10 and several places), or the Israelites being taunted when losing a war (Ps. 44:16). Frequently the psalmist will be taunted by enemies (Ps. 69:19–20).

   A separate category may be made for the meaning reproach, as in the object of reproach or the person being reproached, but this category is more of a grammatical emphasis and does not yield a different meaning for the word. "Reproach of man" (Psalm 22:6) fits here, meaning others were taunting the suffering psalmist. There are many passages that describe someone as being a reproach or the object of reproach (e.g., Ps. 31:11; 39:8).

   Another clear category fits passages where the reproach rests on someone as a condition of shame or disgrace. The barren woman (Gen. 30:23), widowhood (Isa. 54:4), a disease (Job 19:6), or injuries from an enemy (Lam. 3:30) all bring a sense of reproach or disgrace, whether anyone was taunting or not. In the episode at Gilgal when Israelites were circumcised and entered the land of promise they exclaimed that God had rolled away the reproach of Egypt (Josh. 5:9). Until then the they felt the shame of the world's mocking their plight.

treated as worthless. The word can be illustrated with Esau who "despised" his birthright (Gen. 25:34).[29]

Verse 7 describes how the enemies expressed their contempt. They were making all kinds of gestures and facial expressions (metonymies of adjunct) as they taunted his faith. They laughed him to scorn, or mocked him; and they shot out the lip and shook their heads.[30] The other gestures are insulting gestures of astonishment and mockery.

The next verse (8) records the kinds of things that they said: they called on him to trust in the LORD for he would deliver him. The first verb in their taunt is the imperative "trust" ("cast yourself," גֹּל, from the verb גָּלַל, "to roll").[31] All the words related

---

29. בָּזָה means "to despise" in the sense of raising the head loftily and disdainfully, that is, looking down the nose at others and treating them with contempt, or considering them worthless. In Psalm 22:6 the sufferer is said to be despised by the people, for no one cared whether he lived or not.

The sense remains the same in most of the uses of the verb. Genesis 25:34 has already been mentioned; the story is explained at the end: Esau considered the birthright worthless and so that is why he traded it for a meal. In other uses Malachi accuses the priests of despising the name of the LORD (1:6) because they showed no reverence and made no commitment to obey. They did not value the LORD or the ritual. Their worthless offerings were the result, for as Malachi indicates, whatever is despised is considered worthless (1:7). In Isaiah 53:3 the suffering servant is despised, because no one esteemed him as the Messiah—they "wrote him off."

The word is used in Psalm 51:17 in an understatement: God will not despise the broken hearted penitent. The meaning is the opposite: God will joyfully receive him.

30. For the translation of the verb "they mock" the Greek used ἐξεμυκτήρισάν με, which is the exact wording used in Luke 23:35.

31. The verb גָּלַל most commonly refers to the act of rolling. Its related words all have to do with rolling or circles; for example, גֻּלָּה is a "bowl," מְגִלָּה is a "scroll," גַּלִּים are "breakers, rollers [waves]," and גֻּלְגֹּלֶת is a "skull"; there are also names such as Gilgal and Galilee.

There are three categories of meaning. First is the activity of "rolling," as Jacob rolled the stone off the well (Gen. 29:10), or Amasa lay rolling around after he was stabbed (2 Kings 20:12), or a garment rolled in blood (Isa. 9:5). The interesting uses in this group are figurative, such as rolling away (removing) the reproach of Israel (Josh. 5:9). It is also used in Amos 5:24: "let justice roll on like a river." God desired justice to spread as quickly as a rushing torrent.

to this root have something to do with circles and rolling. The meaning "trust" must have in it the idea of rolling or casting burdens on to the LORD, an image that the New Testament picks up in speaking of casting burdens on Christ (1 Peter 5:7). The meaning "trust" would have been a figurative development (an implied comparison). The fact that an imperative was used adds to the taunt: they were putting him to death and challenging him to trust God to escape from them.

The passage is included in Matthew 27:43, which uses a perfect tense (πέποιθεν), "he trusted." It is like the Old Greek in the interpretation, but not the same. In fact this use in Matthew is not a direct quote from the passage, but a general paraphrase: "He trusted in God, let him deliver him now, if he will have him, for he said, I am the Son of God." What was happening there is that Jesus' enemies were taunting him at the cross. They knew that he had claimed to be the Messiah, and they knew that Psalm 22 was in their tradition a messianic psalm about the suffering Messiah.[32] And so they simply used a line from the psalm to mock him on the cross—not realizing that at that very moment they were fulfilling the psalm. It is an amazing case of spiritual blindness.

A second category means "attack, crush, destroy." The guilt-ridden brothers of Joseph thought that their brother would attack them (this particular verbal stem indicating a meaning "roll himself" on us, or overpower us). In Job 30:14 the verb is used in a rare stem to describe enemies who come rolling in, meaning attack and overpower.

The third category is "cast, commit, trust." In Psalm 37:5 we read, "Commit (גּוֹל) your way to the LORD; trust in him and he will do this." "Commit" ("roll") is then parallel to trust (בְּטַח). The same use appears in Proverbs 16:3, "Commit to the LORD whatever you do, and your plans will succeed." The idea is that of rolling it onto God, giving it over to him. And here in Psalms 22:8 we have: "Commit (גֹּל) yourself to the LORD." Again the idea would be that of giving all the burdens and cares over to God, i.e., rolling them over to him. This would be the point whether the form is taken as an imperative or a perfect tense. The imperative would fit the taunt more boldly.

32. A remarkable comment appears in Yalkut 60, applying this passage to Messiah, and using the same words to describe the mocking of the people. Yalkut applies verse 15 to the Messiah.

D. Confidence: Mature believers can draw on a lifetime of trusting when they find their faith challenged (9–10).

The development of the introduction follows these ideas: God seems to have abandoned him (vv. 1–2), but God has a history of not abandoning his people (vv. 3–5); others were taunting his faith (vv. 6–8), but his faith has gotten him through life so far and so he would not abandon it now (vv. 9–10). So verses 9 and 10 now provide this second source of confidence for the psalmist. It was God who "took me ["pushed me"] out of the womb. The expression is literally "my pushing forth (גֹחִי), probably a participle with the objective genitive "me," and certainly a metonymy of cause for the birth. From the time he was at his mother's breasts he was brought up to trust the LORD: "making me trust" (מַבְטִיחִי, s.v. Ps. 4:5) means that from the very start of his life he was taught to trust the LORD and was put in positions where he had to trust the LORD. He concludes the introduction by saying that from the womb he had been cast on the LORD, and throughout his life the LORD has been his God ("my God" forms an inclusio, a bracketing effect, with verse 1). Since God had made him trust throughout life, this event was another opportunity to trust in him. Therefore, he would not give in to the taunts of the wicked.

II. The Lament Proper: Those who trust in the LORD with all their hearts will pour out their laments to the LORD (11–18).

There are two cycles also in this lament section, following the basic pattern of the lament that speaks first of the enemies ("they") and then the sufferer ("I") and finally of God ("you"). The attack of the wicked and the suffering it brought were bad enough, but when God also seemed to be his enemy—that was cause for great lamentation.

A. Believers who suffer at the hands of powerful, ruthless enemies can appeal to God in their distress (11–15).

1. *The prayer is for help (11).*

The psalmist begins by repeating a major motif of the psalm: "do not be far off"—because trouble is near (contrasting far and near). To pray for God not to be "far off" is to pray for God to be present to help, as the last line of the verse makes clear. The word "trouble" is the word that means a bind, a strait, some kind of distress (צָרָה, from צָרַר). The problem, of course, is that there is no one to help (the word "helper" [עוֹזֵר] meaning one who can do for the person what that person cannot do for himself; s.v. Ps. 29:1). Without such "help" the sufferer will die. If God is far off (meaning, not intervening), there is no helper (meaning, no deliverance); but if God is near, trouble cannot be near. Verse 19 will repeat this prayer as part of the petition proper.

2. *The lament describes the enemies: first, the "they" section (12–13).*

The lament now describes the enemies as powerful and inhumane by comparing them to animals (implied comparisons). First, "bulls" have surrounded him; they were mighty (s.v. Ps. 8:1) bulls of Bashan, where everything seemed to grow bigger and better. There were no bulls present of course; but by calling his enemies bulls the psalmist was saying that they were powerful, brutish, senseless, and dangerous. They surrounded him victoriously, as the word "encircled" (כִּתֵּר) suggests, for it is related to the word for "crown." These powerful enemies had sensed they triumphed over him.

Next, they are compared to lions. Again, there were no lions—it is an implied comparison with his fierce enemies who are like lions. The verb begins the sentence before the subject is identified: "they open wide (פָּצוּ, either an instantaneous perfect, or present perfect) their mouth upon me, [as] a lion, tearing and roaring" (the two participles modifying "lion"). They are powerful; they have caught him and are ready to finish him off ("Will a lion roar when it has no prey?" [Amos 3:4]). The word "roaring" (שֹׁאֵג) is the same word used in the beginning of the psalm for his roaring cry to God; perhaps the choice there of this word was to match the prayer with the intensity of the dilemma.

3. The lament describes the sufferings: second, the "I" section (14–15).

In verse 14 there is a description of his physical weakness and then his failing spirit. Hyperbole is used to get the point of his intense sufferings across to the reader. "I am poured out" is figurative (an implied comparison) for his weakened condition. It is like saying, "I am drained" of energy; it implies a comparison with a vessel that is now empty. The simile "like water" makes this clear. Next the psalmist tells of his incoordinated and painful physical condition with hyperbole: "all my bones are out of joint." He was racked with pain and felt as if all his bones were disconnected.

Then he speaks of his spirit—he has almost lost his will to fight for life; his heart has melted like wax. The "heart" means his spirit or will (metonymy of subject). Saying that it has "melted" extends the comparison with wax. Just as under heat or pressure wax will melt, so under the pressure of the attacks of these people David's spirit has almost completely melted away— he has no will left to fight.

And in verse 15a–b he focuses on his emaciated and weakened condition as dried up and withering away. His "strength" has dried up like a potsherd, the simile using the dryness of something like an old, dry flower pot. His vitality, his life-juices, have turned dry—there was no moisture at all, a symptom of failing energy. Consequently his tongue stuck to the roof of his mouth because of the dryness (the term מַלְקוֹחָי is literally "my jaws," and so it has to be taken as a metonymy of subject or adjunct to gain the meaning "the roof of my mouth").

4. The lament includes God's apparent rejection: third, the "you" section (15c).

The last line of verse 15 expresses the most troubling part of the lamentation, that God seems not only to have abandoned him but is involved in his destruction: "and in the dust of death you are laying me (תִּשְׁפְּתֵנִי)." In the final analysis, if God did not do anything to deliver him, then it was God who was putting him in the grave. The nuance of the imperfect tense (a progressive imperfect) stresses that God was now doing this. The grave is referred to as "death's dust" (a metonymy of adjunct) because of the dusty dryness of the place that would receive his body that was becoming dry and emaciated and would now quickly turn to dust in the grave.

Of course the typological fulfillment is to be noted here as well. Jesus was suffering on the cross while the wicked were surrounding him and taunting him, but ultimately it was God the Father who was laying the Messiah in the grave (see Isa. 53:10; Acts 2:23).

B. Believers suffering at the hands of malicious enemies must continue pouring out their complaint to God until there is an answer (16–18).

Now begins the second round of the lament, continuing first with the description of the enemies (a "they" section). The psalmist has used bulls and lions; now he uses dogs (another implied comparison) to describe them. Such dogs were not domesticated pets; these were jackals that went in packs, more like vultures in other cultures, nipping at the remains of carcasses, and nipping at the extremities, the hands and feet. To describe his enemies as dogs was to portray them as nasty predators and scavengers; but it also indicated that he was as good as dead, or appearing lifeless, for the "dogs" would not come around otherwise. That he was not talking about dogs is clear from the parallelism that identifies them as "a band of evil men."

The expression "they pierced (punctured)" the hands and the feet fits the contextual description of scavenging dogs. They nip and bite, and in the process puncture the extended limbs. As discussed earlier, it appears that the idea of piercing was changed slightly to read, "like a lion (my hands and my feet)." The original reading had a verb, probably "they pierced."[33]

---

33. It is important to note that this clause from the psalm is not quoted in the New Testament. While this fact could be taken as an argument against the reading's authenticity, that is not very compelling for it is a well-attested reading. It is more likely that since the psalm is quoted in several places in the New Testament the apostles simply accepted that the whole psalm referred to the suffering and exaltation of the Jesus, the Messiah. In other words, the reference was so obvious that it did not need to be singled out.

In verse 17 the psalmist continues with a description of his suffering (another "I" section): "I can count all my bones" (a potential imperfect). It means that he was so emaciated, so thin, that he could easily count the bones, certainly his ribs (the expression is hyperbolic). Counting the ribs is a poetic way (metonymy of effect) of saying he had lost a lot of weight—this is the effect of the suffering. And so he notes that people stare at him and mock him.

Not only that, he had to endure the last and greatest indignity: "they divide my garments" (v. 18). The last possession a person would retain was the garment—that was his until he died. Here they were dividing up his property because they considered that he was as good as dead. This verse was fulfilled literally at the cross (John 19:24). The parallelism of the verse ("garment" // clothing") would seem here to be synonymous, but the Gospels imply they are separate things.

III. The Petition: Believers must pray with confidence for God to rescue them—until he answers (19–21).

Now the psalm records the actual prayer: it is simply that God rescue him from his enemies and deliver him from death. He begins with the repetition of the motif of distance: "But you, O LORD, do not be far off; / O my strength, hasten to help me." He addresses God as "my strength" (a metonymy of effect), for God is the one who gives him strength. And he pleads with the LORD to do so quickly, for he is about to die.

Then the sufferer pleads for deliverance: "deliver[34] me" and

---

34. The word "deliver" (נָצַל) is another key word for saving and rescuing in the Old Testament. The word has the active meaning in the *piel* verbal system, where it can mean "strip off, spoil, tear away, deliver," and in the *hiphil* verbal system where it can mean "snatch away, take away, deliver, rescue." These meanings also occur in passive verbal formations. There are derivatives and cognate forms that provide an interesting array of uses and developed meanings, but the usage of the verb in the Bible is most instructive. Sawyer suggests that the basic idea of this common word is separation, often in the sense of separating something from something else (*Semantics in Biblical Research*, p. 96). All the uses appear in contexts of a somewhat violent stripping off or snatching away, even in legal contexts where it might refer to taking a person's property without payment.

"save me" (s.v. Ps. 3:2) stressing the urgency simply and clearly. In his petition he uses a series of figures. The first figure is the "sword," the second is the "hand" (paw, meaning power) of the dog, the third is the "mouth" of the lion, and the fourth is the "horn" of the oxen. These figures are metonymies of cause or adjunct, being the means of the harm; but some are also part of the figures of comparison already used (dogs, lions, and bulls).[35] The main idea is his concern with the things about his enemies that will cause him harm; from these he wants to be delivered.

What is interesting about the section is that the parallelism is broken with the last word of the petition section (v. 21). The last

---

One group of uses conveys the sense of "escape." It can describe a slave who has escaped (Deut. 23:15), or an enemy who escapes (2 Sam. 20:16). More frequently it has the meaning of "rescue," as in the account of Moses' delivering the daughters of the priest from the shepherds (Exod. 2:19), or David's telling Saul how he rescued lambs from lions and bears (1 Sam. 17:35), or David's rescuing his wives from the Amalekites (1 Sam. 30:18). The verb can also be used with the nuance of "recover" (Judg. 11:26).

The idea of "plunder" or "spoil" has the same idea of separation, but the separation is more sudden and violent. E.g., Israel would plunder Egypt when they left (Exod. 3:22), and Jehoshaphat plundered the defeated armies of Ammon and Moab (2 Chron. 20:25). The idea seems to be that of snatching something away or stripping it off someone.

In the uses where God is the subject of the verb the general meaning "deliver" is workable, but in some places the idea of snatching away or rescuing is more precise. It refers to God's taking away wealth or possessions that belonged to Jacob's wives (Gen. 31:9), but it also refers to God's taking people away from enemies or disaster (Jer. 15:21). David wrote his psalm of thanksgiving when the LORD delivered him from all his enemies (2 Sam. 22:1). In contrast, pagan gods cannot deliver their own people (2 Chron. 25:15).

In Psalm 56:13 the psalmist says God delivered him from death. Likewise, God delivered the psalmist from the grave (Ps. 86:13). Psalm 34:4 says the LORD delivered the psalmist from all his fears. In many places we read how the LORD delivered people from distress and death. The idea of separating them from enemies or death is at the heart of the word, and the deliverance could be sudden or violent as in the setting of a war.

35. The imagery of the lament is reversed in the petition. The order in the lament was bulls-lions-dogs; now the prayer refers to the dog-lion-oxen/bull. It should be noted also that if the textual difficulty was interpreted to include another reference to lions, the symmetry would be disrupted.

word is not another imperative like "deliver" and "save"; rather, it is a perfect tense: "you have answered me" (עֲנִיתָנִי from עָנָה). Some commentators have argued for an imperative use of the perfect tense ("answer me"); that would finish out the petition with another parallel verb of request, and so many modern translations take it this way. Yet if the psalmist had wished to use another imperative, it would have been easy to do so. Moreover, the Greek text has a noun, "my lowliness" (reading "and [deliver] my lowliness from the horns of the wild ox"), indicating uncertainty about the form since it was not an imperative. Briggs translates the form as a noun: "my afflicted one," meaning "me."[36] The point is that we have a clear perfect tense here right at the very end of the petition section (even in the word order of the line the verb is at the end of the sentence: "from the horns of the wild ox—you have answered me"); and from this point on in the psalm there is not one word of lament or petition of any kind; from this point on the psalm is filled with praise. The perfect tense may have been chosen to begin the transition to the praise section. In the middle of the petition, while asking God to deliver him from his enemies, the suffering psalmist received an "oracle of salvation," that is, some indication that the prayer had been heard and that he was or would soon be delivered; and so he broke off the petition (the figure would be aposiopesis, a breaking off in the middle of the sentence what was to be said) and declared that God had answered him.[37]

IV. Declarative Praise: Committed believers praise God for answers to prayer so that others may be encouraged in their faith (22–31).

A. Praising God in the congregation will encourage others to keep on praying (22–26).

1. Praise is the immediate response to deliverance (22–23).

---

36. Briggs, *Psalms*, p. 190.

37. Kraus says that the makeshift emendations of the form "cannot avoid the odd fact that even before the beginning of the song of thanksgiving (vv. 22ff.) the certainty of being heard is definitely expressed. The verbal form עניתני closes the lament and forms a transition to the song of thanksgiving" (*Psalms 1–59*, p. 292).

The psalmist now decides to praise God in the assembly. Somehow in the midst of all his troubles, and in spite of that fact that it appeared that God had abandoned him, God did break through and answer his prayer so that he was delivered from death. Because of that he will praise in the sanctuary, for praise is the completion of the cycle of prayer (Ps. 50:15). Verse 22 provides this natural response—"I will declare your name to my brethren, in the congregation I will praise you." These verbs (cohortatives) express his resolve to praise God, which he will do immediately.

The "name" (s.v. Ps. 20:1) refers to the nature of God, his attributes or perfections ("name" is a metonymy of subject). It means the psalmist will declare what God is like, i.e., how this divine intervention revealed God's nature; and because praise is a communal act, he calls on the congregation to join him in this praise (23). He invites all who "fear the LORD" (s.v. Ps. 2:11) to praise him. These are the faithful who make up the heart of the congregation; they are willing to praise the LORD on behalf of others. They are the covenant people, for the next two lines use the poetic couplet of "seed of Israel" and "seed of Jacob" ("seed" is metonymy of cause, meaning the effect of the seed, the descendants). They are called on to honor and revere the LORD, joining the psalmist in his praise for being rescued from death.

2. Praise focuses on the LORD (24).

The psalmist reports that God did not forsake him in his affliction after all. The expressions "He has not despised" and "He has not abhorred" are understatements (tapeinosis); the intended meaning is that God valued him and gloriously saved him. These expressions are used because for a while it seemed that God had despised him and his affliction. The object of the verbs is "the affliction of the afflicted" (עֱנוּת עָנִי), the "afflicted" being a reference to himself. The second line of the verse ends up stating the point positively: "He did not hide his face from him, but when he cried to him, he heard" (שָׁמֵעַ). This means that God answered the prayer and not simply that he listened to it. Still referring to himself in the third person, David proclaims that

God did not withhold favor from him (the figure of "hiding the face" is anthropomorphic for withholding favor). The evidence of this was that he answered the prayer.

3. Praise benefits the people (25–26).

The psalmist offers his praise, saying, "From you comes my praise." What this means is that the reason for the praise, i.e., the deliverance, came from God ("praise" is then a metonymy of effect, the cause being the deliverance).

He will pay his vows in the assembly; the vow refers to the praise that he owes to the LORD for the answer to prayer (see Ps. 66:13–20). Answers to prayer must lead to public praise so that God will be glorified in the sanctuary and others will be edified. The praise was to be delivered along with a peace offering (Lev. 7), a sacrifice that would actually become a communal meal. While the animal was roasting on the altar, the one who brought it would stand beside the altar and tell people what God had done. Then, all the people would eat together (it was the only sacrifice that Israelites could eat in the sanctuary). They would eat because God had blessed this person.[38] And so we read in verse 26 that the "poor will eat and be satisfied; those who seek him will praise the LORD." The poor people (עֲנָוִים, s.v. Ps. 9:12), those in need who are seeking help from the LORD themselves, would actually eat (יֹאכְלוּ) because God intervened in David's plight and David faithfully paid his vows and brought the animal for the communal meal. The people would share in his praise, not just because they would have something to eat, but because they were devout believers and could rejoice in what the LORD did for others, knowing that God does answer prayer and will answer their prayers if they keep on praying.

That is the point of the instruction: "Let your hearts live forever." In the lament section (v. 14), David reported that his heart, his will to live, his determination to keep on praying, was

---

38. See my discussion of this aspect of worship in *Recalling the Hope of Glory* (Grand Rapids: Kregel, 2006), chapter 17, "Offering the Sacrifice of Praise," pp. 269–275.

melting like wax within him—he had almost given up. He did not, and now he could tell people not to do that either, but to be encouraged, to keep on praying, because God does not despise the affliction of the afflicted. This is one example of how praise is to be edifying.

B.Spreading the word about how God delivers from death will bring many people to the faith (27–31).

The rest of the psalm records the anticipation that when people hear what kind of God this is they will want to become part of the covenant.

1. People all over the world will enter the kingdom (27– 28).

"All the ends of the earth" will turn to the LORD, that is, the people who live in the ends of the earth (a metonymy of subject). The text says that they will remember (s.v. Ps. 6:5) and turn; that is, they will act by faith on what they hear and turn to the LORD. They will bow down before God; the word "bow down" (הִשְׁתַּחֲוָה) is used to represent worship, the act of bowing down signifying submission, obeisance, and prayer. The psalm anticipates that people will come to faith and become true worshipers when they hear what the LORD has done.

The reason for this is stated grandly in verse 28: "For dominion (מְלוּכָה) belongs to the LORD, and he rules (מֹשֵׁל) over the nations." The idea is that when God prevented the enemies from killing the psalmist, he demonstrated his sovereign reign over people in the world. To Israel this signified the dominion of God. In fact, to the psalmists any answer to prayer was seen as an expansion of God's sovereign rule over people and nature.

2. People of all kinds from age to age will enter the kingdom (29–31).

The psalmist also anticipates that when people understand the sovereignty of this God they will want to enter his kingdom. These verses are fraught with textual difficulties, but the ideas are essentially clear. People who are not even born yet will hear and come to faith. Verse 29 begins with a repetition of the idea of feasting in worship,[39] but now includes everyone from the healthy to the dying. On the one hand, it includes those who are prosperous: "all the healthy of the earth" is literally "all the fat ones of (דִּשְׁנֵי) the earth," a symbol for abundance and wealth (like the "fat of the land"); but it also includes on the other hand those "who are going down to the dust" (יוֹרְדֵי עָפָר), those who are dying. The two descriptions form a merism, meaning people in all kinds of physical and emotional conditions. The last line of verse 29, which in the MT reads "and [even] he [the one who] cannot keep his soul (i.e., himself) alive," seems to restate the description of the one who is dying.

The last two verses announce that people in the future will serve him by telling their children what the LORD has done. They are called a "seed" (metonymy of cause) and they will spread the report to a future "generation," that is, people yet to be born. Their message will concern the LORD's "righteousness" (s.v. Ps. 1:5), the attribute of God that lies behind his actions (so a metonymy of cause): righteousness is the cause, and the deliverance is the effect. The LORD is a God who champions righteousness, and he delivers his righteous servants from the persecution of the wicked (cf. Ps. 98:1). In this psalm we have the righteous prayer of a righteous man for deliverance from the wicked who mock him and his faith. In the end the psalmist can proclaim that God is righteous—he does not abandon his people who call on him for deliverance from death.

The psalm concludes with a summary note on the proclamation that will go forth: "He has done *it*." All that is in the text is the simple verb, "he has done" (עָשָׂה). In the context of this psalm, it refers to God's answering the cry of the suffering psalmist and saving him from certain death. When people hear that the one true and living God actually answers prayers and saves people from death, they will turn to him in faith and become his witnesses to their generations. From the perspective

---

39. The verb אָכְלוּ may be classified as a prophetic perfect since the vision is for a future realization. The second verb, וַיִּשְׁתַּחֲווּ, would then have the same nuance. So, "they will eat and they will worship." The two verbs may form a hendiadys, indicating that the worship will be in their eating.

of the application of the psalm in Christ, when people hear that God delivered him from death, that is, raised him from the dead, they will want to put their trust in such a saving God who has power over the grave.

MESSAGE AND APPLICATION[40]

The psalm provides encouragement for those who feel forsaken by God because their prayers seem to go unanswered. For the longest time this was the psalmist's problem; he was suffering at the hands of his enemies who were trying to put him to death. His situation was lamentable; but what made it almost unbearable was the fact that God seemed to have abandoned him. Nevertheless, he found ways to build his confidence in the midst of such a frightening and frustrating experience, and at the right moment God did deliver him from death. Not only could he then praise, but he could also encourage others to keep on praying (v. 26). So we may provisionally write an expository idea to capture all this: *Those who suffer persecution and scorn for their faith must persevere in praying to God to deliver them, knowing that he does not abandon his afflicted people but will hear their prayer and give them reason to praise in the congregation.*

In addition to this clear message, the New Testament provides another focus for the study of the psalm, the prayer of the suffering Savior. Jesus, then, becomes the perfect example of the message of the psalm. Even a simple reading of the psalm reminds the reader that Jesus appropriated this passage when dying on the cross. The Gospel writers and the apostles recognized, then, that many of the details of Christ's suffering were already laid down in the psalm, and to Christians the psalm finds its divinely intended meaning in Jesus Christ. How this worked was that the Spirit of God inspired the psalmist in the writing of this psalm so that he used many vivid and at times hyperbolic expressions to describe his own suffering that would ultimately be true in a greater way of David's greater son, the Messiah.[41]

---

40. See also S. B. Frost, "Psalm 22: An Exposition," *CJT* 8 (1962):102–115.
41. The statement by Delitzsch is in my opinion still valid. He says that the hyperbolic element of the psalm is changed into the prophetic by the Spirit

What makes the connection so strong is that the lament is not about an illness, or sufferings in a war, but an execution, a deliberate attempt by adversaries to put the psalmist to death as if he were a worthless criminal. The language of the psalmist is natural for someone enduring intense agony at the hands of enemies and the apparent abandonment by God, but it is excessive. It did not seem excessive to the suffering psalmist, or to anyone in such pain. This all ended when he was delivered at the last moment by the LORD, and his lament turned to joyful praise for the whole world to hear.

One of the amazing things about the excessive language of the psalm is that it fits a death by crucifixion very well, and what makes the use of the psalm by Jesus even more fitting is the unique nature of this lament—the suffering psalmist never curses his enemies for their attacks and he never confesses sin as the reason for his suffering. There is not a word of remorse or penitent sorrow. By all appearances the sufferer is an innocent man suffering unjustly at the hands of his enemies—because God seemed to have abandoned him to the grave.

The New Testament provides us with the details from the psalm that apply to Christ. The writers knew that David was a prophet and did speak of the Messiah, whether he understood it all or not. The following list includes citations of or allusions to Psalm 22 in the New Testament:

Matthew 27:46 // Ps. 22:1	My God, my God, why have you forsaken me?
Matthew 27:39 // Ps. 22:7	Those who passed by hurled insults at him, shaking their heads, saying . . .
Matthew 27:43 // Ps. 22:8	He trusts in God. Let God now rescue him if he wants him

---

of God: "For as God the Father moulds the history of Jesus Christ in accordance with his own counsel, so His Spirit moulds even the utterances of David concerning himself the type of the Future One, with a view to that history" (*Psalms*, I:307).

John 19:28 // Ps. 22:15	I am thirsty
John 19:23–24 // Ps. 22:18	They divided my garments among them
Heb. 5:7 // Ps. 22:24, 31	He heard
Heb. 2:12 // Ps. 22:22	I will declare your name to my brethren

In the typological fulfillment of the psalm we see how Jesus also was being put to death by wicked people, and he too cried out for deliverance from death, beginning with the agony in the garden. Hebrews 5:7 says that in the days of his flesh he prayed earnestly with strong crying and tears and was heard for his godly piety. He prayed to be delivered from dying this death ("Let this cup pass from me"). But he died. And yet the book of Hebrews says that he was heard—his prayer was answered. The solution to this tension is found in Hebrews 2:12 which applies verse 22 of the psalm to Christ as well: "I will declare your name . . . ." In the context of Hebrews, this was fulfilled in heaven; and so with regard to the application of the psalm to Jesus, Christian commentators conclude that between the petition proper (v. 21) and the praise (v. 22) the resurrection would have occurred.

This means that in contrast to David's immediate and direct answer to prayer, the answer to the prayer of Jesus on the cross came at a different time and in a different way than he prayed. He prayed on Good Friday, but he was delivered from death on Sunday—a different time. He prayed to be delivered from dying, but he was delivered from death by resurrection—a different way. If the answer came at a different time and in a different way, it was also a better time and a better way. Being delivered out of death at the resurrection meant that he did not remain in mortal flesh; and being delivered on Easter Sunday meant that his death accomplished our redemption. He arose from the dead and ascended to glory to proclaim his praise in the heavenly sanctuary.

Now if the prayer of Jesus can be answered that way, it ought also to be true of believers as well. And this is what

Scripture leads us to believe. Paul reminds us that we do not know how to pray as we ought (Rom. 8:26). If we do not know how to pray, then it stands to reason that our prayers may be answered in a different way than we asked. Paul also reminds us that God is able to do abundantly more than we can think or ask (Eph. 3:20). If that is true, then it stands to reason that our prayers may be answered in a better way than we ask. The psalm teaches us that we should continue praying to God to meet our needs, whatever they may be. If God seems to have abandoned us, the message of the psalm applies even more: "Let your heart live forever." We should not give up, but keep on praying. From the example of the fulfillment of the psalm with Jesus Christ, we learn that the answer to our prayer may come at a different time and in a different way than we pray, and if so at a better time and in a better way, and if not in this life, then surely in the life to come.[42]

---

42. The ideas for this application of the psalm came from an exposition of the passage by Bruce K. Waltke.

PSALM 23

The Faithful Provisions of the LORD

INTRODUCTION

Text and Textual Variants

1 A Psalm of David.

The LORD is my shepherd,[1] I lack nothing;
2   he makes me lie down in grassy green meadows.
He leads me beside peaceful waters;
     he restores my soul.[2]
3 He leads me in the right paths
     for his name's sake.
4 Even though I walk in the valley[3] of the shadow of death
     I will fear no evil,
          for you are with me;
               Your rod and your staff—they comfort me.

5 You prepare a table before me

---

1. For the participle "my shepherd" (רֹעִי) Greek has "shepherds me" (ποιμαίνει με).
2. For the first verb the Greek translation has "made me dwell," and for the second verb, it has "nourished me."
3. Instead of "valley" Greek has "midst" (μέσῳ).

in the sight of my adversaries.
You anoint my head with oil;
    my cup is filled to capacity.[4]
6 Surely, goodness[5] and loyal love
    will pursue me all the days of my life;
    and I shall return[6] to the house of the LORD
    for the remaining days of my life.

---

4. Greek reads "your cup cheers me like the best [wine]" (τὸ ποτήριόν σου μεθύσκον ὡς κράτιστον).
5. "Goodness" is not reflected in the Greek translation; it simply reads "And your mercy will follow me."
6. The Hebrew has a *qal* perfect from "return" (שׁוּב), 1csg with a *waw* consecutive (וְשַׁבְתִּי), translated "and I will return (to the house of the LORD for the length of days)." This is the same verbal root that was used in verse 2, translated "he restores" my soul. The difficulty here is the preposition "in" after the form; it could not have a simple translation value—"I will return in the house of the LORD."

The Greek has "and my dwelling (τὸ κατοικεῖν με) (will be) in the house of the LORD," or, "I will dwell in the house of the LORD." This assumes ושבתי was from a different root, probably a *qal* infinitive (וְשִׁבְתִּי) from יָשַׁב with a suffix; Symmachus, the Syriac, and the Old Latin all follow this reading with "and I dwell." Probably Psalm 27:4 influenced the reading; it has שִׁבְתִּי בְּבֵית־יְהוָה כָּל־יְמֵי חַיַּי, "my dwelling (I will dwell) in the house of the LORD all the days of my life" (not: for the length of days as in Ps. 23:6). Because of the parallel verse, the difficulty with the preposition, and the idea of dwelling with a gracious host, one can see what prompted the Greek translation.

Many modern commentators likewise conclude that the MT form is difficult, if not impossible, and so simply change it to make a smoother reading. That may be an easy solution, but it ignores the basic procedure of textual criticism. If the smooth reading found in the Greek version was the original reading, it is hard to explain why the MT would have come to its reading. One would also note that the variants, while following the same idea, are not identical. The reading in the MT is the more difficult construction, easily leading the Greek translation to change it, and this it did after 27:4. The preposition does not have the clear meaning "to" and so the construction might assume a meaning "return (and dwell) in." Briggs lists a pregnant meaning for the verb, "return to dwell" (*Psalms*, p. 212). If the translator of the Greek was troubled with the use of the preposition and was familiar with the contents of the psalm, he may have assumed the form was the same as that in 27:4. Therefore, it is most likely that the psalmist concluded with the idea that he would "return" to the house of the LORD. Such an idea of "returning" would lead to "dwelling" in the sense of worshiping; but the idea of "returning" brings the sense of a spiritual renewal to his conclusion.

Composition and Context[7]

Of all the psalms in the Bible perhaps none is better known than the 23rd psalm. This passage is loved by people who love the LORD as well as by those who have little to do with the faith. And yet, in spite of its frequent use by worshiping communities little time is given to discovering its full meaning. A close analysis of the text will show that it is a meditation on all that the LORD does for the one who trusts in him.

It is difficult to classify the psalm because it does not fit the major classifications. However, the description by Gunkel that it is "a psalm of confidence (the laments and entreaties having receded into the background)"[8] is workable. The work focuses on the LORD's demonstration of his loyal love and the delight of the faithful in that love. It gives little attention to a specific crisis other than to refer to enemies, or a dangerous valley, or the comfort the LORD provides in such places. Accordingly, it has become the song of trust *par excellence*.

It is far more difficult to determine a setting for the psalm. Traditionally it has been attributed to David, and there is no reason to reject this note of authorship.[9] Delitzsch suggests that "this psalm belongs to the time of the rebellion under Absalom" when David was in the wilderness; he bases this on similarities with Psalm 3, which is said to be connected with that time.[10] Lundbom also concludes that the psalm was set in the wilderness at that time.[11] Without a clear historical reference or convincing internal evidence it is impossible to know exactly when the psalm

---

7. See P. D. Miller, *Interpreting the Psalms* (Philadelphia: Fortress Press, 1986), pp. 112–19; and Dennis Pardee, "Structure and Meaning in Hebrew Poetry," in *Sopher Mahir* (Fs. for S. Segert), ed. by E. M. Cook (Winona Lake: Eisenbrauns, 1990):239–80).
8. Hermann Gunkel, *The Psalms* (Philadelphia: Fortress Press, 1969), p. 35.
9. Goldingay comes close to saying this; he says the heading ascribing it to David "invites us to imagine David using the psalm," especially since he was a shepherd. It is not clear what he means by David's using the psalm. But he adds that the imagery of verses 1–4 and the reality of 5–6 resonate with David's story (*Psalms 1–41*, p. 347).
10. Psalm 3 has a forceful section of confidence in the LORD, but other similarities are less compelling. See Delitzsch, *Psalms*, I:329.
11. Jack R. Lundbom, "Psalm 23: Song of Passage," *Int* 40 (1986):6–16.

was written. All that can be said is that the motifs of the shepherd in the field and the host in the banquet hall, as well as the desire to commune with the LORD in the sanctuary, were all familiar to David.

Other theories seem to be more imaginative. Kraus suggests that the setting is cultic since it focuses on the house of the LORD; he allows that it could be pre-exilic. He adopts the idea that the psalmist may have been unjustly accused and then acquitted. The meal in the psalm then would have been the thanksgiving banquet in the presence of those who accused him.[12] Merrill says the psalm described a royal coronation ritual that involved a procession from the temple to the spring, perhaps making the pilgrimage around the city.[13] Vogt takes the view that the psalm is linked to the thanksgiving sacrifice offered by the pilgrim, perhaps in gratitude for recent protection when he passed through a dark valley.[14] Several writers suggest that there is a pilgrimage behind the psalm, perhaps a symbolic cultic journey by the king through the valley of the shadow of death.[15] In response to this idea, Anderson says the speaker may have been a royal head and representative of the community originally, but that idea would not apply to its use in the post-exilic community.[16] Others have reasoned that the original song was creatively reworked in the exilic community so that they might enjoy the same covenant blessings that David experienced.[17] It would be just as easy to say an ancient psalm was applied to subsequent experiences without saying it had to be revised.

The psalm is written as a song of confident trust in the LORD and gives every indication it represented an individual's

---

12. Kraus, *Psalms 1–59*, pp. 305–6.
13. A. L. Merrill, "Psalm XXIII and the Jerusalem Tradition," *VT* 15 (1965):354–60.
14. E. Vogt, "The 'Place in Life' of Psalm 23," *Bib* 34 (1953): 195–211.
15. See for example, J. H. Eaton, *Psalms: Introduction and Commentary.* Torch Bible Commentary (London: SCM, 1967), pp. 76–7.
16. A. A. Anderson, *Psalms 1–72*, p. 196.
17. Michael L. Barré and John S. Kselman, "New Exodus, Covenant, and Restoration in Psalm 23," in *The Word of the LORD Shall Go Forth,* ed. by Carol F. Meyers and M. O'Connor (Winona Lake: Eisenbrauns, 1983), pp. 97–127.

personal faith. The way that it was written allows for many applications,[18] and so it is not surprising to find so many suggestions.

The poem itself is a rich mixture of figures and emblematic parallelism, attesting to the vivid scenes and full development of its ideas. The ideas of the psalm can be traced in different stages, each presenting a different setting for the meditation. Briggs takes verses 1–3a (in trimeter) as the revelation of the shepherd-feeder, verses 3b–4 (in tetrameter) as the shepherd-guide, and verses 5 and 6 (in pentameter) as the banquet host.[19] This corresponds to Perowne's division of the psalm in accordance with the three verbs "I lack nothing," "I shall not fear," and "I shall return."[20] Perhaps a little different threefold arrangement fits the scenes better: the shepherd in the field (vv. 1–4), the host in the banquet hall (v. 5), and the LORD in the sanctuary (v. 6). Verse six actually forms the conclusion: after meditating on the LORD as shepherd and host, the psalmist is eager to return to the sanctuary; so there is a pilgrimage movement towards the end of the psalm, but it is overshadowed by the meditation on the LORD and the display of his loyal love.

Exegetical Analysis

Summary

Using the settings of a pasture and a banquet hall, David meditates on several important ways that the LORD provides for his spiritual and physical well-being and concludes that this persistent loyal love of the LORD draws him back to full communion in the house of the LORD.

---

18. Mark S. Smith, "Setting and Rhetoric in Psalm 23," *JSOT* 41 (1988):61–66. Kirkpatrick says, "Each sheep can claim the care which is promised to the whole flock (Luke xv. 4ff)" (*Psalms,* p. 124).
19. *Psalms,* I:207.
20. *Psalms,* I:257.

Outline

I. Using the image of a shepherd and his sheep, David meditates on how the LORD provides for all his needs even in dangerous circumstances (1–4).

   A. Under the emblem of feeding, he affirms that the LORD provides him with all he needs so that he is both satisfied and developing (1–2a).

      1. Truth: He declares that when the LORD provides there is nothing he lacks.

      2. Emblem: Using the image of lush green meadows, he asserts that the LORD provides only the best provisions.

   B. Under the emblem of washing and resting, he affirms that the LORD leads him to full restoration (2b–3a).

      1. Emblem: Using the image of placid waters, he asserts that the LORD leads him to a place of rest.

      2. Truth: He declares that the LORD restores his soul.

   C. Under the emblem of guiding in the right paths, he affirms that the LORD leads him because of his reputation (3b).

      1. Truth: He declares that the LORD leads him in the right way.

      2. Reason: He explains that the LORD's reputation depends on it.

   D. Under the emblem of a shepherd protecting the sheep, he affirms that the LORD leads him safely through dangerous circumstances (4).

      1. Danger: He explains that he may go through life-threatening circumstances.

      2. Truth: He declares that the presence of the LORD dispels fear.

      3. Emblem: Using the imagery of a rod and staff he asserts that the LORD will comfort him.

II. Using the image of a gracious host and his guest, David reflects on how the LORD provides for all his needs even in dangerous circumstances (5).

   A. Using the emblem of preparing a banquet table for him in the presence of his enemies, he affirms that the LORD sustains him in time of need.

B. Using the emblem of a host anointing the head with oil, he affirms that the LORD welcomes him into his presence with joy.

C. Using the emblem of a full cup, he affirms that the LORD makes his lot in life full with good things.

III. David concludes that since the goodness and loyal love of the LORD will follow him always he shall return to full communion in the sanctuary (6).

A. Conclusion: The goodness and loyal love of the LORD will persistently follow him everywhere.

B. Decision: He shall return to the house of the LORD for the length of his days.

COMMENTARY IN EXPOSITORY FORM

I. The LORD provides for his people's spiritual and physical well–being as a shepherd (1–4).

Psalm 23 begins with the well-known metaphor, "The LORD is my shepherd." This figure dominates the first four verses of the psalm as David examines the different provisions of the divine Shepherd, and he was fully able to do this because of his experiences as a shepherd (1 Sam. 16:11; 17:34).

A. The LORD provides spiritual nourishment (1–2a).

The first line of poetry focuses on the feeding that a shepherd provides for the sheep.[21] "Shepherd" is an active participle used substantively, stressing the meaning of the word: "my shepherd" or even "my feeder" (רֹעִי from the verb רָעָה, "to pasture, tend, graze, feed"). This word can simply describe animals grazing or feeding, such as in Genesis 41:2 which mentions cows that grazed in the marsh grasses. It is also used of the spiritual relationship between

---

21. The first line does not match the English verse division. On the basis of the parallelism the line may be read as follows: "The LORD is my shepherd; I lack nothing. // He makes me lie down in green pastures." The second half forms emblematic parallelism.

God and his people: "we are the people of his pasture, the flock under his care" (Ps. 95:7). Of course the people are not sheep, and the LORD is not literally a shepherd. The metaphorical usage of a shepherd feeding the flock presents the LORD as a spiritual leader and teacher. Similarly, Ezekiel 34:2 speaks of Israel's leaders as "shepherds"—feeding themselves instead of the flock. These under-shepherds were to take care of the people and teach them the word of the LORD; and the people, the "sheep," were to receive the teaching and grow spiritually. As a shepherd feeds the sheep, so the LORD, provides spiritual food for the spiritual growth of his people, often through his servants who are also called shepherds.

This meaning of the metaphor finds support throughout Scripture. In the New Testament Peter is instructed by Jesus, "Feed my sheep" (John 21:16); and then under the authority of Jesus, the Chief Shepherd, Peter instructs the elders to feed and care for the flock (1 Pet. 5:1–4). Accordingly, Hebrews 5:12–14 uses the imagery of food for the word of the Lord. These samples confirm that the "shepherd" image signifies teaching.

Immediately following this introductory metaphor the psalmist announces the quantity of this provision: "I lack nothing." The verb (< חָסֵר) means "lack, need, be lacking, decrease" (the old translation "I shall not want" is fine, but the meaning of "want" has changed).[22] Here David affirms that there is no lack or deficiency in the LORD's provision.

Two grammatical observations are necessary. First, the verb (אֶחְסָר) should be taken as a habitual imperfect, translated "I lack nothing" or "I do not lack," in view of the participle preceding it as well as the nature of the meditation.[23] And second, the juxtaposition of this clause with the preceding shows that "I

---

22. The derivatives shed significant light on this verb. A nominal form (חֶסֶר) means "poverty" in Proverbs 28:22, where it is the antithesis of "wealth." An adjectival form (חָסֵר) means "needy" in 1 Samuel 21:16 where we read, "Am I needy of madmen?" Interestingly, a noun form (חֶסְרוֹן) bears the nuance of "deficiency"; Ecclesiastes 1:15 refers to a deficiency of money or material items. And a noun (חֹסֶר) denotes "lack" as in Amos 4:6 which speaks of a "lack of bread."

23. This idea may have been implied in the old translation "I shall not want"; but that wording placed it more in the future.

lack nothing" is a result clause (without *waw)*—the result of the LORD's provision is that he lacks nothing.

Not only is the quantity of God's provision without lack, but the quality is the best. The parallel colon "He makes me lie down in grassy green meadows" provides the emblem for the first half of the verse. Therefore, the whole colon could be explained as a continuation of the metaphor, or an implied comparison. In the emblem the term "grass" (דֶּשֶׁא) indicates the rich, abundant grass of springtime.[24] In Deuteronomy 32:2, for example, the term is used for the fresh grass on which falls the morning dew.[25] Here it is an attributive genitive, describing the meadows as grassy. The verb (יַרְבִּיצֵנִי, a causative *hiphil*) is also used as a habitual imperfect—a shepherd regularly leads the sheep to lie down in such grassy meadows. This emblem underscores the truth that God was at work in David's life, leading him to the best provisions where he can "feed" to his heart's content. Since the line is based on the beginning figure (and so an implied comparison), the psalmist is saying that the LORD meets his spiritual needs—and in the process gives him the very best. As grass would be food for the sheep, the word of the LORD would be provision for the "hungry" spirit. This "feeding" could come through personal meditation, but it would regularly be done through the ministry of the priests, the "under-shepherds," who were to teach people the word of the LORD (see Mal. 2:1–9). The LORD could provide the psalmist with spiritual food at any time, anywhere; but it would be a regular provision in the sanctuary.

B. The LORD provides spiritual refreshment (2b–3a).

The second line of the psalm draws upon the care of the shepherd refreshing the sheep with cleansing and rest. The verb (יְנַהֲלֵנִי) means "lead, guide to a watering place or station, refresh";

---

24. In much of the land the grass all but disappears in the heat of the summer, but in the spring time even the normally barren hills have fresh grass. The Sabatean cognate bears out the connotation of "springtime" (see BDB, p. 206).
25. Interestingly, the context of Deuteronomy 32:2 is that teaching is like the gentle rain and the falling dew on the fresh grass.

it is normally used with reference to guidance to water (Isaiah 49:10 states, "And [He] will guide them to springs of water").

The waters to which the LORD leads are "restful," literally "restfulnesses" (מְנֻחוֹת from נוּחַ), meaning places of complete rest and refreshment. The word is an attributive genitive after "waters," describing the kind of waters in view. The sheep are not taken to a rushing stream, but to still, calm lagoons. Flocks in the ancient Near East were watered at least once a day, usually around noon;[26] but this leading was not limited to finding water to drink. It included finding a place for cleansing and refreshment. Here the placid waters could wash the wounds and cleanse the soiled spots. Throughout the Old Testament tempestuous waters speak of distress (cf. Isa. 43:2; 28:2; and 2 Sam. 5:20), but calm waters for washing represent spiritual cleansing (cf. Lev. 11:32; 16:4; 17:15; Num. 19:7; and Exod. 30:18). The point is that the LORD cleanses people from sin and provides spiritual refreshment and renewal from the chaos of life.

That this is the point can be seen from the parallel clause that gives the reality behind the emblem: "He restores my soul." The verb "restores" (שׁוּב, here יְשׁוֹבֵב, a *polel* [habitual] imperfect, meaning "cause to turn back, restore"; s.v. Ps. 126:1) is a common verb with a wide range of uses. In the basic *qal* verbal system it can mean simply "return," or it can mean "repent." In causative formations it has a wide range as well: it is used in 1 Kings 13:6 for the "restoring" of a withered hand; it is used in Isaiah 52:8 for the "restoring" of the captives to their land; in Isaiah 58:12 it refers to the "repairing" of the walls, and in Daniel 9:25 for the "rebuilding" of a ruined city. It therefore bears the idea of returning something to its original state. David's words are general enough to mean that the LORD restores him to his proper spiritual and physical condition by forgiving him and renewing him (see Pss. 32 and 51).

Why would he need this provision? Some possible answers come from passages that describe spiritual waywardness under the figure of sheep. For example, Ezekiel 34 tells why "sheep" may need restoration: they may be scattered by bad shepherds

---

26. *International Standard Bible Encyclopedia*, see under "Shepherd," by James A Patch, IV:2763.

with false teaching; they may catch a scent of fresh grass somewhere across a dangerous ravine; or they may be frightened by
the storms of life. Of course, one of the best-known pictures of
this provision of the LORD is that of Jesus the shepherd retrieving the lost sheep who needed to repent (Luke 15:3–7). The
spiritual healing and refreshment to which David refers could
have come through his prayers and meditations, but it would
have been most effectively communicated through the restor-
ative ritual in the sanctuary.

C. The LORD provides guidance in the right way (3b).

The third line of the poem affirms that the LORD leads in
the right paths. The verb "he leads me" (יַנְחֵנִי) continues with
the imagery of the shepherd. This leading could also have been
effected through circumstances caused by the LORD directly, or
through the written and spoken word for general guidance, or
through spiritual guides and counselors in the sanctuary.[27] The
point is that ultimately God has sovereign control over David's
life to direct him where he should go.

The leading is in "the tracks of righteousness" (בְמַעְגְּלֵי־צֶדֶק); if
the second word is taken as an attributive genitive it would be
translated "in right tracks." Briggs notes that such tracks "lead
directly and safely to the destination, as distinguished from wrong
tracks that would lead astray."[28] The "tracks" are literally "wagon
tracks"; an alert shepherd would seek out those tracks in order
to find the way home safely. The qualifying word "righteousness"

---

27. נָחָה simply means "lead, guide." The word is not used in non–theological
contexts very often. It does occur often with the imagery of the shepherd
in reference to the LORD (see for example Pss. 31:3, 77:20; 78:72). The
word may have been drawn from the setting of shepherding to refer to
divine guidance. In a number of passages the idea of God's leading is an
expression of the believer's confidence in God's presence. In the Exodus
and wilderness wandering the leading took a clear form in the pillar of
cloud (Exod. 13:17) and in the instructions from the LORD to Moses. In
Genesis 24:27 and 48, the circumstances that resulted from a prayerful
dependence on the LORD were referred to as the leading of the LORD.
Some uses look forward to a future when the LORD would lead the nations
on earth as sovereign Lord (Ps. 67:4).
28. *Psalms*, p. 209.

or "right" in the psalm would indicate that the path chosen is the right one, but if God was leading it was also the righteous one. There is a double meaning to the expression. The point is that God never leads anyone in an unrighteous way; he always leads in the righteous way, which is the way home. He leads in the right way because his reputation is at stake. The term "name" (שֵׁם) is used frequently in the Bible for the idea of "reputation" (s.v. Ps. 20:1). In the ancient world a shepherd's reputation depended on his ability to lead the sheep in the right direction. If he lost the sheep, or lost the way home, he would gain a bad reputation and be a worthless shepherd. David affirms that the LORD's reputation depends upon his ability to guide the sheep safely home, which he does.

The Lord's ministry of leading is confirmed in the New Testament as an evidence of salvation. Jesus says that his sheep follow him, and he could declare that of all that the Father had given to him he should lose none (John 6:39). Paul writes that "as many as are led by the Spirit of God are the children of God" (Rom. 8:14). The Lord leads his people in the right path and will bring them safely home to the Father.

Note the progression of ideas for the spiritual meaning: the psalmist receives the teaching of the LORD, and this teaching leads to spiritual renewal, and the spiritual renewal ensures that he will follow the LORD in righteousness.

D. The LORD defends his people in times of danger (4).

Verse 4 states that even in the most dangerous situations the LORD protects his people. The verse begins with the concessive clause, "Even though I may walk in the valley of the shadow of death." The idiom of walking through a valley signifies the dangerous way that his course of life might take him, including the possibility of actually walking in a deep valley. Briggs explains, "The hill country of Judah is broken up by narrow and precipitous ravines, or wadis, difficult to descend and ascend, dark, gloomy, and abounding in caves, the abode of wild beasts and robbers."[29] Here it is likely that the psalmist had a number of such gorges in mind from his time in the wilderness, but he was

---

29. *Psalms*, p. 209.

using the idea of such a "valley" as an image for life-threatening experiences, or difficult places (an implied comparison; see also Ps. 130:1).

That this is the point is suggested by the following genitive, "shadow of death" (צַלְמָוֶת). The word is etymologically difficult because it appears to be two words joined together, "shadow" (צֵל from צָלַל, "to be dark, to grow dark"), and "death" (מָוֶת). It could be rendered "deathly darkness" or "darkness of death," or even interpreted to mean "deep darkness." The word would be a figure describing terrors in the valleys (so a metonymy of adjunct). It is used in Amos 5:8 for the deep darkness of the night. Job 24:17 states that the adulterer "is familiar with the terrors of thick darkness." Jeremiah uses the term figuratively for "distress" (13:16), and "extreme danger" (2:16). Job 10:21 uses the expression "land of darkness" as a label for the world of the dead. The "valley of death darkness" is therefore a vivid depiction of the dangerous places where life is threatened, as if death casts its shadow over the traveler. David had often found himself in such dangerous places, perhaps even retrieving sheep; the places were so dangerous that he might not have gotten out alive if God had not been with him. Even though he walked there, he would fear no harm (רַע, s.v. Ps. 10:15).

The reason that David would not fear was because the LORD was with him. Here the focus of the psalm changes from talking about the LORD to talking directly to the LORD.[30] And the affirmation of the LORD's presence is what makes all the difference in his outlook in dangerous places. Just as a shepherd abides with his sheep always, so the LORD is with his people, even in the dangerous places. Since the LORD is always present everywhere (cf. Ps. 139:7–12), the special statement "you are with me" means something more specific. It means that the LORD intervenes in his life for protection as well as provision. This is one of the major themes of the Bible. God first introduced it to Jacob at Bethel—"I will be with you" (Gen. 28:15). It was expounded by the LORD to Moses—"I am with you" (Exod. 3:12). It found full expression in the prophecy of *Immanuel*—"God is with us" (Isa.

---

30. The pattern is worth noting: he (v. 1), he (v. 2), he (v. 2), he (v. 3) and then you (v. 4), you (v. 5), you (v. 5).

7:14). And, likewise, in the New Testament we have the promise of Jesus that he would be with us always, even to the end of the age (Matt. 28:20).

The psalm continues the shepherding image by associating God's protection with "rod and staff." The "rod" (שֵׁבֶט, from a verb "to smite, slay") is used in Leviticus 27:32 as a rod for counting sheep, and figuratively in Ezekiel 20:37 for a chastening rod. The "staff" (מִשְׁעַנְתֶּךָ , from a verb שָׁעַן, "to lean, support") was for support as well as protection. In Zechariah 8:4 it is an old person's cane. In Isaiah 36:6 it is used figuratively for the support of Egypt to Israel—a nuance of protection. The rod and staff are figures here of course (implied comparisons), for there is no actual rod and staff that God will use. Accordingly, these words refer to the care and the defense of the LORD (of which these were signs). They bring him comfort in difficult times.[31]

II. The LORD provides for his people's spiritual and physical needs as a gracious host (5)

In verse 5 the scene changes from the pasture to the banquet hall, and the image of the LORD from shepherd to host.[32] Here David reflects on the provisions of a host to his honored guest.

He begins: "You prepare a table before me in the presence of my enemies." The idea is another implied comparison; the LORD provides for his guests the way a banquet host would provide. And to "prepare a table" means to lay out food and drink on a table (so "table" is a metonymy of subject). The setting and circumstances that the psalmist intended are not immediately obvious. The verse probably refers to the provision of actual food, for the LORD provides all good gifts (and the feeding in verse 1 referred to teaching spiritual things). It would still

---

31. The verb "comfort" might seem to be a personification in this line; but since "rod" and "staff" are figurative of care and defense, the comfort would come from these divine activities. The point would be about the same in either case.

32. Some interpretations carry the image of the shepherd in this verse as well, making the table mean tableland, and the anointing a treatment of the sheep, but that is forced. The language is more at home in the setting of a banquet hall.

be considered a spiritual provision here, especially if it were a thanksgiving feast eaten in the sanctuary, the house where the LORD welcomed his guests. That food would be most clearly a divine provision,[33] but the image of the host may not carry such specific attachments.

The qualifying phrase supports the idea that it is physical food—"in the presence of my enemies." The prepositional phrase (literally "in the face of") introduces the enemies, those who oppose and harass him. According to customs, the honored guest was safe because the host was obliged to protect a guest at all costs.[34] Sitting down to eat and drink in the midst of danger from enemies is a marvelous picture of safety and security. David is saying that God provides food and safety for his people.[35]

The second half of the verse continues the image of the host, now with the anointing oil.[36] It was the duty and delight of the gracious host to give the guest scented, perfumed oil to freshen up (especially after being in the sun and sand; modern skin lotions may be similarly refreshing). The word "oil" is common (שֶׁמֶן); it means "fat, oil, olive oil." In Ecclesiastes 9:8 it is a token of happiness (cf. 9:7). In Ezekiel 16:20 it is symbolic of prosperity. II Kings 20:13 presents it as a royal treasure. In Hosea 12:2 it is a tribute given to Egypt. It signified wealth, prosperity, happiness, and honor. Here it is a pleasing provision of hospitality for an honored guest. In the New Testament Jesus stopped the criticism of the woman anointing him by reminding his host that he had given him neither water or oil when he entered his house (Luke 7:44–5).

The verb "anoint"(דִּשַּׁנְתָּ) is from the verb "be fat," which in the causative *piel* stem can mean "make fat" and "anoint." This

---

33. Arno C. Gaebelein, *The Book of Psalms* (Wheaton: Van Kampen Press, 1939), p. 115.

34. Briggs, *Psalms*, p. 210. Compare Lot's attempts to protect the angels who came to stay with him. The prophet Isaiah employs the same components of eating and drinking in the presence of enemies, but in that context the participants seem unaware of the enemies outside who are poised to attack (Isa. 21:5).

35. There is no basis and no need for changing the word "table" to a word for some kind of weapon just because the passage mentions the enemies.

36. Here the perfect tense must harmonize with the imperfects throughout; it would be characteristic perfect or gnomic perfect.

anointing is not the ceremonial anointing of a king (מָשַׁח), but a symbol of festivity and joy. It is used in Proverbs 15:30 to report how "good news puts fat on the bones," that is, brings joy to the whole person. By ascribing such lavish treatment to God as a host, David is saying that God is the source of his joy, in that he welcomes him and provides for his comfort and refreshment.

Finally, David exclaims, "My cup is filled to the brim." The old translation of "My cup runneth over" captures the point as well, for the idea (of רְוָיָה) is that it is well-filled, filled to satiety. The "cup" in the Bible is a symbol of one's portion or lot in life. It may be bad, such as a "cup of his fury" that would forewarn judgment (Isa. 51:17), or of fire and brimstone (Ps. 11:6). The judgment motif is also present in such uses. The Father gave Jesus such a cup to drink, the crucifixion, from which he prayed to be delivered (Matt. 26:39). But the cup may also be good, as here in Psalm 23 (and in Ps. 16:5; 116:13). In a banquet hall the cup would be filled with choice wine, so David is saying that the LORD has filled his life with good things. In a way this line summarizes all that has gone before in this meditation on the provisions from the LORD; but specifically it highlights the physical provisions of the LORD in life.

III. Those who enjoy the provisions of the LORD desire continued communion with him (6).

Verse 6 provides the conclusion of the psalm; "surely" (אַךְ) marks the change from what has gone before. The change will be twofold. First, he changes from meditating about the LORD with images of a shepherd and a host to focusing directly on the LORD in his holy house. And second, he will now draw the conclusion from his meditations that he desires more communion with the LORD.

The critical word in David's concluding observation is "loyal love" (חֶסֶד, often translated "mercy" or "lovingkindness"). The addition of the word "goodness" (טוֹב וָחֶסֶד) probably forms a hendiadys with the word: "Surely, goodness and loyal love will follow me" would then be translated as "good loyal love will follow me." It is a way of emphasizing the value of the loyal love and focusing all attention on it. The two words work well together. "Goodness" or "good" refers to that which promotes, protects, produces, and enhances life (s.v. Ps. 34:8).[37] And "loyal love" is the well-known covenant word that describes God's faithful love to keep his covenant promises.[38] No other term could more adequately summarize the provisions of the LORD enumerated in Psalm 23.

---

37. See also Michael Fox, "*TOB* as Covenant Terminology," *BASOR* 209 (1973):41, 2.
38. The word translated "loyal love" (חֶסֶד) is usually translated "mercy" or "lovingkindness." It is defined in the dictionaries as "goodness, kindness" and also "mercy, affection, lovely appearance." Nelson Glueck (*Hesed in the Bible*) demonstrated that the term describes the faithful and loving care of the covenant God for his people and their faithful love in return to him and other covenant members. There are related words as well. There is the verb (חָסַד); "to be good, kind"; there is an adjective (חָסִיד), "kind, pious, faithful" (used as a substantive for the saints, the godly who are loyal to the covenant); and there is a noun (חֲסִידָה), "a stork" or "love." The stork may be so-named because of its kind and affectionate care for its young (Ps. 104:17). There is a helpful illustration for our word in the usage of this noun. In Job 39:13–15 the LORD compares the ostrich to the stork (or to "love" as some versions translate it). The ostrich is not like the stork (or love) because it does not have that caring, faithful love for its young.

According to Glueck (and others before him), the word חֶסֶד does not refer to a spontaneous, unmotivated kindness, but to a kind of behavior that arises from a relationship which has rights and obligations (marriage, the household, the government). When the word is used with God, the relationship is defined in terms of the covenant. Translations such as "loyal love" or "covenant faithful love" are wordy, but they are more precise than "lovingkindness." A survey of the uses of the word and its related forms is in order

First, the word seems to mean "lovely in appearance" in Isaiah 40:6. The text says, "All flesh is grass, and all its beauty (חַסְדּוֹ) is like the flower of the field." The word is questioned in this context and emendations offered.

One major category of meanings is "general kindness, favor." In Genesis 40:14 Joseph said, "please do me the kindness to mention me to Pharaoh." Likewise, Rahab wanted the spies to treat her kindly (Josh. 2:12). 1 Kings 20:31 refers to Israel's kings as merciful. And Proverbs 11:17 refers to a man who is kind.

Another category is "kindness based on a relationship." Abraham appealed to his wife to show him kindness in what she said (Gen. 20:13). In the Book of Ruth the word frequently has this meaning. For example, Ruth displayed loyal love to the family into which she was married (3:10).

The most important category is "faithful covenant love." God demonstrates his covenant love to his people by all that he does for them, sometimes in spite of their unfaithfulness. Deuteronomy 7:12 promises

It is significant that the psalmist uses the verb "pursue" in this line. This could be a personification, but it is more likely that "loyal love" refers to God and his loving acts (so a metonymy of cause). It is God who will pursue him and extend his loyal love to him every step of the way. He will not let David out of his faithful loving care. Why does this love "pursue" him? Was he trying to escape? (cf. Psalm 139:7). No matter where he went, or why, David knew that God would follow him with his love. He had been pursued often in his life; but no man chased him as persistently and effectively as the LORD.[39]

And so David's conclusion is that he would return to the house of the LORD for the length of days. The word used here, "return," is the same word that was used earlier to say "he restores my soul." Was David in need of spiritual renewal? Or was he simply separated from the place of formal worship by circumstances? Whatever David's spiritual condition was, God's loyal love followed him and seemed to draw him back to the place where all God's provisions could be fully realized, the sanctuary. As he meditated on all the provisions of the LORD for his spiritual and

---

that the LORD will fulfill the covenant promise he made and the loyal love he swore. Solomon acknowledges that there is no one like the LORD in "keeping covenant and showing loyal love to his servants" (1 Kings 8:23). God's "loyal love" brings redemption and guidance to his people (Exod. 15:13). In times of war or famine the covenant people may look to the faithful love of the LORD (Ps. 33:22). God's "loyal love" also preserves life (Ps. 6:4). God's "loyal love" is the basis of forgiveness of sins (Ps. 51:1). God's "loyal love" brings restoration to life (Ps. 109:21–26). In fact, this attribute of God appears frequently in selected lists of his attributes (Ps. 36:5; Jon. 4:2; Exod. 34:7 and Ps. 118:1,2). In fact Psalm 118 uses an expression that became common in Israel's praise: "O give thanks to the LORD for he is good, his loyal love endures forever."

Another category is "piety, faithful covenant acts." This category refers to the response of the people of God to their covenant God. Hosea calls on the people to live out their covenant duties because the LORD delights in piety (6:4). The word, and especially the adjective, are used in parallelism with "the righteous" (Isa. 57:1), so people are to display faithful covenant love just as God does.

The word is often paired with "truth" to form a hendiadys: "loyal love and truth" would mean "faithful loyal love" (see the discussion of "truth" with Ps. 15:2).

39. In this light read Francis Thompson's poem "The Hound of Heaven."

physical well-being, he came to the conclusion that he wanted to be in the best place to avail himself of those divine provisions. That place was "the house of Yahweh." The title refers to any place God revealed himself and was worshiped, whether a place in the country where the LORD appeared (see Gen 28:17) or the tent of meeting (1 Sam. 1:7). It is a place of fellowship with and worship of the LORD. There the faithful would be taught God's word; they would find forgiveness and restoration; they would learn of his righteous guidance; they would pray and praise for his protection and provision; and they would be welcomed into his house where they would find provisions in abundance (see Ps. 36:6–8). It is there that the presence of God would be realized. And so David desires to be there, to come into close communion with the LORD for the rest of his days.

Christians now focus on the heavenly temple, the eternal dwelling place of the Lord, and so the words of this psalm are often taken to refer to the place where there is unbroken fellowship with the Lord.

MESSAGE AND APPLICATION

The psalm is primarily a meditation on the spiritual and physical provisions of the LORD. Through the example of David the psalm invites believers to meditate on the many manifestations of the loyal love of the LORD and thereby renew their communion with him in his sanctuary. We could write a full exposition idea in this way: *The righteous desire to be in the presence of the Lord where they will feed on his Word, find spiritual restoration, be guided into righteousness, be reminded of his protective presence, receive provisions from his bounty, and be joyfully welcomed by him.* There is a very practical sequence here: people first need to be taught the Word of God; and when they are, they will see that there are areas of their lives that need cleansing and restoration; and when they are cleansed, they will discover God's guidance in righteousness; and as they follow his guidance, they will find protection; and that protection will be sensed the most in the provisions of his house.

There is another very important meaning of the psalm today. It is clear from the Bible that the Lord Jesus Christ is the "shepherd" in fulfillment of prophecy (Isa. 40:10–11).[40] While on earth he demonstrated these provisions for people who followed him, teaching them, renewing them, guiding them, protecting them, and providing for them. And he fulfills these ministries even now as the Great Shepherd. He does this through the ministry of the Holy Spirit and the agency of under-shepherds, just as he did in the Old Testament through the service of the priests, Israel's shepherds.

The message of this psalm is also instructive for these spiritual leaders. As they minister in the house of the Lord on his behalf, they are reminded that their ministry must include teaching the Word, restoring people spiritually, guiding them into righteousness, defending the flock from physical and spiritual danger, and providing for all the needs, physical as well as spiritual, of those who are given to them.

---

40. In the New Testament Jesus is the good shepherd in John 10:11 who dies for the sheep, the great shepherd in 1 Peter 5:4 who takes care of the sheep, and the chief shepherd in Hebrews 13:20 who will come in glory.

PSALM 24

Preparation to Praise the King of Glory

INTRODUCTION

Text and Textual Variants

A Psalm of David.[1]

1 The earth is the LORD's, and everything in it;
   the world, and [2]they who dwell in it.
2 For he has founded it upon the seas;
   he has established it upon the rivers.
3 Who may ascend to the hill of the LORD?
   Who may stand in his holy place?
4 The one who has clean hands and a pure heart,
     who has not lifted up his soul[3] to falsehood
       and has not sworn deceitfully.[4]
5 He shall receive a blessing from the LORD,

---

1. The Greek adds, "on the first day of the week" (τῆς μιᾶς σαββάτων)
2. Greek adds "all": "and all the inhabitants (καὶ πάντες οἱ κατοικοῦντες)," but the addition is unnecessary.
3. The MT has "my soul," נַפְשִׁי, but most suggest the change to נַפְשׁוֹ , "his soul." This is in harmony with the versions and many manuscripts. But Broyles argues that the MT may be the correct reading because it would be closer to the commandment (not to take "my name" in vain): "who has not lifted up me to falsehood" (*Psalms*, p. 132).
4. The Greek text adds τῷ πλησίον αὐτοῦ, which would reflect לְרֵעֵהוּ, "to his neighbor."

573

and vindication from the God of his salvation.
6 This is the generation of those who seek after him,[5]
Who seek your[6] face, even Jacob. *Selah*

7 Lift up your heads, O you gates,[7]
And be lifted up, you everlasting doors;
And the king of glory will come in!
8 Who is the king of glory?
The LORD, strong and mighty!
The LORD, mighty in battle!
9 Lift up your heads, O you gates,
Yea, lift them up,[8] you everlasting doors;
And the king of glory will come in!
10 Who is the king of glory?
The LORD of armies—
He is the king of glory! *Selah.*

---

5. The MT has the *Kᵉthiv–Qᵉre'* form דֹּרְשׁוֹ; the majority of the manuscripts follow the *Qᵉre'* reading as a plural participle.

6. The MT reads "*who* seek your face, Jacob (probably meaning, "even Jacob," referring to the seekers themselves). Some suggest it would read "O Jacob," but that would make even less sense in the context. The Greek text omits the suffix on פָּנֶיךָ; instead, it (and the Syriac and some Hebrew manuscripts) add "the God of" (= אֱלֹהֵי), reading "seeking the face of the God of Jacob." Two Syriac manuscripts have "your face, God of Jacob." And the Targum has a 3sg suffix, "his face." The variations witness to the difficulty of the line. What is clear is that the worshipers are not seeking Jacob's face, but God's. The MT can be read to clarify that "Jacob" refers to the worshipers who want to ascend the mount to seek God's face (i.e., find his favor).

7. Here and in verse 9 the Greek has "Lift up your gates, O rulers of yours" (οἱ ἄρχοντες ὑμῶν), likely understanding "heads" as a reference to leaders.

8. The verb is וּשְׂאוּ, the simple *qal* imperative, the direct object of the first clause being implied here as well. A few Hebrew manuscripts and the versions harmonize the form with the first refrain, which in 7b has the *niphal* imperative, "and be lifted up," וְהִנָּשְׂאוּ. There is no reason to follow the variant in order to harmonize the two lines; the variant came about because of the desire to harmonize the lines. If it had been the original reading it would be difficult to explain how the simple *qal* found its way into the text.

Composition and Context

Psalm 24 is well-known through musical arrangements and frequent quotations, but sometimes in such uses the main message of the psalm can become obscured. The passage appears to be a liturgy for a festival of praise, frequently associated with a fall festival as suggested by Mowinckel.[9] Most commentators would place the psalm in the pre-exilic, monarchy period, but sometime after Solomon because of the connection to the temple in Jerusalem.[10] There is no question but that the psalm is liturgical, celebrating the victory procession of the LORD into the sanctuary. Broyles says it has strong affinities to the time of David, possibly the bringing of the ark up to Jerusalem;[11] but based on the contents of the psalm, it is more likely that it was written for the procession into the sanctuary to commemorate a great victory in battle. As a liturgical piece, the psalm became an integral part of temple worship (see also the sanctuary liturgies in Pss. 15, 118, and 132) and no doubt used on many occasions.[12]

From the detailed analysis of the psalm we can suggest a reconstruction of the occasion and setting of the piece. The internal evidence suggests that the Israelites had just returned from a victorious battle with the Canaanites. They were proceeding to the sanctuary to give praise to the LORD for the great and mighty victory in battle, carrying with them the glorious ark of the covenant, the symbol of the LORD's presence with them. As they approached the gates they were met by the Levitical gatekeepers. It was the worshipers' part to ask who could enter the sanctuary of the LORD; and it was the gatekeepers part

---

9. See S. Mowinckel, *The Psalms in Israel's Worship* (New York: Abingdon, 1967), pp. 5, 6, 115.
10. See A. A. Anderson, *Psalms 1–72*, p. 200. Of course, there are a number of suggestions for the date of the psalm, ranging from the time of David down to 164 B.C. when the temple was rededicated (see M. Treves, "The Date of Psalm 24," *VT* 10 [1960]:428–37). The psalm certainly could have been used at that time, but was probably much earlier.
11. *Psalms*, p. 131.
12. See further the treatment of the psalm by James L. Crenshaw, "Knowing Whose You Are: Psalm 24," in *The Psalms: An Introduction* (Grand Rapids: Eerdmans, 2001), pp. 155–167.

to answer with the standards set down in the Law—perfect righteousness. The worshipers in this case did not claim to be qualified to enter; rather, they responded that they were simply seeking the LORD's favor—a response that indicates that they wanted to meet the LORD's requirements but had to bring sacrifices to do that. The psalm concludes with the procession of the people into the sanctuary with shouts of acclamation for the LORD's greatness expressed in the form of an encouraging refrain.

Exegetical Analysis

Summary

In preparation for the exaltation of the glorious King, the sovereign LORD of creation who has shown himself mighty in battle, the worshipers in the procession are reminded that those with clean hands and pure hearts may ascend to his holy place.

Outline

I. Introductory Praise: The psalmist acknowledges that everything in the earth belongs to the LORD because he created all of it (1–2).

II. Liturgy at the Gate: The psalmist rehearses the ritual at the gates of the sanctuary which reminds the worshipers that those who are pure in thought and deed may enter God's presence and receive his blessing (3–6).

    A. Inquiry: The people desire to enter the sanctuary and worship the LORD (3).

    B. Instruction: Only those who are without sin in thought and deed may enter God's presence and receive his blessing (4–5).

    C. Identification: The people confess that they are seeking the LORD's favor (6).

III. Procession into the Sanctuary: The psalmist recalls how the acclamation of the LORD's glorious victory in battle was an encouragement to the faith of the people (7–10).

A. Call: He calls people in the gates to be encouraged by the triumphal entry of the King of Glory (7).
B. Clarification: He explains that the glorious King is the LORD, mighty in battle (8).
C. Repeated Call: He calls for people in the gates to be encouraged by the triumphal entry of the King of Glory (9).
D. Repeated Clarification: He explains again that the glorious King is the LORD who is mighty in battle (10).

COMMENTARY IN EXPOSITORY FORM

I. Those who believe in the LORD acclaim his sovereignty over his creation (1–2).

The first two verses of the psalm provide an introductory acclamation: the earth and everything in it belongs to the LORD because he made it all.[13] It is common for psalms to begin with a general word of praise, but this one seems to have a more specific point of reference within the psalm. The psalm appears to be a praise for victory in battle, as the procession indicates; so extolling the LORD's sovereignty over everything in the world would have some specific relevance for the battle. In other words, in a celebration of victory over the enemies of Israel, the Israelites would remind themselves that their God was sovereign over everything in creation.

The acclamation refers to both the territories and the inhabitants as belonging to the LORD. "Earth" and "world" [inhabited land] refer to territory, because the additional expressions add all the things that live in them. The prepositional phrase that begins the verse, "To the LORD [is] the earth," expresses possession—it all belongs to the LORD. He may be the God of Israel, but he is also the God of the whole world—all races belong to him.

---

13. The incomplete parallelism of the line focuses on the LORD: "To Yahweh [belongs] / the earth / and its fullness // the world / and the inhabitants / in it." The holy name receives prominence because it comes first and does double duty in the line.

Verse 2 then provides the explanation of the LORD's sovereign possession of everything: he created it all. The parallelism in the verse stresses this point; two verbs affirm the creation, but in each colon the prepositional phrase comes first: "upon the seas he founded it, and upon the rivers he established it." The first verb is a perfect tense (יְסָדָהּ) which could be a simple definite past, but a present perfect would also fit and stress the continuation of the results ("he has founded it"). The second verb (יְכוֹנְנֶהָ) is obviously a reference to the past as well and is to be translated in the same way as the first verb (it may be classified as a preterite, the past tense use of the form of the imperfect without the *waw*).

With the mention of "seas" (יַמִּים, singular יָם) and "rivers" (נְהָרוֹת, singular נָהָר), we have a picture of the inhabitable earth being created over waters and currents, perhaps a way to explain the fountains, springs, and rivers under the ground. This may seem archaic and quaint to the modern, sophisticated reader, but the unusual verse may have been written primarily as a polemic against Canaanite beliefs, suggesting that if the song was written after a battle it was probably against the Canaanites. In Canaanite mythology the forces of nature were deified, two of them identified as Prince Sea (*Yam*) and Judge River (*Nahar*), the precise words used in the verse. These deities were powerful forces of the underworld to the pagans, but to the Israelites they were simply forces of nature that God had created and controlled when he established the land. Since they were venerated as spirit forces by the Canaanites, Israel could single them out in the praise of the LORD's sovereignty, to stress that in defeating the Canaanites the LORD demonstrated his sovereignty over their gods as well. In affirming the sovereignty of the LORD over all his creation, the psalmist selected these two words to say also that no Canaanite deities or part of the Canaanite world could rival his authority, or even act independently of his will. In general, we find an emphasis in the Old Testament that the LORD establishes his sovereign creation by victory over the waters of chaos. Accordingly, the psalm begins with a shout of victory over the chaos, real or imagined, in the Canaanite world.[14]

14. Broyles, *Psalms*, p. 127.

II. Those who would enter the presence of the LORD must be without sin in thought and deed (3–6).

A. Worshipers must meet God's standards to enter into his holy presence (3).

There is an abrupt change in the psalm now to what may be called a liturgy at the gate, a ritual designed to prepare people to enter the sanctuary and enjoy communion with the LORD. Many of the Levites were assigned to be gatekeepers; their task was to make sure the people who came into the sanctuary met the requirement of holiness and had the proper sacrifices. As the worshipers heard each time the standard for entrance into the presence of God, they would have to acknowledge their need of God's gracious provision of cleansing and atonement through the ritual prescribed in the Law. Even a faithful believer like the psalmist, whom God had blessed with victory on the battlefield, and who was coming to the sanctuary to praise God for it, was reminded by the ritual of the gravity of entering this holy place. The parallelism of the verse stresses this, for "the hill of the LORD" in the first colon is matched by "in his holy place" in the second.[15] Thus, it is the description of the place as holy that is key here—it was a holy place, a place set apart for the worship of God (s.v. Ps. 22:3 for "holy").[16] Only when people sought the LORD's favor through the sanctifying ritual would they be able to enter his courts with praise.

Because of the holy nature of the LORD's dwelling place, the opening question was essential: "Who may ascend to the hill of the LORD? Who may stand in his holy place?" The psalmist leading the procession to the sanctuary probably raised the question, and the answer would have come from the priests. In the questions the two verbs are imperfects of permission: "who may ascend?" This first verb (יַעֲלֶה) fits well with the physical

---

15. The "hill" then is a metonymy of subject, for what is intended is entrance into the sanctuary that is on top of the hill. "Holy place" is an adjectival description of the sanctuary, and so it too would be a figure, a metonymy of adjunct, meaning the holy sanctuary.

16. Broyles says that the temple symbolized the LORD's achievement of world order, and so only those who conformed to his right order could enter (*Psalms,* p. 129).

ascent of the holy mount; and because of that no matter where the pilgrims lived, they would always "go up" to worship the LORD.[17] The second verb "who may stand" (יָקוּם) adds the idea of remaining in the sanctuary.

B. Those who are pure in deeds and thoughts may enter God's holy place and receive a blessing (4–5).

Verse four provides the answer to the question in a summary statement and then gives a specific example. The impact of the summary statement would have been overwhelming because of its scope and finality: "the one who has clean hands and a pure heart" (נְקִי כַפַּיִם וּבַר־לֵבָב). "Hands" and "heart" are figures, the hands are the instruments for doing things and so refers to actions, and the heart is the localization of the will and refers to intentions and choices (the figures are metonymy of cause and a metonymy of subject respectively). In other words, to enter the presence of God and commune with him the worshipers must be perfect—there can be no sinful acts and no improper motives, choices or thoughts, and they must be "clean" in what they do (literally, innocent, free from guilt [נְקִי, s.v. Ps. 19:12]) and pure in what they think or plan (literally, clean, clear, pure [בַּר]). On the face of it this standard would have eliminated everyone from entering God's presence without some divine provision. Its purpose was to remind people of just how holy the LORD is and how they were not qualified to enter his presence without the purification ritual first.

The second half of the verse is a relative clause that provides a specific example of the kind of purity in thought and deed that was required. The line is textually and grammatically difficult; but it reads "who has not lifted up his (Hebrew: my) soul to falsehood, and has not sworn deceitfully." It is referring to a violation of the law concerning false swearing, i.e., swearing an oath to

---

17. If the psalm was indeed written by David, and if the hill refers to Jerusalem, then this event would have occurred after David moved the ark to the holy city. However, it need not refer to Jerusalem. In 1 Samuel 1:3 we read how Samuel's parents "went up" year after year to Shiloh to worship the LORD.

achieve a deceptive end.[18] The first line is cryptic: "who has not lifted up to vanity (אֲשֶׁר לֹא־נָשָׂא לַשָּׁוְא). If the word "name" is understood, then this could be saying, "who has not taken [his name] in vain"; but the clause in the Hebrew text ends with "my soul/life" (= me), which may be explained as a specific reference to the commandment. A good number of manuscripts and versions have rendered it as "his soul/life," which seems to be what is expected here. If the clause refers to taking the LORD's name in vain, then "his soul/life" (meaning "him") has been substituted for "his name."

The third colon of the verse supports this idea of taking an oath for a false or deceptive purpose: "and has not sworn deceitfully" (וְלֹא נִשְׁבַּע לְמִרְמָה [for "deceitfully," s.v. Ps. 5:7]). So one clause would be describing a person who does not take [the name of] the LORD in vain, that is, to a false purpose, and the parallel clause would be explaining further it was a person who does not swear deceitfully. One part looks at the improper use of the divine name in the oath, and the other looks at the intended deceit. This couplet, if it has been interpreted correctly, would make a fitting elaboration on the introductory summary: one who did not raise his hands in a false oath (so clean hands) and one who did not swear deceitfully (so pure hearts).

Verse six then makes a promise that those who qualify to enter the courts of the LORD will receive a blessing. The initial verb (יִשָּׂא, here translated "he will receive," but literally "lift up, bear, carry") does double duty for the line: "He shall receive a blessing from the LORD, // and righteousness from the God of his salvation." The key terms in the line are clearly "blessing" and "righteousness," what the true worshiper hopes to receive from the LORD. The word "blessing" (בְּרָכָה, s.v. Ps. 5:12) has a wide range of meanings, but all are related to the basic idea of a gift, some enrichment or bounty from the LORD, which may be physical or spiritual or both, and may also include the enablement to develop the bounty. The term as used here may refer to the High Priest's blessing (Num. 6:22–27), which would declare the spiritual benefits of grace and peace to the worshiper ("May the LORD bless you and keep you . . . "). To receive the blessing

---

18. Goldingay, *Psalm 1–41*, p. 359.

in the sanctuary would mean that all was well between the worshiper and God.

The parallel word "righteousness" (צְדָקָה, s.v. Ps. 1:5) basically means conformity to the Law, God's standard of righteousness. A simple reading might lead to the interpretation that God was here giving the worshiper righteousness, but the word has other categories of usage as well, such as vindication or victory (a usage based on the figurative use of the word, a metonymy of cause where the intended effect is put for the righteousness). The word could be left as "righteousness" in the translation, but to avoid confusion the intended meaning of "vindication" might be better. "Vindication" makes a close, explanatory parallel to the "blessing" the worshiper receives.

C. Identification: Those who would enter seek the LORD's favor (6).

This verse is difficult in a number of ways. It says literally: "This is the generation of those seeking him, seekers of your face, Jacob" (זֶה דּוֹר דֹּרְשָׁו מְבַקְשֵׁי פָנֶיךָ יַעֲקֹב). The line has a balanced meter, but is at the same time cryptic. The first colon is not too difficult: "This is the generation of seekers of him (דֹּרְשָׁו)." It is a reference to the worshipers, followed by a participle that describes them. The statement may well have been spoken by the people to identify themselves as devout worshipers, people who were seeking the LORD. The verb "seek" (דָּרַשׁ) means "to inquire, seek, investigate." It is a significant word for worshipful acts in the Bible, referring to the diligent pursuit of the LORD, sometime to find out something from the LORD (as in going to inquire of the LORD). To describe this band of worshipers as a "generation" employs a figurative use of the word (an implied comparison); a "generation" is an age, but it often describes a group that have something in common, a class of people, usually clarified by a following genitive (such as "a generation of vipers"). To use it here means that these people all have the same basic spiritual interest and need—they are seekers of the LORD.

The second colon says "seekers of your face (מְבַקְשֵׁי פָנֶיךָ), Jacob." "Seeking your face" ("face" being the objective genitive) is parallel to "seekers of him"; but the suffix "him" is now paralleled with a direct reference to God, "your face." The introduction of the word "face" clarifies the point of seeking, for the idea of seeking God's face is to seek the favor of the LORD (an anthropomorphic expression). Here again we may see an allusion to the priestly blessing: "May the LORD make his face shine upon you and be gracious unto you."

The name "Jacob" added to the line is abrupt. It would make little sense to say "this is the generation seeking your face, O Jacob." It seems more likely that "Jacob" is parallel to "generation" in the earlier part of the verse, forming a cryptic chiasm to the verse: "This is the generation / seeking him, // seeking your face / Jacob" (an ABBA pattern). The choice of the name "Jacob" to describe the people would suggest that they may have stood in need of blessing from God, as indeed Jacob did in the accounts of his pilgrimage.[19] The name "Jacob" here refers to the nation that descended from the patriarch and shared much of his nature (and so is a metonymy of cause). So then, the people were acknowledging they were seeking God's favor, for they knew they were not qualified to enter his presence on their own merits.

III. The acclamation of the LORD's mighty deeds provides encouragement to the people of God (7–10).

It appears that the last few verses record the voices of the worshipers who passed the liturgical process at the gate and were in procession into the sanctuary to praise the LORD. They call for the gates of the sanctuary to open wide enough to let in the glorious king, and then they explain who this king is. The refrain is essentially repeated in verses nine and ten.

Verse seven is a tricolon with a balanced 3 + 3 + 3 meter, with the main division coming between the second and third units:

---

19. Biblical writers frequently refer to the nation as "Jacob" when it was rebellious against God or when it was self-sufficient, and as "Israel" when it was being blessed by God (see 1 Kings 18:31, where the nation was described as Jacob, but the description was clarified with "Israel" in view of the expected revival).

"Lift up / O gates / your heads, /
  and be lifted up / doors / everlasting; //
  and will come in / the king of / glory."[20]

The psalmist addresses the gates[21] and tells them to lift up their heads.[22] Critical to the interpretation of the section is the meaning of the "gates." One possibility is that "gates" would

---

20. So within the first half of the verse there is a clear parallelism: between the first half of the verse (the first two cola) and the last, the relationship is a formal parallelism, because the meaning of the sentence continues into the last clause, which is a causal clause explaining why the gates should be lifted up.

21. The gates are described as ancient or everlasting. This has been taken as one reason why the psalm could not have been Davidic, for it seems to be saying that by the time the psalm was written the doors to the sanctuary were considered ancient. "Gates" could refer to access to the presence of the LORD which was ancient (Gen. 28:17). Dahood suggests taking it as a reference to the LORD: "gates of the Eternal One" (*Psalms,* I:153).

22. The word נָשָׂא, "lift up," is a fairly common word in the Bible (occurring approximately 655 times). It is defined as "lift, carry, take." Its meanings range for the very simple, literal meaning to more figurative uses.

    First, it basically means "to lift" or "lift up." For example, we read that the flood lifted up the ark (Gen. 7:17), or Jacob picked up his heels (i.e., walk enthusiastically; Gen. 29:1), or one lifts the hand to heaven in prayer (Deut. 32:40). In this meaning of "lift up," there are some figurative uses. It is used for "lifting the eyes," meaning look closely (Ps. 121:1), or lifting the voice, meaning speak loudly (Isa. 52:8). One may lift up the name of the LORD in vain, meaning use the name falsely (Exod. 20:7; and perhaps in the earlier part of Psalm 24). One can also lift up the soul to the LORD, meaning direct the mind and will to him (Ps. 25:1). The LORD is said to lift his hand, meaning demonstrate his power (Ps. 10:12). A person might have his head lifted up, meaning be restored to honor (Gen. 41:13), and here in Psalm 24 the call is for the gates to lift their heads.

    Second, the word can also mean "bear, carry." This could be a reference to carrying physical objects, such as bringing an offering (Ps. 96:8); but it can also be used figuratively for bearing a burden of guilt or punishment (Gen. 4:13; Lev. 10:17).

    Third, it can mean "take away, take." It can be used in a fairly literal way, such as taking someone as a wife (Ruth 1:4), or take an enumeration or sum ((Exod. 30:12); but it can also be used for destroying something, i.e., taking it away (Job 32:22). In this category we also have the use for the forgiveness of sin, i.e., the sin and the guilt is taken away, lifted off the person (Ps. 32:1).

mean the elders or people who sit in the gates.[23] This would be a metonymy of subject. This may sound strange at first, but similar idioms occur in our language: we may say that the courts have spoken, meaning those who sit in the courts have decided an issue. The idea would then be that the leaders of the city, the elders who sit in the gates and the people who buy and sell in the adjacent plazas, were worried about the battle almost to the point of depression. Now that the triumphal march was beginning, the word to them was to lift their heads, meaning lift their spirits (so a metonymy of adjunct for the verb) because the glorious king was about to enter.

In line with this idea there may be another allusion here to Canaanite beliefs. In the Ugaritic texts there is a similar sounding poem about Baal and Anath his consort.[24] In this excerpt the emissaries from *Yam* (Sea) and *Nahar* (River) come to seize the god Baal:

Now the gods were sitting down to eat,
the holy ones to dine,
Baal attending on El.
As soon as they see them,
see the messengers of Yamm,
the envoys of Judge Nahar,

There are some related nouns that go with this verb. The most frequently used are: נָשִׂיא is a chief prince (one who is lifted up); מַשָּׂא is either a load, burden or tribute, or a heavy utterance, a burden on the prophet's heart; and מַשְׂאֵת is an uprising, or a burden, or an important offering or tribute.

23. From the earliest periods "gates" became a large complex of gates with rooms on either side of the entrance between the gates. These rooms could be used for stalls for animals, for storage, or for places where the elders would sit to make decisions. The entrance way opened to a plaza, and that is where the business of the town would be conducted. Boaz acknowledged that the whole "gate" of his people knew that Ruth was a virtuous woman, meaning, the people in the gate (Ruth 3:11).

24. See J. Pritchard, *ANET*, Text III AB B, lines 23–30. The precise meaning of the text is open to a number of possibilities, but the point here is simply that a similar idiom is used to encourage people who are discouraged. The connection would be less interesting if it were not for the use of "sea" and "river" at the beginning of the psalm.

The gods drop their heads
   down to their knees
      and on the thrones of their princeship.
Baal rebukes them:
   Why, O gods, have you dropped
      your heads down upon your knees
      and on your thrones of your princeship?
   I see the gods are cowed
      with terror of the messengers of Yamm,
      at the envoys of Judge Nahar.
   Lift up, O gods, your heads,
      from upon your knees,
      from upon the thrones of your princeship.[25]

While this may be a coincidence in expressions used in the languages, it seems that there is more going on than that. The psalm started out with a deliberate use of "sea" (יָם) and "river" (נָהָר). Now in the celebration of victory over the enemies, the psalmist could be using a section of Canaanite phrases expressing their victory of these cosmic forces or deities, the phrases calling for the people in the gates (not gods, but leaders) not to look down in fear or concern, but to look up because the enemy is no match for God. If this is true, the psalmist would be turning the lines around against the Canaanites. He would be taking lines they used at their victory celebrations to speak of Israel's victory over them. It is Yahweh who is mighty in battle, not the Canaanites, and certainly not a god Baal. And Yahweh is mighty in battle not because he defeated Yamm and Nahar—those are just part of nature that God created—but because he defeated the Canaanites and everything they believed. If the Canaanites are defeated, their gods are defeated.

That is one view. A second view is that the gates are actually being addressed by the pilgrim singers, and they are the gates leading to the sanctuary. In this case the figure of speech would be personification, calling gates to raise their tops (see other

---

25. The epic goes on to describe a battle in which Baal defeats Yamm and sends him to his sphere, the sea, and himself to his eternal kingdom, symbolized by his house on the top of his mountain.

samples of such personification: Isa. 14:31; Zech. 9:9) . It would be like saying "make way"—the king of glory should not have to stoop low to go under an archway to enter the sanctuary. The doors should be thrown open wide and their tops lifted away for the LORD. Psalm 118 also focuses on these "gates (of righteousness)" through which the worshipers would pass.

The second view may very well be the primary intention of the writer, but he says it is such an unusual way that he is also probably alluding to the Canaanite mythology. The connections are too close to say it is a mere coincidence.

Who, then, will enter the sanctuary? The king of glory, mighty in battle, Yahweh of armies.[26] All of these are royal military descriptions of the LORD, the God of Israel. The LORD was already dwelling in his sanctuary, and they were entering into his presence. The description of the LORD as the king of glory may suggest that the procession was bringing the ark of the covenant through the gates and to the sanctuary. The use of the word "glory" is occasionally connected to the ark of the covenant, as in the story in 1 Samuel 4 where the Israelites lost the ark to the Philistines, and a child was named "Ichabod" ("inglorious") to signify that the glory, that is, the presence of the LORD represented by the ark, had departed (v. 21; for "glory," s.v. Ps. 19:1).

---

26. The traditional translation of יְהוָה צְבָאֹת is "LORD of hosts," but more specifically it is "Yahweh of armies." The title designates the LORD as the powerful God, as a warrior; the armies that are at his disposal are all the heavenly and earthly hosts, both Israelite forces and those of the nations. The title probably is using "armies" as a genitive of the thing possessed: the LORD possesses the armies.

Usually earthly armies are in mind when the expression is used, for God uses nations to curb or punish other nations. The usage of the title shows that God is sovereign over all nations and is not just Israel's national deity. The LORD can summon Egypt, or raise up the Babylonians, or any other power to do his will. Each usage needs to be studied to determine what armies are meant.

When prophets use the title in delivering a warning to the people, it emphasizes the fact that something has gone terribly wrong, and God with all military forces at his disposal, will deal with it.

The title has a positive significance when Israel celebrates a victory over their enemies in which the LORD of hosts has fought for them. That is the meaning in Psalm 24.

The picture here has all the elements to make a reference to the ark of the covenant being carried back from battle in a procession to the sanctuary. This glorious king (taking "glory" as an attributive genitive) represented by the ark of the covenant was none other than the LORD. He is also described here as "LORD of armies" and "strong (עִזּוּז, s.v. Ps. 29:1) and mighty (גִּבּוֹר, s.v. Ps. 45:3)," "mighty in battle." The repetition of these motifs underscores the idea that the LORD has just shown himself mighty in battle and now returns to his holy hill. Of course they did not have God in a box at the battle; they had the ark that represented their faith that the LORD was with them. Now the people in the procession, probably the victorious armies, came to praise the LORD for the victory.

MESSAGE AND APPLICATION

The expository idea that best expresses the message of the psalm would be something like this: *Those who assemble to praise the sovereign LORD of creation for his mighty and glorious acts of deliverance must be pure in thought and deed (if they are to find God's favor and vindication).* The wording of this statement puts the emphasis on the need for qualification for worship in those who assemble in the sanctuary—even if they had just had a tremendous deliverance by divine intervention! Whenever there is a great deliverance, an answer to prayer, a mighty work, a salvation of any kind, the natural and fitting thing to do is to go with the congregation and offer praise to the LORD. That praise must exalt the LORD as the creator of the world, the possessor of everything, the glorious king, the mighty and powerful conqueror. His victories at times involved actual warfare, and at other times they did not, but always his mighty acts are designed to liberate the world from evil and evil forces.

The psalmist is also saying that first the worshipers have to make sure they are in the proper spiritual condition to do that. It would not be difficult to correlate other passages with the main ideas of this psalm. There are many New Testament passages that praise God for creation, for salvation, or for spiritual victory over the world. The New Testament also reiterates that there are spiritual prerequisites for entering God's presence in worship, any worship, any time. Praise may be given to God, but with holy hands. Worship on earth is a prelude to worship in glory, and the Book of Revelation reminds us that in the final analysis nothing unclean may enter into his presence. Everything must be sanctified and purified, certainly to gain entrance into the heavenly sanctuary, but also here as well for our prayers and praises to be heard. God does not need, neither does he want, praise from disobedient people. There is a standard of holiness for fellowship with the Lord, and the standard is so high that we must acknowledge that the only way we may find acceptance by God is through his gracious provision of atonement. We too come as "Jacob" in need of and seeking divine favor, and he gives it freely, sanctifying us for his presence so that we might praise him with clean hands and a pure heart.

PSALM 25

The Way of the LORD— Forgiveness, Deliverance, and Guidance

INTRODUCTION

Text and Textual Variants

Of David.

א 1 Unto you, O LORD, I lift up my soul; O my God
ב 2 in you I trust,
      do not let me be put to shame;
      do not let my enemies triumph[1] over me.
ג 3 Indeed, none who hope in you shall be put to shame,
      but those who are treacherous[2] without a cause[3]
         will be put to shame.

ד 4 Make me know your ways, O LORD;
      teach me your paths.[4]
ה 5 Lead me in your truth and teach me,
      for you are the God of my salvation,

---

1. The verb עָלַץ followed by the preposition is unusual. The Greek has "laugh me to scorn," καταγελασάτωσάν μου
2. הַבּוֹגְדִים, "those who are treacherous (without a cause)"; the Greek has "who are lawless without a cause (οἱ ἀνομοῦντες διὰ κενῆς)." The treachery can be against God (Ps. 78:57; Jer. 3:20) or against people (Judg. 9:23; Mal. 2:14). In the prophets they are plunderers and oppressors (Isa. 21:2; 24:16; Hab. 1:13).
3. "Without a cause" is רֵיקָם, emptily, or vainly.
4. The Greek version begins the second colon with "*and* your pathways."

591

in you I hope all day long.[5]

ז   **6** Remember your tender mercies, O LORD, and your loyal love,
    for they are from eternity.

ח   **7** Remember not the sins of my youth and my transgressions;[6]
    according to your loyal love, remember me
      for your goodness sake, O LORD.

ט   **8** Good and upright is the LORD;
    therefore he instructs sinners in the way.

י   **9** He leads the afflicted in justice
    and teaches the afflicted his way.

כ **10** All the paths of the LORD are loyal love and truth
    for those who keep his covenant and his statutes.[7]

ל **11** For your name's sake, O LORD,
    forgive[8] my iniquity, for it is great.

מ **12** What man[9] is he who fears the LORD?
    To him he shows the way he should choose.

נ **13** He himself[10] will dwell in prosperity,
    and his descendants will inherit *the* land.

ס **14** The secret counsel[11] of the LORD is for those who fear him,
    and his covenant he makes known to them.

---

5. Some manuscripts have וְאוֹתְךָ instead of MT's אוֹתְךָ supplying a וְ to make the acrostic complete. This is supported by the versions as well.

6. Greek has "ignorance" (ἀγνοίας).

7. NIV takes these words as a hendiadys: "the demands of his covenant."

8. The form in the text is the perfect tense with a strong waw, וְסָלַחְתָּ; it is unusual in that there is no imperative preceding it, but the context requires that it be equal to imperfect of instruction or imperative (Perowne, *Psalms*, I:261; similarly, Ruth 3:3). Greek has "you will expiate," ἱλάσῃ.

9. Hebrew has "Who is this the man," which is rendered by NIV as "Who then is the man."

10. This translation captures the emphasis of נַפְשׁוֹ in the line (cf. Briggs, *Psalms*, p. 224).

11. The word translated "secret counsel" is סוֹד, "council, counsel." BDB (p. 691) explains it here as an intimacy with the LORD (cf. Prov. 3:32). The Greek has "strength," κραταίωμα, as if יְסוֹד.

ע 15 My eyes are ever on the LORD,
    for he will release my feet from the snare.

פ 16 Turn unto me and be gracious to me,
    for I am alone[12] and afflicted.

צ 17 The troubles of my heart have multiplied;[13]
    bring me forth out of my distresses.

ר 18 Look[14] upon my affliction and my trouble
    and take away all my sins.

ר 19 Look upon my enemies, for they have increased,
    and they hate me with cruel[15] hatred.

ש 20 O guard my life and deliver me;
    let me not be put to shame for I take refuge in you.

ת 21 Let integrity and uprightness protect me,[16]
    for I hope in you.

פ 22 Redeem Israel, O God
    from all its troubles.

Composition and Context

This psalm is essentially a lament; it is filled with complaints, petitions and expressions of trust. The psalmist prays for the LORD to show favor by removing his sins and afflictions so that his enemies might be put to shame instead of him. The way the

---

12. Hebrew יָחִיד is "alone, solitary, only"; it is used elsewhere to describe an only possession or an only child. Hence, Greek has "I am only a child" (μονογενής).

13. The perfect tense הִרְחִיבוּ would be translated as "Troubles have enlarged my heart" perhaps meaning they made room for themselves (Ps. 119:32). The Greek has "afflictions are magnified" (ἐπλατύνθησαν). Many suggest emending the text to read the form as the imperative הַרְחֵיב, "set at liberty." The final ו then would become a conjunction on the next word. This change makes a better parallelism and takes away the ambiguity of the verb. Goldingay notes that if the perfect tense were taken as a precative use it would have the same result (*Psalms 1–41*, p. 376). So there would be no need to emend the text.

14. For the acrostic a letter ק is needed. Some suggest emending רְאֵה to something like קְשֹׁב.

15. The word חָמָס is rendered in the Greek as "unjust," ἄδικον.

16. "The harmless and upright join themselves to me" is the Greek (ἄκακοι καὶ εὐθεῖς ἐκολλῶντό μοι).

psalm is written makes it very difficult to find a structure; the repetition of themes throughout the passage hints at the pattern. The repeated ideas are: being ashamed or being put to shame, verses 2, 3, 5, 20, 21; affliction, verses 9, 16, and 18; forgiveness for sin, in verses 7, 11, and 18; and instruction, verses 4, 5, 8, 9, 12, and 14. VanGemeren allows that the psalm could be David's and would fit the time of adversities after his great sin. He does, however, note that there are difficulties with this setting, such as the fact that the psalmist's prayer for forgiveness includes the sin of his youth.[17] Others observe that the ideas in the psalm are very general, making it hard to assign it to a particular occasion. A. A. Anderson suggests it was post-exilic because of the subject matter and the acrostic arrangement.[18] Goldingay concludes that while it is uncertain when it was written it is easy to see how it would have been used in the second temple community,[19] but that would be the case of all the psalms.

The psalm is an acrostic psalm; it follows a structured alphabetic form. This contributes to the difficulty of tracing a structure or clear organization based on any progress of thought.[20] It has lament, but there is no specific lament section. It also has confidence, wisdom, and instruction. While it may be called a lament, it is also a didactic psalm (see Pss. 37, 111, 112, 119, 145); its theme is that God is a teacher of the afflicted and a guide for the erring. Kraus suggests the psalm is an artistically elaborated form of a prayer that combines prayer formulas and wisdom motifs.

The acrostic is not perfectly followed. Verse 2 begins with an א and not a ב, and so many commentators suggest starting the second line with "in you" (בְּךָ) as the Greek version does. There is no letter ו in the sequence, which prompted the addition of a conjunction at the beginning of verse 5c to provide it. The letter ר is repeated in verses 18 and 19, whereas verse 18 should start with ק; some would emend the text to obtain the sequence. The

---

17. VanGemeren, *Psalms*, pp. 263–4. Psalm 51, however, does include in the confession of sin the acknowledgment that the penitent has been in the state of sin since his birth.
18. *Psalms 1–72*, pp. 206–7.
19. *Psalms 1–41*, p. 368.
20. Kraus, *Psalms 1–59*, p. 319.

final verse of the psalm stands outside the arrangement with letter פ. Interestingly, the last verse of both psalms 26 and 34 begins with פָּדָה, which might indicate the two were written by the same author, or at least that one influenced the other. The verse serves as a general collect.

Still, on the whole the psalm should be taken as a lament, but one that is unconventional. It is a plea to be delivered from hateful enemies, to be forgiven for sins, and to be given instruction for the right way to live. None of these motifs are out of place in the life of David. The psalmist apparently is surrounded by numerous malicious enemies, and so he refers to himself as afflicted. He needs deliverance. He knows he is guilty of sin (v. 8) and so prays for forgiveness (vv. 7, 11). He also needs guidance as well and so prays for the LORD to teach him the right way. The prevailing ideas in the psalm are that God is the teacher of the afflicted and the guide to the erring.[21]

The psalm can be divided into two parts: prayer, and then a repeat of the prayer with confident assertions about God.

Exegetical Analysis

Summary

The psalmist confidently turns to the LORD for deliverance and preservation from his enemies, for divine instruction on the right way to live, and for forgiveness on the basis of the LORD's tender, compassionate mercies to Israel.

Outline

I. The psalmist in confidence prays to the LORD for deliverance, guidance, and forgiveness for the sins of his youth (1–7).

    A. He is confident to pray to the LORD for deliverance from his enemies (1–3).

        1. He lifts up his soul to the LORD (1).

---

21. Perowne, *Psalms*, I:258.

2. He does not want to be defeated by enemies because he trusts (2).
3. He is confident that none who wait on the LORD will be put to shame (3).

B. He prays for divine instruction in the truth that will lead him in God's ways (4–5).
   1. He desires to know the ways of the LORD (4).
   2. He waits on the God of his salvation to learn his truth (5).

C. He prays for forgiveness for the sins of his youth on the basis of the loyal love and mercy of God (6–7).

II. The psalmist reiterates his prayer to the LORD for instruction in the true way, pardon for his sins and Israel's sins, and deliverance and preservation from enemies (8–22).

A. He prays for instruction in the true way and pardon for sin as well (8–11).
   1. Out of his goodness the LORD teaches sinners the way (8).
   2. The LORD teaches the afflicted his way (in justice) (9).
   3. The LORD's ways are true and loving to those who keep covenant (10).
   4. Therefore, for the LORD's name's sake he prays for pardon (11).

B. The one who fears God will be blessed with an inheritance and knowledge of God's plans (12–14).
   1. The LORD teaches the God-fearer the way to choose (12).
   2. He one who fears the LORD will inherit the land (13).
   3. The LORD reveals his covenant to those who fear him (14).

C. He prays for gracious deliverance and preservation from all his troubles and sins (15–21).
   1. He faithfully follows the LORD and expects to be rescued (15).
   2. He calls on God to be gracious to him and deliver him from his troubles and forgive his sins (16–18).
   3. He asks for deliverance and preservation from his cruel enemies (19–21).

D. He prays for the redemption of Israel from all its troubles (22).

COMMENTARY IN EXPOSITORY FORM

I. Believers regularly pray for deliverance, guidance, and forgiveness (1–7).

A. They pray for deliverance from enemies (1–3).

The prayers that are arranged in this psalm no doubt came out of the psalmist's personal experience, but they are typical of the prayers of believers of all ages. People must pray, and indeed do pray throughout their lives for protection, guidance, and forgiveness.

The psalmist begins by affirming his dependence on the LORD: "Unto you, O LORD, I lift (s.v. Ps. 24:7) my soul." The word order beginning with "unto you (אֵלֶיךָ) is emphatic and not merely stylistic, for the verb also begins with an א and could have been placed first. The idea of lifting himself up to the LORD signifies his focusing on God by faith. The second verse affirms his trust; it too places "my God" (אֱלֹהַי) first in the sentence for emphasis: "My God, in you I trust (בָּטַחְתִּי, s.v. Ps. 4:5).[22] Then, having affirmed his faith, the psalmist makes his first petition. It is in two parts: that he not be put to shame and that his enemies not triumph over him. The first request is "do not let me be put to shame" (here the cohortative, אַל־אֵבוֹשָׁה). The verb "be ashamed" (בּוֹשׁ; s.v. Ps. 31:1) actually means to be destroyed or ruined, the idea of being put to shame referring to the resultant circumstances. The second appeal is part of this request: "do not let my enemies triumph over me." The main prayer is for God to deliver from enemies; and if he does not do so, then they will triumph and the psalmist will be put to shame.

His petition is balanced by his confidence that the treacherous will be put to shame and not the faithful (v. 3). The faithful

---

22. In the arrangement of the line "my God" is placed at the end of the first line so that "in you" can start the second line with a ב.

are "all who hope in you" (כָּל־קֹוֶיךָ). "Hope" is a word for faith that stresses waiting for or longing for the results, but the waiting is with confident expectation.[23] Here the psalmist is confident that those who hope in the LORD will not be put to shame. The verbal form (יֵבֹשׁוּ with the negative לֹא now) is an expression of his own conviction and not a prayer. And the introductory "indeed" (גַּם, "also, moreover") focuses the reader's attention on the assertion. The faithful will not be destroyed, but "those who are treacherous without a cause" will. This participle (הַבּוֹגְדִים from the verb בָּגַד; s.v. Ps. 78:57) describes enemies as deceitful, i.e., traitors or treacherous people (see Judg. 9:23; Jer. 3:20); and their treachery is "without excuse" (רֵיקָם, literally "emptily, vainly"). Kirkpatrick suggests the word "treacherous" refers to their faithless desertion of God, which is the opposite of patiently waiting on him[24] The psalmist was obviously speaking from his immediate experience because these people were on the verge of triumphing over him, but his prayer not to be put to shame was a confident prayer because he knew how God honors those who hope in him.

B. They pray for guidance from the LORD (4–5).

These next two verses return to petition, but now it is a petition for guidance and not protection. In verse 4 the two imperatives, "cause me to know" (the *hiphil of* יָדַע) and "teach me"

---

23. The verb is קָוָה, "to hope, wait for." It has a related noun "hope," תִּקְוָה. The word is similar in meaning to יָחַל and is often found in parallelism with it. The two words are often hard to distinguish in their meanings. The word קָוָה means "wait for," but it seems to capture something of the tension of waiting. In all the Semitic languages the word and its related forms have meanings that suggest some tension, such as twisting in knots. In fact, the word קַו is "rope, cord" or measuring "line." The positive uses of the verb "hope, wait for" simply emphasize the idea of eagerly waiting for something, hoping for it. But the waiting is an active idea—waiting on the LORD means preparing for the LORD's intervention. When the word is used in passages that do not focus on God, the hope is expressed in negative terms, that is disappointed or lost hope; but when God is the focus of the hope, then confidence is expressed by it. Without exception, hope in God is expressed positively. In fact, the history of the faith is the history of a people whose hope is in the LORD.

24. *Psalms*, p. 133.

(the *piel of* לָמַד), make the petition urgent and direct. What he desires to learn are the ways and the paths of God, that is, the proper conduct of life that would harmonize with the will of God. He would learn this primarily through the word of the LORD. In addition he desires to be led in God's truth (s.v. Ps. 15:2). The verb "lead" is the imperative form built off the noun "way, walk" (literally הַדְרִיכֵנִי is "cause me to walk"). The idiom of walking in the truth means living by it. There are two reasons for this appeal. First, the truth of God is the way to live since God is a saving God. The causal clause refers to God as the "God of my salvation," using objective genitives, meaning "God saves me." This salvation may have come through human agencies for the most part (for "salvation," s.v. Ps. 3:2), but possibly through some divine intervention as well. The second reason for his prayer is his faith, the repetition of the verb in verse 3: "in you I hope all day long." He constantly hopes in the LORD, and the LORD has proven to be his saving God; therefore, he prays to be instructed and led in the right way.

C.They pray for forgiveness from God (6–7).

The psalmist, like all believers, prays for forgiveness. In verse 6 he asks God to remember; in verse 7 he asks God not to remember. The significance of the word has more to do with acting on what is remembered than mere recollection (s.v. Ps. 6:5). In verse 6 he wants God to act in accordance with his "tender mercies" (רַחֲמֶיךָ), the tender compassion that God has for his own,[25] and his acts of "loyal love" (חֲסָדֶיךָ, s.v. Ps. 23:6). Both words are in the plural because the compassion and love of God

---

25. The word is related to a verb רָחַם meaning "to love, have compassion." It carries the emphasis of tender feelings for that which is helpless or dependent. The dictionaries classify the verb as a denominative verb, and so the noun רֶחֶם or רַחַם, "womb," is related more specifically. The verb "have compassion" may have in the meaning the maternal instincts of a mother for the child from her womb. Related is the word רַחֲמִים which is "compassion"; it also has the sense of "brotherly love," the feeling one has for someone from the same womb. The verb and its related nouns are used with both God and humans as subjects, but most occurrences are in reference to the compassion and mercy of God.

are demonstrated in acts. Both of these attributes of God are eternal, literally, "they are from everlasting." The word "eternity" (עוֹלָם; s.v. Ps. 61:5) has to be defined by its context, just as "ever" and "never" would in English. The word means perpetuity, a long time, endless, eternal. Since these attributes describe God they could be said to be eternal; but if they are taken to refer to acts of compassion and love, the word could mean "from old," or as far back as God has been acting in human affairs.

The psalmist also wants forgiveness, and he expresses this with the negated verb: "do not remember" (the jussive). He does not want God to act on his sins, and these sins he describes as the "sins of my youth and my rebellious acts."[26] His concern is that sins of the past (see Job 13:26) remain buried, and his acts of

---

One category of meaning concerns the "deep feelings" of familial love. Isaiah asks if a woman can have no compassion for the son of her womb (49:15). The emphasis in the passage is on the intensity and spontaneity of feeling, pointing to the mother's desire to protect and care for her child,but the word is also used of a father's compassion (Ps. 103:13). Significantly, in both passages God's compassion for his people is viewed as greater. The intensity of the emotion can be seen in Genesis 43:30 when Joseph saw his brother and was so stirred with compassion he had to run from the room.

Another category is for "kind treatment." The focus of this group of uses is more on the dealings with unfortunate people that result from compassion. It can be used negatively, such as referring to the Medes who will not have compassion on children (Isa. 13:17–18). Or it can be positive, as when God granted Daniel favor and compassion in the sight of the leaders—he was treated well (Dan. 1:9).

A third category of meaning is "moving compassion." This is more heightened than "kind treatment." Pardon, forgiveness, and restoration are often associated with God's "tender mercies" (Ezek. 39:25; Isa. 60:10; Jer. 33:26). God's forgiveness is often based on his compassionate character, as Micah 7:18–19 shows. Psalm 51 bases the appeal for forgiveness on God's tender compassion (Ps. 51:1). When God refuses to show compassion, then judgment falls because of sin, as the prophetic message of Hosea's daughter shows (Lo Ruhamah, "not cared for" in Hos.1:6); but this would be changed with the restoration (and the name would be Ruhamah, "cared for").

The word "compassion" became a common attribute for God in the creedal lists of attributes.

26. For "sin," חַטָּאת, s.v. Ps. 51:2; for "rebellious act, transgression," פֶּשַׁע, s.v. Ps. 51:1. "Sin" means missing the mark, coming short, failing to measure up. Goldingay says that what is in view here first is his shortcomings or

---

rebellion be forgotten, forgiven. In this petition as well he prays for God to act on "loyal love" ("remember me according to your loyal love") and "for the sake of your goodness" (s.v. Ps. 34:8). The goodness of God will preserve and provide for his well-being.

II. Because they are confident in God's guidance, believers continue to pray for pardon for their sins and the sins of others and for deliverance and preservation from their enemies (8–22).

A. They pray for forgiveness because God teaches the way (8–11).

In the next four verses the psalmist will continue the petition for forgiveness. He begins by appealing to God's attributes, good and upright. God is good and upright in that he shows sinners the way—exactly what he had prayed that God would do. Now he uses a different word for "teach," a word that means to point in the right direction (יוֹרֶה, the *hiphil* imperfect *of* יָרָה, related to the word for "instruction, law," תּוֹרָה, s.v. Ps. 1:2). If God is good and upright, then the way that he teaches sinners to follow will be the same. The way also is a way of deliverance, for in verse 9 the psalmist affirms[27] that he leads (as in v. 5) the afflicted (עֲנָוִים, s.v. Ps. 9:12) in justice and teaches (as in v. 4) them his way. "Justice" is the word "judgment" or "decision" (מִשְׁפָּט, s.v. Ps. 9:4); it would include here the ideas of a right decision, justice, or vindication.

According to verse 10 all the ways of the LORD are "loyal love and truth," perhaps a hendiadys meaning "faithful covenant love" (s.v. Ps. 23:6). God is faithful to his covenant promises; his people can rely on him for protection, provision, and vindication. The emphasis, though, is that he is faithful to those who keep his statutes, the implication being that those who believe in him need to remain loyal to the covenant. The thought of God's requirements

---

failures when he was young and did not know better, and second his rebellious acts when as an adult he did (*Psalms 1–41*, p. 371).

27. The first verb is a jussive form, and so the verbs in this verse could be a prayer: "May he lead . . . teach."

prompts the psalmist to pray for forgiveness and guidance (v. 11): "For your name's sake," meaning in accordance with your reputation as a faithful, compassion and good God, "forgive my iniquity for it is great" ("iniquity" means going astray; for עָוֹן, s.v. Ps. 32:5). And whatever his iniquity was, it was great. It may have been the reason for the imminent danger of the enemies triumphing over him, and so as part of the prayer that he not be put to shame is this prayer for pardon. The verb translated "forgive" (סָלַח) is well-known from the cultic laws of Leviticus 4. It is used in Psalm 130:4 for the great affirmation of the faith, without which truth nothing else would matter: "for with you there is forgiveness of sin, in order that you might be feared." The word means "pardon, forgive";[28] and if God forgives, then the sin will never be remembered again, not in this life or the life to come.

B. Those who fear the LORD will be blessed with inheritance and knowledge (12–14).

The next three verses shift to confident expectation. The text focuses on any person who fears the LORD ("Whoever is he that fears"; for "fear," s.v. Ps. 2:11). The LORD teaches the devout, obedient worshiper his ways (v. 12). Here we have the same verb used in verse 8, but a new idea is added with the next verb, "he chooses" (יִבְחָר). It is likely that it refers to the way, i.e., the LORD shows him the way that he should choose (the imperfect may be an obligatory imperfect), i.e., the best way.

Moreover, the LORD prospers those who fear him (v. 13). They "will dwell in prosperity" (literally "in good," בְּטוֹב; s.v. Ps. 34:8), the idea of good including anything that promotes, enhances, and enriches life. The verb "dwell" means "lodge, spend the night"; it signifies that he will spend his time in what is good. This goodness will extend to the next generation that will inherit the land (cf. Exod. 20:12; Lev. 26:3; Deut. 4:1). The people who trust and obey the LORD will be blessed in their lives and will find perpetual enjoyment of the good things from God.

Not only will the LORD teach his people and bless them, he

---

28. In modern Hebrew the word is used with the same basic meaning in the expression for "excuse me" or "pardon me" (סְלִיחָה).

will also make known to them his counsel. The psalmist earlier prayed for God to make known his ways (v. 4); now he affirms that the LORD reveals secret things about the covenant to the devout. The word translated "secret counsel" (סוֹד) indicates that there is close, intimate communion between God and his people; he reveals his heart as well as his will to them (see, e.g., Gen. 18:17 where the LORD will not hide from Abraham what he was about to do; see also Prov. 3:22; Ps. 55:14, 15).

C. They pray for deliverance and protection (15–21).

Like all believers who pray for help, the psalmist first affirms that he is a faithful follower of the LORD: "My eyes are ever on the LORD" (this is comparable to "Unto you, O LORD, I lift up my soul" of verse 1). By "eyes" he means his spiritual focus and commitment, as the eyes of a servant would be to a master, waiting for any instruction (cf. Ps. 123:2). Here he is looking for deliverance. It is the attitude of expectant prayer—expecting God to "release" (literally "bring out," יוֹצִיא) his feet from the snare (an implied comparison), meaning the entanglements and perplexities of life, whether due to his own faults or to the enemies alone.[29]

The prayer is more urgent in verse 16. "Turn and be gracious" may form a hendiadys, for a prayer for God to "turn" would mean to look favorably (the opposite of hiding his face) and therefore heighten the verb "be gracious" (s.v., Ps. 4:1). The reason he needs God's favorable response is because he is alone, without a friend or helper for this crisis, and afflicted. He therefore identifies with the afflicted mentioned in verse 9; and the confidence expressed there that God shows the afflicted the way of vindication becomes an implied petition here. Verses 17–19 continue with this prayer for deliverance. The verb "he will release" in verse 15 is now the petition in verse 17, "release me" or "bring me out" (הוֹצִיאֵנִי). His troubles have multiplied, and so he is desperate for God to deliver him from his distresses (מְצוּקוֹת). And then in verses 18 and 19 he appeals for God to look (רְאֵה), first on his afflictions (v. 18) and then on his enemies (v. 19). Calling on God to look means he wants God to intervene ("look"

---

29. Kirkpatrick, *Psalms*, p. 135.

is frequently used in laments in conjunction with a verb like "save"; e.g., Ps.142:4–7). Here he wants God to look on his serious afflictions and forgive his sins. His affliction is a result of his sin, but if God would look on his afflictions he would see how severe they are and have compassion on him (see Ps. 6:1). He also wants God to take away the cause of his problems, the enemies who hate him with a cruel hatred. The description of them is strengthened by a cognate accusative: they hate me with a hatred, and the cognate accusative is qualified by "cruel"—"with a cruel hatred they hate me." If God looks on them, he will see that their animosity has grown far out of proportion; then God will then put them to shame (v. 3).

His prayer is both for protection (שָׁמְרָה, s.v. Ps. 12:7) and deliverance (הַצִּילֵנִי, s.v. Ps. 22:20); it continues the refrain introduced at the beginning of the psalm: "do not put me to shame." His appeal is based on his faith, but now expressed with the verb "I take refuge" (חָסִיתִי, s.v. Ps. 7:1) because he was in need of safety and security.

His prayer includes being protected by integrity (תֹּם; s.v. Ps. 7:8) and uprightness (יֹשֶׁר; s.v. Ps. 67:4), for he hopes in the LORD (קִוִּיתִיךָ). Some take these qualities to be descriptions of the LORD.[30] Others suggest they refer to messengers who have been sent to deliver the afflicted people.[31] It may be that these qualities refer to the psalmist himself; he comes before God praying that integrity and uprightness will protect him.[32] His appeal is that the guilt depart, and in its stead the powers of a new life should enter.[33] If they are the psalmist's qualities, they would still have been taught by God.

D. They pray for complete redemption (22).

The last verse, which is not part of the acrostic sequence (and may be a liturgical addition), is a prayer for complete and ultimate redemption: "Redeem Israel O God, from all its troubles."

---

30. See A. A. Anderson, *Psalms 1–72*, p. 213.
31. See Briggs, *Psalms*, p. 226.
32. See VanGemeren, *Psalms*, p. 271.
33. Kraus, *Psalms 1–59,* p. 322.

The prayer summarizes the concern of the psalmist in his immediate dilemma, but it is a prayer that is timeless as the whole world waits for the day of redemption (Rom. 8:19–22). The verb "redeem" (פָּדָה) means "set free."[34]

MESSAGE AND APPLICATION

The exposition of a psalm like this could take any number of directions: it has emphases on the threat of being destroyed by wicked enemies, confession of youthful sins and rebellious acts,

---

34. פָּדָה is the other major word for "redeem" (compare גָּאַל, s.v. Ps 19:14). The dictionaries define this word as "ransom" or "redeem." It can be used where a price is paid or where the ransom is from violence or death, primarily with God as the subject. There are related nouns: פְּדוּת is a "ransom" (Exod. 8:19, but it seems to mean a distinction or separation), and פִּדְיוֹם, "ransom, ransom money" (Num. 3:49, 51).

One category of meanings concerns "setting free by payment." For example, in Numbers 18:15–16 every firstborn was to be ransomed from God's service by a payment. In Leviticus 27:27 it is used for buying back what had been vowed. Psalm 49:8 uses the word in the same sense, stating that no one could pay a price and ransom himself from death.

The rest of the uses can be listed under the second category, the general meaning of "setting free, redeeming." In these passages there is no mention of paying a price. Rather, the emphasis is on setting free. First, it is used for the redemption of Israel, especially from the bondage of Egypt (Deut. 7:8; 15:15; 24:18). There was no payment of money. It was accomplished by the power of God. Because God redeemed Israel in the past (cf. Micah 6:43), Isaiah says he will redeem Israel in the future (Isa. 35:10). Second, it is used of redemption from iniquity. Although this is not a major use, it does occur. Psalm 130:7 affirms that God will redeem Israel from all its iniquities. Third, it is used for redemption from death and distress. The verb is used in contexts that speak of setting people free from distress, trouble, destruction and death (Pss. 26:11; 44:26; 69:20); this is the meaning here in Psalm 25, for it is a prayer for God to set Israel free from all its troubles.

In one passage the word is used for people redeeming another person: Saul was going to kill Jonathan, but the people rescued him (1 Sam. 14:45).

The word, then, is a general word for "redeem." It refers to the act of freeing or liberating another person from any trouble of danger, and especially from bondage. Primarily, God is the redeemer, which according to this word means that he sets people free from their sins and the consequences of their sins.

the need to learn God's ways to live in this world, and the anticipation of being set free from all trouble and enjoying the good things from God. In the middle of the concern over the trouble, what comes to the fore in the psalm is the persistent thought of God as the teacher of the afflicted and redeemer of the erring. In a way, the psalm looks at the personal effects of adversity on the people of God.[35] As the afflicted cry out to the LORD for deliverance, they are made aware of their need for guidance in the ways of God, and the awareness of his ways makes them aware of the failures of their own ways.[36] The way of the LORD has been fully revealed in his word, and now with the New Testament we have an even clearer understanding of God's ways.

These ideas may be pulled together in an expository statement that will give unity and direction to the exposition; one way to say it would be: *When the people of God are threatened by cruel enemies, they must (or can) pray for deliverance from their troubles along with forgiveness for sins and guidance in the way of the LORD as they try to live in a treacherous world.* Many believers live in very peaceful and quiet settings and therefore might have a hard time identifying with the kind of crisis in a psalm like this; but believers down through history, and even now all over the world, face cruel and treacherous enemies. The antagonism to believers is always there in some subtle way, waiting for the opportunity to lash out at believers, the faith, or the Word of God; so the application to pray for deliverance, to confess sins, and to follow the way of the LORD is never irrelevant. Peter reminds the faithful that they are called on to suffer for the faith, and when that happens they should not be ashamed (1 Pet. 5:16) because such experiences follow in the way of Christ's suffering. Paul in his farewell address to the Ephesians warned of the treachery of opposition to the truth that would come, even through some people they trusted; in preparation for it they needed to focus on the word of God's grace that they would be built up in the faith, knowing that God has prepared a glorious inheritance for those who are sanctified by his word (Acts 20:29–30).

---

35. VanGemeren, *Psalms*, p. 263.
36. Stanley L. Jaki, *Praying the Psalms,* p. 72.

PSALM 26

Separation from Sinners

INTRODUCTION

Text and Textual Variants

Of David.

1 Vindicate me, O LORD, because I walk in my integrity
   and trust in the LORD without wavering.[1]
2 Examine me, O LORD, and put me to the test.
   Indeed, purify[2] my mind and my heart.

3 For your loyal love is always before my eyes;
   and I walk about in your truth.[3]
4 I do not sit with men[4] of falsehood;
   and I do not go in with dissemblers.
5 I hate the gathering of evil-doers;
   and with the wicked I do not dwell.
6 I wash my hands in innocency,
   so that I may go about your altar, O LORD,

---

1. The clause לֹא אֶמְעָד is here subordinated as an adverbial clause, "without moving" or "without wavering."
2. The Kᵉthiv is צְרוֹפָה and the Qᵉre' is צָרְפָה, both being imperatives; but the Kᵉthiv is probably to be read (see similarly Isa. 32:11; Judg. 9:8, 12; 1 Sam. 28:8)
3. The Greek has "I was well pleased (εὐηρέστησα) with your truth."
4. Greek "council" (συνεδρίου).

7 to make the voice of thanksgiving heard[5]
    and to tell of all your wonders.
8 O LORD, I love the refuge[6] of your house,
    and the dwelling-place of your glory.

9 Do not gather me[7] with sinners,
    nor my life with bloodthirsty men,
10 in whose hand are wicked intentions
    and whose right hand is full of bribery.
11 I, however, walk in my integrity;
    therefore, redeem me and be gracious unto me.
12 My foot stands upon a level place;
    among the assemblies I shall bless the LORD.[8]

Composition and Context

Psalms 25–28 seem to have been written during one period of time.[9] The common motifs include the psalmist's undeserved accusation and opposition by unidentified enemies, consistent

---

5. Two manuscripts and the Greek version have "to hear" (reading לִשְׁמוֹעַ for ἀκοῦσαι) in place of the MT's "to make heard." The form in the text is לְשַׁמִּעַ, which without vowels could certainly be read as a *qal* verb, because there has been syncopation of the ה and a defective writing of the word without the י. One would have expected the form to be לְהַשְׁמִיעַ. The translation takes בְּקוֹל with the preposition as the object of the verb (for the construction with the preposition, see Ezek. 27:30)
6. Greek has "majesty" (εὐπρέπειαν), perhaps confusing מָעוֹן, "place of safety, refuge," with עָיֵן, "pleasant, delightful" or נֹעַם in Psalm 27:4.
7. Literally, "my soul."
8. The Greek text reads: "I will bless you, O Lord."
9. If a link can be made between these psalms and events in the life of David, as the more historical approaches to the psalms suggest, then the time of Absalom's rebellion would be one possible setting (Delitzsch, *Psalms,* I:349). There are several reasons to link that event with the psalm: the enemies were hypocrites, they agreed on a bloodthirsty counsel, they threw off their disguise, and they had been won by bribery. If this is correct, it would also explain the psalm's reference to the desire to go to the sanctuary again, although this is not a strong point in the interpretation (vv. 6–8); but these motifs are not limited to any single event—they characterize the wicked of all ages. This makes the attempt to link the psalm to one event difficult, but it also makes the psalm relevant at all times.

loyalty to the LORD, prayer for vindication and deliverance, and confidence that God will answer the prayer. There are hints that some of the enemies were part of the ruling class (such as the reference to bribery in Ps. 26:10). What distinguishes this psalm is that David supports his appeal for vindication with a convincing affirmation of his loyalty to God alone.

It is difficult to classify this psalm. It appears to be a lament, but it does not have some of the basic characteristics of a lament, notably the description of enemies who are attacking the psalmist.[10] Yet it is a prayer for vindication and deliverance—with a strong emphasis on his separation from the wicked people around him. It is certainly a prayer for protection if not a full lament; for whatever the historical occasion the psalmist was under tremendous pressure from enemies. As Kraus puts it, his very existence was under the threatening sign of accusation and indictment by bloodthirsty people.[11] He was sure of his own innocence and therefore appealed to the LORD to vindicate him by delivering him.[12] In addition to being convinced of his own integrity, the psalmist was sure of the righteousness of God, i.e., that he does that which is just and fair for his people. In the psalmist's mind, then, it was fitting for the LORD to vindicate him.

The concerns of the psalmist flow naturally and smoothly through the psalm. Verses 1 and 2 form his appeal, a plea to God for vindication because of his integrity and loyalty. Then, verses 3–5 demonstrate how his integrity was manifested in his separation from the sinful and malicious enemies. Verses 6–8 on the other hand, describe his integrity by his positive attitude and love for the place of worship. Finally, verses 9–11 form the petition proper, that the upright not be gathered to the same fate as the wicked. Verse 12 could be taken as a separate section, but it fits well enough at the end of the petition. It expresses a confidence that expects to praise the LORD in the sanctuary and therefore becomes something of a vow to praise.[13]

---

10. Broyles, *Psalms*, p. 137
11. *Psalms 1–59*, 329.
12. See W. H. Bellinger, "Psalm 26," *VT* 43 (1993):452–61.
13. For a more detailed discussion of the interplay between the psalmist's prayer for vindication and separation from evil, see Paul G. Mosca, "Psalm 26: Poetic Structure and the Form-Critical Task," *CBQ* 47 (1985):21–37.

Exegetical Analysis

Summary

Those who keep separate from sinful, malicious people and openly and obediently identify with the worship of the LORD can pray with confidence that the LORD will separate them from the destiny of the wicked.

Outline

I. The plea for vindication: the psalmist petitions the LORD to examine him and vindicate him because he maintains his integrity (1–2).

II. The protest of innocence: the psalmist affirms his integrity by demonstrating that he keeps himself separate from sinful, malicious people but faithfully and willingly identifies with the worship of the LORD (3–8).

  A. He affirms that he remains separate from sinful people and their gatherings because the loyal love of God inspires him to obey the truth (3–5).

  B. He affirms his innocence and his love for the dwelling-place of the LORD where he will proclaim the wonderful works of the LORD (6–8).

III. The plea for deliverance: the psalmist petitions the LORD to deliver him from a common fate with sinful people and expresses his confidence that he will be delivered to praise God in the congregation (9–12).

  A. He petitions the LORD not to gather him with sinners to their fate but to redeem him (9–11).

  B. He expresses his confidence that he will be delivered to praise the LORD (12).

COMMENTARY IN EXPOSITORY FORM

I. When faced with serious opposition those who are truly righteous may appeal to God to vindicate them (1–2).

The first two verses introduce the subject and set the tone for this psalm: it is an urgent appeal for vindication of the righteous, whom malicious enemies were bent on destroying. The appeal is introduced with the imperative, "vindicate me." This verb (שָׁפְטֵנִי) means "to judge." The judgment might be a decision for acquittal, so it can be rendered " declare righteous, vindicate" or "do justice" (s.v. Ps. 9:4). The translation "vindicate me" emphasizes help for the innocent, and so better expresses the contextual nuance for this passage. It is a common prayer of the righteous in the psalms for God to set things right, and the plea for vindication necessarily includes condemnation on the wicked adversaries who bring false accusations.

There are two reasons for this plea. The first is that he walks in his integrity. The verb "I walk" (הָלַכְתִּי, a characteristic perfect, or possibly a present perfect) is idiomatic for the way that he lives his life, and that is with integrity (תֹּם, here "my integrity" [תֻּמִּי]; s.v. Ps. 7:8). This word not only describes a balanced and blameless life, but one with proper motives as well (see 1 Kings 9:4; Ps. 7:8; 25:21; 41:12; and 78:72). The psalmist is therefore claiming that his life is in order, in thought, and in deed. The description does not mean that the psalmist lives a sinless life; but what it does mean is that he is free from sin or forgiven for sin—when this is true he is blameless.

The blameless life is the effect of an unwavering trust in the LORD. The main verb of the second colon, "I have confidence in" or "I trust" (בָּטַחְתִּי; s.v. Ps. 4:5), like the verb "walk," may be taken as a characteristic perfect (or a present perfect). Whereas the verb "I walk" was qualified with "in my integrity," this verb is qualified with an adverbial clause, "without wavering" (the negated verb forming the clause: "I do not waver," לֹא אֶמְעָד). The verb has the sense of "slip, slide, totter" (see 2 Sam. 22:37; Ps. 18:36; Job 12:5); so the psalmist's life of trust in the LORD is steady—there are no false steps, no sliding as it were (this verb is also figurative, an implied comparison between walking and living by faith).

His appeal for vindication based on his faith and obedience is now intensified by an appeal to God to test him and see that his claim is correct. The verb that forms the first imperative, "examine me" (בְּחָנֵנִי; s.v. Ps. 139:23), means "to prove, test, try." It is an appeal for some empirical testing of his claims (see Job 12:11 and 34:3, "Does not the ear try words as the palate tests food?"). The second verb has a similar emphasis: "and test me" (וְנַסֵּנִי).[14] The verbs are figurative (making an implied comparison with human testing) for divine omniscience does not need to examine in order to discover. David wants the LORD to confirm that he is loyal to God; and the LORD could do this by making him aware of any flaws. God could do this through his word: as David meditated on it God would bring to light things that needed to be changed. Another way for the LORD to do this was to bring circumstances to play in his life that would give him the opportunity to demonstrate the integrity of his faith.

The third verb used (צְרְפָה) means "to refine, smelt, test." Perhaps the best translation in this context would be "purify," for that includes the act of testing and its intended purpose.[15] In the refining of silver, the dross will be removed and pure silver will remain (and so we have another implied comparison). By analogy, then, the LORD refines his people by putting them in

---

14. This verb נָסָה is used in a good sense for testing someone or something to approve it. It can be used for trying something out, as David tried to use Saul's armor (1 Sam. 17:39). It is also used for God's testing Abraham's obedience (Gen. 22:1), or Israel's faith in following the LORD's commands (Exod. 15:25), or Hezekiah's heart with the Babylonian envoys (2 Chron. 32:31).

It is also used in a bad sense, such as Israel's rebellion in the wilderness where they tested the LORD because they did not trust him (Exod. 17:2).

In all the uses there is some doubt that needed to be resolved (for the Israelite's testing of God, their doubt is tantamount to unbelief). When the LORD tests people, it usually involves his bringing together various circumstances that demand that those being tested trust in him in spite of the situation. This usage of the verb in Psalm 26, as well as the first verb "examine," does not have the intention of testing to ensnare (as the Queen of Sheba did with Solomon in 1 Kings 10:1), but to approve. The psalmist willingly submits himself to divine scrutiny to validate his claims of integrity.

15. The refining process was designed to purify a precious metal. For example, the ancient refiners reduced lead sulfide ore (rich in silver) to a metallic condition; the lead was separated from the silver then by blowing hot air over the surface of the melted metal. The lead changed to lead oxide, which, in a powdered condition, was blown away. In the Bible this process proved a good picture (an implied comparison) for the LORD's refining of his people's faith by putting them through trials.

situations or trials that will test their faith, and in the process anything that is worthless or deleterious will be removed and only what is pure, i.e., the life of faith, remains. In this line the psalmist wants the LORD to purify the spiritual inclinations that lie behind his activities. The objects are "my mind and my heart." "Mind" is literally kidneys. Kidneys were used by the ancients for the activities of the conscience, determining what is right and what is wrong, and "heart" refers to the seat of the will and the affections.

A similar prayer occurs in Psalm 139:23–24, which says, "Search me O God, and know my heart! Try me and know my thoughts! And see if there be any wicked way in me, and lead me in the way of everlasting life."

II. Those who pray for vindication must be able to demonstrate their integrity (3–9).

A. Loyalty to God requires separation from evil (3–5).

The central section of the psalm is the protestation of innocence. The psalmist's general claims were not enough; he wanted to detail how he lived. He was confident in his appeal to God to examine his life because he knew how he lived.

1. Loyalty to God must be affirmed (3).

The psalmist first lays down the guiding principles of his life (v. 3). On the one hand, the LORD's loyal love (s.v. Ps. 23:6) is always before him. The clause emphasizes a fixed and enduring condition. It indicates that this has been his permanent state of mind—his focus is continually on the LORD's faithful covenant love. By referring to God's love he includes the effects of this love, how the love was made manifest to him in God's care and provisions (so "loyal love" is a metonymy of cause).

On the other hand he asserts that his daily activities harmonized with God's truth. The verb "walk" (here the *hithpael* perfect, הִתְהַלַּכְתִּי, "walk to and fro, go about") signifies general conduct and behavior, the characteristic patterns and routines of life (it is a comparison that became idiomatic). This behavior, he claims, harmonized with divine truth. In the expression "in accordance with your truth" (בַּאֲמִתֶּךָ), the preposition indicates the norm or standard, and that standard is God's truth. "Truth" (אֱמֶת) is that which is reliable or dependable; and because it is God's truth revealed to mankind, it provides the guidance and instruction for life as well as the promised results of obedience (s.v. Ps. 15:2). The psalmist based his life on God's faithful love and truth; every thought and every action conformed to these spiritual guides.

2. Loyalty to God requires separation from evil (4–5).

Now the psalmist lists what he does not do, which is essentially anything opposed to God's truth. First, he does not associate with sinners (4). "I do not sit" (יָשַׁבְתִּי. a characteristic perfect or present perfect) is figurative (a metonymy of adjunct) for participating in the activities of the wicked. The claim is a reminder of the standard of blessedness in Psalm 1:1. He remains separate from wicked people (literally, "men of falsehood" or "vanity," שָׁוְא; s.v. Ps. 127:1), i.e., those characterized by false or worthless activities. Parallel to this is the statement that he also avoids ("I do not go," the progressive imperfect לֹא אָבוֹא) those who are deceptive, dissemblers, literally, "who conceal themselves" (נַעֲלָמִים, the niphal of עָלַם, "to conceal"). They may present themselves as pious or good, but they only conceal their true nature. Falsehood and hypocrisy repel those who are truly spiritual.

These affirmations are supported with the testimony of the psalmist's attitude behind the decisions. He says, "I hate the gatherings of evil-doers." The verb "hate" includes the effect with the feeling of abhorrence—he rejects their gatherings with loathing (s.v. Ps. 139:21). And the reason is obvious, for as evil-doers they bring pain to others (מְרֵעִים from רָעַע, s.v. Ps. 10:15). David is expressing a healthy and proper response to evil and those who plot it; and this is the inevitable result of one who lives by the truth. This is not a personal vendetta; as a devout believer he cannot tolerate those who despise and reject the LORD.

To this he adds that he does not sit with the wicked (רָשָׁע, s.v. Ps. 1:1), the godless people who are not part of the covenant and therefore do not follow the standard of righteousness that the believer does. Such people lack stability in life, as if tossed in a stormy sea (Isa. 57:20). The verb "I do not sit" (אֵשֵׁב) is also a progressive imperfect—it is the psalmist's continual practice to refuse to join them.

B. Loyalty to the LORD finds full expression in worship in the sanctuary (6–8).

Now we have the positive evidence of the psalmist's loyalty to the LORD. He begins by saying, "I wash my hands in innocency."[16] Washing one's hands was originally a symbolic act to signify innocence of serious charges or separation from some activity (Deut. 21:6; see also Matt. 27:24). With this in mind the expression came to be used figuratively to attest innocent conduct (Job 9:30; Ps. 73:13). The verb could be given a present tense translation as a protestation of his innocence, but in this context it seems to be part of the preparation for entering the sanctuary to praise the LORD. In either case he is affirming his innocence (נִקָּיוֹן has the sense of being free or clear of guilt; s.v. Ps. 19:12).

The purpose of this firm declaration is expressed in the next colon, the conjunction on the verb serving to express the purpose: "I wash . . . that I may go around your altar" (perhaps in a festal procession;[17] cf. Ps. 42:4). If he had been guilty of participation with evil-doers, he would not be free to draw near to the LORD's altar in worship; but he affirms his innocence so that he may draw near to the altar, and the purpose of his being there was to praise the LORD (v. 7). Both halves of this verse use infinitives expressing this purpose. The first, "to cause to be heard," is a little unusual in form (לַשְׁמִעַ for the normal form לְהַשְׁמִיעַ) and function—this verbal stem would normally mean "to cause [someone] to hear," but here the prepositional phrase "with the voice of praise" completes the infinitive: to make the voice of praise be heard." "Praise" (תּוֹדָה) refers to the public acknowledgment in the sanctuary accompanied by the peace offering (s.v.

---

16. The idea that this indicates he was a priest is not very compelling; see P. G. Mosca, "Psalm 26," *CBQ* 47 (1985):212–37.

17. Briggs says it means he will march around the altar in festal procession, with music and song, while the sacrifice was being made by the priests. He adds there is no reason to doubt the ceremonial among the Hebrews, although the direct evidence for it is slight (see Pss. 42:4; 118:27; 1 Sam. 16:11; 30:16; Briggs, *Psalms*, p. 233).

Ps. 6:5). The expression "the voice of praise" means the praise is what the voice proclaims (an objective genitive). Only those who are walking with the LORD and enjoying his blessings will offer such public praise in the sanctuary, and so this intent is part of his claim of integrity.

The second colon uses the infinitive "to tell" (לְסַפֵּר), and now the content of the praise is specified: "your wonders" (נִפְלְאוֹתֶיךָ from פָּלָא; s.v. Ps. 139:5), i.e., the marvelous, extraordinary, supernatural things that the LORD does (which would be everything that God does according to Ps. 139:14). His innocence gives him the privilege of entering the courts to worship the LORD, and his loyalty to the LORD naturally leads him to praise.

Verse 8 captures the essence of this section: he hates the assemblies of the wicked but loves the sanctuary of the LORD (for אָהַב s.v. Ps. 11:7). The sanctuary is here given a twofold description: it is a true sanctuary and a glorious dwelling place. The first word (מְעוֹן) means a refuge, and here specifies God's house: "the refuge (place of safety) of your house." This word is used in the Psalter to stress refuge (Ps. 71:3; 90:1; 91:9), and has such a connotation here, making the house of the LORD a place of protection—a true sanctuary. The second description stresses the importance and wonder of the place—it is the place of "the dwelling of your glory" (מִשְׁכַּן כְּבוֹדֶךָ). People would go to the sanctuary to behold the power and the glory of the LORD (Ps. 63:2), i.e., to witness his wonderful works that confirmed his presence in their midst and to renew their confidence in him as the incomparable and almighty God. The evidence of the divine presence dwelling there made it a glorious place, but they also knew that in the Holy of Holies the glory of the LORD dwelt (for "glory," s.v. Ps. 19:1).

III. The faithful may pray with confidence that they be spared the fate of the wicked (9–12).

A. They may pray to be kept separate from malicious and wicked people (9–11).

In the beginning of the psalm the plea was for vindication. Now, in the petition section we see what the psalmist meant. In his life he has tried to remain loyal to the LORD by avoiding evil and evil-doers; his vindication will come when the LORD spares him from a common fate with them. When the LORD begins to judge the wicked, whether in his lifetime or at the end of the age, he does not want to be judged with them. His prayer is urgent: "Do not gather (אַל תֶּאֱסֹף, the negated jussive) me (my life) with sinners." These are not harmless unbelievers, for the parallel petition clarifies that they are "bloodthirsty men" (אַנְשֵׁי דָמִים, "men of bloods")—men characterized by shedding blood. His description of them continues in verse 10 with two relative clauses: "in whose hands are evil intentions and whose right hand is full of bribery" ("hands" being a metonymy of cause for what they put their hands to, what they do). "Evil intentions" (זִמָּה) refers to their schemes to destroy the innocent, including the psalmist (s.v. Ps. 10:2); the reference to "bribery" (שֹׁחַד) may indicate that they could be bought or in some way induced to carry out the wicked plans.

As for the psalmist, since he walks in his integrity he is free to pray, "Redeem me (פְּדֵנִי, s.v. Ps. 25:22) and be merciful (וְחָנֵּנִי, s.v. Ps. 4:1) unto me." It is a prayer to be rescued from them by God's grace (as when the LORD redeemed Israel from Egypt when he was destroying the oppressors). Being set free from them by God's grace both now and in the future will be the vindication of the righteous.

B. They may be confident they will praise the LORD (12).

In verse 12 the psalmist reiterates his integrity and determination to praise the LORD. The verse could be taken as a fourth section of the psalm, forming a vow to praise; but since it parallels what he has already said in the psalm, it seems to be a restatement of his loyalty to the LORD demonstrated in his faithfulness and worship. He uses the image of his foot standing in a level place to signify that his faith is firm (as opposed to his foot slipping). "In a level place" (בְּמִישׁוֹר; s.v. Ps. 67:4) is a place that is right or equitable; it describes a firm faith that is consistent with the truth of God. This is in contrast to the crooked and devious ways of the wicked; and in his integrity his enemies cannot assail him. Therefore he will fulfill his resolve to praise the LORD in the assemblies of the righteous. Now, however, the word is "I shall bless" (אֲבָרֵךְ, s.v. Ps. 5:12), a word that refers to praise but perhaps with the sense of enriching the LORD with praise so that others will have a greater appreciation of who he is and what he has done.

MESSAGE AND APPLICATION

We have in this psalm the fervent prayer of the righteous for vindication of their loyalty to God. The prayer is an appeal to the LORD's justice, for it is an appeal supported by affirmations of loyalty and integrity, affirmations that the LORD himself can prove through closer examination. Because the psalmist remains untarnished by the wickedness of those around him, he can pray with confidence that the LORD will deliver him from a common fate with them. The way he maintains his spiritual life is by hating the gatherings of the wicked and loving the sanctuary of the LORD. This is true for believers of all ages: *The righteous who are loyal to God and remain separate from evil sinners may pray with confidence that the LORD will vindicate them and redeem them from a common fate with the wicked.*

All the people of God may pray of course, but those who live righteously will have more confidence when they pray. Goldingay emphasizes the implication of the psalm that "ideally, people who pray need to be able to claim moral integrity and religious commitment, and must dissociate themselves from the faithless."[18] After all, James says that it is the prayer of a righteous person that is effectual (5:16). Jesus said the blessing was for those who suffer because of the faith and not their own faults: "Blessed are you when people insult you, persecute you, and falsely say all kinds of evil against you because of me" (Matt. 5:11).

Even if people cannot protest innocence they may still pray for the LORD to deliver them from the wicked, for they belong to God and he will deliver them when he judges the wicked. The reference in the psalm may be to judgments carried out in this life, but it most certainly applies to the end of the age when

18. Goldingay, *Psalms 1–41*, p. 388.

the saints will be vindicated. Even the souls under the altar in heaven pray, "How long, Sovereign Lord, holy and true, until you judge the inhabitants of the world and avenge our blood?" (Rev. 6:10). In addition to the martyrs, all the faithful anticipate the time when their avoidance of wickedness and faithfulness to the Lord will be vindicated; and that anticipation is based on the love of God in Christ that cannot be set aside (Rom. 8:31–39). In the meantime, Psalm 26 is a reminder for the righteous to maintain their innocency in this corrupt world, to keep their attention on the loyal love of the LORD, and to enter his courts with praise for his wonderful acts.

PSALM 27

A Prayer Song
of Courageous Trust

INTRODUCTION

Text and Textual Variants

Of David.[1]

1 The LORD is my light and my salvation;[2]
   whom shall I fear?
 The LORD is the strength of my life;
   of whom shall I be afraid?

2 When evil-doers came against me
   to devour my flesh,
 my adversaries and my enemies,[3]
   they stumbled[4] and fell.
3 Though an army camp encamp[5] against me
   my heart will not fear;
 though war rise against me,
   even in this will I be confident.
4 One thing I have asked of the LORD;

---

1. The Greek text has also "Before he was anointed" (πρὸ τοῦ χρισθῆναι).
2. The Greek has "savior" (σώτηρ).
3. "They (were) to me" is pleonastic.
4. The Greek has "became weak" (ἠσθένησαν).
5. The noun "camp" and the verb "encamp" form a paronomasia.

this shall I seek:
That I may dwell in the house of the LORD
    all the days of my life,[6]
to see the delightfulness of the LORD
    and to seek[7] *him* in his temple.

5 For he will hide me in *his*[8] shelter
    in the day of trouble.
He will hide me in the shelter of his tabernacle;
    he will put me high upon a rock.

6 Now, therefore, my head will be exalted[9]
    above my enemies round about me;[10]
and I will sacrifice in his tabernacle
    sacrifices of joyful shouts.
I will sing, yes, I will make music to the LORD.

7 Hear my voice, O LORD, *when* I call;
    and be gracious to me and answer me,

8 Of you my heart says, "Seek his face!"[11]
    Your face, O LORD, I shall seek.

9 Do not hide your face from me.
Do not turn your servant away in anger,
    you have been my help.[12]
Do not abandon me nor forsake me,

---

6. Editors of BHS suggest this was added and refers to 23:6.

7. Greek has "survey (ἐπισκέπτεσθαι) his temple." Goldingay says this rare Hebrew word has a distinct meaning here of "make request" (*Psalms 1–41*, p. 390).

8. Pronominal suffix "his" from *Qᵉreʾ*. If the pronoun is not added here it would be implied from the following lines. Greek has "in a tent."

9. The MT has "my head will lift high." The Greek and a few other versions read "he will lift my head high" as if the form were *hiphil*.

10. MT has סְבִיבוֹתַי; Greek renders it as "I went around" (ἐκύκλωσα, which would represent אֶסֹבְבָה)

11. The MT has בַּקְּשׁוּ פָנָי, the plural verb: "seek my face." Most suggest the words should be changed to the singular verb and a different suffix: בַּקֵּשׁ פָנָיו, "seek his face." If the MT is retained, it would mean have to mean a command of the LORD was being quoted; Kraus suggests: "My heart holds up [your command] "Seek my face" (*Psalms 1–59*, p. 331). The Greek has "my face sought (ἐζήτησεν)." B has, "I have sought your face."

12. Greek has "Be my helper."

O God of my salvation.[13]

10 For my father and my mother have abandoned me;
    but the LORD will gather me up.

11 Teach me, O LORD, your way,
    and lead me in a level path
        because of my watching enemies.

12 Do not give me over to the desire of my adversaries,
    for false witnesses rise up against me,
        breathing out violence.[14]

13 I am confident[15] of this:
    I will see[16] the goodness of the LORD
        in the land of the living.

14 Wait for the LORD;
    be of good courage, and may your heart be strong;[17]
and wait for the LORD.

Composition and Context

The major issue concerning this psalm is whether or not it is two distinct psalms. The old critical view is that the first part is an

---

13. Greek has "savior."

14. The MT has יָפֵחַ, the construct of the adjective יָפֵחַ, meaning something like "breathing" or more graphically "snorting" violence. Some suggest a different root for the form, perhaps פִּיחַ, וְיָפִיחוּ "and they rouse (injustice)"; but this is unnecessary as the MT makes sense as it stands. The Greek text has καὶ ʼεψεύσατο, "and (injustice) lied to itself."

15. The line begins with לוּ לֹא הֶאֱמַנְתִּי. The particle לוּ introduces a conditional clause, "if not . . . then"; but here the apodosis has been omitted (aposiopesis; see a similar construction in Deut. 32:29). The verb following is the perfect tense, "I believe"; and so the sentence emphasizes the certainty of the belief. See Jeffrey Niehaus, "The Use of *lûlē* in Psalm 27," *JBL* 98 (1979):88–9. It is not in the Greek, Aquila, Symmachus, or the Syriac.

16. The form in the text is the infinitive construct לִרְאוֹת, "to see"; it probably serves as the direct object of the verb, answering the question of what he believes, that he will see.

17. The two verbs in this line, חָזַק and אָמַץ are synonyms, making the translation more challenging. The first is the imperative, "be strong, be firm" (חָזַק), and the second the *hiphil* jussive, "may he/it strengthen" (וְיַאֲמֵץ). It could be "may (the LORD) strengthen your heart" or "may your heart be bold." NIV smooths it out to "Be strong and take heart." The Greek text has "take courage and let your heart be strong."

individual song of trust (vv. 1–6) and the second part is an individual lament (vv. 7–14).[18] Part of the difficulty is the unusual sequence of trust before the lament.[19] To explain this as well as the change in circumstances and tone in the second part many have simply posited two psalms.

Not everyone is convinced that two separate psalms have been joined together for there are many terms that occur in both sections, as the exposition will show.[20] And as far as the composition is concerned, Mowinckel argues that the psalm was deliberately composed with a lengthy hymnic introduction.[21] Having a lament introduced with a hymn of adoration is not without parallel. Laments normally begin with an introductory cry to God, and the introductory cry can easily be expanded into an ascription of praise (for example, see the beginnings of Pss. 9, 41, 44, and 62; and see Psalm 40 which has a praise section and then the lament section). So the way Psalm 27 is put together does not require the explanation that it was compiled from two separate works.

Nearly everyone agrees that the second half of Psalm 27 is a lament,[22] but it is a lament with an extended laudatory introduction. In addition to the structure we may note that the expressions and ideas found here fit laments, as a comparison with Psalm 31 would show (e.g., there are similarities between 27:1 and 31:5, 13; 27:13 and 31:20; 27:5 and 37:21, and 27:14 and 31:25).

The classification of the psalm as a lament then leads to the question of the occasion for its writing. Here we have less certainty. Some have suggested that it is part of the royal liturgy,

---

18. For example, see Bernard Anderson, *Out of the Depths,* pp. 169–71. Because of the differences between the sections Kirkpatrick concludes if they were written by one author they were written at different times and under different circumstances (*Psalms,* p. 140).

19. A. A. Anderson, *Psalm 1–71,* p. 219.

20. Broyles, *Psalms,* p.142. See also A. H. Van Zyl, "The Unity of Psalm 27," in *De Fructu Oris Sui* (Fs. for A. Van Selms), ed. by I. H. Eybers et al (Leiden: E. J. Brill, 1971), pp. 233–51.

21. *The Psalms in Israel's Worship,* I:95.

22. Kraus does not think the psalm fits the category of a lament well enough and so he calls it a prayer song of a person persecuted and accused (*Psalms 1–59,* p. 332).

perhaps an anniversary celebration of the king's coronation. Craigie accepts the unity of the psalm and places it in a royal liturgical setting: the king would publicly declare his faith (vv. 1–6), make his sacrifice (as v. 6 implies), then offer his prayer (vv. 7–13), and receive an oracle form the priest (v. 14). The psalm may have been written as part of a royal collection, but there is insufficient evidence to identify the occasion. In fact, the expressions in the psalm point more to a personal crisis that formed the lament. Attempts to fit it into a particular crisis in the life of David are not convincing, although there is nothing in the psalm that would argue convincingly against Davidic authorship.

The psalm begins with a strong statement of the psalmist's confidence (vv. 1–3); and this is followed by the expression of his desire to be in the sanctuary (vv. 4–6). The second part of the psalm records the petition for the LORD's protection (vv. 7–10) and guidance in the right way (11–12). The psalm ends with a strong statement of the psalmist's confidence (v. 13). The last verse is an exhortation to wait for the LORD (v. 14). This exhortation at the end may have been added as a cultic exhortation in view of the needs and confidence expressed in the psalm.

Exegetical Analysis

Summary

The psalmist, expressing great confidence in the LORD in spite of a host of enemies who threaten his life, prays for help and comfort in his time of need and rejoices in the hope of waiting on the LORD.

Outline

I. Because the LORD has given him the victory in the past, David affirms his confidence in the LORD in spite of the host of enemies and then expresses his desire to find safety and celebration in the house of the LORD (1–6).

A. He states that he is not afraid because the LORD will protect him and give him victory as he has done in the past (1–3).

B. He expresses his desire to abide in the sanctuary where he will find a place of safety and an opportunity for the celebration of praise (4–6).

II. Because he is confident of the LORD's blessings, David prays for help and guidance in his time of need as he is encouraged to wait for the LORD (7–14).

A. He asks that the LORD not forsake him since he is his servant in need (7–10).

B. He petitions the LORD to teach him the way to go because of his enemies and to deliver him from false witnesses who breathe out violence against him (11–12).

C. He expresses his confidence that he will be blessed by the LORD (13).

D. He is encouraged to wait patiently for the LORD (14).

COMMENTARY IN EXPOSITORY FORM

I. Those who trust the LORD and long for his presence will find confidence in the midst of life-threatening situations (1–6).

A. Confidence in the LORD's protection is based on what the LORD has done (1–3).

The psalm begins with a memorable expression of confidence in the LORD. It uses two figures: "light" and "salvation." The metaphor of "light" signifies the joy of life, the perfection of holiness, and the illumination of the way of truth. Light dispels darkness, and darkness represents evil, confusion, gloom and despair, often because of war (see Isa. 8:20–9:2). The same metaphor is used in Micah 7:8–9 in a context that describes how the enemies will be put to shame as the LORD brings his people into the light, meaning a joyous victory. The second figure used here therefore flows from the image of the light: the LORD is his salvation (a metonymy of effect), meaning the LORD brings him victory or deliverance (for "salvation," s.v. Ps. 3:2). Then the second line of the first verse uses the metaphor of "stronghold" (מָעוֹז), comparing the LORD to a place of safety and protection—the LORD securely protects the psalmist's life. All this being

626

true, there is no one that the psalmist (or we) should fear, as the rhetorical questions assert (for "fear," s.v. Ps. 2:11).

The psalmist bases his affirmations on past experiences; the LORD has demonstrated consistently that he is the light and salvation and stronghold.[23] Verse 2 begins with the temporal clause "when (evil-doers) drew near" (using the infinitive of קָרַב). This drawing near was hostile (the preposition "against me" (עָלַי), NIV translated it: "when evil-doers advanced against me." Their purpose was "to devour" his flesh, the figure (an implied comparison with predatory beasts) clearly affirming that they wanted to annihilate him. Describing these people as "evil-doers" (מְרֵעִים; s.v. Ps. 10:15) indicates their activities caused pain and destruction. This was the nature of his "adversaries and enemies," but they stumbled and fell before him (probably referred to in verse 9, which reports that the LORD had been his help; see the use of these verbs in Jer. 46:6, 16; Isa. 3:8; 31:3).

Because of this the psalmist reiterates his unwavering faith in the LORD. Verse 3 sets up hypothetical future situations (introduced by אִם), but situations that could become reality in a moment. The expressions concern warfare: "though an army camp encamped" against him, he would not be afraid (see v. 1); and "though war rose up" against him, even then he would be confident (literally: "in this I trust"). The word "army camp" refers to the warriors in the camp (a metonymy of subject); and the word "war" refers to the army in the war (a metonymy of adjunct).[24] In either case the psalmist says he would not be afraid but remain confident.

B. Confidence is strengthened by being in the LORD's sanctuary (4–6).

In verses 4–6 we read of the desire of the psalmist to abide in

---

23. Some commentators take this verse as a continuation of the confidence for the future and treat the perfect tenses as prophetic perfects, but that change to the future comes between verse 2 and 3, verse 3 looking to the hypothetical future.
24. The fact that the psalmist might be surrounded by an army or attacked with war indicates he is not an ordinary individual; this is what happened to royalty, or at least military leaders.

the sanctuary where he will behold the glorious LORD and find security and celebration in worship. He begins by announcing there is one thing that he has asked from the LORD; it is a single-minded quest. The verb "have asked" (שָׁאַלְתִּי, a present perfect) would include the past and the present; the next verb (אֲבַקֵּשׁ, an imperfect) looks to the future, "I shall seek."[25] So his quest has been and will continue to be to dwell in the sanctuary. This is clarified by a series of infinitive clauses in the second half of the verse. The first is "to dwell" ("my dwelling," שִׁבְתִּי) in the house of the LORD all the days of his life.[26] The infinitive serves as the object of the verb—it is what he seeks. Dwelling in the sanctuary would mean participating in the worship activities,[27] and participating in sanctuary worship would also mean being preserved by God's covenant provisions (Ps. 61).

This desire to dwell in the sanctuary is explained by the next two infinitive clauses. The first is "to see" (gaze upon, from חָזָה) the delightfulness of the LORD. This idea may be contrasted with the pagan culture in which people gazed on the beautiful statues of their gods; but in Israel they did not actually see God nor a statue of him. Rather, they would perceive his graciousness in his wonderful works.[28] The psalmist wanted to see the LORD's "delightfulness" (נֹעַם). This word is used in Psalm 90:17 in conjunction with having the works of one's hands established; in that psalm it comes in a sequence of petitions for God's loyal love, gladness, and deeds of splendor. In Psalm 27 the desire to see the delightfulness of the LORD would be the desire to see the things that God does for his people that are delightful (metonymy of adjunct), and those things would be primarily in answer to prayer.[29]

---

25. Both verbs could also be given a present tense translation to stress his present desire to dwell in the house of the LORD.

26. Kraus says that the clause syntactically and in terms of content fits poorly into this context (*Psalms 1–59*, p. 334). The line is so similar to Psalm 23:6 that the editors of the text suggest it was added to Psalm 27, but there is no evidence for that. Moreover, it would have to be original here if this verse is taken as a resource for the variant reading in Psalm 23:6.

27. Perowne, *Psalms*, I:267–8.

28. A. A. Anderson, *Psalms 1–72*, p. 222.

29. See J. D. Levenson, "A Technical Meaning for *n'm* in the Hebrew Bible," *VT* 35 (1085):61–7.

In line with this the infinitive "to see" ("gaze upon") is figurative; it means to focus attention on the wonders of God. In the sanctuary this would happen as one heard about God's amazing works (expressed in Ps. 63:2 as seeing God's power and glory).

The last infinitive "to seek" or "inquire" (וּלְבַקֵּר) is probably a reference to seeking the LORD's will for guidance.[30] To do this in the temple in God's presence would inspire greater confidence for an answer, because in the sanctuary he would hear the praises and be reminded of God's covenant blessings and promises. He could recall these anywhere, but in the sanctuary he would be surrounded by a cloud of witnesses to these blessings as well as priests who would assist his inquiry with appropriate sacrifices and words of assurance that God accepted him.

Verse 5 offers an explanation for this desire to be in the LORD's presence: it is the place of refuge and security. The synonymous verbs "he will hide" (צָפַן and סָתַר) express the psalmist's confidence in the protection he will receive in the sanctuary.[31] The LORD will hide him in a "shelter" and in the "secret place of his tent," both places referring to the sanctuary in general. In the presence of the LORD where he hears the proclamation of the power of God in the lives of people and receives assurances of being accepted by God from the priests, the psalmist would become more aware of God's provisions of safety and security. The feeling of safety would be like being set high upon a rock (an implied comparison) like a stronghold (see Psalm 18:1–2).

The concluding verse of this first section adds an additional desired benefit of being in the house of the LORD—the celebration of praise. Verse 6 begins with "and now" (וְעַתָּה), which may be taken to announce the immediate liturgical moment that the king was about to offer his sacrifice.[32] If this is the case, then one would conclude that the psalmist must have received

---

30. Kraus says it means he is longing for a sign of salvation in the temple (*Psalms 1–59,* p. 334). Mowinckel suggests a more spectacular interpretation of seeking omens, as in interpreting signs in the sacrifices (*The Psalms in Israel's Worship,* II:54).
31. It is possible that the psalmist might be referring to actual sanctuary at the horns of the altar (1 Kings 2:29), or that the expressions might have become idiomatic based on such ideas.
32. Craigie, *Psalms,* p. 233.

some indication his prayer was answered, perhaps an "oracle of salvation."[33] It is not likely that the prayer has been answered, because the petition is in the second half of the psalm. Perhaps "and now" introduces a practical conclusion of what has been said: on the basis of all he has said (the extended praise for the LORD and what he does for his people), the psalmist anticipates victory in this case as well (so NIV reads, "then"). The image of the victory is that his head would be high or lifted up above all his enemies who surrounded him (see Ps. 3:4 for the image of lifting the head). Because he anticipates the victory, he resolves to offer the sacrifice of praise. The line uses the cohortative, "I will sacrifice" (אֶזְבְּחָה), with a cognate accusative "sacrifices" (זִבְחֵי) as the direct object to intensify the resolution. Instead of the expected "sacrifices of praise" (תּוֹדָה) he has sacrifices of "shouts of joy" (תְּרוּעָה). He substitutes the word "shout" for the praise, emphasizing that his praise would be enthusiastic, loud and clear. His shouts of acclamation would also be accompanied by singing and making music (two more cohortatives of resolve). His praise would be with great celebration (cf. Ps. 69:3).

II. Those who trust in the LORD and wait patiently for him may pray with confidence for his protection and guidance (7–14).

A. It is a prayer for the LORD's continued presence (7–10).

Part two of the psalm opens with a general petition for God to "hear" his voice when he calls, "be gracious" (s.v., Ps. 4:1), and "answer" him. These expressions are often found in the introductory cry and petition of lament psalms. In this verse the parallelism clarifies that "hear" means "answer" (see also Ps. 34:7, 18).

Verse 8 is a difficult verse. It begins clearly enough with "of/to/concerning you my heart says" (לְךָ אָמַר לִבִּי); but the rest of the verse is more problematic: "Seek my face" is the translation of the MT (בַּקְּשׁוּ פָנָי), and this is followed by "Your face, O LORD, I seek" (אֶת־פָּנֶיךָ יהוה אֲבַקֵּשׁ). Some commentators work with the text as

---

33. Claus Westermann, *The Praise of God in the Psalms,* p. 70.

it stands, translating it "To you, says my soul, [belongs the command], 'Seek my face.'" Perowne explains that the words "Seek my face" are the words of God. The psalmist has taken them and laid them before God to make his appeal more irresistible. It is as if he said, "You said, 'Seek my face'; my heart takes them and responds, 'I seek your face.'"[34] Others emend the imperative to a singular form and change the suffix on "face" to a third person, "seek his face" (בַּקְּשׁוּ פָנָיו; see the NIV). This would mean that his heart was encouraging him to seek his face. There is not a great difference in the resultant meaning, not enough to change the text. Other proposals are more extensive. Craigie says that the problem stems from the repetition of "face" and of the verb "seek"; he simplifies it to read "I have sought your face" with the Greek version.[35]

The psalmist's decision to seek the LORD's face harmonizes with his desire to see the LORD's delightfulness. Seeking the face of the LORD means praying for his grace. Psalm 105:4 uses it in conjunction with trusting in the LORD's powerful presence. Similarly, the shining face signifies the LORD's gracious intervention (Ps. 31:16; Num. 6:25). The expression signifies that the psalmist was looking for the LORD's gracious intervention. This fits with the first half of the psalm where the presence of the LORD emphasizes his favor and protection.

The petition is spelled out in verse 9 with four negative requests (four uses of אַל followed by jussives). The first, "Do not hide your face from me," flows naturally from verse 8 which records his decision to seek the LORD's face. To hide the face (an anthropomorphism) would mean to refuse favor and blessing (Pss. 22:24; 143:7) and the result would be terrifying (Ps. 30:7). This initial request is then clarified with the next three. The first is "Do not turn your servant away in anger," meaning do not reject my prayer with anger. The basis for this appeal is that God has been (present perfect) his help. The next two requests are that God not forsake him and abandon him because he is the God of his salvation. If the LORD abandoned him now he would be on his own, and that would certainly mean destruction (compare Pss. 44:9ff. and 78:60)—there would be no light, and

---

34. *Psalms*, I:269; see also Kraus, *Psalms 1–59*, p. 331.
35. Craigie, *Psalms*, p. 232.

there would be no protection like a stronghold. The appeal not to forsake is actually an appeal to intervene to deliver him.

The reason for this appeal not to be abandoned is stated in verse 10: his parents abandoned him in some way.[36] This probably does not mean his parents abandoned him as one might think. It could be a proverbial expression indicating that he is friendless and forsaken like a deserted child,[37] but it may be a reference to their death.[38] If this is the case, then the psalmist felt that he had no one to turn to for advice or support; and so the appeal to the LORD is more urgent. He would be saying to the LORD, do not abandon me because I am already alone. Then he concludes by abruptly affirming his faith that the LORD will gather him up (the clause begins with the strong disjunctive, "But the LORD"). He is quick to assert that the LORD will take him into his care (אָסַף with the meaning "take up, take care of" rather than simply "gather"; e.g., this nuance finds support in 2 Samuel 11:27 which says that David took Bathsheba into the palace to care for her as his wife).

B. It is a prayer for the LORD's guidance in dealing with malicious false witnesses (11–12).

The next petition is expressed with an imperative: "Show me (הוֹרֵנִי from יָרָה, s.v. Ps. 1:2) your way, O LORD." The "way" of the LORD is the revealed will of the LORD expressed in the commandments. The request is for the LORD to guide him in keeping the covenant so that he might receive God's blessings. The parallel colon supports this general meaning: "Lead me (נְחֵנִי; s.v. Ps. 23:3) in a level path." A way of life that is "level" (מִישׁוֹר; s.v. Ps. 67:4) is one that is straight, steadfast and firm; it is free of obstacles and difficulties. The level path will lead to a place of safety and prosperity.

The reason he needs this guidance is on account of his

---

36. The clause is a causal clause, "because." It is possible to take it as a concessive clause, "though" (see NIV), making the line hypothetical.
37. Kirkpatrick, *Psalms*, p. 143.
38. Shalom Paul notes a similar use in the Babylonian theodicy which explains that the parents had died ("Psalm XXVII 10 and the Babylonian Theodicy," *VT* 32 [1982]:489–92).

enemies. Here they are described literally as "my watchers" (שׁוֹרְרָי, "watchers of me"), and so watchful antagonists. These people were watching for any occasion to accuse and any weakness to exploit.

His prayer concludes the request not to be given over to such enemies: "Do not give me (אַל תִּתְּנֵנִי) . . . because false witnesses arise . . ." (This is the same construction of clauses that was used in verses 9c, 10.[39] The request is that God not give him over to the "desire" of the enemies ("soul" [נֶפֶשׁ] can mean appetite or here "desire"; NEB has "greed"; s.v. Ps. 11:5). Their desire was to find something in his life they could use against him, because they were false witnesses and determined to bring him down with violence. The last expression seems to repeat the point that they are witnesses who are malicious (חָמָס; s.v. Ps. 58:2).[40]

C. It is a prayer that is confident of the LORD's blessings to come (13).

The verse begins with a construction (לוּ לֹא) that generally introduces a protasis in the negative, "if not . . . ." The extraordinary points written around the word in the text indicate the Masoretes considered the meaning uncertain. The normal solutions include either assuming the apodosis or eliminating the expression altogether (after the versions). It is also possible that the expression is rhetorical with the meaning "surely."[41] The point of the line is that the psalmist was affirming his confidence. Perhaps a translation "Certainly I believe (הֶאֱמַנְתִּי) that I will see (the infinitive "to see" expressing what he believed) the good things of the LORD in the land of the living. The word

---

39. The difference is that the final part of verse 10 is an expression of confidence, but the last part of verse 12 is a further clarification of the malicious enemies. Because there is no statement of confidence in verse 12, verse 13 will supply it.

40. The word יָפֵחַ is normally taken as the adjective meaning "breathing out" violence. It is possible it is from a different root that has the meaning of "witness" because it is so frequently used in parallelism to "witness," עֵד. The verse then describes the enemies as witnesses that promote violence for which they would be condemned (Deut. 19:16–21). See D. Pardee, "YPḤ 'Witness' in Hebrew and Ugaritic," *VT* 28 (1979):204–13.

41. KBL, p. 477.

"good" (טוֹב; s.v. Ps. 34:8) refers to the concrete blessings of the LORD, good things (see Isa. 63:7 for acts of the LORD, and Jer. 31:12, 14 for flocks and crops). He is confident that he will see (=experience) God's blessings in this life (as the days of his life mentioned in verse 4) when the LORD comes to help him.

D. Those who pray are encouraged to wait patiently for the LORD (14).

The last verse is an exhortation to wait patiently with bold courage for the LORD's deliverance. The word "wait" (קָוֵּה, s.v., Ps. 25:3) indicates confident expectation, albeit with some tension or restlessness as part of the waiting. The imperative is repeated in the verse, but its two occurrences are divided by the exhortation to be strong. The second colon reads "be strong (חֲזַק) and let your heart be strong (וְיַאֲמֵץ)." Although it is possible to understand "the LORD" as the subject of the jussive ("may he strengthen your heart"), "your heart" is probably the subject because it would harmonize better with the line.

But who is the speaker of the verse? It could be interpreted as an oracle of a priest or a prophet given to exhort the psalmist (e.g., 1 Sam. 1:17).[42] Or, it could be the psalmist speaking to himself to strengthen his faith (e.g., Ps. 42:5, 11; 43:5;),[43] or speaking to someone else to encourage a strong faith and hope in the LORD. The fact that the forms are singular would rule out the verse's being a general exhortation to the congregation. In lament psalms it is not unusual to see self-exhortation. Either possibility fits the passage and leads to the same meaning, the building up of confident expectation.

MESSAGE AND APPLICATION

This psalm has several emphases that appeared in Psalms 25 and 26, but the particular emphasis here is on the confidence of the psalmist. In the midst of the trouble caused by false witnesses he remains confident in the LORD who has delivered and

---

42. See A. A. Anderson, *Psalms 1–72*, p. 226; Craigie, *Psalms*, p.234.
43. Weiser, *Psalms*, p. 254.

protected him many times before. He desires to go to the sanctuary where he will be reminded of all the wonderful works of the LORD through the praise of the people. There he will seek the LORD's favor to deliver him and guide him yet again, and there he will be encouraged to be strong in the faith as he waits for the LORD's response. It is in the safety of the sanctuary that he witnesses the reality of divine intervention, and this is what rekindles his confidence to seek the LORD's favor.

The exposition needs to capture the emphasis on confidence and the importance of the sanctuary in order to do justice to this psalm. One way to express the message of the psalm is to say: *When faced with false accusations the faithful will find the sanctuary of the LORD the place to strengthen their faith and seek with confident expectation divine protection and guidance.* The desire of the psalmist to go to the sanctuary is not a desire to go to an empty place. It will only be a place of safety and encouragement if the presence of the LORD is evident. That will only happen if people are there praising the LORD for his wonderful works and encouraging one another to pray with confident expectation. The message of this psalm will not work if the sanctuary is empty and the people are silent.

The experience of the apostle Paul with the Corinthian church captures the tension of this psalm (although here much of the opposition seemed to come from believers). According to his second epistle to that troubled church, false teachers were spreading lies about Paul to discredit him. Paul had to deal with the problem, but he did not deal with it in his own power. His "boast" was in the LORD; when he depended on the LORD, the LORD proved to be strong (see 2 Cor. 12:9–10). To defend himself all he could do was point to what God had done through him in establishing and building up the church. He prayed; he sent messengers; he expressed his love and concern in an effort to bring about reconciliation. In it all, it would be God who would resolve the crisis and build up the faith. Paul, like David, could confidently seek the LORD's favor in resolving the difficulty because he was doing the work of the LORD.

PSALM 28

A Confident Cry for Deliverance from the Wicked and Their Destiny

INTRODUCTION

Text and Textual Variants

Of David.

1 To you, O LORD, I call;
   my rock,[1] do not be deaf to me;
 lest if you remain silent from me
   then I will become like those who go down to the pit.
2 Hear the voice of my supplications
   as I cry out to you for help,
 as I lift up my hands
   toward your inner[2] holy place.
3 Do not drag me[3] away with the ungodly,
   or with those who work evil,
 who speak peace with their neighbors

---

1. Instead of "my rock" the Greek text has "my God."
2. The Greek translation renders אֶל־דְּבִיר as "temple" (πρὸς ναὸν), "unto your holy temple." This word for the innermost sanctuary, the holy of holies, is not related to "word," דְּבָר, as if a place of oracles.
3. The Greek has "my soul" instead of a pronominal direct object. It then adds a verb to the parallel expression: "do not destroy me" (μὴ συναπολέσῃς με) which would represent אַל־תְּאַבְדֵנִי.

but have malice[4] in their hearts.
4 Repay them according to their activity
 and in accordance with the evil of their practices;
according to the work[5] of their hands repay them;
 bring back on them what they deserve.
5 Because they do not give heed to the acts of the LORD
 and to the work[6] of his hands,
he[7] shall tear them down
 and not build them up.

6 Blessed be the LORD
 for he has heard the voice of my supplication.
7 The LORD is my strength and my shield;
 in him my heart trusts, and I am helped.
My heart[8] leaps for joy[9]
 and I will acknowledge him with my song.[10]
8 The LORD is their[11] strength,
 and he is a saving stronghold for his anointed one.

9 Save your people and bless your inheritance;
 and shepherd them and carry them forever.

---

4. MT has רָעָה, "evil" in the sense of causing pain. The Greek text has it plural: "evils."
5. The Greek and other versions as well as two Hebrew manuscripts have a plural "works."
6. The Greek and other versions as well as two Hebrew manuscripts have a plural "works."
7. The Greek text has the 2msg verbs, "you will tear down" and "you will not build up."
8. The Greek translation has "flesh" (σάρξ).
9. The Greek has "revived" (ἀνέθαλεν); see also Theodotion and the Syriac.
10. The Hebrew is וּמִשִּׁירִי, "and with my song"; the Greek has "and out of my will" (καὶ ἐκ θελήματός μου), probably reading "my heart" again.
11. The MT has לָמוֹ but the editors suggest reading with the Greek, Syriac, and a few Hebrew manuscripts "his people" (τοῦ λαοῦ αὐτοῦ) which would reflect a Hebrew לְעַמּוֹ. The MT probably preserves the correct reading; it is certainly the harder reading. Additionally, "people" is used in the next verse and the scribe may have tried to harmonize the two lines.

Composition and Context

As an individual lament, the psalm includes a cry to the LORD to be heard, a prayer to be delivered from the wicked and their destiny, a proclamation of praise to the LORD for answering the prayer and providing strength, protection and salvation, and an additional prayer for the LORD to take care of the nation. There is not a pronounced lament section; but the lamentable situation is certainly discernible in the psalm: the psalmist is surrounded by hypocritical evil-doers bent on destruction—and God does not seem to be responding to the prayer! The work is closely connected to Psalm 27 by common motifs such as the description of the LORD as a stronghold, the emphasis on salvation or deliverance, reference to the sanctuary, as well as similarities in the prayer formula. Psalm 28 also is arranged in the reverse order of Psalm 27: there the hymn of praise came first and then the lament, but here it is the prayer and lament before the confident praise.[12]

It is difficult to know what the exact situation was, for the descriptions are timeless. The psalm refers to the LORD's anointed, but it is not a royal psalm or a messianic psalm; it simply shares the concern for the LORD's reign over the land through his anointed. The psalmist is probably the king (although "anointed" could refer to a priest or even the whole nation). He appears to be confronted by people who pretend to be peaceful but are planning to harm or destroy him; his only recourse is to seek refuge in the sanctuary where he earnestly prays for God to respond to them according to what they deserve—but to do it in such a way that he would not be swept away in their judgment. Kraus concludes that the psalm was from the time of the monarchy and could be very ancient; it would then have found application for any number of afflictions.[13] A. A. Anderson is firm that the psalm is hardly as early as David,[14] but there is nothing in the psalm that precludes Davidic authorship. The reference to the temple as noted earlier could apply to the tabernacle; the imagery of

---

12. VanGemeren, *Psalms*, p. 287.
13. *Psalm 1–59*, p. 340.
14. *Psalms 1–72*, p. 228.

the shield, stronghold, strength, and salvation are common in other Davidic psalms; and the prayer for the LORD to shepherd and carry his people is certainly appropriate for David. If the psalm was not written by David, it would have been written by someone like him early in the monarchy.

The psalm has a link with Psalm 29 as well. In Psalm 28 the writer describes the LORD as his strength; and in Psalm 29 the LORD will be praised because of his great strength that he gives to his people. In Psalm 28 the writer prays for the LORD to bless his people, and that prayer is answered in Psalm 29:11.

This lament may be divided in different ways. It could simply be divided into two, the lament (1–5) and the hymnic thanksgiving (6–9); but verse 9 is a prayer for the nation, so it should be taken as a third part. Verse 5 is an expression of confidence delivered to the congregation and may fit with the praise section which also addresses the congregation (vv. 6–8); but verse 6 begins with the actual praise to the LORD, and so it should begin the praise section leaving verse 5 as the confidence section in the petition.

Exegetical Analysis

Summary

Because the LORD protects and delivers him, the psalmist confidently prays that the LORD will separate those who do wickedly from him by overthrowing them, and continue to protect and care for his people.

Outline

I. The psalmist petitions the LORD to hear his prayer to deliver him from a common fate with the wicked (1–5).
  A. He cries out to the LORD to hear his prayer and separate him from those whose prospect is death (1)
  B. He petitions the LORD to be favorable to him and not draw him away with the hypocritical sinners who will be judged for their works (2–4)
  C. He is confident that the wicked will be utterly destroyed because they disregard God (5).

II. Confident of an answer to his prayer, the psalmist praises the LORD as the one who gives him strength, protection, and victory (6–8).

III. The psalmist petitions the LORD to deliver and care for his people (9)

COMMENTARY IN EXPOSITORY FORM

I. The people of God desire to be separated from the ungodly when God destroys them because of their wicked works and their disregard of his work (1–5).

A. They pray for the LORD to deliver them from a common fate with the ungodly (1).

In the first five verses the psalmist expresses his great need of an answer to his cry for help, even though he does not specify what the difficulty was. His main concern was that if the LORD did not answer him he would die like his enemies who were responsible for his trouble. Verse 1 may be understood as the introductory cry in the lament and verses 2–5 the petition proper, with verse 5 expressing his confidence.

The psalm begins with a direct appeal: "To you, O LORD, I call" (אֶקְרָא has the progressive nuance—I am now calling). The appeal is strengthened by the request that God, addressed as his "rock," not be deaf to him (the negated jussive אַל־תֶּחֱרַשׁ expressing the immediacy of the request). The figure of being deaf (an implied comparison) signifies a failure to respond to his prayer—if God did not answer it would seem as if he did not hear the prayer. The idea is expanded in the second half of the verse: if God remained silent the psalmist would be like those who go down to the pit. The line begins with "lest" (פֶּן) expressing a conditional clause: "if you remain silent" (תֶּחֱשֶׁה), which means if you do not answer my prayer. Because these middle two clauses in the verse are similar, deaf and silent, the emphasis of the verse is the fear that God would not respond. Since God does not hear the prayers of the wicked and the sinner (Isa. 59:1–2), the psalmist was afraid that he was being treated as if he were ungodly too.

And if God did not respond, he would be like those who go down to the pit. The verb "I shall be like" (וְנִמְשַׁלְתִּי, from מָשַׁל; s.v. Ps. 49:3) expresses the consequence of the silence. This word is used mainly when the two objects compared form a contrast that is unacceptable. He does not want to be like those who go down to the pit (יוֹרְדֵי בוֹר) because the pit connotes darkness and gloom. The word "pit" can refer to any kind of hole, cistern, or dungeon; but it is often used synonymously with the grave or death (see Pss. 30:3; 88:6; Prov. 1:12; Job 7:9; for she'ol, s.v., Ps. 6:5). Those going down to the pit are not just dying, but dying without hope. In this simile David is comparing himself to the ungodly; if his prayer goes unanswered, he will not appear to be different. He will die as they die, without any reprieve from the LORD. The opposite idea is expressed in Psalm 30:3 where David praises God for delivering him from death: "You have kept me alive that I should not go down to the pit." His fear was to die with no word from the LORD. His concern was genuine; but his appeal to God was confident, for he calls God his rock, a figure for security and stability (an implied comparison). The use of this designation indicates he has a history of being secured by the LORD. It also indicates that in previous experiences it was God alone who protected him from his enemies. God was the only one who could deliver him now.

B. They pray that the LORD will spare them from the judgment of the evil-doers (2–4).

The ungodly deserve to be judged for the things that they do, but the righteous do not want to be drawn into that judgment because they do not do the same things. "Hear the voice of my supplications as I cry out to you for help." This verse fills out the idea of the first verse: "hear" and "do not be deaf." What he wants God to hear (i.e., respond to) is termed "the voice of my supplications."[15] "Voice" stands for what he says (metonymy of cause), and "my supplications" is the description of what he says. The word "my supplications" (תַּחֲנוּנַי) is an appeal for divine

---

15. The word may be plural to reflect several related requests, or it may be an abstract plural for his supplication.

favor (the word is related to חָנַן, "to be gracious, show favor"; s.v. Ps. 4:1).

The following temporal clauses add to the intensity of his praying. The first is "as I cry out (בְּשַׁוְּעִי) to you," the verb meaning to cry for help out of desperation (cf. Jon. 2:2). The second is "as I lift my hands to your innermost holy place." Lifting the hands signified focused prayer (a metonymy of adjunct because the gesture went with the prayer; see a similar expression in Isaiah 1:15). They could stand (1 Kings 8:22) or kneel (Ezra 9:5) with their hands lifted. The prayer is directed to the sanctuary, but it means to the LORD in the sanctuary (a metonymy of subject). And the "innermost place" (דְּבִיר) is a reference to the Holy of Holies, the enclosed room in the back of the holy place. The term is used only here in the psalms (see 2 Chronicles 5:7). The picture is that of the suppliant standing in the courtyard of the sanctuary with uplifted hands facing the Holy of Holies, where the LORD dwelt among his people, crying out for deliverance.

The petition proper is recorded in verses 3 and 4. He wants God to separate him from the wicked enemies when he judges them (similar to Abraham's prayer in Genesis 18). His description of them shows why. They are "the wicked" (or ungodly; s.v., Ps. 1:1); this identifies them as people who are guilty before God and stand condemned. They are "evil-doers" (doers or practitioners of evil, פֹּעֲלֵי אָוֶן).[16] This description could fit almost any

---

16. The word "evil" (אָוֶן) means "wickedness, trouble, sorrow." The meaning of "sorrow" is illustrated with the naming of Benjamin first as "son of my sorrow" (אוֹנִי) because of the difficulty of his birth. Proverbs 22:8 says the sower of iniquity shall reap "trouble." A second group of passages uses it to describe idolatry (Hos. 12:12). In fact, Hosea plays with the name Bethel because of its idolatry and calls it בֵּית אָוֶן in 4:15. The third category is the common use for trouble of iniquity, wickedness. Psalm 7:14 says the ungodly conceive "misery" and bring forth a lie. It is used in Isaiah 1:13 to describe the hypocritical worship of Israel that the LORD could not bear.

The frequent expression "doers of iniquity" may emphasize people who cause trouble by their wicked acts (see Job 34:36; Ps. 5:6). There has been a good deal of speculation over the identity of the "doers of iniquity." Briggs says in Psalm 28 it refers to the Babylonians (*Psalms,* p. 247), but the context suggests they are within Israel. There is no evidence to conclude they are foreigners; in a lament psalm it is more likely that they are the psalmist's countrymen, or at least people in the land in constant contact

enemies of the faith; here their evil is not the open antagonism of enemy nations, but of people known to the psalmist who proved to be hypocrites. They characteristically speak peace ("speakers of peace," דִּבְרֵי שָׁלוֹם) to their neighbors, but evil (רָעָה, s.v. Ps. 10:15) is in their heart. They speak as if they wish people well, all the while planning to do something that will harm them, either with a deliberate plot to destroy them or with a plan for their own benefit at the expense of the righteous.

These are the people God will judge; and David's prayer is that he be not dragged off with them (אַל־תִּמְשְׁכֵנִי). The picture may be that of a military context in which the conqueror drags people away to their fate. Kirkpatrick suggests the language may have referred to criminals being dragged off to judgment.[17] Whatever the specific significance of the expression was, the point is clear: when the LORD judges these wicked people, the psalmist does not want to perish with them. Why? Because he is not one of them. If God judged the wicked with a national calamity such as a military invasion and he fell with them, it would appear that he was also being judged. He knows that a certain kind of death is the prospect of the wicked; it is a death that leads down to the pit and is clearly different from the prospect of the righteous (see Ps. 1:6; Prov. 12:3, etc).

With that concern expressed, he also prays that the LORD punish them: "give to them according to their activity" and their evil practices. By wording his prayer this way the psalmist is appealing to the justice of God. Because the activities of the ungodly are evil in the sight of God, they deserve God's judgment. The punishment should fit what they actually do, which is the outworking of what was in their heart (v. 3). Since they were called "evil-doers" (< פָּעַל), the prayer is that they be dealt with according to their deeds (< פָּעַל). This word "deeds" simply refers to what they do, activities and the like; but what they do is said to be evil. The same word will be used in verse 5 for the "acts" of

---

(see A. A. Anderson, *Psalms 1–72*, p. 230; Westermann, *Praise and Lament in the Psalms,* pp. 188–94). Bernhardt says they are personal enemies of a private worshiper who want to harm him by misusing their power, especially with slander, false accusations, and cursing (*TDOT,* I:147). See further, G. W. Anderson, "Enemies and Evildoers in the Book of Psalms," *BJRL* 48 (1965, 6):18–29.

17. *Psalms*, p. 145.

the LORD, but because it is the LORD those acts are righteous. That their deeds are evil is emphasized in the next colon: "according to the evil of their practices" (מַעֲלָל, "deed, practice," normally refers to the practices of bad people, although it can refer to the practices of the LORD [Ps. 78:7]). The verse concludes with "bring back on them what they deserve." The verb changes from "give" (תֵּן) to "bring back" (הָשֵׁב from שׁוּב; s.v. Ps. 126:1) because it will be a just recompense—their sins and the results of their sins will come back on them. The word translated with "what they deserve" (גְּמוּל) means "dealing," but it includes the idea of recompense. The prayer, then, is a prayer for judgment on sin.

C. They know that God will destroy those who have no regard for him (5).

The righteous know that God will judge the wicked, so verse 5 expresses the psalmist's confidence that God will do this. It begins with the reason for the judgment: they do not give heed to the works of the LORD. The word "give heed" (יָבִינוּ from בִּין; s.v. Ps. 49:1) literally means "understand, perceive, discern." The psalmist was not basing his appeal only on how these people treated him, but on the fact that they failed to respond by faith to the LORD. By not giving attention to what the LORD has done, they did not concern themselves with his sovereign majesty or his covenant (in Psalm 8:3, 6 "work" is used for God's handiwork in creation). They knew about it, but they did not seek to understand it or to live by it. Kirkpatrick says, "Atheists in practice if not in profession, they deny that Jehovah governs the world, and refuse to discern His working in creation, in providence, and in judgment. Unbelief lies at the root of all their sin. The works of the LORD and the operation of His hands stand in strong contrast to their work and the operation of their hands in v. 4."[18] They may disregard the works of his hands, but God will not disregard the works of their hands.

The expectation of judgment is affirmed in the second half of the verse. The subject of "He shall tear them down" is the

18. *Psalms*, p. 146.

LORD (and so some wish to add the name as the subject). He will destroy them and not build them (up again). Tearing down is a figure for judgment and ruin, and building up would be a figure for establishing and making secure (both are implied comparisons). It is as if the ungodly are a building that will be demolished and not rebuilt (see Mal. 1:1–5). The figure is very realistic; in wars it was often the case that when people were destroyed their houses were decimated (see Jer. 24:6). Defeat was therefore devastating and humiliating.

II. The people of God express their confidence that the LORD will answer their prayer by praising him for giving them strength, protection, and deliverance (6–8).

A. They praise the LORD because they are convinced he has answered their prayer (6).

The tone of the psalm shifts now to praise, a praise that is the natural expression of the confidence in verse 5. The praise begins with "Blessed be the LORD" (s.v. Ps. 5:12) and then gives the summary reason—the LORD heard the voice of his supplication. It is clear that the psalmist has been transformed by realizing God answered his prayer.[19]

B. They praise the LORD for giving them strength, protection, and deliverance (7–8).

In verse 7 he describes the LORD as "my strength and my shield."[20] By affirming that the LORD is his strength (a metonymy of effect), he is saying that his true strength comes from the LORD (cf. Ps. 29:11). By affirming that the LORD is his shield (a

---

19. It could be that it has happened or has begun to happen, and he has received an oracle of salvation; but the verb could also be expressing his confidence in the certainty that God will answer.

20. The poetical arrangement of verse 7 is awkward with the dichotomy (//) coming after "helped": "The LORD is my strength and my shield / in him my heart trusts, and I am helped // my heart leaps for joy / and I will acknowledge him with my song."

metaphor), he is saying that the LORD is his protection. The images in this psalm may suggest a military setting ("rock, "shield," and "stronghold""); or, it may be that these expressions were so common in his thinking he could apply them in a non-military setting as well. God gives him strength to deal with all opposition and protects him in the process. Because the LORD is his strength and shield, he trusts in him (< בָּטַח, s.v. Ps. 4:5), and as a result is helped ("and I am helped," וְנֶעֱזָרְתִּי; s.v. Ps. 46:1). The verb "trusts" may be classified as a characteristic perfect—he has been and still is trusting; and the verb "helped" (וְנֶעֱזָרְתִּי) expresses the result.[21] The idea of God's helping or being a helper emphasizes that he does for people what they cannot do for themselves. The word can be used in military battles (see 1 Sam. 7:12 and Ps. 46:1, 5) as well as in other types of divine intervention, such as delivering the orphan (Ps. 10:14). The help in this case looks at God's answer to his prayer for deliverance from the enemies and their fate. If the LORD had not "helped" (intervened), there would be no deliverance (as the account in 1 Samuel 7 makes clear).

The second half of the verse expresses his joy at divine help: "my heart leaps for joy" (וַיַּעֲלֹז). This is the second time in the verse the psalmist mentions his own heart; and it is a striking contrast to the heart of the enemies (v. 3): their heart was wicked, but his trusts and rejoices. The verb used here (עָלֹז) signifies the expression of joy through singing and shouting. His praise is exuberant! The tense, an instantaneous perfect (here a preterite with the *waw* consecutive), expresses the joy he feels at the moment.

His joy will find expression in the public acknowledgment he will give to the LORD with song.

The verb "I will acknowledge him" (אֲהוֹדֶנּוּ, from יָדָה, s.v. Ps. 6:5) is an imperfect tense (although it could be a cohortative with a suffix); it indicates what he anticipates doing (or what he resolves to do if it is cohortative) when he brings his sacrifice of praise and declares how the LORD answered his prayer.[22]

---

21. Goldingay prefers to translate this as a future, "so I will be helped" (*Psalms 1–41*, p. 408); and Kraus reads the line and the next verb as "I was helped, then my heart exulted" (*Psalms 1–59*, p. 339).

22. It is possible to take the verb as a progressive imperfect and give it an English present tense translation, which would mean he was now acknowledging the LORD with this song.

Verse 8 concludes this section of praise by restating that "the LORD is their strength." The shift from "my strength" to "their strength" has prompted some commentaries to suggest the text is wrong and should read "the strength of his people" (with the support of the Greek and Syriac and a few manuscripts). The form in the text is unusual (לָמוֹ, "to them" = "their"), but probably is saying the same thing that the variant reading (לְעַמּוֹ, "to his people") is saying.

To this is added the affirmation that the LORD "is a saving stronghold" of "his anointed one," most likely the king. The text says literally "the stronghold of salvation" (מָעוֹז יְשׁוּעוֹת). The metaphor "stronghold" is related to the word "strength" (s.v. Ps. 29:1); it is a strong place of safety. The word "salvation" (s.v. Ps. 3:2) may be taken as an attributive genitive, "a saving stronghold"; or it could indicate the effect of the stronghold, salvation. Because the LORD was his place of safety, he was delivered again and again. By the expression "his anointed one" (מְשִׁיחוֹ), the psalmist is referring to himself in the third person. This adjective is an objective genitive ("saving stronghold of his anointed"), meaning the LORD saves his anointed king.

III. The people of God pray for continued blessing and care (9).

The last verse of the psalm is a concluding prayer for the nation. God has shown him salvation, and so he prays "Save your people" (הוֹשִׁיעָה, the alternate hiphil imperative form). His request is for the LORD to deliver the nation from all its enemies and troubles, as he did him. They may not be in danger at the moment, but there was every reason to expect they would be. Then, to the prayer for their deliverance he adds, "Bless your inheritance." By "inheritance" he means the people (an implied comparison), signifying that they now belong to the LORD as his possession (Deut. 4:20). The word captures the special relationship between Israel and the LORD and their value to him. The psalmist prays for divine blessing on them, i.e., that the LORD would enrich and empower them in every way (s.v. Ps. 5:12).

The last colon of the verse asks God to be a shepherd to his people: "and shepherd them (וּרְעֵם from רָעָה) and carry them

(וְנִשָׂא; s.v. Ps. 24:7) forever" (עַד־הָעוֹלָם, "unto eternity"; s.v. Ps.
61:5). The prayer for the LORD to shepherd them draws on the
well-known image that likens the LORD to a shepherd (here an
implied comparison), something that David would have been
very familiar with in his experiences (cf. Ps. 23:1 for the metaphor). The prayer to "shepherd them" is a prayer asking God to
provide for them, lead them, care for them, and defend them.
As a shepherd he will carry them safely through danger (see
Isa. 40:11). The contrast could not be clearer: God will drag the
wicked away to judgment, but the faithful he will tenderly carry
and protect from the enemies.

MESSAGE AND APPLICATION

The message is a reminder that even in the midst of difficult
circumstances the LORD protects and delivers his people. They
therefore can pray for him to continue to defend them from wickedness and to take care of them as their faithful shepherd. At
times, however, it may seem that the LORD does not hear their
prayer; but that should not be interpreted to mean that he has
disowned them, no matter what fears and uncertainties his silence might prompt. When the wickedness of the world becomes
so oppressive that the lives of the people of God are endangered,
they may pray confidently for the LORD to deal with the wicked
according to what they deserve, but to do it in a way that separates the righteous from a common fate with them. If they do
not have such confidence, then they must cultivate and develop
their spiritual growth in the word by their growing faith.

The psalm may be summarized for the exposition in these
words: *Because the LORD is our defender and deliverer we can
rely on him to separate us from the wicked in their judgment
and to care for us forever, a salvation that will inspire great joy
and everlasting praise.* The pattern to follow is, of course, Christ
Jesus, who when he suffered uttered no threats but kept entrusting himself to God who judges righteously (1 Peter 2:23).
God may judge wicked people from time to time even now, but
he certainly will do it in the future when Christ puts all enemies
under his feet (1 Cor. 15:25).

Some people may not feel it is appropriate for modern

believers to pray for God to judge people, but the kind of prayer that we have in Psalm 28 is an appropriate prayer to pray and does not conflict with Christian teaching. David is praying for the LORD to judge a particularly wicked group of people, people who have no regard for God and his will but are bent on harming and destroying other people. He is not praying for God to do something he has never done, or to do something he has not said he was going to do. His prayer is not a personal vendetta; it is a prayer that they be judged according to the wicked deeds they perform and that the judgment be accomplished in a way that would separate them from the righteous. As the king, his concern is to defend the faith and the people of God. Even today all over the world there are people who are so evil they plunder and destroy the lives of innocent people. If malicious people who terrorize and ruin the lives of other people, especially people who are devout believers, were stopped in their tracks, then many would be spared suffering and death. However else we may pray with regard to wickedness in the world, it is proper to pray for justice and righteousness to prevail, and that may require divine justice being enforced. Besides, to pray for the kingdom to come and God's will to be done on earth, or to pray that the Lord come quickly, is to pray for judgment on those who refuse God and reject his word.

PSALM 29

The Powerful "Voice" of the LORD

INTRODUCTION

Text and Textual Variants

A Psalm of David.[1]

1 Ascribe to the LORD, you sons of the Mighty,[2]
  ascribe to the LORD glory and strength,[3]
2 ascribe to the LORD the glory due to his name,
  worship the LORD in holy attire.[4]

3 The voice of the LORD is over the waters.
  The God of glory thunders;

---

1. Some Greek translations add "at the leaving of the tabernacle" (ἐξοδίου σκηνῆς).
2. The phrase "the sons of the mighty" (בְּנֵי אֵלִים) is difficult. The comparable expression, "sons of God" (בְּנֵי אֱלֹהִים) refers to angels in Job 2:1 and Psalm 84:7, and that is probably the meaning of the phrase used here. אֵלִים is not found alone meaning "God"; the plural means "the gods" (see Exod. 15:11; Dan. 11:36). The Syriac has "young rams" as the translation. Some Greek translations have "Give to the Lord, sons of God (υἱοὶ Θεοῦ), give to the Lord young rams" (υἱοὺς κριῶν), repeating the first part of the verse and thereby adding a line to the verse.
3. Greek text has "honor" (τιμὴν). It does translate "strength" in verse 11 with ἰσχὺν.
4. Greek has "in his holy court" (ἐν αὐλῇ ἁγίᾳ αὐτοῦ), perhaps reading בְּחַצְרַת, "in the court of," instead of בְּהַדְרַת.

The LORD is over many waters.

4 The voice of the LORD is mighty;
   the voice of the LORD is majestic.
5 The voice of the LORD breaks the cedars,
   yes, the LORD breaks the cedars of Lebanon.
6 He makes them skip[5] like a calf—
   Lebanon and Sirion like the young of the wild ox.[6]
7 The voice of the LORD splits the flames of fire.
8 The voice of the LORD shakes the wilderness;
   the LORD makes the wilderness of Kadesh shake.
9 The voice of the LORD causes the hinds[7] to calve,
   and strips the forests;[8]
   and in his temple all that is therein says, "Glory!"

10 The LORD sat enthroned at the flood;
    yes, the LORD sits as king for ever.
11 The LORD gives strength to his people,
    the LORD blesses his people with peace.

Composition and Context

Psalm 29, one of the most beautiful psalms, deals with the power of God revealed in nature and available to his people, if they respond with genuine faith. The passage is entirely praise; there is no request at all. A descriptive praise psalm is about the person of God and his works in life, or more simply, his greatness and his grace. In this psalm the emphasis on his greatness is caught up with the power and majesty of the LORD revealed

---

5. Greek has "beat them small" (λεπτυνεῖ).
6. For this line the Greek text reads "and he that is beloved like a young unicorn" (καὶ ὁ ἠγαπημένος ὡς υἱὸς μονοκερώτων).
7. The MT has יְחוֹלֵל אַיָּלוֹת, meaning, "causes the hinds to travail" (in birth pangs). Because this does not make an exact parallel with the next colon, some propose reading אֵילוֹת instead, meaning "oak trees." This makes a good parallelism, of course, but it has two difficulties: it requires an unusual use for the verb, and no manuscript or version has this different reading. The Greek has "prepares the hinds" (καταρτιζομένου ἐλάφους).
8. The Greek has "will uncover/cut off (ἀποκαλύψει) the thickets."

in a thunderstorm, and the emphasis on his grace is found in the declaration that he gives power and peace to his people.

The focus on a thunderstorm is interesting because it is not located in Israel. The psalmist traces the movement of the storm as it crosses Lebanon and Syria to the north, Canaanite territory. The location of the storm and some of the language of the psalm indicate that the piece is a polemic against Canaanite religious beliefs. In that northern region the storm god was the god Baal (Hadad), but to the psalmist it was not the voice of Baal causing the storm, but the voice of Yahweh, the God of Israel.

To form this polemic it is possible that part of a Cannanite hymn may have been taken over and used polemically against the worship of Baal, affirming for the Hebrews the sovereignty of their God Yahweh over all nature and the nations.[9] It is equally possible that the psalm was composed in Israel rather than adapted, because no Canaanite original hymn has been found. There is no evidence to support the idea that an older form of a Canaanite hymn was used by David and this psalm was a later revision of it. It makes just as good sense to say that the writer used old literary conventions that had been developed by the myths of Canaan but made certain they were attributed to the LORD (Yahweh) and not Baal. These ideas and expressions of the psalm could fit a Davidic authorship. The point the psalm makes is clear enough, no matter who wrote it or what the circumstances were behind its composition—Yahweh sits enthroned over all forces of nature.

---

9. The relationship between this psalm and Canaanite ideas is variously explained by scholars. For a few of the treatments, see T. H. Gaster, "Psalm 29," *JQR* 37 (1946,7):55–65; F. M. Cross, Jr., "Notes on a Canaanite Psalm in the Old Testament," *BASOR 117* (1949):19–21; P. C. Craigie, "Psalm xxix in the Hebrew Poetic Tradition," *VT* 22 (1972): 143–51; John Day, "Echoes of Baal's Seven Thunders and Lightnings in Psalm xxix . . . ," *VT* 29 (1979):143–51; and F. C. Fensham, "Ugarit and the Translator of the Old Testament," *Bible Translator* 18 (1967):71–74. Kraus accepts the idea that the psalm goes back directly to a Canaanite Baal hymn, but says the name Yahweh was substituted for the name Baal-Hadad: "The polemical meaning that overcomes the Canaanite myth in this conception will have to be worked out in the interpretation" (*Psalms 1–59*, p. 347).

Exegetical Analysis

Summary

Having witnessed the awesome manifestations of the LORD's power in a terrifying thunderstorm over Lebanon and Syria, the psalmist calls on the angelic hosts to glorify him who sovereignly rules over nature, displaying his ability to give power and peace to his people.

Outline

I. Call to praise: The psalmist calls upon the angelic hosts to glorify the LORD in holy array (1–2).
  A. He calls the hosts to ascribe glory to the LORD (1–2a).
    1. They are to ascribe glory and strength to him (1).
    2. They are to ascribe to him the glory due his name (2a).
  B. He calls the hosts to worship him in holy array (2b).
II. Cause for praise: The psalmist describes the LORD's omnipotent control of nature in a terrifying storm over Lebanon and Syria (3–9).
  A. He attributes the rise of the storm to the "voice of the LORD" (3–4).
    1. The "voice of the LORD" is manifested in the building storm at sea (3).
    2. The "voice of the LORD" is powerful and majestic (4).
  B. He witnesses the "voice of the LORD" in the height of the storm (5–7).
    1. The "voice of the LORD" breaks the cedars of Lebanon (5).
    2. The "voice of the LORD" quakes the great mountains (6).
    3. The "voice of the LORD" flashes forked lightening (7).
  C. He attributes the passing of the storm to the "voice of the LORD" (8–9).
    1. The "voice of the LORD" shakes up everything that is in the wilderness (8).
    2. The "voice of the LORD" is responsible for the effects of the storm (9).
      a. Hinds prematurely calve out of fright.

b. Forests are stripped bare by the storm.

c. All creatures in the heavenly courts shout "glory" to the LORD at the demonstration of his power.

III. Conclusion: The psalmist declares that the LORD rules over all nature and is able to share his strength and peace with his people (10–11).

A. Alluding to the flood, he declares that the LORD sits as king forever (10).

1. The LORD sat (in authority) at the flood.

2. The LORD sits as king forever.

B. Referring to the storm, he also declares that the LORD is able to give strength and peace to his people (11).

1. The one who can call up a storm can give strength to his people.

2. The one who can cause the storm to cease can give peace to his people.

COMMENTARY IN EXPOSITORY FORM

I. God deserves to be praised by his servants for his majestic power (1–3).

The first three verses of the psalm form the call to praise; it is a call to attribute glory to the LORD which is befitting his character and reputation. The form of the call is put in climactic parallelism; three lines are very similar, but the fourth changes to make the important qualification: "Ascribe to the LORD . . . , ascribe to the LORD . . . , ascribe to the LORD . . . , worship the LORD in holy array."

The first three imperatives are "ascribe" or "give" (הָבוּ from יָהַב). This repeated call is to give the LORD "glory and strength," the "glory due his name." The expression basically means to proclaim the glory and strength of God in praise, i.e., to give God the credit that he deserves. The word "glory" (כָּבוֹד, s.v. Ps. 19:1) refers to God's importance, and the word "strength" (עֹז) refers to his power.[10] His power actually displays his glory (cf. Isa. 6:1–3;

---

10. עָזַז means "to be strong"; there is an adjective "strong" (עַז), a noun "strength" (עֹז), a less common noun (עֱזוּז), and an adjective (עִזּוּז), "mighty."

for "glory" s.v. Ps. 19:1). The call is to give God the praise that is fitting for his "name," or, his nature. Everything about the nature of the LORD deserves praise, but especially his strength, i.e., his supernatural power. In this psalm that strength will be evidenced in his sovereign control of nature.

The call is addressed to "the sons of the mighty" (בְּנֵי אֵלִים). The expression is difficult but probably means "sons of God," even though elsewhere that is written differently (בְּנֵי אֱלֹהִים). In the Old Testament these would be angels (Job 2:1).[11] In the Canaanite texts the expression "the sons of El (God)" refers to the pantheon of the gods.[12] It may very well be that the polemic nature of the psalm includes an allusion to pagan mythology. As the psalmist called on the "sons of the mighty" to praise Yahweh, he used language that was familiar to the Canaanites but had the true meaning of the expression—angels. To the pagans he would seem to be calling for the gods of their pantheon to give the praise to Yahweh, the God of Israel, but in his own thinking they were not gods at all, but angelic beings. His words had a

---

The noun "strength" can refer to anything physical or spiritual that is strong or powerful, such as a stronghold, or a strong arm, or a mighty voice. It can be used in a negative sense of an impudent look, i.e., a strong face (Deut. 28:50). Proverbs 21:29 says a wicked man makes his face firm (show boldness).

It is an essential attribute of the LORD for which he is praised. His strength is demonstrated in his creation (Ps. 29:1), his acts of deliverance (Ps. 68:28), his destruction of enemies (Exod. 15:13). His mighty presence is connected to the ark, which is referred to as "the ark of your strength" (Ps. 132:8) or just "strength" (Ps. 78:61) because it became the central focus of the powerful presence of the LORD.

The word has several close synonyms and it is not easy to make a sharp distinction between them.

11. In the expression "sons of the Mighty," "Mighty" is a reference to God and not to the mighty ones on the earth, such as princes of lands. It is not impossible that "the sons of the mighty [God]" refers to the Israelites. But the only place where the phrase refers to humans is Hosea 2:10, which says, "you are the sons of the living God." The Hebrew there uses the singular form of the noun (בְּנֵי אֵל), "the sons of God" (Perowne, *Psalms*, I:277–8).

12. Interestingly John Milton in Book I of *Paradise Lost* identifies the fallen angels as the gods of the ancient Near East. The connection between the biblical "sons of God" as angels, and Canaanite "sons of God" as lesser gods, harmonizes with this insight.

double reference: in calling angelic hosts to worship the LORD in holy array he was in effect calling their gods, or the spirits behind them, to give him the glory, to bow down to Yahweh, and to worship him (הִשְׁתַּחֲווּ). For the idea of pagan gods bowing down to Yahweh, see Psalm 97:7. Worship is the only response of creation to the sovereignty of the LORD.

The psalmist was calling to the hosts of heaven to praise the name of Yahweh, but they were to worship the LORD "in holy array" (בְּהַדְרַת־קֹדֶשׁ; for "holy" s.v. Ps. 22:3). Several commentators note that the language is descriptive of priests who were to array themselves for service in the sanctuary.[13] The priests were to have on pure white linens to signify holiness and purity to the LORD, but at times they wore festive garments to exalt the LORD. Accordingly, in the heavenly courts those worshiping the LORD, both saints and angels, are described symbolically as arrayed with priestly clothes for their unending service to the LORD. The point of this connection would be that while praise may be appropriate for the LORD it has to be from those who are arrayed in holiness that is necessary in the heavenly sanctuary. There is another way to interpret this expression, and that is that it refers to the LORD: worship the one who is arrayed in holiness.[14] The word "array" (בְּהַדְרַת־קֹדֶשׁ, "in array of holiness") usually refers to the LORD's glorious appearance.[15] The relation of God's holiness and the worshipers' appropriate condition would go without saying, but the psalmist included it in his call for praise in order that we mortals see the requirement for offering pleasing praise to God.

II. God is to be praised for his control of nature by his powerful word (3–9).

The psalm now gives the reason for the call to praise: the LORD's omnipotent control of nature by his word. What is

---

13. See e.g., Perowne, *Psalms*, I: 276.
14. Kidner, *Psalms 1–72*, p. 125.
15. The suggestion that the word is not "array" (a word related to "ornament") but related to a Ugaritic word that means "appearance" is not compelling (see Kraus, *Psalms 1–59*, p. 346; P. R. Ackroyd, "Some Notes on the Psalms," *JTS NS* 17 [1966]:392–99).

described here is a tremendous thunderstorm that sweeps across the land. The psalmist traces its path and development, and each step of the way attributes it to the voice of the LORD ("the voice of Yahweh," קוֹל יהוה). The voice occurs seven times in the passage (compare Rev. 10:3 with its seven thunders).

The provenance of the storm, as we shall see, is north of Israel, in Canaanite country. The passage has expressions and concerns that approximate the Canaanite texts (Ugaritic) that attribute the rise and fall of storms to the god Baal, a god of Canaan. The pictures of Baal clearly portray him as the storm god, standing on waves of water with a spear of lightning flashes in his hand and a club, for thunder, in the other. When people wanted it to rain they would cry out to Baal (see 1 Kings 18); when it did rain and thunder, they would credit Baal. In fact, the Canaanite texts refer to the seven peels of thunder from Baal, perhaps represented in this psalm with the seven occurrences of "the voice of the LORD."[16] The psalm, then, takes Canaanite expressions and beliefs to describe a storm in Canaanite country, but to affirm that it is Yahweh and not Baal who is sovereign over nature—even over Baal country.

This section can be broken down into three parts: the rise of the storm in its fury (3–4), the full force of the storm (5–7), and then the passing of the storm off into the desert (8–9).

A. God brings up the storm by his majestic word (3–4).

This section of the psalm begins with the statement that "the voice of the LORD is upon the waters." It is possible to interpret the expression "voice of the LORD" (קוֹל יְהוָה) as a figure of comparison (an implied comparison) referring to the sound of thunder, especially in view of the next colon that states that "the God of glory thunders." "The LORD" (Yahweh) is thus paralleled by "the God of glory" (or "glorious God") and "the voice" is paralleled by the verb "thunders," although in the third colon

---

16. See John Day, *God's Conflict with the Dragon and the Sea: Echoes of Canaanite Myth in the Old Testament* (Cambridge: Cambridge University Press, 1985).

the expression "the voice of the LORD" is paralleled simply with "the LORD" (Yahweh). Comparing thunder to a voice makes a simple interpretation of the verse, but in the rest of the psalm the expression does not seem to be a figure of comparison, and so the psalmist probably means that the voice was commanding the elements of nature, causing the storm by his word to develop and then die out (metonymy of cause). Accordingly, the expression could also be given that interpretation for the first verse, namely, that the LORD spoke the thunderstorm into existence.

The "waters," or "many waters," could refer to almost any body of water, above or below the firmament, but in this passage the path of the storm is from the waters inland to Lebanon and Syria. This would mean that "waters" is a reference to the Mediterranean Sea, the Great Sea. It could also be taken as a reference to the waters above the firmament, the dense storm clouds that would be building up; but even so given the path of this storm those clouds would be out to sea.

Verse 4 simply affirms the might and majesty of the voice of the LORD. These two words are prefixed with a preposition (בְּ), which is best taken to indicate the essence of the voice (a *beth* of essence). The translation then would be " . . . [is] strong," and then " . . . [is] majestic."

B. God's powerful word causes the storm to rage (5–7).

The voice of the LORD now breaks the cedars in pieces. These are the pride of Lebanon, but the storm that the LORD causes overpowers them, uprooting and breaking them with the fierce winds that drive the storm. The parallelism joins a participle (*qal,* שֹׁבֵר) and a preterite (*piel,* וַיְשַׁבֵּר), both expressing the continuing progress of the storm: "breaks" and "breaks in pieces." It also parallels "the voice of the LORD" with "the LORD."

Verse 6 then describes an earthquake in poetic form: "he makes them skip" provides the further comparison for the shifting ground; and the similes (e.g., "like a calf") fill out the poetic imagery. The suffix "them" on the verb is anticipatory, referring to Lebanon and Sirion in the next colon; these are two mountains or mountain regions north of Israel (Mt. Sirion probably refers to Mt. Hermon; Deut. 3:9).

Finally, in verse 7, there is a poetic description of forked lightning: "The voice of the LORD splits (hews out) flames of fire.

C. God's powerful word causes the storm to subside (8–9).

Next, the storm passes over the mountains into the eastern wilderness where it dies out. The location is "the wilderness of Kadesh." The name should not be taken to refer to Kadesh Barnea in the south, for the weather pattern would not turn south in that way. This is probably Kadesh on the Orontes River in the north. The word "Kadesh" designates a shrine, a holy place, and so it would be a fairly popular name for cities with temples. The text says that the voice of the LORD shakes (יָחִיל) the wilderness. "Wilderness" refers to the flora and fauna in the wilderness (a metonymy of subject); the storm makes this all tremble or shake and leaves behind it twisted and torn witnesses to its fury.

The last verse of this section of the psalm records the effects of this storm. The first is that it causes the hinds to travail in birth-pangs (יְחוֹלֵל אַיָּלוֹת), probably giving birth pre-maturely.[17] The change of "hinds" to "oak trees" (אֵילוֹת) is not necessary and has no manuscript support (see NIV and others). It does form a nice parallel with the next colon, which reads "and strips the forests bare." There is no necessity for synonymous parallelism here; to have animals in one line and trees in the next is not a problem. In fact, a third colon gives us a different idea altogether.

Verse 9 provides the conclusion to the cause for praise. All that can proceed from the psalmist now is an acknowledgment of the heavenly hosts praising God: everything in his temple says, "Glory!" "Temple" here probably refers to the heavenly temple,

---

17. There are a number of suggestions for interpreting this line. Most accept that there is a reference to animals, but the verb has been translated "go into labor" (Jerome) "squirm in pain" (Kraus), and "convulse" (Goldingay). Goldingay explains this latter rendering as the deer jumping about in fright (*Psalms 1–41,* p. 412), although he allows "writhing in pain" is a legitimate meaning.

because the use of "glory" recalls the beginning of the psalm where the angelic hosts were enjoined to give God the glory.

"Glory" is an acclamation of praise (s.v. Ps. 19:1). Since the word basically means "to be heavy," the developed sense of "glory" refers to importance or worth, and "glorify" to acknowledge through praise the importance of God. Since no one can add to his intrinsic value or glory, glorifying God means to extend his reputation by praise throughout the earth, and that means declaring that he alone is rightly the sovereign, Lord of all nature.

III. Conclusion: God is able to bless his people with power and with peace (10–11).

A. *The LORD reigns over all nature (10).*

In addition to the description of the LORD's demonstrating his power and glory in Canaan, the psalmist recalls the greatest demonstration of it—the flood (Gen 6–8). This word "flood" is only used of the flood in Genesis. Accordingly, the verb that is used (יֵשֶׁב) refers to that time: "he sat (enthroned)." The next colon expands the idea from the flood to all time: "Yes, the LORD sits (enthroned) as King for ever." The psalmist envisions the LORD's sovereign control over all nature, then, in a universal event, and now in a localized storm.

B. *The LORD meets the needs of his people (11).*

Drawing upon the description of the movement of the storm, the psalmist now expresses the lesson for the people of God. Because the LORD displays his strength by bringing up a fierce storm, he is to be praised for his strength, but he grants that strength to his people as well.[18] In other words, the power of

---

18. There is no reason to make the verbs in this verse jussives on the basis that psalms often end with prayers or that these words continue the words of 9c–10 (Goldingay, *Psalms 1–41,* p. 421). There is also a didactic component in praise psalms, and the traditional understanding of this verse fits that.

God is made available as the resource for the people of God to overcome the world. And then, just as the LORD can command the storm to die out in the wilderness, he can give peace to his people. There is no fury in life that he cannot calm.

MESSAGE AND APPLICATION

Since the psalm provides the lesson for us in the last verse, the direction of the exposition is clear: *God displays his majestic power and perfect peace in nature and makes them available to his people, who with the angels in heaven should praise him and worship him in holiness.* The content of the psalm gives us the full illustration of what that power can do, and how calming that peace is; and the call to praise in the first part of the psalm, although addressed to angels, provides guidance for all God's creation to ascribe to him the glory due his name. That ascription of praise is to come from those who are spiritually prepared to enter into his holy presence. One could say that the implication of all this is that if people want to avail themselves of his power or his peace, they must demonstrate their faithfulness by acknowledging that all glory and power belongs to him—but they must do this in holiness. The apostle Paul told the Philippian church that he had removed everything that was in the way of knowing Christ and the power of his resurrection (Phil. 3:1–11). Arrayed in holiness the saints on earth join the company of angels and archangels in heaven to offer endless praise to the one who is worthy to receive praise, for by his powerful word he not only created everything but sustains it (Heb. 1:3).

The New Testament in many ways identifies the Lord Jesus Christ as the LORD of the Old Testament, and specifically with reference to the subject of this psalm because he demonstrates the same power over all creation. In the New Testament one reads of Jesus calming the storm, walking on water, changing water into wine, and even of his death being accompanied by storms and earthquakes. Such acts were used by Jesus to authenticate his claims to be the Lord of heaven and earth, and to this same Lord believers look for power and for peace throughout their lives.

PSALM 30

A Moment in His Anger— A Lifetime in His Favor

INTRODUCTION

Text and Textual Variants

A Psalm,[1] A Song for the Dedication of the House, Of David.

1   I will exalt you, O LORD, for you lifted me up
       and have not let my foes rejoice over me.
2   O LORD my God, I cried to you for help,
       and you healed me.
3   O LORD, you brought me[2] up from the grave;[3]
       you preserved me alive from those who go down to the
          pit.[4]

4   Sing praises to the LORD, O you his saints,

---

1. The Greek version has εἰς τὸ τέλος "regarding fulfillment," the translation
    it usually has for the Hebrew "for the Chief Musician."
2. Hebrew has "my life."
3. Hebrew: *sheʾol*, a place of certain death in this text.
4. This translation follows the more widely accepted *Kethiv* reading, מִיּוֹרְדִי,
    "from those going down to (the pit)." It is supported by the Greek, Theodo-
    tion, and the Syriac. The *Qʿre'* has an infinitive form, מִיָּרְדִי, "from my going
    down (to the pit)." It is supported by Aquila, Symmachus, the Targum, and
    a few other manuscripts

663

and give thanks to his holy name;[5]

5 for his anger is *but* for a moment,[6]
and[7] his favor is for a lifetime;
weeping may tarry in the evening,
but in the morning *there is* a shout of joy.

6 As for me, I said in my ease,[8]
"I can never be moved."

7 In your pleasure, O LORD, you made my mountain stand
strong;[9]
you hid your face; I was terrified.

8 To you, O LORD, I cried,
and to the Lord[10] I made supplication,[11] *saying:*

9 "What profit is there in my blood,
if I go down to the pit?
Will the dust praise you?
Will it tell of your faithfulness?

10 Hear, O LORD, and be merciful to me!
O LORD, be my helper!"[12]

11 You have turned for me my mourning into dancing;
you have removed my sackcloth and clothed me with
gladness,

---

5. Hebrew has "memorial of his holiness," or "his holy memorial [name]," the word "memorial" often meaning the name by which one would be remembered (see Exod. 3:15; s.v. Ps. 6:5). The Greek version makes a literal translation: "for the remembrance ($\mu\nu\acute{\eta}\mu\eta$) of his holiness.

6. The Greek version says, "anger ($\grave{o}\varrho\gamma\acute{\eta}$) is in his wrath" instead of "a moment," apparently thinking of רֶגַ instead of רֶגַע.

7. The "and" is not in the Hebrew, but in the Greek and Syriac.

8. Or "prosperity" or "self-sufficiency."

9. The MT has "(you made) my mountain (לְהַרְרִי) stand strong." The Greek version apparently understood it to read לְהַדְרִי because it has "(you added strength) to my beauty ($\tau\tilde{\omega}$ $\varkappa\acute{\alpha}\lambda\lambda\epsilon\iota$ $\mu\sigma\upsilon$)."

10. Some manuscripts change אֲדֹנָי to the holy letters יהוה; the Greek has "my God."

11. The Greek translations takes these verbs in the common future translation.

12. All the verbs in this verse are imperatives in the MT, but in the Greek translations they all translated as definite past.

12 that my[13] glory might sing praises to you and not be silent.[14]
O LORD my God, I will give thanks to you forever.

Composition and Context

Because of its beautiful and appropriate imagery and its clear
and powerful movement this psalm is one of the finest pieces of
poetry in the collection. It is a praise psalm that seems to have
been written after a recovery from a nearly fatal illness; as a
result of being healed the psalmist calls other believers to join
him in praise as he relates his experience and God's answer. It is
clear from the passage that his dilemma was the result of God's
anger, and that leads to the most likely interpretation that the
affliction was divine discipline for pride or presumption ("I said
in my self-sufficiency, 'I can never be moved'; You hid your face,
I was terrified"). While some do not think this is a case of divine
discipline,[15] the psalm clearly indicates that his sense of self-
sufficiency was followed by God's hiding his face and causing
terror in the psalmist's spirit—and this is called God's anger.
Perowne suggests he had begun to trust in himself and so paraphrases his thinking: "I seemed so strong, so secure, I began to
think within myself, I shall never be moved; Thou hadst made
my mountain so strong. And then, Thou didst hide Thy face and
I was troubled."[16] If this is the proper understanding, then the
psalmist's healing was more spiritual than physical.

The superscription records the tradition that the psalm was
Davidic and that it was for the "dedication (חֲנֻכָּת) of the house."
Most commentators would say that the psalm could not have
been written by David because it mentions the dedication of the
temple (interestingly taking one part of the superscription to

---

13. The pronoun "my" is in the Greek translation but not the MT.
14. The verb יִדֹּם is "will (not) be silent"; the Greek version has "I may not be
    pierced *with pain* (κατανυγῶ), perhaps representing a Hebrew form like אֶדְדֹּק.
15. Goldingay thinks that the psalm simply describes the normal life of a be-
    liever spent between the downs and ups of life (*Psalms 1–41,* p. 433). But
    as the exposition will show, the language of the psalm hardly describes the
    normal events in life.
16. Perowne, *Psalms,* p. I:280.

deny the other part), the reason being that the word "dedication" implies the completion of the temple. The various commentaries suggest different occasions for such a dedication of the temple. One is that it refers to the rededication of the temple in the days after Antioches Epiphanes, about 165 B.C. (1 Macc. 4:52). The connection to the feast of Hanukkah is intriguing, but there is no reason to place the psalm so late. Besides, the word "dedication" is not normally used for "rededication." Another view would be to take it to refer to the dedication of the temple in 515 B.C. (Ez. 6:16–17). Among those who allow that David may have written it is the suggestion that it was written for the dedication of his own house (2 Sam. 5:11–12), which he understood to be a sign of his security and the strength of his kingdom; but there is no evidence of illness preceding that. Less likely is the view that it was for the purification of his house after the trouble with Absalom (2 Sam. 20:3). VanGemeren suggests that the psalm was "associated with David" but the superscription was added when the psalm was nationalized as an expression of the suffering of the exile and the restoration.[17] He may be saying that David wrote it and later it was adapted for the dedication in 515 B.C., but it is not clear. It is certainly possible that a psalm by David was put to a more significant use later and a superscription added to note it. Goldingay also notes that the heading probably refers to a reuse of the psalm, possibly after the exile, or even after the desecration of Antiochus.[18]

There is also the possibility that the psalm could have been written by David for the dedication of the temple as the superscription simply says. That would not mean David built the temple, only that among all the other things he did to prepare for it he wrote a psalm for its dedication. Interestingly, just prior to acquiring the site for the temple, David sinned in numbering the people, for which the LORD brought a severe plague on the land (2 Sam. 24 and 1 Chron. 21). David did not personally fall sick in that plague (2 Sam. 24:17); and so if that is the original occasion, then the healing mentioned would have to have been more spiritual than physical. It is impossible to say with certainty what

---

17. VanGemeren, *Psalms*, p. 296.
18. Goldingay, *Psalms 1–41*, p. 425

the original occasion for the psalm was, but setting aside the superscription for the moment, the psalm itself could easily be Davidic. Whatever one decides on these issues, the message of the psalm is clear and relevant at all times. The attempt to find the occasion is of limited value other than to offer an illustration of the kind of situation the psalm mentions.

The passage follows the pattern of a declarative praise psalm. There is the introductory praise with summary explanation (vv. 1–3), a call for the congregation to join in the praise because the LORD's anger is brief but his favor lasts a lifetime (vv. 4–5), the report of the dilemma and his prayer (vv. 6–10), and finally the praise itself (vv. 11–12).

Exegetical Analysis

Summary

From his experience of deliverance from chastening for his sin of self-sufficient pride, the psalmist and the congregation praise the LORD for turning his grief to gladness and acknowledge that even though his anger is but for a moment, his favor lasts for a lifetime.

Outline

I. The psalmist acknowledges that the LORD delivered him from certain death and calls for the congregation to join him in praising God that his discipline is brief but his favor lasts a lifetime (1–5).
  A. He resolves to extol the LORD for delivering him from his enemies (1).
  B. He declares that the LORD delivered him from dying and restored him (2–3).
  C. He calls for the congregation to acknowledge that the LORD's discipline is brief but his favor lasts a lifetime (4–5).
II. The psalmist recalls his discipline for his sin of self-sufficiency and his prayer for deliverance (6–10).
  A. He reports how God terrified him with discipline when he acted in self-sufficiency (6–7).

B. He recalls how he prayed for help from that discipline (8–10).
   1. The prayer for God's favor reasoned that God would not profit from his death (8–9).
   2. The prayer was for God to be gracious and help him (10).
III. The psalmist declares that the LORD answered his prayer so that he would praise him forever (11–12).
   A. He tells how God removed the discipline that was causing him grief and restored him to health which resulted in joy (11).
   B. He acknowledges that God did this so that he would praise him forever (12).

COMMENTARY IN EXPOSITORY FORM

I. When God delivers believers from life-threatening trouble, they must lead the congregation in praise for his lasting favor (1–5).

A. Penitent believers acknowledge God's deliverance from life-threatening trouble (1–3).

The first section of the psalm is the summary praise for deliverance from dying. There is no clear indication in this beginning section that the dilemma was divine discipline; it simply reports that God answered the psalmist's prayer and delivered him from death. The first word establishes the purpose of the psalm: "I will exalt you" (אֲרוֹמִמְךָ is a *polel* cohortative from the verb רוּם, "to be high"; s.v. Ps. 46:10), expressing resolve to exalt or extol the LORD through praise—this is what devout believers do. The praise that he will offer will lift the LORD up in the minds of the congregation; it will not exalt the psalmist, because if it were not for the grace of God he would have died. Only the LORD is worthy of praise—always, but especially in this situation. If the first word establishes the purpose of the psalm, the first line gives the reason for the praise: the LORD rescued him from death to the disappointment of his enemies. The rescue is termed "you lifted me up" (דִּלִּיתָנִי). The word means "to draw up," as with a bucket; it is therefore a figurative use (an implied comparison), meaning "you saved me from death." The additional explanation is: "you did not allow my enemies to rejoice over me." The verb (שִׂמַּחְתָּ, the *piel* perfect) could also be translated "you did not cause to rejoice"—you gave them no reason to celebrate ("gloat" may be too trivial; for the word study, s.v. Ps. 48:11). If he had died his enemies would have celebrated, but the LORD prevented the enemies from realizing their expectation.

That this was the result of an answer to prayer is the point of verse 2: "I cried for help" (שִׁוַּעְתִּי) and "you healed me" (וַתִּרְפָּאֵנִי). The word "heal" (רָפָא)[19] suggests healing from an illness or an

---

19. רָפָא essentially means "to heal," but it has a wide range of nuances. It is used mostly of God as the subject, but does have some references where humans are the healers. There is a related noun מַרְפֵּא that means "healing, cure, health" (e.g., Jer. 14:19). The noun can refer to healing words (a soothing tongue, Prov. 15:4) or a healthy mind (Prov. 14:30). It can also be used for the healing of a disease (2 Chron. 21:18).

The verb can be used literally for healing, mending or fixing people or things, such as skin diseases (Lev. 14:3, 48), salty water (2 Kings 2:22) or broken pottery (Ezek. 47:8). It can be used in general for any kind of healing of wounds, diseases, or infections. Since the Hebrews understood that so much of disease was the result of divine discipline, there was a spiritual component to the healing as well—only God could heal, even if they used remedies and physicians. For example, God afflicted and then cured Miriam of a skin disease (Num. 12:9ff.).

The verb can be used figuratively for healing people of their hurts and distresses, and this usually involves the restoration of the LORD's favor, often with forgiveness of sin. Isaiah 6:10 uses it this way, for divine judgment was to follow lest the people be healed (spiritual restoration and deliverance from invasion). In Exodus 15:26 the LORD made the bitter water sweet so that the people could drink, declaring "I am the LORD, your healer." Since the episode was a test, their faith was being strengthened through it. The LORD healed them by changing the water; but it was a sign he could heal them of diseases as well. The use in Psalm 30 probably falls into this classification; because whatever physical healing might have been included, it was essentially a spiritual healing from his pride. In this way the healing almost becomes the equivalent of forgiveness (see Ps. 103:3 where it is paralleled with forgiving guilt and Ps. 147:3 where it refers to healing broken hearts). According to Jeremiah 3:22, God will heal apostasy. 2 Chron. 7:14 states that forgiveness is the prerequisite for restoration. If there is no forgiveness, there is no healing. Probably both are combined in Malachi's revelation of the coming of the Messiah with

injury; but the psalm does not develop either of these ideas and so the word "heal" must refer to some other restoration.[20] Here it more than likely includes the idea of forgiveness. In fact, the Hebrews generally thought that pain and trouble were connected to divine discipline in some way. The rest of the psalm will confirm this idea here because the psalmist will acknowledge that his presumptuous attitude was met with God's anger. The psalmist did not have to be physically ill to say God healed him; it probably was a restoration to a healthy spiritual and physical life with God's blessing.

The deliverance is explained more clearly in verse 3: God prevented him from dying. The first half of the verse says God brought him up from *sheol*. This word *sheol* can mean the grave, death, or the realm of the departed; but it can also mean the place of certain, imminent death, and since the verse will add that God prevented him from dying, this must be the meaning here (s.v. Ps. 6:5). The main verb in the parallel colon is "You preserved me alive" (חִיִּיתַנִי, the *piel* perfect) is from the verb "to live." The form could be translated "give life," "revive," or "preserve alive," but the idea of being kept alive (see also Ps. 22:29; Exod. 1:17, 22) fits best with the following phrase, "from those going down to the pit," meaning the dying. Others were dying, but God prevented him from dying by lifting him up and healing him.

B. Penitent believers invite others to acknowledge that God's discipline is brief compared to his favor (4–5).

The psalmist turns to exhort the congregation to join him in praising the LORD. Here we see the liturgical development from the event, that the praise would be offered in the sanctuary in the company of the righteous who would not only participate in the praise but confirm the belief expressed in the praise. The people are addressed as God's "beloved" (חֲסִידָיו), a word related to "loyal love" (s.v. Ps. 23:6). These are people who are faithful to the LORD and his covenant; they will rejoice when the LORD

---

healing (Mal. 4:2). The prophecy of the suffering servant states that by his suffering we are healed (Isa. 53:5).

20. Goldingay, *Psalms 1–41*, p. 426.

answers the prayer of another. They are invited to sing praises
(זַמְּרוּ) to the LORD and to give thanks or acknowledge (הוֹדוּ, s.v.
Ps. 6:5) his holy memorial (i.e., name; s.v. זָכַר, Ps. 6:5).

The substance of their praise is expressed in the lesson of
verse 5. The English translations usually read smoothly, but the
Hebrew is a little more cryptic, as if the ideas were being proclaimed ecstatically: "For a moment in his anger, a lifetime in
his favor; in the evening weeping may lodge, but in the morning
a ringing cry" (רִנָּה; s.v. Ps. 33:1). The line uses a number of figures of speech: "anger"[21] refers to the suffering he has endured

---

21. אַף (s.v. אָנַף) in the Semitic languages means "nostrils, nose" as well as
"anger." For example, in Genesis 2:7 the text says the LORD "breathed
into his *nostrils* the breath of life." Then, the word in the dual came to
mean "face," as in Genesis 19:1 which says "he bowed his *face* to the
ground." The development to the meaning of "anger" may be because of
the excited breathing of the nose which is characteristic of anger. The word
"wrath, anger" is used both of God and humans, but mostly of God. When
used of God the language is anthropomorphic, but the attribute of wrath it
communicates is real. Because the description draws on human qualities,
it will be helpful to start with human anger.

Anger is an expression of strong feelings of displeasure. It is one of the
strongest emotions, usually stimulated by some threat to one's concerns
and interests or by some affront or actual attack. For example, it is used
for Esau's rage against Jacob for taking his blessing (Gen. 27:45), Jacob's
anger with his wife (Gen. 30:2), and Saul's rage against Jonathan that
almost led to the death of the son (1 Sam. 20:30). Even among friends the
anger can surface: Elihu was angry with Job for vindicating himself (Job
32:2–5), and Moses became angry with the people of God for their wickedness (Exod. 32:19, 22).

The causes of anger are many and varied. For example, Esau was
angry over the loss of his blessing; Potiphar over hearing his wife had
been shamefully treated (Gen. 39:19); and Simeon and Levi were angry
because the family honor was damaged (Gen. 34:28). Sometimes the anger
might be righteous anger, as when Moses was angry over the hardness of
Pharaoh's heart (Exod. 11:8). While human anger could be without much
provocation, it is usually justified or at least understandable by some violation or perceived wrong.

The effects of anger range from reasoned rebukes to open hostility. In
some cases the power of words said in anger is also destructive; but human
anger is also controllable, and that is a concern of the teachings of wisdom
(e.g., Prov. 14:17; 16:32).

Most of the uses of the word, however, refer to God's anger (divine wrath is a biblical teaching in spite of modern views that attempt

because of God's anger (so a metonymy of cause); "favor" refers to the healing it caused (so a metonymy of cause also); "weeping" is the result of the suffering (and so is a metonymy of effect), and the ringing cry is the result of the healing (also a metonymy of effect). Also, "evening" is the time of darkness and danger and so it represents the time of suffering (an implied comparison); "morning" is the time of light and life, a new day, and so it represents the healing (another comparison). The time of suffering is described as a "moment" to contrast it with the lifetime in God's favor; and the experience of the suffering "spends the night" (a comparison with a brief stay). Kraus observes, "Distress and weeping turn out to be events of yesterday, of the past. With the new morning, the point in time of Yahweh's intervention (cf. Ps. 46:5; 90:14; 143:8), jubilation breaks out as the spirit that determines the meaning of life henceforth."[22]

The "moment" (רֶגַע) refers to a very brief time (so it is an understatement); the background of the word retains some of its sense of movement, such as the twinkling of an eye (thus, a denominative verb, "make a twinkling"). The meaning of the word is relative; in Isaiah 54:7 it is used for the duration of the captivity in comparison to God's dealings with Israel in history. Here the word is to be interpreted in comparison to the duration

to minimize this important attribute). God's wrath against sin is found throughout the Old Testament. It appears early in the sin of the golden calf (Exod. 32:10–12, 22) but is used most frequently by the prophets Hosea, Isaiah, Jeremiah, and Ezekiel. The wrath of God is always warranted by some violation or rebellious act.

In many passages the wrath of God is the necessary correlation to divine love (Exod. 4:14; Ps. 30:6). The favor and love of God for his people necessitates dealing with their rebellion, and the human-sounding description of flared nostrils and intense breathing, i.e., "anger," is the description used for the attribute that judges and punishes sin. It cannot be given the full human aspect of a sudden outburst of rage, for God is not capricious and never out of control.

We also read how God is slow to anger (Exod. 34:6; Num. 14:18) because there is always the desire that people come to repentance, but he will not clear the guilty. It is as if the judgment for sin, that is what the wrath of God produces, is the last resort (See Thomas Edward Finch, "A Study of the Word 'ap and the Concept of Divine Wrath in the Old Testament," unpublished thesis, Dallas Theological Seminary, May, 1975).

22. Kraus, *Psalms 1–59*, p. 355.

of his lifetime. Out of a lifetime in God's favor, this discipline was a mere moment. The "favor" of God (רָצוֹן)[23] for the psalmist would be the gracious things God had given him or done for him throughout his life. That divine favor brought him peace and joy, but it was abruptly interrupted by this event, as his report of the dilemma explains.

So this verse forms the subject of the praise, but it is also didactic. Other believers who were in pain would be encouraged to know that it was temporary, a brief moment in the eternal plan of things. At such times it is profitable to rehearse what a lifetime in his favor has meant to help people endure the pain.

II. When penitent believers praise God for restoring them they must acknowledge their sin that brought the discipline (6–10).

A. Confession of sin is part of the confession of faith (6).

There is an abrupt change now to the report of the dilemma. Verse 6 gives us the only clue to what might have caused the problem. The psalmist says, "As for me, I said in my ease, I can never be moved." In this statement the interpretation of the word (שַׁלְוִי) is critical; it could be translated "prosperity" or

---

23. The noun means "goodwill, favor, acceptance, will"; it is related to the verb רָצָה which means "to be pleased with, accept favorably." The basic meaning of this word, though, seems to be "accept"; it also had the idea of finding something good, or being pleased with something. The pleasure can be in the receiving of a gift, or as the motivation for giving things.

    The noun most often indicates pleasure, that is, the mercy and grace and goodness of the sovereign God. In its uses the related ideas overlap. In one category God's "favor" means his general goodwill to his people as opposed to his harsh treatment of them, and that is the meaning here in Psalm 30. In a second category it indicates his acceptance of people. It is used this way for his acceptance of people offering sacrifices (Exod. 28:38; Lev.1:3), and for righteous words and thoughts as acceptable to him (Ps. 19:14). In a third category the word also refers to God's will, i.e., his pleasure or desire (Ps. 40:8).

    The verb's usage carries essentially the same meanings: be favorable to someone; accept someone or someone's sacrifice or gift; be pleased with them.

"ease" or "self-sufficiency." He apparently had been given success and security by the grace of God, and in reflection on that he
asserted that he was "safe and secure" and could never be moved
(בַּל־אֶמּוֹט; s.v. Ps. 62:2). Several commentators like Broyles do
not think the word "prosperity" needs to be construed as self-
assured arrogance since the psalmist attributes his security to
God's favor.[24] The psalm would just be describing the ups and
downs of life, but there are two problems with this interpretation. First, it does not account for God's anger that almost ended
his life—that is not a normal down in life. And second, the statement that his security came from God is in contrast to his statement of self-sufficiency. The anger of God was not inexplicable to
the psalmist. As Kraus says, his statement "Never will I waver"
is an unworried trust in oneself; it is attributed to the ungodly
in Psalm 10:6 and to the fool in Proverbs 1:32.[25] A. A. Anderson
says that in the state of affluence the psalmist lost sight of the
Giver of all prosperity. The Israelites were warned not to become
too self-confident in their good fortune so that they forget the
God who blessed them (Deut. 8:10–20). There is a common temptation to interpret the blessings of God as exclusively human
achievements, and the result is ingratitude.[26] At the very least
the psalmist was presumptuous—to think that because of his
circumstances he was secure. If he meant that his security was
based on self-sufficiency, then it is pride. He thought he could
never be moved; so Anderson concludes that while the statement "I can never be moved" could be that of an arrogant man's
confidence or a righteous man's faith, in this verse it refers to
arrogance.[27] This is the only interpretation that does justice to
the central theme of the psalm, that God was so angry that the
psalmist had to pray to be kept from dying.

Verse 8 develops the result of this statement. The first half
of the verse is difficult to interpret. He says, "O LORD, in your
pleasure you made my mountain stand strong." The expositor
has to decide if this is a positive statement or a negative one. If

---

24. *Psalms*, p. 155.
25. *Psalms 1–59*, p. 356.
26. *Psalms 1–72*, p. 243.
27. Ibid.

by "mountain" we are to understand Mount Zion, i.e., the central location of the kingdom, David would be saying that God had been pleased to establish his monarchy firmly on Mount Zion (see Ps. 2:6). The expression "my mountain" would then be a figure of substitution (metonymy of subject) for what was located on the mountain. God gave him a strong monarchy. This would then be a positive statement; and the rest of the verse would be a contrast.

If by "mountain" he meant an obstacle that God had made to stand firmly against him, then it would be a negative statement, elaborated by the rest of the verse. The expression "my mountain" would then be a figure of comparison (implied) for the discipline God had given.

Depending on which interpretation is taken, the meaning of "pleasure" must be explained. If the clause is positive, then it would mean God in his goodwill and favor made his life and his kingdom strong. If it is negative, then it would mean God's will was to put an obstacle before him for his spiritual benefit as in the words of the prophet, "It pleased the LORD to bruise him"—it satisfied God's will for the intended purpose of the suffering (Isa. 53:10). The fact the word "pleasure" has just been used to represent a lifetime of blessing would probably lend support to the first idea and say God was pleased to give him a wonderful life and a strong monarchy.

The second clause focuses clearly on the dilemma: "you hid your face *and* I was terrified." The figure of God's hiding his face (an anthropomorphism) signifies the withholding of favor, as opposed to God's face shining on people which would mean being gracious to them. The result of God's withholding his favor was that the psalmist was terrified (not "troubled," at the hiddenness of God; for בָּהַל s.v. Ps. 83:16). The point is that he thought in his time of prosperity he could never be moved; and because he had this sense of self-sufficiency, God withdrew his favor and he was terrified. His only recourse was to pray that God would not let him die.

B. The rehearsal of the prayer for restoration both honors God and edifies the people (8–10).

The psalmist now reports his prayer for restoration from the terrifying experience. He does this as an integral part of his praise to God for answering prayer; but he also intends for the prayer and its answer to instruct people how to pray and praise. In verse 8 he introduces the prayer: "To you, O LORD, I called, and to the Lord I made supplication." The verbs in this line are in form imperfect tenses (אֶקְרָא and אֶתְחַנָּן). They may be explained in one of two ways. Verse 8 could be part of the report itself: in the time of suffering he said, "I will call unto you, O LORD, to the Lord I will make supplication." Or, the verse could be a description of what he did at the time: "I called . . . I made supplication." In this sense the verbs would be taken as preterites (without the *waw*).

The prayer begins with the motivation in verse 9 and then records the petition itself in verse 10. The motivation is in the form of rhetorical questions: "What profit is there in my blood if I go down to the pit?[28] The point is that there is nothing to be gained by his death. Even if his death were the result of punishment for sin—how would God benefit from that? The way God would profit would be in rescuing the penitent from death so that praise might be offered in the congregation. That is the point of the rhetorical questions in the second half of the verse: "Will the dust praise you? Will it tell of your faithfulness?" By "dust" he means himself, a dead man in the grave turning to dust (so a metonymy of effect, the cause being death). No, if he were to die, he could not go and make a public acknowledgment in the sanctuary. God would receive no praise over this. The idea is repeated with a more pointed emphasis: "Will it tell of your faithfulness?" (Literally, "your truth" with the sense of faithfulness; s.v. Ps. 15:2). If God is faithful, people can rely on him to keep his promises, promises that included forgiveness and healing. Dying would be no witness to the faithfulness of God; it would indicate God was not faithful in this case. So his appeal to God is essentially this: "You will gain nothing, and lose a worshiper."[29]

The psalmist is not engaging in crass bargaining here with God, but he is saying that if God delivers him from dying then he would have every reason to go to the sanctuary and tell everyone

---

28. The word for "pit" is now שַׁחַת, as in Ps. 16:10; earlier in this psalm "pit" was the word בּוֹר. Both refer to the grave.
29. Kidner, *Psalms 1–72*, p. 129.

of God's faithfulness. This is then a motivation for God to deliver him—if God wants people to hear about his faithfulness, then he must show himself faithful.

In verse 10 he recalls his petition. Three imperatives were used to convey the urgency of the petition: "Hear" and "be merciful to me" and "be" (my help). The verb "hear" (שְׁמַע; s.v. Ps. 45:10) was an appeal for God to respond favorably to his prayer, the verb "be merciful to me" (חָנֵּנִי; s.v. Ps. 4:1) was an appeal for divine favor even though he did not deserve it, and the verb "be (a help to me)" was an appeal for God to help him, meaning, to do for him what he could not do for himself (for "help" s.v. Ps. 46:1). If God did not show him favor and help him, he would die. The psalm began by proclaiming that God had rescued him from dying, so this is a record of what he prayed before that deliverance, and that proclamation (the whole psalm) is the report of the answer to this prayer.

III. When believers praise God for restoring them to a joyful life, they must acknowledge that he did it in order that they might praise him forever (11–12).

Here, in the last two verses of the psalm, we have the praise proper. The psalmist has declared in his introductory praise that God had healed him, and he has invited the congregation to join him in that praise. Now he will actually offer the praise himself. Verse 11 is filled with poetic language so much so that if it were not for the information in the psalm itself it would be hard to explain the meaning. He says, "You have turned for me my mourning into dancing; you have removed my sackcloth and clothed me with gladness." By "mourning" he means the grief he experienced under God's anger (so a metonymy of effect), and by "dancing" he means the great joy he had when he was restored and renewed from his trouble (likewise a metonymy of effect). The two images form a wonderful contrast: mourning is associated with sadness and death, dancing with celebration and life. Then, by saying God removed his sackcloth, he means that God's restoration to life gave him reason to remove it (so a metonymy of effect, God forgave and restored, and he removed the sackcloth, if he was actually wearing it, the clothing of lamentation

677

and grief). When he says that God clothed him with joy, he is using a different figure, a figure of comparison: God had made his life so joyful that it was like being clothed with joy. In the Bible being clothed with joy, or with righteousness, or with salvation, are expressions that describe the nature and condition of the person. To see the psalmist now was to see joy.

God did all this for a purpose: "(to the end) that [my] glory might sing praises to you and not be silent." Here is the great benefit for God in delivering his servant from death. The psalmist refers to himself as "glory" (כָּבוֹד), meaning his own spirit; but the choice of this word emphasizes his value, his true nature (s.v. Ps. 19:1). This is appropriate terminology because when the human spirit sings praises to the LORD God, that reflects the real value of the human spirit—it is the person at his or her best. To be silent would be to deny the intrinsic value of the human spirit and rob God of his glory.

The psalmist, restored to his life in God's favor, vows to praise him forever: "O LORD my God, I will give thanks to you forever." The verb (אוֹדֶךָ; s.v. Ps. 6:5) is probably to be taken as a cohortative, emphasizing the will, although the suffix obscures the ending. He is declaring his resolve to acknowledge the LORD forever.

MESSAGE AND APPLICATION

The central focus of this psalm is the content of the praise: God's anger is but for a moment, but his favor lasts a lifetime. This truth has to be treasured in the minds of the people of God, so that whenever God withholds his favor and there is suffering and trouble they may keep things in proper perspective as they sort through their trouble. This is what kept the apostle Paul ministering when he encountered severe trouble on every side— he looked on things eternal and not temporal (2 Cor. 4:16–18). Even if the trouble is a result of pride or some other sin, the believer knows that the lifetime in God's favor includes and requires divine discipline. If God disciplines his people, it is to restore them to the celebration of being in fellowship with him. So this central point could be worded to bring the exposition of the whole passage together: *God heals and restores his people whom he has chastened so that they might declare to the congregation that the lifetime in his favor overshadows the time of suffering.*

Having the proper understanding in mind of what it means to be in God's favor for a lifetime will certainly keep things in perspective. There is also in this psalm the major application of praise. When people are restored from their trouble to a good life, no matter what the reason for the difficulty was, they are by duty bound to praise the LORD in the congregation. The psalm makes it clear that God delivers people from illnesses and dangers in order that they might praise. This is not because God needs to have our praise; it is because praise is edifying, and in a praise like this people would learn a great truth about God's dealings with his people, and also an important warning about becoming self-sufficient. In so many places today believers do become self-sufficient, until God does something in their lives that brings them to their knees. Those moments are often very troubling, but understood in the light of his favor, will lead to greater devotion and greater glory for God.

PSALM 31

Trust in the Time of Trouble

INTRODUCTION

Text and Textual Variants

To the Chief Musician. A Psalm of David.[1]

1 In you, O LORD, I have taken refuge;
      let me never be put to shame;
      deliver me in your righteousness.[2]
2 Incline your ear to me;
      deliver[3] me quickly;
   be for me for a rock of refuge[4]
      for a fortress dwelling to save me.

3 Because you are my rock[5] and my fortress,
      and for the sake of your name,[6] you will lead me and
        guide me.
4 You will bring me out from the trap that is set for me
      because you[7] are my refuge.

---

1. The Greek manuscripts add ἐκστάσεως, "alarm" or "extreme fear."
2. The Greek has another clause, καὶ ἐξελοῦ με, "and rescue me."
3. Syriac has "answer me."
4. The Greek interpets this as Θεὸν ὑπερασπιστὴν, "a protecting God."
5. Greek interprets as "my strength," κραταίωμά μου.
6. One manuscript and the Syriac add "LORD."
7. Some Greek manuscripts add "O LORD."

5 Into your hand[8] I commit my spirit;
    you have redeemed me, O LORD, God of truth.
6 I hate[9] those who observe lying vanities;
    but as for me, I have trusted in the LORD.
7 I will exult and be glad in your loyal love
    for you have seen my affliction,
    you have known the troubles of my life.[10]
8 You have not given me over into the hand of the enemy;
    you have caused my feet to stand in a wide place.

9 Be merciful to me, O LORD, for I am in distress;
    my eye grows weak with[11] grief,
    (also) my soul and my body.[12]
10 For my life is consumed with anguish,
    and my years with groaning;
    my strength fails because of my iniquity[13]
    and my bones grow weak.
11 Because of all my enemies[14]
    I am a reproach even to my neighbors exceedingly,
    and a dread to my friends;
    those who see me outside flee from me.
12 I am forgotten as though dead, out of mind;

---

8. Greek has "your hands."
9. For MT שֹׂנְאָתִי the Greek (as well as one Hebrew manuscript, Jerome and the Syriac) has "you have hated," ἐμίσησας. This was apparently understood because of the strong contrast in the second half of the verse.
10. The Greek version has "you have saved" (ἔσωσας) me from troubles. This may be an interpretation of the LORD's knowing his troubles rather than a different text.
11. There is some manuscript and version evidence to read "from."
12. There is a tendency for commentators to delete this last part as a supplementary addition (see Kraus, *Psalms 1–59*, p. 360).
13. The word בַּעֲוֹנִי, "because of my iniquity" or "my guilt" is problematic because there is no other indication of sin in the psalm. The Greek has "poverty," πτωχεία. This may reflect reading בְּעָנְי. Symmachus has διὰ τὴν κάκωσίν μου which reflects בְּעָנְיִי, "my sorrow."
14. This verse is rather difficult in its construction; some suggest taking this first prepositional phrase with the last verse, leaving a clearer parallelism. The Greek version reads it as "I have become a reproach among all my enemies, but exceedingly so to my. . . ."

I have become like a broken vessel.
13 For I hear the saying of many,
     "Terror is on every side";[15]
in their conspiring together against me
     they plot to take my life.

14 But as for me, I have trusted in you, O LORD,
     I said, "You are my God."
15 In your hand are my times;
     deliver me from the hand of my enemies
     and those who pursue me.
16 Cause your face to shine upon your servant;
     save me in your loyal love.
17 O LORD, do not let me be put to shame
     because I have called upon you.
Let the ungodly be put to shame
     and be silent[16] in the grave.
18 Let their lying lips be silent,
     the ones that speak against the righteous boldly
          with arrogance and contempt.

19 How great is your goodness[17]
     which you have treasured up for those who fear you,
     which you have wrought for those who take refuge in you,
          in the sight of people.[18]
20 You hide them in the shelter of your presence
     from the conspiracies of man;
you keep them in a tabernacle[19]
     from the strife of tongues.
21 Blessed be the LORD

---

15. The word מָגוֹר has been rendered παροικούντων by the Greek version, reading for the colon: "who dwell round about me." The translation misunderstood the line.
16. Greek reads καταχθείησαν, "and brought down" (וְיִרְדּוּ perhaps) instead of יִדְמוּ.
17. The Greek adds "LORD" (along with a few Hebrew manuscripts).
18. Literally, "the sons of men."
19. A few versions have "your tabernacle."

because[20] he has made his loyal love wonderful to me[21]
    when I was in a fortified city.
22 And I said in my haste,[22]
    "I have been cut off[23] from your eyes."
  Yet[24] you heard the voice of my supplications
    when I cried to you for help.
23 Love the LORD all *you* his beloved.
  The LORD preserves the faithful,[25]
    but the proud he pays back in full.
24 Be of good courage, and let your heart be strong,
  all you who hope in the LORD.

Composition and Context

Psalm 31 is a fascinating work that brings together a variety of images and expressions about affliction and assurance that may be found in other passages in the Bible, such as the Pentateuch, Job, Jonah, Jeremiah and Lamentation. Because of this most scholars today have concluded the work is composite in which two or more authors have drawn on common literary expressions to form this psalm; its arrangement seems to reflect two parallel prayers that move from affliction to assurance (vv. 1–8 and 9–24).[26] Because of the literary expressions that are similar to Jeremiah and Lamentation, some commentators (e.g., Kraus and Kirkpatrick) suggest it was compiled by Jeremiah, or a prophet like him, but in cases like this the question remains whether the psalm was written by Jeremiah because of similarities to things he said, or Jeremiah used older passages and expressions such as are found in Psalm 31.

The older commentators accepted the psalm as Davidic, and in some cases made the connection to 1 Samuel 23:24–26.

20. A few manuscripts and Jerome have "who."
21. "To me" is not in the Greek or Syriac.
22. Greek has "extreme fear" as in the superscription.
23. Since this word occurs only here, some suggest that the verb should be נֶגֶד instead of נִגְרַז; the meaning is the same essentially (see Lam. 3:54).
24. The Greek version has "therefore," διὰ τοῦτο.
25. The Greek version has "the LORD seeks truth," ἀληθείας ἐκζητεῖ.
26. See Anderson, *Psalms 1–72*, pp. 246–7.

The connection links the superscription in the Greek version that says it was written in "alarm" or haste, to the Hebrew word in the psalm ("I said in my haste") and in 1 Samuel where David was fleeing from Saul. Such a thin connection based on the use of a word in two passages is not compelling. Besides, the psalm seems to describe a prolonged suffering by the psalmist as people were speaking maliciously about him and those close to him were abandoning him. The picture of Job is much more in harmony with the themes of this psalm. This is not to say that David could not have written the psalm, only that the occasion could not be specified on the evidence that is available.

The psalm seems to be a lament in its general form, although the motifs of lamentation and thanksgiving recur throughout. The expressions are often general, leaving it unclear whether the psalmist was physically ill or spiritually depressed, or both. It is also unclear whether his troubles were because of enemies trying to kill him or to ruin him with false accusations. There is even some question concerning his guilt as a factor in the suffering. Whatever the situation, the expressions he uses are familiar descriptions of life—threatening afflictions, necessitating his crying out to the LORD for help. In writing the expressions of confidence and hope, the psalmist used covenant expressions as well, words that would be familiar to the faithful. This shows that the psalm had a didactic purpose of encouraging people in obedience to the covenant in spite of all kinds of afflictions and persecutions. By compiling so many familiar expressions, the psalmist (whether a David or a Jeremiah) was presenting the epitome of assurance in affliction. Such an epitome is an abridgment or a summary of the essentials important to the issue at hand; it provided the faithful who learned this psalm with an inventory of the sufferings and afflictions in life as well as the almost creedal statements of those who commit their lives to the LORD in such times. Yet this does not mean the psalm was necessarily a didactic composition. There probably was an experience in the life of the psalmist that prompted its writing in the form of a lament; but in the writing an array of expressions was used to form a summary of the relevant laments, statements of faith, and prayers. The final verse exhorts the faithful to strengthen their faith to meet such difficulties; knowing and praying this psalm would help them to do just that.

Exegetical Analysis

Message

Because the LORD to whom he commits his life is faithful and good, the psalmist prays confidently for the deliverance from and defeat of his malicious enemies and exhorts the faithful to be strong in the LORD who protects his people.

Outline

I. Introductory Cry: The psalmist prays that he will not be put to shame but delivered quickly and made secure (1–2).
II. Confidence: The psalmist entrusts his life to the LORD because he is confident that the LORD will deliver and guide him so that he might offer praise for his loyal love (3–8).
   A. He is sure the LORD will deliver him and guide him because he is his refuge and defense (3–4).
   B. He entrusts himself into the LORD's care and not to worthless idols he despises (5–6).
   C. He expects to praise the LORD's loyal love because the LORD will respond to his afflictions and deliver him (7–8).
III. Lament: The psalmist is in need of God's grace because he is in great distress and constantly reproached while his enemies plot to kill him (9–13).
   A. He needs God's help because he is at the point of perishing (9–10).
   B. He is reproached and rejected by his friends more than his foes (11–12).
   C. He is aware of the malicious plotting against his life (13).
IV. Petition Proper: Reaffirming his faith the psalmist prays to the LORD to save him and to silence his enemies (14–18).
   A. He reaffirms his faith in the LORD (14).

B. He prays that God will show him loyal love by delivering him (15–16).

C. He prays that his enemies be put to shame in silence forever instead of him (17–18).

V. Praise and Exhortation: The psalmist praises the LORD for his protection of the faithful and exhorts all who hope in the LORD to love him and be strong in their faith (19–24).

A. He praises the goodness of the LORD for protecting the faithful (19–20).

B. He blesses the LORD for answering him in spite of his hasty conclusions (21–22).

C. He exhorts those who hope in the LORD to love the LORD and to be strong in their faith (23–24).

COMMENTARY IN EXPOSITORY FORM

I. The faithful will pray for deliverance and defense when wicked people try to ruin them (1-2).

The psalm begins with a summary in the introductory cry: the address to the LORD, the affirmation of faith, and the plea. "In you, O LORD, I have taken refuge" (s.v. Ps. 7:1) makes it clear from the very outset that the psalmist has placed his life in the LORD's care. And his prayer is for deliverance, first stated negatively: "let me never be put to shame" (אַל־אֵבוֹשָׁה לְעוֹלָם). The use of "put to shame, be ashamed" (בּוֹשׁ),[27] refers to the disgrace

---

27. The verb בּוֹשׁ has the meaning of "shame" and "dishonor." There is also a common noun בּוֹשֶׁת, "shame," and a couple of rare nouns with similar or related meanings. The verb and its derivatives are found mostly in the Psalms and Jeremiah. The word can be used for ordinary things that would be embarrassing (such as the use of the word for "private parts") or the activity of the unwise fool (Prov. 10:5), but the meaning is most often more serious. Seebass summarizes the meaning by saying that the word carries the idea that someone or something underwent an experience in which a former respected position and importance were overthrown. The writers used the words to describe devastating catastrophes, and in the case of Jeremiah the destruction of the nation. Along with the idea of something being overthrown is the emphasis on being disgraced or shamed. Jeremiah announced that the nation would be put to shame by

and humiliation of having everything that was once honored and valued overthrown and brought to nothing; and that would include the psalmist's faith, for if God allowed the enemies to destroy him, what he believed would be considered worthless in the eyes of his enemies. The prayer will be that the enemies be put to shame instead of him, that God would show their beliefs and actions to be false. His introductory prayer also has the positive request, that God deliver him in righteousness (s.v. Ps. 1:5), meaning that God's nature would be displayed as he destroyed malicious idolaters and defended his covenant people. A just God cannot destroy those who trust him.[28]

There was no time to lose, and so the appeal in verse 2 is for God

---

foreign powers (see e.g. Jer. 2:36–7). The people had rejected the LORD and so their former estate under his care was to be overthrown and they would be disgraced. In the ancient world such a defeat and exile often did carry with it a shameful display as prisoners were shaved and stripped of all honor and led away (e.g., Mic. 1:16). The shame comes mostly because the people had forgotten their God, and so their God rejected them. See the full discussion of H. Seebass, "בּוֹשׁ, bôš" in *TDOT*, ed. by G. J. Botterweck and H. Ringgren, II:50–60).

Seebass lists four uses of the words in the Book of Psalms: (1) one time it is used in a lament, expressing that shame covered their faces when losing a war (Ps. 44:15); (2) twice it is used in affirmations of trust (Pss. 22:5 [not put to shame] and 44:7); (3) 13 times it is used in petitions, such as "let me not be ashamed" (as here); and (4) 16 times as a wish concerning the enemies, that they be put to shame (Ps. 71:24). The prayer for enemies to be put to shame is not simple revenge, but an appeal that people who live and believe a lie will be exposed by the God of truth. The gods of the Babylonians are said to be put to shame because they fail to deliver (Jer. 50:2). Priests and prophets who know the truth but teach a lie bring shame on themselves (Jer. 10:14). Similarly, people who abandon the righteous way and fall to depths of degradation in sin bring shame on themselves (Hos. 2:5).

The noun בֹּשֶׁת is used synonymously with the name Baal in the prophets (Jer. 3:24; Hos. 9:10) because the mere mention of the name Baal had become a disgrace. The word is also inserted into proper names that may have had at one time the word "baal" ("lord") in them (2 Sam. 2:8). It is also likely that the divine name "Melek" was spelled with the vowels for "shame" to form the name of the pagan god "Molech." The sense goes beyond embarrassment to dishonor or disgrace (see "בּוֹשׁ *bôš*, "to be ashamed," by F. Stolz, in *Theological Lexicon of the Old Testament*, ed. by E. Jenni and C. Westermann, I:204–07).

28. Alexander, *Psalms*, p. 132.

to listen and deliver him speedily. "Incline (or turn, הַטֵּה from נָטָה) your ear" is a bold figure (anthropomorphism) for God to pay very close attention. The prayer itself is for God to deliver him (s.v. Ps. 22:20) speedily (the noun מְהֵרָה, "haste, speed" is used adverbially; in Josh. 8:19 it has the sense of an immediate action). The psalm will explain that his weakened condition is the reason for the urgency.

The second half of verse 2 clarifies what such a deliverance would mean; here the imperative" be" is an appeal for God to demonstrate that he is these things. "Be for me for a rock of refuge (לְצוּר־מָעוֹז), for a strong fortress (לְבֵית מְצוּדוֹת, literally 'for a house of fortresses')." These metaphorical expressions indicate that he wants the LORD to provide for him strength and safety (see the use of these images in Ps. 18), the genitives clarifying the intent and nature of the rock and the house. The purpose of this is stated very clearly at the end of verse 2: "to save me" or deliver me (לְהוֹשִׁיעֵנִי; s.v. Ps. 3:2).

II. The faithful will entrust their lives to the LORD because they know that he will deliver them and guide them so that they will have reason to praise him (3–8).

A. Their confidence in the LORD is based on his reputation of delivering and guiding his people (3–4).

The section of confidence in the psalm begins with a restatement of the ideas expressed in the metaphors of verse 2. Verse 3 is not a prayer for God to demonstrate that he is these things; it is a statement of conviction that he is a rock (a different word for "my rock," סַלְעִי) and a fortress (repeating the second metaphor of v. 2b, "my fortress," מְצוּדָתִי). This assertion is based on previous experiences when God provided strength and safety for him. Because God is his rock and fortress, he knows he can trust him to guide him. The expectation of the LORD's leading is also based on the nature of God: "for your name's sake (for "name," s.v. Ps. 20:1). Because God has a history of doing this, and because it is in harmony with his nature, the psalmist expects guidance and deliverance from the LORD.

The two verbs in verse 3, "you will lead me (s.v. Ps. 23:3) and guide me" are both imperfect tenses. Some commentators choose to classify them (and the next verb in verse 4) as imperfects of injunction and translate them as imperatives (see the NIV). Although the psalm does weave petitions in frequently, this section seems to be more one of confidence, and so a simple future tense serves the best. He expects God will lead, guide, and rescue him. The verb for rescue is "you will bring me out" (תּוֹצִיאֵנִי, from the verb "go out," יָצָא); he expects that God will bring him out (set him free) from the trap (or snare, רֶשֶׁת) that "is set" for him (the verb "they set" has no expressed subject and may then be translated as a passive). The figure "trap" (an implied comparison) draws on the world of hunting to convey the deceptive plot of his enemies to destroy him. He will need guidance from the LORD not to walk into their trap. The reason he knows God will do this is because God is his refuge (the first metaphor of v. 2b is repeated here).

B. Their confidence in the LORD inspires them to entrust their lives to him and to no other god (5–6).

Because of all that the LORD means to him, the psalmist can state without hesitation, "Into your hand I commit my spirit" (v. 5a). The verse is well known because of its use by Jesus on the cross just before he died. The faithful can give their lives, body and spirit, to the LORD for his care, in this life, and in the life to come. The emphasis is on "into your hand" because it is placed first in the Hebrew text ("hand" being the anthropomorphic representation of God's powerful acts). The verb "I commit" (אַפְקִיד, from פָּקַד) here has the meaning of entrust (s.v. Ps. 8:4); and the nuance of the verb fits well as an English present tense (progressive imperfect) because he is here entrusting himself to the LORD. But the use of "spirit" (רוּחִי) is a little unusual, because it does not on its own signify the whole person, body and soul, as other words (such as נֶפֶשׁ) would; it means "breath, wind, spirit." It does represent the whole person (as a synecdoche), but with the emphasis on the spirit. In a way it means that whether he lives or not his spirit is being entrusted to God. The reason that he is doing this is because God has redeemed him ("you have redeemed me," פָּדִיתָה, a present perfect from פָּדָה [s.v. Ps. 25:22]). Perowne says he is saying, "Thou hast been, and Thou art, my redeemer," which implies furthermore that "because Thou changest not, I confidently anticipate redemption from this present calamity."[29] Therefore, he is willing to entrust his life to him. The final expression of the verse further explains his confidence and the focus of his trust—the LORD is "God of truth" (אֵל אֱמֶת). This may have a double meaning to it. "Truth" (s.v. Ps. 15:2) carries the sense of faithfulness or trustworthiness—a God characterized by faithfulness can be trusted. It could also be taken as "the true God" as opposed to lesser objects of faith. The pagan gods he will immediately describe as worthless vanities are not worth trusting.

His commitment to the LORD is contrasted with his total rejection of those who follow false gods: "I hate" (שָׂנֵאתִי, s.v. Ps. 139:21) not only includes the idea of rejection but also the emotional response of despising. He will have nothing to do with the pagans and their worthless gods. They are described as "lying vanities" (הַבְלֵי־שָׁוְא, "vanities of falsehood," the second word being an attributive genitive). The expressions are figurative descriptions of the deities (metonymies of adjunct—pagan gods are empty vanities). False gods are worthless, they are a lie (see Isa. 44:20). People who worship them are deceived because they cannot save (see Ps. 115:2–8), but those blinded by them meticulously observe their religious practices ("those who observe," הַשֹּׁמְרִים, s.v. Ps. 12:7). But not the psalmist! He strongly affirms: "But as for me, I have trusted (s.v. Ps. 4:5) in the LORD."

C. They expect to praise the LORD because he knows their troubles (7–8).

Their confidence now is expressed in the expectation of praising the LORD. The cohortatives (אָגִילָה, s.v. Ps. 6:13; and וְאֶשְׂמְחָה, s.v. Ps. 48:11) convey his determination to praise, but with exultation and joy. It will be a celebration of the LORD's loyal love (חֶסֶד being a metonymy of cause, the word referring to the deliverance and guidance God's faithful love will bring to him).

It is that faithful love that lies behind God's taking notice

---

29. Perowne, *Psalms*, I:285.

of his trouble and rescuing him from it. Verse 7b begins with a pronoun (אֲשֶׁר) that can be taken in an explanatory sense "for" or a relative sense "by which." The two clauses it introduces use perfect tenses (רָאִיתָ and יָדַעְתָּ), which probably should be present perfects, "you have seen" and "you have known," to express his conviction that God has been aware of his difficulties from the outset.[30] This finds support from verse 8 since it specifically applies his confidence to the present situation: "You have not given me over to the hand of the enemy, you have caused my feet to stand in a wide place." The psalmist is convinced that God has not abandoned him but is watching over him; and his certainty that God will deliver him is described as if it has happened (the perfect tense verbs in verse 8 may be perfects of confidence, expressing what he is convinced is going to happen shortly).

III. The faithful will offer their distressing lament to the LORD in a prayer for his gracious intervention (9–13).

A. They tell the LORD about their distress and grief (9–11).

The lament is introduced with an appeal for divine favor: "Be merciful to me" (חָנֵּנִי, the cry is familiar in the psalms: 6:9; 30:10; 51:1; 56:1; etc. for the meaning of the verb, s.v. Ps. 4:1). The point of this section is the lament that makes the cry for the LORD's impartation of favor necessary. The psalmist first describes his own condition in the current crisis. He has trouble (צַר) and his eye grows weak with grief (כָּעַס). The verb "grow weak" or "be consumed" (עָשַׁשׁ) conveys the deterioration from his extreme grief and weakness; the verb expresses essentially that he is falling apart (it is used of garments falling apart in pieces from use or from being moth-eaten). The eye is singled out as it is often the indication of general well-being or grief and anxiety.

---

30. They could be classified as definite past tenses, "you saw" and "you knew," or, they could be given an English present translation, "you see" and "you know" to express the general truth of God's care for his people, the present case being no exception.

Added to this verse is "my soul and my body" (literally, belly), which must signify that in spirit and body he is growing weak.

The evidence his strength is failing and his life fading away is to be seen in his anguish (יָגוֹן) and heard in his groaning (אֲנָחָה). These two words describe the effect of the trouble on his life (and so they are metonymies of effect). Whatever the actual difficulty was, his life had been reduced to anguish and groaning. In the second half of the verse he more specifically says his strength fails because of his iniquity. Because this word suddenly appears here and is not explained anywhere else in the psalm, many commentators wish to emend it to something like "my affliction" or "my misery" in line with the Greek version's translation "poverty."[31] If the word is retained in the line, it could be interpreted to mean guilt feelings or a sense that the affliction comes from his waywardness. This need not be taken to mean that all affliction is a result of iniquity. It may express something of the feeling of Naomi who in her bitterness thought the hand of the LORD had gone out against her (with no explanation there was a sin that caused it). Of course, there may have been some sin to which the psalmist attributed his distress. If so, it is not a major issue in this psalm which focuses on the LORD's love for and faithfulness to his people. The real issue here is that his strength failed and his bones grew weak. By bones he may mean his whole physical body (a synecdoche), or he might mean his spirit encased in a bony framework (metonymy). The latter may be what is in mind because it would be hard to separate physical weakness and spiritual depression in the psalmist's plight.

---

31. A. A. Anderson suggests that "misery" fits the context better and can be derived from the consonants in the text *b'wny* written as *scripta plena* (*Psalms 1–72*, p. 250). VanGemeren says that in the sequence of the other words describing his condition this word should be taken to express the harshness of his condition without a confession of guilt; he refers to the NIV translation "affliction" with a note clarifying it is the word "guilt" (*Psalms*, p. 306). But identifying the meaning as affliction or harshness based on the extended meanings of "iniquity" still indicates a connection with sin. Goldingay says the word could be left as the MT has it and translated "waywardness," or it could be translated with the Greek as "weakness"; and then he makes an application from each one (*Psalms 1–41*, p. 443).

B. They tell the LORD what friends and enemies say about them (11–13).

The lament turns now to describe how other people add to the distress (the "they" part of a lament). His misery is compounded by the misgivings and suspicions of acquaintances and friends. What the enemies were doing to him caused his neighbors to reproach him. The enemies in this line are described with a word (צֹרְרַי, "my enemies, my harassers") related to "distress" (צַר) used at the beginning of the lament. Because of them he has become a reproach to those living nearby.[32] A reproach (חֶרְפָּה; s.v. Ps. 22:6) is a cutting taunt, a sharp criticism. One can only think of the way Job's friends treated him when they came to "comfort" him. The psalmist receives no sympathy or understanding, just criticism and accusation. And to those who know him, he has become a "dread thing" (פַּחַד), something to be feared and avoided (see Ps. 36:1). In fact, when he is outside people who see him run away from him (11b). His only conclusion is that people have forgotten him as if he had died—he is out of mind (literally "out of/from heart," מִלֵּב). The point would be that people have put him out of their minds—they do not want to think about him. He has become like a broken vessel (a "perishing" vessel, אֹבֵד), something that is wearing out and is no longer useful.

Behind the reproach and the avoidance of friends and neighbors is the whispering about him. He hears the slanderous (דִּבָּה), subdued talk about him by many people. Goldingay suggests a meaning of "defamation."[33] This talk is a reminder of the danger he is in: "terror on every side" (מָגוֹר מִסָּבִיב). The expression is used by Jeremiah (20:3) to rename Pashhur in view of the terrifying judgment that was about to fall on him, and it became somewhat of a motto to sum up Jeremiah's message of doom.

---

32. The line ends with the word "exceedingly" (מְאֹד), which seems awkward. The word has been reinterpreted to make better sense. Dahood suggests the word is "calamity" (אֵיד with a prefixed *mem*). He then rearranges the lines to say, "Because of my enemies I am a reproach, and to my neighbors a calamity" (*Psalms* I:189). Delitzsch proposes on the basis of etymology and usage that there is a noun with the sense of "burden," the noun with the letters *m'd*, perhaps מָאוֹד (*Psalms*, I:387–8).
33. Goldingay, *Psalms*, p.435.

There would be no place of safety, no place to hide, and certainly no one to help.

The people who are saying such things are actually conspiring against him. They come together in conclave and plot (יָֽזְמוּ, s.v. Ps. 10:2) to take his life. So now we discover what is at the heart of the distress—malicious enemies who while planning to kill him were spreading word of the terror that surrounds him, and this made him a dread to other people so that they either avoided him or reproached him. In the process he was filled with grief and despair so that he grew weaker by the day. Only the LORD could rescue him from this terrible crisis.

IV. The faithful will pray for the LORD to demonstrate his loyal love by delivering them and silencing their malicious enemies forever (14–18).

A. They pray for the LORD to deliver them by his loyal love (14–16).

In spite of the great danger around him and the rejection by friends and neighbors, the psalmist remains loyal to God. "But as for me, I have trusted in you, O LORD; I said, 'You are my God.'" Both verbs could be translated as present tenses as part of his statement of faith, but if the first one is taken as a present perfect it encompasses what he has said in the psalm already, that he has trusted the LORD and has been delivered so many times that God is his rock and his refuge. He will not now waiver in his faith. His trust in the LORD brings him comfort, for he knows that his times are in God's hand. By "times" he not only means how long he lives but what takes place in the time that he lives (a metonymy of subject). In a way, then, when he prays for deliverance from those who pursue him, he is asking for God to act in accordance with his will for his life. He can pray—and pray earnestly—but will commit his life to the will of God. His prayer is strengthened by his faith: because he knows his times are in God's hands, he prays that his life be delivered from the hands of his enemies. He does not want his enemies to determine what happens to him.

His petition then is based on the loyal love of the LORD (v. 16). This line clearly draws on the high priestly benediction

(Num. 6:25) which says, "May the LORD cause his face to shine upon you and be gracious unto you." He prays for God to do what the oracle of the priest said God would do: "Cause your face to shine upon your servant." This figure (anthropomorphism) signifies divine pleasure and favor extended to people—the shining or beaming face being symbolic of divine favor as the second verb of the priest's blessing makes clear. Here the psalmist makes his appeal with the proper attitude of prayer for he refers to himself as the servant. To call himself God's servant certainly acknowledges humility, but the usage of the word also describes one who is a devout and obedient believer. Because he is an obedient believer, he can appeal to the LORD to save him (הוֹשִׁיעֵנִי) because of his faithful covenant love. Others may avoid the psalmist, or turn on him in his distress, but not the LORD who is his God.

B. They pray for the LORD to shame and silence their enemies (17–18).

The psalmist repeats his cry that the LORD not allow him to be put to shame because he has called out to him for help. Rather, he prays that the wicked people be put to shame and be silenced in the grave.[34] As mentioned earlier, this is not a prayer of personal revenge. To pray for God to put the wicked to shame means that in destroying them God will prove once more that he is the true God. They with their beliefs and their actions claimed to be in the right, implying that the way of the LORD was a lie. When God destroys them, they will bear the shame and disgrace of having believed and lived a lie; and when they are in the grave, they will no longer spread their views or maliciously attack the righteous. Accordingly, in verse 18 he specifies that their lying lips should be silenced. "Lying lips" is literally "lips of falsehood" (שִׂפְתֵי שָׁקֶר); "lips" refers to what they say with the lips (a metonymy of cause), and "falsehood" is the attributive genitive that describes what they say—it is false. He is not referring to every word they say, but what they say against the righteous.

---

34. The word *she'ol* can also mean the realm of the departed spirits of the wicked, or hell, but since this passage emphasizes their silence it probably here simply means the grave (s.v. Ps. 6:5).

This would include denial of the truth, ridicule of the faith, false accusations, taunts and threats. What they say is antagonistic because it is said boldly against the righteous with arrogance and contempt. The word boldly (עָתָק) describes them as assertive, lofty, and impressive. Their words have an authoritative ring. What they say is "with arrogance and contempt." In their attitude of superiority they look down on the righteous as worthless (בְּזֹה; s.v. Ps. 22:6). By answering the psalmist's prayer God would be showing his faithful love to all the righteous who are maligned and threatened by the arrogant ungodly of the world.

V. The faithful will prepare to offer their praise to God and exhort others to love the LORD and be strong in the faith (19–24).

A. Their praise is for God's goodness and protective care (19–22).

This is the praise section of the psalm. On the one hand it seems to be a continuation of the psalmist's strong confidence in the LORD's faithful love; but on the other hand because he explains the LORD answered his prayer in spite of his own hasty conclusion, it is the praise for the deliverance. If it is the actual praise, then the LORD has acted, or begun to act on his behalf, and that prompts the praise. It is praise that is given in the sanctuary because it will encourage others to be strong in their faith as well.

"How great is your goodness" begins the praise. By goodness (s.v. Ps. 34:8) the psalmist means the sum of all good things the LORD has treasured up for the use and enjoyment of his people.[35] By stating that it is treasured up he means that there is much more that God will give to those who fear him and take refuge in him in addition to what he has done for them. All of this is open for people ("the sons of man") to witness.

Specifically the goodness of God in this praise concerns the protective care he gives his people. "You hide them in the shelter of your presence" may be a reference to the sanctuary and the presence of the LORD. It may also refer to God's being with his

---

35. Delitzsch, *Psalms*, I:390

people anywhere to protect them (like a shelter). The protection is "from the conspiracies of man" (מֵרֻכְסֵי אִישׁ). The word occurs only here; it may be linked with the verb "bind," and convey the idea of people banding together, i.e., a conspiracy, or the plotting of such a conspiracy. It is paralleled in the second half of the verse with "from the strife of tongues" (מֵרִיב לְשֹׁנוֹת), and "strife" is often a conflict, legal charge or accusation (s.v. Ps. 95:8). The attack is verbal, as the use of "tongues" makes clear; and it is from mere mortals, as the use of "man" says. God protects his people in his presence with his pavilion (סֻכָּה). If the reference is to the tabernacle, it does not mean that a place is providing the shelter, but the God who is in that place.

The praise continues in verse 21 for the LORD's great deliverance and protection: "he has made wonderful his loyal love." The LORD demonstrated his loyal love in a way that was marvelous and extraordinary—in a wonderful way he showed me his love.[36] The additional prepositional phrase, however, is unclear: "in a city fortified" (בְּעִיר מָצוֹר); so it is deleted by some. It probably means that God protected him as if he were in a fortified city.[37]

The greatness of God's loyal love is magnified all the more since the psalmist had doubts and impatience (חָפְזִי). What he means is that in his alarm he had given himself up as cut off from the sight of the LORD. The word "haste" is used for the hurried flight of one escaping pursuers, so alarm and impatience are connected. He spoke prematurely, probably in a panic, thinking that he had been cast out from the LORD's presence. He had heard so much ridicule and accusation he had almost come to believe God was through with him. Nevertheless he still prayed, and now he had to acknowledge that his conclusion was premature because God heard the voice of his supplication when he cried out to him.

B. Their encouragement is for believers to be strong in the faith (23–24).

The psalm ends with an exhortation to loyalty to the covenant.

---

36. VanGemeren, *Psalms*, p.310
37. The expression could also be translated "in a besieged city," referring to his trouble.

The appeal is for all "his beloved" (חֲסִידָיו), all those who have become the people of God and live by his loyal love. They are exhorted to love (אֶהֱבוּ; s.v. Ps. 11:7) the LORD. This is the fundamental command of the covenant: "You shall love the LORD your God" (Deut. 6:5). It is a call to worship and serve the LORD in a way that will demonstrate obedience to the covenant stipulations. It is a life of submission to the will of God. The reason this is so important in this context is that the LORD preserves the faithful but pays back the proud in full. To refuse to obey the LORD is pride, and it will receive its just punishment; to love the LORD is faithfulness, and the LORD preserves the faithful. To appeal to God for deliverance and protection in this life on the basis of the covenant will be futile if the people are not faithful to that covenant.

And so he addresses the faithful, i.e., people who hope (הַמְיַחֲלִים)[38] in the LORD. The psalmist exhorts them to be of good courage ("be strong") and also strengthen their heart (i.e., will).

MESSAGE AND APPLICATION

This psalm reminds us that opposition to the faith and especially to the righteous is a perennial problem. Some believers in the West may be blessed to live in relative freedom, but in most places in the world the persecution and opposition is

---

38. The word יָחַל means "hope for, wait"; it is a synonym of קָוָה (s.v. Ps. 25:3) but has a slightly different emphasis. There have been a number of etymological suggestions: one is to connect the word to an Arabic word "stuck," indicating waiting for help; another links it to Arabic "be strong," giving it the idea of firm, powerful; and still another links it to Hebrew "be in labor" or birth pangs (חִיל or חוּל) and so waiting for delivery. These are attempts to get at a central idea, but they are not convincing. To hope in the LORD, or wait for the LORD, is a common idea because the LORD is the source of all good. The passages seldom say exactly what they are waiting for, just that they are waiting for the LORD. It seems that the hoping or waiting is for a favorable response to prayer, i.e., waiting for his word. And if that prayer is for the destruction of the wicked, the hoping could take on eschatological significance. Hoping in the LORD requires faith and courage (as here in Ps. 31:24). Faith and courage will be needed because hoping implies the need for endurance, but the endurance is based on a relationship, and so is part of the faith.

strong, especially where the Christian faith is growing. Even in our peaceful places the growing antagonism to the faith is becoming more and more of a problem. There is a growing evil in the world, and it wants to destroy the Christian faith. It may come from other religions, or from atheistic and secular sources. It may begin with malicious words and reproaches, but it will fester into open hatred and opposition. While many people might read psalms like this and not see the relevance, they need to look again at history, at the world, and at the not–so–subtle attempts to rid the culture of the faith.

This is nothing new; it is certainly no surprise to God. He has been delivering his people for ages and will continue to do so if they trust in him. This psalm reminds us that we need to entrust our lives to his care, knowing that our times and circumstances are in his hands, not the hands of the enemies. Entrusting our lives to his care means entering into a vigilant prayer life in which we appeal to God to deliver us from evil, to lead us by his truth, and to vindicate the truth by silencing the wicked who serve false vanities, whether gods or philosophies.

The psalm has many ideas woven together that will have to be addressed in the exposition. While it is hard to summarize a psalm like this into one propositional theme, the following statement at least will keep the exposition focused on the main things: *In a world that despises the truth and seeks to destroy the righteous, God's faithful people may entrust their lives to his care and remain confident as they pray for deliverance from affliction, guidance through life, and judgment on malicious enemies.* The tone the exposition needs to capture is positive, because although there is lament here, this psalm stresses the movement from affliction to assurance.

There is another practical application in that the psalm uses some covenant language. To entrust oneself to the LORD's care carries with it the reminder that his care is his loyal love for his people. Therefore to be recognized as "his beloved" requires that people love the LORD and remain loyal to him by remaining untarnished by pagans and false religious or philosophical ideas, and by fixing their hope in him to bring ultimate victory.

No one has lived out the meaning of this psalm better than Jesus Christ. He was opposed and persecuted by the wicked more than any other person; he suffered at their hands more than any other person; and he had greater faith and confidence in the plan of God than any other person. On the cross he chose the central theme of this psalm and applied it to himself: "Into your hands I commit my spirit" (Luke 23:46). Whereas the psalmist meant by these words that he put himself and all his hopes and cares into the hand of God, the Lord Jesus meant by them that by his own act he gave up his spirit and therefore his life to the Father.[39] He had accomplished what he had come into the world to do, and now it was time to lay down his life. These words have also been used for centuries by saints who have given up their lives for the faith, for entrusting one's life into God's care does not last for a moment or for time, but for all eternity.

---

39. Perowne, *Psalms*, I:284.

PSALM 32

The Joy of Forgiveness

INTRODUCTION

Text and Textual Variants

Of David. A Contemplative Poem.[1]

1 Blessed is the one whose transgression is forgiven,[2]
  whose sin is hidden!
2 Blessed is the one to whom the LORD does not impute
    iniquity,
  and in whose spirit[3] there is no guile!

3 When[4] I kept silent, my bones wasted away
  with my groaning all day long.
4 For day and night your hand was heavy upon me;

---

1. Hebrew מַשְׂכִּיל, related to the word שָׂכַל, "to be wise," may mean a "skill-fully constructed" poem (see Introduction). The Greek version reads "instruction" (συνέσεως), which is understandable since the *hiphil* verb, "I will instruct you," is used in verse 8.
2. The word נְשָׂא is spelled נְשׂוּי as if it were III *he'* verb: "forgiven of transgression." This is parallel to the form of the word "hidden."
3. The Greek translation interpreted the guile to be deceptive speech and rendered "spirit" as "mouth" (ἐν τῷ στόματι αὐτοῦ): "and in his mouth there is no deceit."
4. Or "because" (כִּי).

my vitality[5] was dried up as with the heat of summer.
Selah.

5 Then I made my sin known to you,
    and I did not hide my iniquity;
I said, "I will acknowledge my transgressions[6] to the
LORD";
    and you—you forgave the guilt of my sin![7] *Selah*.

6 Therefore, let all who are devout pray to you
    in a time *when you may* be found.[8]
Surely, when many waters flow
    they shall not reach them.

7 You are my hiding place;

---

5. לְשַׁדִּי is a very rare word, occurring in Numbers 11:8; here it is usually translated "my strength" (a metonymy for "my moisture"). The Greek version (with the later revisions and Jerome) has for it εἰς ταλαιπωρίαν, "to misery, wretchedness," which would reflect לְשֹׁדִי. The translator had other difficulties in the line as well, reading "thorn" (קוֹץ) for "summer" (קַיִץ) and taking the noun "drought," חֶרְבוֹן ("in the drought of," בְּחָרְבֹנֵי), as an infinitive with a suffix from a different root חָרַב, "to attack, smite" (connected to the well-known word "sword"). The result is a translation that reads: "I was turned to misery (= became thoroughly miserable) when a thorn was stuck in me." The fact that the line has a rare word for "moisture," a word for "summer" that could be confused with "thorn," and a noun in the construct plural for "drought" that could be confused with a homonym, all account for how the Greek translation attempted to make sense out of it. The more difficult MT reading is the accepted reading.

6. A few manuscripts, the Greek, Aquila and Jerome all have the singular form.

7. The literal rendering would be "the iniquity of my sin," but "iniquity" can (by metonymy) mean the guilt for the iniquity, or the punishment for the iniquity. Guilt would be forgiven. The Greek version stayed more literally with the word, but some manuscripts varied the end of the verse: "the ungodliness (ἀσέβειαν) of my sin."

8. The Hebrew literally says "in the time of finding" (לְעֵת מְצֹא); this ends the first half of the verse (as indicated by the Masoretic dichotomy). The word רַק, "certainly, surely," is written on the same line, and so some commentators suggest emending the text to רַע, "trouble," to read something like "at a time [you] find trouble," or "at a time trouble finds [you]." But there is no support for the change. The Greek translation has εὐθέτῳ, "at a fit time." If the MT is retained the meaning would be "at a time of finding," and "surely" would start the next line.

you preserve me from trouble;
you surround me with shouts of deliverance.[9] *Selah*.

8 I will instruct you and teach you in the way that you should
    go;
  I will counsel[10] you with my eye upon you.
9 Do not be like a horse or a mule which have no
    understanding;
  whose harness[11] is with bit and bridle to control them
    or they will not come near you.
10 Many will be the troubles for the ungodly;
    but those who trust in the LORD–loyal love will surround
    them.
11 Be glad in the LORD, and rejoice you righteous people,
    and shout for joy all you who are upright in heart.

Composition and Context

Psalm 32 is one of the penitential psalms (see also Pss. 6, 38,
51, 102, 130, and 143). The distinctive message in this passage
is the great joy and relief that comes from being forgiven; and
this is presented in stark contrast to the spiritual depression
and sorrow under divine discipline that comes from stubbornly
refusing to confess sin. In view of the great sorrow for unconfessed sin, and the great joy of forgiveness, the psalmist appeals
to the people to avoid the mistake he made and seek the LORD's

---

9. The Greek translation of the verse is very different; it comes close to paraphrasing the verse, but repeats the idea of "surround." For "you are my
   hiding place, you preserve me from trouble," it reads "you are the refuge
   from the affliction that surrounds me." For "with shouts of deliverance you
   surround me," it reads "my joy, deliver me from those who have compassed
   me about."
10. For the MT's "I will counsel you (אִיעָצָה) with my eye upon you," the Greek
    version has "I will fix my eye on you" (ἐπιστηριῶ, the equivalent of אָעִיצָה).
11. The word עֶדְיוֹ literally would mean "its ornament," but it has the de-
    rived sense here of "trappings" for a horse, i.e., "harness." This makes
    good sense: "whose harness is bit and bridle." The Greek version has τὰς
    σιαγόνας αὐτῶν, yielding "their jaws (cheeks) with bit and bridle," perhaps
    reading לְעֵיהֶם, "their throat."

forgiveness. Thus, the second half of the psalm takes on a didactic tone—it is the urgent advice from one who learned the hard way.

Tradition has ascribed the psalm to David, accepting that he wrote many psalms, and aware that after his great sin there was a long period of time before he was confronted and confessed his sin. Because this psalm speaks of a time of refusing to acknowledge the sin, the connection was made to the sin with Bathsheba, and Psalm 32 became a sequel to Psalm 51. But there is no clear indication of this. Were there no other occasions when David sinned and was slow to confess? And were there no other people who experienced something like this? There are no compelling reasons to make the setting so specific—although there is no reason to reject it either. We cannot be certain. The connection at least gives us a good illustration of the kind of thing the psalmist was addressing.

Psalm 32 is close to a thanksgiving of an individual, but it adds a confession of sin, an oracle, and a didactic emphasis.[12] In fact, the psalm has a few motifs that fit wisdom literature as well, leading to the conclusion that the psalmist may have adapted a thanksgiving psalm to the wisdom tradition.[13] The psalm would have been recited or expressed in the sanctuary during worship, the ideal time to give thanks to the LORD for the forgiveness of sins and for the instruction of the congregation.[14] It has been used down through the centuries to give believers the assurance of the forgiveness of sins.[15]

The psalm may be divided in a number of ways, but the contents of the sections provide the easiest arrangement: verses 1 and 2 record the praise for the forgiveness of sins; verses 3–5 report the dilemma and the deliverance; verses 6–7 form an encouragement; and verses 8–10 are instruction. The biggest change comes with verse 6, and so the first 5 verses may be taken

12. Broyles, *Psalms*, p. 161.
13. VanGemeren, *Psalms*, pp. 310–11.
14. Anderson, *Psalms 1–72*, p. 254.
15. See further R. W. Jenson, "Psalm 32," *Int* 32 (1979):172–76.

together, and then verses 6–7 as a second section, and the rest as the final part.[16]

Exegetical Analysis

Summary

Having experienced divine chastening and then forgiveness for sin, the psalmist encourages others to seek the LORD who deals graciously with sinners, because the bliss of forgiveness is life changing.

Outline

  I. The psalmist declares that he has found the joy of forgiveness when he confessed his sin, but only after enduring divine chastening (1–5).
- A. David declares the heavenly bliss of those who do not conceal their sin but find complete forgiveness (1–2).
- B. David reveals how severely he was chastened when he did not confess his sin (3–4).
- C. David reports how when he confessed his sins he was forgiven (5).

 II. The psalmist encourages others to seek the LORD, because he deals graciously with those who trust in him (6–7).
- A. Lesson: The faithful should pray to God while he can be found, so that they may find safety when trouble comes (6).
- B. Praise: The LORD protects and preserves his people from trouble, surrounding them with shouts of deliverance (7).

III. The psalmist instructs others not to refuse submission to the LORD until he forces them to it, but rather to come willingly with their confession to God (8–11).
- A. David gives the instruction and counsel to others (8).
- B. David instructs the people to follow the LORD and not

---

16. See additionally Jack Barentsen, "Restoration and Its Blessing," *GTJ* 5 (1984):247–69.

be stubborn, because those who trust the LORD will be protected by his loyal love (9–10).

C. David calls on the righteous to rejoice in the LORD (11).

COMMENTARY IN EXPOSITORY FORM

I. The forgiveness of sin brings great joy and relief (1–2).

A. There is great joy in forgiveness (1).

The first two verses announce the grand theme of this contemplative poem: "Blessed is the one who is forgiven by God" (the text simply has: "Blessed is the forgiven of transgression"). The composition to follow develops the theme through a crisis, a crisis that everyone has experienced and will continue to experience, namely, the refusal to confess sin until the feelings of guilt and the disruption of their lives brings them to their knees. And then, to their amazement, God is quick to forgive. There are few feelings that are as troubling and crippling as guilty fears over unconfessed sin; and there are few that are as freeing and relieving as knowing that all has been set right with God. The principle is also true in human relationships; a refusal to apologize for wrongs committed leaves wounds and tensions and divisions that depress the spirit and hinder worship and service.

The psalm states the reason for the blissful joy in two different ways, one that declares the removal of sin, and the other that declares sins have not been recorded. The first is the initial announcement: "Blessed is the one whose transgression is forgiven,[17] whose sin is covered." The joy is so great because sin is so defeating. David describes his sin with a couple of key words. The first is "transgression" (פֶּשַׁע), a word that refers to "open rebellion," such as a military rebellion which turns into an open

---

17. The Hebrew word order is more powerful: "Blessed is [the one who is] forgiven of transgression," that is, forgiven with respect to transgression. The construction throws "forgiven" forward to get attention and then specifies it with the genitive "transgression."

confrontation (s.v. Ps. 51:2). This sin was no accidental sin, no failure to do what ought to be done. It was a willful sin: he went into it knowing full well that what he was doing was wrong.

The second word is the common word for "sin" (חָטָאת), a failure, missing the mark or the way (s.v. Ps. 51:2). The way is the divine revelation, so any act that does not measure up to the divine standard is "sin." The word could refer to any sin, whether a sin of ignorance or a premeditated sin. Likewise the apostle Paul would write that "all have sinned and come short of the glory of God" (Rom. 3:23). Because people fall short of God's standard, they must find forgiveness.

The Bible teaches again and again that there is forgiveness for those who truly repent. Psalm 130:4 says, "There is forgiveness with you, in order that you may be feared." The word that David used for "forgiven" in Psalm 32 is a word that gives the sense that the sin was "lifted away" (נָשָׂא, "to lift up, lift off, take away"; s.v. Ps. 24:7). The word stresses the idea that the sin was completely taken away, and with it the burden of guilty fears. The parallel line says that the sin was "covered" or "hidden" (from כָּסָה), meaning that it was concealed, out of sight and no longer able to cause guilt or fear.[18] When God forgives sin, the sin is removed. God will never bring it up again, not in this life nor the world to come.

Believers of all ages have continually come before God to confess their sins, and have gone away filled with joy and relief because they have been assured that God has put away the sin. They have the word of God on that.

---

18. Some teach that in the Old Testament sins were not truly forgiven but only covered over until the atoning work of Christ. The passage states clearly that the sin was forgiven, and Paul quotes this verse in Romans 4 to stress that certainty. The Old Testament believers may not have understood how the sin would finally be paid for, but in the meantime they had the sure word from God that they would be forgiven if they confessed their sin. They would demonstrate their faith by concluding the process with the prescribed ritual, the killing of the sacrificial animal to signify that there was atonement. The penitents simply took God's word for their forgiveness. We too take God's word of forgiveness by faith; and even though the ritual was fulfilled in Christ, we still appeal to God for cleansing on the basis of the blood of the Lamb of God.

And this is what brings such great joy. The psalm began with the expression of this happy estate—"blessed" (אַשְׁרֵי), or more specifically, "O the blessednesses of (the one whose sin is forgiven)." The word describes the real joy and delight that comes from knowing that one is right with God (see also Ps. 1:1). It is that feeling of heavenly bliss, or eternal joy, over the spiritual release from sin. Even in the midst of physical difficulties and perhaps opposition, one can truly feel blessed by God. The word, therefore, transcends the common idea of being "happy," even though some translations use that as the translation, or something else such as "good fortune."

B. There is great relief in knowing there will be no further condemnation (2).

Not only does forgiveness mean that God takes away the sins, but it also means God does not "impute" iniquity to the penitent: "Blessed is the one[19] to whom the LORD does not impute iniquity." The verb (חָשַׁב)[20] means "impute, reckon, credit"; it is the language of records, of accounting—in fact, in modern

---

19. The line uses the singular noun, "blessed is the man (אָדָם) who is forgiven"; I have translated it "Blessed is the one" to avoid having it sound like it applies to men only because it does not. It could also be put in the plural since "man" means anyone: "Blessed are those whose sins are forgiven."

20. The verb חָשַׁב has meanings in the semantic field of calculation, i.e., compute, account, charge, reckon, as well as in the field of thinking something out, i.e., conceiving and inventing, and often carrying it out. We may survey the usage in several areas. First, there is the meaning "think." In Genesis 38:15 the word is used with this meaning in the sense of taking someone to be a certain kind of person—he thought she was a prostitute. In Jonah 1:4 it is used figuratively to say that in the storm the boat thought it was about to break up.

More commonly are uses with the sense of "plan." Proverbs 16:9 says the mind plans the way, but the LORD directs the steps. A common use of this meaning concerns people who make plans or devise evil things, plans that turn into action (Hos. 7:15).

A third meaning is "consider, value." It is used in Isaiah 40:15 and 17 with the sense of weighing or regarding the nations as all but worthless. 1 Kings 10:21 says that silver was not counted because it was not considered valuable in Solomon's day, and Malachi uses the word to

710

usage the word is related to "computer." Here the psalm is using
an implied comparison, as if there were record books in heaven
that would record the sins. If the forgiven sins are not imputed,
it means that there is no record of them—they are gone and forgotten.[21] Because God does not mark iniquities (Ps. 130:4), there
is great joy.

This same verb is used in Genesis 15:6 as well, which says
that Abram "believed in the LORD, and he reckoned it (וַיַּחְשְׁבֶהָ)
to him *as* (or, *namely*) righteousness." The apostle Paul brings
that verse and Psalm 32:2 together in Romans 4 to explain the
meaning of justification by faith: when people believe in the
Lord, God *reckons* or credits them with righteousness (Paul
will say, the righteousness of Jesus Christ), and *does not reckon*
their sin to them. Thereafter as believers confess their sins, they
know that God will forgive them just as he did the first time they
asked for forgiveness.

The psalm adds "in whose spirit there is no guile" (רְמִיָּה, s.v.
Ps. 5:7). The word refers to deceit or duplicity, here concerning
one's sins; if the guilty sinner holds back or denies the sin, there is
no genuine repentance and therefore no forgiveness. Those who
are truly penitent will have no such deceit in their confession—
they will fully acknowledge their sin. The absence of "guile" is
a qualification for the forgiveness. God knows whether the confession is genuine or the individual is simply going through a
confessional but without remorse for the sin or desire to change.
There is full forgiveness for the one who confesses, but the confession must be honest.

---

describe people who esteem (by faith and obedience) the name of the
LORD (3:16).

Finally, the word is used in passages with the meaning "reckon,
account." Genesis 15:6 uses the word this way: Abram believed in the
LORD and the LORD reckoned to him righteousness. Here in Psalm
32 true forgiveness means that the LORD does not reckon or impute
iniquity.

21. To say that sins are "forgotten" or "remembered no more" by God is anthropomorphic, for God knows all things equally well. But the expressions
have to do with acting on what is remembered: God will not remember
them against the penitent (for "remember," s.v. Ps. 6:5), meaning, he will
never bring them up again or deal with them again if they are forgiven.

II. The misery of guilt is removed with the confession of the sin (3–5).

A. Refusal to confess brings divine discipline (3–4).

In spite of the fact that God stands ready to forgive, and in spite of the fact that people know from his word what sin is and that they need to confess, all too often they are reluctant or refuse to do so. Sometimes they convince themselves that what they have done is not sin; sometimes they tell themselves that there is no need to make confession since they are already the people of God; other times they know what they are doing is sin but cannot stop doing it. Whatever the reason, God will not let them get away with it, not for long anyway. God is very patient, desiring that his people come to their senses and seek forgiveness; but if they refuse, he has ways to bring them to that point.

In this psalm David witnesses to the fact that God disciplined him in some way. We do not know what it was because he expresses it in poetic terms so that other sinners could use the words of this psalm in their particular experience. He simply says, "When I kept silent [about my sin], my bones wasted away with my groaning all day long; for night and day your hand was heavy upon me."

The cause of David's spiritual depression and agony was twofold. First, he kept silent—this is the ultimate cause. The silence has to be considered the opposite of the confession (v. 5). He kept silent about his sin, meaning that he did not confess it.[22]

And so the LORD disciplined him. This is the immediate cause of his suffering. David says that God's hand was heavy upon him.[23] The figure of God's "hand" (anthropomorphism) often refers to his power, but in a very direct and personal way. The hand of God may protect, lead, hold secure, or support people; but it may also go out against people and inflict suffering or death (cf. Ruth 1:13).

---

22. For example, in the sin with Bathseba and the killing of Uriah, David lived in denial or self-deception for the better part of a year, until Nathan appeared in court to expose the sin.

23. The verb form here is תִּכְבַּד. It may be interpreted as a preterite without the *waw* consecutive; or it may be a customary use, expressing the frequency of God's discipline in the past.

What happened to the psalmist is hard to say. The poetic expression that his bones wasted away could be taken in one of two ways. If it refers to his physical body, then the "bones" would be a part for the whole, i.e., the body and its strength. (synecdoche); but if "bones" means the boney framework that houses his spirit (a metonymy of subject), then the distress was more spiritual than physical. The context sounds like the latter is meant, for all his days were filled with groaning as he weakened in his spirit, and his vitality for living, literally his life juices, dried up like the heat of summer. This comparison with the summer heat (simile) is vivid; it drains the energy and immobilizes the will to live life to the full. David's zest was not there; he was not motivated. He felt drained all the time. Basically, he was depressed, and it affected his physical energy and health. God was not allowing the psalmist to live life to the full when he was in rebellion against him, for it was God who gave him the full life to begin with.

B. Confession brings forgiveness (5).

The psalmist's condition would not have gotten any better if he had continued to ignore the main cause, sin; but he attests here that he came to the realization that it was his sin that was keeping him in spiritual depression. So he confessed.

There are two words for confession used in verse 5. The first is "acknowledge," which is a causative form of the verb "to know" (אוֹדִיעֲךָ from יָדַע); "My sin (חַטָּאתִי) I caused you to know" or "I made known to you."[24] Of course God knew all about the sin, but before there was any forgiveness the sinner had to agree with God on this matter, that is, make it known that he had sinned. To this he adds "and my iniquity[25] I did not conceal."

---

24. The verb is the imperfect form, but may be a preterite. It is parallel to a perfect tense, definite past, and so that is probably the nuance here. Some suggest that "I said" in the second colon was misplaced and should be here, yielding, "I said, 'I will make known . . . .'" Others suggest it is implied here as well as stated in 5b. The simple report of confession is preferable.

25. The word "iniquity" is עָוֹן. There are two views concerning the possible etymological connection of this word, and they both involve Arabic cognates. There are two Arabic words with letters that correspond to the Hebrew word (Arabic has two consonants that correspond with the one Hebrew

The other word used in the verse is "confess": "I said, 'I will confess my transgressions to the LORD" (make a public acknowledgment concerning my transgressions [פְּשָׁעַי]). This verb is a similar sounding verb (אוֹדֶה from יָדָה) but different in meaning, although some translate it as acknowledge too (s.v. Ps. 6:5). It signifies a clear and unambiguous confession, most likely made in public, or at least with people to hear and witness it, and be edified and encouraged by it. In the sanctuary people might not know the details of the confession that were in the mind of

---

letter עַ). One means "to go astray" and the other means "to twist, bend." Some lexicographers connect Hebrew עָוֹן to the Arabic word "bend, twist," deriving a definition for the noun as "perversion," i.e., bending the Law in disobedience; others connect it to the Arabic word "go astray, err from the way," and derive the meaning "waywardness" or "iniquity." The iniquity could be deliberate and perverted, or it might be accidental—but the word only would mean erring. In tracing through all the uses of the noun in Hebrew there is no passage where the word must have a meaning of perverted action. The context might portray what "iniquity" is referring to as perverted, but the meaning of the word is more general. So it probably means "to err, go astray" from the right way.

The noun is most often used for a specific act of sin. The Israelites wanted pardon for their iniquity (Exod. 34:9). The iniquity of the house of Eli had gone beyond being atoned for (1 Sam. 3:14). David's confession of sin acknowledges iniquity (Ps. 51:2). These passages, and many more, use the noun to describe any going astray from the LORD's revealed will; so one category means "iniquity, waywardness."

The word can also be used for the result of the sinful act, guilt. In Israel's ritual the worshiper following the divine instructions would be free of "iniquity," i.e., guilt. In Psalm 32:5 the psalmist states that God forgave "the iniquity/guilt of my sin." The word can also be used for another result of the sin, the punishment or consequence. In Genesis 4:13 Cain says, "My iniquity/punishment is too great to bear." He was not confessing sin or appealing for forgiveness; he was complaining about the punishment being too severe. Leviticus 5:17 says if a person sins he will bear his iniquity/punishment. These two categories developed as metonymies of effect.

Sometimes the word is used with all the aspects in mind. Zechariah 3:9 says, "I will remove the iniquity of that land in one day." God will remove the sin and with it guilt and punishment. Often the words for sin are used together in a passage, each bringing some aspect of the sin to attention. The most common word for sin (חַטָּאת) has to do with missing the mark and falling short of the standard; but iniquity, the second most frequently used word, describes the act as erring or going astray from the right way.

the confessor, but they would know that a confession of sin was being made.

The delight was that God immediately forgave. The dramatic reversal is highlighted by the pronouns in the Hebrew text: my sin I acknowledged, my iniquity I did not cover, I said, I will confess, but as for you, you forgave. The pronoun "you" is added to the verb to emphasize the change. God forgave the "iniquity of my sin" (עֲוֹן חַטָּאתִי). This could be interpreted in one of two ways. One would be to take the two words as expressing a superlative genitive (like "king of kings" or "song of songs"); this would stress the sinfulness of the sin. The other way, and the way I would take it, is to define the word "iniquity" in one of its derived senses, "guilt" or "punishment." This would mean that God took away all the effects of the sin when he took away the sin.

III. People may avoid such misery by seeking the LORD's favor (6–7).

The psalmist's immediate thought was to tell other people about his experience to spare them the grief and pain of unconfessed sin. They should pray to the LORD—for divine favor in this context—while he may be found. God's gracious dealings with them will prevent disaster.

The "devout" in verse 6 are the godly, the pious people (חָסִיד). The term used is related to the common word "loyal love" (or "lovingkindness," חֶסֶד; s.v. Ps. 23:6) used throughout the psalms. The devout are the people who are in covenant with God, who desire to love and serve the LORD, but who often find that they need forgiveness in order to maintain a proper relationship with the LORD. David admonishes them to pray, but the cryptic expression "in a time *when you may be found*" (literally, "in a time of finding") raises some questions. When can the LORD *not* be found? One would say theologically that God is always present and can always be prayed to in any time of need, but the Bible uses language like this to describe our situation more than God's availability, that is, the circumstances that would prompt us to pray, a window of opportunity, as it were. God prompts his people to act, either because he has opened a way for them to act, or because he is moving them by his Spirit to respond; but if people do not respond to pray, the opportunity might end and the LORD might no longer prompt confession. When people are made aware of their sins, then they should pray for forgiveness. If they do not, then divine discipline may fall on them. In other words, "at the time of finding" refers to our conviction (by the Spirit) that we need to pray to him; and that sense may be intense or it may grow cold, depending on whether we pray or rebel. When God prompts people to deal with sin in their lives, that is the time for finding him. Psalm 95:7b–8a warns "Today, if you hear his voice, do not harden your hearts."

If people pray to God when they are made aware of their sin (by a prophet in David's case, but often by God's Spirit or God's Word) they will find relief from the misery of guilt and divine discipline. The text uses the imagery of "waters" rushing out for the idea of the discipline.[26] One can think of river beds in the land of Israel that are dry most of the year but in a rainy season can turn into torrents in flash floods. The psalmist means that like such a flood all kinds of troubles can hit suddenly, but those who pray when prompted to do so will avoid the devastation of discipline for sin. He does not say troubles (i.e., waters) will not come in life, but they will not overtake the devout.

This leads David to praise the LORD with several powerful images. God, he says, is his hiding place (סֵתֶר). This figure (metaphor) speaks of divine shelter, protection, and care. Second, he says that God preserves him (תִּצְּרֵנִי) him from trouble. There is divine protection from any of the calamities of life that would press in on him. And third, he says that God surrounds him with shouts of deliverance. The word "shouts" (from רָנַן, "to give a ringing cry"; s.v. Ps. 33:1) is often used for the jubilation of great victory; here the shouts are qualified by the word "deliverance" (פַּלֵּט).[27] The reference may be to the congregation of people in the sanctuary who will sing and shout of God's great protection and

---

26. Isaiah 8 also makes an implied comparison between flood waters covering the land up to the city of Jerusalem and the invasion by the Assyrian army.
27. The genitive could be interpreted in various ways. It could be an objective genitive, meaning they were shouting about the deliverance; or, it could be an attributive use, indicating that these were victory shouts; or it could be subjective genitive, the deliverance caused the shouts.

salvation. A similar result is expressed in Psalm 51 where forgiveness would enable the penitent to enter the sanctuary once
again and hear the joy and gladness.

IV. (Therefore) it is better to submit to the LORD than to resist with stubborn pride (8–11).

A. People must lay aside stubborn pride (8–9).

Verse 8 introduces the resolve of the psalmist to instruct
people in the way that they should go. But is God speaking, or
the psalmist? The sudden shift in verse 8 provides no clear solution to the question. It sounds like an oracle that God delivered
to the psalmist, except that in verse 9 the verb is plural ("Do not
be"); it could be the psalmist speaking to the people, except the
suffixes in verse 8 are singular. Perhaps the solution is that the
psalmist was employing something God said to him and using it
in his advice to the congregation (whom he addresses collectively
as "you," singular); he then expanded on it in verse 9. In any
case, it would not change the meaning, because even if he was
the speaker in verse 8, God would be speaking through him. The
instruction ultimately comes from God.

The verbs used in verse 8 are common in wisdom literature: "I
will instruct you" (אַשְׂכִּילְךָ; s.v. Ps. 36:4) means give understanding,
"I will teach you" (אוֹרְךָ, s.v. Ps. 1:2) means to show the way (and
is related to *torah*, the law), and "I will counsel" (אִיעֲצָה) means
to give advice. This last verb does not have a pronominal suffix,
but the expression "my eye upon you" expresses the manner of
the counsel—watching you with me eye. All of these are used to
impart proper understanding and successful guidance based on
revelation—that is the way that people should go. In this psalm
the wise instruction most certainly is concerned with forgiveness
through repentance and confession, but wisdom goes beyond that
for the way that people should live is the way of righteousness.

Accordingly, stubborn pride must be dealt with. Using two
memorable similes, David warns people not to be like the horse
or like the mule. These animals had to be controlled with bit and
bridle to force them to come along the way. God will do that to
his people if he has to do it; but he would rather have a willing

spirit that does not need it.[28] He would rather have people who will choose the right and reject the wrong, and who will confess their sins when they sin and not try to conceal them.

B. People will find great joy in the LORD's loving care (10–11).

Finally, David offers a little truism, a little proverb, in verse 10: "Many will be the troubles for the ungodly (or wicked), but those who trust in the LORD—loyal love shall surround them." The contrast here is between the "ungodly" (s.v. Ps. 1:1) and those who trust (s.v. Ps. 4:5) in the LORD, between the unbeliever and the believer. For the ungodly there will be many troubles or woes (literally sorrows). He does not specify what they are or when they come, but the word "many" recalls the use of "many waters" in verse 6, the swift catastrophe. Wisdom literature in general teaches that the ungodly have no prospect of divine help for the difficulties of this life, and in the next life they will be judged for their sins.

Believers have a great prospect; God's loyal love will surround them. There may be difficulties to overcome, but God's faithful covenant love will always be there. Even if divine love chastens believers, that love will always have their best interests at heart (see Ps. 30).

What a choice! One can be stubborn like the mule and refuse to acknowledge sin, and so endure divine discipline that will increase guilty fears and spiritual depression. Or, one can confess sin and immediately find relief and joy in divine forgiveness through the loyal love of God.

The last verse of the psalm forms a balance with the first verse. In the first David was lauding the bliss of the forgiven believer; in the last verse he is calling for the righteous, the upright in heart, to praise and shout for joy.

---

28. Similarly in Psalm 51 David will say that God is looking for the broken heart. The imagery of a horse that is broken of its self-will comes readily to mind. The horse does not lose any of its strength or enjoyment—it is simply controllable.

MESSAGE AND APPLICATION

The psalm is a thanksgiving for the joy of forgiveness. Its admonition is clear: confess your sin and find this forgiveness, because there is great joy and relief in forgiveness, and because if you do not, there is great sorrow and grief in divine discipline. God desires that we pray when the time is right; but if we refuse, then God will do something to change us. The point of the psalm is so clear that it will not need much explanation in the conclusion, but I would word an expository idea in two antithetical statements, beginning with the negative and ending with the positive:

Because living with unconfessed sin brings spiritual depression and oppressive guilt, it is foolish to refuse to acknowledge sin.

Because forgiveness of sin brings joyful bliss with God and relief from guilty pain, it is wise to confess sin and not conceal it.

If we deny that we have sinned, we lie. If we confess our sins, he is faithful and just to forgive us our sins, and to cleanse us from all unrighteousness (1 John 1:9). As Psalm 51 will explain, to live with unconfessed sin ruins our joy in the LORD, disqualifies us from participation in worship, and prevents us from teaching others the way of the LORD; but forgiveness is so immediate, so certain, and so joyful, that to refuse to seek it regularly is utterly foolish.

PSALM 33

A New Song of Praise for His Word and His Faithfulness, His Righteousness, and His Love

INTRODUCTION

Text and Textual Variants[1]

1 Rejoice in the LORD, you righteous;
   praise is fitting for the upright.
2 Give thanks to the LORD with the harp;
   sing praises to him on the ten-stringed lyre.
3 Sing to him a new song;
   play skillfully with a loud sound.

4 For the word of the LORD is upright;
   and all his work *is done* in faithfulness.
5 He loves righteousness and justice;
   the earth is full of the loyal love of the LORD.

6 By the word of the LORD were the heavens made,

---

1. The Greek translation attributed the psalm to David: τῷ Δαυίδ. The evidence is insufficient to make a strong case for Davidic authorship.

and by the breath of his mouth all their host.

7 He gathers the waters of the sea like a heap;[2]
    he lays up the deeps in storehouses.

8 Let all the earth fear the LORD;
    let all the people of the world be in awe of him.

9 For he spoke, and it[3] came to be;
    he commanded, and it stood firm.[4]

10 The LORD brings the counsel of the nations to nothing;
    he makes the purposes of the peoples to be of no effect.[5]

11 The counsel of the LORD stands firm forever,
    the purposes of his heart through all generations.

12 Blessed is the nation whose God is the LORD,
    the people whom he has chosen for his inheritance.

13 The LORD looks down from heaven;
    he sees all mankind;[6]

14 from his dwelling–place[7] he watches
    all who live on the earth—

15 he who forms the hearts of them all,[8]
    who considers all their works.

---

2. "Like a heap" is כַּנֵּד. The Greek has "as in a wineskin" (ὡς ἀσκόν), perhaps reading כְּנֹ(א)ד instead of נֵד (from נָדַד). The Greek reading is supported by the Targum, Syriac, and Old Latin. Some commentators suggest reading the form כַּנֵּד, "jar," which would make a good parallel with "store-houses" (see the NIV rendering); but the MT reading is close to Exodus 15:8 and Psalm 78:13.

3. The Greek has this verb, and the last verb in the plural: "they came to be" and "they were created."

4. The Greek version has "created," ἐκτίσθησαν.

5. The Greek version has added a third colon, which duplicates 10a by and large: "and brings to nought the counsel of princes" (καὶ ἀθετεῖ βουλὰς ἀρχόντων).

6. The text literally is "the sons of man" (בְּנֵי הָאָדָם).

7. The text has מִמְּכוֹן־שִׁבְתּוֹ, "from the place of his dwelling." There is some manuscript evidence to read קָדְשׁוֹ in place of שִׁבְתּוֹ; but the Greek and Qumran both support the standard MT reading.

8. יַחַד, "all" or "together," is difficult in this sentence, so the Greek has "alone" (κατὰ μόνας = יָחִיד). A. A. Anderson takes it in the sense of "alone," meaning the LORD alone fashions the hearts (*Psalms 1–72*, p. 265).

16 There is no king saved by the strength of his army;
   no warrior[9] escapes by *his*[10]great strength.
17 A horse is a vain hope for deliverance,
   neither does it deliver[11] *any* by its great power.
18 But the eye[12] of the LORD is on those who fear him,
   on those whose hope is in his loyal love,
19 to deliver them[13] from death,
   and to keep them alive in famine.

20 We wait in hope[14] for the LORD;
   he is our help and our shield.[15]
21 In him our hearts shall rejoice,
   for we have trusted in his holy name.
22 May your loyal love rest upon us, O LORD,
   because we have put our hope in you.

Composition and Context

Psalm 33 is a declarative praise psalm; it has the call to praise
(vv. 1–3), the cause for the praise (vv. 4–19), and the conclusion
(vv. 20–22). Such compositions usually extol the greatness of the
LORD as it is revealed in creation and history, and the grace of
the LORD as he makes his greatness available to his people.
In Psalm 33:4–5 there is a summary statement of the cause for
praise listing four themes, the first three reveal his greatness,
and the last his grace. They are the directness of God's word,
the faithfulness of his work, his righteousness decisions, and his
loyal love for his people. Each of these themes is then developed
in the body of the psalm: the word of the LORD is developed in
verses 6–9, the faithfulness of God in verses 10–12, his love for

---

9. Greek "giant" (γίγας).
10. Some of the versions insert "his" into the text.
11. The verb (a *piel* imperfect in the MT) is rendered passive (= *niphal*) in the
    Greek, σωθήσεται, as in the Targum. It would then read: "neither shall he
    be delivered."
12. One manuscript, as well as the Greek and Syriac make this plural.
13. Literally, "their life."
14. Literally, "Our soul waits."
15. Greek has "defender" (ὑπερασπιστὴς).

righteousness in verses 13–15, and his loyal love for his people in verses 16–19. This deliberate pattern should guide the organization of the exposition.

There is not much evidence to determine the authorship of the composition. This psalm along with Psalms 1, 2, and 10 are the only psalms in Book I that have no superscription. There is, however, an ascription of the psalm to David in the Greek translation and some versions as well as Qumran. There are some Hebrew manuscripts that connect Psalm 33 to Psalm 32, but these may be attempts to supply a missing superscription.

The occasion for the psalm is equally obscure. Because of the emphasis on creation and redemption, the work has been connected with the autumn festival,[16] but the praise of God was never separated from the historical experiences and faith of the people and limited to a specific time.[17] The psalm was probably an independent composition reflecting some crisis in the nation before becoming part of the temple collection. It may have been used for various festivals in Israel's ritual, but its central place remained in the faith of the people. Psalms such as this made creedal statements relevant and memorable.

Exegetical Analysis

Summary

The psalmist calls upon the righteous to praise the LORD because they can trust in him for salvation, knowing that his word is true, his sovereign works are faithful, his judgment is righteous, and his loyal love to those who trust in him is eternal.

---

16. See for example A. A. Anderson, *Psalms 1–72,* p. 260. For Sigmund Mowinckel it was part of the New Year's festival (*The Psalms in Israel's Worship,* I:89, 94–95). Weiser also puts it with the fall festival, but to him it is a covenant festival (*Psalms,* p. 289).
17. See Claus Westermann, *Praise of God in the Psalms,* p. 155.

A New Song of Praise for His Word and His Faithfulness, His Righteousness, and His Love

Outline

I. Call to Praise: The psalmist calls upon the righteous to praise the LORD anew with musical accompaniment and shouts of joy (1–3).

  A. The righteous are called to rejoice (1).

  B. They should praise with musical accompaniment (2).

  C. Their new song should be sung well (3).

II. Cause for Praise: The LORD should be praised because his word is right, his works are dependable, his judgment is righteous, and his loyal love to those who trust in him is eternal (4–19).

  A. He declares and demonstrates the certainty and clarity of the word of God (4a, 6–9).

    1. Summary: The word of the LORD is upright (4a).

    2. Demonstration: The LORD created everything by his word (6–9).

  B. He declares and demonstrates the faithfulness of God's works (4b, 10–12).

    1. Summary: All his works are done in faithfulness (4b).

    2. Demonstration: He frustrates the plans of world and accomplishes his plan (10–12).

  C. He declares and demonstrates that the LORD's judgment is righteous (5a, 13–15).

    1. Summary: The LORD is righteous and just (5a).

    2. Demonstration: The sovereign LORD observes and evaluates humans (13–15).

  D. He declares and demonstrates that the LORD's loyal love is faithful (5b, 16–19).

    1. Summary: The earth is full of evidence of his loyal love (5b).

    2. Demonstration: It is the loyal love of the LORD that saves and preserves the lives of those who trust in him (16–19).

III. Conclusion: The people of God demonstrate their faith in him (20–22).

  A. They wait eagerly for the LORD (20).

  B. They rejoice because they trust in him (21).

  C. They petition him to continue to manifest his loyal love for them (22).

725

COMMENTARY IN EXPOSITORY FORM

I. Call to Praise: The righteous must praise God afresh with great joy and skill (1–3).

A. It is fitting for the righteous to sing joyfully to the LORD (1).

The call is for the "righteous" (צַדִּיקִים) and the "upright" (יְשָׁרִים) to sing praises to the LORD. The word "righteous" refers to believers in the LORD who seek to live according to his standard (Deut. 6:25; s.v. Ps. 1:5); and "upright" refers to those who follow the LORD faithfully and seek to do what is right in his eyes.[18] These two descriptions prepare the reader for what is to follow in the psalm, namely, that the word of the LORD is "upright," i.e., straight or direct, and that the LORD loves "righteousness"(vv. 6–9) and therefore evaluates everyone righteously (vv. 13–15).

In calling the faithful to praise God, the psalm uses six different words for praise, the first two being in verse 1. The first verb, translated "sing joyfully" means "give a ringing cry" (רָנַן). It is often a loud sound of rejoicing, such as was used in cultic shouting (Lev. 9:24), or on joyous occasions such as the deliverance from exile (Isa. 52:8–9).[19] The second word is the noun

---

18. The word "upright" (יָשָׁר) has the idea of going straight or direct (s.v. Ps. 67:4). The upright look straight ahead, i.e., there is no deviation (Prov. 4:25); the upright do what is right in the eyes of the LORD, i.e., they keep his commands (Exod. 15:26; Deut. 6:17–18).
19. The word רָנַן is one of the many words for praise in the Bible. It basically means "to rejoice, cry out." The most common derivative is the noun רִנָּה which is a "loud shout." The verb occurs 53 times in the Bible, 25 of them in the Psalms; the noun occurs 33 times, 15 in the Psalms. Even when it is in other books of the Bible the words are found most often in poetic, psalm-like passages. This may indicate that the words are predominantly part of cultic terminology.

Essentially, רָנַן refers to a loud expression, usually of joy, but in some passages of lament and pain (Lam. 2:19). In some passages it simply refers to a loud shout (Prov. 1:20; 8:3). The idea of its referring to a loud shout has prompted the conclusion that the word is onomatopoeic, sounding like a "ringing cry." The word does not simply refer to a shrieking shout, because

"praise" (תְּהִלָּה). This word, and its verb (הָלַל) refer to spontaneous praise, the natural description of something praiseworthy,
such as in the glowing report about the beauty of Sarai given
by the princes of Egypt (Gen. 12:15). God is praised for so many
things, but especially for his person (Pss. 48:10–12; 106:1), his
creation and its preservation (Ps. 148:1–6), and his acts of salvation (Pss. 22:26; 34:2).[20]

---

in some passages it is used for verbal communication (Prov. 8:3), but in
many passages it refers to a loud shout, a raised voice, or expressions of
a musical nature.The noun is used in similar ways. The element of great
joy is the most common meaning, but it too can be a loud cry of lament or
supplication (e.g., Pss. 17:1; 61:1; 88:2). It is used for loud shouts directed
to God either in praise or in an attempt to gain an answer. Some passages
also indicate the cry has verbal content (Ps. 35:27; Ps. 118:15).

Interestingly not only people give the shouts but personified concepts
shout out, such as wisdom in the streets (Prov. 1:20), the daughter of Zion
(Zeph. 3:14), Zion (Lam. 2:19) and the ruins of Jerusalem (Isa. 52:9). Also,
creation shouts (Jer. 51:48), the entire earth too (Ps. 98:4), and trees (Ps.
96:12). Each of these will have to be interpreted within the contexts. And
of course, angels, the morning stars (Job 38:7) shouted at creation.

The vast majority of uses calls for praise of God. In their cultic use
there is a reason given for the praise, some justification for the shout of
joy. This is usually some act of the LORD that calls for an enthusiastic
response, but it can also be based on his nature, his name, his righteousness, his judgments (See R. Ficker, "רנן *rnn* **to rejoice**," in *Theological
Lexicon of the Old Testament,* ed. by E. Jenni and C. Westermann,
III:1240–1243).

20. By far the best known word for praise from the Old Testament, the word
הָלַל is usually translated "praise" but can also mean "glory in" or "boast";
and there are a few unusual uses that have to be dealt with separately.
There is some disagreement over the etymological identification of the
word, whether it is related to a verb meaning "to be bright, to shine" or
simply to a word "to be boastful, to praise." More helpful is the connection
to Ugaritic where the word means "shout," and Akkadian where it means
"shout, jubilation," and Arabic where the cognate word means "sing joyfully to someone." The Hebrew verb occurs 142 times; the vast majority of
the cases concern praise for the LORD, with only about nine uses for other
objects.

There are a number of related terms that have essentially the same
meaning. There is the most common word תְּהִלָּה which means "praise," but
there are a couple of others too, such as a "celebration at a festival" (הִלּוּל,
Judg. 9:27).

Such praise, the psalmist says, is "fitting" (נָאוָה) for the upright.[21] It is appropriate to the nature and experience of believers to praise, for they have received everything by God's grace. A believer without praise is like a person who is not properly dressed for the occasion.

B. Their songs of praise should be with musical accompaniment (2).

Both halves of verse two call for praise with musical accompaniments. The first imperative, usually translated "praise" or "give thanks" (הוֹדוּ, from יָדָה), is primarily a public praise accompanied

The basic idea of the verb and the common noun is praise or recommendation of someone's attributes or actions. It is a spontaneous expression of joy or appreciation. A classic example is in Genesis 12:15 where the princes praised Sarai to the king. It can be used for other natural responses, such as a husband praising his noble and capable wife (Prov. 31:28), maidens who praise the bride (Cant. 6:9), or the king praised at his coronation (2 Chron. 23:12–13). Even the wicked are praised by those who forsake the Law (Prov. 28:4).

The religious use of the words is the most important here. The same meaning applies here as well, namely, that all spontaneous enjoyment of something finds expression in lavish descriptions, so the devout praise the LORD for his word (Ps. 119:164), for his works (Ps. 113), and for his attributes. People will boast or glory in the LORD (see Ps. 44:8; Isa. 41:16). The most common expression is the plural imperative, "Praise Yah" (הַלְלוּ־יָהּ). This expression (and other uses of the word) indicates that the locus of the praise was in the sanctuary among the congregation of the righteous (Pss. 22:22; 107:32). The call to praise usually includes songs (Ps. 69:30), dancing (Ps. 149:3), and music (Ps. 150:1–5). When David organized temple worship, he designated certain clans to praise the LORD (1 Chron. 16:4, 36; 25:3). The call "Halleû-Yāh" became a brief cultic shout, as witnessed by its use in the New Testament.

Another use of the word is of the action of boasting or taking glory in oneself, such as in Psalm 75:4, "I said to the boastful, do not boast." Then there are passages where it describes the actions of someone that appear foolish, such as judges that appear foolish (Job 12:17), or of laughter that is foolishness (Eccl. 2:2). Other stems of the verb will have the idea of going mad (Jer. 25:16; 1 Sam. 21:13). Whether these are of the same family of words or not is questionable.

21. The meaning of the word is "fitting, appropriate." We can see the meaning best by looking at things that are not fitting. Proverbs uses it to show that excellent speech (17:7), luxury (19:10), and honor (26:1) are not fitting for the fool—they are out of character for the fool. But praise is appropriate for the upright—it fits.

728

by ritual sacrifice (s.v. Ps. 6:5). The word may be better understood as "acknowledge" since it can be used for confessing faith or confessing sin (Ps. 32:5). A confession of faith is an acknowledgment in praise of God and his attributes and his works (Ps. 89:5; and Pss. 105, 106 and 145). The praising was to be done with the harp (כִּנּוֹר), an instrument shaped like a harp, having from 3 to 12 strings.[22]

The other verb in the verse is "sing [praises]" (זַמְּרוּ, from זָמַר).[23] It has the basic idea of making music or singing a melody to the LORD; and it often is used where musical instruments accompany the singing. The verb, and its related noun "psalm" (מִזְמוֹר), would signify singing a melody to the LORD, often to the accompaniment of musical instruments, most likely stringed instruments. Here this was to be done with a ten-stringed lyre (נֵבֶל). Whatever the shape and sound of these instruments, it is clear that the call to praise included the use of stringed instruments; other psalms list different instruments, but this one prefers the lyre and harp.

C. They should play skillfully with a new song of praise (3).

Verse 3 has two more verbs for praising. In the first colon the verb is simply "sing"; and parallel to it is the expression "play skillfully."

---

22. See Eric Werner, "Musical Instruments," in *IDB*, 3:474–75; see also Joachim Braun, *Music in Ancient Israel/Palestine* (Grand Rapids: Eerdmans, 2002).

23. זָמַר means "to make music" in praise of God. It has an Arabic cognate that means "play on a reed," or "pipe." In biblical usage there are two general categories of meaning. First, the verb can be used for singing, that is, praising God with a song (e.g., Ps. 30:12 and many other passages). The singing may or may not be accompanied by instruments. Where it is clearly the case, we have the second category of meaning, playing musical instruments (e.g., here in Ps. 33:2).

The derived noun זִמְרָה, "melody, song" in praise of God, has the same categories: instrumental music (Amos 5:23), singing (Exod. 15:2), and then passages where this distinction is unclear (Ps. 81:2).

The common title in the Book of Psalms is מִזְמוֹר, translated "psalm." It may be understood as "melody"; in titles it is usually followed by the personal name, such as "a psalm/melody of David." It refers to a song that may or may not be accompanied by musical instruments. Many of the psalms specify the use of instruments in the singing of the psalm.

The word "sing" (שִׁיר) is a general term used for individuals (Exod. 15:2), Levitical choirs, or the assembled people who might sing antiphonally or in unison on an anthem. The second command is a little more involved. It literally says "make good to play a stringed instrument." This construction is a verbal hendiadys using an imperative and an infinitive; in it the imperative becomes an adverb and the infinitive the main verb, hence, "play (a stringed instrument) skillfully." The verb "play a stringed instrument" (נַגֵּן) is used of David playing the harp before Saul (1 Sam. 16:23).

All the congregation is called on to sing "a new song" (שִׁיר חָדָשׁ).[24] This would mean more than a new composition; it is a call for a new experience for praise (so a metonymy of effect). The motif of a new song is used seven times in the Old Testament. In Psalm 40:1–3 David explains his recent deliverance by saying that God "put a new song in my mouth." The new song there is clearly a figure of speech (metonymy of effect), the "new song" being put for the deliverance that inspired it. The other references (Pss. 96:1; 98:1; 149:1; Isa. 42:10) as well as this passage (Ps. 33:3) are set phrases in calls to praise with renewed enthusiasm resulting from a new experience of deliverance or a new appreciation of the LORD's presence. Calling people to sing a new song was a way of calling people to enjoy God's presence and his benefits, so that they would have something new to sing about in the sanctuary.

II. The righteous should praise God for his powerful word, his faithful works, his righteous supervision, and his loyal love (4–19).

In the second section of the psalm we have the reason for the praise. It begins with a four-part summary (vv. 4–5) listing four attributes of the LORD. Each of these themes will then be developed in the subsequent sections of the psalm.

---

24. The word שִׁיר, a noun meaning "song," with a denominative verb meaning "to sing," is rather straightforward in its uses. It can be used for any kind of song or singing, love songs, drunken songs, workers' songs, whether noisy or joyous. It can also be used for religious songs or singing to the LORD, whether of the Levitical choirs or the congregation, or individuals. It is used in the headings of the pilgrim songs, "song of going up" (Pss. 120–134). It too can be used for singing that is accompanied by musical instruments.

The first line of the summary declares that "the word of the LORD is upright (s.v. Ps. 67:4)." Then verses 6–9 develop the theme with the most compelling example, the creative pronouncements of the LORD. Those pronouncements were clear and direct; they did not contain uncertainty, they were not inadequate, they did not digress from the point.

The second theme is "all his work is *done* in faithfulness" (v. 4b). "All his work" is much broader than creation—it refers to everything that God does. That it is done in faithfulness means that his revealed plan is completely dependable (s.v. Ps. 15:2). To develop this theme the psalm simply focuses on the plan of God for human history, for that is the most relevant summation of "all his works." God's plan will be fulfilled in spite of many human plans to oppose it.

The third idea (5a) is that the LORD "loves righteousness and justice."[25] The verse begins with the participle (אֹהֵב), but omits the subject pronoun: "he [referring to the LORD] loves." "Righteousness" and "justice" refer to the righteous acts and just deeds that flow from these attributes (so they are metonymies of cause; see also Ps. 98:2 and 99:4). The word "righteousness" refers to that which conforms to the standard—the LORD himself is the standard and he has revealed it in his word (s.v. Ps. 1:5). Since the LORD loves righteousness, he requires it in his people (Ps. 11:7). The other word "justice" applies to all aspects of governmental activities, but primarily decisions (s.v. Ps. 9:4). Legal acts are just when they are in harmony with the justice of God revealed in his word. And so these ideas are explained more fully in verses 13–15. There we read how the LORD who fashioned the human heart examines it in his quest for righteousness in the human race.

And the fourth theme (5b) is the presence of God's loyal love in all the world. Here too the word translated "loyal love" (חֶסֶד, s.v. Ps. 23:6) refers to what this love produces, salvation and care (so it is a metonymy of cause). This is the point of the elaboration

---

25. These two words, "righteousness and justice," may be interpreted as a hendiadys, the one modifying the other: "righteousness in justice," or "righteous justice."

in verses 16–19: by his loyal love the LORD delivers his people in battle and spares their lives in famine.

A. Praise the LORD because his word is direct (4a and 6–9).

The first theme, then, that "the word of the LORD is upright" (v. 4a), is illustrated by the directness of God's word in creation. From this the psalmist will conclude that the LORD should be obeyed and feared.

Verse 6 repeats the summary statement's expression, "the word of the LORD," forming a link with that statement and introducing the contents of the next few verses. The best example of the theme is the proclamation of God in creation, specifically first the heavens and the earth (Gen. 1:1–8). Then, the parallel colon refers to the formation of the heavenly host (Gen. 1:14–19; see also Isa. 40:12ff, and Ps. 147:4). Now it is "his breath" that forms the decree (a metonymy of cause, rephrasing the statement about the "word" in the first colon). The point is that all of creation came about by the powerful word of the living God, delivered effortlessly and directly.[26]

Verse 7 presents the creative acts of God in rich poetic expressions. Most likely, the waters being gathered like a heap refers to the events on the third day of creation when the lands were separated from the seas. Other texts say that God set a boundary for the sea which it could not pass (see Jer. 5:22; Pss. 104:9; 148:6; Job 26:10; Prov. 8:27–29).[27]

There are some connections between the language of Psalm 33 and the Song of the Sea in Exodus 15 (which warrant further study). The expression stating that the waters of the sea

---

26. The account of creation was no magical text, as in the ancient religions. In the pagan religions there are parallels. In Egypt the god Ptah conceives the elements in his mind and brings them into existence by his word (see J. Pritchard, *ANET*, p. 5). The difference is that in the Bible the power is in the LORD and not in the word as some magical element. Genesis 1 therefore also forms a polemic against pagan beliefs.

27. The mythological account of *Enuma Elish* (IV:139, 40) also has Marduk setting a limit to the waters of Tiamat (see Alexander Heidel, *The Babylonian Genesis* [Chicago: University of Chicago Press, 1974], p. 42).

were gathered as a heap (v. 7), appears in Exodus 15:8. Psalm 33:7 mentions the "deeps" which in Exodus 15:5 and 8 are the instrument of destroying the Egyptian army. Moreover, Psalm 33:7 says that the LORD gathered the deeps into store-houses, an idea we have in other related passages (see Deut. 28:12; Job 38:22). Although good things come from God's store-house, the "deeps" are dangerous and destructive, and so the deeps in the storehouses may suggest an arsenal of weapons for God to use (Jer. 5:25). God controls the seas by his word and can use them as he sees fit. In fact, God often uses the elements of creation as weapons as he did at the exodus, so the Song of the Sea is drawing on elements of creation. Psalm 33:6–9 is using similar expressions to praise God for creating these elements.

The natural response to all of this is fear: "Let all the earth fear the LORD; let all the world's inhabitants be in awe of him" (v. 8). The "earth" refers to the people in the earth (metonymy of subject), as the parallelism clarifies. Upon realizing the truths of this psalm, all people should now acknowledge the sovereignty of the LORD—as they will sooner or later. A. A. Anderson notes, the LORD has a special relationship with the people of the world because he is their creator and sustainer, whether they acknowledge this or not.[28]

The exhortation (the verbs are jussives) is for people to revere (worship) and obey the LORD. It is a call for the only appropriate and reasonable response to the absolute authority of the universe: reverence and submission. The parallel verb is even stronger: "be in awe" (יָגוּרוּ); it means to fear in the sense of being intimidated by something superior and more powerful (see Deut. 1:17; 18:22; 1 Sam. 18:15). So not only are people called to acknowledge God as their creator, but also that acknowledgment should fill them with a fear that will prompt reverence and obedience.

The reason for this call is given in verse 9, and it is disarmingly simple but overwhelmingly deep. Here is where we come back to the idea of the directness and clarity of God's word: "For he spoke, and it came to pass; he commanded and it stood firm." The LORD simply spoke, and what he said brought the universe

---

28. *Psalms 1–72*, pp. 263–4.

and everything in it into existence. "He spoke" is literally "he said" (וַיֹּאמֶר), which makes a direct connection to the verb used throughout Genesis 1. And the verb "and it was/came to pass" (וַיְהִי) certainly recalls "and there was (וַיְהִי) light" in Genesis 1:3. The second line uses "he commanded" and "it stood firm." The idea of standing is often used for the action of a subordinate to a superior (e.g., Joseph standing before Pharaoh in Gen. 41:46). This report of his commanding and everything standing firm emphasizes that all creation endures by God's decrees and stands before the LORD to do his bidding. Delitzsch says, "He need only command and it stands forth like an obedient servant, that appears in all haste at the call of the Lord."[29] The same emphasis is found in Psalm 119:89–90.

All people are called on to praise God for his direct and powerful word, for by it he made and sustains everything. When people in their modern sophistication, even in religious circles, ignore or even deny the word of God that reports creation, they not only rob God of his glory but they also undermine true worship. For if there is no sovereign Lord of all creation, there is no reason for worship or obedience.

B. Praise the LORD because his work is dependable (4b and 10–12).

This section focuses on the LORD's sovereign plan in history as the development of the theme that all his work is dependable (v. 4b). Verses 10 and 11 go together as the plan and intentions of the nations (v. 10) are contrasted with the plan and intentions of the LORD (v. 11). The two key words here are "counsel" (or plan) and "purpose" (or intention). The first word (עֵצָה) means "plan, counsel, advice" (see Ps. 1:1; and Exod. 18:19 where Jethro gave Moses advice). The second word (מַחֲשָׁבָה; s.v. Ps. 32:2), often translated "purpose," looks to the idea of intention (see Gen. 15:6 where the verb is used to say God "reckoned" righteousness to the believer; or Gen. 50:20 where it is said the brothers "intended" [planned] evil in their treatment of Joseph). Now, as for the plan and intentions of the nations, the psalmist

---

29. *Psalms* I:42.

says that the LORD "annuls" (פָּרַר) and "thwarts" (נוא) them. This second term has the idea of stopping an action (as in forbidding someone from carrying out a vow; see Num. 30:8).

On the other hand, the counsel and the purposes of the LORD endure forever. Here we find the verb "stand firm, endure" (עָמַד) repeated. As the LORD's creation stood firm at his decree (v. 9), so his counsel stands firm forever (v. 11). It cannot be shaken or interrupted by the antagonistic plans of the world. As the sage says, "There is no counsel, no wisdom, no plan against the counsel of the LORD" (Prov. 21:30). And to make his plan stand, as the psalmist says, "He brings to nothing the plans of the nations." The certainty of the plan of the LORD is not temporary—it is eternal. This is stressed by "for ever, to the farthest time" (the use of עוֹלָם with the preposition; s.v. Ps. 61:5), and reiterated in the parallel colon that affirms that the purposes of God's heart are "until endless generations" (דֹּר וָדֹר). The plan of the LORD can be trusted completely because it is carried out in faithfulness.

Verse 12 appropriately pronounces a blessing on those who are in covenant with the LORD, who live according to his plan and purposes. They are called a "people" (עַם) and a "nation" (גּוֹי); the words are used here in contrast to their usage in verse 10. In other words, there is a nation, a people, who are not trying to destroy the plan of God, for they are at the heart of it. The verse uses the covenant language to make the point that at the heart of God's plan is the choice of Israel in accordance with the covenant made to Abraham to bring blessing to the world. The endless variations of the plan of the nations to oppose the divine plan by opposing Israel will come to nothing. Craigie says, "the 'nation whose God is the LORD' (v. 12) is blessed precisely because its national existence is based upon the divine *plan,* not merely upon human aspirations."[30] The nation whose God is the LORD is not only blessed but also occupies an enviable position among the nations.

How did the LORD become Israel's God? He chose them for his own inheritance (v. 12). Through election the LORD made Israel his own. Deuteronomy 32:8–9 say that when the LORD

---

30. *Psalms,* p. 273.

gave the nations their inheritance he set up boundaries for them according to the number of Israel (or the sons of God), for Israel was his allotted inheritance. Caird explains that when God divided the world up into provinces, he appointed angels to be governors of each of the nations; but he decided to govern Israel himself. Thus, one can conclude with the biblical writers that God was sovereign over the whole world, but uniquely and recognizably sovereign over Israel where his rule was acknowledged and followed.[31]

Thus, Psalm 33 affirms that the LORD is sovereign Lord of history. He has a plan for the world that he will certainly carry out, most often by canceling out the plans and purposes of the world. His plan includes his nation Israel, whom he has chosen for his own possession. All the plans of the world to destroy Israel or the Messiah (see Ps. 2:1–3) that have surfaced from generation to generation have failed, because those plans are contrary to his plan. His plan is eternal.

C. Praise the LORD because in righteousness he evaluates all mankind (5a and 13–15).

In the third section the psalm presents the LORD as the righteous ruler who observes and evaluates all people according to the standard of his righteousness. Verses 13 and 14 are parallel, each verse containing three ideas: the LORD's exalted position ("from heaven" // "from his dwelling place"), his observing ("he looks down" and "he sees" // "he watches"), and the objects of his investigation ("all humans [the sons of man]" // "all who live on earth").

The most telling contrast is that the place from which the LORD looks is "the heavens," and his observation is the dwelling place of humans, "the earth" (v. 13). The next verse adds that it is "his dwelling place," or more precisely, the place of his "sitting/ dwelling" (שִׁבְתּוֹ). The language of sitting applied to the LORD is figurative (anthropomorphic); it usually signifies his kingship (see Pss. 9:7; 29:10; 55:19; and 107:13). It describes the LORD as

---

31. G. B. Caird, *The Language and Imagery of the Bible,* p. 179.

the sovereign ruler who has an exalted position from which he observes all creation.

Three verbs are used in these two verses for LORD's observation: "gazes intently" (נָבַט), "sees" (רָאָה), and "watches" (שָׁגַח). Since the LORD is never an indifferent observer, the meaning of the verbs must be either supervision or evaluation. Verse 15 supports the idea of evaluation by its use of the verb "discern" (בִּין; s.v. Ps. 49:1), i.e., to make distinctions between things. The LORD is "he who considers" (הַמֵּבִין, the participle with the article functioning nominally and standing in apposition to the formal subject of verses 13–14, the LORD). The form clarifies that the LORD is the one who evaluates—his watching is constantly discerning. The first colon of verse 15 parallels this construction with the participle "he who forms" (הַיֹּצֵר). The two halves of the verse both explain who the LORD is in practical terms: the one who sees all is "he who forms" and "he who discerns." The connection between these two participles is clear: the one who forms the heart, i.e., fashions it according to his plan (as יָצַר signifies[32]), evaluates its activities.

The verse says that he forms the heart of them "all." The word (יַחַד) usually means "together" or "all-inclusive" or "all." It refers to individuals doing something or going somewhere together (e.g., Isa. 44:11, "let them be put to shame *together*"). It is sometimes just a synonym for "all" (כֹּל), and is found in parallelism with it as it is here. So the verse may be interpreted to say, "He who forms the hearts of all, who considers all their works." Since the LORD is the sovereign creator of everyone,

---

32. The word means "form, fashion" by design. It is a word appropriate to the work of an artist, as the participle is used for "the potter." The verb can be used for the LORD's creative acts, such as in forming the man from the dust of the ground (Gen. 2:7). The verb is used in Psalm 139:16 for God's forming of the life in the womb with a plan: "the days that were ordained/planned for me."

It can be used of humans as well, such as the participial use for a potter indicates. The emphasis is on creation by design. The related noun יֵצֶר means "intention" or "imagination"; it can refer to the evil inclination of the human heart (Gen. 6:5) or simply the intent of a person in general. The verb means "create, form, fashion" (it is translated "ordain" in Ps. 139:16).

he knows the acts and the intentions of them all. And since he created with a design (as the verb indicates), then his knowledge of the race he created is evaluative. And furthermore, since the summary statement says the LORD loves righteousness and justice (v. 5), then the standard of this evaluative observation is to determine if people are righteous.

The sovereign LORD is the righteous judge; he thoroughly evaluates all human actions. Because he created mankind, his evaluation can penetrate even to motivations behind actions. He understands completely what we are, what we do, and why we do it, and the standard by which he evaluates us is his righteousness.

D. Praise the LORD because he demonstrates his love by saving his people (5b and 16–19).

This fourth section explains how the loyal love of God works in the affairs of people. The summary statement (v. 5b) says that the earth is full of the loyal love of the LORD, meaning that his love manifests itself throughout the world in his dealings with his people (so the attribute is a metonymy of cause). The elaboration of the point begins in verse 16: no king is saved (נוֹשָׁע, s.v. Ps. 3:2) by the greatness of an army (בְּרָב־חָיִל; for חַיִל s.v. Ps. 49:6), and a mighty man (גִּבּוֹר, s.v. Ps. 45:3) is not delivered (יִנָּצֵל, s.v. Ps. 22:20) by the greatness of his strength (בְּרָב־כֹּחַ). The verse is set forth as a general principle, essentially a universal truth. It may appear at times that the victory belongs to the mighty army—and at times God may choose to use the mighty army—but the reality is that the victory comes only if the LORD wills. Those who trust in their military might alone will be dismayed when the LORD fights against them (see Ps. 20:7). The point is that ultimately that victory does not come through military strength alone (as the Egyptians learned; see Exod. 15:1–11).

The idea is developed further in verse 17 as the writer focuses on the horse, the embodiment of military might in the ancient world. He says it is a "vain thing" (שֶׁקֶר). The word means "false, empty" and so "vain." The use of this word is significant in this section of Psalm 33 that focuses on the faithful covenant love (חֶסֶד) of the LORD, because it, and especially its related verb, is often used with reference to broken covenants (cf. Ps. 44:17; 89:33; Gen. 21:23; Isa. 63:8; and Lev. 19:11). For example, Psalm 89:33 says, "I will not take my loyal love (חַסְדִּי) from him, nor will I *betray* (וְלֹא אֲשַׁקֵּר) my faithfulness." The LORD will display his loyal love for his people, but the war horse or the chariot will be a false hope for deliverance—people who trust them will feel betrayed, because in spite of its great strength, it cannot save.

In contrast to the hopelessness of putting one's trust in military force (the "horse" represents the weapons and machines of warfare), the psalmist announces the expectation of deliverance that hoping in the loyal love of the LORD brings. Verse 18 begins with the particle (הִנֵּה) which historically was translated "behold." It is a particle that points out something important here, "the eye of the LORD"; and by doing this in this context, it also expresses a contrast, such as "but, on the contrary." This mention of the "eye of the LORD" (an anthropomorphism) recalls the evaluative looking reported in verses 13 and 14. Now the LORD watches over those who fear him, the faithful covenant believers. And if, according to verse 15, the LORD knows the hearts of the people, he certainly knows those "who hope for his loyal love."

"Hope" (יָחַל; s.v. Ps. 31:24) includes the ideas of waiting with some tension until the thing hoped for arrives (see Gen. 8:2) and of a confident expectation of trust (Ps. 42:5). It is not a last resort, a hoping against hope, as it were. Rather, it is an expectant faith, but a faith that struggles with the tensions in life.[33] Here the object of the hope is "the loyal love" of the LORD, i.e., the faithful, loving acts done in accordance with the covenant promises.

The double purpose of the LORD's watchful care for believers is expressed in verse 19 by two infinitives. The first is "to deliver them from death." "Deliver" (נָצַל; s.v. Ps. 22:20) means "to snatch away, rescue, deliver" (what the warrior in verse 16 could not do). And "death" may be a reference to the result of war (a metonymy of effect; see verses 16 and 17). It may also be taken in the general sense of death for any reason, as the parallelism

---

33. The word יָחַל is a synonym of קָוָה, "wait, hope" (s.v. Ps. 25:3); the two have very similar meanings.

suggests. That parallel clause provides the second purpose infinitive, "to keep them alive in famine." The famine may have been part of a military siege (as the military language in the psalm might suggest); but it could also simply be a natural disaster (see Job 5:20).

The reasons for praising God started with his powerful word, illustrated by creation. The next reason was God's faithfulness in bringing about his sovereign will in history—revealed to us in his word. This focus on his sovereign will prompted the meditation on his sovereign evaluation of humans in his search for righteousness and justice. Finally, this sovereign and righteous God is to be praised for his loyal love that delivers from danger and death.

III. The righteous should remain confident in their faith as they wait for his loyal love (20–22).

In the final three verses the psalmist speaks on behalf of the congregation, using the plural forms of the verb. Normally descriptive praise psalms end with a praise, or a renewed call for praise; but here we have a confession of confidence in the LORD by those waiting for his protection (v. 20), joyfully trusting in his holy name (v 21), and calling in hope for his continued loyal love (v. 22).

In short, the response of the people is one of confident waiting on the LORD. The first verb is "we wait patiently" (חָכָה means "wait, await")—it is a word for patient expectation. For example, Hosea uses the verb for bandits waiting for a victim (6:9). In this psalm the objective of the waiting is good—they wait for the LORD. The two key words, "help" and "shield," provide a clue to the reason for their waiting. The first word, "help" (עֵזֶר, s.v. Ps. 46:1) refers to the victory that only God can give (and so it is a metonymy of cause). The word essentially means that he will provide for them what they do not have, or cannot do themselves. For example, it is used in this sense in Deuteronomy 33:26–27, where the LORD "helps" by driving out the enemies. The other word, "shield" (מָגֵן), is a metaphor signifying protection. It is a term belonging to a military context; in general it means that LORD defends his people.

In verse 21 we have the second part of the conclusion, the expectation of rejoicing. This rejoicing will be based on faith in the "name of the LORD," i.e., the attributes and acts of the LORD (s.v. Ps. 20:1). The line has the imperfect tense first, "our heart will rejoice" (יִשְׂמַח; s.v. Ps. 48:11), and then the perfect tense, "we have trusted" (בָּטָחְנוּ, s.v. Ps. 4:5) in the causal clause. While they both could be translated as present tenses, it seems better in the context to make a distinction. Because they have trusted (present perfect, meaning they came to faith at some point and continue to trust) in the LORD, they are confident they will rejoice. The word for "trust" expresses the security that comes from having such a God in whom to place confidence, and this is what is meant by "his holy name," his divine attributes revealed in his actions.

Finally, in verse 22, the confidence of the people turns to prayer in the form of a request for the LORD's continued loyal love because they have put their hope in him. The psalm suddenly shifts to address God directly (an apostrophe, a closing prayer). The use of "loyal love" (חֶסֶד) in the first half (again a metonymy of cause for the effect) recalls verse 18; here they are wanting what that loyal love produces, further acts of deliverance and protection. The second half of the verse reaffirms their faith: "even as (or because as כַּאֲשֶׁר may indicate) we hope in you." Their appeal is based on their hope in him, for he delivers and sustains believers (vv. 18–19).

MESSAGE AND APPLICATION

The reasons for the righteous to praise the LORD are many; but this psalm singles out four very basic characteristics of the person and work of the LORD. In elaborating on these four themes, a world of theology is opened up—creation, the eternal plan of God, the evaluation of all mankind by the righteous ruler in heaven, and the love of God that delivers and defends those who trust in him. The order of the themes builds to a climax with the loyal love of the LORD; and this emphasis is confirmed by the prayer that expects the loyal love of God to continue to act on their behalf. After all, they are the covenant people because the LORD chose them, gave his word to them, built his plan for human history around them, evaluates everyone in righteousness and delivers by his faithful covenant love. The exposition of the psalm, which will surely focus on the cause for the praise (vv. 4–19), must also build to this climax with the love of God. We may provisionally word an expository idea for this psalm as follows: *It is fitting for God's people to praise him for his exact word, his sure plan, his righteous judgment, and most of all his faithful love that sustains them in times of great danger and deprivation.*

It will not be too hard to find New Testament passages that speak to these themes. Praise for the *creator* is found in the heavenly choirs of Revelation 4 and 5, but also in the treatises of the apostles (Col. 1). John 1, which is written in the style of a psalmic composition, focuses on the creative word. The New Testament has many references to the *faithfulness* of the Lord. 2 Timothy 2:13 reminds us that even if we are unfaithful the Lord remains faithful because he cannot deny himself. It is his nature to be faithful, and because he is faithful, he will strengthen and protect his people from the evil one (2 Thess. 3:3). After all, his name is Faithful and True (Rev. 19:11). Paul reiterates how the plan of God through the ages cannot change but comes to fruition in Christ and will in the end be characterized by his putting all things under his feet and delivering up the kingdom to the Father (1 Cor. 15:20–28). The Lord is also the *righteous* judge who will reward his people but destroy the ungodly (2 Tim. 4:8). Peter quotes from Psalm 34:12–16 to affirm that the eyes of the Lord are on the righteous and his ears attentive to their prayers, but his face is against the wicked (1 Pet. 3:12). If believers sin, they know they have an advocate, Jesus Christ the righteous (1 John 2:1). His righteousness will preserve his covenant people, and destroy the enemies of the faith. All of this is a demonstration of his great *love* for his people which will sustain them in this life and in the life to come (Rom. 8:37). John reminds us that we love the Lord because he first loved us (1 John 4:19), and that love is a saving love (Rev. 1:5).

For all of this believers should be filled with praise as they await further displays of his love. After all, he demonstrated his love and grace in redeeming us in order that we might bring praise to him (Eph. 1:12).

Edifying Praise for the Goodness of God

INTRODUCTION

Text and Textual Variants

Of David. When he changed his behavior before Abimelech, so that he drove him out, and he went away.[1]

א 1 I will bless the LORD at all times;
   his praise *shall* continually *be* in my mouth.
ב 2 In the LORD my soul[2] will make its praise;
   let the humble hear and be glad.
ג 3 O magnify the LORD with me,
   and let us exalt his name together.

ד 4 I sought the LORD, and he answered me

---

1. The superscription sets the occasion at the time David "changed his appearance" (בְּשַׁנּוֹתוֹ אֶת־טַעְמוֹ) before Abimelech so when he (Abimelech) drove him away he left. The reference is 1 Samuel 21:12–15, but the king's name is Achish and not Abimelech. Commentators differ on how to deal with this discrepancy. Some say it is an error, showing how unreliable the superscriptions are; some suggest this is the Semitic name for the man; and some say it is a dynastic title and not the personal name. The psalm shows no specific link to the event other than in the most general of terms.
2. MT has נַפְשִׁי, "my soul," which means "I [will praise]," but since the verb agrees with the noun I have left it as "my soul will make its praise."

and delivered me from all my terrors.[3]

ה 5 *Those who* look[4] to him are radiant,
    and their faces shall never be ashamed.

ז 6 This afflicted man cried, and the LORD heard *him*
    and saved him out of all his troubles.

ח 7 The angel of the LORD encamps around those who fear him
    and delivers them.

ט 8 Taste and see that the LORD is good!
    Blessed is the one who takes refuge in him!

י 9 Fear the LORD, you his saints,
    for those who fear him have no lack.

כ 10 The young lions[5] suffer want and hunger;
    but those who seek the LORD lack no good thing.

ל 11 Come, O children, listen to me;
    I will teach you the fear of the LORD.

מ 12 What man is there who desires life
    and loves many days, that he may see good?

---

3. MT has מְגוּרֹתַי from מָגוּר, "terror." The Greek version mistook the word for the similar verb גּוּר, "to sojourn," translating the form with παροικιῶν, "sojournings."

4. The MT has the perfect tense, הִבִּיטוּ, "they look," but since there is no subject, it has been translated "[Those who] look." A few manuscripts have an imperative, הַבִּיטוּ; and the Greek has "Draw near," προσέλθατε (= גְּשׁוּ). See also Aquila, the Syriac, and Jerome. This reading also required that the next verb be taken as an imperative as well, "and be enlightened," φωτίσθητε (= Hebrew וּנְהָרוּ instead of the perfect tense in the MT, וְנָהָרוּ). And in harmony with these readings the pronoun on "faces" in the Greek is "your [faces]." Kraus notes the problem in the MT is over the subject of the verb "they look," and concludes that a correction is unavoidable; he suggests "look to him and be radiant," after the Greek, Aquila, and Jerome (*Psalms 1–59*, pp. 381–2). But the lack of an expressed subject in a psalm is not an insurmountable problem.

5. כְּפִירִים are "young lions." For this word the Greek has "the rich," πλούσιοι, perhaps thinking of כְּבֵדִים or כַּבִּירִים, "honorable" or "mighty," although Briggs suggests it is an interpretation of the "young lions" (*Psalms*, p. 300). For the retention of "young lions" and its metaphorical meaning, see J. J. M. Roberts, "The Young Lions of Psalm 34,11," *Bib* 54 (1973):165–7. Goldingay suggests a translation "apostates," but it is based on later Hebrew (*Psalms 1–41*, p. 476).

ב 13 Keep your tongue from evil
and your lips from speaking deceit.

ס 14 Turn away from evil and do good;
seek peace and pursue it.

ע 15 The eyes of the LORD are toward the righteous
and his ears toward their cry.

פ 16 The face of the LORD is against those who do evil
to cut off the memory of them from the earth.

צ 17 When *the righteous*[6] cry for help the LORD hears
and delivers them out of all their troubles.

ק 18 The LORD is near to the brokenhearted
and saves the crushed in spirit.

ר 19 Many are the afflictions of the righteous,
but the LORD delivers him out of them all.

ש 20 He keeps all his bones;
not one of them is broken.

ת 21 Affliction will slay the wicked,[7]
and those who hate the righteous will be condemned.

22 The LORD redeems the life of his servants;
none of those who take refuge in him will be
condemned.

Composition and Context

This psalm falls into two major sections, declarative praise
(1–10) and then descriptive praise with the instruction (11–22).
Such a composition using two types of praise is not uncommon
in the collection. Mowinckel says this is due to the influence of
wisdom literature, making the psalm a didactic poem like much
of the learned psalmography.[8] At least we may observe that this
praise psalm has many instructions and exhortations for the
congregation. In fact, verse 8 might capture the theme of the

---

6. "The righteous" is added by the Greek and Syriac to overcome the difficulty of the subject change.

7. The MT has תְּמוֹתֵת רָשָׁע רָעָה, "affliction (i.e., evil) will slay the wicked." The
Greek version has a noun for the *polel* imperfect: "the death of sinners is
evil," θάνατος ἁμαρτωλῶν πονηρός. See T. H. Robinson, "Notes on Psalm
xxxiv. 21," *ExpT* 52 (1940, 41):117.

8. S. Mowinckel, *The Psalms in Israel's Worship*, p. 38.

whole psalm, "O taste and see that the LORD is good." It reflects his prayer, for he has experienced this; and it summarizes his instruction, for he wants others to trust the LORD and experience his goodness. Kraus concludes that the psalm is not a thanksgiving, nor a hymn, nor a wisdom psalm; but its intentions as a psalm of thanksgiving are unmistakable even though it is caught up in a didactic poem under the influence of wisdom.[9]

The psalm has a historical note in the superscription, connecting this psalm to the time David changed his behavior in the Philistine camp (1 Sam. 21:10–15). The support for this connection includes the emphasis on fear (1 Sam. 21:10, 12); the play on the word "taste, appearance, face" in both passages; the emphasis on the contrast between those who fear the LORD and those who hate the LORD; the frequent mention of "face" in the psalm that may hint at his changing his facial features, and perhaps the subtle penitent note in verse 6 of the psalm. However, not many modern commentators would attribute the psalm to that period. A. A. Anderson says its acrostic arrangement implies to some extent that it is post-exilic.[10]

The acrostic, or alphabetical, arrangement of the psalm makes the identification of the structure difficult.[11] In the arrangement the line for the letter *waw* is not included, leaving one line over, and that extra line focuses attention on the redemption of the LORD. So to support the didactic nature of the psalm there is this mnemonic arrangement.

The structure of the passage is not impossible to outline however. : In the declarative praise portion (vv. 1–10) we have the psalmist's vow to praise and call for others to praise with him (vv. 1–3), the report of the deliverance (vv. 4–7), and an exhortation for others to trust the LORD for protection and provision (vv. 8–10). In the second half of the psalm we have the didactic section, exhortations, and instructions (vv. 11–22). In this part there is the exhortation for people to learn about God

---

9. *Psalms 1–59*, p. 383. See also L. J. Liebreich, "Psalms 34 and 145 in the Light of their Key Words," *HUCA* 27 (1956):181–92.

10. *Psalms 1–72*, p. 268.

11. See further Anthony R. Ceresko, "The ABC's of Wisdom in Psalm xxxiv," *VT* 35 (1985):99–104; and Victor A. Hurowitz, "Additional Elements of Alphabetical Thinking in Psalm xxxiv," *VT* 52 (2002):326–33.

by personal experience (vv. 11–12), and then a series of instructions (vv. 13–22).

Exegetical Analysis

Summary

The psalmist invites the people to join him in praising the LORD for delivering him from all his troubles and to experience the LORD's goodness for themselves by following the instructions he gives them.

Outline

I. The psalmist calls the congregation to join him in praising the LORD for delivering him from all his troubles and to experience the goodness of the LORD for themselves (1–10).

   A. He calls the people to praise the LORD with him so that the afflicted will be glad (1–3).

   B. He tells how the LORD answered his prayer and delivered him from his troubles (4–7).

   C. He urges the people to experience the protection and provision from the LORD for themselves (7–10).

II. The psalmist instructs the congregation on how to achieve a long life with the LORD's blessing (11–12).

   A. He urges the people to learn from him (11–12).

   B. He instructs the people on how to achieve a long life under God's blessing (13–22).

      1. They must not speak treacherously but seek peace (13–14).

      2. They must know that the LORD shows favor to the righteous but not to the wicked (15–16).

      3. They will be encouraged to know that the LORD hears the prayers of the righteous who are brokenhearted (17–18).

      4. They will be encouraged to know that he delivers the righteous unharmed (19–20).

      5. They will be encouraged to know that those who hate the righteous will be destroyed and condemned, but the servants of the LORD will be redeemed and never condemned (21–22).

COMMENTARY IN EXPOSITORY FORM

I. People should join in the praise of God for his acts of deliverance and be encouraged to experience the goodness of the LORD personally (1–10).

A. Individual praise should be joined by congregational praise (1–3).

Typical of declarative praise psalms the psalmist begins with his determination to bless the LORD at all times (אֲבָרְכָה is a co-hortative of resolve: "I will bless"; s.v. Ps. 5:12). The second colon parallels the emphasis on continual praise: "his praise (תְּהִלָּתוֹ, s.v. Ps. 33:1) *shall* continually *be* in my mouth" (mouth being a metonymy of cause for what he says). The psalmist's declaration will be a glowing report of the LORD's person and works.

The verb for "praise" (תִּתְהַלֵּל) is used in the first part of verse 2, and the word order ensures that the focus of the praise is not missed: "In the LORD my soul will make its praise." This verbal stem (the *hithpael*) emphasizes the intensive, iterative nature of the word. He will praise regularly and repeatedly, so that many who are afflicted (עֲנָוִים, s.v. Ps. 9:12) will hear his words and be glad. Their joy will not only be for him, but they will also be encouraged in their own faith by hearing the LORD answers prayers. The two verbs "hear" and "be glad" or "rejoice" may be taken as jussives; although future tense translations would also fit: "they will hear" "and they will rejoice." The point of their benefit from hearing the praise would be the same in either case.

In verse 3 the psalmist calls for the people to join him in praise. The first imperative (of invitation) is "magnify" (גַּדְּלוּ, the causative stem of the word "to be big, great").[12] Everyone should participate

---

12. The word גָּדַל, "to be big, great," and its related adjective גָּדוֹל, "big, great," are common in the Old Testament. There are a couple of other words that are related as well, such as מִגְדָּל, "a tower," and גֹּדֶל, "greatness."

The verb occurs in most of the stems: *qal*, "be, become great"; *piel/pual*, "make great, magnify"; *hiphil*, "make great, do great things"; and *hithpael*, "boast, magnify oneself." The common uses concern the meaning of growing large, getting big, or maturing, and the figurative use is in the semantic field of praise for magnifying the LORD.

in telling the deeds of the LORD because telling them focuses attention on the greatness of the LORD, hence, he is magnified in the hearing of the people. Parallel to this is the cohortative "let us exalt, make high" (וּנְרוֹמְמָה) his name together. "Name" is the term used for the totality of the attributes of the LORD, who he is and what he does (s.v. Ps. 20:1). To talk about the LORD is to talk about greatness, and thus the praise will exalt and magnify him.

B.Individual praise exalts the LORD in reporting the deliverance (4–7).

The heart of the declarative praise is the report of the deliverance—this is what the LORD did for him that is to be praised. Verse 4 simply states, "I sought the LORD and he answered me." The verb "I sought" (דָרַשְׁתִּי) figuratively refers to earnest prayer, for the verb has the idea of searching carefully (a metonymy of adjunct, for the praying was an intense seeking for an answer). The

---

In the first category the idea is growing up or becoming great. Genesis 21:8 uses it simply to say the child grew. In Hosea 9:12 it is also used for bringing up children. The idea of greatness could be in number and influence, as the LORD promised to make Abram into a great nation (Gen. 12:2). It also refers to people becoming great (Jer. 5:27). In a similar sense the house of David would be made great (Zech. 12:7).

There is also a group of passages that use the *hiphil* primarily to mean "do great things," i.e., describing the type of things that God has done. In Psalm 126:3 it refers to the deliverance from exile: "the LORD has done great things," literally "he made great to do" (Ps. 126:3).

Of greater interest for the study of the psalms is the group of passages that use the word in praise. There is a basic overlap between *piel* and *hiphil* uses, for both can mean "cause to be great, magnify." God can magnify man (Job 7:17) by increasing his possessions and reputation. But how can one make God great, since God is already great? It can be done by extending the reputation of God through praise. When asserting the greatness of God in praise with specific details, the person and the works of the LORD will be magnified in the understanding of the congregation. People may know that God is great; but through praise they will come to appreciate how great God is, and that may be greater than they ever realized.

When people are the subject of these verbs, especially in the *hiphil* and *hithpael* stems, it usually refers to empty boasting (Dan. 11:36). When the *hithpael* is used with God as the subject, as in Ezekiel 28:23, it means "I will magnify myself," i.e., cause myself to appear greater in your eyes.

report is that God answered the prayer. The second colon specifies what that was: "he delivered me (הִצִּילָנִי, s.v. Ps. 22:20) from all my terrors" (מְגוּרוֹתַי, related to מָגוֹר in Ps. 31:14; גּוּר is "dread").

There is no explanation at this point what the terrifying trouble was, but the end of the psalm speaks of afflictions and relates them to the wicked who hate the righteous–but that still does not clarify what it was.

The seeking is next explained by looking: "*Those who* look to him" is literally "they look [gaze intently] to him," the verb being the perfect tense (הִבִּיטוּ). No subject is expressed; so the verb may be interpreted as the subject for "be radiant." "They look and they are radiant" means "*those who* look are radiant." The verb "are radiant" (נָהָרוּ) means "to shine, beam, be radiant." The idea of beaming, e.g., a shining face, is figurative of joy (an implied comparison), as other words for "light" often are as well. The two verbs may be taken as gnomic perfects, general truths, and so the English present tense is the appropriate translation. People who are looking intently to the LORD reflect the joy of his presence. And as a result, "their faces shall not be ashamed" (אַל־יֶחְפָּרוּ).[13] The form appears to be a negated jussive, "let them not be ashamed," but that does not fit the flow of the passage. This construction is sometimes used to express the conviction that something cannot or should not happen. The negative may have an energetic nuance, and the idea be "their faces are not able to be ashamed," or better, "their faces shall never be ashamed." They will not be destroyed; everything that they regard as valuable in life, even their belief in the LORD, will be preserved. "Faces" are singled out to form a contrast with the first colon: their faces are radiant, their faces will not have the expression of being put to shame.[14]

Now the psalmist breaks from all the figures and clearly reports his own deliverance: "This afflicted man (עָנִי) cried, and the LORD heard and saved him from all his troubles." The description he gives himself could also be translated "humble, poor."

---

13. The verb חָפֵר, "to be ashamed," is usually paralleled with בּוֹשׁ, "to be ashamed." The same connotations apply for these words.

14. Some commentators point out that this line could have some connection to David's feigning madness in the camp of the Philistines instead of showing his faith and confidence with an unashamed face.

The self description is like Lamentation 3:1, "I am the man who has seen affliction." The verbs are past tense, simply reporting the basic facts that the LORD "answered" (i.e., "heard") and "saved" (delivered, s.v. Ps. 3:2) him.

Verse 7 could be taken as part of the next section, the invitation for people to experience the goodness of God; but the change at the beginning of verse 8 is dramatic, and so verse 7 probably should be part of the report of the deliverance. It explains the reason for the deliverance: "The angel of the LORD encamps around those who fear him and delivers them." The verse forms the principle to be learned through the praise, that the LORD protects and delivers those who are devoted to him. The "angel of the LORD," or "messenger of the LORD" (מַלְאַךְ־יהוה) is probably a title for the LORD himself here as it is in other passages (see Gen. 16:7; Josh. 5:14; and Judg. 6:11–33 to name a few). The expression is a description of the manifestation of the LORD on earth, sometimes visible and sometimes not, to defend and deliver his people. According to Joshua 5:14 he is identified as the captain of the LORD's army; and if he is the leader of a host of angels as in 2 Kings 6:17, then that would explain how he encamps around those who fear him. When it says he "encamps" (חֹנֶה) around them, the image is of a military camp (an implied comparison). One thinks of the angels of God who met Jacob on the way, and he named the place Mahanayim ("two camps"; Gen. 32:1). The expression that the angel encamps around the people of God indicates the ever present protection of the LORD. So in reporting the answer to prayer the psalmist manages to keep the focus on the LORD.

C. Individual praise must exhort the congregation to experience the goodness of God for themselves (8–10).

Praise is designed to be edifying: other people may hear the praise report from an individual, and they may even join in the praise; but the purpose of the praise is to exhort them to trust in the LORD so that they too will experience the goodness of God. In verse 8 this exhortation begins. They have heard his praise, but now they are told, "Taste and see that the LORD is good!" The two imperatives, "taste (טַעֲמוּ) and see (וּרְאוּ)" are figurative. Tasting means experimenting with food, trying it, and so here the word forms an implied comparison. It signifies deciding, judging (see Prov. 31:18). The psalmist wants them to discover the goodness of God by acting on their faith in the LORD, i.e., seeking him and praying to him. They may never have experienced an answer to prayer, or a provision of blessing, because they never asked ("you have not, because you ask not" [James 4:2; see also John 16:24]). Kidner notes, however, that the tasting is to be more than a casual sampling; the idea is used in Hebrews 6:5 and 1 Peter 2:3 to describe the beginning of a life of faith.[15]

And if they do experience ("taste") this way, they will "see," meaning realize by experience, that the LORD is good. There is a sequence between the imperatives: taste (and as a result) see. What they will see is that the LORD is good (טוֹב).[16] This word

---

15. *Genesis 1–72*, p. 140.
16. The word "good," טוֹב, and all its related forms occur over 700 times in the Old Testament, indicating how wide the range of meanings would be. A survey of dictionaries and concordances will show it can mean "pleasant, agreeable, satisfying, favorable, useful, right, pretty, handsome, fragrant, joyous, healthy, worthy" and a number of other possible translations. The word essentially describes anything that is beneficial for life—anything that produces, promotes, enhances, or adorns life. It is the opposite of "evil," which describes that which brings pain and destruction to life. Here we have the fundamental problem with human nature—the knowledge of good and evil (Gen. 2:9); people have the capacity to protect and preserve life, but they also can cause great pain to life and destroy it.

One common use is to express the suitability of an object for a person or a purpose, such as the tree being good for food (Gen. 3:6), or Ruth being better than seven sons (Ruth 4:15). This includes things that are not just suitable but beneficial or appropriate for the situation, such as the king's graceful speech (Ps. 45:2) or good news (Prov. 25:25).

A second category uses the word to describe the quality of something or someone, such as a good land, or a good tree, meaning one that produces fruit and not just shade (2 Kings 3:19, 25). This quality will often describe people as happy or good, and then also ethical, righteous or moral (1 Sam. 15:28). It can also describe the appearance or the health of someone, such as a healthy child (Moses, Exod. 2:2), or a beautiful person (several times in Song of Solomon). In the sense of being healthy, the word will often describe "heart," a good heart is healthy spirit (Prov. 17:22). Most of the descriptive uses involve a decision, an opinion by the writer, based on the circumstances. For example, a word (Jethro's advice) is good if it is beneficial (Exod. 18:17). Sometimes the sage will make a fine distinction, that one thing is better than another (Prov. 21:9, 19; 25:24).

embraces everything that is beneficial for life, pleasing to life, and harmonious with life. Here it is an attribute of God, so how would people see that he is good? The word must be a metonymy of cause: they will experience the LORD's provisions for life that demonstrate he is good. He is good because what he creates and what he gives is all good.

To enjoy the goodness of God is a blessed life; therefore the line adds, "Blessed (אַשְׁרֵי) is the one who takes refuge in him." This is the word that was used in Psalm 1:1 (see there for the discussion); people who trust the LORD and experience the goodness of God will also enjoy the heavenly bliss of knowing they are right with God.

The second exhortation is for the congregation to fear the LORD (v. 9). They are addressed here as "his saints" (קְדֹשָׁיו, "his holy ones," s.v. Ps. 22:3), people who belong to the LORD as part of the holy nation (Exod. 19:6). This is the only place they are called "his holy ones," although the description "holy" is used of them frequently (e.g., Lev. 11:44,5). The saints, then, are called on to fear the LORD, which is a call for obedient devotion (s.v. Ps. 2:11) rather than simply an emotional response, because those who fear have no lack. They lack nothing because fearing the LORD means trusting him, obeying him, and worshiping him.

Verse 10 continues the theme of divine protection, showing that those who fear the LORD seek him and lack no good thing. This is in contrast to "the young lions" that do lack food and go

---

The word is also used for religious ideas, such as "the way of the good" (Prov. 2:9), which means the right way to live. In fact, seeking "good" and seeking "God" express almost the same thing. A person can be called good in a greater sense than suitable or appealing; it refers to righteousness (1 Sam. 2:26; Ps. 125:4).

And finally, the word describes God. The liturgical formula calls for people to praise the LORD, because he is good, because his loyal love endures forever (see Ps. 118:1), or because he is a stronghold in the day of trouble (Nah.1:7); or because he can turn evil into good (Gen. 50:20). The fact is that God is intrinsically good or he would not do good things. Everything that God created was very good (Gen. 1:31). He also gives good gifts to his people (Ps. 145:15, 16). For example, he gave the Law to Israel (Deut. 6:24); he gave them the good land (Deut.9:4, 5); he gave them the prophets (Deut. 18:18–22); in fact, every good and perfect gift comes from God—"O that people would praise the LORD for his goodness" (Ps. 107:9).

hungry. If the reference is to the wicked who were afflicting him, then the figure (an implied comparison) describes them as dangerous and destructive (see especially Ps. 35:17, and Ps. 22:13). But they go hungry, i.e., the predators do not get what they want, whereas the people of God lack nothing. The difference is that they seek the LORD, and he provides for them.

II. People who are strong in the faith must include instruction for the congregation when they praise the LORD (11–22).

A. The exhortation is for people to learn how to achieve a long and blessed life (11–12).

The first two verses of this section is the exhortation for people to learn. In Proverbs-like fashion they are addressed as "children" (literally, "sons," בָּנִים, meaning younger, less experienced dependents, learners). They are exhorted to "come" (לְכוּ could be an interjection here) and listen (שִׁמְעוּ meaning to respond to the teachings, to obey, and not just give a hearing; s.v. Ps. 45:10). What he will teach them is the fear of the LORD. The earlier call to fear the LORD will now be detailed step-by-step. The appeal is for people who desire life, that is, loving many days to see good things ("many days" means length of days, a long life; see Prov. 3:2; 10:27). The appeal is presented in a rhetorical question: "Who is the man who desires life," meaning, if people desire life, as opposed to the way of death and destruction, they should follow these teachings. Here the basic issue of wisdom literature is presented as a reasoned question. The basis for a long life with God's blessing of good things is the fear of the LORD (Prov. 1:7).

B. There are five basic lessons to be learned (13–22):

1. Do not follow evil in word or deed but pursue goodness and peace (13–14).

The first instruction has a preventive side and an instructive side. The preventive is "Guard (נְצֹר) your tongue from evil and your lips from speaking deceit." Wisdom literature has much to say about speech (see Prov. 4:24; 13:3; and Matt. 12:36); but the basic teaching is for the wise to control what they say so it is not harmful to others ("evil," רָע; s.v. Ps. 10:15) or deceptive ("treacherous," מִרְמָה; s.v. Ps. 5:7). Their speech must be harmless and honest, but it will take diligence to preserve this. The next verse broadens the instruction from words to deeds. The warning is to turn away (סוּר) from evil and do good (Prov. 16:17). This will involve actively pursuing peace (שָׁלוֹם; s.v. Ps. 38:3). Peace, meaning harmony and well-being as well as the absence of hostility, does not come easily; it must be pursued. So the first instruction calls for the faithful to avoid all evil because it is sinful and harmful, and to follow a lifestyle that is characterized by goodness and peace. Against these there is no law.

2. Live righteously because the LORD honors this and not evil (15–16).

The next instruction is by implication. The principle is that God honors the righteous (s.v. Ps. 1:5) but not those who do evil (רָע), and so the wise listener will conclude that the way of righteousness should be followed. The figures of the LORD's "eyes" and "ears" (both anthropomorphisms) vividly show the LORD watches over the righteous and answers their prayers, but "the face of the LORD is against those who do evil." Here the "face of the LORD" (also anthropomorphic) represents the LORD's determination to judge, because his face is "against" (the preposition בְּ in this context) those who do evil, and because it has the purpose of cutting off their memory from the earth. "Their memory" (זִכְרָם, s.v. Ps. 6:5) may refer to their name, for to cut off their name would be to destroy them from the earth so that they would not be remembered. Therefore, if people choose to do evil, the LORD is against them; but if they choose to do what is good, the LORD protects them.

3. Pray to the LORD in times of trouble because he is compassionate (17–18).

Once again the instruction is in the form of a principle, namely, that God hears the prayers of the righteous and delivers them from their troubles. They need not pray polished or precise prayers—they may simply cry out to the LORD in distress, and he will take it from there. The reason for this is that he is compassionate. The text explains this profoundly in verse 18:

"The LORD is near to the broken-hearted ("to the broken ones of/ in heart," לְנִשְׁבְּרֵי־לֵב), and saves those who are crushed in spirit ("and the ones crushed of/in spirit he saves," וְאֶת־דַּכְּאֵי־רוּחַ יוֹשִׁיעַ). The heart represents the will (metonymy of subject); to be broken in the will means the fight is gone, all hopes and expectations are dashed, and the afflicted one is resigned to devastation. Parallel to that is the "crushed of spirit." "Broken" and "crushed" are figures (of comparison) that describe the person's will and outlook on life as hopeless. People who are broken by circumstances are the very ones that God is near, for he delights to heal and restore those who cry to him from the most difficult situations.[17] Kraus says, "The nearness of God is never anything static, anything metaphysically at rest above humans, but a movement emanating from God, who intervenes on earth and demonstrates his liberating salutary presence."[18]

4. Remain true to the LORD because he delivers the righteous unharmed (19–20).

This instruction also lays out an instructive principle that the LORD delivers the righteous, so the logical conclusion would be to remain righteous. It is interesting that the verse does not say the righteous are prevented from experiencing afflictions— they have many afflictions (רָעוֹת, from רַע, meaning painful experiences, calamities, disasters); but it does say the LORD delivers them from them. The common word "deliver" (נָצַל; s.v. Ps. 22:20) emphasizes that it is a rescue out of the difficulties, as if the LORD plucks them out of the trouble. The resultant description is that they are preserved unharmed. Here the text says "he preserves all his bones; not one of them is broken." The language is poetic (symbolic, and probably hyperbolic) for God's preservation

---

17. The Bible is filled with samples of people in despair crying to the LORD for help. Hagar, for one, saw no hope as she wandered in the wilderness, but was provided for by the LORD when he heard the cry (Gen. 21:17). And even a sinner whose stubborn will is broken will find acceptance from the LORD, for a broken spirit is the only offering a sinner can present to him (Ps. 51:17). But the epitome of this verse is in Isaiah 61:1 where God anoints his servant to bind up the brokenhearted. The reference is to people in exile who were destitute and hopeless.
18. *Psalm 1–59*, p. 386.

so that the afflicted escapes the difficulties unscathed. However, the verse was recognized as being literally true of Jesus at the crucifixion when it was noted that his bones were not broken (John 19:33). That is a specific application of the literal idea of the psalm; but the original meaning was the righteous would be delivered unharmed. Jesus died, of course, and so the deliverance for him would be a greater deliverance from death. In wisdom literature, statements like this form general principles, for there are exceptions to the rule; they teach that the righteous have every expectation of surviving the difficulties of life unharmed.

5. *Take refuge in the LORD because those who do will not be condemned (21–22).*

The last instruction should inspire obedience because it contrasts the destiny of the wicked with that of the righteous. For the wicked, those who do wickedly and hate righteousness, there is condemnation (יֶאְשְׁמוּ)—they will bear their guilt. There is no condemnation (וְלֹא־יֶאְשְׁמוּ) for those who take refuge (s.v. Ps. 7:1) in the LORD—because the LORD redeems (פּוֹדֶה, s.v. Ps. 25:22) the lives of his servants.[19]

---

19. The verb "condemn" is אָשַׁם. It is used in Leviticus as the name of one of the sacrifices, traditionally called the "trespass offering" (AV) or the "guilt offering" (RV), but more precisely called the "reparation offering" because it covers sins that required financial restitution as well as the animal sacrifice.

There are three basic meanings for this verb and its related forms, such as the nouns אָשָׁם and אַשְׁמָה, or the adjective אָשֵׁם; they are 1) an offense or sin, 2) guilt for the sin, and 3) compensation that was part of the reparation offering.

The first category is an offense or a sin that renders the person guilty. This use occurs in Leviticus 5:19 to establish the need for the sacrifice: "he has surely sinned against the LORD" (אָשֹׁם אָשַׁם). It is also used in Psalm 68:21 which says that God will crush those who go on in their sins (בַּאֲשָׁמָיו). Likewise Proverbs 14:9 says that fools mock at making amends for sin.

A second category is the guilt that the sin incurs. Genesis 26:10 uses it clearly in this sense: "What is this you have done to us? One of the men might have slept with your wife and you would have brought guilt upon us." Also, the adjective is used in Genesis 42:21 when the brothers say, "We are truly guilty concerning our brother." Also, Leviticus 6:4 [5:23] uses it for guilt: "When he sins and becomes guilty (אָשֵׁם)." If someone is

MESSAGE AND APPLICATION

This passage includes a number of very practical instructions that will be part of the application of the message, but they are connected to the main idea of the psalm, that praise offered for some act of divine intervention must include exhortations for the people of God. It is what makes praise edifying. In trying to capture the basic ideas of this psalm in an expository idea we will have to be thorough to do justice to it, but concise enough for it to be a unifying theme: *The troubles of life should not overwhelm the people of God, but through prayer they will be delivered out of them, and through praise they will instruct others to live by faith and experience the goodness of God.* This statement captures the setting of answered prayer from trouble, the praise for the deliverance, and the instruction for the people.

There are many ideas here that are repeated in Proverbs and in the New Testament. Perhaps the most direct connection would be to the writings of Peter. In 1 Peter 2:9–17 the apostle describes the believers as holy and then gives all kinds of practical instructions on how to live the faith. Then, in 3:10–13 he quotes from Psalm 34 and applies it to Christians. To this we may add the capstone from Paul, that for the faithful there is no condemnation (Rom. 8:1, 33f.).

---

found guilty, then he is condemned to the punishment for the sin. If people do not repent of their sins and put their faith in the LORD, they remain "guilty" and will have to pay for their sins. But those who trust in the LORD are forgiven, they are not any longer guilty, and will not be punished for their sins. God would take care of their sins, and this is what the sacrifice signified.

A third category concerns the reparation sacrifice, which included the payment for restitution with the sacrifice. It was a reparation for the sin. Here we have the cultic provision for restoration. Leviticus 5:6–7 says the person who sinned was to bring a reparation offering, an אָשָׁם. Leviticus 5:15 also refers to it as the payment to set things right. So the word is used for the crime and the reparation for it (or, the sacrifice matches the crime). These are cases where a monetary value can be placed on the offense and then paid back with a 20 percent surcharge.

PSALM 35

Hated Without a Cause

INTRODUCTION

Text and Textual Variants

Of David.

1 Contend, O LORD, with those who contend[1] with me;
     fight against those who fight against me.
2 Take hold of shield and buckler
     and rise as my help.
3 Draw out[2] the spear and javelin[3] against my pursuers;
     say to my soul, "I am your salvation."
4 Let them be put to shame and dishonor
     who seek after my life;
   let them be turned back and disappointed

---

1. The MT has יְרִיבַי, cognate with the imperative "contend," רִיבָה, meaning "those who contend with me," but the Greek version reads "who do me injustice" (ἀδικοῦντάς).
2. The Hebrew word would mean to draw a weapon out of a case or sheath, but lacking such it probably just meant to get ready to use the weapon (see Gen. 14:14).
3. The Hebrew סְגֹר would be translated as a verb, "stop" or "block" with an assumed ellipsis "the way" against my pursuers. This is the translation in the AV, RV, NEB, and the note in the NIV. Many commentators interpret it as a weapon, pointing it as either סָגָר or סֶגֶר, perhaps a loan word meaning something like a double ax or a javelin. The Greek translation also has "block" (σύγκλεισον).

759

who devise evil against me.

5 Let them be like chaff[4] before the wind,
   with the angel of the LORD driving them away.
6 Let their way be dark and slippery,[5]
   with the angel of the LORD pursuing them.[6]

7 For without cause they hid the pit[7] of their net for me,
   without cause they dug for my life.
8 Let destruction[8] come upon him
     when he does not know it;[9]
   and let the net that he hid ensnare him;
 let him fall into it to his destruction.

9 Then my soul will exult in the LORD,
   rejoicing in his salvation.
10 All my bones[10] shall say, "O LORD, who is like you,
     delivering the poor from him who is too strong for him,
       the poor and needy from him who robs him?
11 Malicious witnesses[11] rise up
     whom I do not know.[12] They question me.
12 They repay me evil for good;

---

4. MT has "like chaff" (כְּמֹץ), but the Greek version reads "dust" (χνοῦς).
5. The form is an emphatic form by reduplication, חֲלַקְלַקּוֹת, exceeding slipperiness (see Jer. 23:12).
6. The Greek text has καταδιώκων, possibly "pursuing", but perhaps "persecuting."
7. This would mean a pit lightly covered over with a net. Many commentators believe the word is out of place: the first colon should have "hid their net" and the second "dug a pit." The Greek version in the first colon has "destructive snare" (διαφθορὰν παγίδος), and in the second colon for "they dug" it reads "reproached" (ὠνείδισαν).
8. In both occurrences in verse 8 in the place of Hebrew "destruction" (שׁוֹאָה) the Greek has "snare" (παγὶς).
9. This clause is here taken as an adverbial clause, "when he does not know," or even shortened to "unawares."
10. Or, "my whole being."
11. Literally, "witnesses of violence."
12. VanGemeren notes that this could mean that he did not know the accusers who interrogated him, either because he did not recognize them now as they had changed, or because they were new messengers (*Psalms*, p. 332).

760

I am bereft.[13]

13 But I, when they were sick,[14] wore sackcloth,
     I afflicted myself with fasting;
     I prayed with head bowed down on my chest.[15]

14 I went about as though I grieved[16] for my friend or my
          brother;
       as one who laments his mother, I bowed down in
          mourning.

15 But at my stumbling they rejoiced and gathered;
     they gathered together against me;
   wretches[17] whom I did not know[18]
     tore me apart without ceasing;

16 as profane mockers at a feast,[19]
     they gnash at me with their teeth.

---

13. For "I (my soul) am bereft," the Hebrew literally has "childlessness (שְׁכוֹל) of my soul"; NIV has "I am forlorn." The editors of BHS suggest reading שָׁכוּ, "they lie in wait" for my life (see Kraus, *Psalms 1–59*, p. 426).

14. The Greek version interprets this section differently, beginning with the reading here of "when they troubled me" (παρενοχλεῖν).

15. The Greek has "my prayer shall return (ἀποστραφήσεται) to my lap."

16. Greek has "like a neighbor, like a brother of ours, so I would please them."

17. The Hebrew נֵכִים is an adjective, meaning "smitten ones," perhaps "cripples," and so an interpretation of "wretches" might capture the idea that the accusers themselves had fallen ill. Others suggest it should be read as a participle and translated "smiters" (נֹכִים). Another suggestion is to emend the text to נָכְרִים, "foreigners." The Greek has "plagues" (μάστιγες), connecting the word to the idea "smitten" from the root נָכָה; but the verse was redivided, so we have "When I fell they rejoiced against me / and plagues were brought [reading the verb as a passive] plentifully against me, / and I knew it not; / they were scattered [reading the verb as a passive], but not stunned."

18. Perowne observes that this could mean that he was claiming to be innocent, or that he was unaware, as the expression in verse 8 (*Psalms*, I:308).

19. This line is very difficult; the MT has בְּחַנְפֵי לַעֲגֵי מָעוֹג, which basically says "as profane mockers/derisions of cake/feast." One suggested emendation is to read the last two words as לַעֲגֵי לָעַג, yielding something like "derisions of the derision," an adverbial idea. The NIV reads it, "like the ungodly they maliciously mocked." This interpretation to intensify the mocking adverbially seems to be in the Greek: "they tempted me, they sneered at me most contemptuously." The suggested emendations, while they make good sense, are not very convincing. The meaning of something like festal food could identify a type of mocker at a feast, or a mocker performing for food.

17 Lord, how long will you look on?
   Rescue me from their destruction;
      my precious life from the lions.
18 I will acknowledge you in the great congregation;
      in the mighty throng I will praise you.
19 Let not those rejoice over me
      who are my foes for no reason;
   and let not those wink the eye
      who hate me without a cause.
20 For they do not[20] speak peace,
      but against those who are quiet in the land
         they devise words of deceit.
21 They open wide their mouths against me;
      they say, "Aha, Aha, our eyes have seen it."

22 You have seen, O LORD; do not be silent.
      O LORD, do not be far from me.
23 Awake and rouse yourself for my vindication,
      for my cause, my God and my Lord.
24 Vindicate me, O LORD, my God,
      according to your righteousness;
   and let them not rejoice over me.
25 Let them not say in their hearts,
      "Aha, our heart's desire."
   Let them not say,
      "We have swallowed him up."
26 Let them be put to shame and disappointed altogether
      who rejoice at my calamity.
   Let them be clothed with shame and dishonor
      who magnify themselves against me.

27 Let those who delight in my righteousness
      shout for joy and be glad
   and say evermore, "Great is the LORD,

We simply do not know exactly what the line was intended to say, except
that it describes mockers who attack him.
20. The Greek has a prepositional phrase "to me" in the place of the negative:
"they spoke peaceably to me."

who delights in the welfare of his servant."

28 Then my tongue shall tell[21] of your righteousness
and of your praise all the day long.

Composition and Context

Psalm 35 is an individual lament, but with a different arrangement—there are actually three laments in one psalm. The
composition begins with an introductory cry to the LORD for
protection and vindication from the attacks of his enemies and
follows with the lament, prayer and vow of praise (vv. 1–10).
Then in a second section the focus is on the lament (vv. 11–18),
and in the third section the petition dominates (vv. 19–28). All
three units may have the basic elements of individual laments,
but not in the set order. In fact, this psalm leans more to petition than lament and confidence, although the vow of praise
expresses confidence. Westermann observes there is a tendency
in laments for the petition section to expand and the lament to
become shorter and disappear.[22]

The psalm is ascribed to David, but most commentators
would say it was written much later, or at least in its present
form it would be later, such as the early post-exilic period. There
is little evidence in the psalm itself to date the composition; it
could fit any number of situations, and probably was applied to
many situations down through the centuries. It is a prayer for
vindication from a false accusation; the imagery of the psalm
shifts between legal, military, and hunting terminology.[23] But
the descriptions and the prayers in the composition are essentially timeless.

The prayer of this psalm takes the form of an imprecation.
There are a number of imprecatory psalms that raise some
difficulties for the modern believer in praying the psalms (see
Introduction). But the psalmist is not here asking God to do anything that he would not do eventually anyway, nor is he simply

---

21. The Greek version takes the verb in its basic sense, "meditate" ($\mu\varepsilon\lambda\varepsilon\tau\acute{\eta}\sigma\varepsilon\iota$).
22. Claus Westermann, *The Praise of God in the Psalms,* p. 55.
23. VanGemeren, *Psalms,* p. 328.

seeking revenge for mistreatment. No, the psalmist represents the righteous who are attacked and maligned and occasionally falsely accused by people who hate their very existence. To pray for God to defend his people and the faith by destroying them is within the bounds of prayer, although in the New Testament the prayer would focus more on their repentance and salvation—except in cases where believers may be undergoing great persecution and destruction and their prayers for deliverance might include the destruction of the oppressors. The prayer for that kind of difficulty to stop often has an urgency that many believers in the West do not fully appreciate.

Exegetical Analysis

Message

In three stanzas, each emphasizing one element of a typical lament psalm, the psalmist petitions the righteous LORD to destroy his adversaries and deliver him from them because they hate him without a cause and falsely accuse him in order to ruin him.

Outline

I. With emphasis on the introductory petition, the psalmist petitions the LORD to deliver him from his enemies by destroying them for they hate him without a cause (1–10).
   A. Turning to the LORD in his time of need, he petitions him to set his enemies down in battle (1–6).
   B. He asks that they would fall in their own traps they had prepared for him for no reason at all (7–8).
   C. He promises to praise the LORD for delivering the weak (9–10).
II. With emphasis on the lament, the psalmist describes how he has suffered under the animosity of his adversaries without a cause and therefore asks for help (11–18).
   A. He laments that his adversaries have repaid him with evil even though he had extended every kindness to them in their time of need (11–16).

B. He laments that the LORD has not yet helped him and so petitions him to deliver him (17).

C. He promises to praise the LORD in the great congregation (18).

III. With emphasis on petition, the psalmist asks the LORD to vindicate him by destroying those who stir up strife by their malicious accusations against peaceful, quiet people (19–28).

A. He appeals to the LORD not to allow the enemy to triumph because they stir up strife by their vicious words (19–21).

B. He asks the LORD to be favorable to him, to judge according to righteousness, and to humiliate the enemy (22–26).

C. He promises that the righteous will praise the LORD continually (27–28).

COMMENTARY IN EXPOSITORY FORM

I. The righteous appeal to the LORD to deal with the wicked who hate them without a cause (1–10).

A. The appeal is for the LORD to defeat the wicked (1–6).

The psalmist's immediate cry to the LORD is that he contend (רִיבָה) with his adversaries, those who contend with him (יְרִיבַי, s.v. Ps. 95:8). His cry is the cry of all righteous people who have had to deal with the same thing, and the appeal is in harmony with the LORD's words: "I will contend with him who contends with you" (Isa. 49:24–26). The cognate word in the line adds to the poetic justice of the prayer: those who cause strife will receive it—from God. The parallel colon indicates that the contention with them could be on the battlefield, or in a battlefield type of conflict: "fight those who fight me" (לְחַם אֶת־לֹחֲמָי). The language is figurative, for unless there was some spectacular independent deliverance the LORD would contend or fight through the efforts of the psalmist and his supporters (so a metonymy of cause). The repetition of the words reminds us of the biblical principle of talionic justice, such as in the expression that those who live by the sword will die by the sword.

The military imagery continues in verse 2 as the psalmist calls on God to "take hold of (הַחֲזֵק) shield and buckler." The first noun refers to a small "shield" and the second to a body shield, so that with the two he would be completely protected. Here too these figures could be taken to describe some intervention (as implied comparisons, meaning it would be a miraculous victory as if the LORD seized weapons), but the idea is probably that the LORD would enable his people to take hold of the weapons (metonymy). The parallel request explains this further: "and rise as[24] my help." The meaning of the word "help" is that the LORD would do for the psalmist what he could not possibly do for himself (s.v. Ps. 46:1). The victory would only come if there was divine "help." The call for God to rise up (קוּמָה; s.v. Ps. 3:1) is an (anthropomorphic) expression for the LORD to begin to act, to move against the enemies in some way. On occasion when the LORD hears the cries of his people and intervenes on their behalf, it begins with "Now I will arise."

The military imagery in verse 3 continues with "draw out *the* spear and javelin" (unless the form in the text is left as a verb "stop," in which case it would read "draw out the spear and close up [the way]").[25] The verb "draw out" (הָרֵק, from רִיק) literally means "empty out" of a casing or sheath. The LORD again would be the divine cause of a successful unsheathing of weapons against those who were pursuing the psalmist. The expression may be general for mobilizing forces, for there may not have been sheaths for the weapons. If the weapons were to be used by the psalmist, then the expression would mean that the LORD would enable them to fight. However the details of the

---

24. The preposition בְ is a "beth of essence," indicating that the LORD is the helper: "arise as my helper."

25. The form in the text reads "close up" (סְגֹר), but most commentators think it is a weapon. Perowne says there is no reason that we should not take the form as the verb with an ellipsis of "the way," even though "to meet" indicates going forth to meet an enemy rather than resisting by barring the way (*Psalms*, I:307).

victory were to be accomplished, the encouragement is that the victory would come from God: "I am your salvation."

In the next three verses the prayer concerns what this divine intervention should do to the wicked. The first request is that they be put to shame and dishonor (v. 4). There are four jussives in the verse, two in each half: "let them be put to shame" and "dishonor"; and "let them be turned back" and "disappointed." Those who should be humiliated are truly evil: they seek his life, meaning trying to kill him, and they devise evil against him, meaning they are planning ways to harm him and destroy his life. Then, in verse 5, the psalmist draws a familiar image from the agricultural world to continue the prayer: "let them be like chaff before the wind." As seen in Psalm 1, the image of chaff indicates that they are worthless to God because of their wickedness and will be removed in judgment. He is praying here for that judgment that separates the chaff from the wheat, the wicked from the righteous. In the simile the wind (רוּחַ) will drive the chaff away, but it will be the LORD who drives them away: "the angel of the LORD thrusting." The form of this verb is the participle (דּוֹחֶה), "thrusting away." Because there is no object expressed, the editors suggest the form should be "thrusting them" (דֹּחָם, as with the Greek version). This would make a better parallel with verse 6 that ends with "the angel of the LORD pursuing them (רֹדְפָם)." The clause is an adverbial clause explaining how the wicked will be blown away, "*with* the angel of the LORD thrusting." This is probably a reference to the LORD himself, as the "angel of the LORD" is often the description of the LORD when he directly intervenes in the human realm. It is used here and in Psalm 34 in the Psalter; and it is repeated in verse 6 as the means of that request as well: "let their way be dark and slippery, with the angel of the LORD pursuing them." The metaphors "dark" and "slippery" indicate that they will be confused and hindered as they try to flee and do not find an easy way.

B. The appeal is based on their unjustified hatred of him (7–8).

The psalmist bases his appeal for deliverance on the fact that there was no reason for his enemies to treat him as they did. It was "without a cause" (חִנָּם, from חָנַן; s.v. Ps. 4:1), for no reason at all. Kidner adds that the psalm makes us sensitive to the hurt of injustice.[26] The psalmist did not deserve their hatred. In fact, the way that he had treated them, as the psalm will detail, deserved just the opposite response. Nevertheless, they hid the pit of their net for him, and "without a cause" they dug it to destroy his life. The figurative language (implied comparisons) draws upon hunting practices. To dig a pit with hostile purposes signifies a plan to capture and destroy the prey. In verse 8 the psalmist prays for talionic justice, that the trap they laid entrap them instead, that they would fall into destruction (שׁוֹאָה). The first verb "let it enter" has "destruction" as the subject, "let destruction come upon him"; the next verb is masculine singular, and may be taken adverbially, "when he does not know," meaning "unawares." The destruction should be his own trap, catching him so that he should fall into destruction.

C. The appeal includes a vow to praise the LORD (9–10).

The result of such an amazing victory over unjust, malicious enemies would be praise. In verse 9 the psalmist says, "Then my soul will exult in the LORD" (meaning "I will exult"), the verb (וְגִיל) being a cultic shout of joy (s.v. Ps. 13:4). And, "It will rejoice (תָּשִׂישׂ) in (or more likely, because of) his salvation." This is the expected and natural result of being delivered; he will rejoice enthusiastically, but it will be clear that it is a celebration of the LORD's deliverance. In fact, his declaration will be with all that he can muster—"all my bones will say," "bones" probably being a figure (a metonymy of subject) for what is within the boney framework, that is, his spirit, his mind, his will, his enthusiasm. With all that he has he will declare the incomparable nature of God. That declaration is here expressed as a rhetorical question that demands a negative answer: "LORD, who is like you" means "LORD, there is no one like you," and to make his point he declares how the LORD delivers the "poor (or afflicted) and needy" (וְעָנִי וְאֶבְיוֹן; s.v. Ps. 9:12) from those who are too strong

---

26. *Psalms 1–72*, p. 143.

for them. The fact that the enemies were strong would not have been a problem if they had been righteous people, but their strength was used to plunder vulnerable people (מִמֶּנּוּ, "from him who robs him"). The LORD delivers (מַצִּיל, s.v. Ps. 22:20) people in desperate need from those who try to destroy them. This is the righteousness and goodness of God displayed.

II. The righteous demonstrate that they are hated without a cause and lament that they have not been delivered (11–18).

A. The lament is that the enemies repay good with evil (11–16).

In the second little lament psalm the psalmist emphasizes more the lament itself, but still includes a petition and a praise. His basic complaint is that people have slandered his character and then repaid his good deeds with evil ones. He first mentions their slander: "Malicious witnesses rise up" against him—making it necessary for the LORD to rise up against them. These witnesses are violent and destructive (חָמָס; s.v. Ps. 58:2). The verb is an imperfect tense with a progressive nuance—their action was going on as he spoke.

The parallel colon is a little unclear: "which/who I do not know they question me" (the verb "ask/question" is another progressive imperfect nuance; the verb "know" is a perfect tense, either characteristic or gnomic). Either they were demanding answers from him about charges he knew nothing about, or, the people asking questions were people he did not know. The whole legal confrontation was a surprise to him.

The lament next turns to a lengthy description of how they repaid his kindness with evil. He summarizes the point in verse 12: "They repay evil instead of good." Delitzsch says what he is complaining about is a reminder of the experience with Saul who tried to kill David even though David treated him with respect (1 Samuel 24:18).[27] The verb "repay" (יְשַׁלְּמוּנִי; s.v. Ps. 38:3), also progressive imperfect, describes their ongoing treatment of him;

---

27. *Psalms*, I:424.

the word usually refers to recompense or a reward for deeds. As a result, the psalmist says that he is all alone, the literal meaning of the expression in the text is "childlessness (שְׁכוֹל) of his soul"—he is alone, bereft, forlorn.

In the next few lines he shows why his complaint of unjust treatment is valid. In short, he says that when they were in trouble he mourned for them and grieved with them as if he were a brother or a friend, but when he fell they rejoiced over it, attacked, and mocked him. The statements are made in amazement, for the contrast in treatment of someone in great need could not be stronger. In verses 13 and 14 he relates how he had compassion on them: "But I, when they were sick (בַּחֲלוֹתָם) wore sackcloth." He showed true empathy with them in their need—which they seemed to have forgotten. He also says, "I afflicted myself with fasting (עִנֵּיתִי בַצּוֹם נַפְשִׁי)." By "afflicting" he means depriving himself of luxuries and comforts and pleasures (cf. Lev. 16:31) for the purpose of focusing on the need of the sick. In other words, his expressions of care were not superficial; he put everything aside to tend to them.

His attitude was that of a sympathetic intercessor. The last colon in the verse is difficult: "and my prayer upon my chest returns (תָשׁוּב)." There are several ways this line can be explained: 1) his prayer was continual; 2) his prayer was with humility; 3) his prayer might redound to his own advantage; or 4) a prediction, my prayer will not be lost but will return in blessing, although it could also mean the prayer would return unanswered. The idea of humility may be what is meant here. Delitzsch, comparing this passage with the account of Elijah on the ground in deep prayer in 1 Kings 18:42, says "his head was lowered upon his chest so that which came forth from the inmost depths of his nature returned again as it were in broken accents to his bosom."[28] But Kidner argues for the idea that the prayer would return either unanswered or as a blessing (cf. Matt. 10:13).[29] At least we can say he prayed for them.

Then, in verse 14 the psalmist describes his grieving for them as if he were a member of the family or a close friend. The

---

28. *Psalms*, I:424.
29. *Psalms 1–72*, p. 142.

word order stresses this: "like a friend, like a brother to me, I went around as one who mourns for *his* mother, bowing down in my mourning." The word "bowing down" (קֹדֵר) has the idea of dark or dirty, probably alluding to the practice of neglecting the appearance in mourning and even using dust and ashes.

The contrast with their actions toward him begins in verse 15. "But at my stumbling" (וּבְצַלְעִי), "to limp, stumble" (< צָלַע) is a temporal clause, "when I stumbled." The expression is probably figurative (an implied comparison) for his experiencing trouble now, perhaps an illness. What did they do when he was in need? "They rejoiced and gathered; they gathered against me!" These people were delighted that the psalmist was in trouble, and so they assembled to plot against him now that he was vulnerable. Here is where he calls them "wretches" (נֵכִים). The word is an adjective (נֵכֶה) from the verb "smite, attack," and has the meaning "smitten ones," i.e., "cripples." If this reading is retained it would have to be broadened in its meaning to something like "wretches." The psalmist would be saying that they had the same infirmities as he, but they responded to his differently than he did to theirs. Some commentators would change the word to "smiters" because they are enemies bent on destroying him.[30] If that meaning is taken it could refer to smiting with the tongue, i.e., slander (cf. Jer. 18:18). Other suggestions in the commentaries involve greater emendations.

After referring to them this way, the psalmist says "and I did not know." This could be subordinated as a relative clause, "whom I did not know," or perhaps a contrast, "and I did not know," meaning their wretchedness against him took him by surprise. Their aggression came in that they tore him apart and did not cease. The verb as it stands would be figurative of their attack; it was as if they tore him to pieces. The violent description continues in verse 16 with "as (among) profane mockers at a feast." The first word, "among the profane of" (בְּחַנְפֵי), probably has a superlative idea since it is in construct to "mockers" (a partitive genitive)—among mockers, these are the profane(st). The mockers (or mockery, לְעֵגֵי) are those who ridicule with their stammering outlandish sayings (it occurs in Isa. 28:11 with the

---

30. Perowne, *Psalms 1–72*, p. 143.

meaning of a stammering, or a barbarism, the confused unintelligible speaking of foreigners). The last word of the clause (מָעוֹג) is rare; it occurs in 1 Kings 17:12 for "cake, festal food." This is somewhat problematic, so commentators suggest that the word may come from a cognate verb (עוג) that would mean "twist, turn." It would be an attributive genitive describing their mocking as crooked. Other commentators retain the connection with food and describe it as festal mocking, or "cake mockers," the genitive being in apposition to "mockers." This could refer to flatterers and mockers who were favorites chosen to mock the psalmist at a festal occasion, or perhaps to obtain food and drink.[31] Then, "gnashing" with their teeth would be figurative of their snarling, mocking, facial expressions to go with the words (metonymy of adjunct). So the picture the psalmist paints of their treatment of him when he was down is amazing for its heartless cruelty and unjustified attacks.

B. The lament focuses on the need for the LORD to deliver (17).

Such vicious mocking and personal attacks can only lead to one recourse, prayer; and the form of the prayer is a familiar one: "Lord, how long will you look on?" ("according to what, will you look?"). It is a rhetorical question, lamenting the fact that the LORD has yet to intervene. The verb "you look" (תִּרְאֶה) probably means that the LORD was only watching and not intervening, for the next colon prays for action: "Rescue me (my life) from their destructions, my precious life from the lions." "Rescue" means "bring back" or "restore" (הָשִׁיבָה). In referring to his life (נַפְשִׁי) he describes it as his dearest possession (יְחִידָתִי; "darling" in older translations). It is the one thing that he had that no one else did—his life; and that is his dearest possession because if he lost his life he would have lost everything.

Significantly, the enemies in this verse are described as "lions" (כְּפִירִים). This clarifies the meaning of "lions" in Psalm 34: 10, since it probably is one of the threads the final editor of the collection used as he stitched the psalms together.

---

31. Moll, *Psalms*, p. 245.

C. The lament includes a vow to praise the LORD in the congregation (18).

This section of the psalm also closes with the psalmist's determination or expectation to praise the LORD. "I will acknowledge you" (אוֹדְךָ, from יָדָה, s.v. Ps. 6:5) indicates his anticipation of making a public acknowledgment of the LORD in the sanctuary, in the midst of the congregation. The mighty throng (עַם עָצוּם) refers to the great assembly, a large congregation, who will hear his praise (the parallel verb is אֲהַלְלֶךָ; s.v. Ps. 33:1).

III. The righteous petition the LORD to render justice to those who stir up strife against those who live at peace (19–28).

A. The petition is to stop the wicked from stirring up strife by their vicious words (19–21).

In the last section of the psalm the emphasis is on petition, first for God to deal with the wicked. He begins by asking the LORD not to let them rejoice over him. This expression (a metonymy of effect) is a request for God not to let them triumph. The subject of this sentence is clarified with "my enemies falsely" (אֹיְבַי שֶׁקֶר). The word "false" (שֶׁקֶר) serves as an adverbial accusative describing the enemies as false enemies (s.v. Ps. 144:8). This reiterates the previous emphasis that they had no reason to be his enemies, so dishonesty and treachery made them enemies. This meaning is confirmed by the parallel line "who hate me without a cause" (שֹׂנְאַי חִנָּם, "my haters without a cause"). Now the request is "let them not wink the eye" (יִקְרְצוּ עָיִן), i.e., wink maliciously. The one who winks the eye is conveying one thing but planning something evil.[32] So in addition to their rejoicing, their winking would be an expression of superiority over the vulnerable psalmist as well as contempt for him.

Verse 20 says these people do not speak peace, but against those who live quietly in the land they plot deceit. The implication of this is that they may appear to speak peace (with a

---

32. See Sir. 27:22.

wink), but as the psalmist rightly discerns they are not speaking peace because they are planning (not speaking) deceit (or deceitful things). Deceit (מִרְמוֹת, s.v. Ps. 5:7) affirms they pretended to be offering peace, but were planning the opposite. The focus of their malicious planning is against the quiet in the land, people who want to live in peace and quiet, and who trust those who proclaim it. What might this deception be? Perhaps it includes what the psalmist has already said, that the deceivers would accuse them of doing things they never knew about. This fits well with verse 21, which says they open wide their mouths and say, "Aha, Aha, our eyes have seen it." If these people were false witnesses, then what they claimed to have seen was untrue, but it was enough to destroy people.

B. The petition focuses on the LORD's deliverance of the righteous (22–26).

The next five verses ask for vindication by divine intervention. The petition is introduced with "You have seen, O LORD; do not be silent" (אַל־תֶּחֱרַשׁ). In the last verse the enemies claimed they had seen victory; in this verse the psalmist knows the LORD has seen his plight. The word "seen" has a different connotation in each verse. Then, the figure of God's being silent is anthropomorphic to say that God was not answering prayer (see also Pss. 50:3; 83:2; 109:1). It is paralleled with "do not be far off," another figurative expression for God's not involving himself in the psalmist's life (Pss. 22:1, 11,19). The prayer is worded positively in verse 23, but with further bold anthropomorphic expressions: "Awake and rouse yourself" (הָעִירָה וְהָקִיצָה). The two verbs are synonymous, so they intensify one appeal—God should wake up, i.e., act on his behalf and not appear to be asleep (i.e., be indifferent or unaware). The appeal is for God to act for his vindication (מִשְׁפָּטִי, s.v. Ps. 9:4), i.e., to decide this case. He is confident in asking this because he knows he is innocent. The parallel prepositional phrase is "for my cause" (לְרִיבִי), the word recalling the petition of verse 1 for God to "contend" or "strive" for him. His confidence is also evident as he addresses his prayer to "my God and my Lord." Then, verse 24 uses the actual verb, "Vindicate me (שָׁפְטֵנִי) according to your righteousness," an appeal he addresses to "LORD, my God," stressing the covenant relationship he has with the righteous God. Because his cause is just, the righteous God will vindicate him. Then he repeats the request of verse 19, "let them not rejoice over me," but adds in verse 25 how they would like to rejoice over him: "Let them not say in their hearts, 'Aha, our heart's desire'; let them not say 'We have swallowed him up.'" If the LORD did not answer his prayer for vindication, they would triumph and be able to proclaim that they had their heart's desire by destroying him. The verb "swallow" is figurative (an implied comparison, perhaps from the animal world—after all, they were compared to lions, and they did open their mouths wide against him); it means utterly destroy so there would be no trace of him.

Finally, he prays in verse 26 that they would be put to shame (s.v. Ps. 31:1) and be disappointed (וְיַחְפְּרוּ) together. Why? They are the ones who were rejoicing at his calamity, and would have loved to rejoice at his defeat. However, his prayer is for the contrary, that they be clothed with shame and dishonor (וּכְלִמָּה). The figure of being clothed (an implied comparison) means that they should be covered with shame as with clothes—it would be the first thing people would see. The punishment would be deserved, for these were people who exalted themselves against the psalmist, i.e., bragged about themselves while slandering him. The psalmist is calling for the LORD to vindicate him by exalting him to his proper place and bringing them down to their proper place.

C. The petition promises that both he and the people of God will praise the LORD continually (27–28).

The last two verses of the psalm once again concern praise; they express the psalmist's desire for the faithful people to praise the LORD (v. 27) and his determination to tell of the LORD's righteousness all the time (v. 28). The first verse is a petition regarding the people: "Let those who delight in my righteousness," that is, those who want me to be declared right or vindicated, "shout for joy and be glad." The petition uses a figure (metonymy of effect), for to let them praise means deliver me in order that they may praise—give them the reason to praise.

The content of their praise should be, "Great (יִגְדַּל) is the LORD who delights in the welfare of his servant" ("welfare" is peace, שָׁלוֹם, what the enemies appeared to be promising deceitfully). The faithful supporters of the psalmist could only say this when the LORD showed his delight in his servant by vindicating him and putting the enemies to shame.

Finally, the psalmist declares that the outcome of this deliverance will be his praise: "Then my tongue (a metonymy of cause for what he says) will tell of your righteousness." The verb translated "tell" is elsewhere "meditate" (תֶּהְגֶּה; s.v. Ps. 2:1); it is an audible speaking, sometimes under the breath, sometimes louder, that rehearses and explains and ponders the works of the LORD. Here its subject matter is "your righteousness." The word in this expression means what God's righteousness would do for him (so it is a metonymy of cause), that is, vindicate him by setting things right. And "your praise" in the second half of the line refers to the praise he will give God (the suffix being an objective genitive). Here too "praise" refers to the cause for the praise, what the LORD will do that is to be praised (a metonymy of effect now). The righteousness of God will bring about the just deliverance, and the just deliverance will issue forth in praise.

MESSAGE AND APPLICATION

Here we have another psalm about the suffering of the righteous at the hands of malicious enemies who try to ruin them by false accusation. The psalm is essentially a prayer to the LORD for protection and vindication. The petition for vindication takes on a very specific tone of imprecation for the wicked, that they would be utterly destroyed. So the exposition will have to be clear in describing the issues: the righteous are here innocent of all the false charges; the enemies hate them without a cause, they pray for God to render justice on those who cause trouble for people wanting to live quietly. If we stay with the theme of the prayer, we may write an expository idea like this: *When righteous people who seek to live peacefully in the world are hated and falsely accused, they should pray to the LORD for protection and vindication.* If we want to get to the theological idea that informs the prayer, we could simply say, *The LORD will destroy the wicked and vindicate the saints.* Then the application would be to pray.

There is a good deal of material in the Bible about suffering, and so many passages could be correlated. We may start with Matthew 10:22 in which Jesus warned that since people hated him without a cause, they would hate us for his name sake. His instruction was to endure so that in the end we would be saved. Peter picks up on this point and offers instructions for the people of God. First, we are to have a good conscience (meaning that the suffering was truly without a cause) so that those who revile our good behavior will be put to shame (1 Pet. 3:16–17). Second, if we suffer now, we should rejoice insofar as we share his sufferings, and we will rejoice when his glory is revealed (1 Pet. 4:13). In the meantime, we are to entrust our lives to God to see us through (1 Pet. 4:19). Believers therefore must be sure that accusations against them are false, that they are indeed innocent. They then may pray for the LORD's protection as they endure the suffering in this world, and they may pray for vindication even now, so their false accusers are put to shame. They do know that when the LORD appears in glory, he will vindicate his people and take revenge on the wicked. It is not wrong to pray for justice to be done, but in the spirit of the New Testament it is appropriate to pray that malicious evil-doers will repent before it is too late for them.

PSALM 36

God's Preserving, Fulfilling Love

INTRODUCTION

Text and Textual Variants

For the Chief Musician. Of David, the Servant of the LORD.

1   An oracle[1] concerning the transgression of the wicked
    is within my heart:

---

1. The word נְאֻם, "oracle" (also at times "says"), has created difficulties for the meaning of the line. The MT has for the first clause: נְאֻם־פֶּשַׁע לָרָשָׁע, "an oracle of transgression concerning the wicked." The problem is linked to the following words, "in the midst of my heart." The whole line in the Greek version reads: "Says the transgressor of the law in himself, that he may sin" (παράνομος τοῦ ἁμαρτάνειν [reflecting a reading פֹּשֵׁעַ לְרָשָׁע]). The MT construction occurs only here. Some commentators have accepted some of the Greek version's readings and change "my heart" to "his heart," and the noun "transgression" to a participle "transgressor": "The rebel speaks wickedly deep in his heart" (see A. A. Anderson, *Psalms 1–72*, p. 287). Kraus suggests changing the word "oracle" to נָעִים, "pleasing is transgression to the wicked deep in his heart" (*Psalms 1–59*, pp. 396, 7). But changing the text and the meaning without strong support to solve the problem is not convincing. Some make only a modified change to "his heart" and read: "An utterance of transgression belongs to the wicked, within his heart" (see VanGemeren, *Psalms*, p. 337). And then there is the suggestion that the word should be in the superscription, or a heading, and not part of verse 1 at all (Broyles, *Psalms*, p. 174; Craigie, *Psalms*, p. 290).The proposals are not without difficulty themselves. The text can be read and interpreted as it is and have a meaning just as plausible as these: "an oracle of/about transgression of the wicked is in my heart"—the psalmist has received a deep understanding of the nature of the wicked.

> There is no fear of God
>> before his eyes.
> 2 For he flatters himself[2] in his own eyes
>> concerning finding his iniquity and hating *it*.[3]
> 3 The words of his mouth are wickedness and deceit;
>> he has ceased acting wisely with respect to doing good.
> 4 Even on his bed he devises wickedness;
>> he stations himself on a way *that* is not good;
> *and* he does not despise evil.
>
> 5 O LORD, in the heavens is your loyal love,
>> your faithfulness[4] is to the skies.
> 6 Your righteousness is like the mightiest mountains,[5]
>> your justice[6] is a great deep.
> Man and beast you preserve, O LORD.
> 7 How precious[7] is your loyal love, O God,[8]
>> that humans[9] may take refuge
> under the shadow of your wings.
> 8 They feast from the abundance of your house;
>> you give them drink from your river of delights.
> 9 For with you is the fountain of life;
>> in your light we can see light.

---

2. הֶחֱלִיק is literally, "he makes smooth"; Kraus translates the line: "For he smooths things out for himself before him" (*Psalms 1–59*, p. 397).

3. The clause simply reads "to find his iniquity to hate" (לִמְצֹא עֲוֺנוֹ לִשְׂנֹא). The Greek and Syriac add a conjunction to the last word "and hate," perhaps reading a finite verb instead of the infinitive.

4. Greek and Syriac have a conjunction: "and your faithfulness."

5. The MT has "like the mountains of God" (כְּהַרְרֵי־אֵל); the word "God" may be interpreted as a superlative, mightiest mountains or greatest mountains.

6. Several manuscripts and versions have the word in the plural, "your decisions/judgments."

7. The Greek reads, "How have you multiplied" (ἐπλήθυνας) instead of "precious" (יָקָר).

8. The word "God" at the end of the colon and "even sons of man" on the next, has prompted some commentators to propose the reading: "unto you they come" (אֵלֶיךָ יָבֹאוּ), which is closer to Ps. 65:2. There is no reason for the change.

9. The MT has "and *the* sons of man."

10 Continue your loyal love to those who know you,
      and your righteousness to the upright in heart.
11 Do not let the foot of pride come against me,
      nor the hand of the wicked drive me away.
12 See[10] how the evildoers have fallen[11]—
      thrown down, not able to rise!

Composition and Content

Kirkpatrick says, "The psalm presents two contrasted pictures: one of the godless principles and conduct of the man who has made deliberate choice of evil; the other of the universal and inexhaustible lovingkindness of God. From the prevailing wickedness around him (to which he is in danger of falling victim, v. 11), the psalmist turns for relief and comfort to contemplate the goodness of God."[12]

This psalm is a beautiful meditation on the blessings of God on the righteous who must live in a world that is characterized by unrighteousness. All around are people who do not believe in God and therefore live by different standards. They may not call what they do "wicked," but if it is godless, selfish, and creates hardships for other people, there is no other way to describe it. It is the fruit of a philosophy that denies any retribution from God.But the psalmist draws strength from his faith in the Lord God who is loving, righteous, and faithful, who blesses his people with all kinds of spiritual provisions and in the end will bring them to eternal life, while the wicked fall in judgment. In this the psalmist takes on a number of the motifs that are to be found in wisdom psalms—the inequities of life, the final retribution, and the blessings of God on the righteous.

The psalm is difficult to classify for it has elements of

---

10. The MT has "there," שָׁם, which is difficult to interpret unless it may be given a temporal meaning. The translation "See how" is the suggestion of Dahood (*Psalms*, I:224). Others emend the text, usually to שָׁמֵמוּ, "they are desolate" (e.g., Kraus, *Psalms 1–59*, p. 397).
11. The perfect tense may be taken as a prophetic perfect, an expectation of what is certain to happen.
12. *Psalms*, p. 183.

different kinds of psalms; it is a mixed type. Verses 1–4 are like an individual lament but with some wisdom elements; verses 5–9 sound like a hymn to God; and verses 10–12 are a prayer. In general the psalm could be classed as a wisdom psalm because it reminds us of Psalms 1 and 14. It could also be a lament since it includes the report of the difficulty and the prayer. It is essentially a meditation that combines motifs from hymns, laments, and wisdom psalms.

The writer is a person who is in danger of persecution by the godless people around him, but who has built his confidence in the person and work of the LORD, to whom he prays for protection. The psalm certainly includes material that is pre-exilic since it speaks of the blessings the righteous enjoy in the sanctuary. Although some would date the psalm late, older traditions are here expressed in the song.[13] It is not impossible that the meditation was actually composed earlier as well, at least in some form.

The psalm can be divided into three parts: the first is the revelation about the philosophy of the wicked and the fruit of that philosophy, a revelation that is reported with the tone of a lament (1–4); the second is the testimony of the psalmist's faith in the revealed nature of God and the way that those attributes apply to his life, a testimony that is hymn-like (5–9); and the third is the confident prayer growing out of this meditation, asking God to continue to demonstrate his loyal love to the redeemed and to prevent the wicked from making him wander from his faith (10–12). The psalm lends itself nicely to an expository development, moving from the negative (the wicked) to the positive (the faith) and ending with a practical prayer.

Exegetical Analysis

Summary

Having received an oracle concerning the philosophy and practice of the unbeliever as he plots his wicked schemes, and having found comfort in his own experiential knowledge of the glorious

---

13. Kraus, *Psalms 1–59*, p. 398.

attributes of the LORD, the psalmist prays that the LORD would continue to preserve him with his loyal love and righteousness so that the wicked will not destroy his integrity.

Outline

I. Lament: The psalmist receives an oracle concerning the philosophy and the practice of the wicked who schemes evil (1–4).
  A. His basic belief assumes that there is no fear of God (1).
  B. His lifestyle is only evil continually:
    1. His conscience is soothed to hide iniquity (2).
    2. His speech is licentious and deceptive (3).
    3. His life has ceased to be worthwhile to God (4a).
    4. His plans are established on an evil course (4b).
II. Hymn: The psalmist finds comfort in a meditation of the attributes of the LORD which bring abundant blessings to the believer (5–9).
  A. His basic belief is based on the revealed nature of the LORD (5–6).
    1. The LORD's loyal love and faithfulness are insurmountable.
    2. The LORD's righteousness and decisions are unfathomable.
    3. The LORD preserves life.
  B. His life enjoys the blessings of God's protection and provisions (7–9).
    1. People can take refuge in the loyal love of the LORD (7).
    2. Believers are satisfied with the best provisions of the sanctuary (8).
    3. Believers receive life and truth from the LORD (9).
III. Petition: The psalmist prays that the LORD continue this protective love so that his integrity will be preserved (10–12).
  A. He prays for the continued benefits from the LORD's love (10).
  B. He prays for preservation from the wicked (11).
  C. He foresees the destruction of the wicked (12).

COMMENTARY IN EXPOSITORY FORM

I. God's revelation uncovers the evil ways of the unbeliever (1–4).

A. *Their basic belief is that there is nothing to fear from God (1).*

The first line of the psalm says, "An oracle of the transgression of the wicked is in the midst of my heart." The word "oracle" (נְאֻם) can be translated "revelation, oracle, divine utterance" and even as a verb, "says." Usually it is followed by its subject ("an oracle *of*/*from* the LORD," i.e., "the LORD says"), but here the expression following it is the object ("an oracle *about* the transgression")—it gives the content of the oracle.[14] The psalmist is saying he knows about the transgression of the wicked because God has revealed it to him. He, or anyone else for that matter, would be aware what the ungodly do; but he is here enabled to penetrate to their beliefs and motivations. And since it is a revelation from God, it is not merely the thinking of the writer but of God.

This revelation will focus on the "transgression" of the "wicked." The "wicked" (or "ungodly," רָשָׁע; s.v. Ps. 1:1) refers to people who are unbelievers. They are guilty before God because they have never repented or sought forgiveness; they are deserving of punishment. In their standing before God they are "wicked"; but in life they may appear to be nice people, so they are sometimes just called the "ungodly." The revelation is about their "transgression" (פֶּשַׁע; s.v. Ps. 51:1). The related verb of this noun is used in military contexts for rebellion against a government or nation, indicating the sin is premeditated. The English word "transgression" means "passing over a boundary"; but the idea of "rebellion" adds the idea of willful and aggressive action to the crossing over. Unbelievers live their lives in rebellion to God and his will—they would deny this, or deny God, but the fact remains that people who choose not to obey God are rebellious.

---

14. Some versions have suggested the translation "wickedness says," following the normal use of the word; but that is a rather difficult concept to explain.

The second half of the verse is the summary of the oracle he has received: "there is no fear of God before his eyes." The key word here is "fear" (פַּחַד, s.v. Ps. 119:120). It is not the usual word for "fear"; it means "dread," or something that is feared, "a dread thing." It describes something that happens that terrifies people and stops them in their tracks. For example, in Psalm 31:12, David says that because of his enemies he has become a dread thing to his friends. Job also says that the calamity from God is a dread thing to him (31:23). It is a word that describes something terrible that causes fear and loathing. Here the meaning would be that the unbeliever may go through life without any "dread thing" from God that would make him stop and consider his ways. His attitude might be that if God did not like what he was doing he would have stopped him, but since he did not, either he approved, or he did not exist at all. As complacency grows, the wicked lose all consideration of God; they become "practical atheists," living their lives as if there were no God. This is the belief at the core of all sin; it clears the way for people to do what they want, no matter what the effects might be on others.

B. The lifestyle of people who think this way is a rationalized sinful life (2–4).

The meditation now will sadly consider what some of the transgressions of the wicked are. The first topic is how the wicked deal with the conscience. Verse 3 literally says, "For he deals smoothly to himself in his own sight, concerning the exposing of his iniquity so as to hate it." It is not an easy verse to translate and interpret, but once we sort out the meanings of the words and the grammatical constructions we will see that he is saying basically that the wicked cover over what they do in their thinking, because if they did not do so they would see what they really are and hate it. The verse begins with "for," which has the force here of "no, rather." It marks a strong contrast. He has no dread of God—rather, he deals smoothly. It has been said that the one who makes little of God makes much of self, and that is what we see here. This slippery character (as the verb implies) "smooths over" (חָלַק) the rough spots in his life so that the sin cannot be found. This is rationalization, self-deception and false flattery. He justifies himself in all things to soothe his conscience, so that he will not see what an unpleasant character he is. God-fearing people see their own sins and deal with them correctly, but this type of person conceals sin.

The rest of the verse is made up of two infinitives, "to find" and "to hate." The first one explains the preceding verb: "he deals smoothly . . . *concerning finding* his iniquity," his going astray or waywardness (s.v. Ps. 32:5). The second infinitive provides the result of this finding, "*and so to hate it*," that is, loathe it and reject it (s.v. Ps. 139:21). The verse says then that if he did not cover over his sins he would discover them and hate them, but in the way he smooths things out, to him his actions may simply be shrewd policies or competitive business, even if they harm or ruin other people.

Verse 3a focuses next on what he says: "the words of his mouth are wicked and deceit." Here the evil begins to affect other people; no longer is it a matter of convincing himself he is a good person. Rather, his words betray him. The first description of what he says is that it is painful or troubling "evil" (אָוֶן; s.v. Ps. 28:3), that is, evil that produces sorrow and trouble. It is not an internal wickedness, such as evil thoughts, but acts that cause grief. The second description of what the wicked say is "deceit" (מִרְמָה; s.v. Ps. 5:7). This term needs little explanation; what they say is deceptive—it cannot be believed. The two words could be taken together (as a nominal hendiadys), "deceitful acts that cause trouble." This would explain the cause of the pain and trouble in their words—they deceive people. In the world of unbelievers, now as well as then, whether business, law, politics, education or even religion, lies predominate and are justified by the liars if they accomplish their goal.

The second half of verse 3 adds another idea about the transgression of the wicked: "he has ceased to act prudently with respect to doing good." The parallelism is either formal or synthetic, because this verse, and the next, list one description after another of the wicked. This verse also uses infinitives to make the point. After the initial verb "he has ceased" (a present perfect of חָדַל) we have an infinitive supplying the direct object (answering what it is he has ceased), "acting prudently" (לְהַשְׂכִּיל from שָׂכַל). This is a wisdom word; it refers to fitting conduct that is in harmony with the wisdom of God and is therefore successful.[15] The last infinitive, "to do good" (לְהֵיטִיב from יָטַב, to be/

---

15. The word שָׂכַל in its various contexts has been translated with "deal wisely, be prudent, have insight, be insightful, be reasonable," and "be successful." The word may be a denominative of the noun "insight," giving it the basic idea of "to have insight" (see K. Koenen, שָׂכַל in *TDOT*, ed. by Botterweck, Ringgren and Fabry, XIV:112–128). In general use it may simply refer to common sense, but in religious contexts it has to do with living wisely according to God's will, which will bring success with God.

The first category of meanings would then be "have insight." We see this sense in Genesis 3:6 in the temptation narrative where eating from the forbidden fruit was said "to make one wise" like God, i.e., to have the insight and wisdom God has ("to be in the know"). There is a legitimate use of this wisdom that should be inspired not by disobedience but by the fear of the LORD. Psalm 32:8 says the LORD gives insight—it comes with divine revelation and divine enablement. According to Proverbs the "prudent" person (as the word may be translated) knows how to act in the different situations (Prov. 10:5; 10:19). In fact, one of the purposes of the Book of Proverbs is to give people discipline that will produce this prudence, and it will be characterized by righteousness, justice, and equity (Prov. 1:4). Psalm 119:99 says that keeping God's commandments distinguishes the prudent person. In Psalm 2:10 the psalmist exhorted the kings of the earth to be wise, perhaps to have common sense, because they were opposing God and God was about to destroy them. In Psalm 36 the ungodly person has ceased acting wisely to do good things—he lives like the fool.

A second category has the meaning "to understand" something. Psalms 14:2 and 53:2 say that the foolish, ungodly human race does not understand. If they did, they would not live such wicked lives and ignore the warnings of judgment to come. Psalm 106:7 explains the ancestors' rebellion against God by saying that they did not understand the works of God. But on the positive side, a blessing is announced for the one who takes note of the poor (Ps. 41:1), meaning that he has compassionate understanding of people in need. The idea is that his understanding is acted upon.

A third category is "be successful." People who have this prudence, this insight, will make the right choices and be successful. 2 Kings 18:7–8 tell how the LORD was with Hezekiah so that he prospered in everything he did.

The use in Isaiah 52:13 probably belongs here, although different versions translate it differently: "My servant shall deal wisely," or "my servant shall prosper." The prophecy foretells how the suffering servant will live wisely in accordance with the will of God so that in the end he will succeed. In the world's opinion, he was a failure, and they did not esteem him;

do good/well; s.v. Ps. 34:8), provides the explanation for acting prudently, "in doing what is good/right."

So the word "act prudently" means to be wise, have insight or understanding, or to show good skill. But the wicked have been in their own ways so long that they have left off acting prudently concerning doing what is right. They may have skill or wisdom in worldly matters, but not in doing what is right. They have been trained to do the right thing for their profession or their success, but not to do what is right.

Verse 4 then focuses on the plans that the wicked make, how they sort out their policies and procedures within their belief system. It begins with "he schemes (< חָשַׁב; s.v. Ps. 32:2) iniquity on his bed." To him what he plans may not seem to be iniquity, i.e., trouble-causing evil, because he has deceived himself. His plans do not take into consideration the requirement of righteousness revealed by God and so they are simply evil. The text then affirms "he stations himself upon a way that is not good." He takes a position in his way of life that is not helpful for people, but brings more harm to them than good (s.v. Ps. 34:8). Finally, the verse says "he does not hate evil" (s.v. Ps. 10:15). The verb "hate" is actually "reject" (< מָאַס); even though what he does might be morally wrong or harmful to other people, he will persist in it because it is pleasing or beneficial to him. The wicked do not reject anything that might cause pain to people (such as putting them out of work, or ruining them financially), for they are often driven by the desire to win, to be successful. The picture here is probably not of murderers lying in bed trying to decide who to ruin, but worldly people who make their plans with no concern whatever for people. It is not hard to look around today, especially in the world of finance, and see what greed has done to the livelihood of millions of people. What the culprits do may not be illegal by the standards of the country, but by God's standard it is sin.

This then is the revelation of the wicked. One may note that the verbs are in the singular, suggesting that the psalmist may have had one person in mind. Many illustrations of what is

---

but in the final analysis he will be exalted over them all so that they will be dumbfounded. It is success with God that is the fruit of godly wisdom.

described here come to mind from biblical history, but the descriptions in the singular are also representative of the type of people who live this way—there are many like this.

II. Faith in the Lord brings deliverance and blessing (5–9).

A. *The Lord's nature has been revealed in his great acts of love (5–6).*

In contrast to the (un)beliefs and acts of the wicked, the psalmist describes the faith of the righteous—his faith. He does not compare the righteous with the wicked; rather, he compares the object of the faith of the righteous—the nature of the LORD—with the beliefs and practices of the unbelievers. He does not elaborate on this contrast; it becomes self-evident as the description of the faith unfolds. Believers cannot put forth their virtues as contrast to the wickedness of unbelievers, for they do many of the same things. The difference is the life they enjoy because they have entered into covenant with the LORD. The first couple of verses in this section describe the key attributes of the LORD. Kidner says:

> Here is a whole world to explore, a 'broad place' to be brought into (cf. 18:19): unsearchable (*heavens, clouds*), impregnable (*mountains*), inexhaustible (*the great deep*); yet, for all that, welcoming and hospitable (6c–9). It is only man's world that is cramping. Human fickleness makes a drooping contrast to this towering covenant-love and *faithfulness* (5); human standards, where all is relative, are a marshland beside the exacting, exhilarating mountains of His *righteousness* (6); human assessments are shallowness itself in comparison with His *judgments*. . . .[16]

Verse 5, then, focuses on his "loyal love" and "faithfulness." These two attributes often go together in the psalms. The "loyal love" (חֶסֶד; s.v. Ps. 23:6) is the faithful covenant love that God

---

16. *Psalms 1–72*, p. 147.

has for his own—he has made a covenant with his people and is faithful to keep it because he loves them. So this word, while often translated "lovingkindness" by Bibles, is more the idea of "loyal love" or "faithful covenant love." "Faithfulness" (אֱמוּנָה; s.v. Ps. 15:2) is a natural parallel for it. This word emphasizes the reliability or dependability of what God has promised (Pss. 33:4; 100:5; 89:50; 88:12). It can be illustrated by its many cognate words, such as "master craftsman," or "pillar," or "trustee" and the like. All these words refer to people or things that are reliable.

What the psalmist says about God's faithful covenant love is that it has no limits. He uses figures comparing the extent of the attributes to the highest heavens: the loyal love is in the heavens, and the faithfulness is to the clouds. The fact that the LORD is seated enthroned in the heavens may have influenced the choice of the description of the attributes, but the main point is that his faithful love is unsearchable, beyond comprehension, unlimited. Is there a limit to God's faithful love? Or is there a limit to the heavens? What God has promised, he is faithful to do, because he loves his people, without limit.

Then in verse 6 the psalmist considers God's righteous decisions, or, in the poetry, his righteousness and his decisions. The parallelism again puts two attributes together that often work together in the poetry. The word "righteousness" (צֶדֶק; s.v. Ps. 1:5) refers to that which conforms to the standard, what is right. God, of course, is the standard, and so whatever he does is right. Parallel to this is the word "judgments" (מִשְׁפָּטִים; s.v. Ps. 9:4), which refers to the decisions that God makes. So the subject matter of this verse is God's righteous decisions. The figures here describe his righteousness as insurmountable (the simile is "like the mountains of God") and unfathomable (the metaphor is that they are "a great deep"). The description "the mountains of God" is an interesting expression. The divine epithet "God" is occasionally used in the Bible to express the superlative. If that is the use here it would mean "the greatest mountains." Great mountains are immovable and inflexible objects, conspicuous and evident to all, and as natural boundaries not easily surmounted. This truth is at the heart of divine revelation: God's righteousness is the obvious and certain standard of all his works. Someone has said that across the path of every unholy person who dreams of heaven stand the touring Andes of divine righteousness, which no sinner can climb.

Calling the judgments a great deep stresses what the Bible says elsewhere, that his wisdom and knowledge are unsearchable. The use of "great deep" (תְּהוֹם רַבָּה) may have a reference to the flood in the days of Noah when the fountains of the deep were broken up, especially since the parallel line affirms that God "saves man and beast." Be that as it may, he is saying that no one can possibly get to the bottom of God's decisions, let alone understand them.

The significance of all this is that the LORD saves ("you save," תּוֹשִׁיעַ; s.v. Ps. 3:2). The verb "you save" (a habitual imperfect since it is God's nature to save) may have the sense of "deliver" in this passage, especially since it refers to man and beast. With regard to people, the deliverance cannot be separated from the spiritual dimension because they trust in him for their deliverance. The point of this whole section is that the evidence of God's faithful love and righteous decisions is salvation.

B. The Lord's nature is manifested in his blessings on the righteous (7–9).

These attributes of God are at first glance abstract; but they are the descriptions of the nature of God who delivers man and beast, and so they are the causes of his acts. In other words, if God is known as faithful it is because he has shown himself faithful in his dealings; likewise with his love and his righteousness. In the next few verses the psalm focuses on the "loyal love" of God—what the faithful, covenant love of God produces in the life of the believer.

The section begins with the exclamatory "How precious is your loyal love, O God, that even humans can take refuge under the shadow of your wings." That which is precious (יָקָר) is rare, and therefore prized. It is choice, like a costly pearl. God's faithful love is the most prized possession any one can receive. The reason for that is that in his loyal love there is safety and security. "Humans" (literally "the sons of man") can take refuge in him.[17] Taking refuge (יֶחֱסָיוּן; s.v. Ps. 7:1) is figurative (an implied comparison), comparing trusting in the LORD to finding a refuge in a storm, a place of safety. Here the object of the faith is "the shadow of your wings" (a zoomorphism). Jesus used the same figure when he said he wanted to gather the people to himself as a hen gathers its chicks, but they refused (Matt. 23:37). The picture is one of God's provision of safety and security in the covenant—this is what the love of God means to the believers. It is their salvation from sin and their deliverance from judgment as well as their security through this life, and this is why it is so precious to them.

Then, in verse 8, the psalmist uses sanctuary and priestly imagery to speak of the spiritual blessings that God has given to his people.[18] The first colon says that the believers "feast from the fatness (דֶּשֶׁן; s.v. Ps. 20:2) of your house." The "house" is a reference to the sanctuary; and the "fatness" refers to the fatty portions of the meat, the oily best portions (see Isa. 55:2; here it is a synecdoche) that normally would be the portions of the priests. It as if what God provides for his people is the best food of the sanctuary. What is in mind is the sanctuary ritual where the worshipers would actually eat the peace offering as a communal meal.[19] It may have been an actual meal, but it was also a symbolic act signifying that they were at peace with God. This blessing has in mind the spiritual benefits of receiving God's grace and being at peace with him, but also the ways those benefits affect their daily life. In the presence of God they are satisfied physically and spiritually.

They also will drink to their satisfaction. In the second colon we have "you make them drink from the river of your pleasures." The word "your pleasures" (עֵדֶן > עֲדָנֶיךָ) is an allusion to Eden

---

17. Some interpretations take "O God" in conjunction with "sons of man" and derive the idea that high born and low born among humans are referred to here (see the NIV). But there is insufficient evidence in this passage for making that distinction for the word "God." Besides, it would limit "sons of man" to low born people.

18. For a detailed study of how these images are connected both to the account of creation and to sanctuaries, see my discussion in *Recalling the Hope of Glory,* chapter 4.

19. Anderson, *Psalms 1–72,* p. 290.

and the river flowing there. The sanctuary was a reminder of the garden in Eden; and the water symbolized God's provision of life. In the sanctuary ritual it was as if in receiving God's blessings believers were once again in Eden drinking of the river of life. It was a practical provision of water, but it had a symbolic meaning of the provision of spiritual life. And the food and drink that God provided for worshipers in the sanctuary also had a typological meaning for the future messianic age, as other passages will show.

The climax of the section comes in verse 9. The psalmist has made the point that the loyal love of God is precious, so precious that believers can take refuge in him. When they take refuge in him they find safety and security, and the abundant life that God provides, spiritually and physically. The underlying reason for all this is "For with you is the fountain of life; in your light we can see light." The word "fountain" is another allusion to creation; it refers to the laver of water in the sanctuary in terms of a spring or a well, but means the provision of all life is God, the Creator. He is life; and he is the creator and sustainer of all life. The expression "in your light" could refer to divine revelation, but might be abbreviated for "the light of your countenance,"[20] meaning divine favor. In the favor of God, people can see light. "Light" is used figuratively in the Bible for truth, righteousness, life, joy, and illumination. Here it may convey the fullness of life which would be spiritual life as well as physical life, and that would include spiritual understanding. When people trust in him they find life by his grace. They come to know what life is because they are in communion with the giver of life.

Life and light go together in the Bible because the first characteristic of life in creation was light. There would be no life without the light; and in the New Testament John says of Jesus, "In him was life and the life was the light of men. And the light shines in darkness, and the darkness did not apprehend it" (1:4). Light is the essence of life; darkness represents death and chaos. When God saves people he delivers them from darkness into light. The light illumines the way, and so in God's light the believer is able to understanding things spiritually. Because

---

20. Anderson, *Psalms 1–72*, p. 290.

God gives his people life by his grace, that life includes spiritual understanding. This oracle that the psalmist received is a part of the light that enabled him to discern between good and evil.

III. The continuation of God's loyal love will enable the righteous to persevere in this wicked world (10–12).

The final three verses of the psalm form a prayer for the LORD to continue this loyal love. The positive side is expressed in verse 10: "continue (or draw out) your loyal love to those who know you, and your righteousness to the upright of heart." These two words, loyal love and righteousness, were introduced in verses 5 and 6; but because "loyal love" comes first in the couplet, and because "loyal love" was the only focus of verse 7, that is the primary interest of the petition. The psalmist wants God to extend all the effects of his attributes to the upright, but primarily the "loyal love" combined with "righteousness."

The negative side of the petition is that God protect the upright from the "foot of pride." The "foot" is singled out (synecdoche) because of the swift movement of the proud ("pride" being a metonymy of adjunct, giving the attribute for the person). These are the destructive wicked who in their arrogance have schemed the evil plans and set themselves on a destructive way of life. It is possible the image in the psalmist's mind is that of a proud conqueror putting his foot on the neck of the subjugated foe. At any rate, the psalmist wants God's loyal love to protect him from them.

The psalmist finishes with a word of confidence, which is a general anticipation of what God's word predicts for the wicked. The text has "there" (שָׁם), but the word is not usually used for future time but for location. No explanation is given concerning its meaning. Unless it is taken to mean "there" in the future, another interpretation is required. Dahood translated it "see." This would capture the idea that the psalmist was looking as if in a vision at the destruction of the wicked—the wicked will fall and not get up (the verbs are perfect tenses and so classified as prophetic perfects in this section of confident anticipation). Their wickedness will find an end, and so the prayer for protection is based on the nature of God who loves his people and delivers them and is expressed with the full confidence that it is only a matter of time before those who are wicked will be destroyed.

MESSAGE AND APPLICATION

In Matthew 13 we have Jesus' parable about the wheat and the weeds. The servants wanted to root out the weeds, but the owner said to leave them until the time of harvest, and then they would be separated. What this means is that for now the righteous must live among the unrighteous. In the world, and in our own little worlds, there are two kinds of people, living according to two different philosophies of life. There are those who have no fear of God and live in defiance of his laws; and there are the righteous who live by faith in the LORD. The apostle Paul spends a good deal of time contrasting the two. In Romans 1:28–32 he describes the people of the world: they did not acknowledge God; so he gave them up to their own devices, and some of their characteristics match the descriptions in this psalm—haughty, deceitful, foolish, inventors of evil. On the other hand there are the believers: they have received access into God's grace by faith, and so God's love has been poured into their hearts (Rom. 5:1–5). As a result, they have been blessed with every kind of spiritual blessing (Eph. 1:3–14), and they know that nothing can separate them from the love of God in Christ Jesus our Lord (Rom. 8:39). What a contrast in philosophies of life, lifestyles, and destinies. An expository idea could be written to reflect the contrast and lay open the two ways of life: *The world rejects God and lives in defiance to his laws, but believers trust in his faithful love and receive abundant physical and spiritual blessing.*

The point of this psalm is timeless, both in its message and its emphasis. The only hope that we have for safety and security in a world that is dominated by godless evil people is the faithful love of the Lord. This psalm gives us the opportunity to think through as David did the nature of this love and what it brings to us in this life and in the life to come. Like David we can pray, we must pray, that God will continue to extend the benefits of his love to us, because that is our life, and in that life we can have the spiritual understanding so necessary to live the faith in this world.

INTRODUCTION

Text and Textual Variants

א   1   Fret not yourself because of evildoers;
         be not envious of wrongdoers;
   2   for they will soon fade like the grass
         and wither like the green herb.

ב   3   Trust in the LORD and do good;
         dwell in the land and feed on faithfulness.[1]
   4   Delight yourself in the LORD
         and he will give you the desires of your heart.

ג   5   Commit[2] your way[3] to the LORD;
         trust in him and he will act.
   6   He will bring forth your righteousness as the light
         and your justice[4] as the noonday.

---

1. The MT has וּרְעֵה אֱמוּנָה, but the Greek version has καὶ ποιμανθήσῃ ἐπὶ τῷ πλούτῳ αὐτῆς, "and you will be fed with the wealth of it," perhaps reading הֲמוֹנָה.
2. MT reading is גּוֹל, "commit," as in Psalm 22:8. The Greek version has ἀποκάλυψον, "disclose," perhaps for גַּל.
3. The Targum and a few manuscripts have the plural, "your ways."
4. The Targum and a few manuscripts have the plural, "your judgments/ decisions."

ד 7 Be still[5] before the LORD and wait patiently[6] for him;
      fret not yourself over the one who prospers in his
         way,
      over the man who carries out evil devices.

ה 8 Refrain from anger and forsake wrath;
      fret not yourself, it surely leads to doing evil.

9 For the evildoers shall be cut off,
      but those who wait for the LORD shall inherit the
         land.

ו 10 But in just a little while the wicked will be no more;
      though you look carefully for his place, he will not be
         there.[7]

11 But the meek shall inherit the land
      and delight themselves in abundant peace.

ז 12 The wicked plots against the righteous
      and gnashes his teeth at him,

13 but the LORD laughs at him,
      for he sees that his day will come.[8]

ח 14 The wicked draw the sword and bend their bow
      to bring down the poor and needy,
         to slay those whose way is upright.[9]

15 Their sword shall enter their own heart
      and their bows shall be broken.

ט 16 Better is the little that the righteous has
      than the abundance of many[10] wicked.

---

5. דוֹם is "be still"; this is interpreted in the Greek version as ὑποτάγηθι, "submit."

6. The verb in the MT is וְהִתְחוֹלֵל. The Greek reads καὶ ἱκέτευσον, "and suppli-cate him," but Aquila reads ἀποκαραδόκει (and the Targum). The editors of BHS suggest reading וְהוֹחֵל.

7. The Greek gives a paraphrase here: μὴ εὕρῃς, "you shall not find *it.*" whereas the MT has "and he is not," וְאֵינֶנּוּ.

8. The form is the imperfect tense, יָבֹא. A few manuscripts and Qumran have בָּא, the perfect tense, meaning "their day has come."

9. The Hebrew literally is "upright of way," "way" being a genitive of speci-fication. The Greek and some other manuscripts have the more common expression, "upright of heart." The MT preserves the correct reading.

10. In the MT "many" (רַבִּים) modifies the "wicked," but the reading in the Greek, Syriac, and Jerome says "abundant wealth (or great abundance) of sinners," the form probably being רַב to work with "wealth."

17 For the arms of the wicked shall be broken,
    but the LORD upholds the righteous.

י 18 The LORD knows the days[11] of the blameless,
    and their heritage will remain forever.

19 They are not put to shame in the time of calamity,
    and in the days of famine they are satisfied.

כ 20 But the wicked will perish;
    the enemies of the LORD are like the glory of the
        pastures;[12]
  they vanish,
    like smoke they vanish away.

ל 21 The wicked borrows but does not pay back,
    but the righteous is gracious and gives.

22 For those blessed[13] by the LORD shall inherit the land,
    but those cursed by him[14] shall be cut off.

מ 23 The steps of a man are established by the LORD,
    and he delights in his way.

24 Though he fall, he shall not be cast headlong,
    for the LORD upholds his hand.

נ 25 I have been young, and[15] now am old,
    yet I have not seen the righteous forsaken

---

11. For "days of" (יְמֵי) the Greek translation has τὰς ὁδούς, "ways," no doubt recalling the familiar expression of the first wisdom psalm, Psalm 1.

12. This verse has some variations in the versions that are difficult to explain. The MT has כִּיקָר, indicating they are like the best, the prized part of the pastures, but the line in the Greek text says, ἅμα τῷ δοξασθῆναι αὐτοὺς καὶ ὑψωθῆναι, "at the moment of their being honored and exalted they have utterly vanished like smoke." The word for "glory, prized" has been taken as a verbal form; and the rare word for "pastures," כָּרִים, has been understood as כָּרוּם. Symmachus has ὡς μονοκέρωτες, the equivalent of כְּרֵמִים, "wild oxen."

13. The form in the MT is the passive, the *pual* participle מְבֹרָכָיו, but the Greek version makes it active, οἱ εὐλογοῦντες αὐτὸν, "those who bless him," as if the form was the *piel* מְבָרְכָיו. The MT preserves the more rare and difficult form and should be retained.

14. Likewise the Greek has the active καταρώμενοι αὐτὸν, "those who curse him," in place of the Hebrew passive "those cursed by him," מְקֻלָּלָיו.

15. The conjunction is from the Greek version and a few manuscripts; it is not in MT.

or his seed begging bread.

26 All the day he is gracious and lends,
and his seed will become a blessing.

ס **27** Turn away from evil and do good,
so you shall always dwell securely.[16]

28 Because the LORD loves justice, he will not forsake his saints;
they are preserved forever;[17]
but the seed of the wicked shall be cut off.

29 The righteous shall inherit the land
and dwell upon it forever.

פ **30** The mouth of the righteous utters wisdom
and his tongue speaks justice.

31 The law of his God is in his heart,
and[18] his steps do not slip.

צ **32** The wicked watches for the righteous
and seeks to put him to death.

33 The LORD will not abandon him to his power,[19]
or let him be declared guilty when he is judged.

ק **34** Wait for the LORD and keep his way,
and he will exalt you to inherit the land;
when the wicked are cut off you will see *it*.

ר **35** I have seen a wicked, ruthless[20] man,
spreading himself like a luxuriant tree.[21]

---

16. Greek: εἰς αἰῶνα αἰῶνος, "for ever and ever" instead of "securely."

17. The Greek version also has ἄνομοι δὲ ἐκδιωχθήσονται, "and the lawless shall be chased away." Some commentators accept the addition because ἄνομοι would be the equivalent of עַוְּלִים, and thus provide the ע for the acrostic. The layout of the text has the second line of text beginning with לְעוֹלָם which would provide the ע if the preposition were not present. In either case the acrostic is not well preserved here.

18. The conjunction is from the Greek and Syriac versions; it is not in the MT.

19. Literally, "in his hands."

20. The Greek version reads ὑπερυψούμενον, "very highly exalting himself, or "being lifted up." The editors suggest changing עָרִיץ to עָלִיץ, "overbearing."

21. The Greek has ἐπαιρόμενον ὡς τὰς κέρδους τοῦ Λιβάνου, "lifting himself up like the cedars of Lebanon." The problem is with the meaning of מִתְעָרֶה, "show itself naked"; it was apparently read as מִתְעַלֶּה, and כְּאֶזְרַח as כְּאַרְזֵי, and רַעֲנָן as הַלְּבָנוֹן. NIV offers an interpretation of "flourishing."

36 But he passed away,[22] and behold, he was no more;
though I sought him, he could not be found.

שׁ **37** Watch the blameless and behold the upright,
for there is a future[23] for the man of peace.

38 But the transgressors shall be altogether destroyed,
the future[24] of the wicked shall be cut off.

ת **39** But the salvation of the righteous is from the LORD;
he is their stronghold in the time of trouble.

40 And the LORD helps them and delivers them;
he delivers them from the wicked and saves them,
because they take refuge in him.

Composition and Context

Psalm 37 is a powerfully didactic psalm that exhibits a proverbial character. Westermann says the psalm is so steeped in the wisdom tradition that it could be included in the Book of Proverbs.[25] Through all its teachings the psalm reveals that the righteousness of God's providence is vindicated in his administration of the world.[26] In discovering this the psalmist instructs people to wait, trust, and look to the end, in order to see how even in this life God manifests his righteousness in rewarding the godly and destroying the wicked.

Typical of wisdom's concerns, the psalm contrasts the prosperity and power of the wicked with the deprivation and suffering of the righteous (because of the wicked). It holds out to

---

22. The Greek version, Syriac, and Jerome all have "I passed by."
23. The Hebrew is אַחֲרִית; the Greek has ἐγκατάλειμμα, "future remnant" or "residue." The Hebrew word means "end, last." Some suggest that it could mean "posterity/offspring," based on the meaning in Jeremiah 31:17 (perhaps behind the interpretation in the Greek version). This would fit the parallelism of verse 38: sinners destroyed // their offspring cut off, but the text makes good sense with the meaning "end": the end of the wicked is destruction, and the end of believers is salvation, end meaning the conclusion of a way of life (see Kraus, *Psalms 1–59*, p. 407). So in the end, i.e., the future, it will be clear how the present conflict will be resolved.
24. Greek: ἐγκαταλείμματα. See n. 23.
25. Claus Westermann, *The Psalms: Structure, Content and Message*, tr. R. D. Gehrke (Minneapolis: Augsburg, 1980), p. 112.
26. Perowne, *Psalms*, I:315.

the righteous the promise of God's protective care now, and his provision of peace in the future—which the wicked will not have. In sum, righteousness not only has its own rewards, it will also be rewarded in the end.[27]

The structure of the psalm is to a large degree concealed by the acrostic arrangement; yet there are signs that are helpful for tracing the different emphases in the psalm. The admonition "fret not" occurs in verse 1 and then in verses 7 and 8 and seems to mark parallel beginnings. The instructions to persevere in the faith, i.e., hope, wait, trust, commit, appear in verses 3, 7, and 34 especially. Verses 1–6 may then be taken together as a call to perseverance in the faith with a promise of blessing; and verses 34–40 may be taken as a concluding call for faith with the promise of future salvation blessings. Verses 7–33 provide the core of the didactic material. Here verses 7–20 seem to go together as a unit with a renewed call to hold fast to the faith because retribution is coming. That leaves verses 21–33, and they extol the life of wisdom to show how the faithful are to demonstrate their faithfulness. These verses can be further subdivided, because verses 21–26 emphasize how the LORD takes care of the righteous, and verses 27–33 instruct the righteous to turn from evil because the LORD loves righteousness and will not abandon the righteous.

Psalm 37 develops some of the ideas introduced in Psalm 1—the contrast between the way of the righteous and the way of the wicked, the focus on the Law, and especially the prospect of future separation in the judgment. Some of these concerns will be picked up in Psalm 73, where the contrast between the prosperous wicked and suffering righteous is more fully drawn, but the emphasis on knowing the Law is less pronounced. That will come later in Psalm 119 (see the Introduction for comments on the organization of the Psalter).

The didactic nature of the psalm, which is close to Torah Psalms (such as Ps. 119) prompted many commentators to date the work as post-exilic, but the concern for righteousness,

---

27. See also Michael Jinkins, "The Virtues of the Righteous in Psalm 37," in *Psalms and Practice,* ed. by S. B. Reid (Collegeville, MN: Liturgical Press, 2001), pp. 164–201.

obedience to the Law, and hope for vindication through divine judgment on the wicked, are not unique to the post-exilic communities. One of the key considerations of the study of Psalm 37 is the intriguing emphasis on the blessing of the land. We read in verse 3 how the righteous will dwell in the land and feed on God's faithfulness, in verse 9 how the wicked will be cut off but the believers will inherit the land, in verse 11 how the meek will inherit the land and enjoy peace, in verse 22 how those blessed by the LORD will inherit the land and those cursed will be cut off, in verse 29 how the righteous inherit and dwell in the land forever, and in verse 34 how the LORD will exalt the faithful to inherit the land when the wicked are cut off. There is no emphasis on returning to the land; rather, it appears that both the righteous and the wicked dwell in the land, but the righteous are under attack from greedy, prosperous enemies. They are enjoined to live faithfully and wait for the LORD to remove the wicked and enable the righteous to inherit the land in peace. The circumstances of the psalm could fit any number of times, and the hope of someday receiving the heritage of the land without oppression from the enemies of the LORD was a constant hope of God's people who were dwelling in the land, but had not realized the promises. The psalm's hope was still relevant in the days of Jesus when he quoted from it to promise the meek that they would inherit the earth (Matt. 5:5; Mark 10:30).

Exegetical Analysis

Summary

Using a collection of proverbial expressions, the psalmist exhorts the righteous to trust in the LORD continually and not to be anxious about the evil person who will ultimately be cast down.

Outline

  I. The psalmist instructs the congregation to persevere in the faith in order to enjoy the blessings of the LORD (1–6).
   A. They should not be anxious about sinful people because they will disappear (1–2).
   B. They should trust in the LORD and do good because he

causes the righteous desires of the heart to be realized (3–6).
II. The psalmist advises the congregation to hold fast to their integrity because the time of retribution is coming (7–20).
   A. They should hope in the LORD and fret not, which only leads to doing evil (7–8).
   B. They should know that the wicked will be judged but the righteous will inherit the land (9–11).
   C. They should note how the LORD prevents and punishes the wicked (12–20).
     1. The wicked devise evil, but the LORD laughs (12–13).
     2. The wicked attack the afflicted, but the wicked shall be broken (14–15).
     3. The righteous may have little, but the wicked will be broken (16–17).
     4. The LORD knows and protects the way of the perfect, but the wicked will be cut off (18–20).
III. The psalmist calls on the congregation to demonstrate their faith with a life of wisdom because the LORD will bless them (21–33).
   A. He describes the way that the LORD takes care of the righteous (21–26).
     1. The righteous give but the wicked keep, and the LORD will recompense each accordingly (21–22).
     2. The LORD establishes and protects the activities of the righteous (23–24).
     3. The LORD provides food for the righteous who care for others (25–26).
   B. He instructs people to turn away from evil because the Lord loves justice (27–33).
     1. They should turn from evil because the LORD preserves and protects those who do good, but destroys the wicked (27–29).
     2. The righteous utter wisdom because the LORD's law is in their hearts (30–31).
     3. The wicked may attempt to destroy the righteous but the LORD will not abandon them (32–33).
IV. The psalmist exhorts the congregation to wait and trust because the LORD brings salvation and peace (34–40).

A. He exhorts them to wait on the LORD obediently because he will exalt them in the end (34).
B. He reminds them that the wicked will be cut off (35–38).
  1. He tells how he witnessed an arrogant person who passed away (35–36).
  2. He affirms that the blameless person has a future, but the wicked will be completely destroyed (37–38).
C. He concludes that the LORD is the salvation of the righteous and saves those who take refuge in him from the wicked (39–40).

COMMENTARY IN EXPOSITORY FORM

I. Perseverance in the faith will bring the enjoyment of God's blessings (1–6).

A. *It is futile to be anxious about sinful people for they will soon disappear (1–2).*

In the first six verses of the psalm the emphasis is on persevering in the faith, especially in view of the promise of blessing for righteousness (see Prov. 24:19; 3:31; and 23:17). The section begins with the admonition "Fret not" (אַל־תִּתְחַר).[28] It is

---

28. "Fret not" is the translation of אַל־תִּתְחַר. The verb חָרָה means "to burn, be kindled (especially of anger)." The noun related to this verb is חָרוֹן, meaning "(burning) anger"; it is often used in parallelism with אַף (see Ps. 2:5). In the *qal* system the word is used for being angry. It may be expressed either as "[anger] was kindled" (Gen. 39:19 and Exod. 32:10 for humans, and Num. 11:1,10 and Exod. 32:10 for God's anger burning), or "it was hot to him" (Gen. 4:5, 6 and Jon. 4:1, 4, and 9 for humans, and Psalm 18:8 for God).

In the *hiphil* stem the word is translated "fret"; it means "heat oneself in vexation." The word occurs four times, three here in Psalm 37 (1, 7, 8) and once in Proverbs 24:19 (where, in fact, the whole first verse of Psalm 37 is found almost word for word). It is hard to find the precise gloss, but "fret" comes closest; the idea is certainly much stronger than "get excited." It expresses a passionate intensity, a consuming indignation. Kraus says that it goes even further than that: it is a passionate frustration and inquiry about the power of the rule of God. It is senseless to fret, for fretting and being angry about the inequities of life are signs of

parizalleled with "do not envy" (אַל־תְּקַנָּא).[29] These warnings understand how easy it is to be affected by the prosperity and
influence of the world, but that is not detailed here. All that is
mentioned is "because of evil-doers" (מְרֵעִים; s.v. Ps. 10:15) and
"wrong-doers (עֹשֵׂי עַוְלָה, s.v. Ps. 43:1). Whatever they do should
not be a worry to the faithful; whatever they have should not be
envied by the faithful. To fret or to envy would be a weakness
of faith, and so the psalm will call on the people of God to trust
in him and live faithfully.

The reason for this admonition is that the wicked are transitory—they have nothing that will last. The image of grass (a
simile) is occasionally used in Scripture for the brevity of life. The
wicked may for a time appear to flourish, but they will fade like
the grass,[30] and wither like the green herb. These comparisons
suggest lost prosperity and influence even before death or divine
judgment. So then, the people of God should fear the one who
determines their destiny, and accordingly, desire things that are
eternal.

B. It is fitting to trust the LORD and do good because he fulfills the desires of the faithful (3–6).

Verse 3 signals the proper alternative to anxious fears and
desires: trust (בְּטַח; s.v. Ps. 4:5) in the LORD and do good (טוֹב;
s.v. Ps. 34:8). The idea is that the believers submit to the will of
the LORD and trust him to sort out the inequities and conflicts
of life. Their faith will be evidenced by their preoccupation with

---

mistrust (*Psalms 1–59*, p. 405). That is why the psalmist will immediately
advise faith and obedience, a faith that turns over all the cares of this life
to the LORD.

29. This verb can be translated as "to envy, be jealous," or "to be zealous." It
describes the passionate intensity in each case, in the positive sense to be
zealous to safeguard an institution or relationship, and in the negative
sense to burn with desire for something. In this verse, "fret not" addresses
the issue of anxiety over what the wicked can and will do, and "do not
envy" focuses on the issue of wanting what they have.

30. To appreciate the intended image one must think of grass in Israel where
water is scarce; the grass all but disappears in most regions once the rainy
season is over.

doing what is in harmony with God's will. This life of faithfulness is explained in practical terms in verse 3b: they are to dwell in the land and feed on his faithfulness. The idea of feeding on his faithfulness (rather than the proposed "tend sheep faithfully"[31]) means they should draw their spiritual strength and security from the faithfulness (אֱמוּנָה; s.v. Ps. 15:2) of God as they live their lives. The contrast presented here between them and the evil-doers is striking: they will enjoy the rich pasture as they live in the land and not fade or wither because God is faithful.

The second command (v. 4) is for the faithful to delight in the LORD and he will give them their petitions (מִשְׁאֲלֹת). As explained in Psalm 1, if the righteous delight in the LORD, then their petitions will be in harmony with his will. This is not a blanket promise that God gives people anything they desire; if their desire is in the LORD their petitions will be fitting. Then they will enjoy his faithfulness.

Verses 5 and 6 expand the call to trust. Here the verb is "commit" (גּוֹל, as in Psalm 22:8); it means "roll away," that is, cast the feelings of resentment, fear, and jealousy onto the LORD.[32] The reason they can and should do this is that he will act (יַעֲשֶׂה). How he will act is the expectation of the faith: he will bring forth their righteousness and their justice "like the light" and "like the noonday." Their righteousness and faithfulness will triumph over the world and its grim prospects. The similes associate the display of justice with the dawning of a new age, when God acts (see Prov. 4:18; Mal. 4:2). This dramatic change in the order of things, the destruction of wickedness and the triumph of righteousness, will display the sovereign rule of God and vindicate the way of faith.

---

31. See the discussion in VanGemeren, *Psalms,* p. 299. The change to "tend sheep faithfully," taking faithfulness adverbially, does make a better parallelism with "dwell in the land" in some ways, but there is no need for it to be somewhat synonymously parallel. As noted before, the Greek version confused the word with "wealth" to read "you will be fed with the wealth of it."

32. VanGemeren, *Psalms, p.* 298.

II. Perseverance in the faith will be rewarded in the day of judgment (7–20).

A. *The righteous must keep the faith to prevent doing evil (7–8).*

In the next section the call to persevere is strengthened by the reminder of the prospect of coming retribution. The first two verses issue the call, repeating the warning "fret not." The first line calls for the people to be still (דּוֹם from דָּמַם) before the LORD and wait patiently (הִתְחוֹלֵל from חוּל, a word that means "writhe," so in the *hithpolel* "waiting longingly")—the silent expectation clearly antithetical to anxieties and frustrated desires. The idea of being still is a calm resignation that leaves itself in the hands of God;[33] the idea of waiting patiently is the expectation of God's intervention. So against the ever present turmoil of anxious living and in contrast to the scheming of evil-doers, which seems to be succeeding, the righteous are to stop and to wait for the LORD to provide for them and protect them. After all, it is as Jesus said, people cannot add a day to their span of life by such anxieties (Matt. 6:27). So the admonition is repeated: do not fret. Now the text explains more about the evil-doers, for they are those who prosper (מַצְלִיחַ)—no one would worry about or envy an evil-doer who was a failure in everything—and those who carry out evil schemes (מְזִמּוֹת; s.v. Ps. 10:2). The evil-doers for a time prosper through their evil schemes; to fret over them is certainly short-sighted.

But the instruction goes beyond this. The righteous are instructed to turn away from anger (אַף; s.v. Ps. 30:5) and forsake wrath (חֵמָה), because it only leads to doing evil (אַךְ־לְהָרֵעַ), the very thing they faced from others (see also Ps. 73:2–3; 15; Gal. 5:20, 21, 26). To live with intense vexation and jealousy can lead to anger, and anger over the wrong things will produce acts that are like those of the evil-doers, or reprisals that use tactics just as evil.

B. *The righteous must know that evil-doers will be destroyed but they will inherit the earth (9–11).*

The righteous must yield to the LORD because he will deal

---

33. Perowne, *Psalms*, I:316.

with the inequities caused by the schemes of wicked people—and only he can. And so verse 9 offers the explanation (כִּי) that evil-doers will be cut off and the righteous will inherit the land. The idea of their being "cut off" (< כָּרַת) probably refers to their death by divine judgment in this context, although in other passages it can be used for excommunication from society or premature death. The point is that divine justice is coming. The point is elaborated on in verse 10, which says that in a little while the wicked will not be (אֵין). The parallel colon adds, "though you look carefully (וְהִתְבּוֹנַנְתָּ) for his place, he will not be *there*." By contrast, the meek (וַעֲנָוִים; s.v. Ps. 9:12), those who are dependent on the LORD and hope in him because of their limited resources and abilities, will inherit the land and delight in abundant peace. The word "delight" is here repeated from verse 4; there they were instructed to delight in the LORD, and here they will delight in peace (a contrast to the turmoil, suffering, and anxiety they faced). So that instruction was a call to live in the expectation of the fulfillment of the promises.

Kraus explains that it is over the land that fate turns in this psalm. Both the righteous and the wicked have the land as a pledge of blessing, but from the wicked it will be taken away because of what they have done. Because they did not receive the pledge of God's grace by faith, they forfeit their life and the land, but believers will inherit the promised blessing, in the present (Ps. 25:13) and in an eschatological sense (see Isa. 60:21; 65:9).[34]

C.The righteous must trust the LORD who prevents and punishes the wicked (12–20).

In this world the righteous are vulnerable to the attacks of the wicked. They are like prey. Verse 12 says the wicked plot (זָמַם; s.v. Ps. 10:2) against the righteous. They have schemes, hoping to ruin people who have faith and integrity. Their gnashing of their teeth may be a figurative description (an implied comparison with beasts of prey); or it may be a reference to their vicious jealousy and greed, as if snarling and gritting their teeth (Ps. 35:16; 112:12). Such is the malice and animosity of evil-doers.

---

34. *Psalms 1–59*, p. 406.

But the LORD laughs at him (them), as in Psalm 2:4. This anthropomorphic expression shows their schemes are laughable, feeble, and destined to fail. Why? Because, the psalmist explains, the LORD sees his (their) day comes (יָבֹא). The LORD already sees the day, i.e., the time and circumstances of their destruction (and so a metonymy of subject) approaching. It is inevitable; it is determined; and it is soon—in God's reckoning. The theme throughout this section is that the life and activity of the wicked has an end.

Verses 14 and 15 portray the attack of the wicked vividly. The sword and the bow are symbols of powerful destruction. The line could be referring to a literal attack by wicked enemies with weapons (synecdoches), or it could be referring to any kind of attack using the military images (implied comparisons). However they try to do it, their goal is to cause the poor and the needy to fall, i.e., to slay those who are upright in the way they live. They are not determined to destroy all who are poor and destitute, just the righteous among them. It is the righteous who pose a threat to the wicked, who are a reminder of coming judgment for sin. There is no place in their world for the upright; so they attack the vulnerable believers, but verse 15 says their attack will be turned back on them and they will be destroyed in their own devices. God is just; he may not act immediately, but he assures his people that there is a day of judgment coming for the wicked, perhaps an immediate judgment, but certainly an eschatological one.

In the middle of this section the psalmist adds a proverbial expression, "Better is the little that the righteous have than the abundance of many wicked." The implication is that the wicked deprived the righteous of most of their substance, but the little they have is better because the wicked will lose everything (v. 17; see Prov. 15:16; 16:8). The arms of the wicked will be broken, signifying that they will have no ability to fight (perhaps a synecdoche), but the righteous will be sustained by the LORD (סוֹמֵךְ). In God's time the wicked will be destroyed and the righteous will inherit the land. The LORD knows "the days of the blameless" (יְמֵי תְמִימִם; s.v. Ps. 7:9). The expression reminds us of the earlier statement that God sees the day of the wicked. Here he knows the ways of the blameless ("days" being a metonymy of subject for their activities as well as length of days). If God knows them it means that he is active in their affairs (see Ps. 1:6).[35] So the righteous are not only meek, poor and needy, they are blameless and upright; and because the LORD knows their ways, their heritage will remain forever (v. 18b).

Their prospects continue in verse 19. Because he knows them, they will not be put to shame (יֵבֹשׁוּ ; s.v. Ps. 31:1), meaning destroyed, and in the days of famine they will be satisfied. Their inheritance, primarily the land but also continued fellowship with the LORD, endures forever, even in the time of trouble or famine. They may not have much, but it will be sufficient. So they should dwell in the land and feed on his faithfulness.

By contrast the wicked will perish (v. 20). The text clarifies that they are "wicked" because they are enemies of the LORD. Earlier they were compared to grass that fades away, now they are compared to the "beauty of the pastures." The word "beauty" (יְקָר) probably describes what is in the pastures (so a metonymy of adjunct); it could refer to plants (Ps. 103:15), or animals (1 Sam. 15:9, 15). At the moment, it is beautiful and rich; but it will end suddenly—and this is all they have. The text then reiterates that "they vanish" (using כָּלוּ twice) in smoke. There is no reason here to see a reference to the smoke of the sacrifices, other than it too is smoke. Smoke vanishes, as indeed they will. The perfect tense may function as a prophetic perfect following the imperfect "they will perish"; or it could be referring to the fact that they also vanish here and now, and so an instantaneous perfect. The images are slightly different, the beauty of the field will disappear, smoke will vanish.

III. Perseverance in the faith will manifest itself in godliness and will enjoy God's protection and provision in this life and the life to come (21–33).

A. The LORD provides for the righteous in this life (21–26).

The psalmist now turns to the blessings of the righteous. A

---

35. See Herbert B. Huffmon, "The Treaty Background of Hebrew *Yada'*," *BASOR* 181 (1966):31–33.

description of one characteristic of the righteous begins and ends this section: they are gracious and giving (חוֹנֵן וְנוֹתֵן) in contrast to the greedy evil-doers who borrow but do not pay back (לֹא יְשַׁלֵּם; s.v. Ps. 38:3). The righteous understand grace, being the recipients of God's grace in so many ways, so they in turn show favor to other people who are in need and give them what they need. Kraus suggests that the evil-doers are unable to pay back what they borrow because of the LORD's judgment on them, but the righteous are in a position to help them.[36] This could be one way that the righteous might act, especially since they are described as gracious, but the line seems to have a broader application. Besides, the characteristic is applied to the righteous in general (Prov. 21:26).

The next verse further describes the blessing of the righteous: those blessed of the LORD (מְבֹרָכָיו; s.v. Ps. 5:12) will inherit the land; but those cursed by him (מְקֻלָּלָיו; s.v. Ps. 109:28) will be cut off. There is no clue that they might receive help from the righteous; rather, they will be removed and never enjoy the land (compare Prov. 10:30).

In verses 23 and 24 the psalmist elaborates on the point that the righteous are secure in the LORD. Their steps are established (כּוֹנָנוּ) by the LORD, and (or when) he delights [in] his way. The image indicates that all his activities are made secure and certain; and they are righteous activities because he delights in the LORD's way, meaning he does righteousness. Even if he falls, perhaps with the sin of envy, or perhaps under the attack of the evil-doers, he will not be cast headlong (יוּטָל). All the images (ways, falling, and being cast headlong) are implied comparisons for the experiences of living: if he gets into difficulties over the evil-doers' attacks, his troubles will not be fatal. This is because the LORD upholds him (סוֹמֵךְ as in v. 17) by the hand (see Prov. 20:24; 16:9).

Then, in verse 25 he reflects on how consistently the LORD provides for the righteous. Now older, he looks back over the experiences of life and says he has not seen the righteous forsaken or their children begging bread. This does not mean the righteous have never been in difficulties, because even in this psalm

---

36. *Psalms 1–59*, p. 406.

they endure famines like other people. But the LORD sustains his people so that they are never abandoned. This observation would certainly be true when the temple was functioning appropriately, because people in need could always go to the sanctuary and receive food from the ritual (Ps. 22:26 says "the poor will eat and rejoice"); and the Law made provision for the righteous to allow people to glean in their fields (Lev. 19:9–10). If everything was in place as God intended, the righteous would never go begging because the LORD made provisions for their needs in many ways.

The section closes with a reiteration of the characteristic of the righteous as generous (v. 26): they are gracious and lend (וּמַלְוֶה). According to Psalm 15:5 they were not allowed to charge interest, and so if they were truly righteous there would be no gain for them in lending to people in need (see Exod. 22:25; Ps. 112:5,9)—it would be a gracious and generous act. The verse adds this cryptic expression: "and his seed for a blessing"; it probably means that God's blessing extends to the next generation, i.e., they will be righteous and blessed and will aid others in the same way.

B. The LORD preserves the righteous from judgment on the wicked (27–33).

In the next seven verses the psalmist tells how the LORD preserves the righteous from the fate of the wicked. Here the section begins with the imperative, "Turn away from evil and do good." Before the calls were to trust in the LORD and do good, and now to turn from anger to avoid doing evil. To persevere in righteousness requires a determined rejection of evil and an intentional pursuit of good, and the result of such faithfulness would be that "you shall dwell forever."

The primary reason for faithfulness is that the LORD loves justice (אֹהֵב מִשְׁפָּט; v. 28) and will not forsake his beloved (חֲסִידָיו, those who have entered into covenant with him; s.v. Ps. 23:6). What is the evidence of their faith? First, we are told in verse 30 they utter wisdom (חָכְמָה; s.v. Ps. 19:7) and speak justice (מִשְׁפָּט; s.v. Ps. 9:4). Wisdom refers to their living a life that is honoring and valuable to God; and justice refers to their making right decisions. The way of wisdom and justice they promote is the way of the righteous in Proverbs (1:3). Second, their words are so characterized because the Law is in their hearts, preserving them from slipping. Since they know and believe the Law (see Ps. 40:6; 49:3; Jer. 31:33) they have good things to say that please God and help others. Righteous people are those who know the word of God, live by it, and readily communicate it. What they say will be wise and just, not malicious and selfish as the evil-doers.

In verse 33 the psalmist reiterates the theme of this section: the LORD preserves the righteous. The case here laid out is that the wicked set an ambush (compare Prov. 1:11–18), not simply intent on hurting or hindering the righteous, but destroying them. The evil-doers referred to here are certainly the worst kind. Their animosity is an adverse reaction in the extreme to wisdom and goodness. But the promise of God is clear: he will not abandon his people to their power.

Finally, he will not let the righteous be made guilty when judged (וְלֹא יַרְשִׁיעֶנּוּ בְּהִשָּׁפְטוֹ). This could mean that in this life God will not let the righteous be tried unjustly, perhaps a reference to the attempt by the evil-doers to slander and destroy the righteous; but history is filled with accounts to the contrary. The point probably is that even if the righteous were hauled into court, they would never be guilty as far as God was concerned (assuming they were truly righteous). As Perowne says, men may condemn, but God acquits.[37] Whatever the exact meaning of the line might be, the argument of the psalm is consistent, i.e., that God will save the righteous and rid the world of the wicked.

IV. Perseverance in the faith guarantees salvation and peace (34–40).

A. The LORD will exalt those who wait obediently on him (34).

Now, in the concluding section, the call is to "wait (קַוֵּה; s.v. Ps. 25:3) for the LORD and keep (שְׁמֹר; s.v. Ps. 12:7) his way."

---

37. *Psalms,* I:319.

Once again the call to persevere in the faith, now waiting for God to resolve the problem of evil, is joined to obedience. To keep the way of the LORD means to obey it, and the promise is that they will be exalted (וִירוֹמִמְךָ; s.v. Ps. 46:10) to inherit the land. They will be transferred from the place of weakness and vulnerability to the place of receiving the promises (Ps. 113:4–5). This will happen when they see the wicked cut off. "You will see" not only means to witness the event, but to look on in triumph. This expectation might be realized from time to time as God delivers his people, but it will be completely fulfilled at the end of time.

B. The LORD guarantees a future for them, but not for the wicked (35–38).

In the meantime, the psalmist describes what he has seen—wicked ruthless people (רָשָׁע עָרִיץ) flourishing. The translation "flourishing" (NIV) is an attempt to capture the meaning of a difficult expression. The verb (מִתְעָרֶה) has the idea of "showing oneself naked," but is interpreted in the sense of "spreading" like a luxuriant tree, i.e., displaying richness and influence. This line was translated into Greek with "lifting himself up like the cedars of Lebanon." The point is that the ruthless wicked people were flourishing, however we translate the difficult word.

Whoever the psalmist was referring to died and was no more (v. 36); and, as mentioned before in such cases (v. 10), he sought him but he could not be found. This incident is meant to be instructive: the wicked will fade away. As Proverbs reiterates, do not envy them for they will be cut off—there is a future yet to be fulfilled (23:17–18).

The psalmist then instructs the people to watch as they wait; for the righteous who live in peace have this future, but the wicked do not (vv. 37–38). The word "future" (אַחֲרִית) could be taken in the sense of a future posterity which would harmonize with the promise of inheriting the land (Jer. 31:17), but it is probably more general than this. Kraus's explanation is to the point: the end of believers is salvation. In this sense "end" or "future" (what comes after) is the conclusion to the way of life. In the future it will be evident how the conflict now in progress will turn out.[38] The end or future of transgressors will be complete destruction—they will be cut off.

C. The LORD saves those who take refuge in him (39–40).

The psalm closes reassuring the believers of their salvation (תְּשׁוּעָה; s.v. Ps. 3:2). The salvation of the righteous is from the LORD—so faith and not fretting is appropriate. He is the stronghold (a metaphor of protection and safety) in the time of trouble (עֵת צָרָה), which in verse 19 was called "an evil time." No matter what the difficulty might be, the LORD helps his people (for עָזַר s.v. Ps. 46:1) and delivers them (וַיְפַלְּטֵם)[39] from wicked people and saves them (וְיוֹשִׁיעֵם). The reason that he does so is their faith, specifically, "they take refuge in him" (חָסוּ בוֹ; s.v. Ps. 7:1).

MESSAGE AND APPLICATION

The exposition of this psalm should be fairly straightforward since it is didactic by nature. The problem behind the instructions is the age-old problem of the prosperity and power of the ungodly versus the deprivation and suffering of the righteous. In this light, then, the psalm instructs believers to trust in the LORD, live out their faith, and look for the final redemption.

---

38. *Psalms 1–59*, p. 407.

39. פלט means "to escape." The basic idea can be seen in the derived noun "fugitive" (פָּלִיט), one who escapes (as in the one who told Abram Lot had been captured; Gen. 14:13). There is also a noun מִפְלָט, a "place of escape" (Ps. 55:8); and a noun פְּלֵיטָה, "escape" in general (Gen. 32:9; Isa. 37:1).

The verb occurs in the causative *piel* system with the meaning "bring into security" or "deliver." The frequent use of the verb in the psalms carries this meaning (Ps. 22:4 and 8 as delivering in answer to prayers; this Psalm 37:40 for complete salvation; and several other passages as well [e.g., 31:1; 71:2]). The participle is used to refer to God as "my deliverer" (Ps. 18:2; 40:17; 144:2).

There are a couple of unusual uses as well. It is used in Job 21:10 in the sense of casting forth (cause to escape?) for calving. And the *hiphil* is used in Isaiah 5:29 in reference to Assyria like a lion carrying the prey away. This seems to be the opposite of "deliver," but it does retain the sense of taking something in security.

The promise is that God's providence will be vindicated, and so the life of righteousness will be rewarded, both in this life and at the end of the age. The immediate and repeated instruction of Psalm 37 is "fret not," but the psalm's collection of proverbial expressions and instructions will give the positive instructions that will enable people to avoid fretting. The main points of the outline will provide the four major summary instructions:

1. Persevere in the faith to enjoy the blessings of God.

2. Hold fast to integrity because a time of retribution is coming.

3. Demonstrate the faith by living a life of wisdom.

4. Wait patiently for the LORD because he brings salvation and peace.

One way to express a unifying expository idea for this full psalm would be in the form of a general statement that informs these instructions: *Those who live by faith and look for the coming of the Lord will not be anxious about this world's inequities but will rejoice in the Lord's blessings on the righteous.*

The apostle Paul instructs us to follow his example and press on in our faith, holding to that which we have received, because we await the Savior (Phil. 3:12–21). He then reiterates the point by instructing us to stand firm in the faith (4:1) and applies it specifically with the instruction to rejoice and to pray rather than be anxious. And the peace of God will guard our hearts (4:4–6).

PSALM 38

Prayer of a Sick Man Suffering Because of Sin

INTRODUCTION

Text and Textual Variants

A Psalm of David. To Bring to Remembrance.[1]

1 O LORD, do not rebuke me in your anger,
   nor[2] chasten me in your wrath.

2 For your arrows have sunk deep into me,
   and your hand has come down[3] upon me.
3 There is no soundness in my flesh
   because of your indignation;
   there is no[4] wholeness in my bones
   because of my sin.[5]

---

1. The word is the *hiphil* infinitive construct, לְהַזְכִּיר. One Greek translation adds περὶ σαββάτου, "for Sabbath."
2. A few manuscripts and the versions repeat the negative וְאַל.
3. The verb in the MT is וַתִּנְחַת, the same verb that is used in the first colon (נִחֲתוּ).The Greek version here reads καὶ ἐπεστήρισας, "clamped down," which would be the equivalent of וַתִּנְחַת. Some commentators believe it unlikely that the same verb would be used in both of the parallel lines, but the repetition of the same verb also occurs in verse 11 (although Kraus says that יַעֲמֹדוּ in that verse is hardly original [*Psalms 1–59*, p. 410]).
4. A few manuscripts and the Syriac have "and there is no."
5. The Greek, Symmachus, and the Syriac all have the plural.

4 For my iniquities have gone over my head;
    like[6] a heavy burden they have become too heavy for me.

5 My wounds stink, they fester[7]
    because of my foolishness.

6 I am utterly bowed down, I am brought very low;[8]
    all the day long I go about mourning.

7 For my loins are filled with inflammation,
    and there is no soundness in my flesh.

8 I am benumbed[9] and utterly crushed;[10]
    I roar on account of the moaning in my heart.

9 LORD, all my desire is for you,
    and my groaning is not hid from you.

10 My heart throbs, my strength fails,
    and the light of my eyes—even that has left me.[11]

11 My friends and my companions stand away from my
        plague,[12]
    and my neighbors stand far off.

12 Those who seek my life lay snares,
    and those who seek my harm discuss destruction;
        they ponder deceits all day long.

13 But I am like a deaf man; I do not hear;
    and like a dumb man who does not open his mouth.

14 I have become like a man *who* does not hear,
    and in whose mouth there are no arguments.

15 But in you, O LORD, do I hope.
    You[13] will answer, my Lord,[14] my God.

16 For I said, "Lest they rejoice concerning me;

---

6. The Syriac and the Vulgate have a conjunction, "and like a."
7. The Greek and the Syriac have a conjunction, "and fester."
8. The Greek and Jerome have a conjunction, "and brought low."
9. The Greek version has "I am afflicted."
10. The MT has נִדְכֵּיתִי, but a few manuscripts spell it נִדְכֵּאתִי.
11. The literal translation is simply "there is not with me."
12. The MT has מִנֶּגֶד נִגְעִי יַעֲמֹדוּ. For this line the Greek version reads ἐξ ἐναντίας μου ἤγγισαν καὶ ἔστησαν, "drew near before me (confronted me) and stood still." This would be equivalent to מִנֶּגְדִּי נָגְשׁוּ וַיַּעֲמֹדוּ.
13. A few manuscripts have the conjunction, "and you."
14. The text has אֲדֹנָי, but most manuscripts have יהוה.

when my foot slips, they boast over me."

17 For I am set to fall,[15]
   and my grief is continually before me.

18 For I declare my iniquity,
   I am distressed because of my sin.

19 But my enemies are living[16] and strong;
   and they that hate me wrongfully are many.

20 And they repay evil in the place of good;
   they oppose me[17] in the place of my pursuing[18] good.[19]

21 Do not forsake me, O LORD;
   O my God, do not be far from me.

22 Hasten[20] to my help,
   O Lord, my salvation.

Composition and Context

This is a prayer. It may be classified as an individual lament psalm, but not in the strict sense of the basic pattern of such psalms. The comparison with Psalm 6 is invited from the very first verse. Here the writer is afflicted with a serious illness. It

---

15. For MT's "for falling" (צֶ֫לַע) the Greek version interprets with μάστιγας, "scourges."

16. The syntax of the MT is difficult with the inclusion of חַיִּים, "living ones"; this reading is supported by the versions. But many commentators follow the suggestion in BHS to read הִנָּם, "gratuitously, without a cause" (Kraus says it is "consonant with the topicality" of the psalm; *Psalms 1–59*, p. 410). This, it is argued, makes a closer parallel with the second colon that describes the enemies as those who hate him for no reason, falsely (compare Pss. 35:19; 69:5). But since there is no textual support for the change, and since parallelism is not always so close, the MT reading should be retained.

17. The Hebrew יִשְׂטְנוּנִי is interpreted in the Greek version as ἐνδιέβαλλόν με, "slander me." The verb means "to be an adversary, to oppose, to accuse."

18. Both the K⁺thiv and the Q⁺re' are infinitives; the Q⁺re' is to be preferred, רׇדְפִי, "my pursuing."

19. The Greek version has "righteousness," and some manuscripts add a colon: "they cast me off, the beloved, like a horrid corpse."

20. The Greek text reads πρόσχες, "draw near, attend."

is such that even his close friends and family avoid him, and his enemies try to take advantage of the situation to ruin him. All of this causes him to examine his relationship to God. As a result he acknowledges that his sufferings are the result of his sin, and so his prayer has the tone of a deeply repentant spirit.[21] Briggs thinks the references to sin are secondary in the psalm,[22] but there is nothing to support that. Besides, the present form of the psalm is the material of the exposition.

There is nothing in the psalm that specifies the sin or the exact nature of the illness; therefore we have no clue as to the occasion. The superscription attributes the psalm to David, and apart from having no record of such an experience, there is no reason he could not have written it. It uses intense descriptions for the suffering, which may be somewhat hyperbolic. The fact that it was deposited in the sanctuary to be part of the collection indicates it would serve a liturgical purpose, at least, for others who similarly suffered, but other than that there is no formal association with cultic or liturgical practice. It probably was a literary composition designed for personal use.[23]

The superscription also says the psalm was "to make memorial" (לְהַזְכִּיר, "to cause to remember"). This note is also found in Psalm 70. It could be understood in the technical sense of the ritual, for in conjunction with the dedication offering the worshiper would offer a portion of the offering as a "memorial" (אַזְכָּרָה). It is possible that the psalm would have been chanted or sung when the "memorial" was being burned.[24]

While the word could suggest a connection to the memorial offering, it may simply be that the heading was intended to be a memorial of his sufferings or a reminder to God of his sufferings. Kidner says, "Since with God to remember is to act, this word

21. There is no reason to doubt that some sin was actually behind the suffering. Many passages show that illness was frequently considered a punishment from God for sin, although there were other explanations as well (see Mowinckel, *Praise of God in Israel's Worship,* II:2). One cannot simply conclude that every illness is the result of sin; but this psalm reminds the faithful that sometimes it is.

22. *Psalms,* I:335, 6.

23. Craigie, *Psalms*, pp. 302–3).

24. A. Cohen, *The Psalms,* Soncino Series, p. 117.

speaks of laying before Him a situation that cries out for His help."[25] Because the psalm belongs to complaints and prayers and not to thanksgivings, this interpretation is more likely.

The psalm begins and ends with prayer (verses 1 and 21–22), but the lament portion takes up verses 2–14. It laments the fact that God was punishing his sin, that he was in serious physical and emotional trouble, and that his enemies were ready to finish him. The confidence comes in verses 15–20 where the psalmist expresses his faith in the LORD to answer his prayer, giving several reasons why God should do it. What distinguishes this psalm from other laments is the extensive section describing his suffering and its cause.

Exegetical Analysis

Summary

Being severely chastened with illness and isolation by the LORD for personal sin, and being grievously attacked by opportunistic enemies, the psalmist pleads with the LORD to deliver him because he has confessed his sin and his hope is in the LORD.

Outline

I. The psalmist appeals to the LORD to stop chastening him in his wrath (1).
II. The psalmist laments his great suffering, isolation, and hostilities that have come upon him because of his sins (2–14).
  A. ("You") He portrays the suffering and anguish he has experienced as a result of God's chastening for sin (2–4).
    1. The LORD's powerful punishment has been heavy on him (2).
    2. The LORD's wrath for sin has brought overwhelming suffering to him (3,4).
  B. ("I") He describes his sickness and isolation that has driven him to seek God (5–11).

---

25. *Psalms 1–72*, p. 153.

1. The chastening has been so severe that he is crushed and feverish (5–8).
2. His pain has not been hidden from the LORD, whom he desires (9).
3. The chastening has depleted his health and weakened his sight (10).
4. His condition has driven his friends and companions away (11).

C. ("They") He laments the hostility of his opportunistic enemies and his inability to reply to them (12–14).
   1. His enemies have seen his suffering as the opportunity to get rid of him (12).
   2. Because of his suffering and sin he is unable to reply to his enemies (13–14).

III. The psalmist is confident that the LORD will answer him because his unjust enemies are ready to gloat, he is about to die, and he acknowledges his sin (15–20).

A. He hopes in the LORD and is confident he will answer his prayer (15).
B. He delineates the reasons for his confident dependence (16–20):
   1. His enemies are ready to gloat when he falls (16).
   2. He is on the verge of death (17).
   3. He acknowledges his sin and guilt (18).
   4. His many enemies, who are healthy and strong, repay his good with evil (19–20).

IV. The psalmist appeals to the LORD to answer his prayer by restoring him (21–22).

A. He entreats the LORD not to forsake him because he is his God (21).
B. He entreats the LORD to hasten to help him because he is his salvation (22).

COMMENTARY IN EXPOSITORY FORM

I. Believers who are being severely chastened for sin can only plead with God for relief (1)

The psalm begins with a plea that God's chastening be not

in wrath, i.e., that the suffering be disciplinary and not penal. The parallelism and word order of the first verse underscores his concern over the severity of God's dealing with him: "O LORD, do not in your anger rebuke me" and "do not in your wrath chasten me." While the text has only one occurrence of the negative (אַל), it is understood in the second colon. The verbs refer to God's rebuke (תוֹכִיחֵנִי) and chastening (תְיַסְּרֵנִי). The two verbs are very close in meaning; "rebuke" (יָכַח) means to correct by word as well as punishment, while chasten (יָסַר; s.v. Ps. 6:1) means to correct by punishment but with instruction as well.[26] He prays that God's anger not be unleashed on him. By acknowledging that it

---

26. The verb יָכַח occurs in the *hiphil* verbal system primarily and has the meanings "decide, adjudge, prove." It is a legal term that may refer to the initiating of the controversy or dispute with rebuke or correction, or the dispute or decision in general, or the result of the conflict, either conviction with rebuke or acquittal.

First, we see it used in the general sense of judging: the Messiah will judge righteously (Isa. 11:3).

Second, there is one use in Genesis 24:14 where the word has the sense of "appoint."

Third, the word is used with the meaning of proving, or showing one to be right (Job 19:5).

Fourth, and much more frequent, is the negative result of the dispute. It has the idea of God's reproving or chiding the people in Psalm 50:8, and of convicting them of their sin in the same passage (v. 21). Humans also can reprove, as Abraham did with Abimelech over the wells of water (Gen. 21:25).

The rebuke of God can also emphasize that the purpose is correction. Proverbs 3:12 tells us that the LORD rebukes those he loves, as a father his son in whom he delights. The LORD warned the kings in the Davidic covenant that he would discipline them when they sinned (2 Sam. 7:14). Such correcting would most often be with pain (Job 33:19), and it is from this that the psalmist's wanted relief so that God's rebuke would not be with wrath (Pss. 6:1; 38:1).

There is a significant use of the *niphal* verb in Isaiah 1:18, traditionally translated "come, let us reason together." A better rendering would be "Come, let us settle this dispute," for the passage is not calling for divine chastening, but an end to it.

There are a couple of nouns related to this verb. תוֹכֵחָה is "rebuke, correction" (Ps. 149:7). And תוֹכַחַת is a "reproof" or "argument." It has the sense of "argument" in Psalm 38:14 where it refers to the psalmist's inability or unwillingness to argue his case (see also Hab. 2:1). The meaning "reproof" is common in the Book of Proverbs (see Prov. 3:11; such reproof

is divine chastening, he is acknowledging that his plight is due to sin. By acknowledging this indirectly, he hopes that God will deliver him from both the sickness and the sin. The psalm will show that he does not simply want a less severe punishment but deliverance from any punishment whatsoever. This initial verse sets the tone for his lament and his prayer.[27]

II. Their plea must acknowledge that their suffering and isolation is due to their sin (2–14).

A. They must acknowledge that their suffering is divine chastening for sin (2–4).

After the initial plea, verse 2 focuses on the severe suffering that the psalmist was experiencing under divine discipline. The first description mentions God's arrows, and the parallel line, God's hand. The arrows are certainly figurative; they could refer to the affliction itself, as illness in the ancient world was often described as arrows from the deity (*Resheph* in Canaan), and the LORD certainly did send such afflictions for sin (Lam. 3:12). The figure would be a comparison between arrows and the "attack" of God. The hand of God is figurative as well (anthropomorphic), signifying his power.

In this verse one verb is used for both the arrows and the hand of God. The first use of the verb (נִחֲתוּ, the *niphal perfect of* נָחַת) means "to penetrate, sink into," fitting for the description of the effect of God's "arrows." The second use of the verb (וַתִּנְחַת, the *qal*) means "and you pressed" your hand heavily upon me. The affliction that was sent by God penetrated his very being, and it weighed heavily upon him.

In verse 3 the psalmist describes his condition as a result of God's discipline. First, we may note his pathetic condition: there was no soundness (מְתֹם; s.v. Ps. 7:8) in his body, meaning

---

is for discipline [6:23] and gives life [15:31]). Finally, it has the meaning of "correction" in Proverbs 29:15 as well as Psalms 39:11 and 73:14.

27. The verse is almost identical to the first verse of Psalm 6, except that here קֶצֶף is used and not אַף for "anger." The use of that verse ties the two passages together; the interpretation of aspects of Psalm 6 will be applicable here as well.

there was no place in his body that was well but that he was afflicted everywhere; and there was no wholeness (שָׁלוֹם)[28] in his

---

28. The word for "wholeness" is שָׁלוֹם. The related participle מְשַׁלְּמֵי, "those who repay," is used in verse 20. A brief survey of this word would be helpful for the study of this and other psalms.

The main verb שָׁלַם means "be complete, sound" in the *qal* stem, and "complete, requite" in the *piel*. There are several related nouns: the most common is שָׁלוֹם, which can mean "completeness, soundness, welfare," and of course "peace"; then there is שָׁלֵם, "complete, safe, at peace"; and שֶׁלֶם, "peace offering."

The verb occurs a few times in the *qal*. It describes something as complete, or ended, such as the temple (1 Kings 7:51); or it means someone is sound or uninjured (Job 9:14).

The verb has a wider range of meanings in the *piel/pual* system. First, it can have the basic causative idea for something being made complete, that is, "to complete" something (the temple, 1 Kings 9:25). A second category has the meaning "to make whole, restore." It is used in this sense in Leviticus 24:18 for making compensation, and in 2 Kings 4:7 for paying a debt. A third use is that of paying vows, or making good on vows (e.g., Psalms 50:14; 66:13). Then, it can also be used with the meaning "reward, requite, recompense." It is used this way in Ruth 2:12 in the desire that the LORD reward Ruth's faithfulness. The reward is a response to works done (2 Sam. 3:39; Ps. 31:23), but on occasion the good seems to be "rewarded" with evil (Gen. 44:4; Psalms 35:12; 38:20).

The *hiphil* meaning is "complete, perform." In Isaiah 38:12–13, the king Hezekiah laments that in his suffering the LORD was making an end of him.

The noun שָׁלוֹם has a similar range of meanings. First, it can mean "completeness," as in referring to Judah being completely carried captive (Jer. 13:19). Second, it can mean "soundness," as in Psalm 38:3, but also in Isaiah 38:17, and in Job 5:24 with the additional sense of safety. Third, it can mean "health," as when someone asks about a person's welfare (Gen. 43:27), or similarly "prosperity" (Ps. 122:6). And fourth, it can mean "peace." This may refer to tranquility in life (Gen. 15:15). It may be used in reference to a relationship, such as a man of peace, meaning a friend. More significantly it is used with God in the covenant (Num. 6:26; Mal. 2:5; Isa. 54:10). It may, of course, refer to peace from war (Isa. 9:5; Mic. 5:4; Josh. 9:15). Within the covenant relationship, peace is often paralleled with "righteousness" (Isa. 53:5; Ps. 125:5); peace and righteousness both refer to right order (72:3, 7).

In the Book of Psalms שָׁלוֹם has a wide range of meanings: security (4:8), calmness or tranquility (29:11; 35:27), possession and enjoyment of the land (37:11), health (38:3), freedom from the threat of enemies (55:18), prosperity (73:3), protection from misfortunes (119:165), and in general,

bones (a metonymy meaning within his boney framework, in his whole person). The word "wholeness" refers to his health and well-being—nothing within him was well.

The reason for this condition is expressed in two clauses that follow these parallel descriptions: there is no soundness, because of God's indignation; there is no wholeness, because of his sin. The word for indignation (זַעַם) has the sense of boiling up; God's anger had reached the point of being poured out on the psalmist because of his sin. Sin is the cause of the indignation, and the indignation is the cause of the bodily derangement. The discipline involved a total affliction that left no part of the psalmist unaffected.

Verse 4 expands the description of his suffering by explaining the effect of his sin on him. He first states that his iniquities have passed over his head. The text does not state the complete image being used here, but it seem most likely he is using the idea of a flood (see Pss. 18:4–5; 69:2). His iniquities would therefore be compared to deep flood waters that have engulfed him and he is drowning. It is possible that "iniquities" means more than his sins; it could also mean the guilt for the iniquities, or the punishment for them (and so a metonymy). It would be difficult in this verse to separate his feeling of being overwhelmed because of his sins from his suffering for them. The second figure of the verse compares his iniquities (and their punishment) to an intolerable burden that presses down on him. The simile indicates that the load of sin and its consequences is too heavy to be carried any further. This verse may not be a confession of sin, *per se*, but it certainly acknowledges that the underlying cause of all his trouble is sin.

B. They will realize their only source of help when pouring out their complaint (5–11).

In the next few verses the psalmist laments his deplorable sickness and again acknowledges that he brought it on himself;

---

the heart of divine blessing (147:14). In general, the term defines the relationship between God and man, linking heaven and earth, and portrays the outworking of that connection in many spheres of existence. See further F. J. Stendebach, "*šālôm*" in TDOT, edited by G. J. Botterweck, H. Ringgren, and Heinz-Josef Fabry, XV:13–48.

because of his condition and because of his sin he is driven back
to God, the only one who can help him.

In verses 5–8 he laments his affliction. He begins by describing his wounds (בּוּרֹת) as giving off an offensive smell. The
verb (הִבְאִישׁוּ from בָּאַשׁ) means "to make something foul and repulsive." Moreover, he says they fester (נָמַקּוּ). The two verbs stress
the excessive distress of his body; the first notes the offensive
smell, and the second the discharge of infectious matter. It is almost impossible to know from this what kind of sickness he had;
the language could be hyperbolic, but need not be. Whatever his
horrible condition was, he makes it clear that it was caused by
his "folly" (אִוַּלְת). His sin was folly because it brought him to this;
and because of this condition, sin is seen in its true light, for all
sin is folly.[29] At least he is spiritual enough to recognize it is folly.

According to verse 6 he has been bowed down and brought
very low. The difference between these two verbs is one of emphasis. The first verb (נַעֲוֵיתִי, the *niphal* from עָוָה) has the sense
of being distorted, writhing, or convulsing. He is basically bent
over, perhaps because of the pain. The second verb (שַׁחֹתִי, the
perfect tense of שָׁחַח) has the idea of being brought down with
sickness, sinking low, or depressing, perhaps prostrate in humiliation. So he says, "I am bent over (with pain) and brought down
(with sickness)." Then, in the parallel colon of the verse he claims
to go about mourning all day long. The verb in this stem (the intensive use of the *piel*, הִלָּכְתִּי) indicates his utter restlessness, and
"mourning" (קֹדֵר) depicts a dark grief over the painful condition.

He tries to explain this in verses 7 and 8, but he cannot do
much more than reiterate his ghastly condition.[30] He first says
that his loins are filled with inflammation (נִקְלֶה),[31] and then repeats his idea from above that there is no soundness in his flesh.
In verse 8 he says that he is feeble (נְפוּגוֹתִי) and utterly crushed
(וְנִדְכֵּיתִי). Along with his moaning within himself (מִנַּהֲמַת לִבִּי), he
says that he "roars." This verb "roars" (שָׁאַגְתִּי) might seem out

---

29. Perowne, *Psalms*, I:322.
30. Briggs says that כִּי could be the intensive "yea" rather than a causal "for"
    (*Psalms*, I:342); but most versions take it to mean "for" in the passage. The
    NIV does not translate it.
31. NIV interprets this as his back had searing pain.

of place here since he would not seem to have the strength to roar but only moan. The word is used for the roaring of a lion, or for the sound of thunder or soldiers; but it also is used for people from whom the pain or grief they experience wrings forth an uncontrolled roaring sound that is incoherent. It is used in this way in Psalm 22:2 for the sufferer's crying to God for help even though near death. This sudden sound that the sufferer emits comes from the moaning in guilt and pain in his innermost being. Beyond his actual physical and spiritual pain, his frustration and fear are expressed in this line of the psalm.

In verses 9–11 the psalmist expresses his desire for the LORD to release him from his plight because he is growing weaker and everyone else has abandoned him. In the midst of describing all his pain and suffering he can muster confidence that his plight is not hidden from God. Verse 9 begins with that statement: "Lord (אֲדֹנָי), all my desire is before you." "My desire" (תַּאֲוָתִי), or "my longing," refers to what he desires (and so a metonymy of cause), i.e., his restoration to health and reconciliation to the LORD.[32] God knows what he longs for because his groaning is not hid from him (the understatement, tapeinosis, meaning just the opposite, that God knows all about his pain and suffering; compare Exodus 2:24). It is a great comfort to him in the time of his affliction that God is intimately aware of every roaring complaint and every soft moan. Therefore, the sufferer will turn to him in confidence.

The LORD is the only one who can help him in his deteriorating condition (v. 10); his condition seems hopeless. He says his heart "palpitates" and his strength "fails." The word translated "palpitate" or "throbs" occurs only here (סְחַרְחַר, a pe'al'al form of the verb; GKC #55e, p. 152). The unusual form of the verb emphasizes movements made in quick succession, here, of the heart beating feverishly.[33] In addition he says that his strength has failed (literally, forsaken him).

The parallel expression focuses on his eyes. The construction

---

32. Dahood suggests the translation "sighing": "all the sighing of my heart," similar to the moaning within his heart (*Psalms*, I:233).

33. Goldingay says it does not mean "palpitate"; rather, it is from a verb that means to go on a journey. So he says the idea is that of taking flight, as in the feeling in suffering that a hole was left in the heart (*Psalms 1–41*, p. 545). Kraus' explanation makes far more sense. He says it means "flit to

is cryptic: "and the light of my eyes, even they are not with me." The image of the loss of the light of his eyes indicates that he no longer has clear perception, but it is not impossible that he is referring to the loss of actual sight. If his strength is fading, his heart racing, and his body weakening in pain, then the loss of clear sight would simply underscore what all the expressions signify, that he is dying.

And to make matters worse, if that were possible, his friends and neighbors have abandoned him (v. 11). He is isolated in his misery. The verse refers to his friends (אֹהֲבַי, "those who love me"), his companions (רֵעַי), and his neighbors (קְרוֹבַי, "those near me"), the very people one would have expected to come to his assistance. Those who love him and are his companions stand away from his plague (stroke, wounds), and those near to him stand far off. The verb (עָמַד) is used twice in the verse, first as the imperfect, and then the perfect tense. While it is possible that a distinction is intended in the two tenses, i.e., that his friends were standing away from his wounds considering what to do, but his neighbors had already stood far off, it is more likely that the two verbs should be given parallel nuances. He is simply describing the aloofness of these so-called intimate friends.

C. They will have nothing to say when their enemies seek to exploit their plight (12–14).

In the last three verses of the lament section the psalmist describes how his opportunistic enemies seize the opportunity of his sickness to destroy him completely. He finds that in his weakened condition and with his realization that his own sin has brought this on, he has no reply for them. He chooses not to respond to their malicious accusations.

Verse 12 describes the hostility of his enemies. His enemies are introduced as people who seek his life. They certainly contributed to his low condition for they added insult to injury, aggravating his trouble by trying to destroy him completely. These people did not cause the sickness, but like vicious animals they

---

and fro," meaning that fear has prompted the disjointed pounding of the heart (*Psalms 1–59*, p. 413).

saw the wounded prey and were ready to take him down. They did not leave him at peace in his misery, but lay snares for him (וַיְנַקְשׁוּ). The second description of them is that they seek his ruin (his painful calamity, רָעָתִי). Not satisfied with killing him, they also want to bring more evil on him, and so they speak of destruction (הַוּוֹת). Finally, the verse says that all day they plot (יֶהְגּוּ; s.v. Ps. 2:1) deception (מִרְמוֹת; s.v. Ps. 5:7). So, from this verse we learn that his enemies were seeking ways to inflict as much damage and destruction on him as they used his plight to destroy his life. The emphasis at the end of the verse suggests that they busied themselves with deceptive accusations and criticisms of the suffering psalmist, all in the attempt to ruin him once and for all.

In contrast to their busy tongues, he is silent. He uses the similes of being like a deaf man who hears nothing, or a dumb man who does not speak. He has become like a man who does not hear them and who has no replies in his mouth. The psalmist feels isolated from his friends and companions and is silently absorbed in his suffering. He does not listen to the destructive comments of his enemies and does not reply to them.[34] His condition is beyond their accusations or their ability to manipulate. The psalmist is waiting for the LORD to restore him to health and reconcile him to himself. There would be no value in taking on deceptive and malicious enemies.

III. Their plea must be based on a confidence in the LORD that is supported by solid reasons (15–20).

A. They must affirm their confidence that the LORD will answer their prayer (15).

The tone of the psalm shifts to confident expectation with verse 15: "But (כִּי) in you, O LORD, do I hope (הוֹחָלְתִּי; s.v. Ps. 31:24); you will answer, my Lord, my God." This verse is distinctive in that it

---

34. It is also possible that because his sickness is the result of his sin he knows that he cannot vindicate himself before their malicious accusations; he can only wait for the LORD to forgive him and set things right.

includes both the praise of God and the confession of trust:[35] his hope is in the LORD, and his confidence is that he will answer his prayer. The subject of the verb in the second colon is made emphatic by the additional pronoun: "You, you will answer."

B. They must have solid reasons for their confidence (16–20).

1. God will not let the wicked gloat (16).

The psalmist now gives several reasons for his confident expectation of answered prayer. The first is that God will not let the wicked rejoice over his destruction (compare Ps. 30:1). Verse 16 says, "For I have said, 'Lest they rejoice over me." The line has an idiomatic use of the word "lest" (פֶּן), meaning "what if they rejoice." His appeal was that they would not rejoice over him." The psalmist knows that if his foot were to slip, meaning if he fell irretrievably in his sickness (that is, die, or perhaps lose his health and be incapacitated), they would boast (הִגְדִּילוּ). They already were delighted over his sickness; the LORD's deliverance would prevent them from celebrating triumphantly over his demise.

2. God will not let him die in grief (17).

A second reason that God will answer the prayer is the fact that he is near death. He says, "I am ready to fall (לְצֶלַע נָכוֹן)," that is, set for a fall. And his grief was continually before him. There was nothing short of divine intervention that would change his constant expectation of death——and God is a saving God.

3. God will receive his confession of sin (18).

A third reason that God would look favorably on him now is his confession of sin: "I declare (אַגִּיד) my iniquities; I am troubled

---

35. Westermann says that praise of God and confession of trust are very intimately related to each other in these types of clauses (that begin with "but"). He adds that the fact that confession of trust, certainty of being heard, and praise of God cannot be clearly distinguished here but merge with one another corresponds to the fact which has been mentioned earlier: no hard and fast boundary can be drawn in the category of petitions of the individual between petitions that have been heard and those that remain open (*The Praise of God in the Psalms,* p. 74).

(אֶדְאַג) because of my sin." Even if "iniquities" were interpreted metonymically here to mean the punishment for the sin, the verse would still be an acknowledgment of his sin. By making known his iniquities (the sin and all its effects), he was confessing. The parallel line does not simply express concern over his present distress but his future as well. The verb means "troubled, anxious, worried" over the future—it stresses that he had a foreboding of the future more than a grief over the past. It is the nature of sin to fill the sinner with guilty fears, but by confessing his sin he gives God the most important reason to bring the chastening to an end.

4. God will not allow the wicked to repay good with evil (19–20).

The wicked are treating him unjustly. They are vigorous and strong (v. 19); they do not appear to be sick and dying as he is (of course, this is what the psalmist sees from his illness; they do die). Rather, they seem to keep on living and remain strong. The text is a little difficult here; it reads, "But my enemies, living ones, are strong" (וְאֹיְבַי חַיִּים עָצֵמוּ). Many commentators have problems with the word "living" in this context; they prefer the word "without a cause" (חִנָּם) instead.[36] This parallels the expression in the second colon that the enemies hate him "wrongfully" (שֶׁקֶר). The suggestion is certainly appealing, but it has no manuscript support. The emphasis on "living" also makes sense in the context. The psalmist looks upon himself as more dead than alive, set to fall completely, while his foes are living and vigorous. And they have no reason to be his enemies, according to the parallel line. The word "wrongfully" means falsely, to a false purpose—they had no reason to oppose him and take advantage of his sickness.

The issue was more fundamental than personal hatred, according to verse 20. It was the age-old conflict between good and evil. The initial participle (מְשַׁלְּמֵי) describes them as people who repay him with evil (רָעָה; s.v. Ps. 10:15) in the place of good (טוֹב; s.v. Ps. 34:8). The second half of the verse reiterates the point: they oppose him because he pursues good. The verb translated "oppose me" (יִשְׂטְנוּנִי) is from a verb (שָׂטַן) that means "to be an adversary"

---

36. See Craigie, *Psalms*, pp. 301–2; Kraus, *Psalms 1–59*, p. 410)

(from which is derived the word "Satan"). In this conflict with his enemies, he pursues good, but they oppose him and try to bring painful calamity on him. He may not always achieve the good, but he pursues it; and they may not achieve the evil they plan, but that is the course they were on. The contrast could not be clearer. To the psalmist, God will not allow evil to triumph over good. He may have sinned and brought this sickness on himself, but he has confessed his sin and can expect God to restore him, if for no other reason than to prevent evil people from doing greater evil.

IV. Their plea for immediate help must be based on their personal relationship with the LORD (21–22).

A. The LORD should not forsake them because he is their God (21).

The psalmist now closes the psalm with a renewed plea. Verse 21 expresses it negatively: "Do not forsake me" (אַל־תַּעַזְבֵנִי) and "do not be far (אַל־תִּרְחַק) from me." The intended meaning is the opposite, of course, because the LORD is his God. It is a plea for God to make his presence known by attending to his needs.

B. The LORD should hasten to help them because he is their salvation (22).

The positive side of the appeal stresses the urgency of the situation: "Hurry to my help" (חוּשָׁה לְעֶזְרָתִי). In verse 21 he addressed his prayer "O LORD, my God"; now he addresses it to "O Lord, my salvation" (אֲדֹנָי תְּשׁוּעָתִי). Calling God his salvation is figurative; God is the Savior who will save him (and so he substitutes the effect, salvation, for the cause, Savior). And salvation is what he means by the word "help" (s.v. Ps. 46:1).[37]

---

37. Craigie reminds us of similar uses of these appeals in Psalm 22. "Do not abandon/forsake" in verse 21a is found in Ps. 22:1; "do not be far off" in verse 21b is found in Psalm 22:11; and "hurry to my help" in verse 22a is found in Psalm 22:19 (*Psalms,* p. 305). The difference between the two laments, though, is that there is not a word of confession of sin in Psalm 22, whereas in Psalm 38 that is the underlying cause of the need.

MESSAGE AND APPLICATION

Among the penitential psalms this passage is unique, in a disturbing way. The suffering psalmist appeals to God for relief from the chastening for sin in only the first and last verses; but he never explains what the sin was, and he gives no hint of the resolution of his dilemma. One would assume the sin was serious because of the extreme nature of the punishment. Perhaps the nature of the sin has been deliberately excluded so that people guilty of any number of sins might appropriate this psalm for relief from chastening.

The bulk of the passage is given over to a detailed description of the chastening he has received for sin: he details his severe illness, his burden of guilt, the estrangement of his friends, and the plots of his enemies. Sections of the psalm are reminiscent of the complaints of Job, but with the mention of the response of his enemies this psalm appeals to God to prevent injustice by bringing relief. The psalmist is confident that God will give him relief because he trusts in God, has confessed his sin, and knows that God will not let the opponents take advantage of this situation to ruin him.

So we may word the central expository idea in this way: *Those who put their hope in the LORD may pray with confidence to be healed from severe chastening when they acknowledge their sin.* The entire psalm may be applied in two ways. First, believers are warned not to take sin lightly. The Bible does make it clear that God will chasten people who persist in sin (see Ps. 6 and Ps. 119:67). Second, believers are encouraged, admonished, to pray to the LORD for relief when there is divine chastening. If they acknowledge their sin and do not try to conceal it or rationalize it, not only will there be forgiveness but also relief from the chastening of God, no matter how severe the sin might be. This psalm is primarily concerned with chastening for sin and not the natural consequences of a sin which may be irreversible.

PSALM 39

The Prayer of a Desperately Sick Man

INTRODUCTION

Text and Textual Variants

To the Chief Musician. To Jeduthun.[1]
A Psalm of David.

1 I said, "I will keep watch over my ways
   to keep from sinning with my tongue;
  I will keep[2] a muzzle[3] on my mouth
     while the wicked are yet[4] before me."
2 I remained silent and still;[5]
    I was silent apart from good,[6]
       but my anguish was stirred up.
3 My heart became hot within me,

---

1. This is the K^e*thiv;* the Q^e*re'* is "Jedithun."
2. The MT repeats the verb "keep, guard"; but the Greek rendering is "I set" (ἐθέμην) which would be the equivalent of אָשִׂימָה; it may have been chosen because of the next textual difficulty.
3. For "muzzle," מַחְסוֹם, the Greek version has "a guard, a watch" (φυλακὴν). The interpretation of "guard" may have influenced the interpretation of the verb to "I set." The Syriac reads "from violence" (מֵחָמָס).
4. The Greek version has "as sinners banded together" (ἐν τῷ συστῆναι); this would reflect a form בַּעֲמֹד instead of בְּעֹד in the MT.
5. The Greek reads "humbled," ἐταπεινώθην.
6. The line in the MT is cryptic: "I was silent from good." The Greek has "good things" (ἀγαθῶν). The various interpretations of the line will be dealt with in the commentary.

in my musing a fire began to burn.
Finally I spoke with my tongue.

4 O LORD, cause me to know my end
and what is the measure[7] of my days;
let me know how transitory[8] I am.[9]

5 Behold, you have made my days as handbreadths,[10]
and my duration as nothing before you;
surely every[11] man standing firm[12] is only a breath.
Selah.

6 Surely as a shadow a man walks to and fro;
surely they are in commotion as a breath.
He heaps up *possessions*
but he does not know who will gather them.[13]

7 And now, what do I wait for,[14] Lord?[15]
My hope[16]—it is in you.

---

7. Greek has ἀριθμὸν, "number."

8. חָדֵל refers to that which ceases, or has an end; and so a translation of "frail" or "transitory" works. The Greek interpreted it with ὑστερῶ, "what I lack."

9. This last clause is simply "how I cease." See further Richard J. Clifford, "What Does the Psalmist Ask for in Psalm 39:5 and 90:12?" *JBL* 119 (2000):59–66.

10. A handbreadth is a little under three inches, about four fingers across. The plural indicates several handbreadths. The Greek manuscripts differ, "old," παλαιάς, or "a span long," παλαιστάς.

11. The MT reads "all vanity every man standing firm." The use of כָּל with "vanity" may have arisen by dittography; it is not in a large number of manuscripts or the Syriac.

12. The form in MT, נִצָּב, "standing firm," has been questioned by a number of scholars (see e.g., D. W. Thomas, "נצב in Psalm XXXIX 6," Studies in the Bible. Fs. for M. H. Segal, *Publication of the Israel Society for Biblical Research* 17 [1964]:10–16). Weiser (*Psalms*, p. 327) interprets it as "self-assured." Kraus (*Psalms 1–59*, p. 416) accepts the repointed form נֶצֶב, "seedling." The Greek has "every man living" (ζῶν).

13. The MT uses the participle with a suffix, "their gatherer," i.e., [who] will gather them. The Greek version retains the subject from the sentence, "for whom he shall gather it" (συνάξει αὐτά).

14. The Greek version has the noun, "my hope," ἡ ὑπομονή μου, reading תִּקְוָתִי.

15. The text has אֲדֹנָי, but many manuscripts have the tetragrammaton.

16. The Greek version may have understood this word to be the ground of hope, because they used "my ground, my existence," ἡ ὑπόστασίς μου.

8 From all my transgressions, deliver me;
  do not[17] make me the reproach of fools.
9 I was silent; I would not open my mouth,
  because you have done *this*.[18]
10 Remove your stroke from me;
  by the blow[19] of your hand I am overcome.
11 With rebukes for iniquity you chasten a man;
  and, as a moth[20] you dissolve his precious things;[21]
  Surely every man is a breath. *Selah*.

12 Hear my prayer, O LORD,
  and to my cry for help give ear;
to my tears[22] do not be silent,[23]
  for I am a sojourner with you,
  a settler like all my fathers.
13 Look away[24] from me,
  that I may be cheerful *again*
  before I go and am no more.

---

17. The Greek does not have the negative אַל translated (perhaps dittography); as a result it has a positive statement, ἔδωκάς με, "you have made me."
18. The MT has the simple perfect tense עָשִׂיתָ; the Greek reads ὁ ποιήσας με, "[you are] he that did it" (= עֹשֵׂנִי), or, "made me."
19. The word תִּגְרָה (occurring only here) means "hostility, blow"; the Greek version has ἀπὸ τῆς ἰσχύος, "from the strength [of your hand]," perhaps thinking of מִגְּבוּרַת.
20. Greek has ὡς ἀράχνην, "like a spider," perhaps a spider's web.
21. חֲמוּדוֹ is a little unclear. It refers to that which is lovely, or precious, perhaps "his beauty" or "his wealth" that is dear to him.
22. The word is literally "my tear," signifying tears; some translations interpret it as "weeping."
23. Because the MT reverses the word order in a couple of places, the word order and line division in the Greek version is different: both have "Hear my prayer, O LORD," but then MT has "and [to] my cries give ear" but the Greek has "and my supplications" to complete the first line; MT then has "to my tears do not be silent," and the Greek has "attend to (for give ear) my tears"; then the Greek is left with "do not be silent." Given the word order and the unusual connections (do not be silent to my tears), it is easy to see how the version made its translation.
24. The MT's הָשַׁע is problematic; it means "smear"—"smear your eyes away"? Kraus says it was surely a slip of the pen for שְׁעֵה, "look" (*Psalms 1–59*, p. 416). The Greek version has ἄνες, "spare" me, or "let me be."

Composition and Context

This psalm is a lament of an individual, and because it contains confession with the lament, it is penitential as well. The prayer is distinct because it has close ties with Job and Ecclesiastes (compare "vanity" in this psalm with Eccl. 1:2 and 12:8, for example).[25] The very personal nature of the expressions in the psalm indicate that it was of private origin and not composed for cultic use, even though when added to the sanctuary collection it would be applicable to other situations. The general thinking is that the poem comes from the Persian period, but Kraus acknowledges that there are no firm clues for the setting, noting that wisdom traditions that can be traced back to Egyptian literature have in later times shaped Psalm 39.[26] Whether the psalm was Davidic or from a later period, its description of suffering under God's chastening hand is timeless.

Here we have a sorrowful prayer of a suffering believer who has been chastened by God for sin. His suffering is so serious that he contemplates the frailty and brevity of life, wondering how many more days he has on earth. He tried to accept the suffering silently, afraid that if he complained too much when unbelievers were around he would sin against God and give fools reason to reproach his faith. As the suffering became more intense and his anguish grew, he could not keep his pent-up feelings to himself; he had to speak. But he spoke to God, not to an unsympathetic world. He wanted to know more about the vanity of life, for it all seemed hopeless to him, except in God's light. There he had hope. His may have been a lament of great sadness, a prayer of desperation; but it was not without hope. Because he hoped in the LORD, he poured out his complaint to him and prayed for help.

The first three verses provide the circumstances of his dilemma, his suffering and his desire not to say the wrong thing about it to the wrong people. The rest of the psalm concerns his feelings: verses 4–6 record his desire to understand the vanity of

---

25. See Broyles, *Psalms*, p. 187.
26. *Psalm 1–59*, p. 417.

life, and verses 7–13 record his prayer for deliverance from sin
and its chastening so that he might enjoy his remaining days in
God's favor.

Exegetical Analysis

Summary

Having accepted that human life is but a vanishing breath on
earth, the psalmist casts himself upon God's care while he lives,
hoping that the chastening would stop so that he might enjoy his
remaining days.

Outline

I. The psalmist relates how he remained silent concerning his
   pain while the wicked were present until his sorrow stirred
   him to speak (1–3).
   A. He resolved to remain silent concerning his pain while
      the wicked were present so that he would not sin against
      God by faulting him (1).
   B. He remained silent but his pent-up emotions were
      stirred up (2).
   C. He was compelled to speak (3).
II. The psalmist presents his petition to understand the
    brevity of life because he knows that God has made it brief
    and frail (4–6).
    A. He prays to be taught about the brevity of life (4).
    B. He bases his appeal on the awareness that God has
       made life brief and frail (5–6).
       1. The span of his days was nothing before God (5a).
       2. Every man is transitory like a vapor even though his
          time is spent in commotion and gathering (5b–6).
III. The psalmist petitions the LORD to deliver him from his
     sin and its chastening so that he might enjoy the rest of his
     life (7–13).
     A. He affirms that his hope is in the LORD (7).
     B. He asks for deliverance from his transgressions to avoid
        the reproach of fools (8).

C. He asks for the chastening to be removed because divine discipline is convicting and all consuming (9–11).
D. He asks for his suffering to end so that he might enjoy what life he has left (12–13).
  1. The LORD should respond to his tearful cry because he is a sojourner (12).
  2. The LORD should let up on the chastening so that his remaining days might be enjoyable (13).

COMMENTARY IN EXPOSITORY FORM

I. Even though believers try to avoid faulting God for their chastening before unbelievers, their pent-up sufferings are hard to contain (1–3).

A. The truly repentant believer will not fault God for his chastening in the presence of unbelievers (1–2).

The psalm begins with the psalmist's report of his effort to avoid sinning by talking about his chastening while ungodly people were present. It was a deliberate decision: "I said" (a definite past verb) fixes the circumstances of this decision prior to the writing of the psalm. That it refers to a time of severe chastening is evident from verses 8–13. He feared that he might bring reproach upon the LORD and those who trusted in him by complaining to unbelievers about the way the LORD was treating him in the chastening. So he resolved (cohortative) to "keep" watch (אֶשְׁמְרָה; s.v. Ps. 12:7) over his ways, and "keep" (the same verb form) a muzzle (מַחְסוֹם) on his mouth while unbelievers were present (literally "yet before me"). If he guarded himself, he would keep from sinning any more. The construction used is an infinitive with a preposition, "from sinning" (מֵחֲטוֹא; s.v. Ps. 51:1). This indicates what he was guarding against—sinning with his tongue, i.e., saying something wrong or to the wrong people. It could also be interpreted as the intended result: "I will guard my ways so as not to sin." He was determined to silence himself, so he used the image of a muzzle (an implied comparison). The word "muzzle" comes from a verb that means "restrain" (חָסַם). He would exercise self-restraint in speaking (similarly, Ps. 73:15 tells how the sage wisely kept his doubts to himself).

According to verse 2, then, he "remained silent in stillness" (נֶאֱלַמְתִּי דוּמִיָּה). The verb refers to past time: "I was silent"; and the noun modifies the verb: "I kept silent in stillness."[27] The two words emphasize that he remained completely silent.

He also says he kept silent "from good" (הֶחֱשֵׁיתִי מִטּוֹב). This prepositional phrase is difficult to interpret. Delitzsch says that the psalmist in his silence was "turning from prosperity," or taking no note of prosperity, i.e., from that in which he saw the evil-doer rejoicing; he tried to silence the troubling disparity between their prosperity and the righteous life.[28] Others say it has the idea of "to no avail" or "no use"—I kept silent apart from good, meaning, it did me no good.[29] Goldingay says it could be rendered "I was silent more than it was good."[30] Perowne argues that the preposition after the verb "be silent" would mean either (1) "far from good" (I silenced myself from comfort and joy, i.e., without comfort and joy—I had no comfort or joy), or (2) as the negative consequence of the silence "so that it was not well with me" or "it did not work."[31] This second option would then be paralleled by "my sorrow was stirred." In other words, he tried to keep silent, but it did not go well for him and so he had to speak. Whatever he meant by the phrase, the point is that he was not able to maintain this decision to be completely silent. The sorrow or pain (כְּאֵב, from the verb כָּאַב, "to be in pain") refers to mental and physical pain (in disappointment and disaster) which the psalmist would surely suffer because he struggled with the problem of his own pain and his distance from the good aspects of life he tried to ignore. Gradually, all this began to stir so he could not control his pent-up feelings.

B. Believers should pour out their hearts to God when their pain is intense (3).

His stress and pain became so severe that he finally had

27. Broyles, *Psalms,* p. 346.
28. *Psalms,* II:28.
29. Kidner, *Genesis 1–72,* p. 156.
30. *Psalms 1–41,* p. 553.
31. *Psalms,* I:327, 330–31.

to speak out—but he spoke to the LORD. His heart became "hot" (חַם) because in his contemplation of things a "fire began to burn." These are figures for his increasing anguish over his painful dilemma (possibly metonymical if he was fevered). Burning within is an idea in Scripture that is connected with passionate intensity that moves people to action (see Jer. 20:9; Luke 24:32)—here it is the pain and anguish that moves him to cry out. The verb "burn" (תִּבְעַר) may be translated "began to burn" or "was burning" because the agitation was increasing to the point of his not being able to remain silent. The burning took place during his "musing," the idea being that the more he thought about it the more painful it became. The word translated "musing" may actually be a word for "sighing" (from הָגָג, "to long for, burn," and not from הָגָה, "to meditate, muse."[32] Finally he could contain himself no longer and spoke out loud ("with my tongue") in complaint to the LORD (v. 4). It may be that this speaking out seemed to be faulting God with his words and was included in his confession in verse 9; or, more likely, the speaking out here is simply his cry to God about his anguish and not directed to unbelievers and so would not need forgiveness. At any rate, the remainder of the psalm comprises what he spoke with his tongue: he spoke to the LORD about his sorrow, his sin, and his remaining years.

II. Believers who suffer want to understand their prospects for life because they know that life is brief and transitory (4–6).

A. Sufferers want to know about the brevity of life (4).

1. They are concerned with the time they have left.

This is a common concern among people who come near to death in their suffering. Beginning with verse 4, the psalmist seeks answers about life, and much of the rest of the psalm is a series of petitions with laments about life intermingled with them. Using an imperative of request, "cause me to know" (הוֹדִיעֵנִי), with a tone of frustration and anxiety, he urgently requests the LORD

---

32. VanGemeren, *Psalms,* p. 359.

to reveal his end and inform him of the measure of his life. "My end" (קֵצִּי) is linked to a verb that means "cut off, end," or "exterminate"; in his suffering he has in mind the end of his life. The parallel expression underscores this with "the measure of his days." "Days" refers to the amount of time he has left to live (a synecdoche); using days makes it seem less than if he had said "the measure of my years." He has become very aware of his mortality.

2. They are concerned about their frailty.

The next portion of the petition is the request (a cohortative) to know how frail he was (מֶה־חָדֵל). This word "frail" is related to a verb that means "to cease, come to an end, cease to be" (חָדֵל). "Transitory" is a good interpretation of the idea. In his grief and frustration the psalmist wants the LORD to let him know how frail he is, which will tell him how long his life will last. He knew his chastening was sufficiently severe to end his life soon. After this emotional outburst, the psalmist presents a comparatively mild lament and gives a wise discourse on the transitoriness of humans.

B. Sufferers realize their life is brief and frail (5–6).

1. Their life span is nothing compared to God (5a).

Here the psalmist laments the shortness of days, especially in view of his personal affliction, and then, with an apparent understanding of God's sovereignty and infinite wisdom, he acknowledges the transitory nature of human life in general. His mood seems to be changing here to one of resignation or confident submission to an all-wise God. He first acknowledges God made his life as "handbreadths." This figure (an implied comparison) expresses the short duration of the psalmist's days; and if the plural form means in brief periods of time, it strengthens the idea that his life is eked out in short time spans. Moreover, the duration of his life (חֶלְדִּי, "my duration") is as nothing before God. His life is brief, made even more brief because of an apparent imminent end; and whatever he has is nothing in comparison to God.

2. They acknowledge that everyone is frail even though they pretend otherwise.

The keen observation on life begins with the particle "surely" (אַךְ). The truth expressed here is that every person "standing firm" (נִצָּב, perhaps "self-assured") is nothing more than a wisp of air, a breath, a vapor (הֶבֶל—a key word in Ecclesiastes).The participle "standing firm" is used to describe people at their best, standing firm for a purpose. Even though when people are at their strongest, or when they present the image of strength, they are but a breath—gone suddenly.

Furthermore, the human is just like a shadow moving about. Once again the particle (אַךְ) begins the clause. The expression (בְּצֶלֶם) is "as a shadow" (it uses the *beth* of essence [as] to signify the nature of the person). The word is an unusual use of the familiar word "image," the word used in Genesis to describe the nature and function of people as God created them; but the psalmist gives it a different twist, saying that due to the brevity of life people appear only as images, replicas of the real thing. The use would stress the nature of the person as somewhere between unreal and presenting a false image, almost ghost-like walking around in daily activities.

The verse continues with the description of human activity that contrasts with reality: people's lives are busy and filled with gaining things, but they are a shadow. "They are in commotion (יֶהֱמָיוּן) vainly" (הֶבֶל again), or, they are filled with activity, but over a fleeting life, a breath as it were. An individual heaps up (יִצְבֹּר) possessions but does not know who will gather them (אֹסְפָם, "their gatherer," the participle with the suffix serving as the objective genitive). People spend all their lives accumulating things, but when they die they have no idea who will have them. How futile! (Ps. 49:10—they leave their wealth to others).

III. Because their hope is in the LORD, suffering believers pray for forgiveness and restoration so that they might enjoy the rest of their lives (7–13).

A. Chastened believers hold fast to their hope in the LORD (7).

The verse begins with "and now," marking a turning point in the psalm. Verse 7, therefore, is a transition to expressions of faith. He addresses God as "Lord" (although other manuscripts have the holy name LORD—Yahweh), and asks, "For what do I wait?" (קִוִּיתִי, s.v. Ps. 25:3). The verb is an instantaneous perfect, and so translated as a present tense. This verb "wait, hope" captures some of the tension in waiting as well as the faith that waits patiently. The psalmist had silently endured the chastening until the burning anguish compelled him to speak out. For what was he waiting? He answers his own question, making his question somewhat rhetorical: "my hope—it is for you, LORD." "My hope" is a synonym of the above verb (תּוֹחַלְתִּי from יָחַל; s.v. Ps. 31:24); it too means a patient endurance. He has no choice but to wait and hope in the LORD, because there is no other deliverer from God's chastening than God himself. The remainder of the psalm will demonstrate this waiting and hoping as he prays to God to intervene on his behalf.

B. Chastened believers pray for relief from sin to avoid the reproach of fools (8).

This verse begins with a request for deliverance (הַצִּילֵנִי; s.v. Ps. 22:20) from his transgressions (פֶּשַׁע; s.v. Ps. 51:1). The word "deliver" here means forgive the sin and remove its consequences. His sins were rebellious acts, committed by a refusal to submit to God's authority. They caused his chastening in the first place; but now this includes his disquieting thoughts and inability to deal with his anguish.

He desires God to deliver him so that he would not be a reproach (חֶרְפָּה; s.v. Ps. 22:6) of fools. A reproach is a cutting taunt, a mockery; and the "fool" (נָבָל, Ps. 14:1) is the one who has no regard for God or his ways—or his people. If the psalmist did not find forgiveness for his sin and relief from his chastening, such fools would have mocked him and his faith.

C. Chastened believers pray for the discipline to end because it is convicting and consuming (9–11).

If believers acknowledge their suffering is a result of

chastening, they in essence have confessed and thus are able to ask for restoration. Here the psalmist repeats from verses 2 and 3 that he remained silent and did not open (a preterite verb) his mouth, because God had chastened him ("because you have done *this*"). His resolution to be silent he says was fulfilled: "I was silent." But then he did open his mouth and speak to God. The silence vowed in the preceding verse had reference merely to disloyal complaints, not prayer.[33] The psalmist seems now to understand his suffering a little more clearly—it was chastening from the LORD, and chastening has the purpose of correcting and instructing. This recognition that it was from the LORD is strengthened in his acknowledgment by the emphatic use of the pronoun "You": "You have done *this*."

He petitions the LORD to remove the chastening because it was consuming him (v. 10). This verse begins with a direct imperative, "remove" (הָסֵר), expressing the urgency of the matter. He appeals for respite because the chastening was so severe that his very life was threatened. He wants God to remove his "stroke" (נִגְעֶךָ), a word that is used figuratively (an implied comparison), especially of diseases regarded as sent by God for chastening for sin. This "stroke" almost killed him: "I am consumed" (אֲנִי כָלִיתִי), i.e., finished. The LORD had brought him to the end of himself, to a place of weakness and complete dependence, so that he might turn to the LORD his only hope.

Just as he earlier made an observation of the transitory nature of people when petitioning God about the frailty he felt, here too he makes an observation about the LORD's chastening when petitioning for it to end (v. 11). God's discipline consumes people. The main verb "you discipline" (יִסַּרְתָּ; s.v. Ps. 6:1) describes God's characteristic or regular activity. His chastening is with rebukes (בְּתוֹכָחוֹת), the synonym for the word for chastening. This intensifies God's corrective purpose.

When God chastens people they find their "precious" things consumed. The word could refer to their life, their appearance, or their possessions, perhaps all of them in one idea—their life, what they cherished and enjoyed. Human nature is frail and

---

33. Alexander, *Psalms*, p. 176.

fleeting; people may build a precious life and hope it lasts, but God can take it down in a single blow.

The word for sin here is "iniquity" (עָוֹן; s.v. Ps. 32:5); it means going astray, waywardness. It here applies generically to the sins of people and is thus appropriate for the observation that includes the LORD's dealings with all people.

D. Chastened believers desire the discipline to end so that they may enjoy the rest of their lives (12–13).

1. Because people are like sojourners they call on God for help (12).

The psalmist now appeals to the LORD to end the suffering, pleading with him to respond to his tearful cry. The reason for his cry is that he is a "sojourner" (גֵּר), a somewhat archaic word that captures the idea well. A sojourner was a temporary dweller in the land with no inheritance rights and only some conceded rights. He was like a passing guest. The parallel word he uses to describe himself is "settler" (תּוֹשָׁב), which may signify a temporary dweller. The psalmist is appealing for help as someone who does not have many rights. Sojourners and settlers were generally poor (except for the patriarchal families) and dependent on the good will of the permanent residents in the land. The idea is fitting for Israel as well, because the land belonged to the LORD and the people were temporary settlers, dependent on his favor (see Lev. 26:23). All believers in this sense are strangers, which is why they pray for favor instead of demanding their rights.[34] As a stranger the psalmist was appealing for special protective care. He was asking God to do what he required his people to do for strangers.

2. They pray for God to let up on them so they can enjoy life (13).

The psalmist does not know how long he has to live, but whatever it is he would like to enjoy it. The verb "look away" is a

---

34. See A. A. M. Beuken, "Psalm 39: Some Aspects of the Old Testament Understanding of Prayer," *Heythrop Journal* 19 (1978):1–11.

figure (anthropomorphism), expressing his desire for God to let up on him—stop paying so much attention to his sin. The reason for this request is "that I may be made cheerful" (וְאַבְלִיגָה). This is a cohortative, but after the imperative it is subordinated as a purpose clause. It is the psalmist's final petition requesting the LORD to end the chastening before it ends him. The last clause of the psalm renews his concern that he might die—go away and be no more.

MESSAGE AND APPLICATION

In the midst of great suffering at the hand of a chastening God, the psalmist was made aware of the brevity of life, his in particular. It is at such times that people realize their lives could end in the suffering. They can only conclude that life is a vapor, a fleeting breath (הֶבֶל); the figure describes the insufficiency of all that is earthy—it is fleeting, it won't last. This lack of permanence and failure of strength is the condition of everyone. The suffering psalmist was faced with the immediate reality; and as time passed his feelings became so intense that his complaints might have sounded like disloyalty to God if expressed in the wrong company.[35] But this believer was responsible; when he could not control his burning anguish he poured out his pent-up frustration—to God. He expressed a desire to learn, a desire for forgiveness, but most of all a desire for the suffering to end so that whatever time he had left could be enjoyable. He never gave up hope.

This psalm provides an essential message for the spiritual life; it will resonate with almost every believer who has had to deal with sin and sorrow.[36] The message could be captured in a number of ways, but one expository idea that will work is this: *Believers who are severely chastened for sin and faced with the frailty and uncertainty of life must pour out their complaint to*

---

35. Kidner, *Psalms 1–72*, p. 156.
36. It will be helpful in the exposition to remind people that this is suffering because of chastening for sin. Not all suffering is caused by sin. People should be reminded of the different reasons for suffering, and perhaps pointed to psalms that deal with sufferings that are not punishment for sin (like Ps. 44).

the LORD (and not to the unsympathetic world) because he is their only hope of deliverance. No one, not the psalmist or the modern believer, can accept suffering like this without being filled with anguish and the need to pour out their complaint. This is human; and it is fine, as long as they speak to the LORD. Oh, they may share their need with other believers and even receive counsel, but ultimately the complaint and the petition have to be addressed to the LORD. No one else can deliver them; no one else can assure them an enjoyable future. The focus on the LORD in this and any suffering is essential, because in the pain all life becomes dubious, but the focus on the LORD transforms it into hope. The New Testament also reminds us that life is transitory, that we are sojourners in this world. But we have a hope in the LORD that transcends all pain, especially pain that we bring on ourselves by sin (see Heb. 11:13; 1 Pet. 2:11).

PSALM 40

The Song of Sacrificial Service

INTRODUCTION

Text and Textual Variants

To the Chief Musician. A Psalm of David.

1 I waited patiently for the LORD;
    he turned to me and heard my cry.
2 He drew me up from the pit of destruction,
    out of the miry clay,
  and set my feet upon a rock,
    making my steps secure.[1]
3 He put a new song in my mouth,
    praise to our God.
  Many will see and fear,
    and put their trust in the LORD.
4 Blessed is the one who makes the LORD his trust,[2]
    and who does not turn to the proud,
      to those who go astray after a lie.[3]
5 You have multiplied, O LORD my God,
    your wondrous deeds and your thoughts toward us;[4]

---

1. The Greek has interpreted this as "he directed my steps."
2. The Greek interprets the verb "makes," שׂם, as the noun "name," שֵׁם: "whose hope is in the name of the LORD."
3. The line is simplified in the Greek text as οὐκ ἐνέβλεψεν εἰς ματαιότητας καὶ μανίας ψευδεῖς, "has not regarded vanities and false delusions."
4. The prepositional phrase "toward us" is not in the Greek version.

they cannot be set in order to you!
I will proclaim and tell of them,
   yet they are too numerous to declare.

6 Sacrifice and offering you have not desired.
   but you have dug ears[5] for me.
Burnt offering and sin offering you have not required.
7 Then I said, "Here, I have come;
   in the scroll of the book it is prescribed for me;
8 I desire to do your will, O my God;
   your law is within my heart."
9 I have proclaimed the glad news of righteousness
   in the great congregation;
Indeed, I have not restrained my lips
   as you know, O LORD.
10 I have not hidden your righteousness within my heart;
   I have spoken of your faithfulness and your salvation.
I have not concealed your loyal love and your faithfulness
   from the great congregation.

11 As for you, O LORD, you will not restrain[6] your mercy from
    me;
   your steadfast love and your faithfulness will ever pre-
    serve me.[7]
12 For evils have encompassed me beyond number;

---

5. The expression in the MT is very precise: "ears you dug for me," but the
Greek translation has σῶμα δὲ κατηρτίσω μοι, "a body you have prepared
for me." This is the text that appears in Hebrews 10:5, 7. The other Greek
versions and some manuscripts of the LXX have ὠτία, "ears." One theory
to explain the change is that the words written in uncials were confused:
the word ΩΤΙΑ changed to ΣΩΜΑ, the sigma being repeated from the
previous word, and the ΤΙ being changed into Μ. The more likely explanation is that the Greek version provided an interpretation for the idiom.
The psalmist used the part, "ears," for the whole, "body." There is also
the theory that the reading in the Book of Hebrews crept into the Greek
manuscript of the Psalm, but this is less likely.
6. Many commentators take the line as a prayer (the verb, an imperfect of
injunction), "do not restrain." This is the interpretation in the Greek version as well. The form will be discussed in the commentary section.
7. The Greek has a past tense translation here.

> my iniquities have overtaken me and I cannot see;
> > they are more than the hairs of my head;
> > my heart fails me.

13 Be pleased, O LORD, to deliver me!
> O LORD, make haste[8] to help me!

14 Let those be put to shame and disappointed altogether
> who seek to snatch away my life;
> let those be turned back and brought to dishonor
> who desire my hurt!

15 Let those be appalled[9] because of their shame
> who say to me, "Aha, Aha!"

16 But let them all rejoice and be glad in you,
> who seek you;
> let them continually say, "Great is the LORD,"
> who love your salvation.

17 As for me, I am poor and needy,
> but the LORD takes thought for me.
> You are my help and my deliverer;
> > O my God, do not delay.

Composition and Content

Psalm 40 provides a good opportunity to address the topic of sacrificial service—dedication to do the will of God. The emphasis on dedication comes in the middle of the psalm as a response to God's great saving acts and as a basis for the prayer for urgent deliverance.

Psalm 40, therefore, seems to be made up of two psalms, a praise and a prayer. The first part is a declarative praise or thanksgiving psalm; it has the report of the deliverance with its lesson and its praise, as well as a vow of dedication. The last part of the psalm is a prayer based on the psalmist's experience

---

8. The interpretation in the Greek version is "draw near (πρόσχες) to help me."

9. The MT has "let them be appalled because of their shame"; the Greek has "let them quickly receive shame for their reward," using κομισάσθωσαν (= יָשֹׁמּוּ), and instead of "because" (עַל־עֵקֶב) παραχρῆμα, "quickly, immediately."

of deliverance expressed in his praise to the LORD. Since he had not failed to praise God for the deliverance, he was confident that God would not fail him in his current crisis. The sequence may be worded as a series of principles: divine intervention inspires genuine praise, and genuine praise leads to personal dedication, and spiritual dedication is essential to prayer.

Not everyone is convinced that two psalms have been put together to form one.[10] It could be an individual unified composition, like Psalm 27, with the praise preceding the petition. There is some overlap of language in the two parts, and a repetitive style. Psalm 40 is part of a liturgy that begins with thanksgiving and a dedicatory vow and moves to lament and then prayer. Craigie follows Eaton in calling the psalm a royal psalm;[11] the appropriate setting to him would be the vow of the king to obey the laws of the kings (Deut. 17:14–20). There is nothing in the psalm that indicates it is a royal psalm; it no doubt could be used by a king, but it would have had a wider use in the worshiping community. Kraus identifies the psalm as a prophetically inspired thanksgiving from the post-exilic times,[12] but the psalm could have come from any time in the Israelite period because prophetic instruction concerning empty ritual can be found in many of the prophets.

As a psalm of sacrificial service, Psalm 40 was also recognized by the apostle as typological of the dedication of Jesus Christ, that is, the psalm finds its fullest meaning in his incarnation and willing obedience to do the will of the Father. So the exposition of the psalm must first deal with the original meaning and application, and then include its use in the Book of Hebrews.

Even if the psalm is a unit, its parts still unfold along the line of a thanksgiving followed by the prayer. The structure of the psalm is identified differently by the commentaries. For example, Kraus divides it in two, verses 1–11 being the praise, and verses 12–17 the prayer. Goldingay has 1–12 as the first part, and 13–17 as the prayer (because it forms Psalm 70). Craigie

---

10. Craigie, *Psalms*, pp. 313–4.
11. Craigie, *Psalms*, p. 315. See also John H. Eaton, *Kingship and the Psalms* (London: SCM Press, 1976), pp. 42–44.
12. *Psalms 1–59*, p. 424.

has 1–10 as the thanksgiving, 11 as the prayer, and 12–17 the lament. In this discussion verses 1–11 are taken as the thanksgiving, ending with the psalmist's affirmation of his loyalty to God and his confidence in future deliverance. Then, verses 12–17 will be taken as the prayer, beginning with the description of the dilemma in verse 12, and the petitions in 13–17. This is one very workable way to deal with the structure, although verses 9–12 could be arranged differently without changing the overall meaning.

Exegetical Analysis

Summary

Having gladly offered himself as an obedient servant to God because of the wondrous acts of deliverance he experienced, the psalmist prays for a hasty rescue from the multitude of present evils.

Outline

I. Because of God's wondrous acts of salvation, the psalmist gladly offers himself as an obedient servant to God, attests his loyalty in praising God, and expresses his confidence in God's continuing protection (1–11).

   A. He joyously tells of his deliverance and exhorts the congregation to put their trust in the LORD (1–4).

      1. He reports that after a long period of prayer God rescued him and gave him reason to praise (1–3a).

      2. Confident that many will trust the LORD through his experience he calls attention to the bliss of those who turn to the LORD and not to some false hope (3b–4).

   B. He offers himself as an obedient servant to the LORD because of his wonderful acts (5–8).

      1. He praises God for his innumerable and wonderful acts (5).

      2. Acknowledging that God desires his life more than a sacrifice, he yields himself to do the will of God (6–8).

        a. Dedication: He gives his life to God.

        b. Direction: He obey's God's word.

   c. Desire: He resolves to do God's will.

C. He attests that he has published the tidings of the LORD to the congregation (9–10).

D. He expresses his confidence that the LORD's faithful love and mercy will preserve him (11).

II. Because the LORD is his help and deliverer, the psalmist pleads for the LORD to deliver him quickly from the evils he must endure from those who would ruin him so that the righteous who seek the LORD might join him in praise (12–17).

A. He laments that he has been overtaken by evils (12).

B. He prays for a quick deliverance from the wicked so that the greatness of the LORD might be declared (13–16)

   1. He prays for a hasty deliverance in which those who were trying to ruin him would be brought to devastating shame (13–15).

   2. He prays that God would deliver him so that all who seek the LORD for deliverance might declare the greatness of God (16).

C. He prays that the LORD not tarry in helping him because he is in great need (17).

COMMENTARY IN EXPOSITORY FORM

I. Because of God's mighty saving acts, the faithful believers owe their lives to him (1–11).

A. God inspires praise by his wondrous acts of salvation (1–5).

In the first five verses we have the psalmist's praise. What is clearly proclaimed here is that God delivers people from their troubles in order that they might declare his works to others.

1. God's acts of salvation are truly amazing (1–3a).

In typical declarative praise fashion, the psalm begins with a report of the deliverance. First, there is a summary statement: "I waited patiently for the LORD, he turned to me and heard my cry." It had apparently been an arduous, persistent prayer, as the verbal construction indicates (קַוֹּה קִוִּיתִי; s.v. Ps. 25:3); the verb "wait" suggests tension and concern but with expectancy, and the infinitive absolute stresses the perseverance. God eventually intervened, and the psalm reports the deliverance with dramatic images. The distress is termed a "slimy pit" (literally, "a pit of destruction," בּוֹר שָׁאוֹן) and "miry clay" (literally, "mud of mire," מִיט הַיָּוֵן). It is not impossible that these were real circumstances. People occasionally got into old, broken cisterns, perhaps hiding there, or perhaps thrown into one by enemies (see, e.g., Gen. 37:14, although there the pit had no water). Broken cisterns would have some water seeping from cracks in the walls and forming muddy footing. If the psalmist had not actually been in such a pit, then he would be using the language figuratively to say it was as if he was mired down in such a horrible pit (and the figures would be implied comparisons). The images of mud and mire in a pit would suggest depressing surroundings, complete helplessness, darkening doubts, and spiritual affliction.[13]

Out of this "mess" the LORD drew him up (וַיַּעֲלֵנִי) and set (וַיָּקֶם; s.v. Ps. 3:1) his feet on a rock, making his standing secure (כּוֹנֵן; s.v. Ps. 93:1). The descriptions are figures as well. If he had been in such a pit and was literally drawn out to stand on solid footing, God would have caused it to happen, perhaps through people who rescued him (so the figures would be metonymies of cause); but if the description of his plight was an implied comparison, then the same would apply here as well—he was delivered from his difficulty by God just as one would draw a victim out of a pit. If this is the interpretation, we do not know exactly what the dilemma was, but it was as hopeless as being in a pit, and as marvelous as being pulled out.

But what a contrast! Not only did God set him free by lifting him out of the pit, but he also made him safe and secure by setting his feet on a rock. The point is that God can deliver people who are in deep trouble, any kind of trouble, unable to free themselves from their difficulties, and oppressed by their

---

13. Kraus says that the two images describe the subterranean chaotic abode of the dead (see 69:2, 14) and here indicate that the life of the psalmist had been almost extinguished as the domain of death had him (*Psalms 1–59*, p. 444). Craigie, who argues for this psalm being a royal psalm, says the images must refer to a military crisis of some kind (*Psalms*, p. 315).

circumstances, and give them security and confidence. Even if the difficulties are the result of foolish choices, or the spiritual life is mired in sin and its consequences, God stands ready to deliver those who wait patiently on the LORD for relief. Waiting patiently is an act of faith; it implies an active faith, watching and praying earnestly until the release comes.

The effect of such an amazing deliverance is public praise to the LORD; so verse 3 says, "He put a new song in my mouth, praise (תְּהִלָּה; s.v. Ps. 33:1) to our God." The "new song" is a new reason for singing praise to God—the deliverance in answer to prayer (and so it is a metonymy of effect). God gave him the reason to sing, or in other words, God delivered him in order that he might praise. Since this was a new deliverance, it was a new song God gave him. Praise is the natural and necessary response to such acts of God.[14]

2. Public praise encourages the faith of others (3b–4).

The psalmist knew full well why God wanted praise—"many will see and fear[15] and put their trust (וְיִבְטָחוּ; s.v. Ps. 4:5) in the LORD." In his praise the psalmist is also teaching that there is no help if they turn to the proud (רְהָבִים) or those who go astray after a lie (שָׂטֵי כָזָב); they will find no such deliverance there. They are deluded, following a lie (a mirage as the term would allow). When people listened to this praise, they would learn the true source of salvation was the LORD—and this was no lie, for the truth was a reality in the psalmist's life. God delivers those who trust in him.

All too often, though, when those with great spiritual needs are looking for help, something to trust in, the people of God are silent—there is no declarative praise.

3. Praise must focus on God's wonderful works (5).

This psalmist now attests that he did not keep silent. In fact, in verses 9 and 10 he affirms emphatically that he was faithful to offer to God the sacrifice of praise. Here he tells of all God's

---

14. Goldingay emphasizes this point by saying that an act of deliverance is never complete until it has led to the worshiper's offering praise (*Psalms 1–41*, p. 570).

15. The verbs form a wordplay on the line: יִרְאוּ רַבִּים וְיִירָאוּ.

works: "You have multiplied, O LORD my God, your wondrous deeds and your thoughts toward us; they cannot be set in order to you.[16] I will proclaim and tell of them, yet they are too numerous to declare." The praise was for God's thoughts for his people as well as for the outworking of those thoughts, his wonderful works. The psalmist determined to declare (a cohortative) them even though they were more than could be told (literally, "too many to tell"). He sees the limits of his powers of expression and so merely refers to the wondrous acts of God in a hymnic style.[17]

One observation to be made here is that divine intervention without the response of declarative praise destroys God's design. God has plans for his people, and those plans provide amazing acts on their behalf. Through it all God desires expressions of praise and thanksgiving because praise will edify and change others.

B. God's wonderful acts of salvation demand personal dedication (6–8).

Gratitude also leads to dedication, which is what God truly desires. The psalmist has offered his praise for God's amazing deliverance, and now he makes the accompanying vow to serve the LORD. In this section it is helpful to recall how Israel's sacrificial worship worked. Whenever people wished to praise the LORD, they brought a "sacrifice" (זֶבַח), a peace offering, to the sanctuary; it was to accompany the praise (see Lev. 7:12). This was the "sacrifice of praise," or the *todah* sacrifice (s.v. Ps. 6:5). Among the accompanying sacrifices they brought was the dedication "offering" (מִנְחָה; see Lev. 2). When thankful worshipers brought this offering, they were in essence saying what David had said, "All things come from you, and of your own hand we have given you" (1 Chron. 29:14). The worshipers would be

---

16. The meaning of the clause is difficult. The MT has אֵין עֲרֹךְ אֵלֶיךָ. These words can be translated, "there is nothing that can be put in comparison to you." The verb can also mean "set in order, set forth": there is no laying forth of them unto you," meaning the thoughts of the LORD towards his people are beyond enumeration.

17. Kraus, *Psalms 1–59*, p. 426.

making the offering as a token of gratitude, and because of what the LORD had done they would make a dedication vow. Psalm 40 provides one such dedication vow, and in the process reveals what God desires from those he saves. He is not interested in ritual alone, but in what the ritual represented. To prepare for this sacrifice of praise and dedication offering, they first would have to bring the sin or "purification offering" (חֲטָאָה) for the removal of impurities and sins, and a "burnt offering" (עוֹלָה) to find complete acceptance by God, or, atonement.[18]

From this section of the passage the exposition may develop three helpful principles for dedication. From the fulfillment of the passage in Christ according to the Book of Hebrews it can find the example of perfect dedication. Since this section of the psalm is written with some parenthetical insertions, the exposition will have to clarify the sequence of thoughts:

Sacrifice and offering you do not desire;
　(Ears you have dug for me)
Burnt offering and sin offering you do not require.

Then I said, "Here, I have come;
　(in the roll of the book it is written for me)
I desire to do your will, O my God,
　(your law is within me)."

1. God is pleased with the dedication of believers.

This first principle is brought out both negatively in what God does not desire and positively in what he has prepared people to do. What did God not want? The psalmist says he does not desire (לֹא־חָפַצְתָּ) the sacrifice (זֶבַח) and the dedication offering (מִנְחָה), neither does he require (לֹא שָׁאָלְתָּ) the whole burnt offering (עוֹלָה) and the sin or purification offering (חֲטָאָה). This text is not repudiating ritual sacrifice; rather, it is affirming that ritual acts in and of themselves are meaningless (see 1 Sam. 15:22). God did not want the sacrifices alone; he never does (so the perfect tenses should be given a gnomic translation, the English present

---

18. For a detailed study of each of these sacrifices, see my work on Leviticus, *Holiness to the LORD* (Grand Rapids: Baker, 2002), pp. 85–154.

tense). Since the Bible makes it clear that God did want these from his people, the point must be that he was not interested in empty ritual; he was less concerned with the sacrifice than the meaning of the sacrifice. When God legislated the sacrifices he intended that the ritual be the outer expressions of inner faith—a sin offering without confession, or a dedication offering without genuine words of dedication, would be worthless.[19] People might make the sacrifices in order to appear spiritual, but without the commitment to the faith the sacrifices would have been an affront to God. The same is true of today's ritual acts, for God primarily wants the worshiper, not just a gift. If he has the worshiper, he will also have the gift given in the right way. Psalm 51:17 says that "the sacrifices of God are a broken spirit, a broken contrite heart." God did not need the animals (Ps. 50:7–14); he desired a contrite heart, which is what the sacrifice was to signify. These statements in Psalm 40 have to be understood in that light. Did God want sacrifices? Yes, for he legislated them; but he wanted what the sacrifices were designed to represent.

The psalmist complies with what God desired: "Here I have come. . . . I desire to do your will." Believers must desire to do the LORD's will or they will not actually be serving him—their will would not be surrendered to his will. The clause "Here I have come" (בָּאתִי) begins with the particle "here" (הִנֵּה), traditionally translated "behold"; it calls attention to what is happening. And what was happening was the psalmist's coming into the presence of the LORD where he declared his desire to do God's will (רָצוֹן; s.v. Ps. 30:5). Because of the repetition of the word one may say that the psalmist's desire was what the LORD desired, the commitment to do what pleased the LORD. In this passage, then, the psalmist has the proper response, for the proper response of someone who has experienced divine deliverance is dedication to serve the LORD.

"Here, I have come! I desire to do your will." Believers in all ages have struggled with this desire throughout their lives; but

---

19. Kraus argues that these verses are the words of the prophets who stressed obedience in contrast to the cult and therefore must be post-exilic (Psalms 1–59, p. 427); but the emphasis on piety in worship was not restricted to that later period.

Jesus was the only person who could ever say that he always did what was pleasing to the Father (John 8:29). He submitted to the Father's will because he came into the world to do the will of the Father.

2. God has prepared every person for his service.

The second principle is given in the parenthetical clause in verse 6: "ears your have dug for me" (אָזְנַיִם כָּרִיתָ לִּי). The focus is on the ears, but it refers to the whole person (a synecdoche); if God has the ear, it means the person is listening to God's instructions. The psalmist's point is that God made him in such a way that he would hear and do what the LORD wanted (similarly Isaiah 50:4 says morning by morning the LORD opens the prophet's ear).[20] This specific expression was interpreted in the Greek version because the idea in the text might not have been understood; it reads "a body you have prepared for me," which, although not as specific, captures the point.

By using this vow all the faithful acknowledged that God made them to do his will. He prepared their bodies and their souls with loving intentions (Ps.139:13–18). Everything they have, every capacity, every member, every function, is therefore to be dedicated to his service. The priests were reminded of this in their ordination, when Moses placed blood on the ear, the thumb and the toe of each of them (Lev. 8:23). In God's service; what they heard, what they handled, where they went, all had to be set apart to the LORD.

Believers today must also acknowledge that their bodies were designed for obedience. The LORD made each of them in such a way that they would hear his instructions and follow them; and once they acknowledge this, their dedication to his service must follow. "Ears you dug for me" should remind believers of Jesus' exhortation to obedience: "Whoever has ears to hear, let him

---

20. This passage in Isaiah is one of the servant songs, which Christian expositors recognize to be prophetic of Christ in the same typological way Psalm 40 is—he hears and obeys is true of the writer but fully realized in Christ. Thus, the emphasis on obedience using the detail of ears, occurs in both messianic passages.

hear" (Matt. 11:15). Believers must be always listening, always ready to use everything God gave them to do his will.

The apostles realized that these words found their fullest meaning in the incarnation of Christ. This Christian doctrine teaches that in some mysterious way the Spirit of God prepared a body for the Son of God whom the Father was sending into the world. That body was prepared for obedient service, as the emphasis on the ears indicates. By his teaching, by his mighty works, and by his love and compassion he would do the will of the Father; and the Father's will for him was that his body be crucified for us.[21]

3. God gives directions for doing his will.

The text says, "In the roll of the book it is prescribed for me" or more literally, "written concerning me" (בִּמְגִלַּת־סֵפֶר כָּתוּב עָלָי). The "roll of the book" refers to holy Scriptures; and so not limited to instructions for sacrifices or rules for kings.[22] To say that something in Scripture was "written for me" is to say it was "prescribed for me"—it was written for me to obey. Like all believers the psalmist knew that there were covenant stipulations for him to follow. God had prescribed in his word how his people were to live and what they were to do with their lives.[23] If this was to be an effective guide for all decisions, it had to become a natural part of one's thinking.

---

21. Perowne explains that the change in the words from "ears" to "body" which is found in Hebrews 10:5, 7 does not materially affect the argument of the Psalm or the passage in Hebrews. The point in Hebrews was not only that the Lord's sacrifice was the sacrifice of a human body, which was already implied in his coming into the world, the incarnation, but that it was the suffering of an obedient will. The writer found these words which once expressed the devotion of a true Israelite to be far more strikingly expressive, indeed, in their highest sense, only truly expressive of the perfect obedience of the Son of God (*Psalms*, I:336).

22. Craigie, following Eaton, suggests that what was written concerned instructions for the king because this is a royal psalm, or, because it is a royal psalm these must be the rules for the king (*Psalms*, p. 315). No doubt if a king used this psalm to express his dedication, he would have included in mind at least the rules for kings; but the psalm shows no clue of such a limited idea.

23. To begin with, the Law said that the redeemed people of God were to be a kingdom of priests and a holy nation (Exod. 19:6). This grand plan immediately settled how they were to live and serve.

The last statement, "your law is within me" (וְתוֹרָתְךָ מֵעָי; s.v. Ps. 1:2), states this point that the psalmist was not just hearing it read, but that he knew it. When devout believers receive the word of the LORD and live by it, then it is said to be in their hearts and in their mouths (see Deut. 30:14). They know it and remember it.

These words also find a greater meaning when applied to Jesus Christ. The line could be interpreted to say that in the word of the LORD "it was prescribed concerning me" or for me. Jesus said that a proper search of the Scriptures would show that they speak of him (John 5:39). Not only did the word instruct in righteousness, but it also revealed through prophecies and types the person and work of the Messiah. Doing the will of God not only means doing what God approves, but doing what he appoints as well. The entire life of Jesus was lived in obedience to the word, but it was also the fulfillment of prophecy. In the final analysis he accomplished what the Father had prescribed for him to do, namely to give his life a ransom for the sins of the world.[24]

With the psalmist all believers accept that "in the roll of the book it is prescribed for" each one of them. God's word informs them what God approves of and what God appoints for them to do. In other words, God's word gives direction to their dedication; and they will need to consult it again and again to know exactly how to please him, for dedication without direction is delusion. All the desire and all the dedication in the world will not do if people do not know what God's will is. It is in his word that God has prescribed his plan for his people—and that plan starts with their becoming just like the Lord.

C. God's righteousness, faithfulness, and love must be proclaimed in the congregation (9–10).

The next few verses form a transition to the second half of the psalm which is a prayer for deliverance from oppressive

---

24. Isaiah 53:10 says, "It pleased the LORD to bruise him." This means he did what the Father wanted him to do. And, to look at the psalm in another way, in the strictest sense the Father did not desire sacrifices from Jesus, for he was sending the Son into the world to be the sacrifice for the sins of the whole world.

enemies. It begins with the psalmist's attestation of faithfulness in giving praise to the LORD for past acts of salvation. This is an important part of the cycle of prayer and praise: God answers prayers in order that the people praise him. In doing this the psalmist is affirming his loyalty and motivating the LORD to answer this urgent request as well.

He begins by stating "I have proclaimed the good news" (בִּשַּׂרְתִּי), but he will stress this point by heaping up words: "I have not restrained my lips," "I have not hidden your righteousness in my heart," "I have spoken of your faithfulness and salvation," and "I have not concealed your loyal love and faithfulness." In the middle of this drum-beat he says, "LORD, you know," meaning, "as you know." He has been faithful to praise God in the congregation.

The subject matter of his praise is rich: "righteousness" (צֶדֶק), "your righteousness" (צִדְקָתְךָ), "your faithfulness" (אֱמוּנָתְךָ), "your salvation" (תְּשׁוּעָתְךָ), "your loyal love" (חַסְדְּךָ) and "your truth/faithfulness" (אֲמִתְּךָ). The two words for "righteousness" are metonymical for the resultant deliverance God gave to the psalmist (the cause of the deliverance was God's righteousness; s.v. Ps. 1:5).[25] "Salvation" is the deliverance for which he has so enthusiastically praised (s.v. Ps. 3:2). The words "loyal love and truth," perhaps a hendiadys meaning "faithful loyal love," describe God's intervention as part of the covenant relationship with God that he enjoyed. These also would be metonymies of cause, for God's loyal love (s.v. Ps. 23:6) brought him salvation. The words "truth" and "faithfulness" are from the same root (s.v. Ps. 15:2); they stress that God's deliverance was evidence of his faithfulness to himself, his word, and his people.

---

25. Many translations put the word "deliverance" in the text to enable people to understand what is meant, but it seems in doing that the emphasis of the writer is lost. He chose to use the words for righteousness because his focus is on the nature of the LORD, even though he meant also what the righteousness of God did. To change it to "deliverance" removes the focus from the LORD and puts it on the experience of the people. It would be far better to explain the text as it was written so that praise is focused on the nature of the saving God. Here Kraus is helpful; he explains that righteousness was in Israel no norm, no principle of justice, but deed, bestowal of salvation, proof of faithfulness of promise and partnership (*Psalms 1–59*, p. 427).

The attributes listed here are theological explanations of the deliverance God had granted him in the past, especially recorded in the beginning of Psalm 40. It is also instructive for believers who wish to offer praise to the LORD: they should be able to describe the nature of God that was made evident in his wonderful acts.

D. God's past acts of deliverance inspire confidence for the future (11).

This verse begins with an address to the LORD: "You, O LORD." The confidence expressed here is that the LORD will not restrain his compassion. The verb "restrain" (תִּכְלָא) is the same verb used in verse 9 (אֶכְלָא): because he did not restrain his lips from praising the faithful love of the LORD, he is confident that the LORD will not restrain his compassion towards him.

The verb in verse 11 could be interpreted as an imperfect of injunction, "Do not refrain," and the line be taken as a prayer.[26] But it is more likely that this is a general statement of confident anticipation connected to the praise just offered (see ESV). The prayer will begin with the lament of verse 12 and be fully expressed in verses 13–17.

What the psalmist expects and desires is the LORD's "compassion" (רַחֲמֶיךָ; s.v. Ps. 25:6), "loyal love" and "truth." He is expecting the deliverance and protection that these divine attributes will produce for him (so they are metonymies of cause). He is totally dependent and helpless, so he needs the LORD's compassion; he is a faithful member of the covenant, and so he expects the LORD's faithful loyal love. He will be preserved through these (יִצְּרוּנִי).

II. Because the LORD is their helper and deliverer, believers may pray for deliverance from the evils of this world on the basis of his faithful love and for the purpose of his glory (12–17).

A. The evils of this world are overwhelming (12).

Verse 12 lays out the lament specifically: he is overwhelmed

---

26. Craigie, *Psalms*, p. 316.

by innumerable troubles, caused largely by his sin. "Evils" (רָעוֹת;
s.v. Ps. 10:15) have encompassed him; these are the painful calamities he was enduring—and they were innumerable. The
parallel colon makes it clear that his iniquities were at fault.
When he says "my iniquities (עֲוֺנֺתַי; s.v. Ps. 32:5) have overtaken
me," he probably means the difficulties his iniquity caused, i.e.,
his troubles (so a metonymy of cause). This interpretation does
not nullify the iniquities; it focuses on the troubles connected to
them. The result is that he was no longer able to see, and this
probably does not refer to his literal sight, but to his perception,
his ability to think straight and understand things.

His troubles are more than the hairs of his head (hyperbole).
Because they are so many, his heart fails him (literally "my
heart abandons/forsakes me"—עֲזָבָנִי). The will to resist, to keep
on going, is not there. His emotional and spiritual resources
have abandoned him.

B. God is able to deliver his people from those who would destroy them so that they might declare his greatness (13–16).

1. They pray for a quick deliverance from evils (13–15).

The last few verses of the psalm record the petition (the section that forms Psalm 70). The psalmist begins with an appeal
to God's will: "Be pleased (רְצֵה; s.v. Ps. 30:5), O LORD, to deliver
me (לְהַצִּילֵנִי; s.v. Ps. 22:20)," but adds a sense of the urgency in
the parallel colon: "O LORD, hurry (חוּשָׁה) to my help." This was
a cry of desperation from someone who knew there was no time
to lose.

Then, in verses 14 and 15 he asks that his enemies be destroyed. There are three petitions[27] for them and their threat
to be ended, and each petition includes a description of the enemies that serves as a reason for the petition. The first request is
that they be put to shame and disappointed (יֵבֹשׁוּ וְיַחְפְּרוּ), and the
qualifying clause is "who seek to snatch my life away" (literally,

---

27. On the other hand, Craigie now takes these verbs as confidence and not
prayers (*Psalms*, p. 316).

"seeking my life to take it," לְסִפּוֹתָהּ). The enemies were blood-thirsty, eagerly looking for ways to kill him, so the prayer is that they be "put to shame" (s.v. Ps. 31:1) and disappointed.[28]

The second petition is that the enemies be turned back and brought to dishonor. They are described as "who desire my hurt" (literally, "desirers of my pain," חֲפֵצֵי רָעָתִי). They were wanting to inflict some painful calamity or ruin on him; for that he prays they will be turned back and dishonored (יִסֹּגוּ אָחוֹר וְיִכָּלְמוּ)

The third appeal is that they be appalled (יָשֹׁמּוּ) because of their shame. They are then described as people who taunt him with the expectation of destroying him: "who say to me, 'Aha, Aha!'" The particle translated "aha" (הֶאָח) indicates a conde-scending, triumphant expression. The psalmist not only wants them to be put to shame, but to be appalled when they are.

2. They pray that God would give them reason to praise (16).

The prayer changes in verse 16 as the psalmist focuses on the desired benefits for the righteous. The destruction of the wicked enemies would not simply give the psalmist relief, but would give the righteous joy. The word order of the petition emphasizes the joy, for the verse reads, "Let them all rejoice and be glad in you, who seek you." The pattern is that the prayer is first expressed, and then the subject of the verbs is clarified with a description. Here the description is of people who seek the LORD, believers who pray to the LORD or seek his counsel. The verbs for re-joicing and being glad (יָשִׂישׂוּ וְיִשְׂמְחוּ) are metonymies of effect, for the cause would be the answer to his prayer for deliverance from and destruction of the murderous enemies (they may also form a hendiadys, "be joyfully glad"; for שָׂמַח, s.v. Ps. 48:11). The prayer is for the LORD to give the faithful reason to rejoice. This idea is enhanced in the second half of the verse: "Let them continually say, 'Great is the LORD,' who love your salvation." People who love the LORD's deliverance are those who watch and pray for it. They are vigilant believers. As in the first half of the verse, the psalmist wants the LORD to answer his prayer so that these

---

28. Broyles argues that the enemies were not trying to kill the psalmist, but his argument is a little confused (p. 192).

people can declare God's greatness. The declaration they will make is "Great is the LORD" (יִגְדַּל יְהוָה). The verb describes his unchanging nature as great, but the proclamation of his greatness comes from the renewed realization of the fact (for the verb, s.v. Ps. 34:3).

C. God has plans for his people so they may pray confidently (17).

The psalm ends in the present with the need for help remaining an urgent need. The shift back to the current dilemma is marked with "But as for me" (וַאֲנִי), and then in a reminder of his lament he states "[But as for me] *I am* afflicted and needy" (וַאֲנִי עָנִי וְאֶבְיוֹן; for עָנִי; s.v. Ps. 9:12). He has no more resources of his own on which he can draw—but he has the LORD. He knows the LORD thinks about him (אֲדֹנָי יַחֲשָׁב לִי). This word "thinks" (חָשַׁב; s.v. Ps. 32:2) means "to consider, reckon, devise." He is not a passing thought to God, nor is he just part of a nation that the LORD protects; God makes plans for him! Here is the comfort: if God made him specifically to do his will, and if God has plans for him, then God will not be willing to relinquish his life to the wicked. In confidence the psalmist can say that God is his help (עֶזְרָתִי; s.v. Ps. 46:1) and his deliverer (מְפַלְטִי; s.v. Ps. 37:40). Even though God has proven himself to be so, the psalmist is becoming anxious here, and so repeats the appeal: "O my God, do not delay" (אֱלֹהַי אַל־תְּאַחַר). Earlier he had implored the LORD to hurry to his help; now he prays that the LORD, his help and deliverer, not delay. The psalmist has confidence in the LORD because of truly amazing interventions in the past, but no matter how confident one may be in the faith, there is no rest until the current crisis is ended.

MESSAGE AND APPLICATION

This passage demonstrates how gratitude for God's great acts of salvation naturally prompts dedication to do God's will and builds confidence for prayer for additional help. In the vow of dedication we also have a typological section of our Lord's incarnation and obedience to the Father. The expository idea of the entire psalm can be developed in a number of ways; this one captures the sequence of the psalm: *God's marvelous acts of salvation inspire praise and dedication, and on the basis of that the faithful continue to pray for the LORD to deliver them so that they might proclaim his greatness.*

If the application is to focus on the dedication of the worshiper, which is the necessary result of praise for divine intervention, and which is essential to effectual prayer in other crises, the following principles might be developed:

First, God requires that his people present their bodies to him as living sacrifices, which is their spiritual service (Romans 12:1). Paul is applying the dedication offering to the Christian life. From the tenses that he uses I understand this presentation to be the main vow of dedication, made once by believers in their spiritual pilgrimages. It is necessary for believers to make such a dedication to the Lord; it means surrendering the whole life to his service. Thereafter, believers must make it their chief concern to remain committed to him.

Second, God has revealed in his word what he approves and what he appoints for us. There is not much profit from unguided dedications. Believers must live in accordance with his word, so that their commitment to obedience will be pleasing to him. There is no other way to know how to find and follow his perfect will.

Third, praise and gratitude are the inspiration for true dedication. God's people call upon the LORD in the time of trouble, and when he answers they must offer their praise. As they praise God for his gracious provisions, they will find their commitment to him and confidence in him greatly strengthened.

Of course, the greatest praise is for Jesus Christ our Savior, who "has lifted us out of the miry clay and set our feet upon a solid rock and put a new song in our hearts." Additionally, by his sacrifice on the cross he has shown to us what it means to surrender to the will of God.

PSALM 41

Encouragement for Help Against Treachery

INTRODUCTION

Text and Textual Variants

To the Chief Musician. A Psalm of David.

1 Blessed is the one who has regard for the weak;[1]
  in the day of trouble the LORD delivers him.
2 The LORD protects him and preserves his life;
  he is *called* blessed[2] in the land—

---

1. The Greek version has καὶ πένητα, "and needy" (the equivalent of וְאֶבְיוֹן). The addition would balance the line metrically (which is why the editors of BHS recommend inserting it), but the addition is not warranted. It may be that the common association of "weak and needy" influenced the Greek translation.

2. The MT has the *pual* form of the verb, יְאֻשַּׁר, "he will be/is blessed," which certainly implies that the LORD will bless him. A number of manuscripts and the Greek version have the active form of the verb, continuing with the LORD as the subject, καὶ μακαρίσαι αὐτὸν, which would be the equivalent of the *piel* form with a suffix: וִיאַשְּׁרֵהוּ. Most commentators conclude that the MT form is corrupt, and the active verb should be followed. The meaning of the verse would not change with this reading; only the consistent flow of the lines with the LORD as the subject would be secured. The more difficult reading is to be preferred, especially since the meaning is clear enough.

873

and do not give him[3] to the desire[4] of his enemies.
3 The LORD sustains him on his sickbed;
    all his bed[5] you change[6] in his sickness.

4 I said, "O LORD, have mercy on me;
    heal me,[7] because I have sinned against you."
5 My enemies[8] speak evil concerning me:[9]
    "When will he die and his name perish?"
6 And whenever *one* comes to see *me*,
    he speaks falsely in his heart,
    he gathers evil for himself,
      he goes[10] outside *and* speaks.

---

3. The MT has a 2nd masculine singular form of the verb, וְאַל תִּתְּנֵהוּ, "and do not give him" (perhaps "you must not give him"). This form does make an abrupt change in the context of the verse from words of confidence about the LORD to a direct address. The 3rd person verb is used in the Greek, Syriac, and Jerome, and most commentators accept it as the preferred reading, changing the initial ת to a י to read "and may he not give him." The poetry of the first three verses may not follow a consistent form, and so the psalmist here may have used the second person to respond to the statements made about the LORD. The meaning of the line is clear in either case.

4. The MT has בְּנֶפֶשׁ; the Greek version has εἰς χεῖρας, "into the hands," which would fit the common expression.

5. The expression may be interpreted as "on his whole bed." If "bed" is taken as a metonymy of subject, then it would mean "all his infirmities" (see RSV); but the meaning is that it is no longer a sickbed because the LORD heals him of his disease.

6. Here too the MT has a 2nd person form of the verb, הָפַכְתָּ, "you turn, change." The MT then shows some flexibility in the style with these different forms. The Greek text has ἔστρεψας, "you turned." Commentators suggest reading this as a 3rd person verb as well to match the flow of the verses. It is not impossible that one colon would say what the LORD does, and the parallel colon address the LORD directly. The change to the 3rd makes a smoother reading, which may be an argument against it.

7. The MT uses נַפְשִׁי, and the Greek version translated it literally as "heal my soul."

8. There is some manuscript support for a conjunction beginning the line.

9. Syriac and Targum suggest עָלַי instead of לִי.

10. The editors of BHS and many commentators suggest deleting the verb "he goes" for metric considerations. The line is rather long; but the manuscript evidence supports its retention.

7 All who hate me whisper together against me;
    against me they imagine my calamity:
8 "A vile disease[11] is being poured out on him,
    and wherever he lies down he will not get up again."
9 Also, my close friend,[12] whom I trusted,
    who ate my bread, has lifted up his heel against me.[13]

10 But you, O LORD, have mercy on me and raise me up
    that I may repay them.

11 In this I know that you are pleased with me,
    that my enemy will not rejoice over me.
12 And as for me, in my integrity you have upheld me,
    and set me before you for ever.
13 Blessed be the LORD, the God of Israel
    from everlasting to everlasting.
    Amen and amen.[14]

Composition and Context

It is difficult enough for believers to have to endure illness along with feelings of guilt for sin, but to be visited by people who say all the pleasantries and then deal treacherously in the hopes of using the situation to destroy them can be devastating. Mercifully, the LORD restores the penitent believers and prevents their enemies from seeing their plans through. This psalm is a celebration of the LORD's intervention on just such an

---

11. The reading in the MT is דְּבַר־בְּלִיַּעַל, "a wicked thing," although the Greek version reads it simply as λόγον παράνομον κατέθεντο κατ' ἐμοῦ, "they put out a wicked word against me." The meaning "a thing of *belial*" means a thing that is wicked and worthless. There is not sufficient evidence to take *belial* as a name of a demon, but Craigie translates the expression as "devilish disease" (*Psalms*, pp. 318–9).
12. The MT is אִישׁ שְׁלוֹמִי, "man of my peace," which the Greek version translated literally.
13. Greek reads the final clause as "magnified trickery against me," ἐμεγάλυνεν ἐπ'ἐμὲ πτερνισμόν. The translation has interpreted "heel" as treachery; the Hebrew literally has "magnified the heel against me."
14. The Greek version translates "amen" (אָמֵן) with γένοιτο, "so be it," which may indicate that "amen" had not yet become a liturgical expression.

occasion. The exposition would certainly emphasize the thanksgiving and the lessons included with it; but the significance of that thanksgiving can only be appreciated against the backdrop of the illness and the treachery the psalmist experienced. Since most believers have experienced similar things in their lives, the message of this psalm will be clearly relevant.

The psalm has three sections that are distinct, making the classification difficult. The first three verses are instruction, the heart of the psalm is the prayer, and the last two verses the thanksgiving. The prayer section of the psalm records what is essentially a lament; but the psalm itself does not follow the pattern of a lament. Craigie, following Mowinckel,[15] describes it as a song of illness; but he takes it further and classifies it as a liturgy, or part of a liturgy, for the ritual when a sick person came to the sanctuary for healing.[16] This would mean that verses 1–3 were the words of the priest to the suppliant (necessitating the changes to the third person throughout). Verses 4–10 would be the words of the ill person praying in the sanctuary, and the approach would necessitate the assumption that there was an oracle of healing between verses 10 and 11 to account for the change to the praise in verses 11 and 12.

It is more likely that the psalm is a thanksgiving. Verses 4–10 are a prayer, but in this type of psalm they represent the psalmist's report of his prayer—it is what he prayed when ill. The last two verses form the actual praise for the restoration. Since this type of psalm often includes a didactic element, verses 1–3 fit nicely. People were to learn from the psalmist's experience.

Some commentators have suggested that the psalm is also a royal psalm. It does not have the distinguishing features of that group of psalms, and so the classification is forced. It may include things that the king was supposed to do, but Scripture does not limit those acts to the king.[17] It may be that the desire to see a royal psalm at the end of Book I has prompted this

---

15. *The Psalms in Israel's Worship,* II:1–9.

16. *Psalms,* p. 318.

17. For example, J. H. Eaton says the first duty of the king was to care for the weak (*Kingship in the Psalms,* pp. 44–46). This is certainly true, and a king would be reminded of that duty with this psalm; but all Israelites were to do this as well (Deut. 10:18–19; 24:17–18).

association. One can say that the psalm certainly could have been used by the king.

The superscription lists this as a Davidic psalm. We have no record that David was ill, although it would be unusual if he never was ill. As Goldingay says, one can imagine David testifying of God's deliverance, but also subsequent kings using it as well.[18] Most commentators, of course, would date the psalm later. Kraus thinks that because the different functions of the speaking parts were no longer alive the psalm in its present form is late; he adds that it must have gone through a long tradition of changes.[19] Of course, there is no compelling evidence for this suggestion; and there is no reason why the psalm could not have been presented originally in its parts by one person.

Exegetical Analysis

Summary

Testifying how the LORD answered his prayer to restore him to health and prevent the treachery of his enemies, the psalmist declares that those who take note of the needy will receive deliverance from the LORD in their time of need.

Outline

I. Instruction: The psalmist instructs believers that God protects and preserves those who take note of people in need (1–3).
   A. He announces that the LORD delivers those who take note of the weak (1).
   B. He delineates how the LORD protects them from their enemies and restores them to health (2–3).
II. Report: The psalmist testifies how the LORD answered his prayer for healing from his illness and deliverance from his treacherous enemies who took advantage of his situation (4–10).

---

18. *Psalms 1–41*, p. 582.
19. *Psalms 1–59*, p. 431.

A. Prayer: He recalls his petition for healing after acknowledging his sin (4).
B. Lament: He reports his suffering over the advantage his enemies and trusted friend took of him during his illness (5–10).
   1. The enemies feigned friendship but spread malicious rumors about him (5–8).
   2. His trusted friend betrayed him (9).
C. Prayer: He recalls his petition for deliverance to repay his adversaries (10).

III. Thanksgiving: The psalmist offers his thanks to God for rescuing him from his enemies and accepting him into his presence on account of his integrity (11–12).

Doxology of First Book: Psalm 41:13

COMMENTARY IN EXPOSITORY FORM

I. Believers who help people in their time of need will find that the LORD delivers and protects them in their time of need (1–3).

A. The LORD delivers those who take note of the weak (1).

The first three verses record the instruction of the thankful psalmist. It begins with the declaration of the maxim that those who take note of the needy will obtain help from the LORD. In a way the line is saying, "Blessed are the merciful, for they shall receive mercy" (Matt. 5:7). The psalm opens with the declaration of the beatitude: "O the blessednesses of" (אַשְׁרֵי, as in Psalm 1:1). The word is usually found in didactic passages, as it is here. Because of this exclamation, the verbs that follow are not prayers but teachings. Those blessed in this case are people who have regard for the weak or needy (דָּל). The verb form used (מַשְׂכִּיל; s.v. Ps. 36:4) is unusual; it is one of the words for wisdom, i.e., dealing wisely or prudently with discernment. In this context it describes practical wisdom, i.e., taking careful thought of the needy rather than looking only at oneself; but it goes beyond taking thought of them—it means acting on their behalf. As the psalmist will make clear, in his own bitter experience people did not do this—even his close friend sinned against him when he was in need.

The lesson is that people who conduct themselves in this right way will not be forsaken in the depth of their misfortune.[20] The text says "the LORD delivers him (יְמַלְּטֵהוּ)[21] in the evil time." To state it negatively one could ask that if people never help others in need what right do they have to ask for help? Or to put it positively, people who seek divine deliverance from their troubles must be people who give active consideration to the weak and the poor.[22]

B. The LORD restores them to health and protects them from their enemies (2–3).

Now the principle is elaborated upon by the psalmist with descriptions of the result of this deliverance. The LORD protects him (יִשְׁמְרֵהוּ; s.v. Ps. 12:7) and preserves him (וִיחַיֵּהוּ). This last verb is the causative of "to live" (חָיָה); it could be rendered "preserve" or "keep alive." The LORD thus ensures that trouble does not overwhelm the believer who extends grace to others.

---

20. Kraus, *Psalms 1–59*, p. 431.
21. The verb מָלַט is another one of the words for deliverance or salvation. It basically means "to slip away" (but does not occur in the *qal* system). It occurs mostly in the *niphal* system. One meaning is simply slipping away or through or past something (1 Sam. 20:29). Its more frequent meaning is "escape" as in slipping through enemy lines or away from danger (as in urging Lot to escape for his life in Gen. 19:17; or the case of the Moabites who did not escape in Judg. 3:29; or when David escaped from Keilah in 1 Sam. 23:13). In Psalm 22:5 it has the passive sense, referring to the ancestors who cried to the LORD and "were delivered."

   In the *piel* it normally means "deliver," as here in Psalm 41:1. Delivering a person or a life means saving him from the midst of peril or difficulty, as if enabling him to slip away and escape. The same meaning is found in the rarer *hiphil* (Isa. 31:5). The couple of *hithpael* forms have the idea of escaping (Job 19:20) or leaping forth (sparks from the jaws of the crocodile in Job 41:11).

   Interestingly, the *piel* is used for laying eggs (letting them slip out; Isa. 34:15), and the *hiphil* similarly is used for giving birth (Isa. 66:7).
22. Craigie, *Psalms*, 320.

The psalmist adds that "he will be blessed in the land." The verb (a *pual* form יְאֻשַּׁר in the MT) probably means that he is praised, that his good name is preserved.[23] The word is related to the first word of the psalm, "blessed" (אַשְׁרֵי), which describes the bliss that comes from knowing one is right with God. The verb means "call blessed, pronounce happy" in several passages (e.g., Gen. 30:13; Prov. 31:28). The line indicates that people will acknowledge his happy estate under God's care. If the alternate reading were taken to make the form *piel*, it would mean God will make him happy or blessed in the land. Clearly, if people call him blessed it is because God blesses him.

The verse then shifts to a direct address to God. The form used is a negated volitive form (וְאַל תִּתְּנֵהוּ) which may be translated directly as an appeal to God: "and do not give him over to the desire of his enemies!" Because a petition like this seems out of place in the immediate context, many commentators have made the change in the text to "may he not give" or "he does not give." The change to a direct address here (and in the next verse) is not that problematic; the form in the text need not be taken as a copyist's slip into the tone of lament with a petition, but may suggest a strong statement appealing to God's will to affirm "you do not give."[24] It would not be in God's will to give the faithful over to the desires of the enemies. In telling others how the LORD delivers the righteous so they will be blessed, he turns to address the LORD to confirm that the righteous will not be surrendered to the desire (בְּנֶפֶשׁ) of the enemies. The text will explain that desire in this case was to destroy him (so "desire" is a metonymy of cause for the attack).

Verse 3 continues the instruction by affirming that the LORD sustains the righteous on his sickbed. The LORD does not simply preserve—he changes things. Caught up in the wonder of this divine care, the psalmist turns to address the LORD: "all his bed you turn in his sickness." The line is cryptic; the bed

---

23. Kraus, *Psalms 1–59*, p. 431.

24. Gesenius says the negative אַל with the jussive is sometimes used to express the conviction that something cannot or should not happen; he lists Pss. 34:6, 41:3, 50:3, and 121:3 (*GKC* #109e, p. 322). Here then the psalmist says "you do not give/do not give" he means "you must not/should not give."

is the place of the suffering (and so it is a metonymy of subject). He means that God transforms the whole place where he lies suffering by healing him. To change the bed in his sickness means to alleviate the sickness so the place is transformed. This statement forms the transition to the testimony about his prayer from his own sickbed. In other words, the psalmist is speaking from experience.

II. The testimony of those whom the LORD preserves and protects will encourage others in similar situations to pray (4–10).

A. *The prayer for restoration may need to acknowledge sin against God (4).*

The central section of the psalm begins and ends with the report of the prayer. That it is a report and not a current prayer is indicated by the initial verb, "I said" (אֲנִי אָמַרְתִּי).[25] There is no reason to take this as a reference to an earlier complaint; it refers to this complaint where he was ill and dealt with treacherously by people. The prayer had two requests: "have mercy on me" (חָנֵּנִי; s.v. Ps. 4:1) and "heal me" (רְפָאָה נַפְשִׁי; s.v. Ps. 30:2). The first is a cry for help which he did not deserve, a petition for mercy; and the second is the specific plea for restoration to health. The second imperative gives clarification for the first— he does not deserve to be healed, but appeals to God's mercy.

The reason that he does so is the explanatory clause, "for I have sinned against you" (חָטָאתִי; s.v. Ps. 51:2). Here then is his acknowledgment of sin. The specific sin is not stated, only that he needs mercy and healing because he sinned. The healing, then, would be of both body and soul, a removal of the illness and the cause of the illness. Of course, not all illness is the result of sinful acts; but in this case it appears to be. This fact explains the response of his enemies—the serious illness brought them to his bedside, all the while hoping for his demise; and some

---

25. Craigie, however, says this is liturgy, vocalized after the words of the priest in verses 1–3 (*Psalms*, p. 319).

awareness of his guilt seems to have given them substance for their accusations against him.

B. The report of the suffering and treachery will encourage others to pray (5–9).

The psalmist was aware of their true motives all along. In verse 5 he says they speak evil (רַע; s.v. Ps. 10:15) concerning him, meaning they talk about harm coming on him, either evil they attribute to him or evil they plan for him—perhaps a little of both in that they see this illness as their opportunity. Ultimately they were not referring to his illness, but to his death for which they longed: "When will he die and his name perish?" For the name (שֵׁם; s.v. Ps. 20:1) to perish would be for him to cease to exist and all memory of him be forgotten. Their words desiring his complete removal are not appropriate words for the punishment for sin. They are malicious.

The psalmist saw through their feigned concern when they visited him. He now uses the singular verb; he may have a particular enemy in mind, or be using it collectively: "When he comes to see me, he speaks falsely in his heart." He says all the appropriate and pleasant things in the visitation, but speaks falsely (שָׁוְא, "empty, vain," to a "false purpose"). He says one thing but in the heart means something else. During the visit he gathers clues for the accusations. The precise interpretation of the line is a little difficult; it reads "he gathers evil (אָוֶן; s.v. Ps. 28:3) for him," i.e., sinful and troubling things, things that could be used maliciously. Does this describe what he is doing, or is it what he says about the sufferer, that he brought it on himself. The verb "gathers" (יִקְבָּץ) suggests the former. In either case the ideas would be given full report outside.

The picture that emerges of the visitor so far includes a lying mouth and an evil heart. To this the report will now add slander. Inside he speaks pleasantries, but outside he changes his words. The text simply says "he goes outside, he speaks." Since the psalmist has described him as speaking falsely and hoping for his death, what he says outside must be in contrast to the false things (kind words) he spoke to the ill man. The psalmist knew what they were thinking and would say outside.

Verses 7 and 8 record what his enemies ("haters of me," שֹׂנְאָי; s.v. Ps. 139:21) whisper together (יִתְלַחֲשׁוּ)[26] against him in the streets. Simply put, they devise (יַחְשְׁבוּ; s.v. Ps. 32:2) evil for him ("his evil"). These verses follow the pattern of verses 5 and 6, first introducing and describing the words, and then reporting them. What they say is then recorded in verse 8: "A vile disease has been poured out on him, and where he lies he will not rise again."[27] The "vile disease" is an interpretive rendering of "a wicked thing" (דְּבַר־בְּלִיַּעַל), perhaps "a thing of *belial*" (s.v. Ps. 18:5). This word usually describes something that is wicked and worthless, and so here something ghastly. The use of the term that is associated so frequently with gross acts of sin would certainly color the report of this illness. There is no evidence in the Old Testament for an interpretation as Belial, prince of demons (but see 2 Cor. 6:15). Kraus suggests that it is a reference to some sinister power of death, as if they were almost using incantation in that their whispering this way turned it into a curse.[28] And Goldingay wonders if they saw themselves as God's servants to see that the sinner was punished.[29] It is doubtful that these suppositions could be proven from the text; they may have simply described his condition in the worst of terms, physically and spiritually. They made sure that everyone knew that his sickbed was his deathbed.

The greatest pain for the psalmist is recorded in verse 9, the betrayal of a close friend. He describes him as "my close friend," or, "a man of my peace" (אִישׁ שְׁלוֹמִי). The use of this description (s.v. Ps. 38:3) indicates the man was, or was thought to be, someone who was committed to his peace and welfare, a close friend who truly cared. Moreover, he is further described as one whom the psalmist trusted (בָּטַחְתִּי; s.v. Ps. 4:5) and with whom he felt safe and secure. Finally he is one who ate bread with him (literally, "eater of my bread/food," אוֹכֵל לַחְמִי). Eating his bread would indicate that there was a genuine trust and

---

26. The word לָחַשׁ means "whisper." Gaster associated it with incantations and gave the interpretation "hiss" (Th. H. Gaster, "Short Notes," *VT* 4 [1954]:73–79). This would further describe their whispering as evil.

27. The MT has "he will not add to rise," which is a verbal hendiadys meaning he will not rise again, i.e., recover from his illness.

28. *Psalms 1–59*, p. 432.

29. *Psalms 1-41*, p. 585.

fellowship with this man who enjoyed the psalmist's hospitality. The wording of three powerful descriptions of the relationship builds to the devastating impact of the betrayal.

"He has lifted up his heel against me." The expression literally says "he has made great" (הִגְדִּיל) his heel. The use of the word "heel" (עָקֵב) is key to the understanding of the treachery. It is best known for its connections to the name "Jacob" in Genesis.[30] The familiar friend, then, turned on the psalmist treacherously and with the enemies tried to gain the upper hand over him to cheat him out of his place. There is no indication as to the identity of this person, although some commentators suggest the likes of Ahithophel. Such betrayal is so common to human relationships that the line no doubt found many applications down through the ages. The verse is appropriately applied to Judas in John 13:18. Jesus does not apply the whole psalm to his situation, only the betrayal. The verse is not a prophecy of Judas; rather, the words find their fullest meaning and significance in his betrayal of David's greater son, Jesus Christ.[31]

C. The prayer for restoration will seek to right the wrongs inflicted on the sufferer (10).

The testimony section of the psalm also ends with a prayer. It reiterates the plea for mercy, "have mercy on me," but instead of the request to be healed it now asks, "and raise me up" (וַהֲקִימֵנִי; s.v. Ps. 3:1), which means the same thing but includes the idea of his full restoration to his position and his power. Whereas the first

---

30. Because the newborn grabbed the heel of his brother, he was named "Jacob" as a commemoration of the event and perhaps a sign of the oracle received (Gen. 25:26). The name "Jacob" (יַעֲקֹב) means "may he protect" or "[the LORD] protects," joining the incident with the heel to the idea of a rear guard. It was when Jacob deceived his brother and took the blessing that his name was given a negative connotation as "heel-grabber" or deceiver (Gen. 27:36). That connotation stuck, as is evidenced by Jeremiah 9:4, "every brother truly overreaches" (עָקוֹב יַעְקֹב), seeks to take advantage by some insidious measures. The word "heel" then signified the treachery of someone overreaching.

31. See M. J. J. Menken, "The Translation of Psalm 41:10 in John 13:18," *JSNT* 40 (1990):61–79.

prayer offered the explanatory confession of sin as part of the appeal, this prayer includes the intended desire "that I may repay them" (וַאֲשַׁלְּמָה לָהֶם; s.v. Ps. 38:3).[32] In other places the psalmist might pray that God would requite them for their wickedness; but here the psalmist desires to do it. Either way the wicked will be repaid for their treachery and malice. Commentators have been troubled by this desire of the psalmist and have tried to play it down.[33] The enemies sought to ruin him by talking about him for evil; they were malicious, treacherous liars. The psalmist wants to be raised up so that he may expose their wickedness, put them to shame for their betrayal, and bring their plans to an end. He will do this by his recovery as an answer to prayer and by his report of their hypocrisy and scheme so that everyone will know of their wickedness. The honor of God and the integrity of the faith and the security of the faithful demands that the righteous do this, for this kind of treachery is no harmless sin. And, if in fact the psalmist was David, then as leader of the nation he had the responsibility to do this, for they tried to get rid of him by wicked lies. This was not personal revenge; it was far more important than that (see the discussion of the imprecatory psalms in the Introduction).

III. The thanksgiving for the deliverance will show that the LORD delights in people who follow him (11–12).

The last two verses of the psalm are addressed to God in

---

32. The word incorporates a word play: his good friend was supposed to be a man of peace, one who cared for his welfare but failed; so the psalmist desires to repay that affront.

33. Kissane says it probably means nothing more than his desire to taunt them with their disappointment (E. J. Kissane, *The Book of Psalms,* p. 184). That is surely too weak; besides, if that is what he meant he could have said it easily enough. Weiser says that the sentiment is understandable, arising out of his indignation and disappointment, but clearly shows that in this passage, under the judgment of the New Testament, Old Testament thought is restricted by emotions which are far too human (*The Psalms,* p. 345). The generalization represents a different view of the nature of Scripture. The words are the expression of the psalmist, but are part of divine revelation, given by divine inspiration.

thanksgiving, but the words are intended for the congregation to hear. The psalmist declares, "In this I know that you are pleased with me." "In this" refers to his healing and restoration.[34] God answered his prayer and healed him. He was able to stand in the sanctuary and declare that this was proof that God was pleased with him, no matter what his enemies tried to say. He knew this because in answering the prayer God did not allow his enemies to triumph over him. The expression literally says "rejoice" or ""shout" over me (יָרִיעַ)—the enemies were not in a place to shout for joy because their hopes for his death had been dashed. They failed in their wicked plan, and they were exposed as well.

This was proof that the LORD upheld him in his integrity (בְּתֻמִּי; s.v. Ps. 7:8). The verb is the perfect tense (תָּמַכְתָּ) which could be taken as a characteristic perfect and translated as a present tense, or it could be a simple perfect, "you have upheld" me, which fits the context a little better. The mention of his integrity as a reason for the LORD's deliverance is not out of harmony with his earlier acknowledgment of sin. Being a sinner does not mean that God was not pleased with him; God was pleased with him because he confessed his sin and appealed for mercy. The fact that he acknowledged his sin is evidence that he was trying to live according to the precepts and provisions of the LORD. Because he held fast to the faith and prayed to the LORD, the LORD healed him and set him in his presence forever. The image of being set (וַתַּצִּיבֵנִי) before the LORD (or in the LORD's presence) may be drawn from the setting of the sanctuary; but it means he now stands firmly in the care of the LORD, forgiven, healed, and restored to communion with God. His position in the presence of God is confirmed forever.

Doxology for Book I

The 13th verse of the psalm is not part of the psalm but a doxology for the collection of psalms in Book I (see the Introduction for the organization of the psalms). It says,

---

34. Craigie says it refers to an oracle given to him (*Psalms*, p. 321).

Blessed be the LORD, the God of Israel
from everlasting to everlasting. Amen and amen.[35]

MESSAGE AND APPLICATION

In this psalm we have a contrast between those who show mercy to people in need and those who deal treacherously with them. This is a psalm of thanksgiving, because the psalmist's prayer had been answered and he had been delivered from his plight and protected from the treachery of his "friends." The point of his praise is that the LORD restores the penitent sufferer and prevents the treacherous plans of the enemies—evidence that the LORD is pleased with him.

What comes to the fore of his praise is that those whom the LORD delivers in the day of trouble are people who help the needy. They are the ones who truly understand the mercy that they seek from the LORD. The flow of the psalm is clear: he first makes the point that God protects and delivers the merciful, then he gives evidence for this by declaring how the LORD delivered him, and finally he offers his thanksgiving for the deliverance that shows the LORD had accepted him. The foundational thought, then, may be reiterated with the beatitude, "Blessed are the merciful, for they shall receive mercy" (Matt. 5:7).

An expository idea for this psalm may be worded as follows: *Because God delights in those who show mercy to people in need, he will deliver them in their time of trouble.* This deliverance includes both the restoration to health and the prevention of treacherous plans being carried out. Just as people who want forgiveness need to forgive others, so people who want mercy need to show mercy to others. The basic application, therefore, must draw out of Scripture instructions for our showing mercy to people in need. This will be blessed by God, especially when we pray for mercy.

---

35. For "blessed" (בָּרוּךְ) s.v. Ps. 5:12; for "amen" (אָמֵן) s.v. Ps. 15:2.

Index of Hebrew Word Studies for All Volumes

בָּקַשׁ	*seek*	83:16
בָּרָא	*create, shape anew*	51:10
בָּרַךְ	*bless, enrich*	5:12

ג

גָּאָה	*rise up in > majesty*	93:1
גָּאַל	*redeem, act as kinsman*	19:14
גָּבַר	*be strong, mighty, >prevail*	117:2
גִּבּוֹר	*mighty, strong*	45:3
גָּדַל	*be great > strong*	34:3
גִּיל	*rejoice*	13:6
גּוֹי	*nation*	43:1
גָּלַל	*roll, roll away, > trust*	22:8
גָּעַר	*rebuke, restrain*	76:6

ד

דָּבָר	*word, speech*	119:9
דִּין	*judge, govern, do justice*	140:12
דַּעַת	*knowledge*	67:2
דָּשֵׁן	*be fat > make fat, accept*	20:3

ה

הָגָה	*meditate, utter, devise*	2:1
הָדָר	*honor, adornment*	96:6
הוֹד	*glory, splendor, majesty*	96:6
הֵיכָל	*temple*	5:7
הָלַל	*praise*	33:1

ז

זֵדִים	*the arrogant, presumptuous*	119:21
זָכָה	*be clean, free, pure*	51:4
זָכַר	*remember, ponder*	6:5
זָמַר	*sing praises, play music*	33:2
זָנַח	*spurn, cast off, reject*	43:2

ח

חָוָה	*bow down, worship*	95:6
חוּס	*have pity, spare*	72:12
חָזַק	*be strong, firm > strengthen*	27:14

חָטָא	sin, miss the mark	51:2
חַיִל	pomp, wealth, power	49:6
חָכְמָה	wisdom, skill	19:7, 49:3
חָלָה	mollify, appease, entreat	119:58
חָלַל	be profane > pollute, defile	74:7
חָמָס	treat violently > violence	58:2
חֵן, חָנַן	be gracious, grace	4:1
חֶסֶד	loyal love	23:6
חָסָה	take refuge	7:1
חֹק	statute, decree	119:5
חָרָה	be hot, angry > fret	37:1
חֶרְפָּה	taunt, reproach, scorn	22:6
חָשַׁב	think, account, reckon	32:2

ט

טָהֵר	clean, pure	51:2
טוֹב	good, goodness, pleasing	34:8

י

יָדָה	acknowledge, praise	6:5
יָדַע	know	67:2
יָחַל	wait, hope	31:24
יכח	correct, rebuke, reprove	38:1
יָסַד	be established > establish	87:1
יָסַר	discipline, admonish	6:1
יָצַר	plan, form, fashion	33:15
יָרֵא	fear, reverence	2:11
יָשַׁע	save, deliver,	3:2
יָשַׁר	be straight > upright	67:4
	מִישׁוֹר, equitable	67:4

כ

כָּבוֹד	glory, honor	19:1
כּוּן	be established, firm	93:1
כָּלָה	be finished, complete	90:7
כִּפֶּר	atone, ransom, propitiate	49:7

ל

לֵב	heart, mind	111:1

לִיץ	scorn	119:51

מ

מוֹט	slip, totter, shake	62:2
מוּל	circumcise, cut to pieces	118:10
מְזִמָּה	purpose, thought, device	10:2
מָלַט	slip away, escape, deliver	41:1
מִרְמָה	deceit, guile, treachery	5:7
מִצְוָה	commandment	119:6
מָשַׁח	anoint	132:10
מָשַׁל	rule, have dominion	66:7
מָשָׁל	proverb, by-word	49:3

נ

נָבָל	foolishness, senseless	14:1
נָגַד	be conspicuous > tell	75:9
נְדָבָה	freewill offering, free	110:3
נוּחַ	rest	95:11
נָחָה	lead, guide	23:3
נָחַם	comfort, be sorry	119:76
נֵכָר	strange, foreign	144:7
נָסָה	test, try	26:2
נָעִים	pleasant	133:1
נֶפֶשׁ	life, soul	11:5
נָצַל	plunder > deliver	22:20
נָצַר	guard, store up, treasure	119:2
נָקִי	clean, free, innocent	19:13
נָקַם	take revenge, avenge	18:48
נָשָׂא	lift up, take away, forgive	24:7
נְשָׁמָה	breath	150:6

ס

| סָלַח | forgive | 130:4 |
| סָמַךְ | lean, sustain | 51:12 |

ע

עָבַד	serve, work	134:1
עֵדוֹת	statute, testimony	119:2
עַוְלָה	iniquity, injustice, wrong	43:1

Selected Bibliography for the Exposition of the Psalms

Introductory Works

Anderson, Bernhard H., with Bishop, Steven. *Out of the Depths: The Psalms Speak for Us Today.* Philadelphia: Westminster John Knox Press, 2000.

Bellinger, W. H. Jr. *Psalms.* Peabody, MA: Hendrickson Publishers, 1990.

Breuggemann, Walter. *The Message of the Psalms.* Minneapolis, MN: Augsburg, 1984.

Bullock, Hassell C. *Encountering the Book of Psalms.* Grand Rapids: Baker, 2001.

Clines, D. J. A. "Psalm Research Since 1955: I. The Psalms and the Cult." *TynB* 18 (1967):103–125; "II. The Literary Genres." *TynB* 20 (1969):105–25.

Cole, Robert L. *The Shape and Message of Book III (Psalms 73–89).* Sheffield: Sheffield Academic Press, 2000.

Crenshaw, James L. *The Psalms, An Introduction.* Grand Rapids: Eerdmans, 2001.

Crim, Keith R. *The Royal Psalms.* Richmond, Virginia: John Knox Press, 1962.

Drijvers, Pius. *The Psalms, Their Structure and Meaning.* New York: Herder and Herder, 1965.

Eaton, J. H. *Kingship and the Psalms.* London: SCM, 1976.

Estes, Daniel J. *Handbook on the Wisdom Books and Psalms.* Grand Rapids: Baker, 2005.

Flint, Peter W. Miller, Patrick D., Jr., Brunell, Aaron, and Roberts, Ryan, editors. *The Book of Psalms: Composition and Reception.* Leiden: Brill, 2005.

Futato, Mark D. *Interpreting the Psalms: An Exegetical Handbook.* Grand Rapids: Kregel, 2007.

Goulder, Michael. *The Psalms of the Sons of Korah. JSOT* Supplement 20. Sheffield: ISOT Press, 1982. Pp. 37–50. (Ps. 84).

Gunkel, Hermann. *The Psalms: A Form Critical Introduction.* Philadelphia: Fortress Press, 1967.

Hayes, J. H. *Understanding the Psalms.* Valley Forge, PA: Judson Press, 1976.

Holladay, William L. *The Psalms through Three Thousand Years, Prayerbook of a Cloud of Witnesses.* Minneapolis: Fortress Press, 1993

Howard, David M., Jr. *The Structure of Psalms 93–100.* Winona Lake, IN: Eisenbrauns, 1997.

Keet, C. C. *A Study of the Psalms of Ascents. A Critical and Exegetical Commentary upon Psalms 120–134.* London, 1969.

Kim, Jinkyu. "The Strategic Arrangement of Royal Psalms in Books IV-V." *WTJ* 70 (2008):143–57.

Kraus, Hans-Joachim. *Theology of the Psalms.* Translated by Keith Crim. Minneapolis: Augsburg Publishing House, 1986.

Mays, James Luther. *The Lord Reigns: A Theological Handbook to the Psalms.* Louisville: Westminster John Knox, 1994.

McCann, J. C., Jr., ed. *The Shape and Shaping of the Psalter.* Sheffield: Sheffield Academic, 1993.

_____. *A Theological Introduction to the Book of Psalms: The Psalms as Torah.* Nashville: Abingdon, 1993

Mowinckel, Sigmund. *The Psalms in Israel's Worship.* 2 Volumes. Translated by D. R. Ap-Thomas. New York: Abingdon Press, 1967.

Sabourin, Leopold. *The Psalms: Their Origin and Meaning.* New York: Alba House, 1974.

Sanders, J. A. *The Psalm Scroll of Qumran Cave 11.* Oxford: At the Clarendon Press, 1965.

Sarna, Nahum M. *The Psalms: Their Origin and Meaning.* New York: Schocken Press, 1993.

Seybold, K. *Introducing the Psalms.* Edinburgh: T. & T. Clark, 1981.

Westermann, Claus. *The Praise of God in the Psalms.* Translated by Keith R. Crim. Richmond, Virginia: John Knox Press, 1965.

_____. *Praise and Lament in the Psalms.* Translated by Keith R. Crim and Richard N. Soulen. Atlanta: John Knox Press, 1981.

Wevers, J. W. "A Study in the Form Criticism of Individual Complaint Psalms." *VT* 6 (1956):80–86.

Whitelocke, L. T. *The rîb Pattern and the Concept of Judgment in the Book of Psalms.* Dissertation: Boston University Graduate School, 1968. DissAbstr 29 (1968f), 1950f-A.

Wilson, Gerald H. *The Editing of the Hebrew Psalter.* Chico: CA: Scholars Press, 1985.

_____. "Editorial Decision in the Hebrew Psalter." *VT* 34 (1984):342–43.

_____. "The Shape of the Book of Psalms." *Int* 46 (1992):129–42.

_____. "Shaping the Psalter: A Consideration of Editorial Linkage in the Book of Psalms." In *The Shape and Shaping of the Psalter.* Ed. by J. C. McCann, Jr. Pp. 72–82. Sheffield: Sheffield Academic, 1993.

_____. "The Use of Royal Psalms at the 'Seams' of the Hebrew Psalter." *JSOT* 35 (1986):85–94.

Commentaries

Allen, Leslie C. *Psalms 101–150.* Word Biblical Commentary. Waco, TX: Word, 1983.

Anderson, J. A. *The Psalms Translated and Explained.* Grand Rapids: Baker Books, 1977 reprint of the 1873 edition.

Anderson, A. A. *The Book of Psalms.* New Century Bible. 2 Volumes. London: Marshall, Morgan & Scott, 1972.

Braude, William B., editor. *The Midrash on the Psalms.* London: The Soncino Press, nd.

Briggs, Charles A. and Briggs, E. G. *A Critical and Exegetical Commentary on the Psalms.* The International Critical Commentary. 2 Volumes. Edinburgh: T. & T. Clark, 1903.

Broyles, Craig C. *Psalms.* New International Commentary. Peabody, MA: Hendrickson, 1999.

Buttenwiesser, Moses. *The Psalms.* Chicago: University of Chicago Press, 1938.

Calvin, John. *Commentary on the Book of Psalms.* Translated by James Anderson. 3 Volumes. Grand Rapids: Eerdmans, 1963 reprint.

Clifford, Richard J. *Psalms.* 2 Volumes. Nashville: Abingdon, 2002, 2003.

Cohen, A. *The Psalms.* Soncino Books of the Bible. London: The Soncino Press, 1945.

Craigie, Peter C. *Psalms 1–50.* Word Biblical Commentary. Waco, TX: Word, 1983.

Dahood, Mitchell. *Psalms.* The Anchor Bible. 3 Volumes. Garden City, NY: Doubleday, 1965.

Delitzsch, Franz. *Biblical Commentary on the Psalms.* 3 Volumes. Translated by David Eaton. Grand Rapids: Wm. B. Eerdmans Publishing Co., reprint.

Eaton, John. *Psalms.* London: SCM Press, 1967.

Gerstenberger, Eberhard S. *Psalms and Lamentations.* 2 Volumes. Grand Rapids: Eerdmans, 1988, 2001.

Goldingay, John. *Psalms.* 3 Volumes. Grand Rapids: Baker Book House, 2006, 2007, 2008.

Goulder, Michael D. *The Psalms of the Sons of Korah.* Sheffield: JSOT, 1982.

Gunkel, Hermann. *Die Psalmen.* Goettingen: Vandenhoeck und Ruprecht, 1926.

Hengstenberg, E. W. *Commentary on the Psalms.* 3 Volumes. Cherry Hill, NJ: Mack, nd.

Hossfeld, Frank-Lothar, and Erich Zenger. *Psalms 3. A Commentary on Psalms 101–150.* Translated by Linda M. Maloney. Minneapolis: Fortress Press, 2011.

Jacquet, L. *Les Psaumes et le couer de l'homme. Etude textuelle, litteraire et doctrinale.* 3 Volumes. Gembloux: Duculot, 1975.

Keet, Cuthbert C. *A Study of the Psalms of Ascent: A Critical and Exegetical Commentary on Psalms cxx–cxxxiv.*" London: Mitre Press, 1969.

Kidner, Derek. *Psalms 1–72, Psalms 73–150.* 2 Volumes. London: InterVarsity Press, 1975.

Kirkpatrick, A. F. *The Book of Psalms.* The Cambridge Bible for Schools and Colleges. 3 Volumes. Cambridge: At the University Press, 1906. Reprinted in one volume by Baker Book House.

Kraus, Hans-Joachim. *Psalms 1–59, Psalms 60–150.* 2 Volumes. Translated by Hilton C. Oswald. Minneapolis: Augsburg Publishing House, 1988.

Leupold, H. C. *Exposition of the Psalms.* Grand Rapids: Baker Book House, 1969.

Mays, James L. *Psalms.* Interpretation. Louisville: Knox, 1994.

McCann, J. Clinton. "The Book of Psalms," in *The New Interpreter's Bible,* Volume 4. Edited by Leander E. Keck. Nashville: Abingdon, 1996, Pp. 639–1280.

Moll, Carl Bernhard. *The Psalms.* Lange's Commentary on the Holy Scriptures. Edited by John Peter Lange. Grand Rapids: Zondervan Publishing House reprint of the 1869 edition.

Oesterley, W. O. E. *The Psalms.* London: S.P.C.K., 1962.

Perowne, J. J. Stewart. *The Book of Psalms.* 2 Volumes. Grand Rapids: Zondervan Publishing House, reprint of 1878 edition.

Rogerson, J. W. and McKay, J. W. *Psalms.* 3 Volumes. The Cambridge Bible Commentary. Cambridge: Cambridge University Press, 1977.

Tate, Marvin E. *Psalms 51–100.* Waco: Word, 1990.

Terrien, Samuel. *The Psalms.* Grand Rapids: Eerdmans, 2002.

VanGemeren, Willem. *Psalms.* The Expositor's Bible Commentary. Grand Rapids: Zondervan, 2008.

Weiser, Artur. *The Psalms: A Commentary.* Old Testament Library. Translated by Herbert Hartwell. Philadelphia: The Westminster Press, 1962.

Wilson, Gerald H. *Psalms 1–72.* NIV Application Commentary. Grand Rapids: Zondervan, 2002.

The Psalms as Poetry

Alden, Robert. "Chiastic Psalms." *JETS* 17 (1974):11–18; 19 (1976):191–200; 21 (1978):199–210.

Alonso-Schökel, Luis. *Estudios de Poetica Hebrea*. Barcelona: Juan Flors, 1963.

_____. "Hermeneutics in the Light of Language and Literature." *CBQ* 25 (1963):371–386.

Alter, Robert. *The Art of Biblical Poetry*. New York: Basic Books, 1985.

Berlin, Adele. *The Dynamics of Biblical Parallelism*. Bloomington: Indiana University Press, 1985.

Blenkinsopp, J. "Stylistics of Old Testament Poetry." *Bib* 44 (1963):352–358.

Boling, R. G. "Synonymous Parallelism in the Psalms." *JSS* 5 (1960):221–255.

Bouzard, Walter C., Jr. *We Have Heard with Our Ears, O God: Sources of the Communal Laments in the Psalms*. Atlanta: Scholars Press, 1997.

Bright, John. *Jeremiah*. The Anchor Bible. Garden City, NY: Doubleday and Company, 1965. Pp. cxxvi-cxxxviii.

Broyles, C. *The Conflict of Faith and Experience, A Form Critical and Theological Study of Selected Lament Psalms*. Sheffield: Academic Press, 1989.

Bywater, Ingram. *Aristotle on the Art of Poetry*. Oxford: At the Clarendon Press, 1909.

Bullinger, E. W. *Figures of Speech Used in the Bible*. Grand Rapids: Baker Book House, reprint of 1898 edition.

Caird, G. B. *The Language and Imagery of the Bible*. Philadelphia: Westminster, 1980.

Casanowicz, Immanuel M. *Paronomasia in the Old Testament*. Boston: Norwood Press, 1894.

Creach, Jerome F. D. *Yahweh as Refuge and the Editing of the Hebrew Psalter*. JSOT Supplement 217. Sheffield: Sheffield Academic Press, 1996.

Cross, F. M., and Freedman, D. N. *Studies in Ancient Yahwistic Poetry*. Missoula, Montana: Scholars Press, 1975.

Driver, G. R. "Poetic Diction." *VT* Supplement 1 (1953):26–39.

Empsom, W. *Seven Types of Ambiguity*. London: Chatto and Windus, 1947.

Engnell, Ivan. "The Figurative Language of the Old Testament." In *Critical Essays of the Old Testament*. Edited by John T. Willis. London: S.P.C.K., 1970.

Gevirtz, Stanley. "On Canaanite Rhetoric: The Evidence of the Amarna Letters from Tyre." *Orientalia* ns 42 (1973):162–177.

_____. "Of Patriarchs and Puns: Joseph at the Fountain, Jacob at the Ford." *HUCA* 46 (1975):33–54.

_____. *Patterns in the Early Poetry of Israel*. Chicago: University of Chicago Press, 1963.

Glueck, J. J. "The Figures of Inversion in the Book of Proverbs." *Semitics* 5 (1976):25.

_____. "Paronomasia in Biblical Literature." *Semitics* 1 (1970):50–78.

Good, Edwin. *Irony in the Old Testament*. London: S.P.C.K., 1965.

Herder, Johann Gottfried von. *The Spirit of Hebrew Poetry*. Burlington, England: Edward Smith, 1833.

Honeyman, A. M. "*Merismus* in Biblical Literature." *JBL* 85 (1966):401–435.

Jackson, Jared J., and Kessler, Martin. *Rhetorical Criticism*. Essays in Honor of James Muilenberg. Pittsburgh: The Pickwick Press, 1974.

Keel, Othmar. *The Symbolism of the Biblical World. Ancient Near Eastern Iconography and the Book of Psalms*. Translated by Timothy J. Hallett. New York: Seabury Press, 1978.

Kessler, M. "*Inclusio* in the Hebrew Bible." *Semitics* 6 (1978):4.

Kikawada, Isaac M. "Some Proposals for the Definition of Rhetorical Criticism." *Semitics* 5 (1977): 67–91.

Kugal, James L. *The Idea of Biblical Poetry*. London: Longman Group Ltd., 1969

Lewis, C. S. *Reflections on the Psalms*. A Harvest Book. New York: Harcourt, Brace and World, Inc., 1958.

Longman, Tremper, III. *Literary Approaches to Biblical Interpretation*. Grand Rapids: Zondervan, 1987.

Lowth, Robert. *Lectures on the Sacred Poetry of the Hebrews*. Translated by G. Gregory. Andover: Codman Press, 1829.

Muilenberg, James. "Form Criticism and Beyond." *JBL* 81 (1969):1–18.

_____. "A Study in Hebrew Rhetoric: Repetition and Style."
VT Supplement 1 (1953):97–111.

Payne, D. F. "Old Testament Exegesis and the Problem of
Ambiguity." *ASTI* 5 (1967):48–68.

Perdue, Leo. *Wisdom and Cult.* Missoula, MT: Scholars Press,
1977.

Preminger, A., Warnke, F. J., and Hardison, O. B. *Princeton
Encyclopedia of Poetry and Poetics.* Revised Edition.
Princeton: Princeton University Press, 1975.

Rankin, O. S. "Alliteration in Hebrew Poetry." *JTS* 31
(1930):285–300.

Robinson, Theodore H. "Hebrew Poetic Form: The English
Tradition." *VT* Supplement 1 (1953):128–149.

_____. *The Poetry of the Old Testament.* London: Duckworth,
1947.

Ryken, Leland. *How To Read the Bible as Literature.* Grand
Rapids: Zondervan, 1984.

Saydon, P. P. "Assonance in Hebrew as a Means of Expressing
Emphasis." *Bib* 36 (1955):36–50; 287–304.

Shepherd, John. "The Place of the Imprecatory Psalms in the
Canon of Scripture." *Churchman* 111 (1997):27–43, 110–26.

Slotki, Israel W. "Antiphony in Ancient Hebrew Poetry." *JQR* 26
(1935):199–219.

Waltke, Bruce K. "Superscripts, Postscripts, or Both." *JBL* 110
(1991):583–96.

Watters, William R. *Formula Criticism and the Poetry of the Old
Testament.* Berlin and New York: Walter de Gruyter, 1976.

Wieder, Laurance, editor. *The Poet's Book of Psalms. The Complete
Psalter as Rendered by Twenty-Five Poets from the Sixteenth
to the Twentieth Centuries.* Oxford: Oxford University Press,
1995.

Wright, Addison G. "The Literary Genre Midrash." *CBQ* 28
(1966):105–138, 417–457.

Additional Resources

Aharoni, Yohanan. *The Land of the Bible: A Historical Geography.*
Philadelphia: Westminster, 1979.

Aharoni, Yohanan, and Michael Avi-Yonah. *The Macmillan Bible
Atlas.* New York: Macmillan, 1993.

Beckwith, Roger T. "The Early History of the Psalter." *TynB* 46 (1995):1–27.

Bonhoeffer, Dietrich, *Meditating on the Word*. Minneapolis: Augsburg, nd.

_____. *Psalms, The Prayer Book of the Bible*. Minneapolis: Augsburg, 1970.

Botterweck, G. Johannes, Ringgren. Helmer, and Fabry, Heinz-Josef, editors. *Theological Dictionary of the Old Testament*. 15 Volumes. Translated by John T. Willis, Geoffrey W. Bromiley, and David E. Green. Grand Rapids : Eerdmans, 1978.

Borowski, Oded. *Agriculture in Iron Age Israel*. Winona Lake, IN: Eisenbrauns, 2002.

Braun, Joachim. *Music in Ancient Israel/Palestine*. Grand Rapids: Eerdmans, 2002.

Bruce, F. F. "The Earliest Old Testament Interpretation," *OTS* 17 (1972):37–52.

Childs, Brevard S. *Memory and Tradition in Israel*. Naperville, IL: Allenson, 1962.

Chisholm, Robert B., Jr. *From Exegesis to Exposition. A Practical Guide to Using Biblical Hebrew*. Grand Rapids: Baker Books, 1998.

Creach, Jerome F. D. *The Destiny of the Righteous in the Psalms*. St. Louis: Chalice, 2008.

Crow, Loren S. *The Songs of Ascent (Psalms 120–134): Their Place in Israelite History and Religion*. Atlanta: Scholars Press, 1996.

Curtis, Edward M. "Ancient Psalms and Modern Worship." *BibSac* 154 (1997):285–96.

Dalglish, Edward R. *Psalm Fifty-One in the Light of Ancient Near Eastern Patternism*. Leiden: E. J. Brill, 1962.

Davies, G. Henton. "The Ark in the Psalms." In *Promise and Fulfillment: Essays Presented to Professor S. H. Hooke*. Ed. by F. F. Bruce. Edinburgh: T. & T. Clark, 1963. Pp. 51–61.

Day, John. *God's Conflict with the Dragon and the Sea: Echoes of Canaanite Myth in the Old Testament*. Cambridge: Cambridge University Press, 1985.

Day, John N. *Crying for Justice. What the Psalms Teach Us about Mercy and Vengeance in an Age of Terrorism*. Grand Rapids: Kregel, 2005.

Dell, Katharine J. "The Use of Animal Imagery in the Psalms and Wisdom Literature of Ancient Israel." *SJT* 53 (2000):275–91.

DePinto, B. "The Torah and the Psalms." *JBL* 86 (1967):154–74.

De Vaux, Roland. *Ancient Israel*. 2 Volumes. New York: McGraw-Hill, 1965

Eichrodt, W. *Theology of the Old Testament*. 2 Volumes. Translated by J. A. Baker. Philadelphia: Westminster, 1961, 1967.

Engnell, Ivan. *Studies in Divine Kingship in the Ancient Near East*. Oxford: Basil Blackwell, 1967 reprint of 1943 Uppsala edition.

Fensham, F. C. "Widow, Orphan, and the Poor in Ancient Near Eastern Legal and Wisdom Literature." *JNES* 21 (1962):129–139.

Field, Fredericus. *Origenis Hexaplorum*. 2 Volumes. Oxonii: E. Typographea Clarendoniano, 1875.

Finkelstein, L. "The Origin of the Hallel (Pss. 113–118)." *HUCA* 23 (1950):319–337.

Fisher, L. R., editor. *Ras Shamra Parallels. The Texts from Ugarit and the Hebrew Bible*. 2 Volumes. Rome: Analecta orientalia, 1972. See especially "Literary Phrases" by Schoors, pp. 1–70; "Ugaritic-Hebrew Parallel Pairs" by Dahood and Penar, pp. 383–452; and "Flora, Fauna, and Minerals" by Sasson.

Flint, Peter W. *The Dead Sea Psalms Scrolls & the Book of Psalms*. Leiden: Brill, 1997.

Gertner, M. "Terms of Scriptural Interpretation: A Study in Hebrew Semantics," *BSOAS* 25 (1962):1–27.

Gillingham, Susan E. *The Poems and the Psalms of the Hebrew Bible*. Oxford: Oxford University Press, 1994.

————. "Studies of the Psalms: Retrospect and Prospect." *ExT* 119 (2008):209–216.

Habel, Norman C. *Yahweh versus Baal, A Conflict of Religious Cultures: A Study in the Relevance of Ugaritic materials for the Early Faith of Israel*. New York: Bookman Association, 1964. Pp. 52–71. (Ps. 93)

Hardin, J. M. *Psalterium iuxta Hebraeos Hieronymi*. London: S.P.C.K., 1922.

Hareuveni, Nogah. *Desert and Shepherd in Our Biblical Heritage*. Translated by Helen Frenkley. Neot Kedumim, Israel, 1991.

Harmon, A. M. "Aspects of Paul's Use of the Psalms." *WJT* 32 (1969):1–23.

Hilber, John W. *Cultic Prophecy in the Psalms.* New York: Walter de Gruyter, 2005.

Holladay, W. L. *The Root ŠUBH in the Old Testament with Particular Reference to Its Usage in Covenantal Contexts.* Leiden: Brill, 1958.

Howard, David M. "Recent Trends in Psalms Study." In *The Face of Old Testament Studies: A Survey of Contemporary Approaches.* Ed. by David W. Baker and Bill T. Arnold. Grand Rapids: Baker Books, 1999.

Hooke, S. H., editor. *Myth and Ritual. Essays on the Myth and Ritual of the Hebrews in Relation to the Cultic Pattern of the ANE.* Oxford: Clarendon Press, 1933.

Human, Dirk J., and Vos, Cas J. A., eds. *Psalms and Liturgy.* London: T. & T. Clark, 2004.

Hvidberg, F. F. *Weeping and Laughing in the Old Testament.* Leiden: E. J. Brill, 1962.

Jaki, Stanley L. *Praying the Psalms, A Commentary.* Grand Rapids: Eerdmans, 2001.

Jenni, Ernst, and Westermann, Claus, editors. *Theological Lexicon of the Old Testament.* 3 Volumes. Translated by Mark E. Biddle. Peabody, MA: Hendrickson Publisher, Inc., 1997 (German edition, 1976).

Johnson, A. R. *The Cultic Prophet and Israel's Psalmody.* Cardiff: University of Wales Press, 1962.

Knight, Jack C. and Sinclair, Lawrence A., eds. *The Psalms and other Studies in the Old Testament,* FS for Joseph I. Hunt. Nashotah, WI: Nashotah House, 1990.

Kohlenberger, John R. III, editor. *The Comparative Psalter: Hebrew-Greek-English.* Oxford: Oxford University Press, 2007.

Kraus, Hans-Joachim. *Worship in Israel.* Oxford: Clarendon Press, 1966.

Lamb, John A. *The Psalms in Christian Worship.* London: Faith Press, 1962.

Laney, J. Carl. "A Fresh Look at the Imprecatory Psalms." *BibSac* 138 (1981):35–45.

Levenson, Jon D. *Sinai and Zion: An Entry into the Jewish Bible.* Minneapolis, MN: Winston Press, 1985.

Lewalski, Barbara. *Protestant Poetics and the Seventeenth Century Religious Lyric.* Princeton: Princeton University Press, 1979.

Lipinski, E. *"Yahweh malak." Bib* 44 (1963):405–460.

Mays, James L. *The Lord Reigns: A Theological Handbook to the Psalms.* Louisville: Westminster John Knox, 1994.

McCann Jr., J. Clinton. *A Theological Introduction to the Book of Psalms: Psalms as Torah.* Nashville: Abingdon, 1993.

McConville, Gordon. "The Psalms: Introduction and Theology." *Evangel* 11 (1993):43–54.

McKeating, H. "Divine Forgiveness in the Psalms." *SJT* 18 (1965):69–83.

McKenzie, J. L. "Royal Messianism." *CBQ* 19 (1957):25–52.

Merton, Thomas. *Praying the Psalms.* Collegeville, MN: Liturgical Press, 1956.

Mettinger, T. N. D. *King and Messiah, The Civil and Sacral Legitimization of the Israelite Kings.* Lund: C. W. K. Gleerup, 1976. (Ps. 110)

Meyers, Carol L. "The Drum-Dance-Song Ensemble: Women's Performance in Biblical Israel." In *Rediscovering the Muses: Women's Musical Tradition.* Ed. by Kimberly Marshall. Boston: Northeastern University Press, 1993. Pp. 49–67.

Miller, Patrick D. *They Cried to the LORD: The Form and Theology of Biblical Prayer.* Minneapolis: Fortress, 1994.

————. *The Way of the LORD: Essays in Old Testament Theology.* Grand Rapids: Eerdmans, 2007.

Moreton, M. J. "The Sacrifice of Praise." *Church Quarterly Review* 165 (1964):481–494.

Morgenstern, J. "The Cultic Setting of the Enthronement Psalms." *HUCA* 35 (1964):1–42.

Pietersma, Albert, and Wright, Benjamin C. Editors. *A New English Translation of the Septuagint.* Oxford: Oxford University Press, 2007.

Pritchard, James. *Ancient Near Eastern Texts Relating to the Old Testament.* Princeton: Princeton University Press, 1969.

Rabinowitz, L. J. "The Psalms in Jewish Liturgy." *Historia Judaica* 6 (1944):109–122 (cf. *CBQ* 1945).

Ringgren, Helmer. *Religions of the Ancient Near East.* Philadelphia: Westminster, 1973.

Rosenbloom, Joseph R. *Conversion to Judaism, From the Biblical Period to the Present.* New York: KTAV Pub. Inc., 1979.

Ross, Allen P. *Recalling the Hope of Glory.* Grand Rapids: Kregel, 2006.

_____. "The Theology of the Psalms: Our Living Hope." *BibV* 4 (1970):126–135.

Ross, J. P. *"Yahweh Ṣebā'ôt* in Samuel and Psalms." *VT* 17 (1967):76–92.

Rowley, H. H. *Worship in Israel.* London: SCM Press, Ltd., 1967.

Sellers, Ovid R. "Musical Instruments of Israel." In *Biblical Archaeologist Reader, 1.* Ed. by George Ernest Wright and David Noel Freedman. New York: Doubleday, 1961. Pp. 81–94.

Sire, James W. *Learning to Pray through the Psalms.* Downers Grove, IL: InterVarsity, 2005.

Smick, Elmer B. "Mythopoetic Language in the Psalter." *WTJ* 44 (1982):88–98.

Snaith, N. H. "Selah." *VT* 2 (1952):42–56.

_____. *The Seven Psalms.* London: Epworth Press, 1964.

Stackhouse, Rochelle A. *The Language of the Psalms in Worship: American Revisions of Watts' Psalter.* Lanham, MD: Scarecrow Press, 1997.

Stec, David M. *The Targums of Psalms.* Collegeville, MN: Liturgical Press, 2004.

Suring, Margrit L. *The Horn-Motif in the Hebrew Bible and Related Ancient Near Eastern Literature and Iconography. AUSS DDS 4.* Berrien Springs, MI: Andrews University Press, 1980.

Terrien, S. *The Elusive Presence.* San Francisco: Harper & Row, 1978.

Thomas, D. Winton. *Text of the Revised Psalter.* London: SPCK, 1963.

VanGemeren, Willem, editor. *The New International Dictionary of Old Testament Theology and Exegesis,* 5 Volumes. Grand Rapids: Zondervan Publishing Company, 1999.

Viviers, Hendrek. "The Coherence of the *ma'ălôt* Psalms (Pss 120–134)." *ZAW* 106 (1994):275–89.

Wallace, Howard N. "King and Community: Joining with David in Prayer." In *Psalms and Prayers.* Edited by Bob Becking and Eric Peels. Leiden: E. J. Brill, 2007.

Waltke, Bruce K., and Houston, James M. *The Psalms as Christian Worship: A Historical Commentary.* Grand Rapids: Eerdmans, 2010.

Walton, John H. *Ancient Israelite Literature in Its Cultural Context: A Survey of Parallels Between Biblical and Ancient Near Eastern Texts.* Grand Rapids: Zondervan, 1989.

Watts, John D. W. "A History of the Use and Interpretation of the Psalms." In *An Introduction to Wisdom Literature and the Psalms.* Edited by H. Wayne Ballard and W. Dennis Tucker. Macon, GA: Mercer University Press, 2000. Pp. 21–35.

Weiss, Meier. *The Bible from Within: The Method of Total Interpretation.* Jerusalem: Magnes Press, 1984.

Wells, C. Richard, and Van Neste, Ray, eds. *Forgotten Songs: Reclaiming the Psalms for Christian Worship.* Nashville: B&H Academic, 2012.

Wenham, Gordon J. *Psalms as Torah: Reading Biblical Song Ethically.* Studies in Theological Interpretation. Grand Rapids: Baker Academic, 2012.

Westermann, Claus. *The Living Psalms.* Translated by J. R. Porter. Grand Rapids: Eerdmans, 1989 (original date, 1984).

Wieder, Laurance. Editor. *The Poets' Book of Psalms.* Oxford: Oxford University Press, 1995.

Wilson, Gerald H. *The Editing of the Hebrew Psalter.* Society of Biblical Literature Dissertation Series 76. Chico, CA: Scholars Press, 1985.

Wolff, Hans Walter. *Anthropology of the Old Testament.* Philadelphia: Fortress Press, 1974.

Wright, G. E. *The Old Testament Against Its Environment.* London: SCM Press, Ltd., 1950.

Yadin, Yigael. *The Art of Warfare in Biblical Lands.* New York: McGraw-Hill, 1963.

Zenger, Erich. *A God of Vengeance. Understanding the Psalms of Divine Wrath.* Philadelphia: Westminster John Knox, 1995.

Specific Studies for Individual Psalms or Motifs

Ackerman, J. S. "An Exegetical Study of Psalm 82." Dissertation, Harvard, 1966.

Ackroyd, Peter R. "Some Notes on the Psalms." *JTS* 17 (1966):392–99. (Pss. 29, 96)

Albright, W. F. "A Catalogue of Early Hebrew Lyric Poems (Psalm LXVIII)." *HUCA* 23 (1950):1–39.

Allen, Leslie C. "Faith on Trial: An Analysis of Psalm 139," *Vox evangelica* 10 (1977):5–23.

———. "Psalm 73: An Analysis." *TynB* 33 (1982):93–118.

———. "The Old Testament in Romans I-VIII," *VT* 3 (1964):11–12. (Ps. 143)

———. "Structure and Meaning in Psalm 50." *Vox evangelica* 14 (1984):17–37.

———. "The Value of Rhetorical Criticism in Psalm 69." *JBL* 105 (1986):577–98.

Alonso-Shökel, Luis. "The Poetic Structure of Psalms 42–43." *JSOT* 1 (1976):4–11.

Althann, Robert. "The Psalms of Vengeance against Their Ancient Near Eastern Background." *JNSL* 18 (1992):1–11.

———. "Atonement and Reconciliation in Psalms 3, 6, and 83." *JNSL* 25 (1999):75–82.

———. "Psalm 58:10 in the Light of Ebla." *Bib* 64 (1983):122–24.

Anderson, G. W. "Enemies and Evildoers in the Book of Psalms." *BJRL* 48 (1965):18–29. (Pss. 5, 28)

———. "A Note on Psalm i 1," *VT* 24 (1974):231–34.

Ap-Thomas, D. R. "Some Aspects of the Root ḤNN in the Old Testament." *JSS* 2 (1957):128–48. (Ps. 4)

Arbez, E. P. "A Study of Psalm 1." *CBQ* 7 (1945):398–404.

Armerding, C. E. "Were David's Sons Really Priests?" In *Current Issues in Biblical and Patristic Interpretation*. Ed. by G. F. Hawthorne. Grand Rapids: Eerdmans, 1975. Pp. 75–86. (Ps. 110)

Auffret, Pierre. *The Literary Structure of Psalm 2. JSOT* Supplement 3. Sheffield: Sheffield Academic, 1977.

———. "Note on the Literary Structure of Psalm 134." *JSOT* 45 (1989):87–9.

———. "YHWH, *qui sejournera en ta tente?*" *VT* 50 (2000):143–51. (Ps. 15)

Barentsen, Jack. "Restoration and Its Blessing." *GTJ* 5 (1984):247–69. (Pss. 32, 51)

Barker, David G. "The LORD Watches Over You." *BibSac* 152 (1995):163–81. (Ps. 121)

Barré, Michael L. "The Formulaic Pair טוב (ו) חסד in the Psalter." *ZAW* 98 (1986):100–105.

————. "Hearts, Beds, and Repentance in Psalm 4:5 and Hosea 7:14." *Bib* 76 (1995):53–62.

————. "Psalm 116: Its Structure and Its Enigmas." *JBL* 109 (1990):61–78.

————. "Recovering the Literary Structure of Psalm xv." *VT* 34 (1984):207–11.

————. "The Seven Epithets of Zion in Ps. 48:2–3." *Bib* 69 (1988):557–63.

————. "The Shifting Focus of Psalm 101," in *The Book of Psalms,* ed. by Peter W. Flint and Patrick D. Miller. Leiden: Brill, 2005. Pp. 206–223.

————. "'Walking About' as a *Topos* of Depression in Ancient Near Eastern Literature and the Bible." *JNES* 60 (2001):171–87. (Pss. 42, 43).

———— and Kselman, John S. "New Exodus, Covenant and Restoration in Psalm 23." In *The Word Shall Go Forth.* Ed. by Carol F. Meyers and M. O'Connor. Winona Lake, IN: Eisenbrauns, 1983. Pp. 97–127.

Bazak, J. "The Geometric-Figurative Sequence of Psalm cxxxvi," *VT* 35 (1985):129–38.

Bee, R. E. "The Textual Analysis of Psalm 132." *JSOT* 6 (1978):68–70.

Begg, C. T. "The Covenantal Dove in Psalm lxxiv 19–20." *VT* 37 (1987):78–81.

Bellinger, W. H. "The Interpretation of Psalm 11." *EvQ* 56 (1984):95–101.

————. "Psalm 26." *VT* 43 (1993):452–61.

————. "Psalms of the Falsely Accused: A Reassessment." *SBL Seminar Papers* 25 (1986):463–69. (Ps. 7)

Bennett, Robert A. "Wisdom Motifs in Psalm 14 = 53–*nābāl* and *'ēṣāh*." *BASOR* 220 (1975):15–21.

Berlin, Adele. "On the Interpretation of Psalm 133." In *Directions in Biblical Hebrew Poetry, JSOT* Supplement 40. Ed. by

Elaine R. Follis. Sheffield: Sheffield Academic Press, 1987). Pp. 141–147.

_____. "Psalm 118:24." *JBL* 96 (1977):567–68.

_____. "The Rhetoric of Psalm 145." In *Biblical and Related Studies Presented to Samuel Iwry.* Edited by Ann Kort and Scott Morshauer. Winona Lake, IN: Eisenbrauns, 1985. Pp. 17–22.

Beuken, W "Psalm 39: Some Aspects of the Old Testament Understanding of Prayer." *Heythrop Journal* 19 (1978):1–11.

_____. "Psalm XLVII: Structure and Drama." In *Remembering the Way.* Ed. by A. Albrektson. Leiden: E. J. Brill, 1981. Pp. 38–54. (*OTS* 21).

Blakeney, E. H. "Psalm 121:1–2." *ExT* 56 (1944, 1945): 111.

Boers, H. W. "Psalm 16 and the Historical origin of the Christian Faith." *ZNW* 60 (1969):105–10.

Boling, R. G. "Synonymous Parallelism in the Psalms." *JSS* 5 (1960):221–255.

Booij, Thijs. "The Background of the Oracle in Psalm 81." *Bib* 65 (1984):465–75.

_____. "The Hebrew Text of Psalm xcii 11." *VT* 38 (1988):210–13.

_____. "Psalm 90:5–6: Junction of Two Traditional Motifs," *Bib* 68 (1987):393–96.

_____. "Psalm ci 2. *VT* 38 (1988):458–62.

_____. "Psalm 104:13b: The Earth Is Satisfied with the Fruit of Your Works." *Bib* 70 (1989):409–12.

_____. "Psalm 109:6–19 as a Quotation: A Review of the Evidence." In *Give Ear To My Words: Psalms and Other Poetry in and around the Hebrew Bible.* FS for N. A. Van Uchelin. Ed. by J. Dyk. Amsterdam: Societas Hebraica Amstelodamensis, 1996. Pp. 91–106.

_____. "Psalm cxxii 4." *VT* 51 (2001):262–6.

_____. "Psalm 127, 2b." *Bib* 81 (2000):262–68.

_____. "Psalm 133." *Bib* 83 (2002):258–67.

_____. "The Role of Darkness in Psalm cv 28." *VT* 39 (1989):209–14.

_____. "Royal Words in Psalm lxxxiv 11." *VT* 36 (1986):117–20.

_____. "Rule in the Midst of Your Foes." *VT* 41 (1991):396–407.

_____. "Some Observations on Psalm lxxxvii." *VT* 37 (1987):16–25.

Bos, J. W. H. "Oh, When the Saints: A Consideration of the Meaning of Psalm 50." *JSOT* 24 (1982):65–77.

Bowker, J. W. "Psalm 110." *VT* 17 (1967):31–41.

Bracke, John M. "*Šûb šebût:* A Reappraisal." *ZAW* 97 (1985):233–44. (Pss. 14, 126)

Brekelmans, C. "Psalm 132: Unity and Structure." *Bijdr* 44 (1983):262–65.

Brooke, G. J. "Psalms 105 and 106 at Qumran." *RevQ* 14 (1989–90):267–92.

Broyles, C. *The Conflict of Faith and Experience, A Form Critical and Theological Study of Selected Lament Psalms. JSOT* Supplement 52. Sheffield: Academic Press, 1989. Pp. 139–44. (Ps. 44)

Brown, W. P. "A Royal Performance: Critical Notes on Psalm 110:3a-b." *JBL* 117 (1998):93–96.

Bruce, F. F. "The Earliest Old Testament Interpretation." *OTS* 17 (1972):37–52.

Brueggemann, W. *Israel's Praise*: *Doxology against Idolatry and Ideology.* Philadelphia: Fortress Press, 1988. (Ps. 93)

_____. "Psalm 100." *Int* 39 (1985):65–9.

Brongers, H. A. "Psalms 1–2 as a Coronation Liturgy." *Bib* 52 (1971):321–336.

Buber, M. "The Heart Determines: Psalm 73." In *Theodicy in the Old Testament.* Ed. by James L. Crenshaw. Philadelphia: Fortress Press, 1983. Pp. 109–18.

Buchanan, G. W. "The Courts of the Lord." *VT* 16 (1966):231–32.

Bullough, Sebastian. "The Question of Meter in Psalm i." *VT* 17 (1967):42–49.

Buss, M. J. "Psalms of Asaph and Korah." *JBL* 82 (1963):382–92. (Pss. 50, 83)

Cahill, M. "Not a Cornerstone! Translating Ps 118, 22 in the Jewish and Christian Scriptures." *RB* 106 (1999):345–57.

Campbell, A. F. "Psalm 78: A Contribution to the Theology of Tenth Century Israel." *CBQ* 41 (1979):51–79.

Carroll, R. P. "Psalm lxxviii: Vestiges of a Tribal Palestine." *VT* 21 (1971):133–50.

Cassuto, U. "Psalm LXVIII." In *Biblical and Oriental Studies,* Vol 1. Translated by Israel Abrahams. Jerusalem: Magnes Press, 1973. Pp. 241–284.

Cazelles, H. "La question du *lamed auctoris.*" *RB* 56 (1949):93–101.

Ceresko, Anthony R. "The ABC's of Wisdom in Psalm xxxiv." *VT* 35 (1985):99–104.

_____. "The Chiastic Word Pattern in Hebrew." *CBQ* 38 (1976):303–11.

_____. "A Note on Psalm 63: A Psalm of Vigil." *ZAW* 92 (1980):435–36.

_____. "A Poetic Analysis of Psalm 105, with Attention to Its Use of Irony." *Bib* 64 (1983):20–46.

_____."Psalm 121: Prayer of a Warrior?" *Bib* 70 (1989):496–510.

_____. "Psalm 149: Poetry, Themes (Exodus and Conquest), and Social Function." *Bib* 67 (1986):179–94.

Charlesworth, James H. "Prolegomenon to a New Study of the Jewish Background of the Hymns and Prayers in the New Testament." *JJS* 1–2 (1982):265–85.

Childs, B. S. "Analysis of a Canonical Formula: 'It Shall Be Recorded for a Future Generation.'" In *Die Hebraische Bibel und ihre zweifache Nachgeschichte,* FS for R. Rendtorff. Ed., by E. Blum, et al. Neukirchen-Vluyn: Neukirchen Verlag, 1990. Pp. 357–64.

_____. "Deuteronomic Formulae of the Exodus Traditions," *VT* Supplement 16 (Leiden: Brill, 1967): pp. 30–39.

_____. "Psalm 8 in the Context of the Christian Canon." *Int* 23 (1969):20–31.

Chinitz, J. "Psalm 145: Its Two Faces." *JBQ* 24 (1996):229–32.

Clifford, Richard J. *The Cosmic Mountain in Canaan and the Old Testament.* HSM 4 Cambridge: Harvard University Press, 1972. Pp. 142–44. (Ps. 48).

_____. "Psalm 89: A Lament Over the Davidic Ruler's Continued Failure." *HTR* 73 (1980):35–47.

_____. "Style and Purpose in Psalm 105." *Bib* 60 (1979):420–27.

_____. "What Does the Psalmist Ask for in Psalm 39:5 and 90:12?" *JBL* 119 (2000):59–66.

Clines, D. J. A. "The Evidence for an Autumnal Year in Pre-Exilic Israel Reconsidered." *JBL* 93(1974):22–40.

Coetzee, J. H. "The Functioning of Elements in Tension in Psalm 44." *Theologica Evangelica* 21 (1988):2–5.

Cogan, M. "A Technical Term for Exposure." *JNES* 27 (1968):133–35. (Ps. 71)

Cohen, M. "'AŠŠŪRÊNÛ 'ATTÁ SEBĀBÛNÎ (Q. *SEBABÛNÛ*) (PSAUME XVII IIA)." *VT* 41 (1991):137–44. (Ps. 17)

Cole, Robert. "An Integrated Reading of Psalms 1 and 2." *JSOT* 98 (2002):75–88.

Condon, K. "The Biblical Doctrine of Original Sin." *ITQ* 34 (1967):20–36.

Cooke, Gerald. "The Israelite King as Son of God." *ZAW* 73 (1960):202–25. (Ps. 2)

Coppens, J. "Les paralleles du Psautier avec les textes de Ras Shamra." *Le Museon* 59 (1946):113–42.

_____. "Les Psaumes 6 et 41 dependent-ils au livre de Jeremie." *HUCA* 32 (1961):217–226.

Costacurta, B. "L'aggressione contri Dio: Studio del Salmo 83." *Bib* 64 (1983):518–41.

Craigie, P. C. "The Comparison of Hebrew Poetry: Psalm 104 in the Light of Egyptian and Ugaritic Poetry." *Sem* 4 (1974):10–21.

_____. "Parallel Word Pairs in Ugaritic Poetry: A Critical Appraisal of Their Relevance for Psalm 29." *UF* 11 (1979):135–40.

_____. "Psalm xxix in the Hebrew Poetic Tradition." *VT* 22 (1972):143–54.

Creach, Jerome F. D. "Like a Tree Planted by the Temple Stream: The Portrait of the Righteous in Psalm 1:3." *CBQ* 61 (1999):34–46.

_____. "Psalm 121." *Int* 50 (1996):47–51.

Crenshaw, James L. "Knowing Whose You Are: Psalm 24." In *The Psalms: An Introduction*. Grand Rapids: Eerdmans, 2001. Pp. 155–67.

_____. "5. Standing Near the Flame: Psalm 73." In *A Whirlpool of Torment*. Philadelphia: Fortress Press, 1984.

Cross, F. M. Jr. "Notes on a Canaanite Psalm in the Old Testament." *BASOR* 117 (1949):19–21. (Ps. 29)

_____. "Notes on Psalm 93: A Fragment of a Liturgical Psalm." In *A God So Near: Essays on Old Testament Theology in*

Honor of Patrick D. Miller. Ed. by Brent A. Strawn and Nancy
 R. Bowen. Winona Lake, IN: Eisenbrauns, 2003. Pp. 73–78.

_____, and Freedman, D. N. "A Royal Song of Thanksgiving:
 II Samuel 22 = Psalm 18." *JBL* 72 (1953):15–34.

Crow, L. D. "The Rhetoric of Psalm 44." *ZAW* 104 (1992):384–401.

Culley, R. C. "Psalm 102, A Complaint with a Difference." *Semeia*
 62 (1993):19–35.

Dahood, M. "The Four Cardinal Points in Psalm 75, 7 and Joel 2,
 20." *Bib* 52 (1971):357.

_____. "The Language and Date of Psalm 48." *CBQ* 16
 (1954):15–19.

_____. "Philological Observations on Five Biblical Texts." *Bib*
 63 (1982):390–94. (Ps. 55)

_____. "A Sea of Troubles: Notes on Psalms 55:3–4 and
 140:10–11." *CBQ* 41 (1979):504–7.

Dalglish, Edward R. *Psalm Fifty-One in the Light of Ancient
 Near Eastern Patternism.* Leiden: E. J. Brill, 1962.

Darby, J. H. "Psalm 44 [45]: The King and His Bride." *Irish
 Ecclesiastical Record* 91 (1959):249–55.

Davidson, R. "Some Aspects of the Theological Significance of
 Doubt in the Old Testament." *ASTI* 17 (1970):44–46. (Ps. 73)

Davies, G. Henton. "The Ark in the Psalms." *ASTI* 14
 (1966–67):30–47.

_____. "Psalm 95." *ZAW* 85 (1973):183–198

Day, John N. *Crying for Justice, What the Psalms Teach Us about
 Mercy and Vengeance in an Age of Terrorism.* Grand Rapids:
 Kregel, 2005. Pp. 62–72. (Ps. 137)

_____. "Echoes of Baal's Seven Thunders and Lightnings in
 Psalm xxix." *VT* 29 (1979):143–51.

DeBoer, P. A. H. "Psalm cxxxi 2." *VT* 16 (1966):287–92.

_____. "Vive le roi!" *VT* 5 (1955):225–31.

Denton, Robert C. "An Exposition of an Old Testament Passage."
 JBR 15 (1947):158–61. (Ps. 130)

DePinto, B. "The Torah and the Psalms." *JBL* 86 (1967):154–74.

Dion, P. E. "YHWH as Storm-god and Sun-god: The Double
 Legacy of Egypt and Canaan as Reflected in Psalm 104."
 ZAW 103 (1991):43–71.

_____. "Psalm 103: A Meditation on the Ways of the LORD."
 Eglise et théologie 21 (1990):13–31.

Driver, G. R. "Reflections on Recent Articles. 2. Hebr. *môqēš* 'Striker.'" *JBL* 73 (1954):131–6.

_____. "Studies in the Vocabulary of the Old Testament. I." *JTS* 31 (1930):274–84. (Ps. 129)

_____. "Studies in the Vocabulary of the Old Testament. V." *JTS* 34 (1933):41–4. (Ps. 58)

_____. "Thou Tellest My Wanderings." *JTS* 21 (1970):402–3.

_____. "Will he not . . .?" *JSS* 13 (1968):37. (Ps. 121)

Durham, J. "The King as 'Messiah' in the Psalms." *Review and Expositor* 81 (1984):425–36.

Durlesser, James R. "A Rhetorical Critical Study of Psalms 19, 42, and 43." *Studia Biblica et Theologica* 10 (1980):179–97.

Eaton, John H. "Hard Sayings: Psalm 4:6–7." *Theology* 67 (1964):355–7.

_____. "Music's Place in Worship." *OTS* 23 (1984):85–107. (Ps. 150)

_____. "Some Questions of Philology and Exegesis in the Psalms." *JTS* 19 (1968):603–9. (Pss. 18, 93)

Eddleman, H. Leo. "Word Pictures of the Word: An Exposition of Psalm 19." *Review and Expositor* 49 (1952):413–24.

Eitan, I. "An Identification of *tiškaḥ yᵉmīnī*," Ps. 137:5." *JBL* 47 (1928):193–95.

Eissfeldt, O. "Psalm 76." *ThLZ* (1957): pp. 801–8.

Emerton, John A. "A Consideration of Some Alleged Meanings of ידע in Hebrew," *JSS* 15 (1970):145–80.

_____. "The Etymology of *Hištaḥăwāh*." *OTS* 20 (1977):41–55.

_____. "A Further Consideration of D. W. Thomas's Theories about *yada'*," *VT* 41 (1991):145–63.

_____. "How Does the LORD Regard the Deaths of His Saints in Psalm cxvi 15?" *JTS* 34 (1983):146–156.

_____. "The Interpretation of Psalm lxxxii in John x." *JTS* 11 (1960):329–34.

_____. "The Meaning of *šēnā'* in Ps cxxvii 2." *VT* 24 (1974):15–31.

_____. "Melchizedek and the Gods: Fresh Evidence for the Jewish Background of John 10:34–36." *JTS* 17 (1966):399ff.

_____."The 'Mountain of God' in Psalm 68:16." In *History and Traditions in Early Israel: Studies Presented to Eduard*

Nielsen. Ed. by A Lemaire and B. Otzen. *VT* Supplement 50 (1993):24–37.

_____. "A Neglected Solution of a Problem in Psalm lxxvi 11." *VT* 24 (1974):136–46.

_____. "Notes on Three Passages in Psalms Book III." *JTS* 14 (1963):374–381. (Ps. 74)

_____. "Notes on Three Passages in Psalms Book III." *JTS* 14 (1963):374–81.

_____. "Sheol and the Sons of Belial." *VT* 37 (1987): 214–18.

_____. "Spring and Torrent in Psalm 74:15." *VT* Supplement 15 (1966):122–33.

_____. "The Syntactical Problem of Psalm XLV, 7." *JSS* 13 (1968):58–63.

_____. "The Text of Psalm lxxvii 11." *VT* 44 (1994): 183–94

_____. "The Translation of Psalm 74:4." *JTS* 27 (1976):391–2.

_____. "The Translation of the Verbs in the Imperfect in Psalm ii. 9." *JTS* 29 (1978):499–503.

Estes, Daniel J. "Like Arrows in the Hand of a Warrior." *VT* 41 (1991):304–11. (Ps. 127)

Feinberg, C. L. "Old One Hundredth Psalm." *BibSac* 104 (1947):43–66.

_____. "Parallels to the Psalms in Near Eastern Literature." *BibSac* 104 (1947):290–97.

Fensham, F. C. "Psalm 68:23 in the Light of Recently Discovered Ugaritic Tablets." *JNES* 19 (1960):292.

_____. "Neh. 9 and Pss. 105, 106, 135, and 136: Post-Exilic Historical Traditions in Poetic Form." *JNSL* 9 (1981):35–51.

_____. "Ugaritic and the Translator of the Old Testament." *Bible Translator* 18 (1967):71–74.

_____. "Widow, Orphan, and the Poor in Ancient Near Eastern Legal and Wisdom Literature." *JNES* 21 (1962):129–139.

Finesinger, S. B. "Musical Instruments in the Old Testament." *HUCA* 3 (1926):21–76.

_____. "The Shofar." *HUCA* 8–9 (1931–32):193–228.

Finkelstein, L. "The Origin of the Hallel (Pss. 113–118)." *HUCA* 23 (1950):319–37.

Fox, Michael. "*ṬOB* as Covenant Terminology." *BASOR* 209 (1973):41–2. (Ps. 23)

Freedman, David Noel. "Acrostic Psalms in the Hebrew Bible: Alphabetic and Otherwise." *CBQ* 47 (1985):624–42. (Ps. 94)

_____. "Psalm 113 and the Song of Hannah." In *Pottery, Poetry, an Prophecies, Studies in Early Hebrew Poetry*. Winona Lake, IN: Eisenbrauns, 1980. Pp. 243–61.

_____. *Psalm 119, The Exaltation of Torah*. Winona Lake, IN: Eisenbrauns, 1999.

_____. "The Structure of Psalm 137." In *Near Eastern Studies*. FS for W. F. Albright. Ed. by H. Goedicke. Baltimore: Johns Hopkins, 1971. Pp. 187–205.

_____. "Who Asks (or Tells) God to Repent?" *Bible Review* 1 (1985):56–9.

Fretheim, T. E. "Psalm 132: A Form Critical Study." *JBL* 86 (1967):289–300.

Frost, S. B. "The Christian Interpretation of the Psalms." *CJT* 5 (1959):25–34.

_____. "Psalm 118: An Exposition." *CJT* 7 (1961):155–66.

_____. "Psalm 22: An Exposition." *CJT* 8 (1962):102–15.

Gaiser, Frederick J. "'It Shall Not Reach You': Talisman or Vocation? Reading Psalm 91 in Time of War." *WW* 25 (2005):191–202.

Gaster, Th. H. "Psalm 29." *JQR* 37 (1946,7):55–65.

_____. "Psalm 45." *JBL* 74 (1955):239–51.

_____. "Short Notes." *VT* 4 (1954):73–79 (Ps. 41)

Geller, S. A. "The Language of Imagery in Psalm 114." FS for W. L. Moran. Ed. by T. Abusch, et al. HSS 37. Atlanta: Scholars Press, 1990. Pp. 179–94.

Gelston, A. "A Note on *YHWH MLK*." *VT* 16 (1966):507–12.

_____. "A Sidelight on the 'Son of Man'." *SJT* 22 (1969):189–96.

Gemser, B. "The *rîb*–or Controversy-Pattern in Hebrew Mentality." *VT* Supplement 3 (1955):122–25. (Ps. 95)

Gertner, M. "Terms of Scriptural Interpretation: A Study in Hebrew Semantics." *BSOAS* 25 (1962):1–27.

Girard, Marc. "The Literary Structure of Psalm 95." *Theology Digest* 30 (1982):55–58.

Glass, Jonathan T. "Some Observations on Psalm 19." In *The Listening Heart*, FS for Roland E. Murphy. Ed. by Kenneth G. Hoglund, et al. *JSOT* Supplement 58 (1987):147–59.

Glenn, Donald R. "Psalm 8 and Hebrews 2: A Case Study in Biblical Hermeneutics and Biblical Theology." In *Walvoord: A Tribute*. Ed. by Donald K. Campbell. Chicago: Moody Press, 1982. Pp. 39–52.

Goldingay, J. "Repetition and Variations in the Psalms." *JQR* 68 (1977):148–9. (Ps. 59)

Goodwin, E. W. "A Rare Spelling, or a Rare Root in Ps. lxviii 10?" *VT* 14 (1964):490–91.

Gordis, Robert. "Psalm 9–10—A Textual and Exegetical Study." *JQR* 48 (1957):104–22.

Gordon, Cyrus H. "The Wine-Dark Sea." *JNES* 37 (1978):51–2. (Ps. 48)

Gordon, Robert P. "How Did Psalm 48 Happen?" In *Holy Land, Holy City*. Carlisle, UK: Paternoster, 2004. Pp. 35–45.

Goulder, Michael. "Psalm 8 and the Son of Man." *NTS* 48 (2002):18–29.

Graber, P. L. "The Structural Meaning of Psalm 113." *Occasional Papers in Translation and Text Linguistics* 4 (1990):340–52.

Gray, John. "Canaanite Kingship in Theory and Practice." *VT* 2 (1952):193–220.

_____. "A Cantata of the Autumn Festival: Psalm LXVIII." *JSS* 22 (1977):2–26.

_____. "The Kingship of God in the Prophets and the Psalms." *VT* 11 (1961):1–29

Greenberg, Moshe, "Two New Hunting Terms in Psalm 140:12." *HAR* 1 (1977):149–53.

Grelot, P. "*HOFŠĪ* [Ps lxxxviii 6]." *VT* 14 (1964):256–63.

Gruenthaner, M. "The Future Life in the Psalms." *CBQ* 2 (1940):57–63

Guillaume, A. "The Meaning of *tôlēl* in Psalm 137:3." *JBL* 75 (1956):143–4.

_____. "A Note on Psalm 109:10." *JTS* 14 (1963):92–93.

Gunnel, Andre. "'Walk,' 'Stand,' and 'Sit' in Psalm i 1–2." *VT* 32 (1982):327.

Habel, Norman C. "'Yahweh, Maker of Heaven and Earth': A Study in Tradition Criticism." *JBL* 91 (1972):321–37. (Ps. 136)

Haran, M. "The Ark and the Cherubim: Their Symbolic Significance in Biblical Ritual." *IEJ* 9 (1959):30–38; 89–94.

Hardy, E. R. "The Date of Psalm 110." *JBL* 64 (1945):385–90.

Harmon, Allen M. "Aspects of Paul's Use of the Psalms." *WJT* 32 (1969):1–23.

_____. "The Setting and Interpretation of Psalm 126." *RTR* 44 (1985):74–80.

Harrelson, Walter. "On God's Care for the Earth: Psalm 104." *CTM* 2 (1975):19–22.

_____. "Psalm 19." In *Worship and the Hebrew Bible*, FS for John T. Willis. Ed. by M. Patrick Graham, et al. *JSOT* Supplement 284 (Sheffield: *JSOT*, 1999):142–7.

Harris, Murray J. "The Translation of Elohim in Psalm 45:7–8." *TynB* 35 (1984):65–89.

Hay, David M. *Glory at the Right Hand: Psalm 110 in Early Christianity.* Nashville: Abingdon, 1973.

Hays, R. B. "Psalm 143 and the Logic of Romans 3." *JBL* 99 (1980):107–19.

Heidel, Alexander. *The Gilgamesh Epic and Old Testament Parallels.* Chicago: University of Chicago Press, 1946. Chapter 3: "Death and Afterlife," pp. 137–223. (Ps. 6)

Heinemann, H. "The Date of Psalm 80." *JQR* 40 (1949/50):297–302.

Hilber, John W. *Cultic Prophecy in the Psalms.* Berlin: Walter de Gruyter, 2005. (Ps. 60)

Hill, David. "'Son of Man' in Psalm 80 v. 17." *NovT* 15 (1973):261–69.

Hillers, D. R. "Ritual Procession of the Ark and Psalm 132." *CBQ* 30 (1968):48–55.

Holman, J. C. M. "Analysis of the Text of Psalm 139." *BZ* 14 (1970):37–71.

_____. "The Structure of Psalm cxxxix." *VT* 21 (1971):298–310.

Holm-Nielsen, S. "The Exodus Tradition in Psalm 105." *ASTI* 11 (1978):22–30.

Honeyman, A. M. "The Evidence for Regnal Names Among the Hebrews." *JBL* 67 (1948):13–25.

Hooke, S. H., editor. *Myth and Ritual. Essays on the Myth and Ritual of the Hebrews in Relation to the Cultic Pattern of the ANE.* Oxford: Clarendon Press, 1933.

Houk, Cornelius B. "Psalm 132, Literary Integrity and Syllable-Word Structures." *JSOT* 6 (1978):41–48.

Hubbard, R. L., Jr. *Dynamics and Legal Language in Conflict Psalms.* Dissertation, Claremont Graduate School, 1980. Ann Arbor: UMI, 1984.

Hubbard, R. L. "Dynamistic and Legal Processes in Psalm 7." *ZAW* 94 (1982):268–79.

Huffmon, Herbert B. "The Treaty Background of Hebrew *YADA'.*" *BASOR* 181 (1961):31–3. (Ps. 37)

Human, D. J. "Psalm 44: 'Why Do You Hide Your Face, O God?'" *Skriff en kerk* 19 1998):566–83.

Hurowitz, Victor A. "Additional Elements of Alphabetical Thinking in Psalm xxxiv." *VT* 52 (2002):326–33.

Hutton, R. R. "Cush the Benjaminite and Psalm Midrash." *HAR* 10 (1986):123–37.

Huweiler, Elizabeth F. "Patterns and Problems of Psalm 132." In *The Listening Heart, Festschrift* for R. E. Murphy. *JSOT* Supplement 8. Ed. by K. G. Hoglund, et al. Sheffield: Sheffield Academic Press, 1987. Pp. 199–215.

Hvidberg, F. F. *Weeping and Laughing in the Old Testament.* Leiden: E. J. Brill, 1962. (Ps. 126)

Iwry, A. "Notes on Psalm 68." *JBL* 71 (1942):161–65.

Janecko, B. "Ecology, Nature, Psalms." In *The Psalms and Other Studies in the Old Testament."* FS for J. I. Hunt. Edited by J. C. Knight and I. A. Sinclair. Nashotah, WI: Nashotah House Seminary, 1990. Pp. 96–108.

Janzen, J. G. "Another Look at Psalm xii 6." *VT* 54 (2004):157–64.

Janzen, Waldemar. "'*Ašrê'* in the Old Testament." *HTR* 58 (1965):215–226.

Jarick, J. "The Four Corners of Psalm 107." *CBQ* 59 (1997): 270–87.

Jefferson, Helen G. "The Date of Psalm lxvii." *VT* 12 (1962):201–5.

_____. "Psalm lxxvii." *VT* 13 (1963):87–91.

_____. "Psalm 93." *JBL* 71 (1952):155–160.

_____. "Is Psalm 110 Canaanite?" *JBL* 73 (1954):152–56.

Jenson, R. W. "Psalm 32." *Int* 32 (1979):172–76.

Jinkins, Michael. "The Virtues of the Righteous in Psalm 37." In *Psalms and Practice.* Ed. by S. B. Reid. Collegeville, MN: Liturgical Press, 2001. Pp. 154–201.

Joffe, Laura. "The Elohistic Psalter." *SJOT* 15 (2001):142–66. (Ps. 42)

Johnson, A. R. "The Psalms." In *The Old Testament and Modern Study*. Ed. by H. H. Rowley. Oxford: Clarendon Press, 1951.

Johnston, W. "YD' II, 'Be Humbled, Humiliated'?" *VT* 41 (1991):49–62145–63.

Jones, G. H. "The Decree of Yahweh."*VT* 15 (1965):335–44. (Ps. 2)

Jones, I. H. "Musical Instruments in the Bible, Part I." *BT* 37 (1986):101–16.

Kaiser, Walter C. "The Promise Theme and the Theology of Rest." *BibSac* 130 (1973):135–150. (Ps. 95)

_____. "The Promise to David in Psalm 16." *JETS* 23 (1980):219–29.

Kapelrud, A. S. "Scandinavian Research in the Psalms after Mowinckel." *ASTI* 4 (1965):148–162.

Keel, Othmar. "Kultische Brüderlichkeit-Psalm 133."*Freiburger Zeitschrift für Theologie und Philosophie* 23 (1976):68–80.

Kelly, S. L. "The Zion-Victory Songs: Psalms 46, 48, and 76. Vanderbilt Dissertation, 1968.

Kenik, Helen Ann. "Code of Conduct for a King," *JBL* 95(1976):391–403. (Ps. 101)

Kilgallen, J. J. "The Use of Psalm 16:8–11 in Peter's Pentecost Speech." *ExT* 113 (2001):47–50.

Kim, Jinkyu. "The Strategic Arrangement of Royal Psalms in Books IV-V." *WTJ* 70 (2008):143–57.

Kimelman, R. "Psalm 145: Theme, Structure and Impact." *JBL* 113 (1994):37–58.

Kissane, E. J. "The Interpretation of Psalm 110."*Irish Theological Quarterly* 21 (1954):103–14.

Kleber, A. "Ps. 2:9 in the Light of an Ancient Oriental Ceremony." *CBQ* 5 (1943):63–67.

Knight, Leonard C. "I Will Show Him My Salvation." *ResQ* 43 (2001):280–92. (Ps.91)

Kselman, John S. "A Note on Psalm 4:5." *Bib* 68 (1987):103–5.

_____. "A Note on Psalm 51:6." *CBQ* 39 (1977):251–53.

_____. "A Note on Psalm 85:9–10." *CBQ* 46 (1984):23–27.

_____. "Psalm 3: A Structural and Literary Study." *CBQ* 49 (1987):572- 580.

_____. "Psalm 72: Some Observations on Structure." *BASOR* 220 (1975):77–81.

_____. "Psalm 77 and the Book of Exodus." *JANES* 15 (1963):51–58.

_____. "Psalm 101." *JSOT* 33 (1985):45–62.

_____. "Psalm 146 in Context." *CBQ* 50 (1988):586–99.

Kuntz, J. Kenneth. "The Canonical Wisdom Psalms of Ancient Israel—Their Rhetorical, Thematic, and Formal Dimensions." In *Rhetorical Criticism.* Ed. by Jared J. Jackson and Martin Kessler. Pittsburgh: Pickwick Press, 1974. Pp. 186–222.

_____. "Psalm 18: A Rhetorical-Critical Analysis." *JSOT* 26 (1983):3–31.

_____. "The Retribution Motif in Psalmic Wisdom," *ZAW* 89 (1977):223–33. (Ps. 112)

Kwakkel, G. "'According to My Righteousness': Upright Behavior as Grounds for Deliverance in Psalms 7, 17, 18, 26, and 44." *OTS* 46. Leiden: E. J. Brill, 2002.

Laato, Antti, "Psalm 132 and the Development of the Jerusalemite/Israelite Royal Ideology." *CBQ* 54 (1992):49–66.

_____. "Psalm 132." *CBQ* 61 (1999):24–33.

Lakatos, E. "Psalm 44." *RB* 76 (1955):40–42.

Laney, J. Carl, Jr. "A Fresh Look at the Imprecatory Psalms." *BibSac* 138 (1981):35–45.

Lange, H. D. "The Relation between Psalm and the Passion Narrative." *CTM* 43 (1972):610–21.

Levenson, J. D. "A Technical Meaning for N'M in the Hebrew Bible." *VT* 35 (1985):61–7.

Leveen, Jacob. "The Textual Problems of Psalm vii." *VT* 16 (1966):439–45.

_____. "The Textual Problems of Psalm xvii." *VT* 11 (1961):48–84.

Lewis, J. O. "An Asseverative לא in Psalm 100:3?" *JBL* 86 (1967):216.

Liebreich, Leon J. "Psalms 34 and 145 in the Light of their Key Words." *HUCA* 27 (1956):181–92.

_____. "The Songs of Ascents and the Priestly Blessing." *JBL* 74 (1955):33–36.

Limberg, J. "The Root *ryb* and the Prophetic Lawsuit Speeches." *JBL* 88 (1969):291–304.

Lindars, B. "The Structure of Psalm cxlv." *VT* 29 (1979):23–30.

Lipinski, E. "Judges 5, 4–5 et Psaume 68, 8–11." *Bib* 48 (1967):185–206.

———. "*Yahweh malak.*" *Bib* 44 (1963):405–60.

Loader, J. A. "A Structural Analysis of Psalms 113." *Die Ou Testamentiese Werkgemeenskap Suid-Afrika* 19 (1977):64–68.

Logan, Norman A. "The Old Testament and a Future Life." *SJT* 6 (1953):165–172. (Ps. 16)

Longman, T., III. "Psalm 98: A Divine Victory Song." *JETS* 27 (1984):267–74.

Loewenstamm, S. E. "*Balloti bešaman ra'anān.*" *UF* 10 (1978):211–13. (Ps. 92)

———. "The LORD Is My Strength and My Glory." *VT* 19 (1969):464–70. (Ps. 118)

———. "The Number of Plagues in Psalm 105." *Bib* 52 (1971):34–38.

Luke, K. "The Setting of Psalm 115." *ITQ* 34 (1967):347–57.

———. "Under the Shadow of the Almighty." *ITQ* 3 (1972):187–93. (Ps. 91)

Lundbom, Jack R. "Psalm 23: Song of Passage." *Int* 40 (1986):6–16.

Luria, B. Z. "Psalms from Ephraim." *Beth Mikra* 23 (1978):151–60. (Ps. 81).

Macintosh, A. A. "A Consideration of Hebrew g'r." *VT* 19 (1969):471–79.

———. "A Consideration of the Problems Presented by Psalm II. 11, 12." *JTS* 27 (1976):1–14.

———. "A Consideration of Psalm vii. 12f." *JTS* 33 (1982):481–90.

———. "Psalms xci 4 and the Root סהר." *VT* 23 (1973):56–62.

Magne, J. "Répétitions de mots et exégèse dans quelques Psaumes et la Pater." *Bib* 9 (1958):177-97.

Magonet, Jonathan. "Some Concentric Structures in Psalms." *HeyJ* 23 (1982):365–69.

Malchow, B. V. "God or King in Psalm 146." *BiTod* 89 (1977):1166–70.

March, W. E. "A Note on the Text of Psalm xii 9." *VT* 21 (1971):610–12.

Marrs, Rick R. "A Cry from the Depths." *ZAW* 100 (1988):81–90.

———. "Psalm 122: 3, 4." *Bib* 68 (1987):106–9.

Martin, Chalmers. "The Imprecations in the Psalms." *PTR* 1 (1903):537–53.

Massouh, Samir. "Psalm 95." *Trinity Journal* 4 (1983):84–88.

Mathys, H. P. "Psalm cl." *VT* 50 (2000):328–44.

Mays, James L. "Worship, World, and Power: An Interpretation of Psalm 100." *Int* 23 (1969):315–30.

_____. "The Place of the Torah Psalms in the Psalter." *JBL* 106 (1987):3–12.

_____. "Psalm 13." *Int* 34 (1980):279–83.

_____. "There the Blessing: An Exposition of Psalm 133." In *A God So Near: Essays on Old Testament Theology in Honor of Patrick D. Miller.* Ed. by Brent A. Strawn and Nancy R. Bowen. Winona Lake, IN: Eisenbrauns, 2003. Pp. 79–90.

McCarthy, D. J. "'Creation' Motifs in Ancient Hebrew Poetry." *CBQ* 29 (1967):395–406.

McKay, John W. "My Glory–A Mantle of Praise." *SJT* 31 (1978):167–72 (Pss. 7, 16)

_____. "Psalms of Vigil." *ZAW* 91 (1979):229–47. (Pss. 5, 63)

McKeating, H. "Divine Forgiveness in the Psalms." *SJT* 18 (1965):69–83. (Ps. 130, 143)

McKenzie, J. L. "Royal Messianism." *CBQ* 19 (1957):25–52.

Mejia, J. "Some Observations on Psalm 107." *BTB* 5 (1975):56–66.

Menken, M. J. J. "The Translation of Psalm 41:10 and John 13:18." *JSNT* 40 (1990):61–79.

Merrill, A. L. "Psalm xxiii and the Jerusalem Tradition." *VT* 15 (1965):354–60.

Meye, R. "Psalm 107 as Horizon for Interpreting the Miracle Stories of Mark 4:35–8:26." In *Unity and Diversity in New Testament Theology.* FS for G. E. Ladd. Ed. by R. Guelich. Grand Rapids: Eerdmans, 1978. Pp. 1–13.

Milgrom, Jacob. "The Cultic שגגה and Its Influence in Psalms and Job." *JQR* 58 (1967–68):115–25. (Ps. 19)

Miller, Patrick D. "Poetic Ambiguity and Balance in Psalm xv." *VT* 29 (1979):416–24.

_____. "Psalm 127– The House that Yahweh Builds." *JSOT* 22 (1982):119–32.

_____. "Psalm 136:1–9, 23–26." *Int* 49 (1995):390–93.

_____. "The Ruler in Zion and the Hope of the Poor: Psalms 9–10 in the Context of the Psalter." In *David and Zion,*

Biblical Studies in Honor of J. J. M. Roberts. Ed. by B. F. Batto and K. L. Roberts. Winona Lake: Eisenbrauns, 2004. Pp. 187–98.

_____. "Trouble and Woe: Interpreting the Biblical Laments." *Int* 37 (1983):32–45.

_____. "*Yāpîaḥ* in Psalm xii 6." *VT* 29 (1979):495–501.

_____. "When the Gods Meet: Psalm 82 and the Issue of Justice." *Journal for Preachers* 9 (1986):2–5.

Mitchell, Christopher Wright. *The Meaning of BRK, "To Bless," in the Old Testament.* SBL Dissertation Series 95. Atlanta: Scholars Press, 1987.

Mitchell, T. C. "The Old Testament Usage of *Nešāmâ.*" *VT* 11 (1961):177–87.

Morag, S. "Light is Sown (Ps. 97)." *Tarbiz* 33 (1963):140–48.

Moran, W. L. "A Note on the Treaty Terminology of the Sefire Stela." *JNES* 22 (1963):173–76. (Ps. 73)

Moreton, M. J. "The Sacrifice of Praise." *Church Quarterly Review* 165 (1964):481–494.

Morgenstern, Julian. "The Cultic Setting of the 'Enthronement Psalms'." *HUCA* 35 (1964):1–42. (Ps. 47)

_____. "The Gates of Righteousness." *HUCA* 6 (1929):1–37. (Pss. 24, 118)

_____. "The Mythical Background of Psalm 82." *HUCA* 14 (1939):29–126.

_____. "Psalm 48." *HUCA* 16 (1941):1–95.

_____. "Psalm 8 and 19A." *HUCA* 19 (1945–46):491–523.

_____. "Psalm 11." *JBL* 69 (1950):221–31.

_____. "Psalm 23." *JBL* 65 (1946):13–24.

_____. "Psalm 121." *JBL* 58 (1939):311–23.

_____. "The Cultic Setting of the Enthronement Psalms." *HUCA* 35 (1964):1–42.

Mosca, Paul G. "Psalm 26: Poetic Structure and the Form-Critical Task.' *CBQ* 47 (1985):21–37.

Mowinckel, Sigmund. "Psalms and Wisdom." *VT* Supplement 3 (1955):204–24.

_____. "Traditionalism and Personality in the Psalms." *HUCA* 22 (1950):205–31.

_____. "The Verb *śîaḥ* and the Nouns *śîaḥ, siḥa.*" *ST* 15 (1961):1–10.

Muilenberg, J. "Psalm 47." *JBL* 63 (1944):235–56.

Mulder, Jan S. *Studies on Psalm 45.* Nijmegen, The Netherlands, 1972.

Mullen, E. T., Jr. *The Assembly of the Gods: The Divine Council in Canaanite and Early Hebrew Literature,* HSM 24. Chico, CA: Scholars Press, 1980. Pp. 226–44. (Ps. 82)

Murtonen, A. "The Use and meaning of the Words *L⁰bārēk* and *B⁰rākāh* in the Old Testament." *VT* 9 (1959):166–68. (Ps. 5)

Nel, P. J. "Psalm 110 and the Melchizedek Tradition." *JNSL* 22 (1996):1–14.

Neuberg, Frank J. "An Unrecognized Meaning of Hebrew *dôr.*" *JNES* 9 (1950):215–17.

Neusner, Jacob. "The Eighty-Ninth Psalm: Paradigm of Israel's Faith." *Judaism* 8 (1959):226–33.

Neyrey, J. H. "I Said: 'You Are Gods': Ps. 82:6 and John 10." *JBL* 108 (1989):647–63.

Niehaus, Jeffrey. "The Use of *lûlê* in Psalm 27." *JBL* 98 (1979):88, 9.

Norin, S. "Zusammenhang und Datierung." *ASTI* 11 (1978):90–95. (133)

North, C. R. "אעלזה אחלקה שכם‎, (Psa lx 8 // Ps cviii 8)." *VT* 17 (1967):242, 3. (Ps. 60)

O'Callaghan, R. T. "Echoes of Canaanite Literature in the Psalms." *VT* 4 (1954):164–176.

Ogden, Graham S. "Joel 4 and Prophetic Responses to National Laments." *JSOT* 26 1983):97–106.

————. "Prophetic Oracles Against Foreign Nations and the Psalms of Communal Lament: The Relationship of Psalm 137 to Jeremiah 49:7–22 and Obadiah," *JSOT* 24 (1982):58–97.

————. "Psalm 60, Irs Rhetoric, Form, and Function." *JSOT* 31 (1985):83–94. (Pss. 60,137)

Ollenburger, B. C. *Zion the City of the Great King. JSOT* Supplement 41. Sheffield: *JSOT*, 1987. Pp. 25–33. (Ps. 93)

Olofsson, S. "The Crux Interpretum in Ps 2,12." *SJOT* 9 (1995):185–99.

Oosterhoff, B. J. "Het Loven van God in Psalm 118." In *Leven en Geloven.* Ed. by M. H. Van Es, et al. Amsterdam: Ton Bolland, 1975. Pp. 175–90.

Owen, John. "A practical Exposition upon Psalm cxxx." In *The Works of John Owen*. Edinburgh: T. & T. Clark, 1862 reprint. 6:325–648.

Palmer, M. "The Cardinal Points in Psalm 48." *Bib* 46 (1965):357–8.

Pardee, D. "*YPH* 'Witness' in Hebrew and Ugaritic." *VT* 28 (1979):204–13.

Parker, N. H. "Psalm 103: God Is Love. He Will Have Mercy and Abundantly Pardon." *CJT* 1 (1955):191–196.

Parunak, H. Van Dyke. "A Semantic Survey of *NHM*." *Bib* 6 (1975):48–87.

Patterson, Richard D. "Psalm 22." *JETS* 47 (2004):213–33.

Paul, Shalom M. "Psalm xxvii 10 and the Babylonian Theodicy." *VT* 32 (1982):489–92.

_____. "Psalm 72:5–A Traditional Blessing for the Long Life of the King." *JNES* 31 (1972):351–54.

Perdue, Leo G. "The Riddles of Psalm 49." *JBL* 93 (1974):533–42.

Pettey, Richard J. "Psalm 130." In *The Psalter and Other Studies in the Old Testament. FS* for Joseph I. Hunt. Ed. by Jack C. Knight and Lawrence A Sinclair. Nashotah, WI: Nashotah House, 1990. Pp. 45–53.

Pinto, B. De. "The Torah and the Psalms." *JBL* 86 (1967):154–74.

Pitkin, Barbara. "Psalm 8:1–2." *Int* 55 (2001):177–80.

Pleins, T. D. "Death and Endurance: Reassessing the Literary Structure and Theology of Psalm 49." *JSOT* 69 (1996):19–27.

Ploeg, J. v. d. "Psalm XIX and Some of Its Problems." *Jaarsbericht v. h. Vooraziatisch-Egyptisch Genootschop 'Ex Oriente Lux'* 17 (1963):192–201.

Porter, J. R. "The Interpretation of 2 Samuel vi and Psalm cxxxii." *JTS* 5 (1954):161–73.

Porúbčan, S. "Psalm cxxx 5–6." *VT* 9 (1959):322–23.

Prasad, J. "Psalm 47: A Case Study in Poetic Techniques in the Psalms." *Bible Bhashyam* 29 (2003):5–25.

Prinsloo, W. S. "Psalm 149: Praise Yahweh with Tambourine and Two-Edged Sword." *ZAW* 109 (1997):385–407.

Rabinowitz, L. J. "The Psalms in Jewish Liturgy." *Historia Judaica* 6 (1944):109–122 (*CBQ* 1945, 353).

Reif, S. "Ibn Ezra on Psalm i 1–2." *VT* 34 (1984):232–36.

Reumann, John H. "Psalm 22 at the Cross: Lament and Thanksgiving for Jesus Christ." *Int* 28 (1974):39–58.

Reynolds, Carol Bechtel. "Psalm 125." *Int* 48 (1994):272–75.

Rice, Gene. "The Integrity of the Text of Psalm 139:20b." *CBQ* 46 (1984):28–30.

Ridderbos, H. "Psalm 51:5–6." In *Studia Biblica et Semitica* (1966):299–312.

_____. "The Psalms: Style, Figures and Structure." *OTS* 13 (1963):43–76. (Pss. 22, 25, 44)

_____. "The Structure of Psalm 40." *OTS* 14 (1965):296–304.

Ridderbos, J. "Jahwah Malak." *VT* 4 (1954):87–89. (Ps. 93)

Riding, C. B. "Psalm 95:1–7c as a Large Chiasm." *ZAW* 88 (1976):418.

Ringgren, Helmer. "Behold Your King Comes," *VT* 24 (1974):207–11. (Ps. 96)

_____. "Enthronement Festival or Covenant Renewal?" *Biblical Research* 7 (1962):45–48.

_____. "Psalm 2 and *Belit's* Oracle for Ashurbanipal." In *The Word of the Lord Shall Go Forth*. *FS* for David Noel Freedman. Ed. by C. L. Meyers and M. O'Connor. Winona Lake: Eisenbrauns, 1983. Pp. 91–95.

Rios, R. "A Call to Worship (Ps. 94, Vulgate)." *Scripture* 1 (1946):74–77.

_____. "Thirst for God (Pss. 41, 42, Vulgate)." *Scripture* 2 (1947):34–38.

Roberts, J. J. M. "The Davidic Origin of the Zion Tradition." *JBL* 92 (1973):329–44. (Ps. 48)

_____. "Of Sages, Prophets, and Time Limits: A Note on Psalm 74:9." *CBQ* 39 (1977):474–81.

_____. "The Religio-Political Setting of Psalm 47." *BASOR* 220 (1975):129–32.

_____. "The Young Lions of Psalm 34,11." *Bib* 54 (1973):165–7.

Robinson, A. "A Possible Solution of Psalm 74:5." *ZAW* 89 (1977):120, 21.

Robinson, A. "Zion and Saphon in Psalm xlviii 3." *VT* 24 (1974):118–23.

Robinson, B. P. "Form and Meaning in Psalm 131." *Bib* 79 (1998):180–97.

Robinson, T. H. "Notes on Psalm xxxiv. 21." *ExT* 52 (1940, 41):117.

Rosenbaum, Stanley N. "New Evidence for Reading *ge'im* in Place of *goyim* in Psalms 9 and 10." *HUCA* 45 (1975):65–70.

Rosenberg, R. A. "Yahweh Becomes King." *JBL* 85 (1966):297–307.

Ross, Allen P. "Anything In My Name." *BibV* 4 (1970):95–103. (Ps. 20)

_____. "Name." In *NIDOTTE*. Ed. by W. VanGemeren. Grand Rapids: Zondervan. (Ps. 20)

_____. "The 'Thou' Sections of Laments, The Bold and Earnest Prayers of the Psalmists." In *The Psalms, Language for All Seasons of the Soul*. Ed. by Andrew J. Schmutzer and David M. Howard, Jr. Chicago: Moody Press, 2013. Pp. 135–150.

Ross, James P. "Psalm 73." In *Israelite Wisdom*. Ed. by J. G. Gammie, et al. Missoula: Scholars Press, 1978. Pp. 161–175.

_____."*Yahweh Ṣebā'ôt* in Samuel and Psalms." *VT* 17 (1967):76–92.

Rowley, H. H. "The Structure of Psalm 42/43." *Bib* 21 (1940):45–55.

_____. "The Text and Structure of Psalm 2." *JTS* 42 (1941):143.

_____. "Melchizedek and Zadok (Gen. 14 and Ps. 110)." FS for A. Bertholet. Tübingen, 1950.

Ruppert, L. "*Zur Frage der Einheitlichkeit von Psalm 114.*" In *Altes Testament: Forschung und Wirkung*. FS für H. Graf Reventlow. Ed. by P. Mommer and W. Thiel. Frankfurt am Main: Long, 1994. Pp. 81–94.

Sabottka, Liudger. "*Rē'eykā* in Psalm 139:17." *Bib* 63 (1982):558–59.

Sanders, J. A. "The Scroll of Psalms (11QPsa) from Cave 11." *BASOR* 165 (1962):11–15.

_____. "Psalm 151 in 11QPsa." *ZAW* 75 (1963):73–86.

Sarna, N. M. "The Psalm for the Sabbath Day (Ps. 92)." *JBL* 81 (1962):155–168.

_____. "Psalm XIX and the Near Eastern Sun-God Literature." *Fourth World Congress of Jewish Studies* 1 (1967):171–75.

Schedl, C. "*Hesed* in Psalm 52 (51)." *BZ* (1961):259–60.

Schenkel, J. D. "An Interpretation of Ps. 93:5." *Bib* 46 (1965):401–16.

Schmidt, W. H. "Gott und Mensch in Ps. 130. Formgeschichtliche Erwägungen." *ThZ* 22 (1966):241–53.

Schmutzer, Andrew J. and Howard, David M. Jr. *The Psalms, Language for All Seasons of the Soul*. Chicago: Moody, 2013.

Schroeder, Christopher. "Psalm 3." *Bib* 81 (2000):243–51.

Seitz, C. R. "The Divine Council: Temporal Transition and New Prophecy in the Book of Isaiah." *JBL* 109 (1990):229–47. (Ps. 82)

Shafer, B. E. "The Root *bhr* and Pre-exilic Concepts of Chosenness in the Hebrew Bible." *ZAW* 89 (1977):20–42. (Ps. 135)

Sharrock, Graeme E. "Psalm 74: A Literary-Structural Analysis." *AUSS* 21 (1938):211–23.

Shepherd, John. "The Place of Imprecatory Psalms in the Canon of Scripture." *Churchman* 111 (1997):27–47, 110–26.

Shoemaker, H. Stephen. "Psalm 131." *RevExp* 85 (1988):89–94.

Skehan, P. W. "Strophic Structure in Psalm 72 (71)." *Bib* 40 (1959):302–8.

Šulj, Edo. "Musical Instruments in Psalm 150." In *The Interpretation of the Bible*. Ed. by Jože Krašovec. *JSOT* Supplement 289. Sheffield: Sheffield Academic Press, 1998. Pp. 1117–30.

Slotki, I. W. "Omnipresence, Condescension and Omniscience in Psalm 113:5–6." *JTS* 32 (1931):367–370.

_____. "Psalm 49:13, 21 (AV 12, 20)." *VT* 28 (1978):361–62.

Smick, E. B. "Mythological Language in the Psalms." *WTJ* 44 (1982):88–98. (Pss. 74, 82)

Smith Mark S. "The Invocation of Deceased Ancestors." *JBL* 112 (1993):105–7. (Ps. 49)

_____. "Psalm 8:2b–3." *CBQ* 59 (1997):637–41.

_____. "'Seeing God' in the Psalms: The Background to the Beatific Vision in the Hebrew Bible." *CBQ* 50 (1988):171–83. (Pss. 42, 43)

_____. "Setting and Rhetoric in Psalm 23." *JSOT* 41 (1988):61–66.

Snaith, H. *Hymns of the Temple (Pss. 42/43; 44; 46; 50–73).* 1951 London: SCM Press, Ltd., 1951.

_____. "The Meaning of Hebrew אך." *VT* 14 (1964):221–25.

_____. "Selah." *VT* 2 (1952):42–56.

Sonne, Isaiah. "Psalm 11." *JBL* 68 (1949):241–45.

_____. "The Second Psalm." *HUCA* 19 (1945):43–55.

Spangenberg, I. J. J. "Psalm 49 and the Book of Qoheleth." *Strif en kerk* 18 (1997):328–44.

Spero, S. "Psalm 50: Prophetic Speech and God's Performative Utterances." In *Prophets and Paradigms*. Ed. by S. B. Reid. Sheffield: Sheffield Academic Press, 1996. Pp. 217–30.

Speiser, E. A. "'People' and 'Nation' of Israel." *JBL* 79 (1960):157–63.

_____. "The Stem *PLL* in Hebrew." *JBL* 82 (1963):301–6.

Steyl, C. "The Construct Noun, *Ešet,* in Ps. 58,9." *JNSL* 11 (1983):133–34.

Strugnell, John. "A Note on Ps. cxxvi.i." *JTS* 7 (1956):239–43.

Tate, Marvin. "An Exposition of Psalm 8." *Perspectives in Religious Studies* 28 (2001):343–59.

_____. "Psalm 88." *RevExp* 87 (1990):91–95.

Thierry, G. J. "Remarks on Various passages of the Psalms." *OTS* 13 (1963):77–82. (Ps. 7)

Thomas, D. W. "נצב in Psalm XXXIX 6." In *Studies in the Bible. FS for M. H. Segal. Publication of the Israel Society for Biblical Research* 17 (1964):10–16.

_____. "Hebrew עֲנִי, 'Captivity'." *JTS* 16 (1965):444–5. (Ps. 109)

_____. "The Meaning of זיז in Psalm lxxx. 14." *ExT* (1965):385.

_____. "A Note on שֶׁנָה יִהְיוּ זַרְמְתָם in Psalm 90:5," *VT* 18 (1968):267–68.

_____. "The Root ידע in Hebrew. 2," *JTS* 36 (1935):409–412.

_____. "Some Observations on the Hebrew Word רַעֲנָן." In *Hebraische Wortforschung. FS for Walter Baumgartner. VT Supplement* 16. Leiden: E. J. Brill (1967). Pp. 387–97. (Ps. 92)

_____. "Some Rabbinic Evidence for a Hebrew Root ידע = (Arabic) *wd'*," *JQR* NS 37 (1946, 47):177–78.

Thomas, M. E. "Psalms 1 and 112 as a Paradigm for the Comparison of Wisdom Motifs in the Psalms," *JETS* 29 (1986):15–24.

Thompson, Thomas L. "From the Mouth of Babes, Strength: Psalm 8 and the Book of Isaiah." *SJOT* 16 (2002):226–45

Tigay, J. H. "Divine Creation of the King in Psalm 2:6." *Eretz-Israel* 23 (2003):246–51.

_____. "Psalm 7:5 and Ancient Near Eastern Treaties." *JBL* 89 (1970):176–86.

Torrance, T. F. "The Last of the Hallel Psalms." *EvTh* 28 (1956):101–108.

Treves, M. "The Date of Psalm 24." *VT* 10 (1960):428–37.

Tromp, N. "The Text of Psalm cxxx 5–6." *VT* 39 (1989):100–103.

Trull, G. V. "An Exegesis of Psalm 16:10." *BibSac* 161 (2004):304–21.

_____. "Views on Peter's Use of Psalm 16:8–11 in Acts 2:25–32." *BibSac* 161 (2004):194- 204.

Tsevat, Matitiahu. "God and the Gods in the Assembly." *HUCA* 40 (1969):123–37.

_____. "God and the Gods in the Assembly: An Interpretation of Psalm 82." In *The Meaning of the Book of Job and Other Studies*. New York: KTAV, 1986. Pp. 131–148.

_____. "Psalm XC 5–6." *VT* 35 (1985):115–17.

Tsumura, David Toshio. "The Literary Structure of Psalm 46,2–8." *AJBI* 6 (1980):29–55.

Tur-Sinai [Torczyner], H. H. "The Literary Character of the Book of Psalms." *OTS* 8 (1950):263–281.

VanGemeren, Willem A. "Psalm 131:2–*kegāmul:* The Problem of Meaning and Metaphor." *Hebrew Studies* 23 (1982):51–57.

Van der Ploeg, J. P. M. "Psalm 19 and Some of its Problems." *JEOL* 17 (1964):193–201.

_____. "Psalm cxxxiii and its Main Problems." In *Loven en geloven, FS* for N. H. Ridderbos. Amsterdam: Ton Bolland, 1975. Pp. 191–200.

Van der Wal, A. J. O. "The Structure of Psalm cxxix." *VT* 28 (1988):364–67.

Van Zijl, P. J. "A Discussion of the Root *ga'ar* (Rebuke)." In *Biblical Essays.* Edited by A. H. Van Zyl. Potchefstroom: Pro Rege-Pers, 1969. Pp. 56–63.

Van Zyl, A. H. "Psalm 19." *Biblical Essays 1966* (1967):142–58.

_____. "The Unity of Psalm 27." In *De Fructu Oris Sui. FS* for A. Van Selms. Ed. by I. H Eybers, et al. Leiden: E. J. Brill, 1971. Pp. 233–51.

Vawter, B. "Post-exilic Prayer and Hope." *CBQ* 37 (1975):460–70. (Ps. 90)

Vogels, Walter. "A Structural Analysis if Ps 1." *Bib* 60 (1979):410–16.

Victor, P. "Note on Psalm LXXX.13." *ExT* 76 (1965):294–95.

933

Vogt, E. "The 'Place in Life' of Psalm 23." *Bib* 34 (1953):195–211.

Volz, P. "Psalm 49." *ZAW* 55 (1937):235–65.

Wagner, N. E. "רִנָּה in the Psalter." *VT* 10 (1960):435–41. (Ps. 142)

Wahl, Harold Martin. "Psalm 90, 12." *ZAW* 106 (1994):116–23.

Waltke, B. K. "Responding to an Unethical Society." *Stimulus* 1 (1993):13–18.

Wanke, D. *Die Zionstheologie der Korachiten. Beiheft fur ZAW* 97 (1966):23–31.

Ward, J. M. "The Literary Form and the Liturgical Background of Psalm lxxxix." *VT* 11 (1961):321–39.

Ward, Martin J. "Psalm 109: David's Psalm of Vengeance." *AUSS* 18 (1980):163–168.

Watson, Wilfred G. E. "The Hidden Simile in Psalm 133." *Bib* 60 (1979):108–9.

Watts, J. D. W. "*Yahweh Malak* Psalms." *ThZ* 21 (1965):341–48. (93)

Watts, J. W. "Psalm 2 in the Context of Biblical Theology." *HBT* 12 (1990):73–97.

Weir, J. E. "The Perfect Way," *EvQ* 53 (1981):54–59.

Weir, T. H. "Psalm 121:1." *ExT* 27 (1915–16):90–91.

Wenham, J. W. "Large Numbers in the Old Testament." *TynB* 17 (1967):19–53. (Ps. 50)

Wernberg-Moller, P. "Two Difficult Passages in the Old Testament." *ZAW* 69 (1957):69–73. (Ps. 12)

Werner, Eric. "Musical Instruments." In *IDB* 3:474–5. (Ps. 33)

Westermann, C. "Psalm 90: A Thousand Years Are But As Yesterday." In *Living the Psalms*. Translated by J. R. Porter. Grand Rapids: Eerdmans, 1989. Pp. 156–65.

————. "Struktur und Geschichte der Klage im Alten Testament." *ZAW* 66 (1954):44–80.

Whitley, C. F. "Psalm 99:8." *ZAW* 85 (1973):227–30.

————. "Some Remarks on *lu* and *lo*." *ZAW* 87 (1975):212–4. (Ps. 100)

————. "Textual and Exegetical Observations on Ps 45,4–7." *ZAW* 98 (1986):277–82.

————. "The Text of Psalm 90, 5." *Bib* 63 (1982): 267–68.

Wildberger, H. "Die Thronenamen des Messias, Jes. 9, 5b." *ThZ* 16 (1960):285–97.

Whybray, R. N. "'Their Wrongdoings'" in Psalm 98:8." *ZAW* 81 (1969):237–39.

Wilfall, W. "The Foreign Nations: Israel's 'Nine Bows'." *Bulletin of Egyptological Seminar* 3 (1981):113–24.

Willesen, F. "The Cultic Situation of Psalm lxxiv." *VT* 2 (1952):289–306.

Williams, W. G. "Liturgical Problems in Enthronement Psalms." *JBR* 25 (1957):118–122.

Willis, John T. "An Attempt to Decipher Psalm 121:1b." *CBQ* 52 (1990):241–51.

_____. "The Song of Hannah and Psalm 113." *CBQ* 35 (1975):139–54.

_____. "Psalm 121 as a Wisdom Poem." *HAR* 11 (1987):435–51.

Willis, T. M. "So Great Is His Steadfast Love: A Rhetorical Analysis of Psalm 103." *Bib* 72 (1991):525–37.

Wolff, Hans Walter. "Der Aufruf zur Volksklage." *ZAW* 76 (1964):48–56.

_____. "Psalm 1," *EvTh* 9 (1949, 50):385–94.

_____. "Psalm 110:4." In *Herr, tue meine Lippen auf.* Edited by C. Eicholz. 2nd Edition. 5 Volumes. Wuppertal-Barmen: Müller, 1961. 5:310–23.

Wolverton, W. I. "The Psalmist's Belief in God's Presence." *CJT* 9 (1963):82–94. (Ps. 139)

_____. "The Meaning of the Psalms." *ATR* 47 (1965):16–33.

Woudstra, Marten H. *The Ark of the Covenant from Conquest to Kingship.* Philadelphia: Presbyterian and Reformed Publishing Company, 1965. (Ps. 63)

Wright, D. P. "Ritual Analogy in Psalm 109." *JBL* 113 (1994):385–404.

Würthwein, E. "Erwägungen zu Psalm 73." *FS* for A. Bertholet. Tübingen, 1950. Pp. 532–49.

_____. "Erwägungen zu Psalm 139." *VT* 7 (1957):165–182.

Yadin, Yigael. "New Gleanings on Resheph from Ugarit." In *Biblical and Related Studies Presented to Samuel Iwry.* Ed. by Ann Kort and Scott Morschauer. Winona lake, IN: Eisenbrauns, 1985. (Ps. 57)

Yaron, Reuven. "The Meaning of *zānah.*" *VT* 13 (1963):237–39. (Ps. 44)

Young, E. J. *A Study of the Omnipresence of God.* London: Banner of Truth Trust, 1965. (Ps. 139).

Youngblood, R. "A New Look at Three Old Testament Roots for 'Sin.'" In *Biblical and Near Eastern Studies. FS* for W. S. LaSor. Ed. by G. A. Tuttle. Grand Rapids: Eerdmans, 1 978. (Ps. 51)

Zevit, Ziony. "Psalms at the Poetic Precipice." *HAR* 10 (1986):351–66. (Ps. 134)

Zimmerli, W. "Knowledge of God according to the Book of Ezekiel." In *I Am Yahweh.* Translated by D. W. Stott. Atlanta: John Knox Press, 1954/1982). (Ps. 100)

Zink, J. K. "Uncleanness and Sin. A Study of Job xiv 4 and Psalm li 7." *VT* 17 (1967):354–61.